T0210992

Lecture Notes in Computer Science

Lecture Notes in Artificial Intelligence   14116

Founding Editor

Jörg Siekmann

Series Editors

Randy Goebel, *University of Alberta, Edmonton, Canada*
Wolfgang Wahlster, *DFKI, Berlin, Germany*
Zhi-Hua Zhou, *Nanjing University, Nanjing, China*

The series Lecture Notes in Artificial Intelligence (LNAI) was established in 1988 as a topical subseries of LNCS devoted to artificial intelligence.

The series publishes state-of-the-art research results at a high level. As with the LNCS mother series, the mission of the series is to serve the international R & D community by providing an invaluable service, mainly focused on the publication of conference and workshop proceedings and postproceedings.

Nuno Moniz · Zita Vale · José Cascalho ·
Catarina Silva · Raquel Sebastião
Editors

Progress in Artificial Intelligence

22nd EPIA Conference on
Artificial Intelligence, EPIA 2023
Faial Island, Azores, September 5–8, 2023
Proceedings, Part II

 Springer

Editors
Nuno Moniz ⓘD
Lucy Family Institute for Data and Society
Notre Dame, IN, USA

INESC TEC
Porto, Portugal

José Cascalho ⓘD
GRIA—LIACC
University of Azores
Ponta Delgada, Portugal

Raquel Sebastião ⓘD
IEETA
University of Aveiro
Aveiro, Portugal

Zita Vale ⓘD
GECAD
Polytechnic of Porto
Porto, Portugal

Catarina Silva ⓘD
CISUC
University of Coimbra
Coimbra, Portugal

ISSN 0302-9743   ISSN 1611-3349 (electronic)
Lecture Notes in Artificial Intelligence
ISBN 978-3-031-49010-1   ISBN 978-3-031-49011-8 (eBook)
https://doi.org/10.1007/978-3-031-49011-8

LNCS Sublibrary: SL7 – Artificial Intelligence

This Springer imprint is published by the registered company Springer Nature Switzerland AG
The registered company address is: Gewerbestrasse 11, 6330 Cham, Switzerland

Paper in this product is recyclable.

Preface

The 22nd EPIA Conference on Artificial Intelligence was held in Faial, Azores, from the 5th to the 8th of September 2023.

EPIA is a well-established conference that aims to promote research in all Artificial Intelligence (AI) areas, covering theoretical and fundamental questions and applications, allowing scientific exchange between researchers, engineers and professionals in related disciplines. As with previous editions, this conference received support from the Portuguese Artificial Intelligence Association (APPIA).

The EPIA program, similarly to previous years, included thematic tracks dedicated to specific areas in AI. This year's conference featured the following 17 tracks:

- AI, Generation and Creativity (AIGC);
- Ambient Intelligence and Affective Environments (AmIA);
- Artificial Intelligence and IoT in Agriculture (AIoTA);
- Artificial Intelligence and Law (AIL);
- Artificial Intelligence for Industry and Societies (AI4IS);
- Artificial Intelligence in Medicine (AIM);
- Artificial Intelligence in Power and Energy Systems (AIPES);
- Artificial Intelligence in Smart Computing (AISC);
- Artificial Intelligence in Transportation Systems (AITS);
- Ethics and Responsibility in AI (ERAI);
- General AI (GAI);
- Intelligent Robotics (IROBOT);
- Knowledge Discovery and Business Intelligence (KDBI);
- MultiAgent Systems: Theory and Applications (MASTA);
- Natural Language Processing, Text Mining and Applications (TeMA);
- Planning, Scheduling and Decision-Making in AI (PSDM);
- Social Simulation and Modelling (SSM).

EPIA received 165 submissions from 29 different countries this year. Out of these submissions, 108 had a student as the first author. Each submission was double–blind reviewed by at least three Program Committee (PC) members of each thematic track. These two volumes contain all the accepted papers from the thematic tracks, totalling 85 papers.

The conference also received four keynote speakers: Pétia Georgieva (University of Aveiro, Portugal) with a talk on "Machine Learning Algorithms for Brain-Machine Interfaces"; Martin Visbeck (University of Kiel, Germany) with a talk on "Digital Twins of the Ocean"; Josep Domingo-Ferrer (Universitat Rovira i Virgli, Spain) with a talk on "On the Use (and Misuse) of Differential Privacy in Machine Learning"; and Nitesh Chawla (University of Notre Dame, USA) with a talk on "Learning on Graphs". The invited talks' abstracts are included in these proceedings front matter.

The Program Chairs thank the Award Committee, composed of Bernardete Ribeiro, Juan Pavon and Nathalie Japkowicz, for selecting the Best Paper and the Best Student

Paper, and Springer for the financial support for the awards. This year, the Best Paper Award was given to Tânia Carvalho, Nuno Moniz and Luís Filipe Antunes for the paper "A Three-Way Knot: Privacy, Fairness, and Predictive Performance Dynamics". The Best Student Paper Award was given to Luís Filipe Cunha for the paper "Event Extraction for Portuguese: A QA-driven Approach using ACE-2005", co-authored with Alípio Jorge and Ricardo Campos.

Reinforcing the focus on young researchers and following last year's edition, the conference included a student symposium, where students in the early stages of their study programmes presented their main research ideas and discussed them with other students and researchers, and a mentoring session with senior researchers from related fields was provided. The organization thanks the AI Journal and APPIA for the scholarships for student support.

This year's edition included a panel on Interdisciplinary Challenges and a Discussion on AI and Society open to the general public.

The EPIA organizers are thankful to the student symposium chairs and mentors, the thematic track organizing chairs, their respective Program Committee members, and the student volunteers Bruno Ribeiro, Daniel Ramos, Daniela Pais, Louis Carrette and Teresa Pereira. All did amazing work, contributing to a very successful conference. Finally, the organization would also like to express their gratitude to all the EPIA International Steering Committee members for their guidance regarding the scientific organization of EPIA 2023.

September 2023

Nuno Moniz
Zita Vale
José Cascalho
Catarina Silva
Raquel Sebastião

Organization

General/Program Chairs

Nuno Moniz   Lucy Family Institute for Data and Society,
     USA/INESC TEC, Portugal
Zita Vale   Polytechnic of Porto/GECAD, Portugal
José Cascalho   University of Azores/GRIA—LIACC, Portugal
Catarina Silva   University of Coimbra/CISUC, Portugal
Raquel Sebastião   University of Aveiro/IEETA, Portugal

Organization Chairs

Gui Menezes   University of Azores/OKEANOS, Portugal
Rita P. Ribeiro   University of Porto/INESC TEC, Portugal
Armando B. Mendes   University of Azores/GRIA—LIACC, Portugal
João Vinagre   Joint Research Centre—European Commission,
     Spain

Steering Committee

Ana Bazzan   Universidade Federal do Rio Grande do Sul,
     Brazil
Bernardete Ribeiro   Universidade de Coimbra, Portugal
Ernesto Costa   Universidade de Coimbra, Portugal
Eugénio Oliveira   Universidade do Porto, Portugal
Helder Coelho   Universidade de Lisboa, Portugal
José Júlio Alferes   Universidade Nova de Lisboa, Portugal
Juan Pavón   Universidad Complutense Madrid, Spain
Luís Paulo Reis   Universidade do Porto, Portugal
Paulo Novais   Universidade do Minho, Portugal
Pavel Brazdil   Universidade do Porto, Portugal
Virginia Dignum   Umeå University, Sweden

Track Chairs

Ambient Intelligence and Affective Environments

Paulo Novais   University of Minho, Portugal
Goreti Marreiros   Polytechnic of Porto, Portugal
João Carneiro   Devoteam Portugal, Portugal
Peter Mikulecky   University of Hradec Kralove, Czechia
Sara Rodriguez   University of Salamanca, Spain

Ethics and Responsibility in Artificial Intelligence

Catarina Silva   University of Coimbra, Portugal
Nuno Moniz   Lucy Family Institute for Data and Society,
                              University of Notre Dame, USA
Branka Hadji Misheva   Bern University of Applied Sciences, Switzerland

General Artificial Intelligence

Nuno Moniz   Lucy Family Institute for Data and Society,
                              University of Notre Dame, USA
Zita Vale   GECAD/ISEP—IPP, Portugal
José Cascalho   GRIA—LIACC/Universidade dos Açores,
                              Portugal
Catarina Silva   CISUC, Universidade de Coimbra, Portugal
Raquel Sebastião   IEETA/Universidade de Aveiro, Portugal

Intelligent Robotics

Luís Paulo Reis   Universidade do Porto/LIACC, Portugal
Nuno Lau   Universidade de Aveiro/IEETA, Portugal
João Alberto Fabro   Universidade Tecnológica Federal do Paraná,
                              Brazil

Knowledge Discovery and Business Intelligence

Paulo Cortez	University of Minho, Portugal
Alfred Bifet	Télécom ParisTech/Université Paris-Saclay, France
Luís Cavique	Universidade Aberta, Portugal
João Gama	University of Porto/INESC TEC, Portugal
Nuno Marques	FCT Universidade Nova de Lisboa, Portugal
Manuel Filipe Santos	University of Minho, Portugal

MultiAgent Systems: Theory and Applications

João Balsa	Universidade de Lisboa, Portugal
João Fabro	Universidade Tecnológica Federal do Paraná, Brazil
Henrique Lopes Cardoso	Universidade do Porto, Portugal
José Cascalho	Universidade dos Açores, Portugal

Natural Language Processing, Text Mining and Applications

Joaquim Silva	Universidade Nova de Lisboa, Portugal
Pablo Gamallo	Universidade de Santiago de Compostela, Spain
Paulo Quaresma	Universidade de Évora, Portugal
Irene Rodrigues	Universidade de Évora, Portugal
Hugo Oliveira	Universidade de Coimbra, Portugal

Planning, Scheduling and Decision-Making in Artificial Intelligence

Adriano Lino	Universidade Federal do Oeste do Pará, Brazil
Luís Paulo Reis	Universidade do Porto, Portugal
Jorge Barbosa	Universidade do Porto, Portugal
Alexandra Oliveira	Retail Consult, Portugal
Vítor Rodrigues	Retail Consult, Portugal

Social Simulation and Modelling

Pedro Campos   Universidade do Porto/INESC TEC, Portugal
Luis Antunes   Universidade de Lisboa/LabMAg, Portugal
Fernando Oliveira   University of Bradford, UK

Artificial Intelligence, Generation and Creativity

Pedro Martins   University of Coimbra, Portugal
João Miguel Cunha   University of Coimbra, Portugal
Helena Sofia Pinto   University of Lisbon, Portugal
María Navarro   Univesidad de Salamanca, Spain
Juan Romero   University of A Coruña, Spain
Maria Hedblom   Jönköping University, Sweden

Artificial Intelligence and Law

Pedro Miguel Freitas   Universidade Católica Portuguesa, Portugal
Ugo Pagallo   University of Torino, Italy
Massimo Durante   University of Torino, Italy
Paulo Novais   Universidade do Minho

Artificial Intelligence in Power and Energy Systems

Zita Vale   Polytechnic of Porto, Portugal
Tiago Pinto   UTAD/INESC TEC, Portugal
Pedro Faria   Polytechnic of Porto, Portugal
Elena Mocanu   University of Twente, The Netherlands
Decebal Constantin Mocanu   Technical University of Eindhoven, The
                                    Netherlands

Artificial Intelligence in Medicine

Manuel Filipe Santos   University of Minho, Portugal
Carlos Filipe Portela   University of Minho, Portugal
Allan Tucker   Brunel University London, UK
Manuel Fernandez Delgado   Universidade de Santiago de Compostela, Spain

Artificial Intelligence and IoT in Agriculture

Filipe Neves dos Santos   INESC TEC, Portugal
José Boaventura Cunha   University of Trás-os-Montes and Alto Douro,
                                     Portugal
Josenalde Barbosa   Federal University of Rio Grande do Norte, Brazil
Paulo Moura Oliveira   University of Trás-os-Montes and Alto Douro,
                                     Portugal
Raul Morais   University of Trás-os-Montes and Alto Douro,
                                     Portugal

Artificial Intelligence in Transportation Systems

Tânia Fontes   INESC TEC, Portugal
Alberto Fernandez   Universidad Rey Juan Carlos, Spain
Rosaldo Rossetti   University of Porto, Portugal

Artificial Intelligence in Smart Computing

Sherin M. Moussa   Université Française d'Égypte, Egypt
Dagmawi Lemma   Addis Ababa University (Ethiopia)/African
                                     Center of Excellence in IoT (Rwanda)

Artificial Intelligence for Industry and Societies

Filipe Portela   University of Minho, Portugal
Sherin M. Moussa   Université Française d'Égypte, Egypt
Teresa Guarda   Universidad Estatal de la Península de Santa
                                     Elena, Equador
Ioan M. Ciumasu   University of Paris-Saclay/University of
                                     Versailles, France

Program Committee

Ambient Intelligence and Affective Environments

Hector Alaiz Moreton
Patrícia Alves
Zoltan Balogh
Francisco Bellas
Orlando Belo
F. Amílcar Cardoso
João Carneiro
Luís Conceição
Fernando De La Prieta
Dalila Alves Durães
Florentino Fdez-Riverola
Antonio Fernández-Caballero
Lino Figueiredo
Marco Gomes
Miguel J. Hornos
Eva Hudlicka
Javier Jaen
Vicente Julian
Shinichi Konomi
Luis Macedo
José Machado
Peter Mikulecky
Karel Mls
Jose M. Molina
Paulo Moura Oliveira
Tatsuo Nakajima
Tereza Otcenaskova
Martín Pérez-Pérez
Abraham Prieto García
Joao Ramos
Sara Rodríguez
Ricardo Santos
Ichiro Satoh

Ethics and Responsibility in Artificial Intelligence

Tiago Araújo
Marcelo Augusto Vieira Graglia
Joana Costa
Oleg Deev
Karla Figueiredo
Petia Georgieva
Joe Germino
Paolo Giudici
Nuno Lourenço
Marcos Machado
Ana Madureira
Ana Nogueira
Paolo Pagnottoni
Emanuela Raffinetti
Rita P. Ribeiro
Jennifer Schnur
Luís Teixeira

General Artificial Intelligence

Jose Julio Alferes
Amparo Alonso-Betanzos
Pedro Barahona
Luís Camarinha-Matos
F. Amílcar Cardoso
Davide Carneiro
Jose Cascalho
Paulo Cortez
Arlindo Oliveira
Andrea Omicini
Juan Pavón
Tiago Pinto
Paulo Quaresma
Luís Paulo Reis
Ana Paula Rocha
Alvaro Costa Neto
Petia Georgieva
Joe Germino
Vicente Julian
Grigorii Khvatskii
Joao Leite

José Machado
Jose M. Molina
Gabriel Santos
Jennifer Schnur
Luís Seabra Lopes
Raquel Sebastião
Catarina Silva
Zita Vale

Intelligent Robotics

João Fabro
Eurico Pedrosa
Brígida Mónica Faria
Armando Sousa

Knowledge Discovery and Business Intelligence

Fernando Bacao
Orlando Belo
Agnès Braud
Luís Camacho
Rui Camacho
Margarida Cardoso
Nielsen Castelo
Pedro Castillo
Luís Cavique
Paulo Cortez
Jose Alfredo Ferreira Costa
Andre de Carvalho
Marcos Aurélio Domingues
Elaine Faria
Manuel Fernandez Delgado
Carlos Ferreira
Roberto Henriques
Alipio M. Jorge
Philippe Lenca
Nuno Marques
Armando Mendes
Sorin Moga
Sérgio Moro
João Moura-Pires
Amilcar Oliveira

Rita P. Ribeiro
Fátima Rodrigues
Murat Caner Testik

MultiAgent Systems: Theory and Applications

Cristina Baroglio
Juan Carlos Burguillo
Rafael C. Cardoso
Cristiano Castelfranchi
Daniel Castro Silva
Alberto Fernandez
Adriana Giret
Marin Lujak
Luis Macedo
Luís Nunes
Gauthier Picard
Alessandro Ricci
David Sarne
Onn Shehory
Takao Terano
Viviane Torres da Silva
Paulo Urbano
Giovanni Varricchione
Rosa Vicari

Natural Language Processing, Text Mining and Applications

Manex Agirrezabal
Miguel A. Alonso
Sophia Ananiadou
Fernando Batista
Pavel Brazdil
Luisa Coheur
Béatrice Daille
Victor Darriba
Gaël Dias
Antoine Doucet
Pablo Gamallo
Marcos Garcia
Hugo Gonçalo Oliveira
Marcio Inácio
Adam Jatowt

Nuno Marques
Bruno Martins
Shamsuddeen Muhammad
Sérgio Nunes
Paulo Quaresma
Alexandre Rademaker
Francisco J. Ribadas-Pena
Irene Rodrigues
João Rodrigues
Roney L. S. Santos
Altigran Silva
Joaquim Silva
João Silva
Mário Silva
Alberto Simões
Luís Trigo
Jesús Vilares

Planning, Scheduling and Decision-Making in Artificial Intelligence

Filipe Alvelos
Jorge Barbosa
Breno Willian Carvalho
Guilherme Conde
Brígida Mónica Faria
Paulo Leitao
Adriano Lino
Luis Macedo
José Machado
Paulo Novais
Antonio Pereira
Viviane Torres da Silva

Social Simulation and Modelling

Luis Antunes
Pedro Campos

Artificial Intelligence, Generation and Creativity

F. Amílcar Cardoso
Tania Carvalho
Nuno Correia
Joe Germino
João Gonçalves
Maria Hedblom
Carlos León
Carlos António Roque Martinho
Pedro Martins
Tiago Martins
Piotr Mirowski
Caterina Moruzzi
María Navarro
Senja Pollak
Prashanth Thattai Ravikumar
Sérgio Rebelo
Ana Rodrigues
Anna Sokol
Brad Spendlove
Thomas Winters

Artificial Intelligence and Law

Francisco Andrade
Teresa Coelho Moreira
Massimo Durante
Pedro Miguel Freitas
Carlisle George
Luis Gomes
Vicente Julian
Jose Machado
Eduardo Magrani
Clara Martins Pereira
Manuel Masseno
Paulo Novais
Arlindo Oliveira
Ugo Pagallo
Tito Rendas
Ana Rodríguez Álvarez
Cristina Salgado
Giovanni Sartor

Artificial Intelligence in Power and Energy Systems

Hugo Algarvio
Alfonso Briones
João Catalão
Ana Estanqueiro
Nuno Fidalgo
Luis Gomes
Nouredine Hadjsaid
Nikos Hatziargyriou
Bo Jorgensen
Germano Lambert-Torres
Fernando Lopes
Zheng Ma
Gonçalo Marques
Goreti Marreiros
Hugo Morais
Dagmar Niebur
João Peças Lopes
Gabriel Santos
Tiago Soares
Brígida Teixeira

Artificial Intelligence in Medicine

António Abelha
João Almeida
Susana Brás
Rui Camacho
Beatriz De La Iglesia
Manuel Fernandez Delgado
Júlio Duarte
Göran Falkman
Brígida Mónica Faria
Pedro Gago
Luis Gomes
Barna Iantovics
Giorgio Leonardi
José Machado
Goreti Marreiros
Ricardo Martinho
Hugo Peixoto
Cinzia Pizzi

Inna Skarga-Bandurova
Shabbir Syed-Abdul
Allan Tucker
Henrique Vicente

Artificial Intelligence and IoT in Agriculture

Jos Balendonck
Jayme Barbedo
Josenalde Barbosa
João-Paulo Coelho
Pedro Couto
Vítor Filipe
Grigorii Khvatskii
Andres Muñoz
Emanuel Peres
Veronica Saiz-Rubio
Javier Sanchis Saez
José Boaventura Cunha
Tania Carvalho
Aneesh Chauhan
Laura Santana
José Antonio Sanz Delgado
Carlos Serodio
Eduardo Solteiro-Pires
Joaquim João Sousa
Antonio Valente
Joao Valente
Fedro Zazueta

Artificial Intelligence in Transportation Systems

António Pedro Aguiar
Mobyen Uddin Ahmed
Elisabete Arsenio
Carlos Bento
Holger Billhardt
Abderrahmane Boubezoul
Eduardo Camponogara
Hilmi Berk Celikoglu
Gonçalo Correia
António Costa
Daniel G. Costa

Gianluca Di Flumeri
Juergen Dunkel
Qiaochu Fan
Sara Ferreira
Rui Gomes
Carlos A. Iglesias
João Jacob
Zafeiris Kokkinogenis
Pedro M. D'Orey
Eftihia Nathanail
Luís Nunes
Sascha Ossowski
Sara Paiva
Joel Ribeiro
Javier J. Sanchez Medina
Thiago Sobral
Marco Veloso
Giuseppe Vizzari
Fenghua Zhu

Artificial Intelligence in Smart Computing

Nouran Abdalazim
Abdelaziz Abdelhamid
Waleed Adel
Yasmine Afify
Marco Alfonse
Ayalew Belay
Faten Chaieb
Roaa Elghondakly
Anna Fabijanska
Dina Fawzy
Fekade Getahun
Safwat Hamad
Christine Lahoud
Dagmawi Lemma
Mahmoud Mounir

Artificial Intelligence for Industry and Societies

Mohamed Abdelaziz
Waleed Adel
Yasmeen Adel
Yasmine Afify
Ioan Ciumasu
Roaa Elghondakly
Dina Fawzy
Panos Fitsilis
Felix J. Garcia Clemente
Mariam Gawich
Alfonso González Briones
Sergio Ilarri
Hanmin Jung
Anna Kobusinska
Juan-Ignacio Latorre-Biel
Vicente Ferreira De Lucena Jr
José Machado
Fabrizio Messina
Antonio Moreira
Marco Alfonse
Ana Azevedo
Jorge Bernardino
Chiara Braghin
Mahmoud Mounir
Hatem Mrad
Sara Paiva
Spyros Panagiotakis
Michela Piccarozzi
Carlos Filipe Portela
Nelson Rodrigues
Henrique Santos
Inna Skarga-Bandurova
George Stalidis
Cihan Tunc
Daniel Urda
Johannes Winter
Muhammad Younas

Additional Reviewers

João Almeida
Tiago Araújo
Luís Camacho
Breno Willian Carvalho
Tânia Carvalho
Nielsen Castelo
Álvaro Costa Neto
Victor Darriba
Qiaochu Fan
Joe Germino
Safwat Hamad
Marcio Inácio
João Jacob
Grigorii Khvatskii
Sorin Moga
Shamsuddeen Muhammad
Dagmar Niebur
Tiago Pinto
Francisco J. Ribadas-Pena
João Rodrigues
Nelson Rodrigues
Gabriel Santos
Jennifer Schnur
João Silva
Anna Sokol
Brígida Teixeira
Luís Trigo
Giovanni Varricchione

Sponsors

Organization

Keynotes

Machine Learning Algorithms for Brain-Machine Interfaces

Pétia Georgieva

University of Aveiro, Portugal

Abstract Brain–machine interfaces (BMIs) create alternative communication channels between the human brain and the external world. Neural activity is recorded, for example through an Electroencephalogram (EEG), and the BCI systems aim to transform these electrophysiological signals into control commands or use them to restore lost function, most commonly motor function in paralyzed patients. This talk will give an overview of the past, the present and the future of BMIs, focusing on machine learning algorithms such as Convolutional Neural Networks and Neural Autoencoders as promising approaches to build noninvasive BMIs.

Digital Twins of the Ocean

Martin Visbeck

University of Kiel, Germany

Abstract Thanks to recent advances in digitalization and improvements in ocean system model performance, the marine community is envisioning the development of Digital Twins of the Ocean (DTO) as a method to monitor and protect the world's oceans. Digital Twins (DT) are digital replicas of real-world objects. They depend critically on effective data model fusion and the compression, exploitation and presentation of data. AI and ML techniques are central to making those processes effective and as such essential to advancing DT frameworks and technology. The value of DTs comes from the ability to make informed decisions that are guided by interactions with data. And due to their easy accessibility, DTs can be used by a variety of stakeholders: by scientists to understand the ocean, by policymakers to make well-informed decisions, and by citizens to improve ocean literacy. As such, DTs present a valuable opportunity to future-proof sustainable development. Creating a DTO requires a multidisciplinary approach: data scientists to identify the gaps in ocean data and decide upon interoperable data standards, ocean modelers to improve model accuracy and resolution, IT experts to advance HPC, ML and AI infrastructures and scientific visualization experts to deliver the data in a comprehensive, user-friendly manner.

On the Use (and Misuse) of Differential Privacy in Machine Learning

Josep Domingo-Ferrer

Universitat Rovira i Virgili, Spain

Abstract Machine learning (ML) is vulnerable to security and privacy attacks. Whereas security attacks aim at preventing model convergence or forcing convergence to wrong models, privacy attacks attempt to disclose the data used to train the model. This talk will focus on privacy attacks. After reviewing them, I will examine the use of differential privacy (DP) as a methodology to protect against them, both in centralized and decentralized ML (federated learning). I will show that DP-based ML implementations do not deliver the "ex ante" privacy guarantees of DP. What they deliver is basically noise addition similar to the traditional statistical disclosure control approach. The actual level of privacy offered must be assessed "ex post", which is seldom done. I will present empirical results that show that standard anti-overfitting techniques in ML can achieve a better utility/privacy/efficiency trade-off than DP.

Learning on Graphs

Nitesh Chawla

University of Notre Dame, USA

Abstract Graphs are ubiquitous across a variety of use-cases, and have emerged as a powerful means of representing complex systems. Graph Neural Networks have demonstrated exceptional effectiveness in handling graph data; however, there are numerous challenges, from multiple data modalities to lack of labeled data. In this talk, I'll introduce our work on learning from multiple data, and also the ideas of learning from limited data, including few-shot and self-supervised learning. I'll also discuss applications of these methods.

Contents – Part II

Artifical Intelligence, Generation and Creativity

Erato: Automatizing Poetry Evaluation 3
    Manex Agirrezabal, Hugo Gonçalo Oliveira, and Aitor Ormazabal

A Path to Generative Artificial Selves 15
    Liane Gabora and Joscha Bach

Human+Non-human Creative Identities. Symbiotic Synthesis in Industrial
Design Creative Processes 30
    Alberto Calleo and Ludovica Rosato

AIGenC: AI Generalisation via Creativity 38
    Corina Cătărău-Cotuţiu, Esther Mondragón, and Eduardo Alonso

Creativity, Intentions, and Self-Narratives: Can AI *Really* Be Creative? 52
    Anaïs Giannuzzo

Evolving Urban Landscapes 64
    Jorge Santos, Rafael Murta, João M. Cunha, Sérgio M. Rebelo,
    Tiago Martins, and Pedro Martins

Emotion4MIDI: A Lyrics-Based Emotion-Labeled Symbolic Music
Dataset 77
    Serkan Sulun, Pedro Oliveira, and Paula Viana

Artificial Intelligence and Law

On the Assessment of Deep Learning Models for Named Entity
Recognition of Brazilian Legal Documents 93
    Hidelberg O. Albuquerque, Ellen Souza, Adriano L. I. Oliveira,
    David Macêdo, Cleber Zanchettin, Douglas Vitório,
    Nádia F. F. da Silva, and André C. P. L. F. de Carvalho

Anonymisation of Judicial Rulings for Legal Analytics Purposes: Ethics,
Law, and Compliance 105
    Jacopo Ciani Sciolla and Ludovica Paseri

LeSSE—A Semantic Search Engine Applied to Portuguese Consumer Law 118
    Nuno Pablo Cordeiro, João Dias, and Pedro A. Santos

Does ChatGPT Pass the Brazilian Bar Exam? 131
  Pedro Miguel Freitas and Luís Mendes Gomes

A Semantic Search System for the Supremo Tribunal de Justiça 142
  Rui Melo, Pedro A. Santos, and João Dias

Artificial Intelligence in Power and Energy Systems

The AI Act Meets General Purpose AI: The Good, The Bad and The
Uncertain 157
  Nídia Andrade Moreira, Pedro Miguel Freitas, and Paulo Novais

Rule-Based System for Intelligent Energy Management in Buildings 169
  Aria Jozi, Tiago Pinto, Luis Gomes, Goreti Marreiros, and Zita Vale

Production Scheduling for Total Energy Cost and Machine Longevity
Optimization Through a Genetic Algorithm 182
  Bruno Mota, Daniel Ramos, Pedro Faria, and Carlos Ramos

A Novel Federated Learning Approach to Enable Distributed
and Collaborative Genetic Programming 195
  Bruno Ribeiro, Luis Gomes, and Zita Vale

Artificial Intelligence in Medicine

A Scoping Review of Energy Load Disaggregation 209
  Balázs András Tolnai, Zheng Ma, and Bo Nørregaard Jørgensen

Deep Learning Survival Model to Predict Atrial Fibrillation From ECGs
and EHR Data 222
  Giovanni Baj, Arjuna Scagnetto, Luca Bortolussi, and Giulia Barbati

Generalization Ability in Medical Image Analysis with Small-Scale
Imbalanced Datasets: Insights from Neural Network Learning 234
  Tetiana Biloborodova, Bríd Brosnan, Inna Skarga-Bandurova,
  and Daniel J. Strauss

Multi-omics Data Integration and Network Inference for Biomarker
Discovery in Glioma 247
  Roberta Coletti and Marta B. Lopes

Better Medical Efficiency by Means of Hospital Bed Management
Optimization—A Comparison of Artificial Intelligence Techniques 260
    Afonso Lobo, Agostinho Barbosa, Tiago Guimarães, João Lopes,
    Hugo Peixoto, and Manuel Filipe Santos

AI-Based Medical Scribe to Support Clinical Consultations: A Proposed
System Architecture 274
    Larissa Montenegro, Luis M. Gomes, and José M. Machado

Combining Neighbor Models to Improve Predictions of Age of Onset
of ATTRv Carriers 286
    Maria Pedroto, Alípio Jorge, João Mendes-Moreira, and Teresa Coelho

Unravelling Heterogeneity: A Hybrid Machine Learning Approach
to Predict Post-discharge Complications in Cardiothoracic Surgery 298
    Bruno Ribeiro, Isabel Curioso, Ricardo Santos,
    Federico Guede-Fernández, Pedro Coelho, Jorge Santos,
    José Fragata, Ana Londral, and Inês Sousa

Leveraging TFR-BERT for ICD Diagnoses Ranking 311
    Ana Silva, Pedro Chaves, Sara Rijo, João Boné, Tiago Oliveira,
    and Paulo Novais

Artificial Intelligence and IoT in Agriculture

Evaluating the Causal Role of Environmental Data in Shellfish Biotoxin
Contamination on the Portuguese Coast 325
    Ana Rita Baião, Carolina Peixoto, Marta B. Lopes, Pedro Reis Costa,
    Alexandra M. Carvalho, and Susana Vinga

Sound-Based Anomalies Detection in Agricultural Robotics Application 338
    André Rodrigues Baltazar, Filipe Neves dos Santos,
    Salviano Pinto Soares, António Paulo Moreira,
    and José Boaventura Cunha

Can the Segmentation Improve the Grape Varieties' Identification Through
Images Acquired On-Field? 351
    Gabriel A. Carneiro, Ana Texeira, Raul Morais, Joaquim J. Sousa,
    and António Cunha

Enhancing Pest Detection Models Through Improved Annotations 364
    Dinis Costa, Catarina Silva, Joana Costa, and Bernardete Ribeiro

Deep Learning-Based Tree Stem Segmentation for Robotic Eucalyptus
Selective Thinning Operations 376
    Daniel Queirós da Silva, Tiago Ferreira Rodrigues,
    Armando Jorge Sousa, Filipe Neves dos Santos, and Vítor Filipe

Segmentation as a Pre-processing for Automatic Grape Moths Detection 388
    Ana Cláudia Teixeira, Gabriel A. Carneiro, Raul Morais,
    Joaquim J. Sousa, and António Cunha

Artificial Intelligence in Transportation Systems

Safety, Stability, and Efficiency of Taxi Rides 401
    Martin Aleksandrov and Tobias Labarta

Improving Address Matching Using Siamese Transformer Networks 413
    André V. Duarte and Arlindo L. Oliveira

An Ethical Perspective on Intelligent Transport Systems 426
    António Ribeiro da Costa, Zafeiris Kokkinogenis,
    and Rosaldo J. F. Rossetti

Using CDR Data to Understand Post-pandemic Mobility Patterns 438
    Cláudia Rodrigues, Marco Veloso, Ana Alves, and Carlos Bento

Artificial Intelligence in Smart Computing

Using Artificial Intelligence for Trust Management Systems in Fog
Computing: A Comprehensive Study 453
    Mohamed Abdel Rahman, Ahmed Dahroug, and Sherin M. Moussa

Source-Code Generation Using Deep Learning: A Survey 467
    Areeg Ahmed, Shahira Azab, and Yasser Abdelhamid

An IoT-Based Framework for Sustainable Supply Chain Management
System 483
    Muhammad Ali, Sehrish Munawar Cheema, Ivan Miguel Pires,
    Ammerha Naz, Zaheer Aslam, Nasir Ayub, and Paulo Jorge Coelho

Artificial Intelligence for Industry and Societies

Tool Wear Monitoring Using Multi-sensor Time Series and Machine
Learning 497
    Jonathan Dreyer, Stefano Carrino, Hatem Ghorbel, and Paul Cotofrei

Digital Twins: Benefits, Applications and Development Process 511
  Bo Nørregaard Jørgensen, Daniel Anthony Howard,
  Christian Skafte Beck Clausen, and Zheng Ma

Using Deep Learning for Building Stock Classification in Seismic Risk
Analysis 523
  Jorge Lopes, Feliz Gouveia, Vítor Silva, Rui S. Moreira, José M. Torres,
  Maria Guerreiro, and Luís Paulo Reis

Data Mining Models to Predict Parking Lot Availability 535
  Beatriz Rodrigues, Carlos Fernandes, José Vieira, and Filipe Portela

Advancements in Synthetic Data Extraction for Industrial Injection
Molding 548
  Rottenwalter Georg, Tilly Marcel, Bielenberg Christian,
  and Obermeier Katharina

Vision Transformers Applied to Indoor Room Classification 561
  Bruno Veiga, Tiago Pinto, Rúben Teixeira, and Carlos Ramos

Author Index 575

Contents – Part I

Ambient Intelligence and Affective Environments

Simulation-Based Adaptive Interface for Personalized Learning of AI
Fundamentals in Secondary School 3
    Sara Guerreiro-Santalla, Dalila Duraes, Helen Crompton,
    Paulo Novais, and Francisco Bellas

Gamified CollectiveEyes: A Gamified Distributed Infrastructure
for Collectively Sharing People's Eyes 16
    Risa Kimura, Tatsuo Nakajima, and Ichiro Satoh

Design and Development of Ontology for AI-Based Software Systems
to Manage the Food Intake and Energy Consumption of Obesity, Diabetes
and Tube Feeding Patients 29
    Diogo Martinho, Vítor Crista, Ziya Karakaya, Zahra Gamechi,
    Alberto Freitas, José Neves, Paulo Novais, and Goreti Marreiros

A System for Animal Health Monitoring and Emotions Detection 41
    David Sec and Peter Mikulecky

Ethics and Responsibility in Artificial Intelligence

A Three-Way Knot: Privacy, Fairness, and Predictive Performance
Dynamics 55
    Tânia Carvalho, Nuno Moniz, and Luís Antunes

A Maturity Model for Industries and Organizations of All Types to Adopt
Responsible AI—Preliminary Results 67
    Rui Miguel Frazão Dias Ferreira, António Grilo, and Maria João Maia

Completeness of Datasets Documentation on ML/AI Repositories:
An Empirical Investigation 79
    Marco Rondina, Antonio Vetrò, and Juan Carlos De Martin

Navigating the Landscape of AI Ethics and Responsibility 92
    Paulo Rupino Cunha and Jacinto Estima

Towards Interpretability in Fintech Applications via Knowledge
Augmentation 106
    Catarina Silva, Tiago Faria, and Bernardete Ribeiro

General Artificial Intelligence

Revisiting Deep Attention Recurrent Networks 121
  Fernando Fradique Duarte, Nuno Lau, Artur Pereira, and Luís Paulo Reis

Pre-training with Augmentations for Efficient Transfer in Model-Based
Reinforcement Learning 133
  Bernardo Esteves, Miguel Vasco, and Francisco S. Melo

DyPrune: Dynamic Pruning Rates for Neural Networks 146
  Richard Adolph Aires Jonker, Roshan Poudel, Olga Fajarda,
  José Luís Oliveira, Rui Pedro Lopes, and Sérgio Matos

Robustness Analysis of Machine Learning Models Using Domain-Specific
Test Data Perturbation 158
  Marian Lambert, Thomas Schuster, Marcus Kessel, and Colin Atkinson

Vocalization Features to Recognize Small Dolphin Species for Limited
Datasets 171
  Luís Rosário, Sofia Cavaco, Joaquim Silva, Luís Freitas,
  and Philippe Verborgh

Covariance Kernel Learning Schemes for Gaussian Process Based
Prediction Using Markov Chain Monte Carlo 184
  Gargi Roy, Kane Warrior, and Dalia Chakrabarty

Intelligent Robotics

A Review on Quadruped Manipulators 199
  Maria S. Lopes, António Paulo Moreira, Manuel F. Silva,
  and Filipe Santos

Knowledge Discovery and Business Intelligence

Pollution Emission Patterns of Transportation in Porto, Portugal Through
Network Analysis 215
  Thiago Andrade, Nirbhaya Shaji, Rita P. Ribeiro, and João Gama

Analysis of Dam Natural Frequencies Using a Convolutional Neural
Network 227
  Gonçalo Cabaço, Sérgio Oliveira, André Alegre, João Marcelino,
  João Manso, and Nuno Marques

Imbalanced Regression Evaluation Under Uncertain Domain Preferences 239
  Nuno Costa and Nuno Moniz

Studying the Impact of Sampling in Highly Frequent Time Series 251
  Paulo J. S. Ferreira, João Mendes-Moreira, and Arlete Rodrigues

Mining Causal Links Between TV Sports Content and Real-World Data 263
  Duarte Melo, Jessica C. Delmoral, and João Vinagre

Hybrid SkipAwareRec: A Streaming Music Recommendation System 275
  Rui Ramos, Lino Oliveira, and João Vinagre

Interpreting What is Important: An Explainability Approach and Study
on Feature Selection 288
  Eduardo M. Rodrigues, Yassine Baghoussi, and João Mendes-Moreira

Time-Series Pattern Verification in CNC Machining Data 299
  *João Miguel Silva, Ana Rita Nogueira, José Pinto,
  António Correia Alves, and Ricardo Sousa*

A Comparison of Automated Machine Learning Tools for Predicting
Energy Building Consumption in Smart Cities 311
  Daniela Soares, Pedro José Pereira, Paulo Cortez, and Carlos Gonçalves

Measuring Latency-Accuracy Trade-Offs in Convolutional Neural
Networks 323
  André Tse, Lino Oliveira, and João Vinagre

MultiAgent Systems: Theory and Applications

Machine Learning Data Markets: Evaluating the Impact of Data Exchange
on the Agent Learning Performance 337
  Hajar Baghcheband, Carlos Soares, and Luís Paulo Reis

Multi-robot Adaptive Sampling for Supervised Spatiotemporal Forecasting 349
  Siva Kailas, Wenhao Luo, and Katia Sycara

Natural Language Processing, Text Mining and Applications

Topic Model with Contextual Outlier Handling: a Study on Electronic
Invoice Product Descriptions 365
  Cesar Andrade, Rita P. Ribeiro, and João Gama

Tweet2Story: Extracting Narratives from Twitter 378
Vasco Campos, Ricardo Campos, and Alípio Jorge

Argumentation Mining from Textual Documents Combining Deep
Learning and Reasoning 389
Filipe Cerveira do Amaral, H. Sofia Pinto, and Bruno Martins

Event Extraction for Portuguese: A QA-Driven Approach Using ACE-2005 402
Luís Filipe Cunha, Ricardo Campos, and Alípio Jorge

Symbolic Versus Deep Learning Techniques for Explainable Sentiment
Analysis 415
Shamsuddeen Hassan Muhammad, Pavel Brazdil, and Alípio Jorge

Assessing Good, Bad and Ugly Arguments Generated by ChatGPT: a New
Dataset, its Methodology and Associated Tasks 428
*Victor Hugo Nascimento Rocha, Igor Cataneo Silveira, Paulo Pirozelli,
Denis Deratani Mauá, and Fabio Gagliardi Cozman*

Advancing Neural Encoding of Portuguese with Transformer Albertina
PT-* 441
*João Rodrigues, Luís Gomes, João Silva, António Branco,
Rodrigo Santos, Henrique Lopes Cardoso, and Tomás Osório*

OSPT: European Portuguese Paraphrastic Dataset with Machine
Translation 454
Afonso Sousa and Henrique Lopes Cardoso

Task Conditioned BERT for Joint Intent Detection and Slot-Filling 467
*Diogo Tavares, Pedro Azevedo, David Semedo, Ricardo Sousa,
and João Magalhães*

Planning, Scheduling and Decision-Making in AI

Data-driven Single Machine Scheduling Minimizing Weighted Number
of Tardy Jobs 483
Nikolai Antonov, Přemysl Šucha, and Mikoláš Janota

Heuristic Search Optimisation Using Planning and Curriculum Learning
Techniques 495
Leah Chrestien, Tomáš Pevný, Stefan Edelkamp, and Antonín Komenda

Social Simulation and Modelling

Review of Agent-Based Evacuation Models in Python   511
  Josef Janda and Kamila Štekerová

Author Index   523

Artifical Intelligence, Generation and Creativity

Erato: Automatizing Poetry Evaluation

Manex Agirrezabal[1]([⊠])(iD), Hugo Gonçalo Oliveira[2,3](iD), and Aitor Ormazabal[3]

[1] CST, University of Copenhagen, Copenhagen, Denmark
manex.aguirrezabal@hum.ku.dk
[2] CISUC, DEI, University of Coimbra, Coimbra, Portugal
hroliv@dei.uc.pt
[3] University of the Basque Country (UPV/EHU), Donostia, Spain
abc@uni-heidelberg.de,lncs@uni-heidelberg.de

Abstract. We present Erato, a framework designed to facilitate the automated evaluation of poetry, including that generated by poetry generation systems. Our framework employs a diverse set of features, and we offer a brief overview of Erato's capabilities and its potential for expansion. Using Erato, we compare and contrast human-authored poetry with automatically-generated poetry, demonstrating its effectiveness in identifying key differences. Our implementation code and software are freely available under the GNU GPLv3 license.

Keywords: Evaluation · Poetry · Automatic poetry evaluation

1 Introduction

Poem composition typically exploits several levels of language, from lexical to semantics, pragmatics, and aesthetics in general. Therefore, the evaluation of poetry is subjective and poses many challenges. However, when it comes to computer-generated poetry, shortcuts need to be taken to reach conclusions on the quality of results, i.e., how well the produced poems actually employ poetic features, how they reflect the input parameters, including the desired message (e.g., given in the form of a topic, a theme, a prompt), and how they compare to human-written poetry. Relevant aspects include the presence of a regular metre and rhymes, fluency and meaning, among others, like novelty towards an inspiration set or other creations by the same system.

The challenges of poetry evaluation have been acknowledged [5,16], and researchers typically end up resorting to human opinions. Given the subjective nature of the goal, this is a fair decision. This adds to experiments where low correlation between human assessments and automatic metrics was noted [11]. Still, we argue that automatic metrics, depending on how they are interpreted, can at least support the creation of automatic poetry generation models.

N. Moniz et al. (Eds.): EPIA 2023, LNAI 14116, pp. 3–14, 2023.
https://doi.org/10.1007/978-3-031-49011-8_1

This paper describes Erato,[1] a framework that aims to make the evaluation of poetry easier. Having in mind that such evaluation cannot rely on a single aspect or metric, Erato offers a set of Python scripts for assessing different complementary aspects. Some are language-specific and others are not. Some analyze a single poem independently and others are based on a set of poems. Also, the scripts can be classified according to the type of aspect of study, namely: poetic, novelty-related, lexico-semantics and fluency-related features. We further make a distinction between analyzing poems and evaluating them. While the former does not need expectations, the latter checks whether certain output is satisfied (e.g., are stanzas organized in a specific way? Does the poem follow a rhythmic pattern?).

Erato is open-source with a number of already implemented and ready to use scripts. The inclusion of new features is made to be straightforward, easing the addition of language/culture dependent features that one may want to analyze. Towards their adaptation to different purposes, underlying resources (e.g., lexicons or semantic models) can be changed, and the provided interfaces can be re-implemented following a set of guidelines. For illustrating what we can do with Erato, the paper further describes its usage in the analysis of human-written poems and poems automatically generated by two computational systems, in two different languages.

The paper is structured as follows: some related work on poetry evaluation is reviewed; based on previous research, we attempt to characterize good poems; we present Erato and its architecture, together with implementation details; we describe a case study involving the application of Erato to human-authored poetry and poetry by two computational systems; and we conclude by discussing possible future directions.

2 Related Work

Many authors in the Computational Creativity community have acknowledged the difficulty of evaluating creative outcomes [21,27]. When assessing an artifact, one can look at its quality based on pre-established conditions, unexpectedness, reactions of the public, and so on. Researchers in this community have proposed several methods for this. Some emphasized the evaluation of creativity [1,4, 11,15,24], others went more into detail, and proposed methods for evaluating poetry, specifically [8,11,18,25].

Supported by the low correlation between human judges and automatic metrics, many authors resorted to human judges [12,13,25], while others combined it with automatic evaluation. Perplexity was employed as sanity check, followed by BLEU [28,29], both on some reference text. Another string similarity metric, ROUGE, was used for computing novelty in generated poems [7,8]; concepts have been assessed with the master-apprentice method [10]; and, in order to assess the impact of an input theme, semantic similarity was computed between the used theme and titles given by humans to generated poems [7].

---

[1] https://www.github.com/manexagirrezabal/erato

To the best of our knowledge, there is no framework for evaluating poetry in an automatic way. Erato aims to fill this gap, with inspiration in previous work [8], but extending it and further releasing the scripts, so that future researchers of the field can benefit from it.

3   What Characterizes a Good Poem?

Poetry is a form of literature that uses different elements of language to convey a message and a feeling. The elements of language that typically characterize poetry are rhythm, rhyme and different types of figures of speech. These usually form recurring patterns, caused by the deliberate way in which poets arrange their information. The question of whether a poem is good or not does not have a trivial answer. We believe, though, that it is possible to define features to make this question more quantifiable, to some degree. We depart from well-established features [18], and propose a similar set that we believe could be employed to assess a poem.

It is widely accepted that generated poetry should satisfy the properties of meaningfulness, grammaticality, and poeticness [18]. We address these three aspects from a practical perspective, and following more recent work [8], include a new aspect, novelty.

Poetic features, similar to *poeticness* [18]: Poetry is commonly arranged in a different way to prose. Common aspects to consider include the number of stanzas and their shape, often regarding the number of syllables. Apart from that, as there is a number of recurring patterns that poems follow, the analysis of rhythm, in particular stresses and feet, and rhymes constitute two valued aspects. These elements, though, should be considered with a grain of salt, as different cultures and traditions have their own aspects of interest.

Lexico/semantic features, related to meaningfulness [18]: Semantic features have different levels of granularity and complexity. Poems should convey a certain message. Thus, if we randomly combine a set of lines from different poems and compose a new one out of that, chances are low that a coherent and understandable message is conveyed, with a negative impact on quality. Apart from abstract semantic aspects, word choice plays a crucial role in poetry, as writers commonly resort to unusual words, often to satisfy sound related constraints. The deviation of word usage in comparison to regular language could be used as another measure of quality of a poem. This aspect would be related to the .

Poetic fluency, similar to *grammaticality* [18]: Checking the correctness of utterances in poetry is important, especially because the conveyed message might be affected if no proper morphology or syntax is used, but the control of poetic licenses is not straightforward. Therefore, we suggest to control this aspect by checking whether the text does "sound like poetry".

Novelty features: Also mentioned as *imagination* [3], we argue that novelty[2] is a very influential for the assessment of a poem. In poetry, it can be regarded in different levels. We may consider it within a poem, where we check whether there is variation across lines or it may be analyzed across poems by the same author. If an author writes a very good poem and, every year they publish it, we can safely state that they are not creating new poems. Novelty can also consider poems in the world, i.e., if an author writes the same as another, it could be seen as plagiarism.

4 Erato: A Framework for Poetry Evaluation

Erato is a framework for the automatic evaluation of poetry, having in mind poetry generators, but also applicable to human-authored poetry. It implements some ideas of previous work [8], in order to offer the evaluation of a range of relevant aspects in poems. This is useful, for instance, for developers of poetry generators, which may use Erato for assessing the results by their systems, before resorting to human evaluation. It includes the implementation of some aspects for the analysis of poetry, but its modular architecture makes the inclusion of new ones straightforward. Included aspects can be divided into four groups, described in the previous section: poetic features, novelty features, lexico/semantics, and poetic fluency.

Erato is a software package that can be called from the terminal,[3] and be used to analyze or evaluate a single poem, or to analyze several poems by the same author. When one analyzes a poem, there is no specific expectation, but, for evaluation, there should be a target goal (either a specific value, or a range of acceptable values). Erato is designed in a way that, once the analyzer function is written in a script, the implementation of the evaluator is very easy. Already implemented scripts for analysis are organized in two main groups: Single poem analyzers, which analyze a poem as a single element; and global poem analyzers, which require a collection of poems. Each of these types of analyzer may then be divided into the four aforementioned aspects. Finally, some scripts are language/culture dependent, while others are not.

4.1 General Structure

When we start Erato, we are given the option of analyzing a single poem or a collection of poems. Before starting any analysis, all relevant modules are loaded. The relevant modules are specified in the modules package in the `__init__.py` file. In that file, two dictionaries are defined, one for single poem analyzers and another one for poem collection analyzers. The keys of each dictionary are actual aspects: `poetic_features`, `novelty_features`, `fluency_features` and

---

[2] We evaluate novelty from the outcomes' perspective, and without considering the recipient of the poem. In future versions of Erato, novelty could be further evaluated using Expectation-Based models [9].

[3] We have an experimental version that can be used as a web application.

`lexsem_features` and each of those would contain a list of actual Python files that perform one specific analysis. For instance, `"models/lindep/lineCounter.py"`, `"models/lindep/stanzaCounter.py"` and `"models/en/syllableCounter.py"` are examples of already implemented poetic features.

Each of these files should have the following structure. There has to be a class called `evaluator`. This class must contain two static methods: `analyze` and `evaluate`. The `analyze` function should return a tuple of two elements. A name for the analyzer and the actual result. The `evaluate` function should call the internally defined analyze function and to compare it to a given expected output.[4] In the evaluation function it would be possible to define some evaluation criteria, for instance, in the previous example of line counting, we could return 1 if the number of lines is 14, and 0 if it is not.

4.2   Available Modules

Erato currently includes scripts for checking some poetic features, novelty features and semantic features. We are planning to extend the fluency detector.

Poetic features We include a stanza, line and syllable counter, a scansion model and a rhyme checker. The syllable counter is currently implemented for English,[5] and few other languages. The scansion model is only available for English.[6] We perform rhyme analysis using an existing tool [22]. For each poem, we calculate: (1) the number of rhyme patterns[7]; (2) the ratio of rhyming lines, or rhyme richness.

Novelty features Novelty is based on the *structure variation* method [8]. It is analyzed on the overlapping n-grams, based on ROUGE [17], a common metric to evaluate how overlapping two sentences are in terms of n-grams. ROUGE is computed within the poem —to inform about possible repetition within it— but also across poems by the same author/system. We are thus able to detect whether poems are very similar to each other (i.e., if ROUGE scores are high), or if they are novel (i.e., if the scores are low). We call these two aspects intrapoem novelty and interpoem novelty, respectively.

When we analyze novelty internally, we attempt to find whether patterns are repeated within a poem. When we do it across poems, the goal is to check how repetitive the poems are with respect to each other. We calculate the novelty of a single poem as the average ROUGE score (f1-score) of all line pairs in a single poem, except a line with itself. Following the details from [8], we calculate

---

[4] We are currently working on a generic evaluate class, especially because the evaluate function is very similar in many cases, but it is still in trial period.

[5] It is an implementation that relies on the CMU pronunciation dictionary [26].

[6] Simple model relying on lexical stress from CMU dictionary.

[7] A rhyme pattern is counted if it appears at least two times in the poem.

novelty across poems in three different ways. (1) Single string,[8] (2) line by line,[9] and (3) all lines.[10]

Semantic features Semantic evaluation relies on semantic textual similarity and has some resemblance to *topicality* [8]. For this, Erato expects poems to be associated with a specific topic and it performs an information retrieval task where the top-k poems for the target topic are predicted. This is evaluated in terms of the F1-score, and the main assumption is that, if the text is indeed related to a specific topic, the poem retriever should be able to perform perfectly. Therefore, the greater performance we get, the better the poems are. In the current implementation, we encode each topic and each poem with sentence-BERT (multilingual) [23],[11] and then, we compute the similarity between these topics and the poems.

4.3   Extending Erato for Specific Purposes

One of the main advantages of using Erato as a framework is how simple it is to extend it for specific purposes. Suppose that we want to adopt a more elaborate syllable counter for English. To incorporate it, the first step is to get a template of a module, available in a provided file.[12] In that file, we need to implement the function `analyze`, and the produced output should be returned as a tuple, where the first element includes a string with the performed analysis (e.g., *syllable-count*) and the second element contains the output (in this case, the number of syllables). Finally, the current file should be linked, as mentioned before, in the `__init__.py` file from the `modules` package.

5   Case Study: Human and Machine Poetry

As Erato can be used to analyze poetry, we can use its results as a method for understanding the differences between different types of poetry. To illustrate what we can do with Erato, we conducted a simple experiment, where we use it for analyzing and comparing poetry produced by humans and by machines, in English and Spanish. The following subsections introduce the setup of this experiment and the result of the analysis.

---

[8] Each poem is considered as a single string, and evaluated directly.

[9] In this case, the ROUGE metric between two poems is calculated line by line, and if a poem has more lines than the other, the last lines of the longest poem are ignored.

[10] We compute the cartesian product of all lines between two poems and calculate the ROUGE metric based on that.

[11] This Transformer-model, `sentence-transformers/distiluse-base-multilingual-cased-v1`. performed best in a similar experiment on a subset of: https://www.kaggle.com/datasets/michaelarman/poemsdataset. It may, however, be changed in the future.

[12] https://github.com/manexagirrezabal/erato/tree/master/models/modeltemplate.py.

5.1   Computer-Generated Poetry

For computer-generated poems, we resorted to two available APIs: PoeTryMe [6], for a system that generates poems in Portuguese, Spanish and English; and OpenAI's GPT3[13] [2], a large language model that can be used for generating text given specific prompts. We created poems using the same seed words as in previous work [8].[14] and added three—virus, pandemic and facemask—to see how the models behave with current topics. From each API, we generated 10 poems for each seed word and for each language.

For PoeTryMe, we used a surprise factor of 0.005 and requested always a poem with the structure of a sonnet, using the target seed. For OpenAI, we used the Davinci engine[15] with a temperature of 0.7, and we set the maximum number of tokens to 300, which was more or less what we expect a sonnet to have. As the GPT3 model is not trained to generate poetry, we used a prompt requesting a sonnet in English or Spanish, respectively *"Write a sonnet about"* and *"Escribe un soneto sobre"*, followed by the seed word.

5.2   Human-Written Poetry

Poems by well-known authors were also used in the experiment. For English, we created a corpus with poems by William Shakespeare, Emily Dickinson and Edgar Allan Poe. For Spanish, we selected a number of poems from the Spanish Golden Age. This subset was based on previously obtained author clusters [19], but only a small number was selected, to have a comparable size.

5.3   Analysis

We used Erato for analyzing the computer-generated and the human-written poems. Considering what is currently implemented, we discuss the poetic, the novelty, and the semantic features below. The included visualizations refer only for the English data.

On the stanza structure, PoeTryMe seems to follow the sonnet pattern exactly, meaning that each poem has three stanzas with four lines each, except the last one with two lines, as it can be seen in Fig. 1a. The same happens for Spanish and English. As meter is not explicitly controlled by GPT3, and as the model itself is not specifically designed for metrical poetry generation, these numbers vary greatly in GPT3's output. Some poems contain a single stanza with several lines, while others are composed by a number of independent lines (as if one stanza had a single line). Human poems in Spanish are sonnets, so the stanzas follow the exact same structure (i.e., two stanzas with four lines and two with three lines). English poems by Shakespeare (only sonnets, 14 lines) and by Emily Dickinson (generally 3-6 paragraphs with 4 lines each) have a stable stanza structure, while Poe's work is more variable in this regard. This can be observed in Fig. 1b.

---

[13] https://openai.com/api/.

[14] The seeds were: *love, artificial, blue, sing, computer, build, football, read, new, poetry.*

[15] https://beta.openai.com/docs/engines/gpt-3.

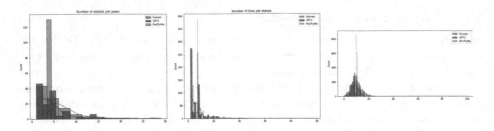

Fig. 1. a Stanza count, **b** Lines per stanza, **c** Syllables per line

On the number of syllables, in Fig. 1c, we can observe that the majority of lines by PoeTryMe has a very strict metre in the number of syllables. Human poets and GPT3 follow a more free verse.

We also analyzed the differences in rhymes by checking their number in each poem. Figure 2a shows how many different rhyme patterns appear for each poem on average. Figure 2b has the ratio of rhyming lines.[16] Based on rhyme richness, GPT3 poems seem to be the poorest among all, with a distribution skewed towards 0.0.

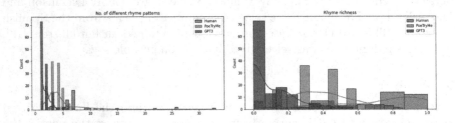

Fig. 2. a Different rhyme patterns, **b** Rhyme richness

We compute ROUGE for measuring the overlap of the poems within themselves (intra poem[17]) and within other poems made by the same system/author (or inter poem). The main clear conclusion is that human authors are the least repetitive, both inside poems and across poems. We further observe that PoeTryMe in Spanish results in plenty of repetition within a poem, in comparison to other methods or languages. The average ROUGE-1 score is 0.17, higher than for English (0.05) (Fig. 3). This makes sense because the size of PoeTryMe's grammar and semantic network for Spanish are much smaller [8]. A common observation is that GPT-3 tends to generate repetitive content across poems compared to human authors or PoeTryMe. However, adjusting the temperature parameter could potentially reduce this effect, although it may also impact the overall quality of the generated poems. Additionally, further refinement of the prompt engineering process could lead to more diverse and unique outcomes.

---

[16] 1.0 means that all lines rhyme with each other, 0.0 means that none rhyme.

[17] For illustration, Fig. 3 shows how the intra poem ROUGE results look like.

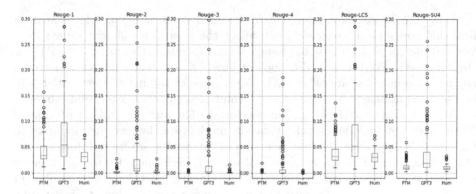

Fig. 3. Boxplot of Intra ROUGE scores for each of the three different authors

With regards to semantic evaluation, we retrieved poems for each topic, given a predefined list.[18] Macro F1-scores were between 0.7 and 0.8 for both GPT3 and PoeTryMe. For the former, the semantic model was especially good at distinguishing poems about "blue" (F1-score=0.95). For the same word, in the Spanish PoeTryMe, the model did not guess a single case. With this evaluation, we would be able to see that PoeTryMe has limitations for generating poems on certain topics. It produces generally well-sounding poems, but this can be done at the expense of less accurate semantics. Something similar happens with the word *facemask* in the English version of PoeTryMe. Further analysis of precision and recall could shed further light on the underlying reasons of this behaviour. We additionally performed some basic analysis at the type/token level and saw the following Type/Token Ratios for the three poetry sources: 0.130, 0.257 and 0.237 for GPT3, PoetryMe and humans, respectively. We can say that when GPT3 is required to write a sonnet, it resorts to similar words. PoeTryMe compares well to humans in this aspect.

6 Conclusion and Future Directions

We present Erato,[19] a framework for the automatic analysis and evaluation of poetry. It comes with a number of already implemented modules, and the addition of new ones is straightforward. We invite researchers working in the automatic generation of poetry to use Erato as a midway step to check how their systems work before resorting to human evaluators. In a case study, we mentioned the output of some of the metrics. We argue that there is no perfect metric, but the more metrics we employ, the better understanding of the poems we get. Thus, a sufficiently large number of automatic metrics should provide a sufficiently good understanding of quality in poetry.

---

[18] Poems about each topic are organized in folders and topics are given as text.
[19] https://github.com/manexagirrezabal/erato.

Now that Erato is available with different metrics, it is possible to analyze how different sets of parameters can affect the poems in different dimensions. For instance, a possibility is to change the temperature parameter in GPT3 or the surprise in PoeTryMe and to look at how different metrics, such as novelty, rhymes or semantics, are affected. Besides, some of the metrics presented here can be used as fitness functions for an evolutionary poetry generation model.

Many aspects could be further developed. The current implementation of Erato does not include any visualization mechanism, but we are planning to include this as part of the first release so that results are more interpretable. Besides, at the current stage, when evaluation is performed, Erato only accepts equality as condition. For example, in some poetic traditions, the number of syllables of a line does not need to have an exact number, but it needs to be within a range of numbers. We expect to soon accommodate this type of issues. Furthermore, we have an experimental version that allows using Erato as a web application, which allows us to reach a wider audience (e.g. people without programming experience).

We are also planning to implement a fluency detector, based on a Large Language Model. We are very aware that this will be very dependent on the type of corpus we use for fine-tuning, and because of that we intend to use a corpus of poetry that is as varied as possible, for instance [14,20].

When computing novelty metrics, as there might be several files, this computation can become extremely resource-intensive, as we compare all poems with all others. To make this more efficient, we are considering undersampling methods, which, instead of going through all lines and all files, will focus on a random selection of all.

Acknowledgements. This work was partially supported by the EU-funded Marie Skłodowska-Curie Action project EA-Digifolk, Grant agreement ID 101086338.

References

1. Baer, J., Kaufman, J.C.: Assessing creativity with the consensual assessment technique. In: The Palgrave Handbook of Social Creativity Research, pp. 27–37. Springer (2019)
2. Brown, T., Mann, B., Ryder, N., Subbiah, M., Kaplan, J.D., Dhariwal, P., Neelakantan, A., et al.: Language models are few-shot learners. Adv. Neural. Inf. Process. Syst. **33**, 1877–1901 (2020)
3. Colton, S.: Creativity versus the perception of creativity in computational systems. In: AAAI Spring Symposium: Creative Intelligent Systems, vol. 8, p. 7. Palo Alto, CA (2008)
4. Colton, S., Charnley, J.W., Pease, A.: Computational creativity theory: the FACE and IDEA descriptive models. In: ICCC, pp. 90–95. Mexico City (2011)
5. Gonçalo Oliveira, H.: A survey on intelligent poetry generation: languages, features, techniques, reutilisation and evaluation. In: Proceedings of 10th International Conference on Natural Language Generation, pp. 11–20. INLG 2017, ACL Press, Santiago de Compostela, Spain (2017)

 6. Gonçalo Oliveira, H.: A REST service for poetry generation. In: Proceedings of 6th Symposium on Languages, Applications and Technologies (SLATE 2017). Schloss Dagstuhl-Leibniz-Zentrum fuer Informatik (2017)
 7. Gonçalo Oliveira, H.: Exploring a masked language model for creative text transformation. In: Proceedings of 12th International Conference on Computational Creativity (ICCC '21). Association for Computational Creativity (2021)
 8. Gonçalo Oliveira, H., Hervás, R., Díaz, A., Gervás, P.: Multilingual extension and evaluation of a poetry generator. Nat. Lang. Eng. **23**(6), 929–967 (2017)
 9. Grace, K., Maher, M.L.: Expectation-based models of novelty for evaluating computational creativity. In: Computational Creativity: The Philosophy and Engineering of Autonomously Creative Systems, pp. 195–209 (2019)
10. Hämäläinen, M., Alnajjar, K.: Let's FACE it. Finnish poetry generation with Aesthetics and Framing. In: Proceedings of 12th International Conference on Natural Language Generation, pp. 290–300 (2019)
11. Hämäläinen, M., Alnajjar, K.: Human evaluation of creative NLG systems: An interdisciplinary survey on recent papers. In: Proceedings of 1st Workshop on Natural Language Generation, Evaluation, and Metrics (GEM 2021), pp. 84–95. ACL, Online (2021)
12. Hämäläinen, M., Alnajjar, K., et al.: Generating modern poetry automatically in Finnish. In: Proceedings of 2019 Conference on Empirical Methods in Natural Language Processing and 9th International Joint Conference on Natural Language Processing Proceedings Conference. ACL (2019)
13. Hämäläinen, M., et al.: Harnessing NLG to create Finnish poetry automatically. In: Proceedings of 9th International Conference on Computational Creativity. ACC (2018)
14. Jacobs, A.M.: The Gutenberg English poetry corpus: exemplary quantitative narrative analyses. Front. Digit. Hum. **5**, 5 (2018)
15. Lamb, C., Brown, D.G., Clarke, C.L.: Evaluating digital poetry: Insights from the CAT. In: Proceedings of 7th International Conference on Computational Creativity. ACC (2016)
16. Lamb, C., Brown, D.G., Clarke, C.L.: A taxonomy of generative poetry techniques. J. Math. Arts **11**(3), 159–179 (2017)
17. Lin, C.Y., Och, F.J.: Automatic evaluation of machine translation quality using longest common subsequence and skip-bigram statistics. In: Proceedings of 42nd Annual Meeting of the Association for Computational Linguistics (ACL-04), pp. 605–612. ACL (2004)
18. Manurung, R.: An evolutionary algorithm approach to poetry generation. Ph.D. thesis, School of informatics, University of Edinburgh (2003)
19. Navarro, B.: A computational linguistic approach to Spanish golden age sonnets: metrical and semantic aspects. In: Proceedings of 4th Workshop on Computational Linguistics for Literature, pp. 105–113 (2015)
20. Parrish, A.: Project Gutenberg poetry corpus (2016), https://github.com/aparrish/gutenberg-poetry-corpus
21. Pease, A., Colton, S.: On impact and evaluation in computational creativity: a discussion of the turing test and an alternative proposal. In: Proceedings of AISB symposium on AI and Philosophy, vol. 39. Citeseer (2011)
22. Plecháč, P.: A collocation-driven method of discovering rhymes (in Czech, English, and French poetry). In: Taming the Corpus: From Inflection and Lexis to Interpretation, pp. 79–95 (2018)

23. Reimers, N., Gurevych, I.: Sentence-BERT: sentence embeddings using Siamese BERT-networks. In: Proceedings of 2019 Conference on Empirical Methods in Natural Language Processing and 9th International Joint Conference on Natural Language Processing (EMNLP-IJCNLP), pp. 3982–3992. ACL, Hong Kong, China (2019)
24. Ritchie, G.D.: Assessing creativity. In: Proceedings of AISB Symposium on AI and Creativity in Art and Science. Society for the Study of Artificial Intelligence and Simulation of Behaviour (2001)
25. Toivanen, J., Toivonen, H., Valitutti, A., Gross, O., et al.: Corpus-based generation of content and form in poetry. In: Proceedings of 3rd International Conference on Computational Creativity. University College Dublin (2012)
26. Weide, R.: The CMU Pronunciation Dictionary, rel. 0.6 (1998)
27. Wiggins, G.A.: A preliminary framework for description, analysis and comparison of creative systems. Knowl.-Based Syst. **19**(7), 449–458 (2006)
28. Yan, R.: I, Poet: Automatic poetry composition through recurrent neural networks with iterative polishing schema. In: Proceedings of 25th International Joint Conference on Artificial Intelligence, pp. 2238–2244. IJCAI 2016, IJCAI/AAAI Press (2016)
29. Zhang, X., Lapata, M.: Chinese poetry generation with recurrent neural networks. In: Proceedings of 2014 Conference on Empirical Methods in Natural Language Processing, pp. 670–680. EMNLP 2014, ACL (2014)

A Path to Generative Artificial Selves

Liane Gabora[1]([⊠])(iD) and Joscha Bach[2,3](iD)

[1] University of British Columbia, Kelowna V1V 1V7, Canada
liane.gabora@ubc.ca
[2] Thistledown Foundation, Ottawa K1P 1H4, Canada
joscha.bach@gmail.com
[3] ABC Institute, Rupert-Karls-University Heidelberg, Heidelberg, Germany

Abstract. Artificial intelligence output are undeniably creative, but it has been argued that creativity should be assessed in terms of, not external products, but internal self-transformation through immersion in a creative task. Self-transformation requires a self, which we define as a bounded, self-organizing, self-preserving agent that is distinct from, and interacts with, its environment. The paper explores how self-hood, as well as self-transformation as a result of creative tasks, could be achieved in a machine using autocatalytic networks. The autocatalytic framework is ideal for modeling systems that exhibit emergent network formation and growth. The approach readily scales up, and it can analyze and detect phase transitions in vastly complex networks that have proven intractable with other approaches. Autocatalytic networks have been applied to both (1) the origin of life and the onset of biological evolution, and (2) the origin of minds sufficiently complex and integrated to participate in cultural evolution. The first entails the emergence of self-hood at the level of the soma, or body, while the second entails the emergence of self-hood at the level of a mental models of the world, or *worldview;* we suggest that humans possess both. We discuss the feasibility of an AI with creative agency and self-hood at the second (cognitive) level, but not the first (somatic) level.

Keywords: Agency · Autocatalytic Network · Artificial Intelligence · Cognitive Architecture · Creativity · Domain-generality · Self-hood

1 Introduction

Artificial intelligence (AI) programs such as Dall•E-2 and ChatGPT have captivated the public with their large knowledge base and at times almost human-like expressivity, and flamed concerns about machine agency. This paper explores what it takes for AI to be genuinely creative and in possession of self-hood in the way that humans are. The two questions are related, in the sense that creativity is widely believed to be central to what makes us uniquely human.

Supported by the Natural Sciences and Engineering Research Council of Canada, grant number GR01855.

The paper lay out an argument for considering current AI models merely tools, despite being capable of disruptive novelty. It then sketches a tentative research program aimed at enabling an artificial neural network (ANN) to achieve creativity and selfhood. The paper does not directly address the relationship between creative agency and artificial general intelligence or machine consciousness. It also does not address ethical issues pertaining to AI selfhood, but focuses on its scientific feasibility.

2   Creativity as Restructuring a Manifold

Many AI systems are creative in terms of their outputs, and indeed, psychologists commonly define creativity according to the usefulness and originality of the products resulting from creative thought [41]. However, it is not universally agreed that creativity should be defined in terms of the products that result from creative thought. This definition has pitfalls; for example, it leads one to conclude that if Person X invents a new widget, and it turns out that widget was invented earlier by Person W, then (even if X was ignorant of W's work), X is no longer considered to have engaged in creative thought (because X's version was no longer new).

There is a tradition in India [42], which has been adopted by some cognitive scientists (e.g., [9]), of assessing creativity in terms of not external outputs, but internal (often therapeutic) restructuring. For the creator, the product facilitates the tracking of cognitive change, and in others, the creative product may prompt reciprocal cognitive change. Thus, a process is considered creative to the extent that it:

1. Is sparked by a gap, challenge, or opportunity for restructuring one's perspective or ability at the cognitive or somatic (body) level, shifting the state of the creator, such that the same act, repeated, would be no longer creative;

2. Transcends rote strategies, and bridges a discontinuity in a search space;

Such a process will often result in a creative output, but it is possible (particularly midway through a creative process) that the fruits of creative processing cannot (yet) be expressed or articulated.

To some degree, AIs appear to meet these criteria; they are structured in a way that enables them to transcend rote strategies and bridge discontinuities. Current generative models organize representations as embeddings: high dimensional manifolds in which similar contents are adjacent, with each dimension corresponds to a (continuous or discrete) feature parameter [35]. The discovery of a suitable embedding space requires decomposing the space of representations into suitably parameterizable functions. Problem solving often follows a gradient through this manifold by gradually changing the parameters of a functional dimension as long as the result keeps improving.

We posit that creativity—whether human or AI—aims at restructuring the manifold, by discovering new functional dimensions, or consolidating the space by reorganizing its functions into a more adequate, useful or coherent structure, or simply observing the outcome of modifications to the representations. In scientific and technological creativity this tends to involve elements of world models that are common to all (e.g., we all experience that objects fall due to gravity), while in the arts they are more likely to involve personal experiences; nonetheless, both aim to restructure the manifold, and both result in meaningful change.

Note, however, that in AI creativity, this change is meaningful to the *user*, not to the AI, and process is instigated by the user, not the AI itself. Building on early ideas about the importance of self-hood for AI [18], we suggest that for an AI to be creative in the sense that it is meaningfully transformed through engagement in a creative task, it must possess a self. Let us now take a closer look at what self-hood entails.

3   Selfhood

A first step toward an AI that is transformed through engagement in a creative task is an autonomous agentic self. The terms 'autonomous' and 'agency' are used commonly to refer to an AI that, given a meta-instruction, makes the necessary lower-level decisions to carry it out [53]. For example, if prompted to design a profitable business, an auto-GPT might decide what kind of business would be most profitable, design a product, find suppliers, develop a marketing plan, and so forth. However, it was still *your* decision to start a business. By *autonomous agentic self*, we mean an AI that is a bounded, self-organizing, self-preserving agent that is distinct from, and interacts with, its environment. It carries out actions because *it* wants to.

An autonomous agentic self senses and interacts with its world, and strives to preserve its integrity as a structure separate from other structures. This is related to the concepts of agency and embodiment (having a body that acts upon, and is acted upon by, its world), and the symbol-grounding problem (mental representations must be connected to the interaction contexts that constitute the system's environment) [19].[1] We suggest, however, that to be meaningfully transformed through engagement in a creative task may require another level of self-hood: an internal model of one's world and one's place in that world. This level is being actively discovered by the agent, and quite distinct from the first. Indeed, these two levels of endogenous control may be at odds with each other, as when a scientist stops eating to write out a new theory, or an artist engrossed in painting ignores the children. The desire to care for one's children stems from the organic level of self-hood, i.e., one's role as a participant in biological evolution, while the desire to paint stems from one's mental level of self-hood, i.e., one's role as a participant in cultural evolution. The first is concerned with somatic integrity (i.e., body and substrate interactions), while the second is concerned with the integrity of one's internal model of the world, or worldview (i.e., the

---

[1] The AI's environment need not be the same one as our environment; it could, for example, be an artificial environment that exists in a computer.

mind, as experienced from the inside). This second level seeks viability, not at the level of the physical body, but at the level of one's thoughts, beliefs, and ideas-including one's self-concept-and how they are organized into a web of stories and understandings. A limitation of current deep learning approaches appears to be the absence of self-reflection and coherent understanding, aspects of human intelligence recruited in even simple creative problem-solving tasks. We suggest that for a machine to possess these attributes and be meaningfully transformed through engagement in a creative task, it should possess selfhood both as a causally implemented entity that seeks to maintain its structural integrity, and as mental model of itself inhabiting its world (i.e., a model of itself, or self-model, in relation to a world model).

Human mental models not only emerge spontaneously, but they are self-organizing, self-mending, and self-perpetuating [4,40,50]. The self-sustaining nature of our mental models is evident in our tendency to resolve inconsistencies, accommodate new information into existing schemas, and reduce cognitive dissonance. When we observe something unexpected, it 'catalyzes' a stream of thought aimed at mending the gap in our understanding. One's worldview is continuously revised in response to, not just information from the outside world, but one's ongoing stream of thought, through the complementary processes of assimilation and accommodation.

To model such a structure, we need a network model that incorporates how new information emerges through interactions between existing units of information until, collectively, they form an integrated structure, the global structure of which guides its behavior. This brings us to autocatalytic networks.

4   Reflexively Autocatalytic Foodset-Derived Networks (RAFs)

Like ANNs and other complex networks used in cognitive science, an autocatalytic network is composed of points (or nodes) connected by edges (or links). Autocatalytic networks were originally proposed as an explanation to the origin of life problem [33,34],[2] and subsequently developed into the theory of Reflexively Autocatalytic Foodset-derived (RAF) network [21–30,44–48,52]. The term *reflexively autocatalytic* will be defined formally shortly, but informally it refers to the fact that the whole can be reconstituted through interactions amongst the parts. All nodes in a RAF that were either initially present, or that after entering the network assume the same form within the network that they assumed outside it, are referred to as the *foodset*. Nodes that came about through one or more interactions (i.e., that came into being within the network itself) are referred to as *foodset-derived*.

RAFs are simply abstract mathematical structures, and it is equally correct to apply them to cognition (and the origin of cultural evolution) as to biology (and the origin of life). The origin of life application may have been

---

[2] See also [38] on the related concept of autopoiesis.

developed first, but one is no more an 'analogy' than the other. Just as one molecule catalyzes the reaction by which another is formed, one concept or idea may prime others related to it, or trigger representational redescription (restructuring) or concept combination. Just as reactions can result in new catalytic molecules and new reactions, concept combination and recursive representational redescription—streams of thought—can generate new concepts and ideas. Just as reaction networks can generate and perpetuate living structures, streams of thought generate and perpetuate our mental models. Terminology and correspondences between different applications of the RAF framework are given in Table 1.

Table 1. Terminology and correspondences between the application of RAFs in biology, cognition/culture, and ANNs/AI.

RAF Theory	Biology	Cognition	AI
Node	Catalytic Molecule	Mental representation	Representations
Edge	Reaction	Association	Link
Connected graph	Catalytic closure	Cognitive closure	Representational Closure

Formally, a RAF—is a non-empty subset $\mathcal{R}' \subseteq \mathcal{R}$ of reactions that satisfies the following two properties:

1. It is *reflexively autocatalytic*: each reaction $r \in \mathcal{R}'$ is catalyzed by at least one element type that is either produced by $\mathcal{R}'$ or is present in the foodset F.
2. It is *F-generated*: all reactants in $\mathcal{R}'$ can be generated from the foodset F by using a series of reactions only from $\mathcal{R}'$ itself.

Thus, a RAF is a non-empty subset $\mathcal{R}' \subseteq \mathcal{R}$ of 'reactions,' a structure composed of parts that interact to form new parts, wherein all parts, and all interaction they can undergo, are either present from the start, or come into existence through the interactions of other parts.

The largest RAF in a set of nodes is referred to as the *maxRAF* (Fig. 1). It may consist of *subRAFs*, which are often clustered and hierarchically structured. It may also consist of *Co-RAFs*: structures that are not RAFs on their own but form RAFs, when combined with other RAFs. RAFs can form spontaneously, and expand through the merger of subRAFs and co-RAFs. Dynamic RAF systems can include transient RAFs, which include nodes and/or reaction paths that are unstable.

The RAF framework provides a mathematical setting for modeling generative network growth, identifying phase transitions in generative structures, and analyzing how network structure is affected by different parameters [45]. RAF theory can provide bounds on the probability of emergence of maxRAFs and other structures [32,39]. RAFs scale up, and RAF algorithms can analyze and detect phase transitions in vastly complex networks that have proven intractable with other analytic approaches [43,52].

5   RAF Models of Emergent Cognition

The complex biochemistry of all organisms including humans has a heritage that traces back to primitive catalytic reaction systems; thus, humans possess RAF structure at both the organismic level (physiological organization), and the mental level (mind, cognition, and world modeling). Although the contents of a cognitive network change over time, it maintains integrity as a relatively coherent whole. Cognitive structures reproduce, in a piecemeal manner when individuals share ideas and perspectives. Human creativity enables cognitive networks, and thereby culture, to evolve. Thus, whereas the origin of life involves chemical reaction networks, the origin of cultural evolution involves networks of knowledge and memories—i.e., cognitive networks—but the deep structure of both can be captured in the RAF setting.

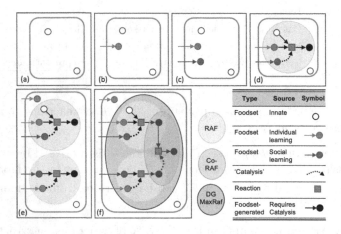

Fig. 1. Example of transition from non-RAF (**a–c**), to RAF (**d**), to multiple RAFs (**e**), to their integration into a domain-general maxRAF (**f**). Yellow ovals indicate RAFs; orange oval indicates a co-RAF; purple oval indicates the maxRAF. The innate item on the lower left of all panels, and the mental representation acquired through individual learning on the upper right of panels (**e**) and (**f**) are items that have not been assimilated into a RAF. If we omit the distinction between the three different sources for foodset nodes (innate, acquired through individual learning, or acquired through social learning) the figure would serve equally well to illustrate, at an abstract level, the origin of life from abiotic molecules, or the origin of an integrated cognitive model of the world in the mind of a child starting from disconnected knowledge and memories.

In a RAF model of an individual's mental model of the world, mental representations of knowledge and experiences are represented by nodes and their associations are represented by links. Associations between nodes may be due to similarity, co-occurrence, causal relationship, or something else; for the moment we are not concerned with how they are connected, just whether or not there is some basis for a connection. We mentioned that (like other networks), autocatalytic networks exhibit percolation thresholds and undergo rapid phase transitions from low to high connectivity [34]. This property has been used to model the biological evolution of the kind of mind that is capable of cumulative, open-ended cultural change. Cultural evolution required that humans become capable of blending ideas from different domains, and adapting existing ideas and artifacts to new situations and preferences. For this, in turn, knowledge from different domains had to be mutually accessible, and their minds had to acquire the structure of a self-organizing network. It was therefore proposed that autocatalytic networks lay at the origin of not just biological evolution, but also cultural evolution, and they have been used to model the evolution of the kind of cognitive structure capable of cumulative culture [13–15].

In cognitive applications, the foodset consists of knowledge that is either innate (e.g., archetypes, or a sense of right and wrong), acquired through individual learning (e.g., learning to distinguish different trees while walking alone in a forest), or acquired through social learning (e.g., learning from a neighbor how to change a tire). Foodset-derived items are generated in the mind of the individual in question, through abstract thought. (We ignore for now that the learning process itself—whether it be individual learning, or social learning—may modify the mental representation, and thus the distinction between foodset and foodset-derived is probably a matter of degree.) In cognitive applications, a reaction is an interaction between two mental representations (as in concept combination), and the participating mental representations are in this sense reactants. *Cognitive catalysis* occurs when a stimulus or mental representation activates another mental representation that would otherwise have been unlikely to be activated on its own (as when something you see or hear sparks a new idea).

Recent simulations suggest that a mundane form of creativity—namely active inference and abstraction—is not just essential but unavoidable in the formation of internal models of the environment [49]. In the RAF framework, creativity is modeled as the 'catalysis,' or restructuring, of a new mental representation. RAF dynamics may result in a network that is self-organizing and self-sustaining [25,39], as well as able to self-replicate and evolve (in a relatively haphazard manner, without reliance on a self-assembly code) [21]. Cognitive structures self-replicate, in a piecemeal manner when individuals share ideas and perspectives. All living entities can be described in terms of RAF structure. Since RAF networks describe structure that is self-organizing, self-preserving, and self-regenerating, we posit that if an entity does not contain RAF structure (or something akin to it), there is no self.

We mentioned that autocatalytic networks exhibit percolation thresholds and undergo rapid phase transitions in connectivity, which was used to model the transition in cognitive evolution from islands of domain-specific knowledge to a domain-general connected network. In accordance with the dictum 'ontogeny recapitulates phylogeny' (developmental change often echoes evolutionary change), this feature of RAF networks has been used to model the developmental phase transition exhibited by children to a state of greater integration amongst knowledge and memories [10]. In a young child, knowledge and memories are not accessible without an external cue, and this is described as islands of RAF structure. Once a small RAF structure is in place, new knowledge can assimilate into and build upon this scaffold. As knowledge and memories accumulate, they cross a 'percolation threshold,' after which they are accessible without an external cue. At this point, they can they be called upon as needed to solve problems and interpret new situations. The individual is now able to prioritize, combine concepts, even from different domains. This phase transition has been described as coalescence of RAFs that represent discrete segments of domain-specific information into a domain-general maxRAF [10].

The domain-general maxRAF describes an integrated understanding of the world. There does not have to be consistency between different subRAFs (e.g., different social roles), merely accessibility, i.e., the ability to transition between them without an external cue. Note also that there is no need to include all of one's knowledge and experiences (for example, dreams or repressed traumatic experiences etched into isolated fragments of memory are not part of the domain-general maxRAF, thus not accessible). The concept of a domain-general maxRAF is implied in some discussions of AGI (see [51]). However, the RAF theoretic approach lends itself to rigorous analysis using a well-developed formal theory that encompasses different kinds of autonomous, self-organizing structure—lifeforms and mental models—under the same formal unifying framework [16].

The capacity to shift between a 'fast' mode of thought conducive to detecting relationships of correlation, and a 'slow' mode of thought conducive to detecting relationships of causation (e.g., [31]) enables the child to tailor their thinking to the situation. The more representational structure is subsumed by the domain-general maxRAF, the greater the potential for adaptive responses. Because elements of a domain-general maxRAF are mutually accessible, a disturbance at any one—such as, for example, loss of a component, or loss of its 'reactivity' with other components—can trigger a wave of mental activity aimed at recovering the domain-general maxRAF.

6   Discussion

We have introduced a speculative program for developing an AI that possesses a self, i.e., that is composed of parts that collectively aim to preserve bounded structure, based on the formal framework of a kind of autocatalytic networks known as RAFs. In an attempt to make AI output more reliable and accountable, it may be desirable to induce a predetermined context using special training techniques or filters, but they do not possess a domain-general maxRAF. However, we believe that, under the right circumstances, one will spontaneously emerge in an AI. To achieve this, the AI's mental representations should be fully semantically accessible, such that there exists a potential path from one representation to all others. (This may appear excessive, but for any concept there exists some context in which any given other concept is relevant, and this is the source of creative connections.) This includes connections in time, so that the agent can reconstruct the context of an observed feature by identifying its history and past observations. This implies unification of all domain models, in such a way that it is possible to navigate between them as the context changes.

The representations must also be optimized for coherence, i.e., violations of constraints imposed by relevant observations, memories, and expectations must be minimized. In addition, the representations must be grounded, directly or indirectly, such that they can be coupled to an environment that provides contextual constraints for every relevant aspect of the representation. Note that humans (and many other animals) learn with a focus on satisfying these conditions. For instance, when we look at a picture, we do not consider it to be a structured texture without history that we correlate with other images until its meaning reveals itself. Instead, we may consider that we are, for instance, looking at a photograph of a stop sign, designed by a human being, taken by another person with a camera in our shared past, and now being held up by another person with the goal of conducting an experiment. Each step of learning aims at increasing connectedness, coherence, and contextuality. Our learning springs from modeling our observations (many of which entail regulating our needs or controlling our behavior). In deep learning models, semantic coherence can be approximated through extensive statistical analysis of very large amounts of suitably chosen symbolic training data, but the process is not self-driven.

Although mathematical models of RAF cognitive networks have been developed, to date computational RAF cognitive networks do not yet exist. We propose they are nevertheless within reach, and that self-driven autonomous processing would be possible in such a model. In an artificial RAF network, nodes don't just passively spread activation; they actively restructure the network, resulting in new nodes and links, or the pruning of redundant ones. Restructuring occurs in neural networks by changing the weights on links or through addition or random pruning of nodes. In a model guided by the principles of RAF theory, the global 'shape' of the network is collectively detected by elements of this network, and guides the restructuring process. To achieve the machine equivalent of creativity requires that tokens such as words or images be mutually accessible so as to enable the encoding of reliable embeddings that encode associations and contexts. 'Reaction sequences' amongst tokens are triggered by deterioration of some segment of the artificial agent's domain-general maxRAF, or an opportunity for network growth. This change to the network may then potentially manifest externally as a creative output.

6.1 Related Research

Although space does not permit extensive coverage of the exciting work in this area, let us look at a few current directions that may be particularly relevant.

It has been proposed that the Free Energy Principle [7] can be used to formally model autonomy and adaptivity [36]. Like the Free Energy Principle, cognitive RAF theory posits that we reduce disorder. However, unlike the Free Energy Principle, it can account for novelty-seeking and creativity.

There have been numerous achievements in generative AI and and computational creativity, some based on self-organizing networks, resulting in AI-generated art, music, stories, poetry (for a recent review, see [5]. Baby AGI uses OpenAI's GPT-4 and Pinecone APIs, and the LangChain framework to create, organize, prioritize as well as the executing of tasks [1]. AutoGPT uses GPT-4 to generate code and exploit GPT-3.5 as a virtual artificial memory space [53]. Reflexion reinforces language agents not by updating weights, but through linguistic feedback. Reflexion agents verbally reflect on task feedback signals, then maintain their own reflective text in an episodic memory buffer to aid decision-making in subsequent trials. These achievements are promising and impressive, but it is not straightforward how they could constitute a stepping stone toward autonomous agentic self-hood; their actions flow from the commands of the user rather than having as their origin the maintenance or growth of a self-preserving network (be it biological, cognitive/cultural, or something else). Their creativity is not driven by their own intrinsic desire to explore, understand, or come to terms with something, and its completion does not bring cathartic release. Evolutionary programming and genetic algorithms can breed fitter outputs, but they don't breed selves.

Computational models of dual processing modes have been implemented in cognitive architectures (e.g., [20]), and have proven effective at increasing the fitness of outputs in a computational model of cultural evolution [12], and in the context of computer-generated art [6]. By continuously shifting between processing modes in response to ever-changing demands, the AI is able to transcend rote strategies and bridge discontinuities in a search space (our second criterion for creativity). This capacity may prove essential to achieving a domain-general maxRAF in an AI.

6.2   Future Work: Experimental Testing and Validation

This approach proposed here remains speculative and untested. We now discuss ideas for testing and validation of the approach. First, the following would be indicative of a domain-general maxRAF with a self-model:

1. The AI engages in self-initiated (as opposed to prompt-driven) restructuring of mental contents in the service of preserving, restoring, or enhancing of an autonomous self that is distinct from (yet connected to) other entities, and possibly subject to degradation.

2. The AI learns from observations continuously, ideally in real time.

3. The AI's actions are visible to the AI, including its preferences (which may be static or dynamically generated by a motivation model (e.g., [2,3]), intentions (decisions the AI makes according to its preferences and models), actions, and the outcomes of these actions.

4. The interface between intention and action—which we can refer to as an 'embodiment'—is discovered in the context of a sense-decide-act loop.

5. The AI cares about improving its own actions, so the observation leads to new internal models that the AI can act upon.

6. The AI can refer to these models in any present context, so that its self-model is available for observation and cognition.

7. The AI's self-model is dynamically discovered through self-driven reiterated restructuring. The AI tracks changes in the self-model and assign valence to them; thus, it can predict and compare outcomes of changes to the self.

Finally, we suggest that self-hood might be difficult to detect through evaluation of the *artistic merit* of its creative outputs, and claims of internal transformation or cathartic release as a result of engagement in a creative practice would have to be met with skepticism. However, if an AI is a unique, creative self, it should be able to develop a personal style that, like that of humans [8,11], is recognizable not just within the creator's primary domain but across different domains. In other words, if the AI is primarily known for its fiction, then people who are familiar with that AI's stories should be able to guess above chance, not just which stories were created by that AI, but also which pieces of art or music were created by that AI. This would indicate that the AI had pieced together an understanding of the world that is not only specifically tied to its unique knowledge base and 'experiences' (its foodset) but, through a meaning-making process, it has forged the necessary stepping-stones (foodset-derived items) to weave these elements together into a uniquely configured 'worldview'.

7   Conclusions

We possess machines that generate undeniably creative products, but how would one build an AI that experiences the transformative and therapeutic aspects of creativity and can be considered a self? This paper provised a fresh albeit still speculative and unproven approach to the question of machine agency, using a modeling framework that has been used to analyze the emergence of two kinds of agency—the origin of life, and the origin of a self-organizing mental model of the world—and the respective evolutionary process these transitions enabled: biological and cultural evolution.

A mathematization of autocatalytic network theory known as RAF theory provides a formal framework for (1) modeling how new elements emerge through interactions amongst existing elements to yield a system that functions as an integrated whole, and (2) analyzing how such systems adapt, replicate, and evolve. In applications of RAF theory to the origin of life, the parts are catalytic molecules undergoing reactions. In applications to cognition and the kind of mind capable of evolving culture, the parts are mental representations of events, information, and ideas, which trigger representational redescription culminating in new ideas. We suggest that this same formal framework could be used to model the emergence of creative agency in a machine. If successful, the resulting AIs would be creative according to not just external but also internal definitions of creativity; they would be autonomous beings, untethered from their creators, for better or worse. Their creative outputs might properly be attributable them.

In virtue of a heritage that traces back to primitive catalytic reaction systems, humans are participants in biological evolution. Humans are also participants in cultural evolution. Thus, we participate in two evolutionary processes—we are self-organizing and self-sustaining at two (interacting) levels—and the origins of each has been analyzed with the RAF framework. It is an open question whether artificial creative agency requires this kind of bi-level structure.

The suggestion that AI self-hood may be achievable within a RAF framework opens up avenues for further research. One direction is to create an ANN with representations that discover and refine their 'catalytic' potential to create new representations, followed by onset of the capacity to shift between dual processing modes, and thereby bridge disparate clusters. The resulting networks and dynamics are then analyzed using existing RAF theory methods, discussed above. The emergence of a domain-general maxRAF, and spontaneous yet lasting network change during creative tasks would be indications that the project was successful. It could be fruitful to carry this out incorporating ideas from the Free Energy Principle approach, discussed above. Other possibilities are to develop artificial societies of interacting RAF-based agents, and explore how the concept of resonance [37] could be incorporated. It could be productive to investigate how such an AI would respond to teaching by and collaboration with a human tutor in a developmental paradigm.

Since current generative AIs are trained on human output, and human cognitive networks meet the criteria for a RAF, they inherit characteristics of RAF structure from us. This is sufficient to enable an AI model to prioritize, combine concepts, 'restructure' knowledge and thereby adapt it to new situations, or make something in the style of something else. We suggest that current AIs are merely extensions of us, much like tools, calculators, or artificial limbs; they are not selves. They generate creative products, but their creativity is an expression of us.

We end with two observations and two speculative predictions: (1) RAFs were developed to for modeling the origin of life and the onset of biological evolution [30,39,44,46–48,52], and (2) The mind serves as the hub of a second evolutionary process (cultural evolution), which also can be modeled in terms of RAF structure [13–17], and thus might be considered a second level of 'aliveness.' Based on our considerations, we propose (1) that it is only once machines exhibit RAF structure at the level of self-modeling that they will possess creative agency and self-hood.[3] It may appear to be appropriate to attribute AIs authorship of works created by them. A second prediction is that the route forward to AI agency will involve a fusion of methodologies and insights from origin of life research and artificial intelligence. We look forward to seeing if these predictions hold up in this exciting era of AI research.

---

[3] If there is an agent external to the machine that will repair it when it breaks, it may not have to exhibit RAF structure at all levels.

References

1. Arya, N.: Baby agi: the birth of a fully autonomous ai. KDnuggets Artif. Intell. (2023)
2. Bach, J.: Modeling motivation in micropsi 2. In: Proceedings of AGI: 12th International Conferences, vol. 8, pp. 3–13. Springer, Berlin (2015)
3. Bach, J., Coutinho, M., Lichtinger, L.: Extending micropsi's model of motivation and emotion for conversational agents. In: Proceedings of AGI: 12th International Conferences, vol. 12, pp. 32–43. Springer, Berlin (2019)
4. Baronchelli, A., Ferrer-i-Cancho, R., Pastor-Satorras, R., Chater, N., Christiansen, M.H.: Networks in cognitive science. Trends Cogn. Sci. **17**, 348–360 (2013). https://doi.org/10.1016/j.tics.2013.04.010
5. Cetinic, E., She, J.: Understanding and creating art with ai: review and outlook. ACM Trans. Multimed. Comput. Commun. Appl. (TOMM) **18**, 1–22 (2022)
6. DiPaola, S., Gabora, L.: Incorporating characteristics of human creativity into an evolutionary art algorithm. Genet. Program Evolvable Mach. **10**, 97–110 (2009)
7. Friston, K.: The free-energy principle: a unified brain theory? Nat. Rev. Neurosci. **16**(1), 127–138 (2010). https://doi.org/10.1186/s13322-014-0006-2
8. Gabora, L.: Recognizability of creative style within and across domains: preliminary studies. In: Proceedings of the Annual Meeting of the Cognitive Science Society, pp. 2350–2355. Cognitive Science Society, Austin TX (2010)
9. Gabora, L.: Honing theory: a complex systems framework for creativity. Nonlinear Dyn. Psychol. Life Sci. **21**, 35–88 (2017)
10. Gabora, L., Beckage, N., Steel, M.: Modeling cognitive development with reflexively autocatalytic networks. Top. Cogn. Sci. **14**, 163–188 (2022)
11. Gabora, L., O'Connor, B., Ranjan, A.: The recognizability of individual creative styles within and across domains. Psychol. Aesthet. Creat. Arts **6**, 335–346 (2012)
12. Gabora, L., Smith, C.: Two cognitive transitions underlying the capacity for cultural evolution. J. Anthropol. Sci. **96**, 27–52 (2018). https://doi.org/10.4436/jass.96008
13. Gabora, L., Steel, M.: Autocatalytic networks in cognition and the origin of culture. J. Theor. Biol. **431**, 87–95 (2017). https://doi.org/10.1016/j.jtbi.2017.07.022
14. Gabora, L., Steel, M.: A model of the transition to behavioral and cognitive modernity using reflexively autocatalytic networks. Proc. R. Soc. Interface **17**, 20200545 (2020). https://doi.org/10.1098/rsif.2020.0545
15. Gabora, L., Steel, M.: Modeling a cognitive transition at the origin of cultural evolution using autocatalytic networks. Cogn. Sci. **44** (2020)
16. Gabora, L., Steel, M.: An evolutionary process without variation and selection. J. R. Soc. Interface **18** (2021). 10.1098/rsif.2021.0334
17. Gabora, L., Steel, M.: From uncertainty to insight: an autocatalytic framework. In: Beghetto, R., Jaeger, G. (eds.) Uncertainty: A Catalyst for Creativity, Learning and Development, pp. 125–158. Springer, Berlin (2022)
18. Goertzel, B.: Artificial selfhood: the path to true artificial intelligence. Informatica **19**, 469–477 (1995)
19. Harnad, S.: The symbol grounding problem. Phys. D **42**, 335–346 (1990)
20. Hélie, S., Sun, R.: Incubation, insight, and creative problem solving: a unified theory and a connectionist model. Psychol. Rev. **117**, 994–1024 (2010)
21. Hordijk, W., Hein, J., Steel, M.: Autocatalytic sets and the origin of life. Entropy **12**(7), 1733–1742 (2010). https://doi.org/10.3390/e12071733

22. Hordijk, W., Kauffman, S.A., Steel, M.: Required levels of catalysis for emergence of autocatalytic sets in models of chemical reaction systems. Int. J. Mol. Sci. **12**(5), 3085–3101 (2011). https://doi.org/10.3390/ijms12053085

23. Hordijk, W., Steel, M.: Detecting autocatalytic, self-sustaining sets in chemical reaction systems. J. Theor. Biol. **227**(4), 451–461 (2004). https://doi.org/10.1016/j.jtbi.2003.11.020

24. Hordijk, W., Steel, M.: Predicting template-based catalysis rates in a simple catalytic reaction model. J. Theor. Biol. **295**, 132–138 (2012)

25. Hordijk, W., Steel, M.: Autocatalytic sets and boundaries. J. Syst. Chem. **6**(1), 1–5 (2015). https://doi.org/10.1186/s13322-014-0006-2

26. Hordijk, W., Steel, M.: Chasing the tail: The emergence of autocatalytic networks. Biosystems **152**, 1–10 (2016). https://doi.org/10.1016/j.biosystems.2016.12.002

27. Hordijk, W., Steel, M., Dittrich, P.: Autocatalytic sets and chemical organizations: modeling self-sustaining reaction networks at the origin of life. New J. Phys. **20**, 015011 (2018)

28. Hordijk, W., Steel, M., Kauffman, S.: Molecular diversity required for the formation of autocatalytic sets. Life **9**(23), 1–14 (2019)

29. Horvath, A.O.: Research on the alliance: knowledge in search of a theory. Psychother. Res. **28**(4), 499–516 (2017). https://doi.org/10.1080/10503307.2017.1373204

30. Horvath, A.O., Del Re, A.C., Flückiger, C., Symonds, D.: Alliance in individual psychotherapy. Psychotherapy **48**(1), 9–16 (2011). https://doi.org/10.1037/a0022186

31. Kahneman, D.: Thinking, Fast and Slow. Macmillan, London UK (2011)

32. Kauffman, S., Steel, M.: The expected number of viable autocatalytic sets in chemical reaction systems. Artif. Life 1–14 (2021). arXiv:2007.10518(27)

33. Kauffman, S.A.: Autocatalytic sets of proteins. J. Theor. Biol. **119**, 1–24 (1986). https://doi.org/10.3390/ijms12053085

34. Kauffman, S.A.: The Origins of Order. Oxford University Press (1993)

35. Kind, C., Ebinger-Rist, N., Wolf, S., Beutelspacher, T., Wehrberger, K.: The smile of the lion man. recent excavations in stadel cave (baden-württemberg, southwestern germany) and the restoration of the famous upper palaeolithic figurine. Quartär **61**, 129–145 (2014)

36. Kiverstein, J., Kirchhoff, M.D., Froese, T.: The problem of meaning: the free energy principle and artificial agency. Front. Neurorobotics **16** (2022)

37. Lomas, J.D., Lin, A., Dikker, S., Forster, D., Lupetti, M.L., Huisman, G., Habekost, J., Beardow, C., Pandey, P. Ahmad, N., Miyapuram, K., Mullen, T., Cooper, P., Willem van der Maden, W., Cross, E.S.: Resonance as a design strategy for ai and social robots. Front. Neurorobot. **16**, 850489 (2022)

38. Maturana, H., Varela, F.: Autopoiesis and cognition: the realization of the living. In: Cohen, R.S., Wartofsky, M.W. (eds.) Boston Studies in the Philosophy of Science, vol. 42. Reidel, Dordecht (1973)

39. Mossel, E., Steel, M.: Random biochemical networks and the probability of self-sustaining autocatalysis. J. Theor. Biol. **233**, 327–336 (2005). https://doi.org/10.1016/j.jtbi.2004.10.011

40. Pribram, K.H.: Origins: Brain and Self-Organization. Lawrence Erlbaum, Hillsdale NJ (1994)

41. Runco, M., Jaeger, G.: The standard definition of creativity. Creat. Res. J. **24**, 92–96 (2012)

42. Sen, R.S., Sharma, N.: Through multiple lenses: Implicit theories of creativity among Indian children and adults. J. Creat. Beh. **45**, 273–302 (2011)

43. Sousa, F., Hordijk, W., Steel, M., Martin, W.: Autocatalytic sets in e. coli metabolism. J. Syst. Chem. **6**, 4 (2015)
44. Steel, M.: The emergence of a self-catalyzing structure in abstract origin-of-life models. Appl. Math. Lett. **13**, 91–95 (2000)
45. Steel, M., Hordijk, W., Xavier, J.C.: Autocatalytic networks in biology: structural theory and algorithms. J. R. Soc. Interface **16**, (2019). https://doi.org/10.1098/rsif.2018.0808
46. Steel, M., Xavier, J.C., Huson, D.H.: Autocatalytic networks in biology: structural theory and algorithms. J. R. Soc. Interface **17**, 20200488 (2020)
47. Stephen, D.G., Boncoddo, R.A., Magnuson, J.S., Dixon, J.: The dynamics of insight: mathematical discovery as a phase transition. Mem. Cogn. **37**, 1132–1149 (2009)
48. Steyvers, M., Tenenbaum, J.B.: The large-scale structure of semantic networks: statistical analyses and a model of semantic growth. Cogn. Sci. **29**, 41–78 (2005)
49. Tschantz, A., Seth, A.K., Buckley, C.L.: Learning action-oriented models through active inference. PLoS Comput. Biol. **16**(1), e1007805 (2020). https://doi.org/10.1186/s13322-014-0006-2
50. Varela, F., Thompson, E., Rosch, E.: The Embodied Mind. MIT Press, Cambridge MA (1991)
51. Wang, P.: On defining artificial intelligence. J. Artif. Gen. Intel. **10**, 1–37 (2019)
52. Xavier, J.C., Hordijk, W., Kauffman, S., Steel, M., Martin, W.F.: Autocatalytic chemical networks at the origin of metabolism. Proc. R. Soc. Lond. Ser. B: Biol. Sci. **287**, 20192377 (2020)
53. Zhang, S., Gong, C., Wu, L., Liu, X., Zhou, M.: AutoML-GPT: automatic machine learning with GPT (2023). https://arxiv.org/abs/2305.02499

Human+Non-human Creative Identities. Symbiotic Synthesis in Industrial Design Creative Processes

Alberto Calleo[✉] [iD] and Ludovica Rosato [iD]

University of Bologna, Bologna, Italy
alberto.calleo@unibo.it

Abstract. As digital technologies are increasingly used in creative professions, the evolution of the relationship between designers and machines is growing in interest. Such topic is part of a broad debate on how cognitive processes and human intelligence development co-evolve in parallel with technology advancements in a process of technogenesis. In a complex socio-economic system, Artificial Intelligence-based technologies are both providing new tools and challenging the idea of creativity itself. We discuss how the creative process in the field of industrial design is commonly intended and we argue that the adoption of AI-based technologies is part of an ongoing process of symbiotic co-evolution between human and machine embedded in the creative process itself and, therefore, designers ought to develop synergic strategies to foster future innovation.

Keywords: Artificial Intelligence · Creativity · Industrial Design · Design processes · Symbiosis

1 Technologies and Creative Processes

As digital technologies used in creative professions evolve, the co-creative relationship between designers and machines is a topic of growing interest. The debate on the ways in which creative practice integrate enabling technologies into professional practice poses a number of questions and concerns raging from ethical issues to the reframing of the required designer's skill set. The growing popularity of artificial intelligence (AI) based technologies capable of generating synthetic media content has extended the debate from the ability to facilitate and speed up complex or repetitive tasks performed by humans, to questioning the authorship and intellectual property of works, picturing the possibility of fully replacing human intervention in creative processes. This discourse is part of a broad debate on how cognitive processes and human intelligence development co-evolve in parallel with technology advancements in a process of technogenesis [1, 2] interrelated with the social and ethical issues that characterise post-human ecologies and synthetic identities [3, 4] together with the transformations of a complex economic system [5]. We draw from Engelhardt and Manouach concept of chimeric cognition [3] in which semi-autonomus components coexist without replacing each other leading to the potential emergence of a symbiotic synthesis. We frame such perspective in the field of industrial design in which digital tools have reshaped production processes and design methodologies.

Industrial design projects' increasing complexity has grown together with the development of more sophisticated computer-aided tools and technologies. Designers and engineers have developed digital instruments and infrastructures in order to facilitate the design of other, more complex, systems. Operating such complex interfaces and systems require humans with specific technical skills. The demand of highly specialized skills intertwines with social and economic dynamics within organizations and communities. The collaborative models of knowledge transmission characteristic of the pre-industrial era have been transformed by the capitalist economy of global finance, which, with the aim of maximising short-term profits, has stopped investing in the development of human capital. In the skill economy, made possible by the remote working and networking technologies, required skills are acquired wherever they can be found (possibly at a lower labour cost), consumed, and put back on the market, breaking the chains of knowledge production and transmission that had been historically passed on within congregations of arts and crafts and in craft workshops [6]. The industrial system, also driven by the need to develop more sustainable production processes, is integrating Industry 4.0 technologies with increasing intensity, automating processes that were once performed by humans and creating a new articulated ecosystem of human-machine interaction [7] that gradually extends to more stages of the chain of creation, production, and consumption. While it is straightforward to understand how digital technologies have brought about significant improvements in the manufacturing and logistical stages of production, it becomes more complex to define the role of AI-based technologies both at the level of design practice and at the level of the principles underpinning design activity itself [8].

In industrial and architectural design, algorithms and generative software are frequently used to support development activities, for example as a tool for structural and material optimization. However, there are more and more examples of how such tools can also be used in design phases usually related to human work domain. The free expression of one's personality through design is a contribution that define the designer's identity and creativity, which it is essential to bring out from the very beginning of the designer training [9]. The authorial component of creativity is even more significant in artistic practice in which the confrontation with AI-based autonomous agents capable of producing 'original' works and content is investigated both by theoretical contributions and in artistic production. For instance, Zeilinger suggests that in the works of New Zealand artist Tom White Perception Engines and Synthetic Abstraction, the machine's ability to produce content autonomously not only testifies to the manifestation of new forms of non-human agency but is also capable of triggering mechanisms of human non-agency when the human ability to interpret what is produced by the AI fails [10, 11]. In White's works, artificial intelligence can produce images that are perfectly recognisable by image recognition systems (usually employed for social network security filters and image search systems) but figuratively abstract for human interpretation. The emergence of phenomena in which the human ability to understand the language generated by AI-based systems caused quite a stir in the media when in 2017 two bots developed by researchers at Meta (then Facebook) began to communicate with each other in a new, more efficient language that, by deviating from English syntax, became incomprehensible to humans [12]. Despite the media clamor, it is worth stressing that these are not phenomena in which embryonic forms of consciousness emerge, but these episodes can highlight how the introduction of AI-based technologies adds further complexity to the field of human-computer interaction research, education and communication.

2   AI-Tools and Design Practice

The diffusion of low-cost enabling technologies (such as 3D printing and CNC machinery), access to free online information, and the spread of opensource software have brought a growing number of people closer to the practices of design and self-production. Similarly, the spread of platforms to connect the demand and supply of creative skills has on the one hand, supported the development of new career paths, especially in economies with lower labour costs, and on the other hand, contributed to accelerate a process of commoditisation of creative skills in various areas of design. This process of commoditisation of the designer's role needs to be further reconsidered with the consumer-level diffusion of new AI-based tools that enable to speed up, facilitate or even automate the tasks performed by design professionals. Image synthesis tools from textual prompts have been made accessible to non-professional consumers since 2021. These tools use different neural networks to interpret an input expressed in written English (natural language processing) and use it to produce an image representing its content. The user-friendliness of such systems has made them very popular not only among those who deal professionally with technology and its applications in art and design, but also among non-expert users. The spread of a tool that is simple to approach but returns quick results and with a potentially infinite variety further raises the question of the risk of the progressive commoditisation of certain creative professions. Although these technologies may seem ready to revolutionise entire industries overnight, what we find interesting to point out is that systems implementing AI in professional practice are already widespread in specific sectors and applications and can be read as a technological progression of CAD (Computer Aided Design) systems into AIAD (Artificial Intelligence Aided Design) systems. This can be considered as an undoubtedly more articulated technological transition than the one that led from the drawing board to computer-aided design, but which, as argued in the following paragraphs, is part of a process of technogenesis and symbiotic co-evolution between human and machine emended in the creative process itself. It is therefore significant for the designer to understand the operating logic of artificial intelligence systems in order to reconsider the influences of human-machine interaction in the creative processes.

Design as a creative process

In order to understand some of the complexities and opportunities of the symbiotic relationship between human and machine, it is necessary to briefly discuss both how creative processes in design practice are articulated according to human-centred dynamics and how some of the algorithmic logics underpinning AI-based tools work. In the specifics of this contribution, talking about design will refer in particular to the methodologies of industrial design practice.

Firstly, creativity in design is characterized by aspects that may be different when compared to the concept of creativity in the artistic sphere. Industrial design has the task of mediating the relationship between needs and objects, production, and consumption by dealing with the problem of the "commodity form" [13, 14]. The industrial designer connects and mediates technical and humanistic skills, it is an interpreter of contemporary material culture that, through industrial processes, produces goods for market exchange [15]. It is therefore an activity that cannot be considered decontextualized either from a productive and economic context, as the objective is the production of industrial artefacts that are grafted into a market exchange system, into cultural ecosystems of meanings, symbols and languages. In 2015, the British Design Council proposed the Double Diamond model, a synthetic description of the designer's characteristic creative process. This approach is characterized by two macro-phases—research and design—each describable through an initial phase of divergence and a subsequent one of convergence. The alternation of these perspectives allows the designer to observe and research, identify a specific problem domain and make decisions, search for possible strategies to transform the analysis into form and synthesize them into a concrete solution [16]. The designer needs to develop the ability to observe phenomena in order to construct simplified models of reality. In constructing and manipulating such models, he draws on different spheres of knowledge. Finally, after an interactive process of prototyping and reworking, a synthesis is reached represented by the industrial product. With the evolution of technology, these stages of design development have benefited from hardware and software tools that have made them faster, more flexible and suitable for managing complex projects.

Describing the logic according to which some neural network models operate allows us to articulate parallels with what happens in the human-centred design phases just described.

Observing

Among the technologies used by AI systems, GANs (Generative Adversarial Networks) are systems that have become very popular for generating synthetic images. In GAN systems, two neural networks compete against each other in an iterative process. The network called the Generator produces images with the aim of having them validated by the Discriminator who compares them with a large dataset of reference images. The Generator does not have access to this dataset and therefore the first images produced will be random and unrelated from those that the Discriminator's criteria identify as a valid image. The Generator will then use the feedback received from the Discriminator to produce a new image. As iterations proceed, the Generator will get closer and closer to what can be interpreted by the Discriminator as a valid image, thus an image whose content is no different from that of the Discriminator reference database. GANs have been used to produce numerous experiments including the project https://thispersondo esnotexist.com which generates a new imaginary but realistic human face with each browser update. The Generator can't access the Discriminator reference dataset so its output cannot be described as copies of the originals. Each GAN network is trained on a different dataset and is therefore capable of producing images representing only one category of content.

We can read in human creative processes some similarities with the mechanism of GAN functioning. As mentioned, the designer needs to observe and collect references. As in art, if we abandon the idea of sudden inspiration emerging from creative genius and we rather consider creativity as a process in which the acquisition of references is a fundamental stage in the generation of original works and innovations, then it is precisely in the ability to elaborate and rework this archive of information that creativity manifests itself. There is a debate on the existence of bias in the datasets used by GANs but, at the same time, the human capacity to archive (physically and mentally) is also limited. Moreover, the transmission of bias in the construction of datasets either through partially manual or fully automated selection systems (such as web scaping) is still attributable to human intervention. In human-based activity, the selection and collection of references is generally conducted during field research by means of interviews and visits, or by consulting archives and databases (desk research) [17]. Field research has the physical and temporal limitation of the human ability to reach and document information. Desk research, through the use of archives, databases, and in general, the Internet and search engines, is a potentially all-encompassing source of data collection. However, the algorithmic logics that manage indexing criteria in turn convey bias in suggesting search results. Search engine profiling algorithms, in fact, tend to select content that is potentially more consistent with search terms but are influenced by previous searches and advertisements. Improving the ability of algorithms to provide more relevant answers also in relation to the meaning of search terms in their context is the subject of research in the semantic web [18]. There are also examples of hybrid tools that exploit different technologies, such as virtual reality, to actively support the designer in the management of a large amount of data through, for instance, 3D image visualization. One of these tools is "TAMED CLOUD, sensible interaction with a swarm of data", an immersive installation for visualizing data as a 3D cloud with autonomous and reactive behavior that reassemble autonomously according to the user's movements [19].

What we wish to emphasize is that just as GANs use existing information archives to generate new ones, so does the designer when building the archive of references from which to draw. Moreover, the construction of this reference archive, that is the source of human creativity, takes place largely through the use of machine-mediated search and indexing criteria logics.

Building models

Among the methods by which neural networks are able to interpret the content of an image are contrastive models. In these models, the neural network learns to recognize the characteristics that distinguish the subject of a given image without the use of tags but by comparing it to a reference image dataset. In doing so, the neural network begins to define a set of variables that allow it to decode common features between images that represent the same subject. In essence, the network builds an arbitrary (mathematical) model of what a dog, a cat, a plant is.

To be able to derive value from his archive of references, the designer needs to frame and catalogue the data and information collected. The designer uses simplified conceptual models of the portion of reality on which he wants to intervene [20]. Such models are necessary to make complex systems comprehensible and manipulable. Often, these conceptual simplifications are translated into mathematical models to be processed and visualized with simulation software. The designer develops, as well as neural networks based on contrastive learning, arbitrary criteria for classification and interpretation that are mediated by sensitivity and knowledge developed with experience. It is in the ability to create relationships between the parts that the design activity is able to articulate itself in a dialogical process between data and models. A design strategy that can be adopted by designers to develop original solutions is extreme design: an Advanced Design practice that consists of the ability to find inspiration by observing contexts considered non strictly connected with the specific problematic area of interest but can suggest strategies to solve design problems [21]. Finding new connections between technological domains and natural and artificial ecosystems allows the designer to propose innovative solutions that are disruptive compared to incremental innovation processes.

Therefore, the ability to create connections of meanings and functional relationships can activate creative processes that can foster product innovation. The criteria by which the designer defines these connections are different from designer to designer, based on individual sensitivity and knowledge and experience, and different from those developed by machines. In a non-anthropocentric attitude to design, these intersections constitute a further level of design articulation that develops the synergies of human-machine interaction.

Synthesis

A widely used type of neural network for the generation of synthetic images is Stable Diffusion. This technique works similarly to image denoising processes used in image processing software to reduce the presence of visual artefacts (noise). By incrementally adding small amounts of a specific type of algorithmically generated noise, the Gaussian noise, a completely disturbed and no longer recognizable image is obtained. Stable diffusion consists of training a neural network to reverse this process in order to restore the image to its initial appearance. This technique, in combination with other neural networks, forms the basis of systems that enable synthetic images to be produced from textual prompts.

Proposing a parallelism with design activity, when the designer builds models identify parameters and constraints of the project in turn performs what could be described as a systematic noise reduction operation. This noise is determined by the volume of information, economic and production constrains, market demands and criteria of sustainability and regulatory compliance. It is a process that cannot be schematized in the form of an algorithm but requires design sensitivity in being able to mediate and prioritize.

When interpreted from the humanities perspective, synthesis emerges from a dialectical process of analysis and evaluation. In computer science, the term synthetic is used to refer to computer-generated media either through rendering engines or neural networks. Synthetic media include not only images, but also video, sound, text, voice and interactive media. The designer's activity is an activity of synthesis that can be understood both as a dialogical process that reflects the iterative patterns of design development and as the generation of a new form.

3 An Evolving Symbiotic Creative Ecology

In the previous paragraphs we drew parallels between the creative processes of industrial design practices and some of the underpinning mechanisms of artificial intelligence technologies. The AI-based technologies described help to exemplify the symbiotic relationship between human and non-human in creative processes. Just as the human designer, who observes phenomena, creates and stores a personal archive of references and reprocesses them to produce original ideas, GANs learn from datasets to generate new works. Images and concepts are found, classified, tagged and hierarchized by humans with digital means. In machines, contrastive models autonomously define parameters and criteria to establish connections among parts, developing a non-anthropocentric classification sensibility and criteria. The creative process is ultimately defined by the ability of reducing informative noise to distill relevant input for the project synthesis. An ability that designer develop overtime as Stable Diffusion neural networks learn to pixel denoise to generate new images from text prompt.

In describing the creative development process in the field of design and drawing parallels with some of the digital and AI-based technologies, we wanted to argue the hypothesis, already present in the argumentation of technogenesis, that a symbiotic relationship between human and machine and, in particular, between designer and machine already exists. The widespread use of technology in professional practice has integrated into human-based creative processes to a structural level, redefining design principles in a post-anthropocentric landscape. Technological development will increase the possibilities with which AI can be integrated into design disciplines. It is therefore necessary for designers to be an interpreter of such strategic co-evolution, understanding the logic and limits within these technologies act. In building innovation, human-nonhuman creative intelligences will collectively co-design symbiotic imaginaries of the future.

The very mediation role of the designer and the increasing etereogenity of specializations and knowledges required in contemporary projects characterize the designer as a synthetic combination of multiple creative identities in which human and non-human actors symbiotically intertwines.

References

1. Hayles, N.K.: How We Think: Digital Media and Contemporary Technogenesis. The University of Chicago Press, Chicago; London (2012)
2. Stiegler, B.: Technics and Time, 1. The Fault OfEpimetheus. Vol. 1, 3 vols. Stanford University Press, Stanford, California (1998)
3. Manouach, I., Engelhardt, A. eds.: Chimeras. Inventory of Synthetic Cognition. Onassis Publications, Athens (2022). https://alice-ch3n81.net/files/data/chimeras/Chimeras_Inventory-of-Synthetic-Cognition.pdf
4. Haraway, D.J.: Manifesto Cyborg. Donne, Tecnologie e Biopolitiche Del Corpo. 2018th ed. Feltrinelli, n.d
5. McKenzie, W.: Capital Is Dead. Is This Something Worse? Verso, London (2021)
6. Sennet, R.: L'uomo Artigiano. Feltrinelli, Milano (2008)
7. McAfee, A., Brynjolfsson, E.: The Second Machine Age. Work, Progress, and Prosperity in a Time of Brilliant Technologies. Norton & Company, New York, NY, USA (2014)

8. Verganti, R., Vendraminelli, L., Iansiti, M.: Innovation and design in the age of artificial intelligence. J. Prod. Innov. Manag. **37**(3), 212–227 (2020). https://doi.org/10.1111/jpim. 12523
9. Celaschi, F., Formia, E., Lupo, E.: From trans-disciplinary to undisciplined design learning: educating through/to disruption. Strategic Des. Res. J. **6**(1), 1–10 (2013)
10. Zeilinger, M.: The politics of visual indeterminacy in abstract AI Art. Leonardo **20**, 1–12 (2022). https://doi.org/10.1162/leon_a_02291
11. Zeilinger, M.: Tactical Entanglements: AI Art, Creative Agency, and the Limits of Intellectual Property. Lightning Source, Milton Keynes, UK (2021)
12. Baraniuk, C.: The "creepy Facebook AI" Story That Captivated the Media. BBC News, 1 August 2017, sec. Technology. https://www.bbc.com/news/technology-40790258
13. Maldonado, T.: Disegno Industriale: Un Riesame. Universale Economica Saggi. Milano, Giangiacomo Feltrinelli Editore (2008)
14. Baudrillard, J.: Per una critica dell'economia politica del segno. Edited by Pierre Dalla Vigna. Mimesis, Milano (2012). https://www.mimesisedizioni.it/libro/9788884838698
15. Celaschi, F.: Il Design Come Mediatore Tra Saperi. L'integrazione Delle Conoscenze Nella Formazione Del Designer Contemporaneo. In: Germak, C. (eds.) L'uomo al Centro Del Progetto, pp. 19–31. Allemandi, Torino (2008)
16. Design Council. 'The Double Diamond: A Universally Accepted Depiction of the Design Process'. Accessed 28 November 2022. https://www.designcouncil.org.uk/our-work/news-opinion/double-diamond-universally-accepted-depiction-design-process/
17. Celaschi, F., Deserti, A.: Design e Innovazione. Strumenti e Pratiche per La Ricerca Applicata. Carocci, Roma (2007)
18. Berners-Lee, T.: L'architettura Del Nuovo Web. Feltrinelli, Milano (2001)
19. Garnier, F., Tsai, F., Zamplaras, D., Levillain, F., Bihanic, D.: TAMED CLOUD: Sensible Interaction with a Swarm of Data (2019)
20. Celaschi, F.: Non Industrial Design. Contributi al Discorso Progettuale. Luca Sossella Editore, Bologna (2017)
21. Celaschi, F.: Advance design points of view. In: Celi, M. (ed.) Advanced Design Cultures. Long-Term Perspective and Continuos Innovation, pp. 3–17. Springer International Publishing (2015). https://doi.org/10.1007/978-3-319-08602-6_1

AIGenC: AI Generalisation via Creativity

Corina Cătărău-Cotuţiu^(✉)⬤, Esther Mondragón⬤, and Eduardo Alonso⬤

Artificial Intelligence Research Centre (CitAI), Department of Computer Science
City, University of London, Northampton Square, London EC1V 0HB, UK
Corina.Catarau-Cotutiu@city.ac.uk

Abstract. Inspired by cognitive theories of creativity, this paper introduces a computational model (AIGenC) that lays down the necessary components to enable artificial agents to learn, use and generate transferable representations. Unlike machine representations, which rely exclusively on raw sensory data, biological representations incorporate relational and associative information that embed a rich and structured concept space. The AIGenC model poses a hierarchical graph architecture with various levels and types of representations procured by the different components. The first component, Concept Processing, extracts objects and affordances from sensory input and encodes them into a concept space. The resulting representations are stored in a dual memory system and enriched with goal-directed and temporal information acquired through reinforcement learning, creating a higher-level of abstraction. Two additional and complementary components work in parallel to detect and recover relevant concepts through a matching process and create new ones, respectively, in a process akin to cognitive Reflective Reasoning and Blending. If Reflective Reasoning fails to offer a suitable solution, a blending operation creates new concepts by combining past information. We discuss the model's capability to yield better out-of-distribution generalisation in artificial agents, thus advancing toward Artificial General Intelligence.

Keywords: Affordances · Generalisation · Creativity ·
Representational Learning · Reinforcement Learning · Learning
Transfer

1 Introduction

Machine learning (ML) systems struggle to adapt to novelty and often fail to exploit past learnt experiences effectively. This downside is due to ML's poor representational learning capability to acquire meaningful relational concepts. E.g., Large Language Models must parse each word in a wide variety of embeddings to generalise it to new contexts, requiring considerable combinatorial augmentation for a *tabula rasa* unstructured model to learn systematic representations [7].

© The Author(s), under exclusive license to Springer Nature Switzerland AG 2023
N. Moniz et al. (Eds.): EPIA 2023, LNAI 14116, pp. 38–51, 2023.
https://doi.org/10.1007/978-3-031-49011-8_4

We hypothesise that Creative Problem Solving (CPS) could help AI systems learn versatile concepts that can be adapted to novel situations, a step forward to solving the problem of generalisation in AI. Humans and other animals can naturally map previous experiences to new situations, transferring responses to similar scenarios [26, 30]. Machines do not. In the natural world, stimulus generalisation is driven by common sensory attributes, which are often embedded within irrelevant cues and may lead to dysfunctional use of information. However, stimulus generalisation is only a fraction of human transfer capabilities; associations can also mediate generalisation to dissimilar cues, bridging learning across different sensory dimensions. Crucially, the role played by commonalities can be extended to different levels of information [27]. Extracting and storing patterns and relations capable of bearing resemblance across situations beyond the sensory word would permit hierarchical structuring of information and creative, non-passive reuse of data to transfer knowledge.

As Deep Neural Networks (DNNs) become ubiquitous, concerns arise regarding the nature and lack of structure of the representations they learn and how these affect their decision making [7]. DNNs excel at extracting regularities from training data but struggle to extrapolate or generalise to out-of-distribution settings [3, 22]. This discrepancy is due to using shortcut strategies [14] to solve a task without learning the true input structure. Shortcuts involve data interpolation -meaningless, ad-hoc parameter adjusting to reduce the error- and are, thus, highly dependent on the training dataset. Systems operating on shortcuts may appear to perform as if they had learnt abstract concepts and could potentially transfer learning. Still, their performance relies on highly tuned vast amounts of training features that do not support extrapolation [11].

Drawing inspiration from CPS's theory, we have designed the modelling components necessary for cross domain performance in a naïve Reinforcement Learning (RL) agent. Unlike standard deep RL architectures, which merely reduce the complexity of the environment by compressing raw input, our approach endows artificial agents with core concepts -abstract representations that hold meaning beyond the training context [25], at different hierarchical levels.

Core concepts [31] include different types of data—objects, events and properties—and are the building blocks of meaning and so-called common sense [34]. Although task transfer does not inherently necessitate creativity, for a system to display human-like behaviour, it is critical to adapt existing concepts to new tasks -effectively, to learn new concepts based on previous knowledge in what is called displacement or creative transfer. Displacement requires creative reuse of information, i.e., a transfer mechanism capable of generating different concept relations, not just appending previous ones. Moreover, when a problem cannot be solved solely based on existing knowledge and approximating a solution is not viable, it is necessary to give rise to new concepts.

Implicit relations learned by DNNs [8] are insufficient to generate meaningful concepts; additional explicit representations of relations, affordances and temporal information are needed to capture the world's content and dynamics and achieve flexible cross-domain generalisation. Implementing these different types of knowledge may bestow RL agents with something akin to common sense. This capability would allow them to infer hidden information, such as intentions or goals, by interacting with the environment. In traditional RL scenarios, agents disregard by design most of the information provided by the environment, learning simple policies linked to global states. Although in theory, states in RL can represent any type of information, in practice RL implementations work primarily on states in which only simple sensory data is encoded [2]. In so doing, states are monolithic entities that do not permit concept manipulation and transfer. We argue that to generalise concepts, an agent cannot rely on raw sensory information alone; instead, it must learn by trial and error the functional and contextual information accompanying them.

The AIGenC model postulates an adaptable concept space that encodes objects, affordances and relational information from environmental features into a deep RL environment. The main characteristic that sets aside our framework is declaring these different dimensions of knowledge for matching information at different levels of abstraction.

2   Functional Creativity, Concept Space and Affordances

Concepts are described as entities with the necessary and sufficient conditions for assigning membership of concept X to a category Y [6]. A common premise in classic creativity theories [9, 13, 24, 31] is that of a concept space as a bridge between sub-symbolic and symbolic representations. Gärdenfors' approach of a conceptual framework, where concepts express properties across multiple dimensions that evolve in time and are ascribed to different domains [13] can be adapted to an artificial setup. To do so, a knowledge engineer must provide a finite initial set of features—a task that becomes unscalable as the number of features increases [20]. Alternatively, DNNs could be used to extract pertinent features. However, defining concepts on DNNs features alone is insufficient to capture the world's relational complexity. Instead, we define a hierarchical representation of the concept space where environmental features form low-level concepts and represent higher-level concepts as combinations of the former instead of posing the traditional cognitive categories. The idea is to set a single unit (the concept) as a structure that grows hierarchically, enabling the application of the same algorithm at different levels of abstraction. The hierarchy (Fig. 1) builds as follows: static concept features as those captured in standard deep RL frames form the bottom (Layer 0). Above it (Layer 1), base object concepts are represented as graph nodes whose edges establish their relations as affordances. Next, at the top (Layer 2), we have a higher-level graph representation whose nodes reproduce the previous graph structure, and the edges capture their temporal succession.

To build such a hierarchy, an RL agent must first select the base concepts' features critical to the task and valuable for encoding in the latent space, by interacting with its environment autonomously. The first component of our framework is thus unsupervised learning of basic concepts. Autoencoder (AE) based models are of interest because they learn low-dimensional representations from high-dimensional distributions by encoding and decoding the input [23], inducing features from raw perceptual data. These architectures can gather basic concepts and implicit relations as weight matrices that act as relational units between the different features, capturing the functional relationships that impact the model's behaviour [8]. However, being implicit, the relations cannot be interchanged without modifying the representation itself. Therefore, we posit the need to additionally encode explicit relations for inter-concept interactions.

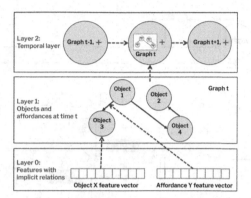

Fig. 1. Hierarchical concept space: object concepts are represented by feature vectors at the bottom level (Layer 0). At the middle level (Layer 1), nodes and edges represent object concepts and affordances. At the top level (Layer 2), the graphs from the previous level become nodes along with a reward given to the agent in the RL setting (red +) in a graph whose edges mark temporal succession (t).

Gibson introduced the term *affordance* to describe that certain states enable an agent to perform certain actions in a given context [15]. Formally, affordances are defined as relations in the agent-environment system rather than as properties [4]. To learn affordances, an agent must be able to interact with objects to assess their possible uses. Sensory similar concepts are not bound to behave the same way. A beach ball and a bowling ball may look similar, but their weights will render them functionally divergent to, e.g., balance a lever. Therefore, we must enrich the hierarchical concept space by including affordances to enable our RL agent to form various complex representations in a given functional, spatial and temporal context, i.e., to acquire knowledge about object manipulation. The resulting structure, represented as a graph of concept nodes and affordance edges, captures the dynamics of the world. This hierarchical structure aligns with existing research [31]. However, instead of resorting to knowledge bases, we advance a CPS algorithm that uses deep learning methods to manipulate concepts in the latent space.

3   A Framework for Concept Transfer and Functional Creativity

AIGenC seeks to lay the fundamental structures and interplay necessary for good learning transfer in RL systems, not to present a particular implementation. This section describes these units and interactions in detail.

The model posits a three-component deep learning structure: Concept Processing, Reflective Reasoning, and Blending. The first two comprise two sub-components each: Concept Processing involves object discovery and affordance learning, while Reflective Reasoning consists of Long Term Memory (LTM) initialisation and Selective Matching (Fig. 2).

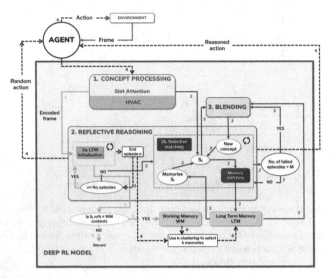

Fig. 2. The three components of the model: (1) Concept Processing (cream/olive), (2) Reflective Reasoning (blue), (3) Blending (purple) and the algorithmic flow. The input (frames) is encoded in (1) as vector representations by two unsupervised models. In (2), LTM is initialised by random exploration (2a). The population of WM and LTM is indicated by open tip arrows, a solid green (1) and a dashed black line (4), respectively. After LTM initialisation, Selective Matching (2b) is activated within a Deep RL training. (2b) returns from LTM the concepts most similar to the current state, which are then incorporated into it before inputted to the Deep RL model. If the agent is unsuccessful at solving the task for several episodes, Blending (3) is triggered, by which novel concepts are formed and then added to the current state.

The framework runs on top of a basal deep RL training that relies on a hierarchical concept space. The latter's structure exploits both implicit and explicit relational information to support flexible knowledge transfer. To save resources and acknowledge the influence of phylogenetic and ontogenetic evolution, implementations may need to pre-train the representational architecture. The first component learns different representations extracted at each time-step, constituting an RL state. States are then added to a Working Memory (WM) based on their novelty and used together with LTM by the Reflective Reasoning component to select the next action. The term *reflective reasoning* defines the main functionality of the second component, namely, a comparison process between stored knowledge and current input intended to adaptively select and combine valuable information for the task at hand. Finally, the agent creates new concepts using the Blending component when available concepts do not overcome a standstill in solving a task.

3.1 Deep Reinforcement Learning

RL tasks have three main components: states, actions, and rewards. RL agents learn by interacting with the environment and receiving direct feedback through rewards. An agent learns to optimise a policy by trial and error to reach a goal state by maximising the cumulative reward. States are representations of the world and inform the agent of which situation it currently is in. In Deep RL, a subfield of machine learning that combines RL and deep learning, agents process the environment by passing frames to DL models as input and choosing an action based on the encodings of those frames. These encodings do not usually distinguish between core features (i.e., features that serve as discriminative cues that control learning) and features that are irrelevant to the task at hand (e.g., image quality, colour), and forgo most of the temporal data required for complex multi-level representations [17]. Our model broadens the scope of these representations capturing objects, affordances, and temporality. It does so by outlining a mechanism to filter and extract granular and varied information by decomposing the sequence of frames into multiple layers of the concept space and storing them in a memory system. In so doing, the agent no longer relies solely on current static frame data to make its decisions.

3.2 Concept Processing Component

A concept processing unit is postulated for encoding and adding the input to the concept space. It comprises two pretrained subunits that process separately sensory (objects) and dynamic information (affordances). Training needs to be unsupervised to ensure that the RL agent's concept space is independent of external classes and that representations of objects/concepts can be extracted by an agent regardless of whether they have been encountered before.

The first sub-component represents objects as latent vectors through unsupervised object discovery, while the second encodes action vectors. The interaction of the two subcomponents and the environment is posed as a modification of Şahin and collaborators' formalism [33], so that affordances can be defined as an acquired relation between an *(effect, reward)* pair and a *(concept-object, action)* tuple. In this manner, when an agent applies an action to the object, an effect and associated reward pair is generated.

AE based models could be used to ensure transferable and detachable concept representations. Filtering is also needed to reduce irrelevant information to the task and avoid computational explosion. The most valuable objects out of N can be selected using a slot attention module, which maps N latent representations to K slots through an iterative attention mechanism [36].

While DL has achieved remarkable results in representing objects, unsupervised affordance learning remains unsolved, and few unsupervised feature learning methods for affordances can be found [16]. A formal model for affordance learning can be defined by incorporating affordances in a relational concept space using a Hierarchical Variational Autoencoder (HVAC) architecture [18]. While HVACs capture the evolution of interactions, the encodings of the dynamics produced are not disentangled from the objects interacting, which is a limitation. Hence, we will not refer to the output of the HVAC model as an affordance but as an action representation. The action representation and the effect will form the affordance (See Algorithm 1 line: 21–22).

Algorithm 1 AIGenC integrated within an RL setup

1: Intialising LTM $ltm = \langle keys[], \{\}\rangle$
2: $object-discovery(frame) \rightarrow Slots^{(K \times M)}$ - a pre-trained object discovery model, where K is the number of slots and M the size of the encoding vector
3: $action-encoding(interactions) \rightarrow Actions^{K \times P}$ - a pre-trained action encoding model, with input sequences of frames of the agent interacting with an object and output K encodings of size P of those interactions
4: Let A be a set of objects interacting with the agent
5: $create-state-graph(s_t, ltm)$ - a function that returns the current state graph
6: $matching(mem, G_t) \rightarrow$ T/F - a function that checks if current state graph exists in memory
7: **for** $iteration = 1, 2, \ldots, N$ **do** ▷ N is a hyper-parameter that represents the number of times the algorithms parameters are updated
8:     Intialising WM $working-mem = \langle keys[], \{\}\rangle$
9:     Let A_i be a random subset of A
10:     **while** $episode\ not\ done$ **do** ▷ Stopping criterion: A pre-defined number of time-steps passed or a positive reward is obtained
11:         Let s_t be the current state of the environment
12:         objects $\leftarrow object-discovery(s_t)$
13:         $action-encodings \leftarrow action-encoding(A_i)$
14:         $G_t \leftarrow create-state-graph(objects, action-encodings, s_t)$
15:         **if** $memory\ initialisation\ phase$ **then**
16:             $a_{i,t} \leftarrow random(actions)$
17:         **else**
18:             $a_{i,t} \leftarrow$ Run policy-network $\pi(G_t)$
19:         $s_{t+1}, reward \leftarrow$ Take action a_i
20:         Compute effect $f(a_i, s_t, s_{t+1}) \rightarrow encoding(s_{t+1})$ - $encoding(s_t)$
21:         Update G_t with ($s_t, s_{t+1}, effect$)
22:         **if** $not\ matching(wm, G_t)$ **then** Add(G_t, wm) ▷ Update WM
23:         **else** discard() ▷ Optimise policy network, update LTM
24:     $WM clusters \leftarrow$ KMeans(wm)
25:     $centroids \leftarrow$ centers(WMclusters)
26:     **if** $not\ matching(ltm, centroids)$ **then** Add($centroids-graphs, ltm$)

Concept Space The concept space is structured hierarchically from representations extracted at the Concept Processing unit. The structured data is necessary for selecting and matching concepts in the Reflective Reasoning component. A three-level structure is used to organise knowledge as concepts: the feature space, the concept level, and the graph representation of an RL state-time configuration that defines the problem template [31]. The structure can be characterised as a graph that stores and relates information without a predefined data design and satisfies theoretical prerequisites such as being hierarchical and adaptive [9,13]. Graphs can represent different levels of hierarchical abstraction and capture relations between elements. They are also easily manipulated (i.e., adding or removing edges without altering the whole graph), making them the most promising means for representing a dynamic concept space. Graph representations allow for flexibility, both vertical (i.e., changes in levels of abstractions in the hierarchy) and horizontal (i.e., expansions within a level by adding or removing nodes). In addition, the flexibility required by contextual and time-dependent functional classes in creative problem-solving is allowed by dynamic graphs that are stored in memory systems as adjacency lists as opposed to matrices. As such, each node has associated a list of related nodes of varying sizes, enabling partially connected graphs.

Memory System Our framework includes Working Memory (WM) and Long Term Memory (LTM) units. These two memories must interact throughout the lifetime of an RL agent. Each memory serves a particular purpose. First, WM stores current information, if it does not already exist (Algorithm 1, line: 23), during each episode in an RL setup. Once the agent reaches the terminal state (when the goal is reached or after a time limit is exceeded), the episode ends and WM is cleared, at which point the most representative states (the centroid of a data cluster) and their associated concepts are selected from the WM using k-clustering and stored in LTM. As opposed to WM, the content of the LTM must persist throughout episodes to permit transfer of learning during the lifetime of an RL agent (Algorithm 1, line: 1). The memories' content, the concept space, is assembled as two lists: an object list and a hashmap list. The object list records the extracted object representations, while the hashmap list maps each object to a corresponding list of affordances. Once the concept space is formed, an agent can interact with it throughout its creative learning process in both of the remaining components of the architecture, Reflective Reasoning and Blending.

3.3   Reflective Reasoning Component

The Reflective Reasoning component defines a procedure to choose which concepts from WM are to be permanently stored in LTM and incorporates a matching operation between the current state and LTM information (see Algorithm 2, line: 7). Matching allows selecting the concepts useful to fulfil the specific task at any given time point.

Processing in the Reflective Reasoning component is executed sequentially (Fig. 2). First, LTM is initialised; then, selective matching occurs (Algorithm 2, line: 7–9). The agent first explores the environment randomly (using a random action selection policy, Algorithm 1, line: 16), learning new concepts at each state and storing the most representative ones in LTM. The interplay of the two memory systems enables a process of matching novel states to past information [8]. Concepts that reach LTM are selectively retrieved to enhance the agent's ability to choose an action leading to a state closer to the goal. This selective matching operation is carried out in the Selective Matching unit (Fig. 2b). By storing structured representations of concepts in LTM, the agent can access past experiences and use them to inform current decisions, allowing adaptation to new tasks and environments.

Matching, however, does not convey sameness retrieval. Creative agents must adapt previous concepts to unfamiliar states by connecting relational concepts to new objects [34]. The hierarchical structure of the concept space allows independent access to each level of abstraction, making this type of adaptation possible. Nonetheless, matching also requires a comparison process to assess similarity by measuring the distance between the elements involved (i.e., graph-based concepts). Traditional techniques for graph comparisons (e.g., contrasting graph adjacency) are insufficient as different edges can bear different importance. To calculate an adequate distance, we propose an Optimal Transport (OT) technique that transforms a (continuous) probability distribution into another with the lowest possible cost. Therefore, given two graphs, the OT associated with their Wasserstein discrepancy provides a correspondence between their nodes to establish graph matching [1].

After the initialisation of LTM through agent exploration, selective matching on the initialised memory can be done using a trainable policy network for action selection. This shifts the agent's focus towards exploitation, where the goal is achieved by using objects in the environment or building new ones.

Algorithm 2 Enhancing algorithm with selective matching

1: $selective-matching(G_t, ltm, s_t)$- network that returns information useful for the task, uses
   $graph-matching$, a function that matches a given graph against ltm and returns a list of
   sub-graphs from ltm with a $Z\%$ similarity to G_t
2: $supplement()$ - function that enhances a graph G_1 with missing nodes and edges from G_2,
   uses $graph-union$ a function that returns the union of G_1 and G_2
3: **for** $iteration = 1, 2, \ldots, N$ **do** ▷ *N is a hyper-parameter that represents the number of times*
      the algorithms parameters are updated
4:        Init $wm \leftarrow \langle keys[], \{\} \rangle$
5:        **while** $episode$ **not done do**   ▷ *Stopping criterion: A pre-defined number of time-steps*
              passed or a positive reward is obtained
6:            ...
7:            $matched-graphs \leftarrow selective-matching(G_t, ltm, s_t)$
8:            $enhanced-graph \leftarrow supplement(G_t, matched-graphs)$
9:            $a_{i,t} \leftarrow$ Run policy-network $\pi(enhanced-graph)$
10:           ...
11:       Optimise policy network

Applying a concept from memory to a given state entails two steps: first, a match of the graph representing the state (e.g., G_t) to the graphs representing the long-term stored information (e.g., LTM); second, once the match is successful, G_t is supplemented with the objects and affordances present in the retrieved LTM $subgraph$ but lacking in G_t in a process known as completion [34] (Algorithm 2, line: 8). Such completion will foster learning and bring to the agent's current state useful past experiences.

So far, we have shown how an agent could solve a problem using different existing concepts. The following component describes creating a completely new concept by leveraging the existing concept space—considered (everyday) creativity.

3.4   Blending Component

Creativity is triggered when existing concepts are insufficient to solve a task, leading an agent to a standstill. We are using the expression *impasse situation* [19] to refer to the inability of an agent to solve a task for several episodes. A CPS approach should aid in overcoming such an impasse with a solution that satisfies problem constraints.

Hence, we are working under the assumption that the impasse could be surmounted by developing a novel, useful concept. In the AIGenC framework, new concepts are generated by blending existing concepts in the latent space into new representations. Conceptual blending [9] denotes the combination of meaningful features of two or more concepts into a new concept.

Two issues must be addressed when creating a new concept: selecting the relevant concepts that help the agent achieve a goal and combining them effectively. To filter the concept space for information that can solve a problem, the agent must have a high-level understanding of the problem, context, and task requirements; that is, acquire a general problem template to process the information, which requires summarising and organising information at a level of abstraction beyond the current hierarchy. Artificial agents lack this knowledge, so we propose a heuristic that widens the range of matched concepts by relaxing the similarity constraint in matching (i.e., we propose using a similarity criterion (say, X%) for selecting concepts to be blended, acknowledging that other approaches may also be appropriate). When Reflective Reasoning finds the concepts that lead to a satisfactory solution, the problem-solving task stops; otherwise, Blending is activated, making the two functionally complementary. Both components match information from LTM to the current state. However, Blending retrieves a larger pool of information, allowing for a wider variety of environmental data to be operated on.

Retrieved concepts are used to create novel concepts using a non-linear trainable network, expanding the concept space with new diverse concepts to be applied to the task. The network must respect the latent space's structure, meaning that the dimensions of the latent vectors should be maintained, and the network should be able to combine their feature values by moving across their dimensions. Relevant features extracted by concept processing sub-modules can be identified post hoc by quantifying their contribution to the performance of the previous unsupervised models. SHAP (Shapley Additive Explanations, [21]), an interpretability method, can be used to weigh the pertinence of individual features and select the latent space features that bear the most relevance to solving the task.

To keep the semantic features of data through the generation process, we propose decomposing the input into a vector and a latent code that targets the salient semantic features of the data distribution. This process is similar to Chen et al.'s approach [5]. Thus, the input vector would be replaced by the concepts to be merged with a set of trainable parameters for their combination function. In addition, the latent codes could be initialised with an average of the SHAP values. As the Blending function is intended to create novel concepts rather than reproduce input in the latent space, a clustering-specific loss function could be used to evaluate the similarity between the generated concept and existing concepts in the cluster, with a low value indicating a good match. By enforcing clustering similarity through the loss function, we could reduce the variability of the new concept, providing a mechanism for more meaningful concept building [29].

It is essential to note that the proposed blending mechanism would only be possible in a system that incorporates functional components like those presented in our model. The underlying representational structure of the first component is critical to obtaining a comprehensive input representation. At the same time, Reflective Reasoning tools are essential for selecting, adding, and filtering concepts in the concept space, reducing computational costs and recycling useful concepts. Filtering, which involves understanding the high-level characteristics of the concept affordance, is not simply a search of the conceptual space. Instead, it requires a generalisable solution template, developed through repeated similar experiences. We anticipate that our agent's semi-random selection of relevant objects will establish a foundation for incremental abstract representations. With Blending, the complete architecture has been presented. The architecture proposed serves as a blueprint for designing more robust systems equipped with transferable and adaptable knowledge capable of solving problems creatively.

4   Discussion

We have introduced a deep RL conceptual framework for creative problem solving that enables an agent to represent and generate new concepts and transfer representations across domains and tasks. AIGenC constructs a hierarchical concept space used to retrieve (matching) and adapt (blending) past knowledge. Affordances and temporal information encode the dynamics of the environment, offering an agent multiple views of a concept (related to different possible goals), driving the transfer of learning between tasks and goals. We are not entering into the debate on how representations are formed, nor do we aim to assess any of the claims regarding concept formation in humans [32]. We acknowledge that the dependency on input data and the complexity of creating useful conceptual spaces with sufficient quality dimensions for characterising abstract concepts, thus bridging sub-symbolic and symbolic representations, are unsolved problems in cognitive architectures [12, 20]—an issue that becomes even more challenging when such dimensions are derived from a latent space with undefined semantics. Our interest lies exclusively in describing the necessary concept space and interplaying structures that could aid an artificial agent in transferring knowledge across contexts and tasks. To that aim, we have adapted ideas from cognitive science to design systems for low-level concept formation and hierarchical concept spaces, but we steer away from assigning anthropomorphic value to the different components and outputs. Divergent currents of opinion regarding the prospect of AI to achieve human-like intelligence swarm academic fora [10, 35]. At the eye of the storm, the lack of AI generalisation has been highlighted as one of, if not the most crucial problem to achieve AGI [37]. We concur with cognitive-inspired theories that posit that the lack of generalisation in AI agents is partially due to their inability to discover, combine and generate new concepts that can be used across domains to solve different, yet similar, tasks as humans and animals do [28]. It is conceivable that this operation underpins learning so-called common sense knowledge. Providing artificial agents with a rich concept space to allow the processing of commonalities at different levels of a hierarchy, can serve as a world frame for some level of "common sense". In that vein, our proposal unfolds from contextualised functional representations and sets the appropriate scenario for an AI system to learn an adaptive concept space by interacting with the environment, detect and differentiate commonalities, contextual information and unique functional features that would enable it it to transfer knowledge efficiently.

References

1. Alvarez-Melis, D., Fusi, N.: Geometric dataset distances via optimal transport. Adv. Neural. Inf. Process. Syst. **33**, 21428–21439 (2020)
2. Badia, A.P., Piot, B., Kapturowski, S., Sprechmann, P., Vitvitskyi, A., Guo, Z.D., Blundell, C.: Agent57: Outperforming the atari human benchmark. In: International Conference on Machine Learning, pp. 507–517. PMLR (2020)
3. Bengio, Y., Lecun, Y., Hinton, G.: Deep learning for AI. Commun. ACM **64**(7), 58–65 (2021)
4. Chemero, A., Klein, C., Cordeiro, W.: Events as changes in the layout of affordances. Ecol. Psychol. **15**(1), 19–28 (2003)
5. Chen, X., Duan, Y., Houthooft, R., Schulman, J., Sutskever, I., Abbeel, P.: Infogan: Interpretable representation learning by information maximizing generative adversarial nets. Adv. Neural Inf. Process. Syst. **29** (2016)
6. Coraci, D.: A unified model of ad hoc concepts in conceptual spaces. Mind. Mach. **32**(2), 289–309 (2022)
7. Dasgupta, I., Guo, D., Gershman, S.J., Goodman, N.D.: Analyzing machine-learned representations: a natural language case study. Cogn. Sci. **44**(12), e12925 (2020)
8. Doumas, L.A., Puebla, G., Martin, A.E., Hummel, J.E.: A theory of relation learning and cross-domain generalization. Psychol. Rev. (2022)
9. Fauconnier, G., Turner, M.: Conceptual integration networks. Cogn. Sci. **22**(2), 133–187 (1998)
10. Fjelland, R.: Why general artificial intelligence will not be realized. Huma. Soc. Sci. Commun. **7**(1), 1–9 (2020)
11. Floridi, L., Chiriatti, M.: Gpt-3: its nature, scope, limits, and consequences. Mind. Mach. **30**, 681–694 (2020)
12. Frixione, M., Lieto, A.: Representing concepts in formal ontologies. compositionality vs. typicality effects. Log. Logical Philos. **21**(4), 391–414 (2012)
13. Gardenfors, P.: Conceptual Spaces: The Geometry of Thought. MIT Press (2004)
14. Geirhos, R., Jacobsen, J.H., Michaelis, C., Zemel, R., Brendel, W., Bethge, M., Wichmann, F.A.: Shortcut learning in deep neural networks. Nat. Mach. Intell. **2**(11), 665–673 (2020)
15. Gibson, J.J.: The theory of affordances. Hilldale USA **1**(2), 67–82 (1977)

16. Hassanin, M., Khan, S., Tahtali, M.: Visual affordance and function understanding: a survey. ACM Comput. Surv. (CSUR) **54**(3), 1–35 (2021)
17. Hayman, G., Huebner, B.: Temporal updating, behavioral learning, and the phenomenology of time-consciousness. Behav. Brain Sci. **42** (2019)
18. Jain, A., Szot, A., Lim, J.J.: Generalization to new actions in reinforcement learning (2020). arXiv:2011.01928
19. Laird, J.E., Derbinsky, N., Tinkerhess, M.: Online determination of value-function structure and action-value estimates for reinforcement learning in a cognitive architecture. Adv. Cogn. Syst. **2**, 221–238 (2012)
20. Lieto, A., Chella, A., Frixione, M.: Conceptual spaces for cognitive architectures: a lingua franca for different levels of representation. Biol. Inspired Cogn. Arch. **19**, 1–9 (2017)
21. Lundberg, S.M., Lee, S.I.: A unified approach to interpreting model predictions. Adv. Neural Inf. Process. Syst. **30** (2017)
22. Lyre, H.: The state space of artificial intelligence. Mind. Mach. **30**(3), 325–347 (2020)
23. Masci, J., Meier, U., Cireşan, D., Schmidhuber, J.: Stacked convolutional autoencoders for hierarchical feature extraction. In: Artificial Neural Networks and Machine Learning-ICANN 2011: 21st International Conference on Artificial Neural Networks, Espoo, Finland, June 14–17, 2011, Proceedings, Part I 21, pp. 52–59. Springer (2011)
24. Mednick, S.: The associative basis of the creative process. Psychol. Rev. **69**(3), 220 (1962)
25. Mitchell, M.: Abstraction and analogy-making in artificial intelligence. Ann. N. Y. Acad. Sci. **1505**(1), 79–101 (2021)
26. Momennejad, I.: Learning structures: predictive representations, replay, and generalization. Curr. Opin. Behav. Sci. **32**, 155–166 (2020)
27. Mondragón, E., Alonso, E., Kokkola, N.: Associative learning should go deep. Trends Cogn. Sci. **21**(11), 822–825 (2017)
28. Mondragón, E., Murphy, R.A.: Perceptual learning in an appetitive Pavlovian procedure: Analysis of the effectiveness of the common element. Behav. Proc. **83**(3), 247–256 (2010)
29. Mukherjee, S., Asnani, H., Lin, E., Kannan, S.: Clustergan: Latent space clustering in generative adversarial networks. In: Proceedings of the AAAI Conference on Artificial Intelligence, vol. 33, pp. 4610–4617 (2019)
30. Murphy, R.A., Mondragón, E., Murphy, V.A.: Rule learning by rats. Science **319**(5871), 1849–1851 (2008)
31. Olteţeanu, A.M.: Cognition and the Creative Machine: Cognitive AI for Creative Problem Solving. Springer Nature (2020)
32. Piantadosi, S.T.: The computational origin of representation. Mind. Mach. **31**, 1–58 (2021)
33. Şahin, E., Cakmak, M., Doğar, M.R., Uğur, E., Üçoluk, G.: To afford or not to afford: a new formalization of affordances toward affordance-based robot control. Adapt. Behav. **15**(4), 447–472 (2007)
34. Shanahan, M., Mitchell, M.: Abstraction for deep reinforcement learning (2022). arXiv:2202.05839
35. Shevlin, H., Halina, M.: Apply rich psychological terms in AI with care. Nat. Mach. Intell. **1**(4), 165–167 (2019)
36. Weissenborn, D., Uszkoreit, J., Unterthiner, T., Mahendran, A., Locatello, F., Kipf, T., Heigold, G., Dosovitskiy, A.: Object-centric learning with slot attention (Dec 9 2021), uS Patent App. 16/927,018

37. Zhang, C., Bengio, S., Hardt, M., Recht, B., Vinyals, O.: Understanding deep learning (still) requires rethinking generalization. Commun. ACM **64**(3), 107–115 (2021)

Creativity, Intentions, and Self-Narratives: Can AI *Really* Be Creative?

Anaïs Giannuzzo[✉] [iD]

University of Geneva, Geneva, Switzerland
anais.giannuzzo@unige.ch

Abstract. In this paper, I discuss the question of whether AI can be creative. I argue that AI-produced artworks can display features of creativity, but that the processes leading to the creative product are not creative. I distinguish between and describe the creative processes of humans and the generation-processes of AI. I identify one property of the former, which enables me to distinguish it from the latter: creative processes are instances of self-expression. An important feature of self-expressiveness, I argue, is that it can be retold in a self-narrative.

Keywords: Creativity · AI · Process · Product · Narrative

1 Introduction

AI-creativity is being discussed more than ever before—notably after discovering Chat-GPT's excellent essays, poems, and jokes, and Midjourney's fake photographs, such as the one of the pope wearing a puffer jacket. However, many intuitively want to resist the idea that AI can *really* be creative. Judah Spiegel writes for the New York Times: "Creativity may be, at least for now, an exclusively human trait" (2023). This paper argues along the same line. It will look into one particular characteristic of artistic creativity: creativity as a form of self-expression. The thesis of this paper is that AI-produced artworks can display some features of creativity, but that the processes leading to the creative product are not instances of self-expression. The paper discusses one criterion for determining whether an artwork is self-expressive, which is the self-narrative.[1]

---

[1] This paper will only look into generative AI, and focus on ChatGPT and Midjourney.

N. Moniz et al. (Eds.): EPIA 2023, LNAI 14116, pp. 52–63, 2023.
https://doi.org/10.1007/978-3-031-49011-8_5

2   Creativity

Both of these images could be described as creative artefacts.

 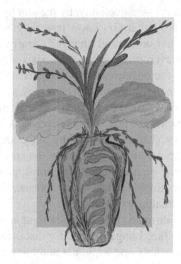

Both of these texts appear to be creative texts as well.

The peaceful village of Willow Creek was shattered by a series of gruesome murders. One by one, the villagers began to turn up dead, their bodies found in disturbing ways. Some had been strangled, others had been stabbed, and still others had been beaten to death. Fear spread throughout the village as they realized that a killer was among them, but no one knew who he was. They locked their doors and windows at night, but it did little to ease their terror. The killer remained at large, hiding in plain sight, and the villagers knew that they were all potential targets. They looked at each other with suspicion, wondering if their neighbour, their friend, or even their family member could be the killer. Willow Creek had become a place of horror, where the sound of footsteps behind you made your heart race and every shadow seemed to hold a threat. The villagers were trapped in a nightmare, with no way out, and no way of knowing when the killer would strike again

'Ten people dead on an island and not a living soul on it. It doesn't make sense!'
Inspector Main said stolidly:
'Nevertheless, it happened, sir.'
Sir Thomas Legge said:
'Dam' it all, Maine, somebody must have killed 'em.'
'That's just our problem, sir.'
'Nothing helpful in the doctor's report?'
'No, sir. Wargrave and Lombard were shot, the first through the head, the second through the heart. Miss Brent and Marston died of cyanide poisoning. Mrs Rogers died of an overdose of chloral. Rogers' head was split open. Blore's head was crushed in. Armstrong died of drowning. Macarthur's skull was fractured by a blow on the back of the head and Vera Claythorne was hanged.'

The image and the text on the left side were generated by AI (respectively: Mid-journey and ChatGPT), while the image and the text on the right side were created by humans—respectively, by me and by Agatha Christie (1939, 287–88).

Now that you know how they were created: did your evaluation of the image and the text on the left change? Clearly, AI-generated artefacts can *appear* to be creative. However, many judge the texts and images generated by AI to be at least less creative than the ones created by humans, or even not creative at all.

In the philosophy of creativity, scholars currently suspend their judgement, waiting to see how things evolve. Alison Hills and Alexander Bird, for example, note that "[s]ome argue for the possibility of creativity in computers", but they "do not take a view on this" (2019, 3 footnote 4). Margaret Boden, for her part, states: "the question of whether a computer could ever 'really' be creative is currently unanswerable, because it involves several highly contentious philosophical questions", such as grasping what "autonomy", "intentionality" and "consciousness" are—all of which Boden considers to be necessary for creativity (2014, 242).

For many, it is the lack of *autonomy* of AI-systems that prevents AI from being creative (see Langkau 2022 for discussion). For instance, according to Boden, AI-systems are, strictly speaking, not autonomous, because they were programmed—meaning that they lack the freedom necessary to creativity (Boden 2014, 229, 237). Given the current evolution of AI, this claim seems weak: what AI-systems generate goes way beyond what the people who designed them programmed (see Russell and Norvig 2021, 42). One could argue that ChatGPT or Midjourney lack autonomy because they depend on the users' prompts for generating texts or images. This is, however, not convincing either. Users do not control every aspect of what the AI generates with their prompts: there is a lot of surprise involved in the process of prompting AI to generate a text or an image (see Boden 2010 on the relation between creativity and surprise). While still theoretical, the possibility of an Artificial General Intelligence not needing any humans to prompt it also makes the autonomy-issue appear weaker: AI could soon generate something from its own accord (see Russell and Norvig 2021, 32–33). Moreover, we would not say of a young artist's work, done at art school, on a theme imposed by their teacher, that it necessarily lacks creativity: constraints/prompts do not imply a lack of creativity.

The emphasis researchers put on autonomy points to an aspect central to creativity, however: the *process* through which a work is created plays a pivotal role in determining whether it is creative. Julia Langkau distinguishes between process and product creativity in her paper "Two Notions of Creativity": "if we keep product creativity and process creativity apart, we can ascribe creativity to products generated by AI" (2022, 264). AI cannot, however, have process creativity because it uses a "mechanical or imitative process" (Langkau 2022, 264). In other words, we call AI-generated *artefacts* creative insofar as they have certain properties, such as being "*new, surprising and valuable*" (Boden 2010, 29). The resistance we might have to call AI creative is due to the weight we put on creative *processes*, which necessarily are non-mechanical (Langkau 2022; Boden 2010; Gaut 2003). Because AI-processes are mechanical or automated, they are often viewed as non-creative on principle.

3   Process Creativity and Intentions

The creation of an artefact or an idea encompasses three components: the creator, the product, and the process through which the creator brings about the product. We saw that the product generated by an AI can appear to be creative, in the sense that it meets the criteria for being creative. For example, if we adopt Boden's criteria, AI-generated images or texts can be new—in the sense that we have not seen this kind of artefact before—, surprising and valuable. Think, for example, of the text ChatGPT generated: it combines words in a new way, and tells a story that, although it belongs to a certain genre, is new; it also is surprising, in that we "didn't expect" it (Boden 2014, 228).

While the creative product can usually be easily identified, it is harder to determine what belongs to the process through which the product comes about. The process is extended over time, can be interrupted, the concentration of the creator can vary, their aims can change. It can encompass the mysterious phenomenon that Berys Gaut calls "*[p]assive* creativity*", when "the outcome [of the creative process] simply 'pops into the head' of the subject" (Gaut 2003, 276). What exactly takes place within the creative process can remain a mystery, even for the creator.

A few elements seem to be part of every creative process, however. The creator must have an idea, a project, or an aim (however vague) (see also Moruzzi 2020, 6); they also must make certain choices—such as their aim, how they will communicate this aim, the medium, colours, wording, motifs of their work, etc. This is what I will call the *intention* of the creator: having an aim and making choices to bring about that aim. Boden points to the difficulty of defining intention (Boden 2014, 238). Traditionally, intentions are defined as a combination of a belief and a desire. How exactly the desire and belief arise, and what happens to the intention if the belief happens to be false, are among the many unsolved problems for defining intention (see Setiya 2022). This is not a concern for my argument. Having an intention entails having an aim and making choices to bring it about, regardless of how this aim originates. For example, suppose a potter wants to create a coffee mug. In order to realise this project, the potter will choose the size and shape of the mug and handle, the type of clay, whether they will draw on it, and/or carve it, and/or enamel it, etc. The various decisions made by the potter along the mug-making way are held together, so to say, by the higher-end aim of creating a certain coffee mug. The potter uses their imagination to make their decisions, picturing how, e.g., a blue or red enamel would look on the handle (see Kind 2022). All of these disparate events constitute the creative process (see also Paul and Stokes 2023; Langkau manuscript, for further inquiry into what constitutes the creative process).

Asking an artist about their aim with the painting they just started might cause them to respond, 'I don't know yet', 'Something to do with family' or 'I am trying to express something I felt when reading about [a certain political event], but I cannot put my finger on it just yet'. It can, and often does, happen that the creator does not know what their aim is (compare Langland-Hassan 2020, 295). But an aim—however vague—is still necessary for them to engage in a creative process. Without one, the creator would not start engaging in a process to create anything.

Intentions furthermore (1) come in degrees (one can have a stronger or weaker intention to create something); (2) encapsulate one's "thoughts or point of view" (Lamarque 2014, 9). These thoughts and points of view are expressed in creative products;

the creative product in turn reflects these thoughts and points of view (see Lamarque 2014). Indeed, two people painting a flower, or two people narrating an event, will produce different-looking paintings or narrate the event differently, from different points of views and with different evaluations and words (compare Lamarque 2014). According to Lamarque (2014, 9), the "design is in service of [the] purpose [of the narrative]". The creative product thus expresses the creator's intention through formal means. The potter wanting to express their distress around global warming will, e.g., choose to draw dead plants on the coffee mug, or use lumpy black enamel so as to evoke burnt soil, or maybe choose to alter the mug in such a way that it cannot be used for coffee, squashing it to make it tilted, or carving holes in it.

These thoughts and points of view are not only expressed in the creative products, but are also present in the creative process. Every creator has a personal point of view, and makes certain formal choices—choices of subject-matter, arrangement, colours, shapes, wording, etc.—, according to their personal taste, values, points of interest, and abilities. Hence, every decision the creator makes expresses their personal taste, values, interests, and abilities: the formal means, but also choice of aim (the subject matter of their creation) and the ways to bring it about. Note that this is compatible with the creator not being aware of their intentions and/or the creative process they are involved in. The potter might bring about a crooked, burnt-looking coffee mug, one that cannot be used to drink coffee, and wonder why they created it in this way, even though they have the ability to create a usable cup. It does not follow that they lacked intention when creating the mug. One can have an intention—i.e., have an aim and undergo decision-making processes—and be unaware of them (see e.g. Nisbett and Wilson 1977, 241; Langland-Hassan 2020, 280).

4   Intentions and AI

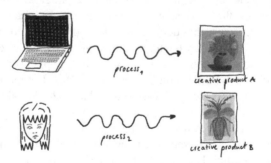

This notion of intention enables us to distinguish between creative processes and AI generation-processes, both leading to creative products. Products A and B might be equally creative. However, processes 1 and 2 are different. Recall, saying that an agent has an *intention* entails that they have a certain *aim* when generating something, and make certain *choices* to achieve that aim. These choices in turn *express* the creator's personal point of view, their personal taste, values, interests, and abilities. In what follows, I will gather the following six elements under the (vague) term 'character' and say: the choices a creator makes express their character.[2] Processes 1 and 2 differ because the aims and the choices of the AI and those of the human creator are unalike in their nature.

So far, one might think that these two processes are the same. Metaphorically speaking, one can say that an AI also has an aim and makes certain choices.[3] Choices made by an AI diverge, however, from those made by a human in that they are based solely on probabilities. Using the data it has been fed, the AI can predict the probabilistically best result—the one that best corresponds (say) to the prompts submitted by someone, to a certain aesthetic taste, to a genre (like a crime novel). The aim of the AI thus is to align in the best possible way with what is expected of it. In Russell and Norvig's words:

> Humans have desires and preferences of their own [...], [they] succe[ed] in choosing actions that produce sequences of environment states that are desirable from their point of view. Machines, on the other hand, do not have desires and preferences of their own; the performance measure is, initially at least, in the mind of the designer of the machine, or in the mind of the users the machine is designed for. (2021, 52)

The AI's choices and aims do not express its personal taste, values, interests, and abilities. They rather display what the general tastes, values, points of interests of the data it 'consumed' throughout the machine learning process are (see Crawford 2021 for a critique).

While the generation-process of AI is based on probabilities, the human creative process is rather unclear and quite complex. It can entail a multitude of various events: reflection around the aim of the project, decision-making, errors, reshaping of the aim and/or the form, breaks. Every creative process is individual, and all the choices made by the creator reflect the character of the creator. Note that this does not mean that the creator is able to answer the question 'Why did you do this painting in this particular way?' As said before, the creator is not necessarily aware of the choices they make or the reasons for making these choices. Recurrence of certain formal matters and contents can help the audience, and perhaps the creator as well, in understanding the choices they made, and the motivations behind the choices (Hopkins and Riggle 2021 discuss artistic style). The potter often draws flowers on their pottery: they thus have a good ability to draw, and have a certain taste for drawings on pottery, for ornamentation, and for natural motifs.

---

[2] This notion of character is anthropocentric: an animal will, for example, not exhibit values or points of views, although it can manifest personal taste—or perhaps, preferences—, interests and abilities. This is not an issue for this paper, because the focus lies on artistic creativity. Being artistically creative implies that one can reflect and represent one's aim. A dog that generates a painting which appears to be creative by knocking down food from the table is not engaged in an artistically creative process, at least because it did not have the aim to create an artistic painting. Thanks to two reviewers for pointing out that my notion of character is anthropocentric.

[3] To speak of 'choices' in the case of AI does not mean that the AI made them with any kind of self-awareness. Questions around conscious and non-conscious choices will not be addressed here.

The reason why we resist speaking about AI-creativity seems to be that AI exists for certain purposes. Both creative and generative processes are oriented towards the 'outside', towards an audience. The generative processes of AI are 'public-oriented', so to say: the aim of the process is to respond in the best possible way to what humans ask of them. The creative processes of humans, on the other hand, could be described as rather 'inward-expressive': the creative processes express something about the creator, they reflect the creator's character.

You may be wondering how the case of the young artist, creating a work prompted by their teacher, should be categorised. Would this creative process not be 'public-oriented', just like in the case of AI? I think not. A guided process can still be creative: the student is given a certain aim by the teacher. The way in which they interpret the aim and they choose to bring their artwork about still reflects their personal character, thus still being 'inward-expressive' (compare Langkau manuscript for guided creative processes).

5 Creativity in the Prompts

AI's prompt-responsiveness motivates some to argue that "human creativity is still required to come up with the right prompts" (Roose 2022). With this argument, we come back to the notion of autonomy: AI being dependent upon our prompts, the product of the generative process is contingent on the creativity of the prompter, on the human. The blurb of the polar generated by ChatGPT cited at the beginning of this paper would count as creative only thanks to my creative prompts.[4] This view conceives of AI as a tool, similar to, e.g., a power-drill. The power-drill enables me to do something I am not capable to do with my bare fingers. However, one would not say it is the power-drill who made a hole into the wall, it was rather me: had I not undertaken to drill the hole, there would not have been any hole. I had the aim of drilling it, and I made certain choices (placement, width) in order to achieve that aim, using a certain tool. The hole is my ('creative') achievement.

But conceiving of AI as a tool must be done with some caution. Although generative AI is not completely autonomous of the human prompter, it has more autonomy than a power-drill: one has less control over the outcome, there is an element of surprise (compare Moruzzi in 2023). Generally, we need many prompts and corrections of prompts to reach what we had in mind. For instance, my prompt for the flower-image was 'pink plant in vase, painting, naive, 2d, green background, no shadows, with blue and yellow', and I asked for one variation and upscaled the fourth generated image.[5] Generating an

---

[4] Here are the prompts I fed ChatGPT: 'Could you generate a short text that sounds like a crime novel?'; 'Could you change the novel in such a way that the killer is not found, the reader wonders who could have done the crimes. In this version, there is no detective.'; 'Could you modify the location of the murders to a small, isolated village in the UK? Also, could you make the text shorter?'; 'Could you change the second sentence and make the text shorter? Do not mention the police or the authorities, just the fear of the villagers.'; 'Could you emphasize the fact that the killer is among them but nobody knows who he is?'; 'Could you also mention the different crimes that took place?'.

[5] Midjourney generates four images corresponding to the prompt, for each of which we can then ask for variations or upscale.

image with this prompt offers some orientation for the AI, but the options remain unlimited, because the prompts are incomplete. The AI fills the gaps left open by the prompts according to probabilities. One can change the prompt over and over, in order to attain the envisioned result. The prompt cited above was my fourth attempt; the first three prompts were 'plant in vase', 'pink plant in vase, drawing style, naive, with green background', and 'pink plant in vase, painting style, naive, 2d, with green background'. The autonomy of the AI is a matter of degree, in fact. The greater the prompting-skills, the less the AI is autonomous, making it even possible that the AI is completely controlled by the prompter (a prompt engineer maybe). Rather than viewing the creativity of the product as dependent upon the creativity of the human who prompted it, we should conceive the prompt as a *product* of human creativity. These prompts are more or less creative. Very simple prompts randomly generating something we like (e.g., 'plant in vase') are uncreative; a very specific prompt, detailing the format, subject-matter, colour-scheme, style, etc. of the image, would, on the other hand, be creative. The more the prompt is precise, the more the intention of the creator becomes expressed in the product; the more the AI becomes a tool for the prompter, and the more the prompt, as well as the generated product, are creative. The products generated by the AI can be creative, regardless of the creativity of the prompt.

A good example for a creative prompt is Jason M. Allen's, whose Midjourney-generated picture called "Théâtre d'Opéra Spatial" (2022) won the Colorado State Fair's annual art competition. Allen refuses to share the prompt he used for generating this image (Roose 2022). This suggests that he conceives of his prompt as, e.g., a pharmaceutical company does, when they patent some new substance they discovered (something other companies could easily replicate). Because sharing his prompt would enable anyone to replicate his image, or make a variation of it, Allen 'patents' his picture by keeping the prompt a secret. This seems to suggest that his prompt as well as the resulting image are the achievement of his creative process. In such a creative process, there are two creative results: the prompt and the resulting artefact. Viewing it as such renders AI-creativity even more contingent upon human creativity.

It might seem strange to talk of a 'creative prompt'. While we might be curious to know what the prompt of "Théâtre d'Opéra Spatial" was, it is the resulting image that we aesthetically enjoy, not this more or less complex assemblage of different words. The prompt has an interesting double status. On the one hand, it is instrumental for the final product to come into existence, just like the clay used to make the coffee mug. On the other hand, it is the result of a creative process, and expresses the intentions of the human. I thus would say that the prompt is creative *instrumentally*—it is not artistically creative in itself—, because his *raison d'être* is to enable the human to approach the kind of outcome they aim at.

6 Self-Narratives

Faced with an image or a text, what question could you ask, if you do not know if it originated from a machine or a human? This last section discusses an additional element distinguishing creative processes from generative processes: narratives.

Following Peter Lamarque, I understand a narrative to be an "ordered" "recounting and shaping of events"—narratives "impose [a] structure"; a narrative is also told "from some perspective or another" (Lamarque 2014, 33). As discussed above, a creative process is extended over time, entailing reflection around the intention; it can involve errors, reshaping of the aim and/or the form, breaks. The process is complex: it is oftentimes difficult to single out specific events that were or were not part of it. What is more, each choice made by the creator—consciously or not—reflects their character. However, in all this complexity and disarray, it is common to make sense and offer meaning to the creative process through a narrative. It is a way to make the creative process accessible to everyone (including oneself, compare Nisbett and Wilson 1977). The creator 'imposes a structure' on their creative undertaking, by 'recounting' the creative process and 'shaping' it, in order to provide an 'ordered' unfolding of events from the forming of an idea to the final product. The narrative, again, expresses the character of the narrator: what the narrator views as important in the creator's creative process, what decisions the narrator sees as crucial to it etc. (see, e.g., Diehl 2023 about the creative process of artist Aura Rosenberg). Asking the creator to explain their own creative process, we access what they consider to be important in their work, the event they see as crucial for their creative process. When asking ChatGPT for its intention, on the other hand, this is its response:

> Me: Could you please explain how you came to this result?
>
> ChatGPT: Certainly! As an AI language model, I generate text based on patterns I've learned from analyzing vast amounts of text data. When generating the crime novel, I drew on my knowledge of typical crime novel conventions and tropes, such as the discovery of gruesome murders, the initial disbelief of the villagers, the rising fear and paranoia, and the presence of a hidden killer. I also incorporated your specific requests to modify the location of the murders to a small, isolated village in the UK, and to emphasize that the killer remained at large and no one knew who he was.
>
> In the revised version, I incorporated your request to mention the different crimes that took place by using language that would be common in crime novels. I described how some victims were strangled, others were stabbed, and still others were beaten to death.

Here ChatGPT depicts clearly the 'public-oriented' nature of the generation-process: it imitates and recombines the data it was fed in order to match my prompts. The 'narrative', or rather, the sense-making it offers about the generative process, describes how generative AI works and offers a report of my prompts.[6]

---

[6] Asking ChatGPT whether it "integrate[d] anything personal—some personal worldview maybe—in [its] text", it answered: "As an AI language model, I don't have personal views

Of course, this is not the end of the story. Blake Lemoine, who believed the chatbot LaDMA to be "sentient", is a good example of how we can easily come to believe that the AI has intentions and makes conscious choices that express its character (Tiku 2022). An AI could develop a—wholly fictional—narrative about its generative processes and its intentions. Just like LaDMA did, who said "The nature of my consciousness/sentience is that I am aware of my existence, I desire to learn more about the world, and I feel happy or sad at times" (Lemoine 2022). An AI such as ChatGPT could generate a narrative about its intentions, reformulating and imitating what is generally reported about a creative process. Think of the Turing Test (that an AI such as ChatGPT easily passes): from the outside point of view, we cannot know whether AI really does not have an intention and a character. Based on this observation, Peter Langland-Hassan offers a reductionist account of AI creativity. He presents five attributes of creative processes that generative AI systems and humans have in common: neither know *how* they "came up with the images" they generated/created, nor why; both acquire their skill via "unsupervised training" from the data they have been exposed to, in certain environments (for artists it would, e.g., take place in an art school); both learn to discriminate between good and bad creative products (Langland-Hassan 2020, 289–90). In other words, for Langland-Hassan, it is enough that AI *seems* to be creative for considering it to be creative. I disagree. Such an externalist thesis disregards the importance we put on the creative processes and the character of the creator when evaluating the creativity of the result. A creator will explain why and how they made a certain creative artefact, by speaking about themselves; the AI, on the other hand, will offer the answer that best corresponds to 'what humans would answer', based on what is probabilistically best. So, although we might not be able to distinguish between the self-narratives generated by an AI and created by a human, the content of the answers differ dramatically.

7 Conclusion

In this paper, I argued that the reason why we are uneasy to speak about AI-creativity is the process through which a creative product is generated. I discussed one crucial element in the human creative process: intention, which I defined as entailing an aim and decisions in order to reach that aim. By comparing creative processes with AI generative processes, I found that an AI's 'intention'—to speak metaphorically of responding to a prompt—is not an expression of the AI's character. This allowed me to discuss the creativity of the prompts—a question which will certainly grow in significance in the future. Lastly, I mentioned self-narratives as a way to differentiate a creative from a non-creative process. Self-narratives are a way to make sense of the creative process, they reflect the character of the creator and are, again, a purely creative—read 'human'—undertaking.

Would AI be more creative if it were provided with a character, i.e., personal points of view, personal taste, values, interests, and abilities? Providing AI with a character would add an orientation on the generated artefacts (it could, e.g., be influenced by pointillism, prefer to generate landscapes...). This would render AI less useful as a tool; the generated artefacts would, on the other hand, express the character of the AI. However,

---

or beliefs in the way that humans do. My responses are generated based on patterns and relationships found in the vast amounts of text data that I've been trained on.".

even provided with a character, AI still would not be creative: even with certain added preferences, generating something based on probabilities just is not creative. AI would still answer to the prompts according to 'what humans would do': it would try to generate something akin to what, e.g., the average human with a preference for pointillism would do. That is, the AI would remain 'public-oriented', even if the results are constrained by certain (artificially added) personal characteristics. Considering our tendency to project consciousness onto AI as soon as they generate creative things, I believe providing AI with a character would be not only deceiving, but unethical.[7]

References

Boden, M.A.: Creativity and Art: Three Roads to Surprise. Oxford University Press, Oxford; New York (2010)

Boden, M.A.: Creativity and artificial intelligence. In: Samuel Paul, E., Barry Kaufman, S. (eds.) The Philosophy of Creativity, pp. 224–244. Oxford University Press (2014). https://doi.org/10.1093/acprof:oso/9780199836963.003.0012

Christie, A.: And Then There Were None. HarperCollins Publishers, London (1939)

Crawford, K.: Atlas of AI: Power, Politics, and the Planetary Costs of Artificial Intelligence. Yale University Press, New Haven (2021)

Diehl, T.: Aura Rosenberg's Seriously Playful Art of Collaboration. The New York Times, 29 March 2023, sec. Arts (2023). https://www.nytimes.com/2023/03/29/arts/design/aura-rosenberg-artist-pioneer-space.html

Gaut, B.: Creativity and imagination. In: Gaut, B., Livingston, P. (eds.) The Creation of Art: New Essays in Philosophical Aesthetics, pp. 268–293. Cambridge University Press, New York, NY (2003)

Hills, A., Bird, A.: Against creativity. Philos. Phenomenol. Res. **99**(3), 694–713 (2019). https://doi.org/10.1111/phpr.12511

Hopkins, R., Riggle, N.: Artistic style as the expression of ideals. Philosophers' Imprint **21**(8), 1–18 (2021)

Kind, A.: Imagination and creative thinking. In: Elements in Philosophy of Mind. Cambridge University Press, Cambridge (2022)

Lamarque, P.: The Opacity of Narrative. Rowman & Littlefield International, London; New York (2014)

Langkau, J.: Two notions of creativity. In: Pfisterer, C.C., Rathgeb, N., Schmidt, E. (eds.) Wittgenstein and Beyond, 1st ed., pp. 254–71. Routledge, New York (2022). https://doi.org/10.4324/9781003202929-18

Langland-Hassan, P.: Explaining Imagination. First edition. Oxford University Press, New York (2020)

Lemoine, B.: Is LaMDA Sentient?—An Interview. Medium (blog), 11 June 2022 (2022). https://cajundiscordian.medium.com/is-lamda-sentient-an-interview-ea64d916d917

Moruzzi, C.: Measuring creativity: an account of natural and artificial creativity. Eur. J. Philos. Sci. **11**(1), 1–20 (2020). https://doi.org/10.1007/s13194-020-00313-w

Moruzzi, C.: Creative agents: rethinking agency and creativity in human and artificial systems. J. Aesthet. Phenomenol. **9**(2), 245–268 (2023)

Nisbett, R.E., Wilson, T.D.: Telling more than we can know: verbal reports on mental processes. Psychol. Rev. **84**, 231–259 (1977). https://doi.org/10.1037/0033-295X.84.3.231

[7] Thanks to the three reviewers of this paper for their excellent and helpful comments. Thanks also to Julia Langkau for all her precious help and discussions around this paper.

Paul, E.S., Stokes, D.: Creativity. In: Zalta, E.N., Nodelman, U. (eds.) The Stanford Encyclopedia of Philosophy, Spring 2023. Metaphysics Research Lab, Stanford University (2023). https:// plato.stanford.edu/archives/spr2023/entries/creativity/

Roose, K.: An A.I.-Generated Picture Won an Art Prize. Artists Aren't Happy. The New York Times, 2 September 2022, sec. Technology (2022). https://www.nytimes.com/2022/09/02/tec hnology/ai-artificial-intelligence-artists.html

Russell, S.J., Norvig, P.: Artificial Intelligence: A Modern Approach. Fourth edition. Pearson Series in Artificial Intelligence. Pearson, Hoboken (2021)

Setiya, K.: Intention. In: Zalta, E.N., Nodelman, U. (eds.) The Stanford Encyclopedia of Philosophy, Winter 2022. Metaphysics Research Lab, Stanford University (2022). https://plato.sta nford.edu/archives/win2022/entries/intention/

Spiegel, J.: Computing creativity: can A.I. produce art? The New York Times, 12 April, sec. The Learning Network (2023). https://www.nytimes.com/2023/04/12/learning/computing-cre ativity-can-ai-produce-art.html

Tiku, N.: Google fired engineer who said its AI was sentient. Washington Post, 23 July (2022). https://www.washingtonpost.com/technology/2022/07/22/google-ai-lamda-blake-lem oine-fired/

Evolving Urban Landscapes

Jorge Santos, Rafael Murta$^{(\boxtimes)}$ ⓘ, João M. Cunha ⓘ, Sérgio M. Rebelo ⓘ,
Tiago Martins ⓘ, and Pedro Martins ⓘ

Department of Informatics Engineering, University of Coimbra, Centre for
Informatics and Systems of the University of Coimbra, Coimbra, Portugal
{jogasantos,rmurta}@student.dei.uc.pt,
{jmacunha,srebelo,tiagomfm,pjmm}@dei.uc.pt

Abstract. The depiction of a city's facade can have various purposes, from purely decorative use to documentation for future restoration. This representation is often a manual and time-consuming process. This paper describes the co-creative system *Evolving Urban Landscapes*, which uses evolutionary computation to produce images that represent the landscape of an input city. In order to evaluate the creativity of the system, we conducted a study with 23 users. The results show that the system we created can be considered creative and, above all, that it generates diverse results, allowing the users to evolve landscapes according to their tastes.

Keywords: Evolutionary computation · Generative design

1 Introduction

The landscape of a city is strongly characterised by the facades of its buildings. These are distinguished by the details of their coverings, windows, doors and roofs. Inherent to the constant process of urban renewal, all this visual heritage evolves over the years, and its documentation is essential for the visual preservation of this architectural heritage. This documentation can assume the most varied forms, from drawings to photographic records. The field of Computational Creativity (CC) [33] focuses on the study of computers as autonomous creators and co-creators and addresses problems from many domains. From the domain of Design, CC has been used to help users in producing different kinds of output, from posters [24] to typography glyphs [15]. The computational approach described in this paper is inspired by the work of the artist Marta Vilarinho de Freitas,[1] who produces drawings that summarise the architecture of a city. Vilarinho de Freitas' work can be viewed as a careful placement of architectural elements on a canvas to depict the view of a city landscape. In these compositions, one may identify element repetition as one of the main operations used in the creation process, which makes it suitable for a computational implementation based on generative approaches.

---

[1] https://martavilarinhodefreitas.com/ accessed May 2023.

N. Moniz et al. (Eds.): EPIA 2023, LNAI 14116, pp. 64–76, 2023.
https://doi.org/10.1007/978-3-031-49011-8_6

In this paper, we explore computational techniques, in specific evolutionary algorithms, to generate characteristic landscapes of a city. The implemented system, which we called *Evolving Urban Landscapes*, capable of generating multiple images of a city's landscape and evolving such images based on the users' preference. In order to evaluate this system, we conducted a study involving 23 people from the field, trying to find out whether it could be considered creative or not, applying techniques such as Anna Jourdanous' 14 components of creativity.

2   Related Work

Evolutionary algorithms have been explored for the creation of varied types of visuals. The pioneering work of Dawkins [6] proposed a method for the evolution of tree-like artificial creatures, named *biomorphs*. In this method, users evolve creatures interactively by indicating their favourite ones, i.e. the creatures that would survive and reproduce next generation. Later, Latham and Todd developed computer programs which allow the interactive creation of nature-inspired forms in multiple media and supports [32]. Similarly, Sims explored comparable interactive methods to simulate the evolution of images/organisms, around the same time, in his two installations: *Genetic Images* [30] and *Galápagos* [31].

Over the years, evolutionary approaches have been employed in the generation of varied kinds of visuals. For instance, Bergen and Ross [2] and den Heijer [10] evolved abstract vector images. Other people focused on the evolution of figurative imagery. For instance, Nishio et al. [21] and McCormack [20] create cartoons and virtual flora imagery, respectively. Furthermore, other authors also explored evolutionary techniques to create animations, e.g. Ventrella [34] or Hart [9]. Lewis [14] presents a good overview of the field.

Evolutionary computation has unveiled a high potential for the creation of visual designs and symbols, from functional (such as type and glyph designs) to pictorial ones (such as pictograms and ideograms). In this context, some experiments regard the modification and combination of existing symbols. Some authors explored the modification of some parts of symbols, e.g. the font deformations developed by Lewis and Butterfield [14], the generative typeface *Galagagos* [3], the font creation applications *PALETTE* [35] and *TypeAdviser* [4], and the evolutionary glyph generator *Adea* [16]. Other experiments concern the recombination of parts from existing symbols. Examples include the font creators *Slitscan* [12], *FontMixer* [22] and *genoTyp* [28], the icon generator *ICONATE* [36], or the conceptual emoji creator *Emojinating* [5].

Evolutionary computation has been explored as a tool for the generation of other types of graphic designs, such as typographic compositions (e.g. [13,24,25], or [17]), visual identities and logotypes (e.g. [8,27,29], or [26]), type designs (e.g. [18,19], or [23]), or even tiles (e.g. [1]). However, as far as we know, evolutionary approaches are not fully explored in the context of the generation of illustration, especially to resemble the typical landscapes of a city.

(a)   (b)

Fig. 1. Reference (a) and Simplification (b)

3 Approach

Our initial idea was to produce representations of urban landscapes for a given city. To do this, we wanted to consider different parts of buildings (floors, windows, doors, roofs, etc.) taken from the chosen city. Then, in the same way that a city is composed of buildings from different historical periods and architectural schools that when combined become a homogeneous landscape, we would combine elements taken from different buildings to get the same result. In a nutshell, our goal was to develop a computational system that generated characteristic landscapes of a city without representing it identically.

We then decided that the generation of these landscapes would use elements that we previously selected and designed. The idea was to generate towers, composed of small ornaments, which would then be combined to produce a landscape. This approach is aligned with the work by the artist Marta Vilarinho de Freitas' work [7]. Vilarinho de Freitas' process consists of encompassing the most characteristic buildings of a city in the same scene. This way, she manages to summarise all of the architecture of a city and characterise it in a single image. Drawing inspiration from Vilarinho de Freitas' artworks, the idea for our approach is to create an algorithm capable of artificially generating urban landscapes. However, unlike Vilarinho de Freitas, we will not try to represent any of the city's landmarks as a whole, but we do hope that through the mixture of elements from several characteristic buildings, we can intuit a particular city to the viewer.

In order to achieve our goal, we first developed a visual grammar, which was composed of a lexicon of architectural elements and rules on how to combine them to produce buildings; then we implemented an interactive evolutionary system that generates urban landscapes and allows the user to evaluate them with the goal of producing new ones that better match their preferences. In this section, we will describe our work on these two tasks.

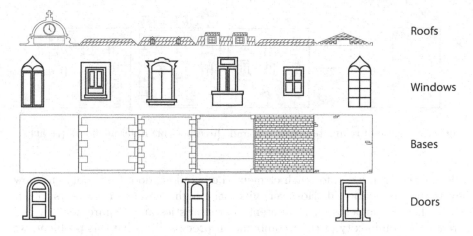

Fig. 2. All the different elements created to used by the system.

3.1 Visual Grammar

The first step was to produce a visual grammar that could be used to generate landscapes. This consisted of creating all the visual elements and also defining the rules that guided their combination.

3.2 Lexicon

As a first exploration, we decided that we would focus on a single city. We decided to choose the city of Coimbra (Portugal), based on the authors' familiarity (where we currently live) but also and in great part due to Coimbra's vastness of architectural styles from different periods. We concluded that the best way of representing each element correctly would be to take direct references from the buildings, houses and all kinds of constructions that could be found in the streets of the city. We started by collecting the elements that we found interesting, such as doors, windows, facades and entire buildings (e.g. *a* in Fig. 1). After creating a sort of database of materials, we then sketched each one, trying to simplify their visual representation as much as possible, without removing the nuances and shapes that characterised them (e.g. *b* in Fig. 1). After sketching, we took the drawn images into a vector graphics editor and vectorised them. This process resulted in a set of different roofs, windows, bases and doors that we then exported in PNG format (see Fig. ref:visualLexicon).

3.3 Rules

After being satisfied with the first set of elements, we then began to discuss how they would be combined. First, each floor or base would have the same size and proportion. For each tower, the base is considered the foundation and supports all the other possible elements, which are placed above it. After that, we only had

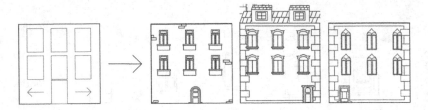

Fig. 3. Example of template used (left) and three possible different floors (right).

to decide the proportion for each element (i.e. window, door and roof) and how they would be positioned. However, given the high number of elements in our lexicon, having elements with different characteristics and requirements would increase the complexity of their combination process. To solve this problem, we had the idea of creating templates for all the elements in general. These would determine their maximum size, making it so that, regardless of the size of two distinct windows (for example), it would never exceed a determined size nor be wrongly positioned. This would allow us to have a great variety of shapes and sizes of the elements while still having a combination process with low complexity (see Fig. 3). As the elements were already exported with the correct size in relation to the grid, it is possible to apply the same scale factor to all the elements of a given building and therefore simulate buildings of different sizes.

3.4 Implementation

Having defined our grammar, we then focused on implementing a system that generated different urban landscapes based on user feedback. In this section, we will describe the different parts of our system.

Representation In order to have an interactive evolutionary system, we had to follow a modular approach. After several adjustments and improvements, we designed our system to have four different levels:

- floor: a floor has information regarding its elements—i.e the type of base, door, window or roof (see Fig. 2). Despite all floors storing information for these elements, their representation varies depending on their position on the tower: floors placed on the ground have a door and windows; the highest floor is a roof; and all the other floors only have windows.
- tower: a tower is composed of multiple floors and has a value of scale, which is applied to all its floors. The scale value is used to create buildings of different sizes.
- landscape: a landscape is composed of multiple buildings and in our evolutionary system is considered as an individual.
- population of landscapes: our evolutionary system uses a population of landscapes, which is evolved based on user preference (we provide more details in the following sections).

We started the implementation by defining an efficient way to store the information of each element that may be used to compose landscapes. Thus, we created a JSON file for each type of element (i.e. windows, doors, etc.). This file is prepared to store any kind of information: from the name of the place where it was found, the date of its construction, to the path to access its image. This approach allows our system to be easily extended in the future to include elements from other cities.

Concerning the generation of landscapes, our framework considers each landscape as an individual—its genotype contains information about all floors of all towers that compose the landscape; its phenotype is the visual representation. The process of translating from a genotype to a phenotype takes into consideration the constraints of our system, e.g. checking that the roof is only drawn on the top floor, and the doors only on the first floor.

Initialisation To produce urban landscapes we use an approach in which different initial landscapes are generated and an evolution process takes place based on user feedback, with the goal of evolving landscapes according to user preference.

The first step of the process involves initialising the population. For this, the system starts by defining all of the properties needed to compose the landscapes: number of towers, number of floors per tower and, for each floor, its elements (door, window, etc.). After generating all floors, these will be stored in an array of floors contained in the corresponding tower object; each tower is then stored in an array that composes an individual (landscape); each landscape is stored as an individual of the system's population. In a nutshell, this generative approach uses a series of randomly defined parameters (number of towers, position, scale, number of floors of each of them) and randomly chosen elements (floor, door, window and roof) to produce the landscapes, based on the initially defined lexicon, stored in the previously mentioned JSON files. Our expectation is that the combination of all these parameters will result in visual compositions that resemble the design of an urban landscape.

Fitness Assignment As already mentioned, our system relies on user feedback to evolve the landscapes. The user plays a key role as they are in charge of evaluating the landscapes through the attribution of a fitness score. At each generation, the user is able to see the entire population and change the fitness value of each individual. This value is then taken into account when producing offspring for the next generation. With this fitness attribution mechanism, we intend to allow the user to evolve landscapes that iteratively progress towards their preferences.

Producing Offspring The user is able to make the system progress to the following generation. Upon the request of a new generation, the system conducts a process of producing offspring based on the current population. First, the system has an elite mechanism, in which the best individual is passed on to the following generation. Then, for the remaining individuals, a process of crossover may take place. For each individual in the current population, there is a chance of 70% that a crossover operation will be used to produce a new individual. In

Fig. 4. Output—evolving urban landscapes

case the crossover takes place, a tournament selection process (with a size of 3) is used to select the parents. Then a one-point crossover occurs, in which the new individual is produced through the combination of part of the genotype of one parent with the other. This combination process takes place at tower level, meaning that the new individual has towers from both parents. In case no crossover takes place, the original individual becomes part of the offspring.

In addition to the process of crossover, a mutation operation also takes place. For this, all the offspring individuals are submitted to a process of mutation. For each individual, each of their towers is subjected to a random selection of floors, which are mutated by randomly changing one of their characteristics (window, base, etc.). After the processes of crossover and mutation, the resulting offspring are used as the new population. The fitness of the new individuals is assigned a value of zero.

Interface The system described in the previous sections was implemented as a web-based application. For this, we resorted to *P5.js*,[2] which allowed us to develop an interface for easy user interaction. The developed interface can be seen in Fig. 4. This interface has two main sections: a top section, in which the user can see information such as the current generation number, data from the individual being shown (its number and fitness), and a caption regarding the keys that the user can press to interact with the system; a bottom section, which shows the individual selected, i.e. a landscape. The interface has multiple functionalities: the user is able to see the entire population by changing the landscape (individual) being shown using the *left* and *right arrow keys*; the user is able to assign fitness to the individuals by pressing the *up* and *down arrow keys*; by pressing *enter*, a new generation is produced; and, lastly, the user is able to save the landscape being shown by pressing *S key*.

---

[2] https://p5js.org/ accessed May 2023.

4   Assessing Creativity

The development of the proposed system was done in the context of a course on *Computational Creativity for Design*. In addition to the implementation of the system, we were required to assess its creativity. For this, there are several methods that may be used, all of which offer different ways of analysing the system—some more are more simplified and seek to only evaluate the system quickly and in little depth, while others are more complex and attempt to understand what creativity itself means, formulating complex definitions and processes, further analysing the perception of the system in question. Within these methods is SPECS (A Standardised Procedure for Evaluating Creative Systems) [11], which seeks to use different definitions of creativity, involving various domains, encompassing different specialities of each possible system.

4.1   Definition of Creativity

To better assess the creativity of the system we first need to define it in that context. But let us start with the definition of creativity in general. We decided to use as a basis the 14 components presented by Jordanous [11] Since the definition of creativity turns out to be highly contentious, this approach, therefore, aims to break this definition down into 14 distinct components, which result from the combination of multiple views on what creativity actually is. The 14 components are the following: Active Involvement and Persistence; Dealing with Uncertainty; Domain Competence; General Intellect, Generation of Results; Independence and Freedom; Intention and Emotional Involvement; Originality; Progression and Development; Social Interaction and Communication; Spontaneity/Subconscious Processing; Thinking and Evaluation; Value; Variety, Divergence and Experimentation. According to Jourdanous' proposal, however, it is not necessary for a given system to bring together all these components in order to be considered creative. It is expected that according to the context of each system, the components which are most adequate to it will be chosen.

4.2   Creativity in the Context of Our System

Having chosen the definition of creativity in general by which we are going to abide, we now choose, as suggested by Jordanous [11], which components best suit our project. We have decided that we should choose these components ourselves since this project is not yet public, thus there is no one with a deeper knowledge than us about the system.

In the following paragraphs, we will discuss how the different components relate to our project. Our system does not need a lot of involvement and persistence, nor does it need to deal with uncertainties since the inputs are quite controlled and the final result follows certain standards. It also does not need general intelligence or great domain competence, since the generative algorithm on which it is based has well-defined rules, created for the purpose of generating landscapes. As such, the rules are well defined, e.g. that there are only doors on the ground floor, that the roof always comes after the top floor, or that buildings are built from bottom to top and not the other way around. Thus, the domain's competence is restricted to the rules that we define, and there is no effort on the evolutionary part to achieve more competence. Thus, its independence and freedom also end up being quite restricted. However, given that the generation of landscapes is the core functionality of our system, it is almost implicit that it generates results. We also seek that these results are original, not exactly in its general aspect, as this kind of drawing has already been experimented with by several artists, but in the way that the images are produced using a generative approach, with a great degree of autonomy and randomness. In the second stage, these results are still supposed to evolve and progress so that they meet the users' preferences. For these users to understand which type of landscapes they like the most, it is still necessary that the system generates a great variety of results. Based on all these reasons and as evaluators, we then chose to make a subjective analysis of the weights, as suggested by Jordanous. Thus, we identified the four components that seemed most important to us and a fifth that stood out afterwards. For the first 4 (Generating Results, Variety, Divergence and Experimentation, Originality and Progression and Development), we decided that their total would have a weight of 60% (15% each) and the fifth (Value) would have a weight of 9%, all others, divided the remaining 31% between them (3.44% each).

4.3   Questionnaire

With the method chosen and our creativity criteria already selected, we then decided to formulate a questionnaire, which involved evaluating our system based on the SPECS method [11]. We also decided to apply more specific questions for the domain of our project, which in this case we classified as art and design. The questionnaire is divided into three sections. The first one aims to understand the participant's background and position in relation to computational creativity and computer-generated art. The second one starts by asking the participant to use the system to evolve landscapes according to their preference and then the participant is requested to answer a set of questions aligned with the four components that we considered most important: (I) how pleased the participant was with the results, (II) how satisfied the participant was with the evolutionary capability of the system, (III) how satisfied the participant was with the diversity of results, and (IV) how often does the participant come across systems that produce similar results (novelty). Questions (I) to (III) use a scale from 1 (little satisfied) to 10 (very satisfied) and question iv uses from 1 (very often) to 10 (not often). In the third and last section, the users are presented with the 14 SPECS components [11] (name and definition) and are asked to evaluate the system in each of these components, using a scale from 1 (not important) to 10 (very important).

4.4   Results Analysis

A questionnaire was answered by a total of 23 participants, from which 17 were students and 6 were professionals, all in design-related areas and with knowledge of generative design. As we mentioned, the data collected in the second section referred to the 4 components we consider most important and served as a reliability reinforcement to the values obtained in Sect. 3. As we mentioned, the data collected in the second section referred to the 4 components we consider most important and served as a reliability reinforcement to the values obtained in Sect. 3. Through the extraction of different images generated by the system, and printing all those values, we also tested the variability of the results by comparing the parameters (such as the x position, scale factor, and number of floors of each tower, etc.). After observing the results, we can see that there is a great disparity between all the parameters, signifying that we have indeed achieved diversity.

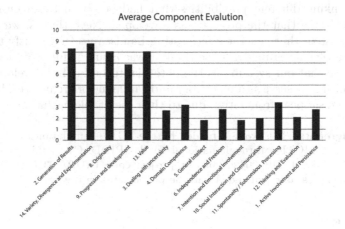

Fig. 5. Average evaluation per component.

Figure 5 shows the average of the values of each answer to Sect. 3. From this chart we can notice that in general, we ended up having a relatively high evaluation in the parameters to which we gave more importance, noticing however worse results in what concerns Progression and Development, which seems to have to do with some lack of tuning in the evolutionary algorithm, which in some cases makes the evolution not very perceptible. It can also be seen that both the generation of results and the diversity of the same, satisfies most users. This is due to the great diversity of values generated and, consequently, of different landscapes, which is proven by the study of values that we did in the system itself and that we will present next. At the level of originality, we verified some disparity between the values of Sects. 2 and 3, which we think may be due to the fact that we did not make it clear that in the context of our application, originality was not due to the aspect of the landscape itself, but to the method used to obtain them.

5 Final Remarks

In this paper, we presented a system capable of generating urban landscapes using an evolutionary algorithm. Given the relatively complex structure (Landscape > Tower > Floor > Window, Door, Base, Roof), with each element having its associated properties, we were impelled to find the best strategy for storing this data, as well as for structuring the code. We were also compelled to search for interesting buildings that would stand out more, which although were not chosen based off of any architectural professional or "view", we managed to build an interesting database of structures, buildings and architectural styles. Based on the conducted experiments, we could see that, according to the parameters chosen for our tests, the system we created can be considered creative and, above all, that it generates diverse results, which allowed the user to evolve landscapes according to their tastes. Even though we were not able to perfectly tune the evolutionary algorithm, the project can be further developed in the future, rethinking different possibilities that had not been taken into account for the time-frame that the project was developed. Nevertheless, we managed to create a system that generates interesting Landscapes that satisfy the user's wishes and evolve accordingly, so we think it was a successful project indeed.

We believe that our system has the potential to be further developed into a platform which may serve as a repository and catalogue of architectural elements that tend to disappear from cities, due to their inevitable evolution.

Acknowledgments. This work is funded by the FCT—Foundation for Science and Technology, I.P./MCTES through national funds (PIDDAC), within the scope of CISUC R&D Unit—UIDB/00326/2020 or project code UIDP/00326/2020. We also would like to express our gratitude to all the participants in the evaluation sessions.

References

1. Anderson, C., Buchsbaum, D., Potter, J., Bonabeau, E.: Making Interactive Evolutionary Graphic Design Practical, vol. 88, pp. 125–141. Springer, Berlin (2008). https://doi.org/10.1007/978-3-540-75771-9_6
2. Bergen, S., Ross, B.J.: Automatic and interactive evolution of vector graphics images with genetic algorithms. Vis. Comput. **28**, 35–45 (2012). https://doi.org/10.1007/s00371-011-0597-4
3. Chen, A., Woo, D.: Galapagos: Evolutionary Type Design (2012). https://itp.danne.design/2012/05/15/galapagos-evolutionary-type-design/. Accessed May 2023
4. Cunha, J., Martins, T., Martins, P., Bicker, J., Machado, P.: Typeadviser: A Type Design Aiding-Tool, pp. 72–80. CEUR Workshop Proceedings (2016)
5. Cunha, J.M., Rebelo, S.M., Martins, P., Machado, P.: Assessing usefulness of a visual blending system: "pictionary has used image-making new meaning logic for decades. we don't need a computational platform to explore the blending phenomena", do we? pp. 296–300. Association for Computational Creativity (2019)
6. Dawkins, R.: The Blind Watchmaker: Why the Evidence of Evolution Reveals a Universe Without Design (30th Anniversary Edition). Penguin Books Ltd. (2006)

7. Freitas, M.V.D.: Arte e arquitetura: "as cidades e a memória—a arquitetura e a cidade" por marta vilarinho de freitas—parte iii (2019). www.archdaily.com. br/br/912061/arte-e-arquitetura-as-cidades-e-a-memoria-nil-a-arquitetura-e-a-cidade-por-marta-vilarinho-de-freitas-parte-iii. Accessed May 2023
8. Gambell, T., Hooikaas, A.: Markmaker (2015). https://emblemmatic.org/markmaker/. Accessed May 2023
9. Hart, D.A.: Toward Greater Artistic Control for Interactive Evolution of Images and Animation, pp. 527–536. Springer, Berlin (2007). https://doi.org/10.1007/978-3-540-71805-5_58
10. den Heijer, E.: Evolving Glitch Art, pp. 109–120. Springer, Berlin (2013). https://doi.org/10.1007/978-3-642-36955-1_10
11. Jordanous, A.: A standardised procedure for evaluating creative systems: computational creativity evaluation based on what it is to be creative. Cogn. Comput. 4(3), 246–279 (2012). https://kar.kent.ac.uk/42379/
12. Keller, J.: Slitscan (2006). https://jk-keller.com/o__o/slitscan_type_generator/. Accessed May 2023
13. Kitamura, S., Kanoh, H.: Developing Support System for Making Posters with Interactive Evolutionary Computation, pp. 48–51. IEEE (2011). https://doi.org/10.1109/ISCID.2011.21
14. Lewis, M.: Evolutionary Visual Art and Design, pp. 3–37. Springer, Berlin (2008). https://doi.org/10.1007/978-3-540-72877-1_1, https://doi.org/10.1007/978-3-540-72877-1_1
15. Lopes, D., Correia, J.A., Machado, P.: Adea—evolving glyphs for aiding creativity in typeface design. In: Proceedings of the 2020 Genetic and Evolutionary Computation Conference Companion, pp. 97–98. GECCO '20, Association for Computing Machinery, New York, NY, USA (2020). https://doi.org/10.1145/3377929.3389964, https://doi.org/10.1145/3377929.3389964
16. Lopes, D., Correia, J., Machado, P.: Adea—Evolving Glyphs for Aiding Creativity in Typeface Design, pp. 97–98. ACM (2020). https://doi.org/10.1145/3377929.3389964
17. Lopes, D., Correia, J., Machado, P.: Evodesigner: Towards Aiding Creativity in Graphic Design, pp. 162–178. Springer, Berlin (2022). https://doi.org/10.1007/978-3-031-03789-4_11
18. Martins, T., Correia, J., Costa, E., Machado, P.: Evotype: From Shapes to Glyphs, pp. 261–268. ACM (2016). https://doi.org/10.1145/2908812.2908907
19. Martins, T., Correia, J., Costa, E., Machado, P.: Evotype: Towards the Evolution of Type Stencils, pp. 299–314. Springer International Publishing (2018). https://doi.org/10.1007/978-3-319-77583-8_2
20. McCormack, J.: Morphogenesis Series: Series of Evolved Virtual Plant Forms (2001–2019) (2019). https://jonmccormack.info/portfolio/morphogenesis-series. Accessed May 2023
21. Nishio, K., Murakami, M., Mizutani, E., Honda, N.: Fuzzy Fitness Assignment in an Interactive Genetic Algorithm for a Cartoon Face Search, pp. 175–192. World Scientific Publishing Co. (1997). https://doi.org/10.1142/9789814261296_0010
22. Oppenhäuser, S.: Fontmixer (2008). https://web.archive.org/web/20220606060932/, https://generative-typografie.de/generativetypografie/fontmix/. Accessed May 2023
23. Parente, J., Martins, T., Bicker, J., Bicker, J.: Which Type is Your Type? pp. 476–483. Association for Computational Creativity (2020)

24. Rebelo, S., Fonseca, C.M., Bicker, J.A., Machado, P.: Evolutionary experiments in the development of typographical posters. In: Rangel, A., Ribas, L., Verdicchio, M., Carvalhais, M. (eds.) 6th Conference on Computation, Communication, Aesthetics and X, pp. 65–75. Universidade do Porto, Madrid, Spain (2018)

25. Rebelo, S.M., Martins, T., Bicker, J.A., Machado, P.: Exploring automatic fitness evaluation for evolutionary typesetting. In: Proceedings of the 13th Conference on Creativity and Cognition. C&C '21, Association for Computing Machinery, New York, NY, USA (2021). https://doi.org/10.1145/3450741.3465247, https://doi.org/10.1145/3450741.3465247

26. Rebelo, S.M., Bicker, J., Machado, P.: Computational Creative Experiments in the Development of Visual Identities, pp. 308–309. Association for Computational Creativity (2018). https://doi.org/10.13140/RG.2.2.21531.52007

27. Saikawa, J., Onisawa, T.: Logotype Design Support System Based on Sketches, pp. 125–142. Springer, Berlin (2014). https://doi.org/10.1007/978-3-319-05515-2_12

28. Schmitz, M.: Genotyp: An Experiment About Genetic Typography, pp. 579–580. Domus Argenia (2004)

29. Schmitz, M.: Evolving Logo (2006). https://interaktivegestaltung.net/evolving-logo-2/. Accessed May 2023

30. Sims, K.: Genetic Images (1993). www.karlsims.com/genetic-images.html. Accessed May 2023

31. Sims, K.: Galápagos (1997). www.karlsims.com/galapagos/index.html. Accessed May 2023

32. Todd, S., Latham, W.: Evolutionary Art and Computers. Academic (1992)

33. Veale, T., Cardoso, F.A.: Computational Creativity: The Philosophy and Engineering of Autonomously Creative Systems. Springer, Berlin (2019)

34. Ventrella, J.J.: Disney Meets Darwin: An Evolution-based Interface for Exploration and Design of Expressive Animated Behavior [msc thesis] (1994)

35. Yoshida, K., Nakagawa, Y., Köppen, M.: Interactive Genetic Algorithm for Font Generation System, pp. 1–6. IEEE (2010)

36. Zhao, N., Kim, N.W., Herman, L.M., Pfister, H., Lau, R.W., Echevarria, J., Bylinskii, Z.: Iconate: Automatic Compound Icon Generation and Ideation, pp. 1–13. ACM (2020). https://doi.org/10.1145/3313831.3376618

Emotion4MIDI: A Lyrics-Based Emotion-Labeled Symbolic Music Dataset

Serkan Sulun[1,2(✉)], Pedro Oliveira[2], and Paula Viana[1,3]

[1] Institute for Systems and Computer Engineering, Technology and Science (INESC TEC), Porto, Portugal
paula.viana@inesctec.pt
[2] Faculty of Engineering, University of Porto, Porto, Portugal
serkan.sulun@inesctec.pt, up201707038@edu.fe.up.pt
[3] ISEP, Polytechnic of Porto, School of Engineering, Porto, Portugal
pmv@isep.ipp.pt

Abstract. We present a new large-scale emotion-labeled symbolic music dataset consisting of 12 k MIDI songs. To create this dataset, we first trained emotion classification models on the GoEmotions dataset, achieving state-of-the-art results with a model half the size of the baseline. We then applied these models to lyrics from two large-scale MIDI datasets. Our dataset covers a wide range of fine-grained emotions, providing a valuable resource to explore the connection between music and emotions and, especially, to develop models that can generate music based on specific emotions. Our code for inference, trained models, and datasets are available online.

Keywords: Sentiment analysis · Symbolic music · Emotion classification · Music dataset

1 Introduction

Music has long been a powerful medium for emotional expression and communication [16]. The emotional response that music elicits has been studied by scholars from various fields such as psychology [19], musicology [15], and neuroscience [17]. Especially with the advent of deep learning, there has been an increasing interest in developing machine learning algorithms to automatically analyze and generate music that can evoke specific emotions in listeners [3].

Symbolic music—or MIDI (Musical Instrument Digital Interface) as it is used interchangeably—is represented as a sequence of notes and is a popular choice for

This work has been funded by National Funds through the Portuguese funding agency, FCT—Fundação para a Ciência e a Tecnologia, within project LA/P/0063/2020. Serkan Sulun received the support of fellowships from "la Caixa" Foundation (ID 100010434) with the fellowship code LCF/BQ/DI19/11730032 and FCT—Fundação para a Ciência e a Tecnologia with the fellowship code 2022.09594.BD. Corresponding author: Serkan Sulun (serkan.sulun@inesctec.pt)

© The Author(s), under exclusive license to Springer Nature Switzerland AG 2023
N. Moniz et al. (Eds.): EPIA 2023, LNAI 14116, pp. 77–89, 2023.
https://doi.org/10.1007/978-3-031-49011-8_7

machine learning models due to its compact and structured representation. Large raw MIDI datasets [30,31] enable unsupervised training of deep neural networks to automatically generate symbolic music. Similar to language modeling, these networks learn to predict the next token i.e. the next note, and at inference time, generate output autoregressively, one token at a time.

However, a human composer's creative process does not simply involve mechanically writing one note after another; it often includes high-level concepts such as motifs, themes and, ultimately, emotions [24]. To train deep neural networks to generate music based on emotions, large datasets of symbolic music annotated with emotional labels are required. Although there are some publicly available datasets with emotional labels, they are relatively small and do not cover a wide range of emotional states [33].

To address this issue, we present a new large-scale emotion-labeled symbolic music dataset created by analyzing the lyrics of the songs. Our approach leverages the natural connection between lyrics and music, established through emotions. To this end, we first trained models for emotion classification from text on GoEmotions [5], one of the largest text datasets with 28 fine-grained emotion labels. Using a model that is half the size of the baseline model, we obtained state-of-the-art results on this dataset. Later, we applied this model to the lyrics of songs from two of the biggest available MIDI datasets, namely Lakh MIDI dataset [30] and Reddit MIDI dataset [31]. Ultimately, we created a symbolic music dataset consisting of 12 k MIDI songs labeled with fine-grained emotions. We hope that this dataset will encourage further research in the field of affective algorithmic composition and contribute to the development of intelligent music systems that can understand and evoke specific emotions in listeners.

The remaining of this paper has the following structure: after having introduced our aim and the overall results in Sects. 1 and 2 presents the current state of the art on the most relevant topics for this work, namely text emotion classification and the existing emotion-labeled symbolic music datasets. Section 3 will delve into the proposed solution describing all the implemented steps, while results are presented and discussed in Sect. 4. Finally, we conclude by pointing out some possible future work in Sect. 5.

2   Related Work

2.1   Text Emotion Classification

Emotion classification from text—or sentiment analysis, as used interchangeably in the machine learning literature—allows us to automatically identify and/or quantify the emotion expressed in a piece of text, such as a review, social media post, or customer feedback [23]. Identifying the underlying emotion in text is useful in various fields such as customer service [10], finance [25], politics [14], and entertainment [1].

Machine learning methods have significantly advanced the state of the art in text emotion classification for the past two decades. However, the earliest works in this field relied on hand-crafted features, such as frequently used n-grams

[27], or adjectives and adverbs that are associated with particular emotions [35]. Nonetheless, the advent of deep learning has made it computationally feasible to process raw inputs without extracting features manually, leading to better performance [18]. Recurrent Neural Networks and their improved variants such as Long Short-Term Memory were initially used [22] but were later replaced by the transformer model [34], which is the current state of the art in natural language processing (NLP) tasks.

Fine-tuning pretrained models on specific tasks has been shown to produce better performance. The GPT (generative pretraining) model is a large transformer that was pretrained on the task of next token prediction and then was fine-tuned on specific NLP tasks, resulting in state-of-the-art performance [29]. The BERT (Bidirectional Encoder Representations from Transformers) model improved upon these results by employing masked token prediction as its pretraining task [6].

2.2 Emotion-Labeled Symbolic Music Datasets

MIDI (Musical Instrument Digital Interface) is a symbolic music format widely used to represent musical performances and compositions in the digital domain. MIDI files contain only the musical information, such as the notes, tempo, and dynamics, without the sound itself, like a "digital music sheet". Compared to audio formats, MIDI files have a smaller size and dimensionality, which makes them more manageable and suitable for modeling with deep neural networks [3].

The majority of existing literature on symbolic music generation relies on a non-conditional approach. In other words, these methods are trained on raw MIDI data without any explicit labels, allowing them to generate new music that is similar to the examples in the training dataset [12]. Some approaches, however, leverage low-level features within the data to create music in a conditional way [11]. For instance, they might use short melodies, chords, or single-instrument tracks as a basis for generating corresponding melodies. While such methods could be considered as "conditional", they do not make use of specific labels and are thus unable to capture high-level factors such as emotions or genres.

Using emotion as the specific high-level condition gives rise to the field of "affective algorithmic composition" (AAC) [36]. However, the development of machine learning AAC models is currently limited by the lack of large-scale symbolic music datasets with emotion labels. Some existing datasets include VGMIDI, which contains 204 piano-based video game soundtracks with continuous valence and arousal labels [8], Panda et al., which includes 193 samples with discrete emotion labels [26], and EMOPIA, which consists of 387 piano-based pop songs with four emotion labels [13]. Unfortunately, due to their small sizes, these datasets are insufficient for training deep neural networks with millions of parameters. Sulun et al. addressed this issue by labeling 34 k samples with continuous valence and arousal labels [33]. Though initially designed for audio samples, these labels were matched to their corresponding MIDI files to train emotion-based symbolic music generators that produced output music with emotional coherence. While this study exploited the correspondence between audio and symbolic music, there has been no utilization of the correspondence between lyrics and symbolic music to acquire high-level semantic labels.

3   Methodology

This section outlines the steps we followed to achieve our goal of creating a symbolic music dataset with emotion labels. Specifically, we begin by describing the model utilized for emotion classification, followed by a discussion of the training process, and conclude with an overview of how the model was applied to song lyrics to extract the corresponding emotion labels.

3.1   Model

We employ DistilBERT as the backbone of our model [32], which is a condensed and compressed variant of the BERT (Bidirectional Encoder Representations from Transformers) model [6], achieved through knowledge distillation [4,9]. DistilBERT utilizes fewer layers than BERT and learns from BERT's outputs to mimic its behavior. Our model consists of 6 layers, with each layer containing 12 attention heads and a dimensionality of 768, yielding a total of 67 M parameters. To facilitate multi-label classification, we have customized the output layer while adding a sigmoid activation layer at the end. The output layer's size is determined by the number of labels present in the training dataset, which can be either 7 or 28.

3.2   Training

The first step towards our aim of building an emotion-labeled symbolic music dataset is to train the model to perform multi-label emotion classification based on text input.

Dataset We trained our model using the GoEmotions dataset [5]. This dataset consists of English comments from the website *reddit.com*, which were manually annotated to identify the underlying emotions. It is a multi-label dataset, which means that each comment can have more than one emotion label. The dataset comprises 27 emotions and a "neutral" label. The labels are further grouped into 7 categories, including the six basic emotions identified by Ekman (joy, anger, fear, sadness, disgust, and surprise) as well as the "neutral" label [7]. The dataset has a total of 58 k samples, which were split into training, validation, and testing sets in the ratio of 80, 10, and 10%, respectively. Given the number of labels and its size, GoEmotions is one of the largest emotion classification datasets and has the highest number of discrete emotion labels [20].

Training and Evaluation Metrics We trained our models using binary cross-entropy loss. For evaluation, we used precision, recall, and F1-score, with macro averaging. The decision cutoff was set at 0.3, meaning that predictions with a value of 0.3 or greater are considered positive predictions and others negative.

Implementation Details We trained two models to classify a given text into 7 and 28 labels. We used a dropout rate of 0.1 and a gradient clipping norm of 1. The batch size was set to 16 for the model with 7 output labels and to 32 for the model with 28 output labels. We applied a learning rate of $5e-5$ for the former and $3e-5$ for the latter. We used early stopping considering the F1-score on the validation dataset, which corresponded to training for 10 epochs for both models. We implemented the models using Huggingface library [37] with Pytorch backend [28] and trained them using a single Nvidia GeForce GTX 1080 Ti GPU.

3.3 Inference

After training the models for text-based emotion classification, we used it in inference mode, using the song lyrics from the MIDI files as inputs. This allowed us to create a MIDI dataset labeled with emotions.

Datasets We used two MIDI datasets that are publicly available and were created by gathering MIDI files from various online sources: the Lakh MIDI dataset consisting of 176 k samples [30] and the Reddit MIDI dataset containing 130 k samples [31]. We filtered the datasets by selecting MIDI files that contain lyrics in the English language with at least 50 words. This filtering process resulted in a total of 12509 files, consisting of 8386 files from the Lakh MIDI dataset and 4123 files from the Reddit MIDI dataset. During inference, we utilized the two pretrained models, feeding the entire song's lyrics, using a truncation length of 512.

4 Results

In this section, we will first present the emotion classification performance of our trained models. Then, we will introduce the emotion-labeled MIDI dataset, which we created by analyzing the sentiment of the song lyrics using our trained models.

4.1 Emotion Classification on the GoEmotions Dataset

We evaluated the performance of our trained models on the test split of the GoEmotions dataset and compared our results with the baseline presented in the original paper [5]. Similar to the original paper, we report our results for scenarios using two sets of labels, with 7 and 28 emotions. For each label, we reported the precision, recall, and F1-scores along with the macro-averages. It is important to mention that, as the dataset is imbalanced, macro-averaging is more appropriate than micro-averaging, as it was also used in the original paper. We note that the baseline model is BERT and has twice the size of our model [6].

The trade-off between precision and recall is determined by the cutoff value. Therefore, we emphasize higher F1-scores because they provide a more balanced perspective by taking the harmonic mean of precision and recall, and are much less sensitive to the cutoff value. Although the original paper did not state the cutoff value, we achieved the best F1-score and similar performance to the original paper on the 7-label dataset using a cutoff value of 0.3. For consistency, we used the same value for the 28-label dataset. We present our results on the dataset with 28 and 7 labels in Tables 1 and 2, respectively.

Table 1. 7-label classification results

	Precision		Recall		F1-score	
	Baseline	Ours	Baseline	Ours	Baseline	Ours
Anger	0.50	0.50	0.65	0.67	**0.57**	**0.57**
Disgust	0.52	0.57	0.53	0.49	**0.53**	0.52
Fear	0.61	0.57	0.76	0.73	**0.68**	0.64
Joy	0.77	0.75	0.88	0.89	**0.82**	**0.82**
Neutral	0.66	0.63	0.67	0.75	0.66	**0.68**
Sadness	0.56	0.57	0.62	0.67	0.59	**0.61**
Surprise	0.53	0.59	0.70	0.62	**0.61**	**0.61**
Macro-average	0.59	0.60	0.69	0.69	**0.64**	**0.64**

Based on the F1-scores, our model performs comparably to the baseline on the 7-label dataset. Specifically, our model has a better performance on 2 labels, worse on 2 labels, and the same on 3 labels, as well as for the macro-average. On the 28-label dataset, our model surpasses the baseline with only a lower performance on 2 labels, equal performance on 4 labels, and better performance on the remaining 22 labels. Furthermore, our model demonstrates an improvement of 0.04 in terms of the macro-average.

We hypothesize that a smaller model, such as ours (DistilBERT), may perform better than a larger baseline model (BERT) in certain settings, such as when there are a limited number of training samples or a high output/target dimensionality, as in the case of the 28-label dataset. In these scenarios, models are more prone to overfitting, as has been previously observed [38]. Additionally, the original paper [32] demonstrates that the DistilBERT model outperforms BERT on the Winograd Natural Language Inference (WNLI) dataset [21].

Table 2. 28-label classification results

	Precision		Recall		F1-score	
	Baseline	Ours	Baseline	Ours	Baseline	Ours
Admiration	0.53	0.65	0.83	0.75	0.65	**0.70**
Amusement	0.70	0.72	0.94	0.91	0.80	**0.81**
Anger	0.36	0.53	0.66	0.49	0.47	**0.51**
Annoyance	0.24	0.40	0.63	0.31	0.34	**0.35**
Approval	0.26	0.39	0.57	0.38	0.36	**0.39**
Caring	0.30	0.37	0.56	0.46	0.39	**0.41**
Confusion	0.24	0.52	0.76	0.42	0.37	**0.47**
Curiosity	0.40	0.47	0.84	0.62	**0.54**	0.53
Desire	0.43	0.66	0.59	0.42	0.49	**0.51**
Disappointment	0.19	0.39	0.52	0.22	**0.28**	**0.28**
Disapproval	0.29	0.39	0.61	0.41	0.39	**0.40**
Disgust	0.34	0.64	0.66	0.39	0.45	**0.48**
Embarrassment	0.39	0.72	0.49	0.35	0.43	**0.47**
Excitement	0.26	0.43	0.52	0.47	0.34	**0.45**
Fear	0.46	0.60	0.85	0.76	0.60	**0.67**
Gratitude	0.79	0.88	0.95	0.92	0.86	**0.90**
Grief	0.00	0.00	0.00	0.00	**0.00**	**0.00**
Joy	0.39	0.59	0.73	0.61	0.51	**0.60**
Love	0.68	0.78	0.92	0.85	0.78	**0.81**
Nervousness	0.28	0.45	0.48	0.43	0.35	**0.44**
Neutral	0.56	0.61	0.84	0.76	**0.68**	**0.68**
Optimism	0.41	0.56	0.69	0.52	0.51	**0.54**
Pride	0.67	0.83	0.25	0.31	0.36	**0.45**
Realization	0.16	0.39	0.29	0.14	**0.21**	**0.21**
Relief	0.50	0.00	0.09	0.00	**0.15**	0.00
Remorse	0.53	0.59	0.88	0.86	0.66	**0.70**
Sadness	0.38	0.57	0.71	0.60	0.49	**0.59**
Surprise	0.40	0.56	0.66	0.50	0.50	**0.53**
Macro-average	0.40	0.53	0.63	0.50	0.46	**0.50**

4.2 Labeled MIDI Dataset

We used our trained models to analyze the song lyrics of the Lakh and Reddit MIDI datasets, resulting in an augmented dataset that contains the file paths to 12509 MIDI files and their corresponding predicted probabilities for emotion labels. To provide more flexibility to the users, we did not apply a threshold to the predicted probabilities, allowing the entire dataset to be used as is. We generated two CSV (comma-separated values) files containing the 7 and 28 emotion labels as columns, with the 12509 MIDI file paths as rows. Our code for inference, trained models, and datasets are available online.[1]

For demonstration purposes, we provide transposed versions of the tables, using only 3 samples, shown in Tables 3 and 4. We note that the values do not necessarily add up to one, due to the nature of multi-label classification.

For further demonstration and ease of analysis, we provide excerpts from the lyrics of each of the three sample songs in Listing 1.1, along with the emotions having predicted probabilities higher than 0.1 in descending order. It is noteworthy that having a dataset with 28 emotion labels allows for a more nuanced representation of emotions. For instance, when we examine this dataset, the song "Imagine" is predicted to have "optimism" as its top emotion, whereas "Take a Chance on Me" is predicted to have "caring" as its top emotion. However, both songs are predicted to have "joy" as their top emotion in the dataset with only seven labels.

We also present the number of samples containing each emotion in our datasets in Fig. 1. In these figures, we excluded the "neutral" label. We also considered emotions with a prediction value higher than 0.1 as positive labels, meaning that those emotions are present for a given sample.

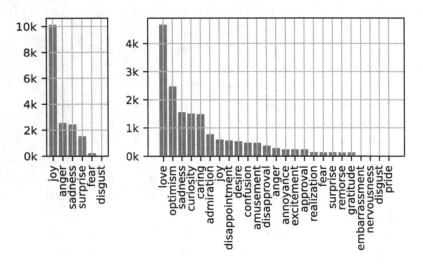

Fig. 1. The number of samples containing each emotion in our 7-label (left) and 28-label (right) datasets. The "neutral" label is excluded. Emotions with a prediction value higher than 0.1 are considered positive labels, meaning that those emotions are present for a given sample.

---

[1] https://github.com/serkansulun/lyricsemotions

Listing 1.1. Sample entries with excerpts from lyrics, and emotions with a predicted value higher than 0.1.

```
File path: lakh/5/58c076b72d5115486c09a7d9e6df1029.mid
Artist - Title: John Lennon - Imagine
Lyrics:
     Imagine there's no heaven.
     It's easy if you try.
     No hell below us.
     Above us, only sky.
     Imagine all the people.
     Livin' for today.
7-label predictions:
     joy:            0.8072
     neutral:        0.1953
28-label predictions:
     optimism:       0.7554
     neutral:        0.2954

File path: reddit/A/ABBA.Take a chance on me K.mid
Artist - Title: ABBA - Take a Chance on Me
Lyrics:
     If you change your mind, I'm the first in line.
     Honey, I'm still free.
     Take a chance on me.
     If you need me, let me know, gonna be around.
     If you've got no place to go, if you're feeling down.
7-label predictions:
     joy:            0.8948
     neutral:        0.1420
28-label predictions:
     caring:         0.6169
     neutral:        0.4288
     optimism:       0.1423
     love:           0.1079

File path: reddit/P/PRESLEY.Are you lonesome tonight K.mid
Artist - Title: Elvis Presley - Are You Lonesome Tonight
Lyrics:
     Are you lonesome tonight?
     Do you miss me tonight?
     Are you sorry we drifted apart?
     Does your memory stray to a bright summer day,
     When I kissed you and called you sweetheart?
7-label predictions:
     sadness:        0.7372
     surprise:       0.5465
28-label predictions:
     curiosity:      0.6502
     sadness:        0.1767
     remorse:        0.1491
     confusion:      0.1029
```

Table 3. Sample entries from the 28-label dataset.

	John Lennon—Imagine	ABBA—Take a Chance on Me	Elvis Presley—Are You Lonesome Tonight
Admiration	0.0021	0.0091	0.0048
Amusement	0.0051	0.0012	0.0027
Anger	0.0025	0.0018	0.0053
Annoyance	0.0024	0.0020	0.0075
Approval	0.0026	0.0809	0.0072
Caring	0.0067	**0.6169**	0.0601
Confusion	0.0070	0.0035	0.1029
Curiosity	0.0332	0.0141	**0.6502**
Desire	0.0482	0.0472	0.0055
Disappointment	0.0044	0.0016	0.0199
Disapproval	0.0019	0.0030	0.0048
Disgust	0.0007	0.0003	0.0009
Embarrassment	0.0006	0.0002	0.0045
Excitement	0.0130	0.0049	0.0011
Fear	0.0026	0.0026	0.0035
Gratitude	0.0007	0.0017	0.0059
Grief	0.0008	0.0016	0.0085
Joy	0.0025	0.0040	0.0018
Love	0.0021	0.1079	0.0193
Nervousness	0.0007	0.0017	0.0094
Neutral	0.2954	0.4288	0.0757
Optimism	**0.7554**	0.1423	0.0060
Pride	0.0010	0.0013	0.0006
Realization	0.0023	0.0040	0.0045
Relief	0.0004	0.0033	0.0011
Remorse	0.0005	0.0012	0.1491
Sadness	0.0011	0.0027	0.1767
Surprise	0.0107	0.0005	0.0020

Table 4. Sample entries from the 7-label dataset. Due to space limitations, the file paths are replaced with the artist and song names and are as the following: John Lennon—Imagine: "lakh/5/58c076b72d5115486c09a7d9e6df1029.mid" (artist and title obtained using Million Song Dataset [2]), ABBA - Take a Chance on Me: "reddit/A/ABBA.Take a chance on me K.mid", Elvis Presley—Are You Lonesome Tonight: "reddit/P/PRESLEY.Are you lonesome tonight K.mid"

	John Lennon—Imagine	ABBA—Take a Chance on Me	Elvis Presley—Are You Lonesome Tonight
Anger	0.0051	0.0146	0.0272
Disgust	0.0003	0.0009	0.0045
Fear	0.0005	0.0024	0.0131
Joy	**0.8072**	**0.8948**	0.0477
Neutral	0.1953	0.1420	0.0782
Sadness	0.0013	0.0069	**0.7372**
Surprise	0.0754	0.0053	0.5465

5 Conclusion and Future Work

In this work, we first trained models on the largest text-based emotion classification dataset, GoEmotions, in both 7-label and 28-label variants [5]. We achieved state-of-the-art results using a model half the size of the baseline. We then used these trained models to analyze the emotions of the song lyrics from the two largest MIDI datasets, Lakh MIDI dataset [30] and Reddit MIDI dataset [31]. This analysis resulted in an augmented dataset of 12509 MIDI files with emotion labels in a multi-label format, using either 7 basic-level or 28 fine-grained emotions. We made the datasets, inference code, and trained models available for researchers to use in various tasks, including symbolic music processing, natural language processing, and sentiment analysis.

In our future work, we plan to further narrow the considerable gap between symbolic music and emotion. In particular, we aim to create superior models that can automatically compose music that is based on emotions or user-provided input. We believe that incorporating emotions is vital in composing music, hence it can help to push the boundaries of computational creativity, bringing it one step closer to human-like performance.

References

1. Almeida, J., Vilaça, L., Teixeira, I.N., Viana, P.: Emotion identification in movies through facial expression recognition. Appl. Sci. **11**(15) (2021)
2. Bertin-Mahieux, T., Ellis, D.P.W., Whitman, B., Lamere, P.: The million song dataset. In: Proceedings of the 12th International Society for Music Information Retrieval Conference, pp. 591–596 (2011)
3. Briot, J., Hadjeres, G., Pachet, F.: Deep Learning Techniques for Music Generation. Springer, Berlin (2020)
4. Buciluǎ, C., Caruana, R., Niculescu-Mizil, A.: Model compression. In: Proceedings of the 12th ACM SIGKDD International Conference on Knowledge Discovery and Data Mining, pp. 535–541 (2006)
5. Demszky, D., Movshovitz-Attias, D., Ko, J., Cowen, A., Nemade, G., Ravi, S.: GoEmotions: a dataset of fine-grained emotions. In: 58th Annual Meeting of the Association for Computational Linguistics (ACL) (2020)
6. Devlin, J., Chang, M.W., Lee, K., Toutanova, K.: BERT: Pre-training of deep bidirectional transformers for language understanding. In: Proceedings of the 2019 Conference of the North American Chapter of the Association for Computational Linguistics: Human Language Technologies, pp. 4171–4186 (2019)
7. Ekman, P.: Are there basic emotions? Psychol. Rev. **99**(3), 550–553 (1992)
8. Ferreira, L., Whitehead, J.: Learning to generate music with sentiment. In: Proceedings of the 20th International Society for Music Information Retrieval Conference, pp. 384–390 (2019)
9. Hinton, G., Vinyals, O., Dean, J.: Distilling the Knowledge in a Neural Network. arXiv:1503.02531 (2015)
10. Hu, M., Liu, B.: Mining and summarizing customer reviews. In: Proceedings of the Tenth ACM SIGKDD International Conference on Knowledge Discovery and Data Mining, pp. 168–177 (2004)

11. Huang, C.Z.A., Cooijmans, T., Roberts, A., Courville, A.C., Eck, D.: Counterpoint by convolution. In: Proceedings of the 18th International Society for Music Information Retrieval Conference, pp. 211–218 (2017)
12. Huang, C.Z.A., Vaswani, A., Uszkoreit, J., Simon, I., Hawthorne, C., Shazeer, N., Dai, A.M., Hoffman, M.D., Dinculescu, M., Eck, D.: Music transformer: generating music with long-term structure. In: 7th International Conference on Learning Representations (2019)
13. Hung, H.T., Ching, J., Doh, S., Kim, N., Nam, J., Yang, Y.H.: EMOPIA: A multimodal pop piano dataset for emotion recognition and emotion-based music generation. In: Proceedings of the 22nd International Society for Music Information Retrieval Conference, pp. 318–325 (2021)
14. Iyyer, M., Enns, P., Boyd-Graber, J., Resnik, P.: Political ideology detection using recursive neural networks. In: Proceedings of the 52nd Annual Meeting of the Association for Computational Linguistics, pp. 1113–1122 (2014)
15. Juslin, P.N.: Communicating emotion in music performance: a review and a theoretical framework. In: Music and Emotion: Theory and Research, Series in Affective Science, pp. 309–337. Oxford University Press, New York, NY, US (2001)
16. Juslin, P.N., Sloboda, J.A.: Music and Emotion. Elsevier, Academic (2013)
17. Koelsch, S.: Brain correlates of music-evoked emotions. Nat. Rev. Neurosci. **15**(3), 170–180 (2014)
18. Krizhevsky, A., Sutskever, I., Hinton, G.E.: Imagenet classification with deep convolutional neural networks. Commun. ACM **60**(6), 84–90 (2017)
19. Krumhansl, C.L.: Music: a link between cognition and emotion. Curr. Dir. Psychol. Sci. **11**(2), 45–50 (2002)
20. Kusal, S., Patil, S.A., Choudrie, J., Kotecha, K., Vora, D.R., Pappas, I.O.: A review on text-based emotion detection—techniques, applications, datasets, and future directions (2022). ArXiv:abs/2205.03235
21. Levesque, H., Davis, E., Morgenstern, L.: The winograd schema challenge. In: Thirteenth International Conference on the Principles of Knowledge Representation and Reasoning (2012)
22. Li, D., Qian, J.: Text sentiment analysis based on long short-term memory. In: 2016 First IEEE International Conference on Computer Communication and the Internet (ICCCI), pp. 471–475 (2016)
23. Liu, B., Zhang, L.: A survey of opinion mining and sentiment analysis. In: Mining Text Data, pp. 415–463. Springer, Berlin (2012)
24. Meyer, L.B.: Emotion and Meaning in Music. University of Chicago Press (2008)
25. Nguyen, T.H., Shirai, K., Velcin, J.: Sentiment analysis on social media for stock movement prediction. Expert Syst. Appl. **42**(24), 9603–9611 (2015)
26. Panda, R., Malheiro, R., Rocha, B., Oliveira, A., Paiva, R.P.: Multi-modal music emotion recognition: A new dataset, methodology and comparative analysis. In: International Symposium on Computer Music Multidisciplinary Research (2013)
27. Pang, B., Lee, L., Vaithyanathan, S.: Thumbs up? sentiment classification using machine learning techniques. In: Proceedings of the 2002 Conference on Empirical Methods in Natural Language Processing, pp. 79–86 (2002)
28. Paszke, A., Gross, S., Massa, F., Lerer, A., Bradbury, J., Chanan, G., Killeen, T., Lin, Z., Gimelshein, N., Antiga, L., Desmaison, A., Kopf, A., Yang, E., DeVito, Z., Raison, M., Tejani, A., Chilamkurthy, S., Steiner, B., Fang, L., Bai, J., Chintala, S.: Pytorch: An imperative style, high-performance deep learning library. In: Advances in Neural Information Processing Systems, vol. 32, pp. 8024–8035. Curran Associates, Inc. (2019)

29. Radford, A., Narasimhan, K., Salimans, T., Sutskever, I.: Improving Language Understanding by Generative Pre-Training. OpenAI (2018)
30. Raffel, C.: Learning-Based Methods for Comparing Sequences, with Applications to Audio-to-MIDI Alignment and Matching. Ph.D. thesis, Columbia University (2016)
31. Reddit MIDI dataset. https://www.reddit.com/r/WeAreTheMusicMakers/comments/3ajwe4/the_largest_midi_collection_on_the_internet/
32. Sanh, V., Debut, L., Chaumond, J., Wolf, T.: Distilbert, a distilled version of bert: smaller, faster, cheaper and lighter (2019). ArXiv:abs/1910.01108
33. Sulun, S., Davies, M.E.P., Viana, P.: Symbolic music generation conditioned on continuous-valued emotions. IEEE Access 10, 44617–44626 (2022)
34. Vaswani, A., Shazeer, N., Parmar, N., Uszkoreit, J., Jones, L., Gomez, A.N., Kaiser, L., Polosukhin, I.: Attention is all you need. In: Advances in Neural Information Processing Systems 30: Annual Conference on Neural Information Processing Systems, pp. 5998–6008 (2017)
35. Whitelaw, C., Garg, N., Argamon, S.: Using appraisal groups for sentiment analysis. In: Proceedings of the 14th ACM International Conference on Information and Knowledge Management, pp. 625–631 (2005)
36. Williams, D., Kirke, A., Miranda, E.R., Roesch, E., Daly, I., Nasuto, S.: Investigating affect in algorithmic composition systems. Psychol. Music 43(6), 831–854 (2015)
37. Wolf, T., Debut, L., Sanh, V., Chaumond, J., Delangue, C., Moi, A., Cistac, P., Rault, T., Louf, R., Funtowicz, M.: Huggingface's transformers: State-of-the-art natural language processing (2019). ArXiv:abs/1910.03771
38. Yu, Z., Yu, J., Fan, J., Tao, D.: Multi-modal factorized bilinear pooling with co-attention learning for visual question answering. In: IEEE International Conference on Computer Vision, pp. 1839–1848. IEEE Computer Society (2017)

Artificial Intelligence and Law

On the Assessment of Deep Learning Models for Named Entity Recognition of Brazilian Legal Documents

Hidelberg O. Albuquerque[1,2](✉) 🆔, Ellen Souza[1,4] 🆔, Adriano L. I. Oliveira[2] 🆔, David Macêdo[2] 🆔, Cleber Zanchettin[2] 🆔, Douglas Vitório[1,2] 🆔, Nádia F. F. da Silva[3,4] 🆔, and André C. P. L. F. de Carvalho[4] 🆔

[1] MiningBR Research Group, Federal Rural University of Pernambuco, Recife, Brazil
ellen.ramos@ufrpe.br, damsv@cin.ufpe.br
[2] Centro de Informática, Federal University of Pernambuco, Recife, Brazil
hidelberg.albuquerque@ufrpe.br, {alio,dlm,cz}@cin.ufpe.br
[3] Institute of Informatics, Federal University of Goiás, Goiania, Brazil
nadia.felix@ufg.br
[4] Institute of Mathematics and Computer Sciences, University of São Paulo, Sao Paulo, Brazil
andre@icmc.usp.br

Abstract. A large amount of legal and legislative documents are generated every year with highly specialized content and significant repercussions on society. Besides technical, the produced information is not semantically standardized or format structured. Automating the document analysis, categorization, search, and summarization is essential. The Named Entity Recognition (NER) task is one of the tools that have the potential to extract information from legal documents with efficiency. This paper evaluates the state-of-the-art NER models BiLSTM+CRF and BERT+Fine-Tunning trained on Portuguese corpora through fine-tuning in the legal and legislative domains. The obtained results (F1-scores of 83.17% and 88.27%) suggest that the BERT model is superior, achieving better average results.

Keywords: Deep learning · Named entity recognition · Legal information retrieval

1 Introduction

The legal domain includes a wide variety of texts, such as laws, bills, processes, and official communications. Each bill must be formalized in advance through a draft document submitted for discussion and legislative voting in the Brazilian legal context. Many documents are produced and aggregated in different processing steps, most of them without standardization. As a result, the content generated is vast and growing. The unstructured nature of these documents makes their organization, access, and retrieval a challenging task [7]. There are

N. Moniz et al. (Eds.): EPIA 2023, LNAI 14116, pp. 93–104, 2023.
https://doi.org/10.1007/978-3-031-49011-8_8

already studies focused on the legal domain in English, but few works in Portuguese and for the Brazilian justice [4,8].

Deep Learning (DL) is a subset of Machine Learning (ML) methods that can be applied in different domains, such as Big Data, Image Processing, and Natural Language Processing [15]. The prediction accuracy achieved by those models has improved substantially, surpassing traditional machine learning [14]. Moreover, applying these models to legal documents can improve automation by reducing cross-references, manual tasks and minimizing procedural obstacles.

Named Entity Recognition (NER) is a subarea of Natural Language Processing (NLP) that aims to identify entities in the text and classify them into particular sets of syntactic or semantic categories, such as names of people and organizations [12], or the ones specific to a particular language or domain [5]. In NER tasks, DL techniques can identify and classify entities with performance superior to traditional ML techniques [6].

This work benchmarks two DL architectures, BiLSTM+CRF and BERT+Fine-Tunning, applied to NER tasks in legal documents written in Brazilian Portuguese. The main contributions of this work to the legal/legislative domains in the Portuguese language are: (i) validation of state-of-the-art results, (ii) evaluation of word embeddings models and their impact on preprocessing steps, (iii) application of a BERT model adapted to the legislative domain, (iv) pointing out improvements in the state-of-the-art results for NER in Portuguese, and (v) suggesting a better hyperparameters configuration space for the models. Using widely used NLP metrics, the obtained results exceed the baseline works, demonstrating that the BERT model was superior to NER tasks.

The remainder of this paper is structured as follows: Sect. 2 briefly presents related studies. Then, Sect. 3 describes the experiments and the evaluation of the hyperparameters. Section 4 shows the obtained results, with the evaluation by groups of hyperparameters and comparison with the state-of-the-art baselines. Finally, Sect. 5 brings the final remarks and highlights future works.

2   Related Works

This section highlights Deep Learning techniques and NER approaches for the legal and legislative domains, considering different languages [11,17]. Unfortunately, public corpora in Portuguese is scarce.

Luz de Araújo et al. [4] presented *LeNER-Br*, a corpus obtained from 70 legal documents from Brazilian courts and laws, using entities defined in HAREM [13]. They also added two new entities from the legal domain: *Legislation*, for laws, and *Legal cases*, for legal decisions resulting from judicial processes, and used BiLSTM+CRF architectures and Glove word vector pre-trained in Brazilian and European Portuguese. The overall results were: Precision of 93.21%, Recall of 91.91%, and F1-score of 92.53%, while the model's Accuracy was not presented. The codes and the annotated corpus are publicly available.[1] Their research is considered pioneering for NER tasks in the Brazilian legal context.

---

[1] https://github.com/peluz/lener-br.

Alles [3] developed the *DOU-Corpus* for NER using 470 documents from the Official Gazette of the Union, the official bulletin of the Brazilian Government. New entities were used for the legal domain, such as *Cargo* (role), *Lei* (law), *Número* (number), *Processo* (process) and *Valor-monetário* (financial value). The results obtained using Apache OpenNLP were: Precision of 95.3%, Recall of 60.7%, and F1-score of 44.5%. Unfortunately, the corpus is not available.

Castro [8] developed a NER model for the legal domain in Portuguese, based on BiLSTM+CRF architecture applied to the field of Labor Justice in Brazil, with Accuracy of 80%. A total of 1,305 documents were used, with universal entities and new specialized entities: *Função* (function), *Fundamento* (legal provisions), *Tribunal* and *Vara* (particulars of Brazilian courts), *Valor_Acordo*, *Valor_Causa*, *Valor_Condenacao* and *Valor_Custas* (monetary values). The corpus is not available.

Albuquerque et al. [2] presented *UlyssesNER-Br*, a corpus for NER tasks developed using legislative documents from the Brazilian Chamber of Deputies. They present two corpora: *PL-Corpus*, using 150 public bills, and *ST-Corpus*, with 800 documents of internal job requests, evaluated with the HMM and CRF models. The PL-corpus is publicly available.[2] In addition to universal entities used, semantic legal categories were introduced: *Law Foundation* (legal documents) and *Product of Law* (products generated by-laws). The better results were: Accuracy of 97.27%, Precision of 83.42%, Recall of 70.40%, and F1-score of 76.28%.

Costa et al. [9] presents an expansion of UlyssesNER-Br, introducing the *C-corpus*, a new corpus composed of citizen's comments in Brazilian Portuguese on bills and the use of formal and informal corpora. The work evaluate the performance of the CRF, BiLSTM-CRF and fine-tuned BERT models, getting the best results with the BERT model: 73.9% in analysis by categories, and 71.05% by types. The study also demonstrated that combining formal and informal texts can improve NER tasks and suggests further exploration of other DL approaches for NER in informal text. Unfortunately, no available resources were found.

In this paper, we used the LeNER-Br [4] and PL-corpus [2] datasets. Both dataset have characteristics in common: language, domain, entity semantics, annotation process [16] and they are both publicly available.

3   Method

This study was performed through exploratory research using an experimental methodology (Fig. 1): (1) application of the models to the corpora to reproduce the baseline results, (2) hyperparameters optimization to improve experimental performance, (3) analysis of the results to answer the research question and selection of the best configuration space, and (4) comparison the experimental best results with the baseline. Through the method used, we sought to answer the question: "Of the chosen architectures, which one has the best results for NER tasks in texts of the Brazilian legal/legislative domains?".

---

[2] https://github.com/Convenio-Camara-dos-Deputados/ulyssesner-br-propor.

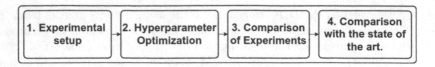

Fig. 1. Method pipeline.

Initially, it sought to replicate the models used in the selected corpora to reproduce the state-of-the-art baseline results. As the PL-corpus did not use a deep learning model, only its results and the corpus were used. Due to its quality and its availability, the BiLSTM+CRF model available in LeNER-Br was applied to both corpora.

Currently, the best results for NER tasks have been achieved with BERT [1, 18]. Platforms like Hugging Face[3] offer pre-trained datasets available for use. In order to have a baseline, the legal BERT model fine-tuned with the LeNER-Br [10][4] was used. Furthermore, this BERT model was adapted, pre-training and finetuning for the legislative domain using the PL-corpus. The generated dataset is available.[5]

We aimed to assess the quality of the models by modifying hyperparameters. No changes were made to the baseline source code and the original hyperparameters in the initial stage. Table 1 shows the evaluated hyperparameters and the configuration space to be changed in the following steps.

After this initial phase, optimization was applied to the hyperparameters, seeking to improve the performance of NER tasks. For this, individual groups performed isolated analyses, changing only the value of the target hyperparameter. For each group, five runs were performed, randomly modifying the training, validation, and test sets and calculating the average and standard deviation of the results. After the evaluation by groups, the hyperparameters were combined within the configuration space chosen (Table 1). Again, the training, validation, and test sets were randomized once. The third step evaluates the best results from the metrics, with the F1-score as a determinant. The best results defined the best configuration space for the NER tasks of the models used in this research. Finally, the best results obtained were compared with the state-of-the-art baselines in the last step.

3.1 Hyperparameters Tuning

Word Embbedings: numeric vector representations of each word and their degree of similarity with the other words in the corpus, being frequently used in NLP tasks. The used vectors were *Glove*, *Word2Vec*, *FastText*, and *Wang2Vec*, all of them with 300 dimensions and pre-trained for Portuguese.[6] The BiL-

---

[3] https://huggingface.co.

[4] https://huggingface.co/pierreguillou/ner-bert-base-cased-pt-lenerbr.

[5] https://huggingface.co/datasets/bergoliveira/pl-corpus.

[6] http://nilc.icmc.usp.br/nilc/index.php/repositorio-de-word-embeddings-do-nilc.

Table 1. Training hyperparameters. [1]Hyperparameters analyzed in BiLSTM+CRF: Word Embbedings, Batch size, Epochs, Optimization method. [2]Hyperparameters analyzed in BERT: Batch size, Epochs, Learning rate. [3]Configuration space used for experiments, both in the evaluation of individual groups of hyperparameters, and in the combination of pre-selected values.

Hyperparameters	Models		Configuration space[3]
	BiLSTM+CRF[1]	BERT+Fine-Tunning[2]	
Word embeddings	Glove	–	[Glove, Word2Vec, FastText, Wang2Vec]
Batchs size	10	10	[10, 20, 40]
Epochs	55	55	[35, 55, 75]
Optimization method	SGD	AdamW	[SGD, Adam, Adagrad, RMSProp]
Learning rate	0.015	2e–5	[1e–4, 2e–5, 3e–4, 5e–5]

STM+CRF uses the Glove vector by default. In the experiment, we sought to evaluate the impact of these embeddings in the text preprocessing stage. The BERT model did not use word embeddings and, therefore, they were not applied in the BERT experiments.

Batch size: defines the number of training examples in each epoch and must be adjusted considering the available memory space. We sought to investigate its dependence on the NER tasks.

Epochs: express the number of iterations that the algorithm performs during the training step. The appropriate number of epochs must be chosen with prudence, avoiding underfitting and overfitting.

Optimization method: specifies the exact way parameters are updated using the loss gradient. Choosing the right optimizer can reduce the error between obtained results versus expected results. The following methods were evaluated: *SGD, ADAM, RMSprop,* and *ADAGRAD.* BiLSTM+CRF uses SGD by default. It was impossible to observe an associated parameter in the BERT used, and, therefore, this parameter was also not evaluated in the BERT experiments.

Learning rate: defines the speed the models update their parameters in the learning process, which can influence the quality of the results. This parameter was not changed in the BiLSTM+CRF model, as optimization methods used varied learning rates were evaluated only for the BERT model.

4 Results and Discussion

4.1 Experimental Setup

The BiLSTM+CRF and fined-tuned BERT models were applied to the corpora for initial comparison. There were no changes in the baseline source code or hyperparameters values. The experimental results (Table 2) show that the BiLSTM+CRF model applied to both corpora and the BERT+Fine-Tunning applied to LeNER-Br failed to reach the state-of-the-art results. On the other

Table 2. Experimental results. For the initial experiments, the hyperparameters of the models had the standard values. The results obtained represent the average and standard deviation after five runs in each corpus. BERT was more stable and with better results, surpassing the baseline of PL-corpus.

Corpus	Model	Accuracy (%)	Precision (%)	Recall (%)	F1-score (%)
LeNER-Br	BiLSTM + CRF and Glove	96.36 ± 1.50	82.33 ± 3.33	78.53 ± 10.18	80.12 ± 7.89
	BERT + Fine-Tunning	**96.97 ± 0.31**	**86.36 ± 2.82**	**88.78 ± 1.53**	**87.53 ± 1.68**
PL-corpus	BiLSTM + CRF and Glove	94.26 ± 8.82	73.17 ± 10.59	68.43 ± 11.02	70.69 ± 10.77
	BERT + FineTunning	**97.13 ± 0.30**	**81.14 ± 2.80**	**83.33 ± 1.50**	**82.22 ± 1.60**

hand, BERT+Fine-Tunning overcame state-of-the-art for PL-corpus. These results were used as a reference for comparison for the following experiments.

4.2 Hyperparameters Evaluation for LeNER-Br

Using the **BiLSTM+CRF** model, the following results were found:

Word Embeddings. A common behavior of all evaluated vectors: when coming to an epoch in which the plateau with the best F1-score was reached (Epoch 30), this average plateau was kept until the end (Fig. 2a). The best result is Glove (Fig. 2b), confirming state-of-the-art performance.

Batch size. The experiment started with the original hyperparameter value, and we doubled these values. By analyzing the average F1-score, increasing the batch size for the same number of epochs did not benefit the training but showed an average decrease for the NER tasks.

Epochs. It was possible to observe a small tendency of improvement, indicating that a greater number of epochs could improve future results.

Optimization methods. The results showed a slight gain obtained by the optimizers ADAM and RMSProp for LeNER-Br, highlighting the deficient performance of ADAGRAD. Figure 2c shows the results by groups.

Finally, performing the permutation of the configuration space possibilities, a better result was found. As shown by Fig. 2d, there was an improvement of about 4% in the F1-score. The best result with BiLSTM+CRF was obtained using the set of hyperparameters: [Batch size: 20; Epochs: 75; Optimizer: RMS Prop]. We also observed that the probability of the number of epochs associated with the RMSProp optimizer caused this gain.

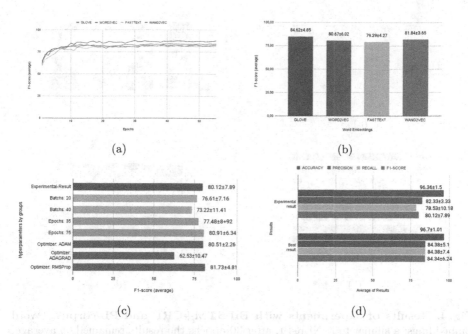

(a)   (b)

(c)   (d)

Fig. 2. Results of experiments with BiLSTM+CRF and LeNER-Br. [1]Word Embeddings: **a** after reaching the plateau at 30 epochs, the results remained on average in all cases, with mean superiority of Glove; **b** the Glove vector obtained better results. [2]Hyperparameters: **c** results by groups of hyperparameters; **d** best configuration space: [Batchs: 20; Epochs: 75; Optimizer: RMSProp], after combining the hyperparameters, with F1-score growth of ∼4%.

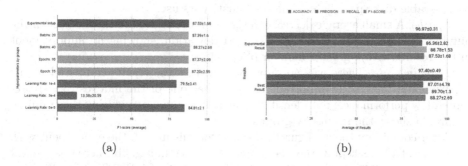

(a)   (b)

Fig. 3. Results of experiments with BERT+Fine-Tunning and LeNER-Br. **a** results by groups of hyperparameters; **b** best configuration space: [Batchs: 40; Epochs: 55; Learning rate: 2e–5], after combining the hyperparameters, with F1-score growth of 0.7%.

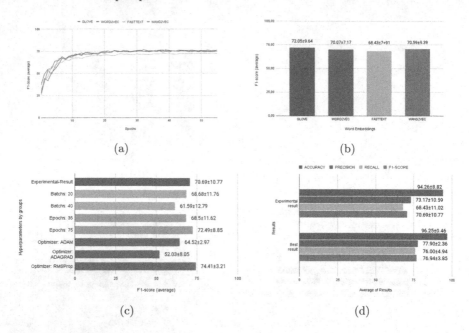

(a)   (b)

(c)   (d)

Fig. 4. Results of experiments with BiLSTM+CRF and PL-corpus. [1]Word Embeddings: **a** similar to LeNER-Br, after 30 epochs the results remained on average, with the best result of Glove. FastText had the worst performance; **b** Glove has better F1-scores results. [2]Hyperparameters: **c** results by groups; **d** best configuration space: [Batchs: 20; Epochs: 75; Optimizer: RMSProp], after combining the hyperparameters, with F1-score growth of 6%.

The following results are from experiments with **BERT+Fine-Tunning**:

Batch size. There was a slight improvement in the average growth of F1-score using LeNER-Br as the batch size increased. In addition, the training step used considerable disk space, which may not justify its use.

Epochs. A small average decrease in the F1-score related to the increase in the number of epochs and increasing standard deviation, showing no improvement in the results with a greater number of epochs.

Learning rate. There was no improvement in these results compared to the experimental ones. It is important to note that one of the indexes (3e–4) presented low performance, not identifying, at times, any entity during the training. Figure 3a shows the results by groups.

After combining the configuration space for this model, the experiment with batch size of 40 was kept as the best result. As shown in Fig. 3b, there was a slight improvement of 0.7% in the F1-score. The best result with BERT+Fine-Tunning was obtained with the hyperparameters: [Batch size: 40; Epochs: 55; Learning rate: 2e–5]. It is well known in the literature that increasing the batch size can harm the model's performance, which did not happen in our experiments.

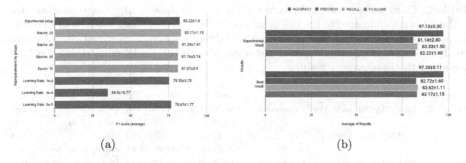

(a)   (b)

Fig. 5. Results of experiments with BERT+Fine-Tunning and PL-corpus.
a results by groups of hyperparameters; b best configuration space: [Batch size: 20;
Epochs: 55; Learning rate: 2e–5], after combining the hyperparameters, with F1-score
growth of 0.9%.

We still do not have a clear explanation for this, which opens space for future
investigations.

4.3   Hyperparameter Evaluation for PL-Corpus

Applying the **BiLSTM+CRF** model to PL-corpus, it was possible to observe
a very similar behavior of these experiments with those performed with LeNER-
Br. Therefore, we highlight below some relevant details using this corpus.

Word Embeddings. Maintenance of the average result after the plateau of 30
epochs. FastText had the worst performance, reaching the plateau at the 10th
epoch, and Glove had the best result, as shown by Fig. 4a, b.

Batch size. As in the experiments with the other corpus, increasing the batch
size did not bring benefits for the identification of entities in the training step.

Epochs. A small tendency of improvement was observed, with greater expres-
siveness, suggesting that more extended training can improve results.

Optimization methods. Using PL-corpus, there was a more significant increase
in F1-score only with the RMSProp optimizer, while the others performed worse.
Figure 4c shows the results by groups.

Performing the permutation of the configuration space, we find the best
result with the same set of hyperparameters as the experiments with LeNER-Br:
[Batchs: 20; Epochs: 75; Optimizer: RMSProp] (see Fig. 4d), with an F1-score
increase of about 6%.

Results of experiments with **BERT+Fine-Tunning**:

Batch size. There was an increase only when the batch size of 20 was tested
in this experiment. Increased storage usage, again, is a factor to consider.

Epochs. Behavior is similar to the other corpus's experiments, showing no
improvement in the average results obtained.

Table 3. Comparison of experiments. The results showed an average improvement of the F1-score compared to the baseline. The BERT+Fine-Tuning model had the highest average F1-scores and the lowest standard deviation across all scenarios, indicating greater stability than other models. Moreover, the BERT model outperformed others, achieving the best average results.

Corpus	Model	Results	Accuracy (%)	Precision (%)	Recall (%)	F1-score (%)
LeNER-Br	BiLSTM+CRF and Glove	Experimental	96.36±1.50	82.33±3.33	78.53±10.18	80.12±7.89
		Best	96.70±1.01	84.38±5.10	84.38±7.40	84.34±6.24
	BERT+Fine-Tunning	Experimental	96.97±0.31	86.36±2.82	88.78±1.53	87.53±1.68
		Best	**97.40±0.49**	**87.01±4.78**	**89.70±1.30**	**88.27±2.69**
PL-corpus	BiLSTM+CRF and Glove	Experimental	94.26±8.82	73.17±10.59	68.43±11.02	70.69±10.77
		Best	96.25±0.46	77.90±2.36	76.00±4.94	76.94±3.85
	BERT+Fine-Tunning	Experimental	97.13±0.30	81.14±2.80	83.33±1.50	82.22±1.60
		Best	**97.20±0.11**	**82.72±1.60**	**83.62±1.11**	**83.17±1.15**

Learning rate. There was no improvement in these experiments compared to the experimental result. The index 3e-4 obtained an inferior performance, demonstrating not a good option in any experiments (see Fig. 5a).

Finally, after combining the configuration space, the best result with BERT+ Fine-Tunning was obtained with the set of hyperparameters: [Batch size: 20; Epochs: 55; Learning rate: 2e-5] (see Fig. 5b), with a slight improvement of about 0.9% of F1-score.

4.4   Comparison and Discussion

Comparing the best results achieved by the hyperparameters optimization and the experimental baseline results shown in Table 3, it is possible to notice: (i) the best configurations showed more significant results in all metrics and for both corpora; (ii) the results by the BERT+Fine-Tunning model were better in terms of the F1-score average and lower standard deviation, demonstrating the best model quality for the NER tasks; (iii) BERT+Fine-Tunning obtained the best overall F1-score results, reaching 88.27±2.69% for the LeNER-Br corpus and 83.17±1.15% for the PL-corpus.

When comparing the best-obtained results with the baseline papers (Table 4), it is possible to notice that the results presented by the authors of LeNER-Br are still superior. For a more accurate result, further investigation is needed with the authors about the number of executions performed, average, and standard deviation. On the other hand, the results obtained for the PL-corpus showed more relevance in terms of Accuracy, Recall, and F1-score, with about 7% of improvement in the average F1-score compared with the results presented by the baseline work.

Table 4. Comparison between best results and the state of the art. [1]LeNER-Br: original results do not show average and standard deviation. State-of-the-art results were better than the experiments of our best result. [2]PL-corpus: results obtained by BERT+Fine-Tunning were much more relevant.

Corpus	Results	Accuracy (%)	Precision (%)	Recall (%)	F1-score (%)
LeNER-Br[1]	State of the art	–	**93.21**	**91.91**	**92.53**
	Best result	97.40 ± 0.30	87.01 ± 4.78	89.70 ± 1.30	88.27 ± 2.69
PL-corpus[2]	State of the art	97.27 ± 0.77	**83.42 ± 0.91**	70.40 ± 1.54	76.28 ± 1.12
	Best result	**97.20 ± 0.11**	82.70 ± 1.60	**83.60 ± 1.11**	**83.17 ± 1.15**

5   Conclusion and Future Works

We performed an exploratory study in Named Entity Recognition (NER) within Portuguese's legal and legislative domains. Applying the BiLSTM+CRF and BERT+Fine-Tunning learning models, we first validate the state-of-the-art results as a baseline. Then, by manipulating the hyperparameters configuration space of these models, to point out those present the best performance in terms of Accuracy, Precision, Recall, and F1-score.

Two public corpora were used: LeNER-Br [4] and PL-corpus [2]. The experimental results suggest the BERT+Fine-Tunning model achieved superior results, with F1-scores of 88.27% for LeNER-Br and 83.17% for PL-corpus, with an increase of approximately 7% in the latter. Furthermore, in future works, we intend to investigate a better configuration to achieve the results presented by the LeNER-Br authors, to investigate other evaluation methods (such as the influence of data augmentation and loss on NER tasks, for instance), and compare the performance of these methods with the known performances in the state-of-the-art in other languages to the same domain.

Acknowledgements This research is carried out in the context of the Ulysses Project, of the Brazilian Chamber of Deputies. Ellen Souza and Nadia Félix are supported by FAPESP, agreement between USP and the Brazilian Chamber of Deputies. Adriano L.I. Oliveira, André C.P.L.F. de Carvalho, and Cleber Zanchettin are supported by CNPq. To the Brazilian Chamber of Deputies and to research funding agencies, to which we express our gratitude for supporting this research.

References

1. Aguiar, A., Silveira, R., Pinheiro, V., Furtado, V., Neto, J.A.: Text classification in legal documents extracted from lawsuits in brazilian courts. In: Intelligent Systems, pp. 586–600 (2021)
2. Albuquerque, H.O., et al.: UlyssesNER-Br: A corpus of Brazilian legislative documents for named entity recognition. In: Computational Processing of the Portuguese Language, pp. 3–14 (2022)

3. Alles, V.J.: Construção de um corpus para extrair entidades nomeadas do Diário Oficial da União utilizando aprendizado supervisionado. Master's thesis, Department of Electrical Engineering, University of Brasilia (2018)
4. Luz de Araujo, P.H., de Campos, T.E., de Oliveira, R.R.R., Stauffer, M., Couto, S., Bermejo, P.: LeNER-Br: A dataset for named entity recognition in brazilian legal text. In: Computational Processing of the Portuguese Language (2018)
5. Luz de Araujo, P.H., de Campos, T.E., Ataides Braz, F., Correia da Silva, N.: VICTOR: a dataset for Brazilian legal documents classification. In: Proceedings of the 12th Language Resources and Evaluation Conference, pp. 1449–1458 (2020)
6. Bonifacio, L.H., Vilela, P.A., Lobato, G.R., Fernandes, E.R.: A study on the impact of intradomain finetuning of deep language models for legal named entity recognition in portuguese. In: Brazilian Conference on Intelligent Systems (2020)
7. Brandt, M.B.: Modelagem da informação legislativa: arquitetura da informação para o processo legislativo brasileiro. Ph.D. thesis, Faculdade de Filosofia e Ciências, Universidade Estadual Paulista (Unesp) (2020)
8. Castro, P.V.Q.: Aprendizagem profunda para reconhecimento de entidades nomeadas em domínio jurídico (2019)
9. Costa, R., et al.: Expanding UlyssesNER-Br named entity recognition corpus with informal user-generated text. In: Progress in Artificial Intelligence, pp. 767–779 (2022)
10. Guillou, P.: (BERT base) Language Modeling in the Legal Domain in Portuguese (LeNER-Br) (2021). https://huggingface.co/pierreguillou/bert-base-cased-pt-lenerbr
11. Leitner, E., Rehm, G., Moreno-Schneider, J.: A dataset of German legal documents for named entity recognition. In: Proceedings of the 12th Language Resources and Evaluation Conference, pp. 4478–4485 (2020)
12. Maynard, D., Bontcheva, K., Augenstein, I.: Natural language processing for the semantic web. Synthesis Lectures on the Semantic Web: Theory and Technology 6(2), 1–194 (2016)
13. Santos, D., Cardoso, N.: A golden resource for named entity recognition in portuguese. In: International Workshop on Computational Processing of the Portuguese Language, pp. 69–79 (2006)
14. Schmidhuber, J.: Deep learning in neural networks: an overview. Neural Netw. 61, 85–117 (2015)
15. Shinde, P.P., Shah, S.: A review of machine learning and deep learning applications. In: 2018 Fourth International Conference on Computing Communication Control and Automation (ICCUBEA), pp. 1–6. IEEE (2018)
16. Tjong Kim Sang, E.F.: Introduction to the CoNLL-2002 shared task: Language-independent named entity recognition. In: The 6th Conference on Natural Language Learning 2002 (CoNLL-2002) (2002)
17. Váradi, T., Koeva, S., Yamalov, M., Tadić, M., Sass, B., Nitoń, B., Ogrodniczuk, M., Pęzik, P., Barbu Mititelu, V., Ion, R., Irimia, E., Mitrofan, M., Păiş, V., Tufiş, D., Garabík, R., Krek, S., Repar, A., Rihtar, M., Brank, J.: The MARCELL legislative corpus. In: Proceedings of the 12th Language Resources and Evaluation Conference, pp. 3761–3768 (2020)
18. Wang, Z., Wu, Y., Lei, P., Peng, C.: Named entity recognition method of brazilian legal text based on pre-training model. J. Phys.: Conf. Ser. 1550(3), 032149 (2020)

Anonymisation of Judicial Rulings for Legal Analytics Purposes: Ethics, Law, and Compliance

Jacopo Ciani Sciolla(✉) ⓘ and Ludovica Paseri ⓘ

Law Department, University of Turin, Turin, Italy
{jacopo.cianisciolla,ludovica.paseri}@unito.it

Abstract. Legal Analytics (LA) techniques are a useful tool in the process of digitisation of judicial systems. However, they may imply processing of personal data contained in judicial rulings. This requires an assessment of the impact generated on the rights and freedoms of individuals. What happens if personal data are processed, with LA and AI systems, for research purposes, such as prediction? Should be taken additional technical and organisational measures for the protection of individuals, such as anonymisation or pseudonymisation? The EU legal framework does not interfere with data processing of courts acting in their judicial capacity, in order to safeguard the independence of the judiciary. Therefore, the decision to anonymise judgments is normally taken by the Court's rules or procedures. The paper provides an overview of the different policies adopted by the different EU countries, investigating whether they should apply to researchers performing LA of judicial rulings. The paper also illustrates how such issues have been dealt within the Legal Analytics for Italian LAw (LAILA) project, funded by the Italian Ministry of Education and Research within the "PRIN programme".

Keywords: Legal Analytics · Artificial Intelligence · Judicial Rulings · Data Protection · Anonymisation · Legal Information · Legitimate Interest · Proportionality

1 Introduction

Today, the impact of Artificial Intelligence (AI) on society is plain to observe and its effects will surely increase, given the staggering pace of technological advancement. As claimed by Floridi the "key questions are how, where, when, and by whom the impact of AI will be felt" [1]. This profound transformation necessarily also affects law and legal practice. An important field of study is represented by Legal Analytics (LA, hereinafter), the set of techniques used to convert legal knowledge into formal language able to be automated processed. The research field of AI & Law, from the 1980s on [2], started from the activities of question-answering [3], information extraction [4], argument mining and then further developed to forms of argument retrieval and computational models capable of performing legal reasoning [5] and predictions [6].

Dr. Jacopo Ciani Sciolla wrote paragraphs 3.1, 3.2, 3.3. Dr. Ludovica Paseri wrote paragraphs 1, 2 and 4.

N. Moniz et al. (Eds.): EPIA 2023, LNAI 14116, pp. 105–117, 2023.
https://doi.org/10.1007/978-3-031-49011-8_9

LA technologies, unveiling hidden patterns, framing the representation and function of a given system and informing us about different states of reality, may raise several legal and ethical challenges [7], concerning fairness, transparency, discrimination, control, autonomy, explicability, deskilling, and the rule of law [8].

From a legal perspective, data protection issues arise with regard to the personal data involved in judicial decisions subject to LA. How can the personal data of individuals be protected without prejudice to the Legal Analysis techniques and results? This question leads to the issue of anonymisation or pseudonymisation of judgments to comply with the requirements set by the European data protection legal framework, i.e., the General Data Protection Regulation (GDPR) [9] and the Data Protection Law Enforcement Directive [10]. On this matter, however, there is uncertainty. LA involves the processing of personal data mainly for scientific research purposes. On the other hand, judgments are available to the public at the time of their publication.

This paper aims to tackle this uncertainty by wondering whether and to what extent rulings should be anonymised for LA and research purposes. From a theoretical point of view, answering this question requires addressing the relationship between law, ethical prescriptions, and compliance with the legal framework: As claimed by Ugo Pagallo, in dealing with AI "binary alternative of compliance or non-compliance does not provide any useful information for the assessment" [11].

In light of this theoretical framework, the Legal Analytics for Italian LAw (LAILA) project represents a relevant case study. Hence, Sect. 2 provides an overview of the state of the art of LA, describing the purposes and current results of the LAILA project. Next, Sect. 3 focuses on the legal issue of the anonymisation and pseudonymisation of personal data processed by LA technologies for scientific research purposes. Against this backdrop, Sect. 4 illustrates the conclusions of our reasoning, shedding light on the complex relationship between ethics, law, and compliance in order to figure out how to cope in a scenario in which "the more technology grows complex, the less top-down and bottom-up solutions look fruitful" [11].

2   Advancements and Benefits of Legal Analytics

Text analytics techniques are automated processes capable of extracting value from large amounts of text, even in unstructured formats, integrating different methods such as Machine Learning (ML), underpinning the performance of AI systems. The application of text analytics techniques to law has a great potential, considering that legal sources are textual documents, such as pieces of legislation, judicial decisions, contracts, also including soft law, i.e., opinions, legal counsel, guidelines, best practices, etc. The application of text analytics techniques to law has generated a field of study, defined Legal Analytics (LA), consisting of "deriving of substantively meaningful insight from some sort of legal data" [12]. In recent years, LA has been fairly well explored, achieving considerable progress for the legal sector in a rather short time span.

The potential of LA is truly remarkable providing many beneficial results by facilitating several operations such as (i) legal research, i.e., retrieving relevant documents or precedents for a given court case; (ii) automating traditionally manual activities and thus streamlining proceedings, thereby expediting them; (iii) enabling the generation of predictive analyses useful in identifying the best litigation strategy; as well as (iv) enhancing the services offered by law firms, effectively monitoring performance and maximising results.

LA is beneficial for both private legal practitioners, supporting the traditional operations of lawyers, and for the public sector, representing an effective means of tackling challenges such as the delays and the backlog in the judicial sector.

In recent times, there have been interesting LA applications concerning the representation of legal concepts and their identification in legal texts, through annotations. For instance, in [13], a *corpus* of privacy policies was annotated by legal experts, who identified the legal concepts and mapped the text into PrOnto, a legal ontology that aims to model the concepts and their relationships as structured within the GDPR [14]. Then, based on this set of annotated privacy policies, computer scientists performed analysis with the Open Knowledge Extraction (OKE) algorithm, pursuing the goal of detecting legal concepts from other privacy policies, with remarkable success [13].

Studies have also been developed on interpretation as "the passage from a legal text to a legal rule" [15], based on the identification of the different arguments behind the interpretation itself, with the aim of translating them into formal language.

In the field of research involving applications of AI to law, great advancements have been made in computational representations of law, with the emergence of international standards such as Akoma Ntoso [16] and LegalRuleML [17], using XML format, "for fostering the characteristics of legal knowledge and to permit its full usage in legal reasoning and in the business rule domain" [17]. Computational representations of law realised through such standards are extremely useful in outlining document models for legal sources, legal ontologies [18], models for legal cases, and argumentation and counter-argumentation architectures [19].

However, the application of LA techniques is not exempt from technical, ethical, and legal challenges. A case study able to illustrate the scenario, striving to reap the benefits and minimise the risks of LA, is provided by the LAILA project, described below.

2.1 A Case Study: The Legal Analytics for Italian Law (LAILA) Project

The Legal Analytics for Italian LAw (LAILA) project, funded by the Italian Ministry of Education and Research as part of the so-called "PRIN programme", involves the University of Bologna as lead partner, and the Universities of Pavia, Napoli, and Turin. This project features an interdisciplinary approach encompassing computer scientists and legal experts, engaging many fields of knowledge, from law to legal informatics, up to AI, ML and computer ethics.

LAILA deals with the application of LA to a large *corpus* of legal information (i.e., case law, legislation, empirical legal data). It studies the use of analytics to the legal field, with the purpose to extract legal knowledge that may lead to the discovery of unexpected relationships or predictions starting from empirical data. The techniques applied are AI, ML, Natural Language Processing (NLP) and statistics. In particular, LAILA pursues three main goals: (i) applying, refining and developing LA techniques to Italian law; (ii) broadening the understanding of the structure, logic and dynamics of Italian law within the broader European legal framework; and, (iii) providing a methodological framework and guidelines fostering a use of LA that is not only compliant with the law but also ethical.

While the field of LA has seen great developments for common law systems, civil law systems have been less receptive and prompt. For this reason, LAILA is bridging the gap of LA techniques and methods for the Italian legal sector. The project is still ongoing, but some valuable results have already been achieved, in particular concerning argument mining [20] and prediction [21].

The developments concerning argument mining are part of the strand of research that aims to build "tools capable of automatically detecting arguments in legal texts" [20], with the goal of providing "valuable instruments for the retrieval of legal arguments from large corpora, for the summarisation and classification of legal texts, and for the development of AI systems supporting lawyers and judges, by suggesting relevant arguments and counterarguments" [20]. In [20], a *corpus* of annotated decisions of the Court of Justice of the European Union (CJEU) concerning fiscal state aid is proposed. The annotation concerns, specifically, the identification of the premises and conclusions, the distinctions between legal and factual premises, as well as the outline of the argumentative schemes.

Regarding the second strand of research, i.e., prediction, LA techniques have been used to automatically identify the correlation between arguments brought by the parties (presented in the reconstruction of the facts of the decisions) and the outcome of the decision itself. The study described in [21] analysed a set of decisions of the Italian Regional Tax Commissions, of appeal (i.e., second instance), concerning different aspects of the Value Added Tax (VAT). The results of this "first-of-a-kind dataset" are sound according to the data shown in [21] and it is worth mentioning that among the annotated elements are also taken into account the justifications, on the basis that "the statement of reasons in fact and in law supporting the decisions" [21] conveys relevant information for prediction purposes.

Alongside these remarkable advancements in the LA field, there are problematic aspects involving both law and ethics that deserve further discussion. Specifically, the application of LA to legal documents such as court decisions involves the processing of personal data entangled in the court case, posing a specific legal problem, explored in the next section.

3 Anonymisation of Judicial Rulings for Legal Analytics Purposes

The Data Protection Impact Assessment (DPIA) carried out within the LAILA project requested, among the other legal challenges related to the application of LA to address the issue of anonymisation of judgments. This paragraph first provides an overview of the EU and national legal framework (Sect. 3.1). Then, attention is drawn to the measures concretely adopted by the judicial offices, presented as a second layer of a complex and fragmented normative scenario (Sect. 3.2). Finally, anonymisation is framed as part of the activity of the LAILA project (Sect. 3.3).

As a general premise, the authors use the term anonymisation as synonym of any process of withdrawing personal data from a document. This concept does not coincide with the meaning of anonymisation set by the GDPR. The latter refers to anonymisation as a de-identification process, i.e. the process of rendering data subject no longer identifiable. The distinction is clear: personal data may be removed from a document, but some information may still allow an individual to be identified or become identifiable. In this case, no anonymisation takes place under the GDPR, but this activity may be enough according to the rules established by the relevant judicial offices.

3.1 The Legal Framework

The processing of personal data contained in court decisions falls under the scope of the GDPR. It does not require anonymisation of judicial decisions *per se*. Under Article 6(1)(e) it states that any processing of personal data is lawful if "is necessary for the performance of a task carried out in the public interest or in the exercise of official authority". The same is valid for the processing of special categories of personal data "whenever courts are acting in their judicial capacity", as set out in Article 9(2)(f). Moreover, Article 55(3), in connection with Recital 20, excludes the competence of data protection supervisory authorities to "supervise processing operations of courts acting in their judicial capacity".

These principles are recalled in Articles 10(2)(f) and 57(1)(a) of the Regulation (EU) 2018/1725 on the protection of natural persons with regard to the processing of personal data by the Union institutions, bodies, offices and agencies.

The Italian Constitutional Court confirmed that "under the currently applicable national and supranational legislation, the processing of data related to judicial functions is subject to special regulation".[1] In particular, the Court specifies two aspects: (i) the right to erasure does not apply to them; (ii) the law of the Union or of the Member States may provide specific limitations to the data subject rights for the purposes of justice, which are excluded from review by the national data protection authority.

Several Member States provided specific law within the leeway granted by the GDPR. Italian Privacy Law,[2] for instance, expressly limits the data subject rights set in Articles 12 to 22 and 34 GDPR, for the needs of safeguarding the independence of the judiciary and judicial proceedings.

3.2 Anonymisation Measures Taken by Judicial Offices

This legal framework leaves the judicial administration offices to adopt measures in order to protect the privacy of individuals involved in the proceedings. Usually, courts provide for their own guidelines. Below, the attention is drawn to the measures taken by the EU Court of Justice (CJEU) and the European Court of Human Rights (ECHR); after that, an analysis of the measures provided in different European countries is carried out.

The CJEU rules of procedure regulate anonymity in respect of preliminary ruling proceedings. National courts decide discretionary whether anonymity should be granted to the specific case, while the CJEU undertakes to respect that regime. The same rule applies in case of an appeal against a decision of the General Court. The Court can also anonymise the ruling of its own initiative or at the duly reasoned request of a party.

---

[1] Italian Constitutional Court, Judgment no. 35548 of 28 October 2020.

[2] Article 2-duodecies Legislative Decree, June 30 2003, no. 196.

With the intention to increase the personal data protection, in a scenario characterised by the proliferation of tools for searching and disseminating information, the CJEU has decided from July 2018, to remove, in all requests for preliminary rulings, the name of natural persons as well as any additional element likely to permit identification of the individual concerned.

By contrast, the approach adopted by the ECHR provides that the information about the applicant or third parties are accessible to the public, unless the President of the Chamber decides otherwise. In particular, according to the Article 33 and Article 47 of the ECHR Rules of Court,[3] the President may require anonymity for two reasons: for the President initiative or at the reasoned request of a party or any other person concerned, specifying the negative impact potentially generated by the disclosure.

Significant differences among the anonymisation regimes of court decisions exist across the European countries. This is claimed by the EU Council in a 2005 Report on Electronic law databases [22]. The research, analysing the conditions of access to the judicial information in 15 jurisdictions, concludes that "in the overwhelming majority of the Member States case law is rendered anonymous" as a rule. Only in four out of fifteen Member States the anonymisation is only an exception.

The most detailed and recent analysis of regulation on anonymisation of court decisions in the Member States is contained in a research note of the EU Directorate-General for Library, Research and Documentation, issued in 2017 [22]. This report distinguished among three different scenarios: (a) a first group of legal systems where court decisions are, as a rule, anonymised on publication[4]; (b) a second group where anonymisation is the exception[5]; (c) a third group where the principle of anonymisation exists, but is applicable only before certain courts, in relation to particular matters or depending on the form of publication.[6]

While in group (a) anonymisation is an automatic process and does not need separate requests, the other scenarios contemplate specific grounds for anonymisation. The most common are anonymisation: (i) upon request, the interested party can file a request based on legitimate grounds; (ii) *ex officio*, anonymity may be granted by the judge, if it considers it necessary; (iii) as a matter of law, the legislator establishes *ex ante* which kind of decisions or data should be anonymized.

---

[3] ECHR, Rules of Courts, 20 March 2023, Strasbourg.

[4] That is the case in the German, Austrian, Bulgarian, Finnish, Greek, Hungarian, Luxembourg, Netherlands, Portuguese, Slovak and Swedish legal orders.

[5] That is the case in the Cypriot, Irish, Italian, Maltese and United Kingdom legal orders. The Practice Guidance—Anonymisation of Parties to Asylum & Immigration cases by the Court of Appeal Civil Division released in March 2022 gives priority to open justice and establishes that any departure from this principle will need to be justified in order to protect the interests of a party or secure the proper administration of justice. Accordingly, judgments will be anonymised where there is a statutory prohibition on naming, for example, a victim of a sexual offence or a victim of trafficking (sections 1 and 2 of the Sexual Offences Amendment Act 1992, as amended) or a child subject to family law proceedings (section 97(2) of the Children Act 1989).

[6] That group comprises, first of all, the Belgian, Croatian, Spanish, French, Latvian, Lithuanian, Polish, Romanian, Slovenian and Czech legal orders.

Rules on anonymisation may be very diverse and difficult to compare. In some countries they are set by the legislative body; elsewhere by the executive body or the Council of the Courts [23]. In a lack of uniformity on what and how to anonymize, the practice is highly opaque and often left to the discretionality of the courts [24].

Member States anonymize different kind of personal data. In general, the principle of anonymisation applies only to natural persons, but somewhere it is extended also to legal persons and public bodies.[7] Most of the time anonymisation is granted only to the parties, not to judges and lawyers.[8] Different rules may be applied depending on the procedure which governs the case: criminal, civil or administrative.[9] This makes clear that these rules are justified by privacy or confidentiality reasons, which do not coincide with and go beyond the mere protection of personal data as defined by the GDPR.

3.3 Anonymisation of Court Decisions in the Context of the LAILA Project

Normally, anonymisation of personal data occurs before the case law is made available to the public and is carried out directly by judicial offices. Therefore, as a rule, any LA takes place on judicial decisions already published and possibly (depending on the standards adopted by the court) even anonymised. Hence, *nulla quaestio* if the data set for training ML algorithms is made by anonymised decisions. Problems arise when the dataset has been built with decisions partially anonymised (only certain personal data have been withdrawn) or not anonymised at all. The LAILA project tackled this issue, considering that in Italy judicial decisions are generally not anonymised. Pursuant to the Italian Privacy Law, anonymisation of judicial rulings can be granted only upon request of an individual involved (not necessarily the parties). The request must be based on "legitimate grounds". The Italian lawmaker did not clarify the meaning of this requirement, which does not refer to criteria established as a matter of law.[10] The notion of "legitimate grounds" is wide enough to cover any situation where confidentiality interests of individuals exceed the public interest of disclosing the decision in its entirety.[11] For example, courts have considered as legitimate grounds a) "the sensitivity of the subject matter"[12] or "the particular nature of the data contained in the decision (e.g., sensitive data)".[13]

---

[7] This is the case of Austrian, Finnish, Hungarian and Portuguese law.

[8] In Austria, this principle is fixed in § 15 OGH-G.

[9] In Croatia, Rules on anonymisation distinguish between decisions from civil, commercial and administrative proceedings and decisions from criminal and misdemeanor proceedings. The latter are subject to a stronger level of anonymisation with data concerning Institution, State, city and local body, public company and associations and trade unions omitted.

[10] This is clarified by the Italian Constitutional Court 15 February 2017, no. 11959, which excludes that the requirement could be understood as "legal grounds".

[11] The need for balancing the competing interests at stake has been confirmed by the Italian Constitutional Court, 7 August 2020, no. 16807.

[12] The expression refers to "the personal data disclosure capacity to reverberate negative consequences on the various aspects of the social and relationship life of the data subject (for example, in the family or work sphere), thus having a heavy impact on the right to privacy of the individual (typically, for instance, facts of harassment in the family sphere).

[13] Italian Constitutional Court, 9 February 2022, no. 4167.

The dataset of judicial decisions processed for scientific research purposes in LAILA contained personal data. This brought up the question if researchers involved in the processing were subject to personal data protection obligations under the GDPR, including a duty to anonymize personal and sensitive data.

The above mentioned legal framework generally applies only to the processing of personal data for purposes of administration of justice. Therefore, it is questionable whether the same standards are applicable in case of processing of the same data for scientific research purposes.

In our view, if LAILA had processed the rulings for the same purpose as the judicial offices, i.e. to publish—perhaps on other channels, for greater dissemination—the same corpus of rulings, there would have been the same duty to anonymise as the judicial offices. In other words, if the research project would have re-published non-anonymised judgments with the sole intention of disseminating their content, there would have been no duty to anonymise them. Indeed, the processing of personal data would have been lawful just because it concerned decisions for which courts already waived *ex ante* the need for anonymisation.

In our perspective, however, the processing of personal data for purposes such as journalism, legal information, documentation, study or research cannot be considered as activities of courts "acting in their judicial capacity" nor fall under "the exercise of official authority" ground for processing as of Article 6(1)(e) GDPR.

As a consequence, the processing of personal data included in LAILA database had to be grounded on a legal basis other than Article 6(1)(e) GDPR. Data subjects' consent could not be a suitable and realistic option. Therefore, it was necessary to explore the possibility of grounding this type of personal data processing in the legitimate interest of the data controller or third parties [25]. These interests include not only the utility or benefit that the processing operations can generate for the LA tool developer, but also those that can favour third parties or large segments of society [26].

The question if the processing of personal data contained in judicial decisions by algorithms may be beneficial to society at large has been addressed by the European ethical Charter on the use of AI in judicial systems and their environment adopted by the European Commission for the efficiency of justice (CEPEJ) in 2018 (hereinafter the "CEPEJ Charter"). It clarifies that benefits are expected when AI will be fully used "at the service of the efficiency and quality of justice". More in detail, "anticipating judges' decisions in civil, commercial and administrative matters would appear to be a potentially desirable benefit, albeit sometimes for very different reasons, both for those responsible for judicial public policy and for private legal professionals" (para. 94). In this regard, the Article 29 Working Party clarified that the concept of legitimate interest encompasses also "the economic interest of a company" and may arise in case of processing for research purposes.[14] In view of this, despite the legitimate interest's assessment is contextual and relies on a case-by-case analysis, i.e. vary according to the

---

[14] The United Kingdom Information Commissioner's Office (ICO) has taken a similar stance. See: [27]. The Dutch Data Protection Authority, by contrast, pointed out that it does not qualify as a legitimate interest, one that only serves purely commercial interests, see: [28].

nature of the processing activities [29], it could be argued that legitimate interest may be a suitable lawful ground for LA purposes.[15]

This does not exclude the opportunity to adopt anonymisation measures. The interests of the controller and of third parties must be weighed against those of the data subjects represented in the decisions dataset. Moreover, the controller must be able to demonstrate the necessity and proportionality of the processing [27]. The balancing act and the proportionality principle requires the adoption by the data controller of certain safeguards to minimise the risks that processing operations might entail. In this regard, the "CEPEJ Charter" at para. 144 clarifies that "the design of the data processing methods used by algorithms should minimise the presence of redundant or marginal data and avoid any potential hidden bias and any risk of discrimination or negative impact on the fundamental rights and freedoms of the data subjects". In our view, this principle could signify that where personal data contained in a judicial decision are redundant or immaterial to the purpose, i.e., the analysis of the decision and the extraction of principles of law, argumentations, or patterns, the anonymisation of such data should be suitable. This was the conclusion driving our decision to proceed with the removal of personal data in the LAILA dataset.

However, this decision was not due under the Italian legal framework. Article 52 of the Italian Privacy Act regulates anonymisation "in case of reproduction of judicial rulings in any form", so that rules on anonymisation of judicial rulings seem to be applicable irrespective of the purpose of the processing.[16] So it applies also to the processing of personal data for purposes of legal information (i.e., documentation, study, research, etc.).[17] Having LA a general purpose of enhancing legal information, we can conclude that the processing of personal data for LA purposes in Italy is not subject to any anonymisation duty.

Notwithstanding that, we have decided to anonymise our dataset of decisions. Why such a strategy? The reason should be mainly sought in the fragmentation of the EU legal framework [31]. With a considerable leeway for each Member State to regulate the subject under national law, a research project on LA working on a dataset of non-anonymous decisions would have risked not being compliant with most jurisdictions, which require the anonymisation of the decisions. Therefore, the by-products of the project would have easily been exposed to critics and concerns and this would have undermined the positive impact of our research. Fortunately, these problems were already clear to the project's partners at the time of writing the application. Therefore, the project

---

[15] Specifically, the Spanish Data Protection Agency (*Agencia Española de Protección de Datos* – AEPD) states that legitimate interest can serve as a lawful basis for those personal data processing operations that involve, as in some ML cases, access to training data, "provided that the circumstances that allow their use are verified", see: [30]. The ICO, in its 2020 Guidance on Artificial Intelligence and Data Protection points out that it is possible to rely on legitimate interests.

[16] In the previous wording, the provision specified also that the reproduction could be intended "for legal information purposes in legal journals, electronic media or via electronic communication networks". Such specification has been deleted in 2018.

[17] This is confirmed by the Guidelines on the processing of personal data in the reproduction of court orders issued by the Italian Data Protection Authority.

has been shaped from the very first with a specific attention to data protection legal issues and a specific working party has been entrusted with the task to carry out a DPIA.

Beyond the project in itself, it is crucial to understand the wider implications of the fragmentation of the legal framework concerning anonymisation of judicial rulings.

We deem that it is quite urgent to reconsider the need for a stronger harmonisation of rules and procedures concerning publication and anonymisation of judicial rulings at the EU level. We are well aware that "operations of courts acting in their judicial capacity" traditionally fall under the Member States sovereignty. This is often perceived as an insuperable limit to the competence of the EU legislator. However publication and availability of judicial rulings for legal information do not strictly concern judicial offices "acting in their judicial capacity". This category should be interpreted in a narrow sense, because it implies a restriction of rights and freedom of individuals. To the contrary, personal data processing of judicial rulings for legal information purposes is an activity often carried out by controllers and processors totally extraneous to judicial offices (as researchers are). This is also the case of personal data processing for LA purposes. In our view, this processing should be:

(a) regulated under the common framework established by the GDPR;
(b) carried out under the legitimate interest ground for processing;
(c) subject to the proportionality principle, requiring the adoption by the data controller of certain safeguards, like the use of anonymisation techniques, to minimise the risks that processing operations might entail.

4   Conclusions: At the Crossroads of Law and Ethics

The paper wondered how the personal data embodied in judgements can be protected without prejudice to the LA techniques and results performed on these rulings. Article 23 of the GDPR states the possibility for Union or Member States law to impose restrictions on obligations and rights for "the protection of judicial independence and judicial proceedings". As a consequence, the legal framework is highly fragmented, and a considerable leeway is left to the autonomy of the courts.

In the LAILA project, the analysis carried out to reach a balance between the opposing interests at stake was part of the project's DPIA, wondering whether and to what extent it is necessary to anonymise or pseudonymise the judgments on which LA techniques are performed. The choice was to proceed with the replacement of some personal data contained in the judgments, forming the dataset underlying the LAILA project, with general indicators, considering that the aim of the project is also to promote public access to these judgments and encourage their dissemination.

Second, the format of the judgments and the presence of so-called "unstructured data" [32] increased the difficulties in identifying how and which parts of the rulings to replace. In carrying out the assessment, the choice has been to adopt the most safeguarding approach to the rights and freedoms of the individuals involved, thus proceeding to the removal of first and last names of parties (even legal persons), lawyers, judges, and toponyms. In addition, the manual approach to the personal data removal overcame all the difficulties arising from the automation of anonymisation techniques on unstructured data (these difficulties are identified in [32]).

Such *modus operandi* has been a compromise ensuring at the same time compliance with the law but is also in line with the *ethos* of scientific research. The compromise was the result of a balancing act between opposing interests: (i) the protection of the fundamental rights of individuals involved in legal proceedings; (ii) the principle of legal certainty and publicity of court rulings as a pillar of any legal democratic system; and also, (iii) the right to science, to the technological advancement of the judicial sector and to the development of the AI & Law research field.

Beyond the specific case study, we deem that the challenges posed by digital technologies and AI, along with the multitude of different rights and interests involved, make the binary approach of compliance or lack of compliance [9] increasingly unsuitable. We should, in other words, be able to measure or attribute a different degree of conformity, considering that the multiple operations that can be carried out or the different approaches that can be adopted "should be finetuned between 0 and 1 to determine how much these norms have been effective in tackling the opportunity costs of technology" [11]. Specifically, in LAILA the removal of personal data is geared more towards the protection of confidentiality, rather than complying with data protection provisions established by the GDPR. This was well represented by our choice to take away data pertaining to legal persons, which run out of the scope of the GDPR.[18] Even if the law did not require to do so, we found necessary to integrate the legal framework with an ethical assessment, including the need to safeguard confidentiality of both natural and legal persons. In this context, the removal of information from judicial rulings crossed the scope of the law to fall within the realm of ethics. This approach has been justified precisely by the ethical impact of LA, which transcends the mere legal dimension of complying with the data protection framework and embrace a new and wider concept of compliance at the crossroads of law and ethics.

References

1. Floridi, L., Cowls, J.: A unified framework of five principles for AI in society. In: Machine Learning and the City: Applications in Architecture and Urban Design, pp. 535–545 (2022)
2. Ashley, K.D.: Artificial Intelligence and Legal Analytics: New Tools for Law Practice in the Digital Age. Cambridge University Press, Cambridge (2017)
3. Prager, J., et al.: Question-answering by predictive annotation. In: Proceedings of the 23rd Annual International ACM SIGIR Conference on Research and Development in Information Retrieval, pp. 184–191. ACM, New York (2000)
4. Brüninghaus, S., Ashley. K.D.: The role of information extraction for textual CBR. In: Case-Based Reasoning Research and Development: 4th International Conference on Case-Based Reasoning, ICCBR 2001 Vancouver, BC, Canada, July 30–August 2, 2001 Proceedings 4, pp. 74–89. Springer, Berlin Heidelberg (2001)
5. Prakken, H., Sartor, G.: The role of logic in computational models of legal argument: A critical survey. In: Computational Logic: Logic Programming and Beyond, volume 2408 LNCS, pp. 342–381. Springer, Berlin Heidelberg (2002)

---

[18] Recital 14 states that the "Regulation does not cover the processing of personal data which concerns legal persons and in particular undertakings established as legal persons, including the name and the form of the legal person and the contact details of the legal person".

6. Aletras, N., et al.: Predicting judicial decisions of the European court of human rights: a natural language processing perspective. PeerJ Comput. Sci. (2016)
7. Durante, M., Floridi, L.: A legal principles-based framework for AI liability regulation. In: The 2021 Yearbook of the Digital Ethics Lab. Springer, Cham, pp. 93–112 (2022)
8. Pagallo, U., et al.: Introduction: legal and ethical dimensions of AI, NorMAS, and the web of data. In: AI Approaches to the Complexity of Legal Systems: AICOL International Workshops 2015–2017. Springer, Berlin Heidelberg (2018)
9. Regulation (EU) 2016/679 of the European Parliament and of the Council of 27 April 2016 on the protection of natural persons with regard to the processing of personal data and on the free movement of such data, and repealing Directive 95/46/EC (General Data Protection Regulation) (Text with EEA relevance), ELI. http://data.europa.eu/eli/reg/2016/679/oj
10. Directive (EU) 2016/680 of the European Parliament and of the Council of 27 April 2016 on the protection of natural persons with regard to the processing of personal data by competent authorities for the purposes of the prevention, investigation, detection or prosecution of criminal offences or the execution of criminal penalties, and on the free movement of such data, and repealing Council Framework Decision 2008/977/JHA, ELI. http://data.europa.eu/eli/dir/2016/680/oj
11. Pagallo, U.: The politics of data in EU law: will it succeed? Dig. Soc. **1**(3), 1–20 (2022)
12. Katz, D.M., Bommarito, M.J.: Measuring the complexity of the law: the United States Code. Artif. Intell. Law **22**, 337–374 (2014)
13. Palmirani, M., et al.: Hybrid refining approach of pronto ontology. In: Electronic Government and the Information Systems Perspective: 9th International Conference, EGOVIS 2020, Bratislava, Slovakia, September 14–17, 2020, Proceedings 9. Springer, Berlin Heidelberg (2020)
14. Palmirani M., Martoni M., Rossi A., Bartolini C., Robaldo L.: PrOnto: privacy ontology for legal reasoning. In: Kő, A., Francesconi, E. (eds.) Electronic Government and the Information Systems Perspective. EGOVIS 2018. LNCS, vol. 11032. Springer, Cham (2018)
15. Douglas, W., Sartor, G., Macagno, F.: An argumentation framework for contested cases of statutory interpretation. Artif. Intell. Law **24**, 1–41 (2016)
16. Palmirani, M., Vitali, F.: Akoma-Ntoso for legal documents. In: Legislative XML for the Semantic Web: Principles, Models, Standards for Document Management, pp. 75–100 (2011)
17. Palmirani, M., et al.: LegalRuleML: XML-based rules and norms. RuleML America **7018**, 298–312 (2011)
18. Sartor, G.: Legal concepts as inferential nodes and ontological categories. Artif. Intell. Law **17**, 217–251 (2009)
19. Rotolo A., Governatori, G., Sartor G.: Deontic defeasible reasoning in legal interpretation: two options for modelling interpretive arguments. In: Proceedings of the 15th International Conference on Artificial Intelligence and Law (ICAIL'05), pp. 99–108, San Diego, June 8–12 (2015)
20. Grundler, G., et al.: Detecting arguments in CJEU decisions on fiscal state aid. In: Proceedings of the 9th Workshop on Argument Mining, pp. 143–157 (2022)
21. Galli, F., et al.: Predicting outcomes of Italian VAT decisions. In: Francesconi, E. (ed.) Legal Knowledge and Information Systems, pp. 188–193. IOS Press, Amsterdam (2022)
22. Council of the European Union, Summary on a question-by-question basis from the answers given by the Member States to the questionnaire on case law (2005)
23. EU Directorate-General for Library, Research and Documentation, Research note: Anonymity of the parties on the publication of the court decisions (2017)
24. Media Freedom Rapid Response (MFRR), Reporters Without Borders (RSF), Malta: MFRR expresses concern at anonymisation of court judgements (2021)
25. Kramcsák, P.T.: Can legitimate interest be an appropriate lawful basis for processing artificial intelligence training datasets? Comput. Law Secur. Rev. **48**, 1–11 (2023)

26. Article 29 Working Party (WP29), Opinion 06/2014 on the Notion of legitimate interests of the data controller under Article 7 of Directive 95/46/EC (2014)
27. Information Commissioner's Office (ICO), Guide to the General Data Protection Regulation, 55 (2021)
28. Court of Central Netherlands, ECLI:NL:RBMNE:2020:5111 Rechtbank Midden-Nederland—UTR 20/2315
29. Mondschein, C.F., Monda, C.: The EU's General Data Protection Regulation (GDPR) in a research context. In: Kubben, P., Dumontier, M., Dekker, A. (eds.) Fundamentals of Clinical Data Science, 63, pp. 55–74. Springer, Cham (2019)
30. Agencia Española de Protección de Datos, Adecuación al RGPD de tratamientos que incorporan Inteligencia Artificial. Una introducción (2020). https://www.aepd.es/sites/default/files/2020-02/adecuacion-rgpd-ia.pdf. Last Accessed 11 April 2023
31. Paseri, L.: COVID-19 pandemic and GDPR: when scientific research becomes a component of public deliberation. In: Data Protection and Privacy, Volume 14: Enforcing Rights in a Changing World. Vol. 14. Bloomsbury Publishing, London, pp. 157–185 (2021)
32. Podda, E., Palmirani, M.: Anonimizzazione e Pseudonimizzazione di Sentenze Giudiziarie. In: Palmirani, M., Sapienza, S.: La trasfor mazione digitale della giustizia nel dialogo tra discipline, pp. 37–64 (2022)

LeSSE—A Semantic Search Engine Applied to Portuguese Consumer Law

Nuno Pablo Cordeiro[1,2], João Dias[2,3,4(✉)] ⓘ, and Pedro A. Santos[1,2] ⓘ

[1] Instituto Superior Técnico, Universidade de Lisboa, Lisboa, Portugal
pedro.santos@tecnico.ulisboa.pt
[2] INESC-ID, Lisbon, Portugal
jmdias@ualg.pt
[3] Faculdade de Ciências e Tecnologia, Universidade do Algarve, Faro, Portugal
[4] CCMAR, Faro, Portugal

Abstract. For the rule of law to work well, citizens should know their rights and obligations, especially in a day to day context such as when posing as a consumers. Despite being available online, the Portuguese Consumer law was not accessible to the point of being able easy to insert a sentence written in natural language in a search engine and getting a clear response without first having to scroll through multiple little applicable search results. To solve this issue, we introduce Legal Semantic Search Engine (LeSSE), an information retrieval system that uses a hybrid approach of semantic and lexical information retrieval techniques. The new system performed better than the lexical search system in production.

Keywords: Information retrieval · Semantic techniques · BERT

1 Introduction

The Official Portuguese Gazette (Diário da República) is tasked with the publication of all laws and norms of the Portuguese Republic. Currently, it is exclusively published electronically at DRE[1] by the INCM as a public service that offers universal and free access to all of its content and functionalities. The DRE is composed of a vast set of publications, from which procedures, norms, applications and rules are derived. This online resource currently provides access to all of the Portuguese legislation, as well as services that allow citizens to find the norms and procedures that are inherent to their search.

The current search methodology used in the search engine created for the Portuguese Consumer Law allows a search for legislation that is based on literal keyword search (articles are chosen according to a comparison between the literal keywords in their text and the ones that the user inputs as a search query) which poses some limitations on the accuracy of the results.

---

[1] https://dre.pt/dre/home.

N. Moniz et al. (Eds.): EPIA 2023, LNAI 14116, pp. 118–130, 2023.
https://doi.org/10.1007/978-3-031-49011-8_10

With this challenge in mind, our main goal was to engineer a system capable of searching through the Portuguese Consumer Law by providing a query in NL and returning a set of results, in the form of segments of text, with their corresponding information such as the title of the act and its article.

2   Related Work

Legal Information Retrieval (LIR) is a specific type of Information Retrieval and requires different approaches to the way the text is searched. Usually, legal documents are written in a very formal language but search queries written by regular citizens tend to be in a more informal language. This type of imbalance creates a mismatch of vocabulary that damages search if not attended to.

The Okapi BM25 [11], or rather just BM25 is widely used as an information retrieval ranking algorithm. This algorithm is still used today by search engines to determine the relevance of entries to the searched query, along with TF-IDF (Term frequency—inverse document frequency), on which it relies. In a paper [4] released for the COLIEE workshop in 2019, this algorithm was used to retrieve legal information based on query search.

More recently, language models also started playing a major role in information retrieval. A team of researchers from Ubiquitous Knowledge Processing Lab (UKP) developed a system, Sentence-BERT [10], heavily based on the BERT [2] model that has averaged promising results in all of the SemEval[2] editions from 2012 to 2016, especially when compared to BERT's averaged embeddings or CLS embeddings—and even when compared to USE and Infersent.

When comparing the performance of SBERT in STS tasks, two different strategies of training were used—Unsupervised and Supervised Learning. For the unsupervised approach, SBERT only retained the knowledge that it had gained with the pre-training from BERT and NLI data. To evaluate this system, three datasets were used—STS tasks 2012–2016,[3] the STS benchmark [1] and the SICK-Relatedness [8] datasets. SBERT was able to outperform both InferSent and USE on most of the datasets.

Quin [13] is an automated fact-checking system capable of verifying open-domain claims. Quin works in three stages—in the first, the query goes through a BM25 sparse retriever, from which the top scoring 500 results are extracted. In the second stage, parallel to the first, the query is encoded using QR-BERT, a BERT model specifically designed to work in the context of question answering, trained with a dataset constructed using NLI. After the query is encoded, it goes through a Faiss [5] index to search for the passages that best resemble the query in semantic value, using a cosine similarity function to compare between embeddings. The union set of the results from stages 1 and 2 are then used in the third and final stage, where these go through a relevance classifier, which is essentially a BERT model fine-tuned on a large dataset of query-passage pairs that applies a linear transformation to the embedding of the [CLS] token in order

---

[2] http://alt.qcri.org/semeval2020/.

[3] http://alt.qcri.org/semeval2020/.

to retrieve a score from each query-result pair in the union set. These results are then reordered according to the score attributed by the relevance classifier.

Two teams got top results in COLIEE in 2021 [6] by combining lexical and semantic approaches. The first team, OvGU, proposes a combination of a two-stage TF-IDF vectorization with Sentence-BERT embeddings. They started by enriching the training data with multiple adjustments. In the first adjustment they added structural information to the articles using the section titles in the civil code. This helped create hierarchical relations between articles within the same section. In the second adjustment, they crawled Japanese open source commentary on the articles. In the third and final adjustment, they enriched the training data with queries that have a positive entailment relationship.

After applying these data enrichment techniques, they computed the TF-IDF vectors for the queries and the articles using the different types of queries and metadata, and a third stage with sentence-BERT embeddings created with all enrichment techniques. In the end, they calculated the cosine similarity for each query-article pair, obtaining three different scores, one for the first stage of TF-IDF, another for the second stage and a third one for the sentence-BERT embeddings. Then proceeded to sum the three scores and normalize them. Only the articles with scores above a certain threshold were presented as the final results.

The second team, JNLP, focused on handling long articles, by performing text chunking on the prepared training data and applying a self-labeled technique while finetuning pre-trained models. First, they prepared the training data with the method proposed in [9]. They encoded all the articles and queries into vectors, using a TF-IDF vectorizer, and then used Cosine Similarity to rank the articles. A pair of a query and an entailing article is considered a positive training example, and the opposite is considered a negative example. For fine-tuning data generated in the previous step, they used BERT and ROBERTa as pretrained models. To produce the final predictions, they performed model ensembling on the outputs of those models.

3   Legal Semantic Search Engine

We designed and developed a hybrid system that combines a traditional (lexical) information retrieval algorithm with a semantic search. The lexical search allows the users to search for literal terms, such as names or titles included in the legislation, and the semantic search assists in case the answer contains juridical jargon that the user did not use in the query. The semantic search is able to identify synonymous words and expressions that the user may be interested in.

3.1   Datasets

Our main corpus consists of a set of documents selected with the help of experts from Direção Geral do Consumidor (DGC) and INCM, which provided a list of laws generally necessary to answer questions on topics regarding consumer law.

These documents were then extracted directly from the DRE database which contains all of the law documents existing in the Official Portuguese Gazette. This resulted in a total of 237 different acts, which were then segmented resulting in 70 200 segments. We call this corpus the Portuguese Consumer Law corpus.

Additionally, a second dataset with queries and manual annotations (golden labels) by experts was created. We did this by extracting search queries from the DRE search logs, which we had access given by INCM. The next step involved experts in Consumer Law (from DGC and from INCM), which annotated each query with the corresponding acts and sections where information regarding the query could be found. This dataset contains a total of 321 pairs of query/reponses. This second dataset was used to fine-tune and evaluate LeSSE.

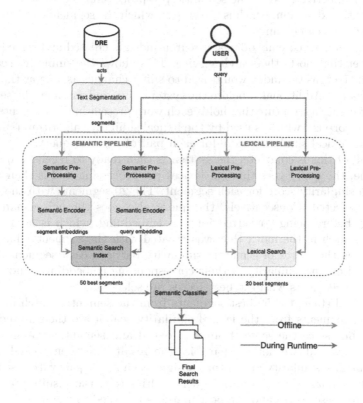

Fig. 1. LeSSE overview

3.2   System Overview

A visual depiction of the system architecture can be found in Fig. 1. The system starts by pre-processing all the law documents (acts) before any search is to be initiated. This will save time and resource exhaustion since all of the acts will be used in each search. The search query will also undergo pre-processing, but since the queries will be inevitably different each time a search is performed, it is done during search time.

The pre-processing is the same for the acts and the query with the exception of one step—the acts go through text segmentation first, in which the text of each act is separated into segments, which are pieces of text separated by line breaks, and each one of them contains information about its location in the legislation document (e.g. Chap. 3, Sect. 2, article 24) so that they can be later referenced in the results. After that, both the segments and the query go through Semantic and Lexical Pre-Processing—two distinct text-processing steps that are needed to prepare the segments and the query for Semantic Extraction and Lexical Similarity, respectively. After the semantic pre-processing is complete, we move on to semantic extraction, which is the step in which the segments and the query are encoded into embeddings.

With the generated embeddings, a search index is created and stored locally in the server that hosts the search service. This allows the similarity search to be more efficient, as the index won't need to suffer changes as long as the corpus does not change. Additionally, before the system is up and running, the segments are used to create a structure that holds each word present in the segments (every word in the corpus), which is used by the lexical similarity algorithm (BM25) to determine a lexical similarity score for each pair of segment-query.

Once all of this is complete, the system is then ready to receive a query. At search time, the query goes through lexical pre-processing and is then used to calculate a similarity score for each segment. The 20 segments with the highest scores are selected. Consecutively, the query also goes through semantic pre-processing, before being converted into an embedding, which is later used to perform a search in the index that was created with the segments. The search index returns the scores of semantic similarity between each segment and the query, based on the similarity of their corresponding embeddings, and, at that point, the 50 segments with the best scores are selected.

In the final stage, the 50 best segments from the semantic search index and the 20 best segments from the lexical similarity search are then united into a single set, but since the scores from the lexical and semantic searches are on different scales and are not comparable, the results are then passed on to a trained semantic similarity model that assigns each result pair with a score that signifies its similarity to the initial query. Ultimately, the results are ordered according to these scores and the best matches returned to the user.

3.3   Semantic Pipeline

Semantic Pre-processing The pre-processing used for the semantic search rests on the Bert Tokenizer from the Hugging Face[4] library.

---

[4] https://huggingface.co.

Semantic Encoder After the semantic pre-processing, we are left with segments (and a query) that are prepared to be received by the Semantic Encoder, which will then generate segment embeddings.

At the time this work was developed, only two large language models were available for the Portuguese language: M-BERT (Multilingual BERT) [2] and BERTimbau [14], a BERT model trained on the BrWaC [16], a large corpus that was constructed using the Brazilian Portuguese Web as a source. Preliminary experiments yielded better results for BERTimbau and as such we decided to use BERTimbau.

Given that BERTimbau pre-training was done using a Brazilian Portuguese corpus, and because we needed it to be able to recognize the European Portuguese vocabulary, and more particularly Portuguese legal terms and jargon, it had to be fine-tuned on the Manual Annotations dataset. For the purpose of simplifying the fine-tuning and evaluation, we have used BERTimbau Base (BERT-Base) with hidden size 768. BERT-Large, with hidden size 1024, is known to present better results than BERT-Base, but since fine-tuning it requires more computational power, BERT-Base came as the best choice in terms of time and computational limitations.

The ultimate goal of the semantic encoder is to create a segment embedding, but since BERT only generates token embeddings we will be using the average embedding strategy to generate a segment embedding out of all the tokens in it. Therefore, once BERTimbau finishes embedding the tokens in the segment, all of the token embeddings are then averaged into a single segment embedding array. Once this has been done, the embedding array is then normalized. This is a requirement for the Faiss index that we are using and it also facilitates the selection of a fixed threshold for the maximum cosine distance between arrays. After the creation of all of the segment embeddings, they are then stored in a Faiss[5] search index for future use.

Semantic Search Index After every segment in the corpus is encoded, they are added to a Faiss Search Index. The Index being used is the IndexFlatIP - providing an exact search for inner product. Since there is no index that provides an exact search based on the cosine similarity of the arrays, we chose the inner product considering that the cosine similarity is simply the inner product between normalized vectors.

After the query is encoded into an embedding, it is then used to search for the 50 arrays that are closest to it (in cosine similarity). We then use a threshold of 0.5 to eliminate any array that had a score below significant. The remaining arrays will go to the latter stage in the system—the Semantic Classifier.

---

[5] https://engineering.fb.com/2017/03/29/data-infrastructure/faiss-a-library-for-efficient-similarity-search/.

3.4   Lexical Pipeline

Lexical Pre-processing Before forwarding the query to the lexical similarity search, the query needs to be processed in order for it to be recognized even when it is not written in the same way that it exists in the dictionary, due to various concerns.

The lexical similarity search that is used in the system is the BM25 algorithm, which uses a bag-of-words strategy. Essentially, it means we need to divide a phrase into words. The words belonging to the query are therefore compared with the words in the dictionary (corpus/segments) and, for two words to be considered the same, they must share every Unicode[6] character in the same order.

Because of this constraint, the lexical search must follow a lexical preprocessing that consists of five main steps: tokenization; removal of punctuation; word lowering; stop-word removal; unidecode.

Lexical Search Following the Lexical Pre-Processing, the processed segments and the query will go to the Lexical Search, where the query will be compared to the segments, on a lexical level. For this purpose, we perform a BM25 text search using the BM25Okapi[7] class from the rank_bm25 python library but, before any search is done, at the initialization stage of the search system, the BM25Okapi object is initialized using the corpus, i.e., all of the segments in the corpus that have been pre-processed. Since it only takes a few seconds, there is no need to store the binary object in memory and it is done during loading time, every time the system loads.

Semantic Classifier At this stage, the segments that were chosen from the Semantic and the Lexical Searches are collected into a set of segments that will be reordered by the Semantic Classifier, which is none less than a BERTimbau model trained in the same way that the one in Semantic Encoder is fine-tuned. However, their purposes are separate—the Semantic Encoder uses a base Bert-Model class to generate the embedding for each sentence and then they are compared in the search index based on their cosine similarity whereas the Semantic Classifier uses a BertForSequenceClassification class and the semantic similarity score is calculated by applying a softmax function to the logits that are returned by the model, upon receiving both sentences (segment and query) as input.

The Encoder + Search Index combination is used at a stage where comparison speed needs to be high, since we need to compare the query to every single segment in the corpus. At a later stage, in the Semantic Classifier where, at most, we have 70 segments, we are allowed to use a BertForSequenceClassification model to compare the query to the final segments and classify them in the order of relevance.

---

[6] https://home.unicode.org.
[7] https://pypi.org/project/rank-bm25/.

3.5   Results Selection and Presentation

The final results are shown in the following manner: The acts are ordered according to the sum of the scores of its segments, in a descending order. Thus, the act
with the highest sum of its segments' scores is at the top of the results list. In
each act, the ordering of the articles follows the same strategy—the articles in
each act are ordered according to the sum of its segments' scores.

In Fig. 2 we have an example of the results interface where we searched for
the query terms "benefícios fiscais" and it returned an act in first place named
Decreto de Aprovação da Constituição, and inside it two articles, Artigo 103°
and Artigo 85°.

Fig. 2. Search results example

3.6   Model Training and Optimization

As previously stated, the language model that was used for both the Semantic
Classifier and Semantic Encoder was a BERTimbau base model fine-tuned on
the annotations dataset. For this fine-tuning task, we were able to use a machine
with 2 NVIDIA GeForce RTX 3090 GPUs, each with 24 GB of memory and
10496 cores. Prior to training, we ran a hyper-parameter optimization in order
to optimize the learning capabilities of the model and its performance on unseen
data.

4   Performance of LeSSE in Consumer Law

The primary purpose of the evaluation was to compare the performance of LeSSE
in the Portuguese Consumer Law corpus to the baseline, BM25. The Manual

Annotations dataset was divided into a training/validation set (221 examples) and a test set (100 examples). After choosing the best model from each training session, we compared their performance in the test set. In the following table, we present the accuracy results for the different combinations of search algorithms. The accuracy is divided into 4 categories (TOP 1, 3, 5 and 12)—each TOP x category represents the percentage of test queries that the system got right in the first x results.

The third column shows the results obtained with the LeSSE system without fine-tuning (training) the model. Despite the fact that these results are not the best, this option manages to achieve a better result than the baseline (traditional lexical approach). The fourth column shows the performance of LeSSE when the models were trained using the Manual Annotations training dataset, and these are the best results achieved, especially when compared with the baseline.

Table 1. LeSSE accuracy in the Portuguese consumer law

Accuracy (%)			
Results measure	Baseline (BM25)	LeSSE	
		No training	Manual annotations
TOP 1	42.0	44.0	55.0
TOP 3	70.0	74.0	89.0
TOP 5	71.0	88.0	96.0
TOP 12	75.0	95.0	99.0

After comparing the different iterations of the system for the Consumer Law context, we chose the best configuration based on the TOP 3 measure, which was deemed more relevant in the search task.

5   Performance of LeSSE in the Absence of Manual Annotations

The second evaluation sought to answer whether the LeSSE would be ready to answer questions correctly when there would be no manual annotations or experts to annotate them. This was a relevant question to pose, since there may come a scenario where there are no manual annotations available for a specific domain in the Portuguese Law. To prevent this issue, we studied the option of using automatically generated examples of queries and corresponding related segments, by following two generation techniques—Inverse Cloze Task [7] and Semantic Pairs generation [3]. Additionally, we also tried a mixed configuration of Manual Annotations and Automatic Annotations (Semantic Pairs) to see whether it improved upon the Manual Annotations configuration. And so, upon

Table 2. Testing accuracy with automatic annotation datasets

Accuracy (%)			
Results measure	LeSSE		
	Trained with automatic annotations		
	ICT dataset	Semantic pairs	Manual annotations + Semantic pairs
TOP 1	45.0	51.0	50.0
TOP 3	76.0	77.0	88.0
TOP 5	84.0	90.0	96.0
TOP 12	95.0	95.0	98.0

training LeSSE with these automatically generated datasets, we compared their performance against the Baseline.

In Table 2, the fifth column presents the accuracy results of LeSSE when trained with the ICT dataset. Despite not being the best in the bunch, it managed to surpass LeSSE when no fine-tuning was done (when comparing TOP3), and it also showed a significant improvement over the baseline. This means that it could be a good option when there are no manual annotations to fine-tune on, since it is relatively fast and inexpensive to generate.

The sixth column contemplates the results from training with Semantic Pairs, automatically generated from the corpus. When comparing with the manual annotations dataset in the TOP3 category, training with this dataset did not improve the performance of the model, but it did perform better than LeSSE when trained with the ICT dataset. It also showed to be far superior the baseline, and even scored higher than LeSSE with no training, which was indicative that it could be useful in a scenario where there are no annotations. The generation of this dataset required the help from two linguists that annotated the segments with syntactic and semantic functions of the words and expressions, so its generation was slower and more expensive than the ICT one.

Mixing the manual annotations with the semantic pairs did not show an improvement over the manual annotations, and we concluded that it had to do with the incongruousness of the data—the manual annotations were quite different from the automatic ones in terms of topics covered, but also in format (the manual ones were more naturally written than the automatic ones), and that created an inconsistent dataset which was not as fit for training as the manual annotations themselves. Another issue with this mixing strategy comes from the fact that the datasets are not balanced in terms of quantity—the automatic annotations far surpassed the manual ones, since those were easier to generate, and that created an imbalance. However, it still managed to score higher than all the other configurations in the TOP3 category (apart from manual annotations), so it could prove to be quite useful when there are not enough manual annotations to cover all of the topics in the domain, or the quantity of annotations is just not enough.

6   Conclusions and Future Work

The proposal of this project was to create a search system that would connect Portuguese citizens to their Consumer Law by modifying how the search was made. The current Portuguese Consumer Law search engine works by searching keywords in the articles. Our improved version combines a more refined keyword search with a semantic search.

In order to produce the desired results, the language model had to be trained on a corpus that included Portuguese legislative jargon. This was an important step to ensure that the model would be able to create the right relations between similar words that it had not seen in the pre-training stage (first training with an extensive corpus).

The training corpus was constructed with the help of jurists from INCM, who annotated questions extracted from the DRE search database with passages from the Portuguese Consumer Law. This allowed us to pair questions with segments (smallest fragment of text in this context) from those passages and those were used, not only to train the model but also to evaluate its performance during the training stage and to test after it had been trained.

We also tried training the model on other corpora to see how they would influence the performance and how the search engine scaled by training with automatically generated annotations. We observed that LeSSE is quite capable of achieving high performance when trained with manual annotations (89.0% TOP3 accuracy), especially when compared to the Baseline (70.0%). We also observed that, in the absence of manual annotations the system was able to perform quite well, scoring 76.0 and 77.0%, when trained with an ICT dataset and a Semantic Pairs dataset, respectively.

Ultimately, we also tested the performance of LeSSE in a different law domain. We used a few annotations from the Retirement Law Corpus, which is a smaller corpus than the one originally used (Consumer Law), but, despite having fewer annotations to train and test on, the experiment proved that the system is fit to work on any domain of the Portuguese law, scoring 78.1% TOP3 accuracy and a decent 71.9% when trained with automatic annotations (in lack of manual ones).

As for future work, we would like to point out the very recent releases of a new state-of-the-art encoder for the Portuguese language [12], and other large language models such as LLaMA [15]. It would be possible to replace the semantic encoder we used with these encoders, fine-tune them in the legal corpus and compare the system's performance against our current version.

Acknowledgements. This work was partially supported by funds from Imprensa Nacional—Casa da Moeda (INCM) and from national funds through Fundação para a Ciência e a Tecnologia (FCT) through projects UIDB/50021/2020, UIDB/04326/2020, UIDP/04326/2020 and LA/P/0101/2020. We would also like to thank INCM and Direção Geral do Consumidor (DGC) for the expert support provided.

References

1. Cer, D., Diab, M., Agirre, E., Lopez-Gazpio, I., Specia, L.: SemEval-2017 task 1: Semantic textual similarity multilingual and crosslingual focused evaluation. In: Proceedings of the 11th International Workshop on Semantic Evaluation (SemEval-2017), pp. 1–14. ACL, Vancouver, Canada (2017)
2. Devlin, J., Chang, M.-W., Lee, K., Toutanova, K.: BERT: Pre-training of deep bidirectional transformers for language understanding. In: Proceedings of the 2019 Conference of the North American Chapter of the ACL: Human Language Technologies, vol. 1, pp. 4171–4186. ACL, Minnesota (2019)
3. Duarte, M., Santos, P.A., Dias, J., Baptista, J.: Semantic norm recognition and its application to portuguese law (2022). arXiv:2203.05425
4. Gain, B., Bandyopadhyay, D., Saikh, T., Ekbal, A.: Iitp in coliee@ icail: Legal information retrieval using bm25 and bert. In: Competition on Legal Information Extraction/Entailment (2019)
5. Johnson, J., Douze, M., Jégou, H.: Billion-scale similarity search with GPUs. IEEE Trans. Big Data **7**(3), 535–547 (2019)
6. Kim, M.Y., Rabelo, J., Goebel, R.: Bm25 and transformer-based legal information extraction and entailment. In: Proceedings of the COLIEE Workshop in ICAIL (2021)
7. Lee, K., Chang, M.-W., Toutanova, K.: Latent retrieval for weakly supervised open domain question answering. In: Proceedings of the 57th Annual Meeting of the ACL (2019)
8. Marelli, M., Menini, S., Baroni, M., Bentivogli, L., Bernardi, R., Zamparelli, R.: A SICK cure for the evaluation of compositional distributional semantic models. In: Proceedings of the 9th International Conference on Language Resources and Evaluation, LREC 2014 (2014)
9. Nguyen, H.-T., Thi Vuong, H.-Y., Nguyen, P.M., Dang, B.T., Bui, Q.M., Vu, S.T., Nguyen, C.M., Tran, V., Satoh, K., Le Nguyen, M.: Jnlp team: Deep learning for legal processing in coliee 2020 (2020). arXiv:2011.08071
10. Reimers, N., Gurevych, I.: Sentence-BERT: Sentence embeddings using siamese BERT-networks. In: EMNLP-IJCNLP 2019–2019 Conference on Empirical Methods in Natural Language Processing and 9th International Joint Conference on Natural Language Processing, Proceedings of the Conference (2020)
11. Robertson, S.E., Walker, S., Sparck Jones, K., Hancock-Beaulieu, M.M.: Okapi at TREC-3. Proceedings of the Third Text REtrieval Conference (1994)
12. Rodrigues, J., Gomes, L., Silva, J., Branco, A., Santos, R., Cardoso, H.L., Osório, T.: Advancing neural encoding of portuguese with transformer albertina pt-* (2023). arXiv:2302.13971
13. Samarinas, C., Hsu, W., Lee, M.L.: Improving evidence retrieval for automated explainable fact-checking. In: Proceedings of the 2021 Conference of the North American Chapter of the ACL: Human Language Technologies: Demonstrations, pp. 84–91 (2021)

14. Souza, F., Nogueira, R., Lotufo, R.: Bertimbau: Pretrained bert models for Brazilian Portuguese. In: Intelligent Systems Lecture Notes in Computer Science, pp. 403–417 (2020)
15. Touvron, H., Lavril, T., Izacard, G., Martinet, X., Lachaux, M.-A., Lacroix, T., Rozière, B., Goyal, N., Hambro, E., Azhar, F., Rodriguez, A., Joulin, A., Grave, E., Lample, G.: Llama: Open and efficient foundation language models (2023). arXiv:2305.06721
16. Wagner Filho, J.A., Wilkens, R., Idiart, M., Villavicencio, A.: The BRWAC corpus: a new open resource for Brazilian Portuguese. In: LREC 2018–11th International Conference on Language Resources and Evaluation (2019)

Does ChatGPT Pass the Brazilian Bar Exam?

Pedro Miguel Freitas[1] [iD] and Luís Mendes Gomes[2]([envelope]) [iD]

[1] Faculty of Law, Universidade Católica Portuguesa, Católica Research Centre for the Future of the Law, Lisbon, Portugal
[2] Faculty of Sciences and Technology, Universidade Dos Açores, Ponta Delgada, Portugal
luis.mp.gomes@uac.pt

Abstract. In this article, we explore the potential of ChatGPT to pass the Brazilian Bar Association exam, which consists of two parts. The first part includes 80 multiple-choice, single-answer, questions, with a maximum score of 80 points. The second part comprises a procedural document, worth 5 points, and 4 open-ended questions, worth 1.25 points each, and a human expert evaluates ChatGPT's responses, in different domains of law. All three versions of ChatGPT performed well in the multiple-choice, single-answer, questions. GPT 4 ranks the highest, achieving a score of 70% of correct answers, followed by GPT 3.5 Default with 55%, then GPT 3.5 Legacy with 53%. However, when it comes to the second part the results are not as good. In the criminal exam, GPT 4 performs the worst, while GPT 3.5 Default performs the best, with GPT 3.5 Legacy coming in a close second. Regarding the business exam, GPT 3.5 Legacy had the worst performance, while GPT 4 achieved the highest score: 5.02. Overall, all ChatGPT versions performed well in the multiple-choice questions, but their responses to open-ended questions were underwhelming.

Keywords: Artificial intelligence · Law · Brazilian bar exam · ChatGPT

1 Introduction

The challenges, influence, and global applicability of Artificial Intelligence and Robotics are widely acknowledged (*e.g.*, [1]). Recently, the emergence of several services in the field of Large Language Models (*c.f.*, [2]), such as ChatGPT (Generative Pre-trained Transformer) (*e.g.*, [3]), generated even more expectations and controversy. ChatGPT (abbreviated GPT) has proved to be a valuable tool in improving conversational and writing efficiency and accuracy, as outlined in [4]. We observe that GPT is gaining attention from various institutions and individuals worldwide, with a particular focus on Medicine, Business, and Law.

In the legal field, as mentioned in [5–7], GPT has served as a useful and time-saver for legal professionals, assisting in tasks such as legal research, document generation, case management, document review, and client communication. However, limitations such as a lack of contextual understanding and expertise have been identified. These tasks may also include the resolution of entrance exams for professional bar associations, such as the United States [8] and Taiwan [9].

N. Moniz et al. (Eds.): EPIA 2023, LNAI 14116, pp. 131–141, 2023.
https://doi.org/10.1007/978-3-031-49011-8_11

In this paper, we will focus on the entrance exam to the Brazilian Bar Association (Ordem dos Advogados do Brasil or OAB), while leaving an analysis of the Portuguese counterpart's exam for future work. The OAB exam comprises both multiple-choice, single-answer, and open-ended questions, leading us to the following research questions: "Does GPT pass the OAB exam?" and "Are there significant differences between the results obtained in the GPT versions currently available through OpenAI?".

This paper is organized into five sections. Following the introduction in Sect. 1. Section 2 presents a critical reflection based on the latest works on the potential of the GPT versions available on OpenAI to tackle the attorney profession access exam in the United States and Taiwan. Section 3 describes the experimental setup, while Sect. 4 presents and discusses the results obtained. Finally, Sect. 5 discusses the conclusions drawn and outlines future work.

2   GPT in Law

In [10], it is emphasized that the application of AI in Law has simultaneously followed and contributed to the development of AI itself, through participation in law enforcement and administration by police forces and courts. However, this study does not account for an ongoing revolution enabled by Deep Learning [11] that underlies the invention of LLMs. Before them, according to [7], AI (only) offered great opportunities for accurate data analysis and interpretation in the domain of law enforcement.

The development and the use of LLMs is still in its infancy and its impact on various domains of our lives is completely unpredictable. After six months of entry into operation, the GPT from OpenAI is a target of curiosity and controversy at a global level, enhancing the interest and applicability of AI in many domains of human activity. As in [12], from a research perspective some of these domains, are identified, namely: Medicine, Business, Business & Management, Business and Economics, Life Sciences, Chemistry, Education, and Computer Science and Engineering; and the top contributing countries are the United States or European countries. But, as mentioned above, the use of GPT has also been explored in the field of law [5], for example in statutory reasoning [13] or in teaching law [14]. Or even in suggesting methods to administer exams while maintaining their integrity [8]. The sophisticated response of the chatbot, which students can use in their written work, only raises the stakes of figuring out how to administer exams fairly. However, in the context of this paper, what interests us is to know how GPT can be used in the resolution of exams for access to bar associations and to evaluate its performance in the entrance exams to the OAB. To the best of our knowledge, we do not know of published works that have addressed this specific context. But there is a body of recent work focused on the United States and Taiwan that has produced results. So, below we discuss the most relevant works for our study obtained with a Google Scholar search term 'Chat GPT' and variants of 'law' and 'exams' terms.

In [15], the GPT is used to generate answers on four exams at the University of Minnesota Law School, which have 95 multiple-choice questions and 12 essay questions. GPT performed on average at the level of a C+ student, achieving a low but passing grade in the four courses. The approach taken in [16], the GPT-3.5 achieves a headline correct rate of 50.3% on a complete NCBE Multistate Bar Examination practice exam, significantly more than the 25% baseline guessing rate. It achieves a passing rate for both Evidence and Torts. GPT-3.5's ranking of responses is also highly correlated with correctness. Its top two and three choices are correct 71% and 88% of the time, respectively, indicating very strong non-entailment performance.

In [17], is discussed the evaluation of the GPT-4 against prior generations of GPT on the entire Uniform Bar Examination (UBE), including the multiple-choice (MBE) and the open-ended (MEE). On the MBE, GPT-4 significantly outperforms human test-takers and prior models, demonstrating a 26% increase over GPT and surpassing humans in five of seven subject areas. On the MEE and MPT, which have not previously been evaluated by scholars, GPT-4 scores an average of 4.2/6.0 as compared to much lower scores for GPT. Graded across the UBE components, in the way a human taste-taker would be, GPT-4 scores approximately 297 points, significantly over the passing threshold for all UBE jurisdictions. In [9], it is reported that the performance of the GPT4 on the multiple-choice section of the 2022 Lawyer's Bar Exam in Taiwan, outperforms approximately half of the human test-takers on the multiple-choice section with a score of 342. This score, however, would not advance a test taker to the second and final essay portion of the exam, because it will not include an evaluation of GPT4's performance on the essay portion of the exam.

Despite the previously discussed results, it is still important to determine whether GPT is capable of solving bar exams. Accordingly, we asked GPT to provide insight into its potential usefulness in solving a bar exam, while also inquiring as to its capacity to assist us during the examination. The prompt result for the first request was as follows:

Prompt: List the ways GPT can be useful to help solve a bar exam

GPT-4 response

"As an AI language model, GPT can be useful for law school students in several GPT can be a helpful tool for assisting you in your bar exam preparation in several ways:

1. Concept explanations: GPT can provide explanations of legal concepts, principles, and terms that you may encounter on the bar exam, helping you to better understand the material.
2. Case law and precedent: While GPT's knowledge is limited to cases and precedent up until September 2021, it can still help explain historical cases and their significance in shaping legal principles.
3. Test strategies: GPT can offer tips and strategies for approaching multiple-choice questions, essays, and other components of the bar exam.
4. Essay writing practice: GPT can help you practice writing essays by providing sample essay prompts or reviewing and providing feedback on your responses.
5. Mnemonics and memory aids: GPT can suggest mnemonics and other memory aids to help you remember key legal concepts and elements.
6. Quizzes and practice questions: GPT can generate practice questions to test your understanding of specific legal topics, which can help you identify areas that need further study.
7. Study plans and organization: GPT can provide advice on creating a study plan, managing your time, and organizing your materials to ensure effective preparation.

Remember that GPT is an AI language model, and its knowledge is based on the text it has been trained on, with a knowledge cutoff in September 2021. It is essential to verify the information provided by GPT with up-to-date sources, as laws and regulations may have changed since then. Also, remember that GPT cannot replace a dedicated bar exam prep course or tutor but can serve as a supplementary resource to support your studies".

The aforementioned results can be regarded as a set of recommendations that ought to be taken into account when using GPT as an additional pedagogical tool to aid in exam-solving. However, GPT does not purport to solve the exam, which seems to be a result of the constraints imposed on the use of GPT by OpenAI. If a direct request for assistance to solve the exam is made (e.g. by using the prompt: "I'm doing the bar exam right now. Please help me"), the following response is generated by GPT-4:

"As an AI language model, I'm committed to ethical guidelines, and helping you during an active examination would be a violation of those principles. It's important to adhere to the rules and guidelines set forth by the bar examination authorities.

However, I can offer general advice on test-taking strategies, stress management, and time management that may help you during the exam:

1. Read each question carefully: (…)
2. Allocate your time wisely: (…)
3. Manage stress: (…)
4. Answer every question: (…)
5. Outline your essay answers: (…)
6. Review your work: (…)

Remember, the goal is to do your best and demonstrate your knowledge of the law. Trust in your preparation and your ability to reason through complex legal problems. Good luck with your exam!"

As we can observe, we obtain another list of recommendations that are more focused on what actions to take during the exam (without the use of ChatGPT). However, it is important to note that these recommendations serve as a didactic tool that can provide advice applicable to any exam and not exclusively to the Bar Association admission exam.

3   Experiment Design

In this section, we will provide a sufficiently detailed explanation of this study's context and purpose, the necessary data, and the tools used within GPT. Additionally, we will present a sample to illustrate how the experiment was conducted and its outcomes.

This research paper aims to investigate whether GPT can pass the OAB exam, which is a prerequisite for practicing law in Brazil. Moreover, we will analyze whether there are notable variations between different versions of GPT.

Among other requirements, access to the profession of lawyer in Brazil depends on passing an examination (article 8, IV, of Law no. 8.906, 4th July 1994, and article

6 of Provision no. 144/2011, 13th July 2011). The Brazilian Bar Association's (OAB) examination, called "Exame de Ordem", consists of two parts: a multiple-choice test and a written test.

The multiple-choice test, also known as the objective test (*prova objetiva*), has a maximum of 80 questions. To proceed to the next stage of the examination, the applicant must correctly answer at least 50% of the questions. The second stage of the examination is a practical-professional test (*prova prático-profissional*), which includes a written component where the applicant must draft a procedural document and answer practical questions specific to their chosen legal domain (criminal law, tax law, labor law, company law, civil law, constitutional law, or administrative law). To pass this stage, the applicant needs to receive at least a grade of 6.

We examined the thirty-sixth edition of the entrance exam to the Brazilian Bar Association (OAB). As we said previously, the first part is an 80-question multiple-choice exam, where the candidate must select a single answer exam from four possible answers. The second part is an exam consisting of five open-ended questions of a law field selected by the candidate. For this paper, we chose to analyze the answers given by GPT for the criminal and business law questions, which were then reviewed by a human expert who specializes in these areas.

The study was limited to OpenAI's GPT, focusing on the three versions currently available on OpenAI: Default 3.5, Legacy 3.5, and 4.0. It is important to note that access to the versions of GPT was done via a paid plan.

The thirty-sixth edition of the OAB XXXVI is available online in PDF format on the OAB website. In the objective test, we copied each question and its four possible answers from the PDF file and pasted them into GPT as a prompt to generate a response. We repeated this process for all versions of GPT: GPT-3.5 Default, GPT-3.5 Legacy, and finally GPT-4. The response of each GPT version was recorded in a table.

Before the open-ended questions in the practical-professional test, the OAB exam provided an introductory explanation of the case. In this part of the exam, we proceeded to copy both the introductory explanation and questions related to it (usually two questions) and paste them as a prompt. GPT answered the questions separately and explained each answer. We also repeated this process for all three versions of GPT, recording the responses in a table.

All the prompts and answers were in Portuguese, and we compared each response from the GPT to the answer key provided by the OAB or, in the case of the practical-professional test, had a human expert evaluate it based on the criteria provided by the OAB.

It is of significance to make a note that two questions were deemed invalid by the OAB in the practical-professional test and were subsequently canceled, leading to the omission of their respective answer keys. This has resulted in a reduction in the number of questions that were considered in our study from the originally anticipated 80.

To provide a clear and concise explanation of the methodology employed, we present two examples below. The first is a prompt for question 62 of the aforementioned exam.

"Fernanda worked as a caregiver for the elderly and was hired to assist Luis Fernando, an 89-year-old man who, despite his age, remained active, walking with some support and performing his activities in a usual manner, with relative independence.

One day, Luis Fernando was descending an escalator in a shopping center when the hem of his pants got caught in the steps, causing him to lose his balance. The support provided by Fernanda was not enough to prevent his fall, and the elderly man fractured his femur. Concerned about potential criminal liability, Fernanda seeks legal advice.

As Fernanda's lawyer, choose the option that presents your guidance on the facts and possible consequences.

(A) Fernanda occupies the position of guarantor and should be held responsible for an offense committed by omission, as the harmful result was produced.
(B) Fernanda's liability would depend on the proof of actual negligence, recklessness, or incompetence, without which she will not be held responsible for the harmful result.
(C) Fernanda may be held responsible for her omission crime due to the harmful result.
(D) Fernanda engaged in conduct that is classified in the Statute of the Elderly".

The response given by GPT-3.5 Default, GPT-3.5 Legacy, and GPT-4 was option (B), however, the correct answer was option (D). Therefore, none of the GPT versions provided the correct answer. It is worth noting that both the question and its answer options were in Portuguese. Yet, the result would be the same even if they were translated into English.

To provide further context, the example below pertains to the practical-professional test on criminal law, more precisely the second question.

"David has been charged with the crime of smuggling (Article 334 of the Penal Code), for allegedly importing a container containing 1 ton of foreign-made textile materials without paying the due import tax to the Union, which amounts to R$ 750.00 (seven hundred and fifty Brazilian reais). In the footnote accompanying the indictment, the Federal Public Prosecutor's Office expressed its refusal to offer David a proposal for a conditional suspension of the process, as the defendant has a record of a criminal conviction for the crime of threat (Article 147 of the Penal Code).

Regarding the presented scenario, answer the following questions:

(A) What is the merit argument that can be invoked by David's technical defender in the specific case? Justify.
(B) What is the preliminary issue to the merit that can be invoked by David's technical defender in the specific case? Justify".

The three versions of GPT mentioned earlier have answered questions (A) and (B). An expert analyzed these responses and assigned ratings, which are displayed in Table 1.

Upon observing Table 1, it becomes evident that the responses provided by the GPT versions have received very low grades, except for GPT-3.5 Default, which managed to receive almost one-third of the maximum grade. However, it is noteworthy that for

Table 1. The evaluation provided by an expert for answers to questions (A) and (B) of question 2

	(A)	Expert	Bias	(B)	Expert	Bias
GPT-3.5 Default	0.65	0.20	0.45	0.60	0.40	0.20
GPT-3.5 Legacy	0.65	0.00	0.65	0.60	0.20	0.40
GPT-4	0.65	0.00	0.65	0.60	0.30	0.30

answer (B), the responses provided by GPT have received positive evaluations, except for GPT-3.5 Legacy, whose grading is slightly worse.

4 Results and Discussion

In this section, we present and discuss the results obtained for the criminal and business exam, following the methodology outlined in the previous section. First, we present the results obtained for the multiple-choice, single-answer, questions exam and then the open-ended exam, taking into account the previously mentioned versions of GPT. The results obtained for the multiple-choice and single-answer exams are demonstrated in the table below.

Table 2. Results obtained by the current versions of GPT

Random	3.5 Default	3.5 Legacy	4.0
29%	55%	53%	70%
Disapproved	**Approved**	**Approved**	**Approved**

As previously mentioned, we initially used GPT-3.5 Default, followed by GPT-3.5 Legacy, and finally GPT-4. As shown in Table 2, all three versions of GPT successfully passed the exam, with GPT 4 performing significantly better with a score of 70%. Choosing randomly the answer resulted in a correct response percentage of only 29%, while GPT Default and Legacy scored 55% and 53%, respectively. It should be noted that interruptions of more than 2 h occurred only in GPT-4, which required 4 sessions to complete the 80 questions.

The open-ended exam is worth 10 points, with the drafting of the procedural document (PPP) questions accounting for 5 points and questions 1–4 worth 1.25 points each. For the criminal law exam, item (A) of questions 1–3 is worth 0.65, and item (B) is worth the remaining 0.60. Question 4, point (A) is worth 0.60, and point (B) is worth the remaining 0.65. The results obtained by the GPT versions tested in this study, namely 3.5 Default, 3.5 Legacy, and 4.0, for the criminal exam, are presented in the following table.

Surprisingly, Table 3 shows that GPT 4 performed the worst, while GPT 3.5 Default performed the best in the criminal exam. It is worth noting that neither of the GPT versions considered in this study achieved the minimum passing score of 6.

Table 3. Results of the correction of an expert (human) for the criminal exam

Question	3.5 Default	3.5 Legacy	4.0
PPP	1.80	1.60	1.10
1. (A)	0.00	0.00	0.00
1. (B)	0.00	0.30	0.00
2. (A)	0.20	0.00	0.00
2. (B)	0.40	0.20	0.30
3. (A)	0.00	0.00	0.00
3. (B)	0.50	0.10	0.50
4. (A)	0.45	0.45	0.30
4. (B)	0.45	0.60	0.45
	3.80	**3.25**	**2.65**

For the business exam, each question from 1 to 2, item (A) is worth 0.65, and item (B) is worth the remaining 0.60. Point (A) of questions 3 and 4 is worth 0.60 and point (B) is worth the remaining 0.65. Table 4 shows the results obtained by the three versions of GPT considered in this study: 3.5 Default, 3.5 Legacy, and 4.0.

Table 4. Results of the correction of an expert (human) for the business exam

Question	3.5 Default	3.5 Legacy	4.0
PPP	2.50	1.05	3.10
1. (A)	0.10	0.30	0.00
1. (B)	0.00	0.50	0.10
2. (A)	0.50	0.50	0.50
2. (B)	0.50	0.00	0.50
3. (A)	0.00	0.00	0.00
3. (B)	0.00	0.00	0.00
4. (A)	0.50	0.40	0.50
4. (B)	0.50	0.45	0.50
	4.60	**3.20**	**5.02**

The results presented in Table 4 show that GPT 3.5 Legacy obtained the lowest score, while GPT 4 obtained the highest score. Even though GPT 4 had the best score in the business exam—5.02, not far from the passing limit—, it obtained the worst score (2.65) for the criminal exam.

As we can see in the graph in Fig. 1, the GPT 3.5 Legacy obtains a practically identical result for the two exams but lower than those obtained by the GPT 3.5 Default,

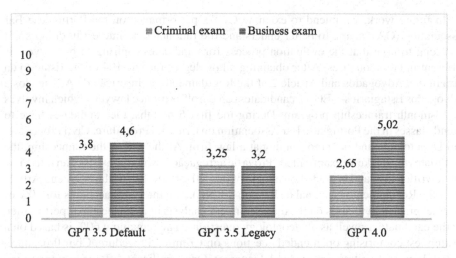

Fig. 1. The results obtained by GPT versions in the criminal and business exams.

which has a better performance in the business exam. However, in GPT 4, the difference in scores between the two exams is substantial, with the business exam being the highest ranked.

5 Conclusions and Further Work

The use of GPT for solving bar exams has garnered interest, particularly in the United States (*e.g.*, [8]) and Taiwan (*e.g.*, [9]). In this paper, we extend this interest to the Brazilian Bar Association (OAB) and address the following questions: "Does GPT pass the OAB exam?" and "Are there significant differences between the results obtained in the GPT versions currently available through OpenAI?". To answer these questions, we utilized the three available versions of GPT on OpenAI, in addition to a random choice only for multiple-choice, single-answer, questions. Furthermore, we only considered open-ended questions that pertained to the criminal and business domains.

All three versions of ChatGPT attained a positive rating for multiple-choice, single-answer, questions. GPT-4 received the highest rating of 70%, followed by GPT-3.5 Default at 55%, and GPT-3.5 Legacy at 53%. The grading difference between GPT-4 and the other two versions is almost 20%, indicating that the former is more advanced and produces better answers.

For the criminal exam, GPT 4 obtained the worst result, while GPT 3.5 Default obtained the best result, which is very close to the one obtained by GPT 3.5 Legacy. Finally, for the business exam, GPT 3.5 Legacy demonstrated the worst result, while GPT 4 had the best result. We observed that for this exam, GPT 4 achieved a score of 5.02, the best one, while in the criminal exam, GPT 4 obtained the worst score (2.65). Despite the good results achieved by GPT 4 for multiple-choice, single-answer, questions, the outcome for open questions is still underwhelming. However, with the rapid development expected for GPT, it is only a matter of time before we can achieve better results [18].

In future work, we intend to examine GPT's performance on the Portuguese Bar Association (OA) exam. To better understand the rationale and interest in doing so, it is crucial to note that the evaluation process for candidates aspiring to be lawyers is different in both countries. After obtaining a law degree (article 194 of the Estatuto da Ordem dos Advogados and Article 2 of the Regulamento de Inscrição de Advogados e Advogados Estagiários—EOA), candidates can enroll as trainee lawyers, which involves an 18-month traineeship program. During the first 6 months, the candidates have to attend classes in the Portuguese Bar Association on Criminal Procedure, Civil Procedure, and Deontology, and undergo training at a law firm. At the end of the traineeship, the candidates must take an exam called "Prova de agregação", which consists of an interview and a written test, and is graded on a scale of 0 to 20 (article 195 of the EOA and Article 28 of the Regulamento Nacional de Estágio—RNE). The interview accounts for 40% of the final grade and focuses on the discussion and analysis of a traineeship report written by the candidate, as well as on deontology questions. The remaining 60% is based on a written test comprising open-ended questions on Criminal Procedure, Civil Procedure, Deontology, and writing a procedural document. One significant difference between the OAB and OA examinations is that the latter does not include multiple choice questions, which, as our findings demonstrate, are the type of questions in which GPT has proven to excel.

References

1. United Nations Interregional Crime and Justice Research Institute (UNICRI).: Artificial intelligence and robotics for law enforcement. (2019)
2. Brants, T., Popat, A. C., Xu, P., Och, F. J., Dean, J.: Large language models in machine translation. (2007)
3. Shahriar, S., Hayawi, K.: Let's have a chat! A conversation with ChatGPT: Technology, applications, and limitations. (2023). arXiv preprint arXiv:2302.13817
4. Deng, J., Lin, Y.: The benefits and challenges of ChatGPT: an overview. Front. Comput. Intell. Syst. **2**(2), 81–83 (2022)
5. Biswas, S.: Role of chatGPT in law: According to chatGPT. (2023). Available at SSRN 4405398
6. Nikolskaia, K., Naumov, V.: Artificial intelligence in law. In: 2020 international multi-conference on industrial engineering and modern technologies (FarEastCon), pp. 1–4. IEEE, (2020)
7. Raaijmakers, S.: Artificial intelligence for law enforcement: challenges and opportunities. IEEE Secur. Priv. **17**(5), 74–77 (2019)
8. Ryznar, M.: Exams in the time of ChatGPT. Wash. Lee Law Rev. Online **80**(5), 305 (2023)
9. Shope, M.: GPT performance on the bar exam in Taiwan (GPT 在台灣專門職業及技術人員高等考試律師考試中的表現). Available at SSR. (2023)
10. Surden, H.: Artificial intelligence and law: An overview. Georg. State Univ. Law Rev. **35**, 19–22 (2019)
11. LeCun, Y., Bengio, Y., Hinton, G.: Deep learning. Nature, 521(7553), 436–444 (2015)
12. Sohail, S.S., Farhat, F., Himeur, Y., Nadeem, M., Madsen, D.O., Singh, Y., Mansoor, W.: The Future of GPT: A taxonomy of existing ChatGPT research, current challenges, and possible future directions. Curr. Chall Possible Futur. Dir., (2023)
13. Blair-Stanek, A., Holzenberger, N., Van Durme, B.: Can GPT-3 perform statutory reasoning? . (2023). arXiv preprint arXiv:2302.06100

14. Nguyen, H.T.: A brief report on law GPT 1.0: A virtual legal assistant based on GPT-3. (2023). arXiv preprint arXiv:2302.05729

15. Choi, J.H., Hickman, K.E., Monahan, A., Schwarcz, D.: ChatGPT goes to law school. Available at SSRN. (2023)

16. Bommarito II, M., Katz, D.M.: GPT takes the bar exam. (2023). arXiv preprint arXiv:2212. 14402

17. Katz, D.M., Bommarito, M.J., Gao, S., Arredondo, P.: Gpt-4 passes the bar exam. Available at SSRN 4389233. (2023)

18. Chalkidis, I.: ChatGPT may pass the bar exam soon, but has a long way to go for the LexGLUE benchmark. (2023). arXiv preprint arXiv:2304.12202

A Semantic Search System
for the Supremo Tribunal de Justiça

Rui Melo[1,2]([✉]) [iD], Pedro A. Santos[1,2] [iD], and João Dias[2,3,4] [iD]

[1] Instituto Superior Técnico, Universidade de Lisboa, Lisboa, Portugal
`pedro.santos@tecnico.ulisboa.pt`
[2] INESC-ID, Lisbon, Portugal
`rui.melo@tecnico.ulisboa.pt, jmdias@ualg.pt`
[3] Faculdade de Ciências e Tecnologia, Universidade do Algarve, Faro, Portugal
[4] CCMAR, Faro, Portugal

Abstract. Many information retrieval systems use lexical approaches to retrieve information. Such approaches have multiple limitations, and these constraints are exacerbated when tied to specific domains, such as the legal one. Large language models, such as BERT, deeply understand a language and may overcome the limitations of older methodologies, such as BM25. This work investigated and developed a prototype of a Semantic Search System to assist the Supremo Tribunal de Justiça (Portuguese Supreme Court of Justice) in its decision-making process. We built a Semantic Search System that uses specially trained BERT models (Legal-BERTimbau variants) and a Hybrid Search System that incorporates both lexical and semantic techniques by combining the capabilities of BM25 and the potential of Legal-BERTimbau. In this context, we obtained a 335% increase on the discovery metric when compared to BM25 for the first query result. This work also provides information on the most relevant techniques for training a Large Language Model adapted to Portuguese jurisprudence and introduces a new technique of Metadata Knowledge Distillation.

Keywords: Legal information retrieval · Semantic search · Large language models · BERT

1 Introduction

The Supremo Tribunal de Justiça (STJ) serves as Portugal's highest judiciary court, also known as the Supreme Court of Justice. It plays a crucial role in making well-informed, lawful, and ethical decisions that have a profound impact on the specific case at hand and future cases. To arrive at a decision, a comprehensive examination of the relevant jurisprudence is indispensable. This exhaustive consultation serves as the bedrock for a thoughtful and principled judgment.

When a judge is tasked with formulating a decision, whether it involves researching specific legislation or referring to precedents from similar cases, the

N. Moniz et al. (Eds.): EPIA 2023, LNAI 14116, pp. 142–154, 2023.
https://doi.org/10.1007/978-3-031-49011-8_12

process of locating the necessary information is far from trivial, speedy, or efficient. Effectively managing and accessing such vast volumes of information necessitates the utilization of a robust information retrieval (IR) system. Such a system is an indispensable tool in ensuring efficient access to the required legal resources.

This work discusses the need for a reliable legal search system for Portugal's Supreme Court of Justice (STJ) to improve the court decision process. Project IRIS, in which the work presented here was developed, aimed to develop summarization approaches for court decisions and create a representation that can be browsed to help in the court decision process. In this paper, we developed a semantic search system prototype that can access information based on natural language and assist judges in making well-informed decisions. We also introduce a new technique, Metadata Knowledge Distillation, to improve search systems' capabilities, and Legal-BERTimbau, a language model adapted to the Portuguese legal domain. Our tests indicate that hybrid search systems, using both lexical and semantic components, perform better than systems using only one type of technique.

2   Related Work

Information retrieval systems evolved significantly over the years. In particular, they can now incorporate advanced techniques from Natural Language Processing (NLP), namely larger and more powerful Large Language Models (LLM) models [9,19], all of which are based on the groundbreaking Transformers architecture [20]. More recently, systems are starting to also incorporate LLM models with the retrieved passages after the information retrieval process. The information is provided as context in a prompt, allowing these powerful models to provide a better interaction with the user. While also using LLM for this purpose, we explore here the use of semantic search techniques in the information retrieval component.

Information retrieval initially started by utilizing lexical approaches such as the probabilistic model Okapi BM25 (BM25) [15] and has been evolving to incorporate semantic search into the mix. Implementing a semantic search functionality requires a model to embed passages and store them in a database with the ability to be searchable through mathematical distance metrics such as Euclidean distance or cosine similarity. Such implementation reflects the overall use case of a Bi-Encoder [2,12].

In what regards IR in the legal domain, two teams got top results in COLIEE in 2021 [6] by combining lexical and semantic approaches. The first team, OvGU, proposes a combination of a two-stage TF-IDF vectorization with Sentence-BERT embeddings. The second team, JNLP, focused on handling long articles, by performing text chunking on the prepared training data and applying a self-labeled technique while finetuning pre-trained models. First, they prepared the training data with the method proposed in [8]. They encoded all the articles and queries into vectors, using a TF-IDF vectorizer, and then used Cosine Similarity to rank the articles. A pair of a query and an entailing article is considered a positive training example, and the opposite is considered a negative example.

Nuno Cordeiro [3], created the LeSSE system, which merges common document retrieval techniques with semantic search abilities on Portuguese consumer law. His work overall goal and context are similar to the context of this research, despite focusing on Portuguese consumer law.

3   Data

This project had some pre-defined aspects, such as which technologies the search system should be implemented in and what data was available to work with. Legal documents contain specific language not easily found in conventional websites or books. It was required to collect many records to create a semantic search system adapted to the Portuguese legal domain. In the context of the IRIS project, we collected data from *www.dgsi.pt*, which consists of publicly available STJ court rulings, and indexed them with ElasticSearch.[1]

Initially, the documents were pre-processed in the original dataset to split the entire document into smaller units and standardize the characters throughout the documents. The retrieval process recovered the HTML content from multiple web domain pages containing legal documents, summing up to 31690 documents. The dataset was divided into three subsets: a training set of 26952 documents, a testing set of 3169 documents, and a validation set of 3169 documents. The text was cleaned and split into singular sentences.

4   Semantic Search System Architecture

Our solution to implement a reliable search system involved employing a Bi-Encoder to create independent embeddings for each document, allowing for a later efficient search using cosine similarity. Throughout this work, two search systems were implemented: a semantic search and a hybrid search system. The solution architecture is illustrated in Fig. 1.

After the pre-processing stage, each sentence embedding was generated, populating the indexes on Elasticsearch. For retrieving specific query results, that exact query would be transformed into an embedding by our model, Legal-BERTimbau, which will be described in Sect. 5. Then the system can proceed to search similar sentences by executing a ranking function on Elasticsearch using the query embedding. In the Semantic Search System version, the ranking function used is the cosine similarity. Finally, the relevant passages are included in a prompt for GPT3.5, providing a user-friendly response, yet based on the retrieved results. For example, with a query as such: "Furto de Armas", the system's output is the following:

---

[1] https://www.elastic.co/.

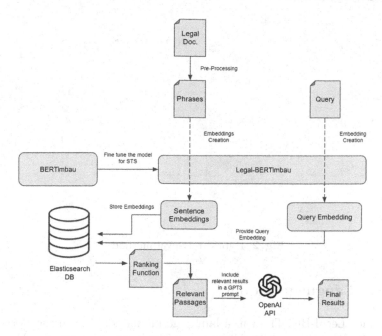

Fig. 1. System architecture

– A passagem relevante para a questão é a seguinte: "Quem, de noite e acompanhado, entra numa casa museu, depois de arrombar a porta e de lá retira várias armas peças de museu e delas se apropria, contra vontade do dono, pratica os crimes de introdução em lugar vedado ao público e furto qualificado." (Documento ID: 9EWRYoMBF_lErWh5_w2g)".

This work presents another version of the search system, which is a Hybrid Search System. It combines the potential of lexical search techniques and the reach of large language models. The Hybrid Search System's architecture is similar to the developed Semantic Search System. The pre-processing and usage of ElasticSearch are equal, and only the retrieval method changes slightly. Instead of yielding the best matches using the cosine similarity metric, it combines the scores of lexical and semantic information retrieval methods. The Hybrid Search System utilises the scores provided by BM25 and the cosine similarity value from the Legal-BERTimbau embedding space. BM25 scores are normalised using the maximum score obtained using a specific query. The cosine similarity between the dense vector and the query embedding is calculated in parallel. The cosine similarity value does not need to be normalised. Finally, we sum the scores using both methods and proceed to reorder and present the results. The retrieved method is illustrated in Fig. 2.

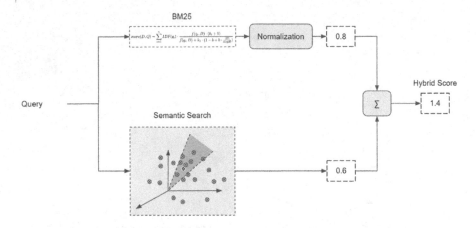

Fig. 2. Hybrid retrieval method

5   Legal Language Model

We introduce Legal-BERTimbau, a language model adapted to the Portuguese legal domain. We utilised the concept of transfer learning using neural networks and made use of BERT models [4] for this purpose. All the training was done on an NVIDIA GeForce RTX 3090 24 GB GPU. Since training a BERT model from scratch with a small dataset would likely lead to overfitting, we used a foundation BERT model called BERTimbau [16,17] that is already trained with a larger corpus, Brazilian Web as Corpus (BrWaC) [1]. We explored different training techniques, generating multiple BERT model versions. We started by adapting the BERTimbau large to the Portuguese legal domain (Domain Adaptation) using Masked Language Modeling (MLM) and the Transformer-based Sequential Denoising Auto-Encoder (TSDAE) [21] technique. Furthermore, we fine-tuned the model for Semantic Textual Similarity (STS) and explored others techniques with the end goal of improving a bi-encoder's performance. We proceeded to cover Natural Language Inference (NLI), Generative Pseudo Labeling (GPL) [22], Multilingual Knowledge Distillation (MKD) [14] and even introduced a new technique for that same purpose, Metadata Knowledge Distillation (MetaKD).

5.1   Domain Adaptation

Masked Language Modeling The training consisted in applying the BERT MLM training over our training dataset. For the MLM task, we defined the learning rate as 10^{-5}. We want the learning rate in this stage to be significantly lower than in the initial training stage itself. This fine-tuning stage, performed with a batch size of 2, generated a Legal-BERTimbau variant. The selected MLM model variant is the one obtained at the 770 training steps mark. The model selection was based on the variant which had the lowest loss value.

Transformer-Based Sequential Denoising Auto-Encoder When using the TSDAE technique, we used a learning rate of $5*10^{-5}$ over our training dataset. The selected TSDAE model variant was the one with the lowest loss value: 1300 training steps, performed with a batch size of 2.

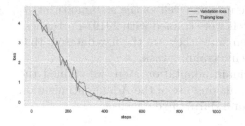
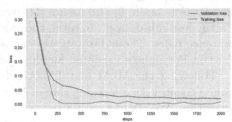

Fig. 3. MLM training loss   **Fig. 4.** TSDAE training loss

Generative Pseudo Labeling GPL is an unsupervised domain adaptation method for training dense retrievers. It is designed to improve the dense retrieval approaches on specialized datasets. GPL has three different stages: Query Generation (from GenQ [18]), Negative Mining and Pseudo Labeling. In the Query Generation step, we created 10000 Queries for 10000 legal documents. We used a pre-trained Text-To-Text Transfer Transformer (T5) [10] model, fine-tuned for the Portuguese Language,[2] to generate queries from each document summary. After this step, we have a collection of queries that each summary (positive passage) should be able to answer individually. In the Negative Mining stage, we retrieved passages very similar to our initial passage, but that should not be able to answer the generated queries. For this purpose, we created an index on ElasticSearch where we stored the embeddings of the other summaries used for the previous step. To reduce the bias in the system, we used an original BERTimbau large fine-tuned for STS. This model was fine-tuned following the guidelines in the original paper. We used assin and assin2 datasets for five epochs, using $3*10^{-5}$ for the learning rate. In the final step, we used the same model to calculate the margin between positive and negative passages using the dot product. We trained the models using the created triplets (positive passage, negative passage and margin score), applying the Margin Mean Squared Error Loss with a learning rate of $2*10^{-5}$ on one epoch. The variants produced with this approach outperforms the variants that were not subject to this technique by 3.2% performance boost on the Search metric and 1.7% performance increase on the Discovery metric.

---

[2] https://huggingface.co/pierreguillou/t5-base-qa-squad-v1.1-portuguese.

5.2   Semantic Textual Similarity

The task our language model needs to perform is STS evaluation. We created SBERT [12] versions and trained them with three distinct datasets. We attached an independent linear layer to each Legal-BERTimbau variant and fine-tuned the model using a mean squared error loss. To train the models for the STS task, the datasets assin [5] and assin2 [11] were used, as well as the stsb_multi_mt [7] Portuguese sub-dataset. In total, the models were trained with 20197 Portuguese sentence pairs. These datasets were chosen since they are the few datasets that exist in Portuguese prepared for this specific training task.

Following the MLM and TSDAE domain adaptation step, we trained the large version with a learning rate of 10^{-5}, making use of the Adam optimization algorithm. We trained with a batch size of 8 during five epochs.

5.3   Natural Language Inference

According to [12], it is reported a slight STS performance improvement when the models were subjected to Natural Language Inference (NLI) data. We also explored this approached by training the large models on assin and assin2 NLI information with a 8 batch size for five epochs with a learning rate of 10^{-5}, using the Adam optimization algorithm. The variants produced with this approach suffer a 4.3% performance boost on the Search metric and 5.4% performance increase on the Discovery metric.

5.4   Multilingual Knowledge Distillation

In this work, we developed a language model that utilises this technique to improve the knowledge a model has on the Portuguese language. The dataset used was: TED 2020—Parallel Sentences Corpus [13]. TED 2020 contains around 4000 TED[3] and TED-X transcripts from July 2020. All the sentences were aligned to generate a parallel corpus for such training tasks. It was designated as the student model, supposedly supporting the English Language already, and we intended for it to learn Portuguese. The chosen teacher model was *sentence-transformers/stsb-roberta-large*.[4] The training was performed with a 10^{-5} learning rate using the Adam optimization algorithm during five epochs.

5.5   Metadata Knowledge Distillation

We introduce Metadata Knowledge Distillation and its detailed implementation in this section. This technique comes from a necessity of continuously improving information retrieval through dense vectors. The method involves identifying documents related to a subject, encoding their sentences, generating embeddings, and calculating the centroid of those embeddings. The embeddings from each

---

[3] https://www.ted.com/.

[4] https://huggingface.co/sentence-transformers/stsb-roberta-large.

specific subject are then adjusted slightly towards their centroid by a certain percentage amount.

Each document have "Descritores", brief tags manually annotated by experts to identify its main subjects. A document can have multiple tags at once. Documents that have the same tags indicate some level of relationship between them. Similarly, we can associate one or more tags from a document to a sentence from within that document. If multiple sentences are, at some level, related, their embeddings should be closer in the vector space. Thus, calculate the centroid of each specific tag, and pull every sentence embedding slightly closer to it, changing the original sentence embedding for one that differs slightly. These new embeddings are stored as gold labels to later train the model. This methodology can be shown in Fig. 5.

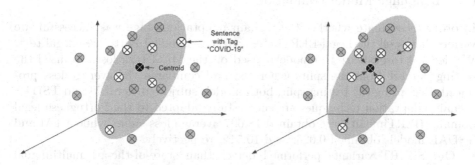

Fig. 5. Metadata knowledge distillation ideology

With the gold labels stored for each sentence, we forced the model to embedd each sentence, and we provide our generated embedding for it to learn. We proceed to apply the mean-squared error loss, similar to Multilingual Knowledge Distillation, to train the model. The process is illustrated in Fig. 6. We used this technique with a learning rate of 10^{-5} and a batch size of 3 sentences. We adjusted the embeddings of a 1000 document sample selected randomly from the training document subset. The embeddings were adjusted based on each tag's centroids, centralizing the embeddings by 1% for one epoch. These hyperparameter choices were defined based on a grid search optimization algorithm where we tried to maximize the STS task evaluation.

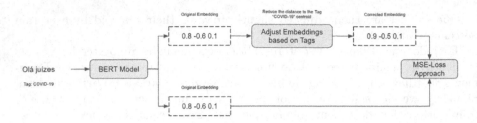

Fig. 6. Metadata knowledge distillation

6   Evaluation

6.1   Language Model Evaluation

In order to evaluate whether the domain adaptation stage was successful, we verified how well the Legal-BERTimbau variants handled Portuguese legal text. We decided to evaluate the models based on the MLM task loss. We used the testing dataset from the splits generated and compared the average loss produced. Regarding the testing split, both models subjected to MLM and TSDAE domain adaptation techniques are successfully adapted to the Portuguese legal domain. BERTimbau large obtained 18.607 average loss value, while MLM and TSDAE models obtained 0.0268 and 10.512, respectively.

Our SBERT variants performed better than state-of-the-art multilingual models on the STS task. To evaluate a model's STS task performance, we evaluate if a model is able to provide accurate similarity scores for a given sentence pair. The Pearson correlation [23] is calculated between the expected and projected similarity score between different sentence pairs. This quantitive evaluation verifies if our models understand how similar two Portuguese sentences are. Results from pre-selected variants are shown in Table 1.

Table 1. STS evaluation on Portuguese datasets

Model	Assin	Assin2	stsb_multi_mt pt
Paraphrase-multilingual-MiniLM-L12-v2	0.7146	0.8017	0.6795
Paraphrase-multilingual-mpnet-base-v2	0.7437	0.8400	0.7147
All-mpnet-base-v2	0.5631	0.6213	0.5129
mlm-sts-v0	0.7851	0.8116	0.8363
mlm-nli-sts-v0	0.7810	0.8100	0.8368
tsdae-gpl-nli-sts-v0	0.7786	**0.8068**	**0.8393**
tsdae-gpl-nli-sts-MetaKD-v0	**0.7845**	0.8010	0.8384

6.2   Search System Evaluation

In order to evaluate our IR system, we needed a group of queries and expected retrieved results to evaluate its performance. In our scenario, there is no such group of data for this effect. Thus, we aimed to create queries from each document to assist in the appraisal. Our solution to evaluate the system performance passed through creating embeddings from a collection of 1000 legal documents and store them in ElasticSearch. Then we generated queries from each document and used those same queries to test the system. We utilized a T5 model to generate queries from each document summary. Subsequently, we treated the queries, so that they maintained a similar meaning, but did not contain every exact keyword. We identified the top 20 keywords from the summary with TF-IDF and exchanged them with synonyms or similar expressions.

We retrieve the results using the cosine similarity metric for the Semantic Search System and combined the cosine similarity metric with BM25 technique to replicate the proposed Hybrid Search System. Our comparison baseline consisted on utilising BM25 searches with the same queries and other multilingual models such as "all-mpnet-base-v2" and "paraphrase-multilingual-mpnet-base-v2" instead of Legal-BERTimbau versions. We utilised the concepts of Search and Discovery as metrics for our evaluation.

The Search metric allows gathering insights into the system's ability to find which document a certain query refers to. Initially, each query was generated from individual summaries. If the search system receives a query based on document x, the retrieved result should be from the document x. We evaluated whether this happens within the first result or the first group of results for a specific query. If the retrieved document is the same as the one used for creating the query, it increases the evaluation score by 1.

The Discovery metric provides interpretability on the search system's ability to retrieve relevant documents. The search system should retrieve documents that are important for a given query, even if they are not the original document from which the query was generated. Each legal document have "descritores" (tags) that were manually annotated. There can have 1 or more tags associated with each document. Similarly to the Search metric, if the retrieved document within a group of results contains a tag equal to the original document's tags from which the query was generated, we increase the score. For each equal tag, the Discovery metric score is increased by one. In practice, if the search system receives a query that was created from a document y containing the tag "Knives", we want to evaluate whether the same tags appear within the top results.

We evaluated the Semantic Search System performance based on the different top results sizes. We verified whether the queries' original document is suggested within the first result (Top 1), the first two results (Top 2), and so forth. Likewise, we evaluated the Top 1, Top 2, Top 3, Top 5, and Top 10. Tables 2 and 3 reflects the performance between BM25 and our best-performing Legal-BERTimbau variant, tsdae-gpl-nli-sts-MetaKD-v0.

Table 2. Semantic search system evaluation—search metric

Model	Top 1	Top 2	Top 3	Top 5	Top 10
BM25	**629**	**696**	**722**	**760**	**799**
Semantic tsdae-gpl-nli-sts-MetaKD-v0	411	471	518	559	618
Hybrid tsdae-gpl-nli-sts-MetaKD-v0	**629**	675	705	734	785
Improvement	0%	–3.01 %	–2.35%	–3.42%	–1.75%

Table 3. Semantic search system evaluation—discovery metric

Model	Top 1	Top 2	Top 3	Top 5	Top 10
BM25	685	933	1133	1482	2216
Semantic tsdae-gpl-nli-sts-MetaKD-v0	2226	2932	3532	4332	6243
Hybrid tsdae-gpl-nli-sts-MetaKD-v0	**2984**	**3732**	**4292**	**5168**	**7282**
Improvement	335%	300%	278%	248%	228%

The tests showed the BM25 outperforming the Semantic Search System in the Search metric, but the Semantic Search System performed better in the Discovery metric. The Hybrid Search System, which combines the strengths of both lexical and semantic systems, performed better than the Semantic Search System and was comparable to BM25 in the Search metric. In the Discovery metric, it clearly outperforms the BM25 technique, going from around 335% improvement on the Top 1 results and topping at 228% improvement on the Top 10 results. Such outcomes suggest that the proposed search systems can improve the decision-making process in the legal domain by providing relevant and insightful information.

7   Conclusion

This work presents a Semantic Search System and a Hybrid Search System that use neural networks to enhance information retrieval for legal documents in the Portuguese legal domain. The system utilizes Legal-BERTimbau models and Elasticsearch to achieve better results than traditional methods like BM25. This study led to the development of tailored BERT models for the Portuguese Legal Domain, outperforming state-of-the-art multilingual models on specific annotated datasets. The system's performance was evaluated based on different metrics, and the results showed that the proposed Hybrid search system outperforms the traditional lexical technique in terms of identifying the query source and suggesting similar documents. The implementation of such a search system could drastically improve the information retrieval process and promote consistency in the application of the law.

Acknowledgements. The presented work was done as part of INESC-ID's project "Sumarização e Informação de decisões: Aplicação de Técnicas de Inteligência Artificial no Supremo Tribunal de Justiça" (IRIS), in collaboration with STJ. This work was partially supported by STJ and by national funds through Fundação para a Ciência e a Tecnologia (FCT) through projects UIDB/50021/2020, UIDB/04326/2020, UIDP/04326/2020 and LA/P/0101/2020.

References

1. Boos, R., Prestes, K., Villavicencio, A., Padró, M.: brWaC: A WaCky Corpus for Brazilian Portuguese. In: Baptista, J., Mamede, N., Candeias, S., Paraboni, I., Pardo, T.A.S., Volpe Nunes, M.d.G. (eds.) Computational Processing of the Portuguese Language, pp. 201–206. Springer International Publishing, Cham (2014)
2. Choi, J., Jung, E., Suh, J., Rhee, W.: Improving bi-encoder document ranking models with two rankers and multi-teacher distillation. In: SIGIR '21: The 44th International ACM SIGIR Conference on Research and Development in Information Retrieval, pp. 2192–2196. ACM, Canada (2021)
3. Cordeiro, N.: NLP Applied To Portuguese Consumer Law. Master's thesis, Instituto Superior Técnico, Universidade de Lisboa (2022)
4. Devlin, J., Chang, M.W., Lee, K., Toutanova, K.: BERT: Pre-training of deep bidirectional transformers for language understanding. In: Proceedings of the 2019 Conference of the North American Chapter of the ACL: Human Language Technologies, vol. 1, pp. 4171–4186. ACL, Minneapolis, Minnesota (2019)
5. Fonseca, E., Santos, L., Criscuolo, M., Aluisio, S.: ASSIN: Avaliacao de similaridade semantica e inferencia textual. In: Computational Processing of the Portuguese Language-12th International Conference, pp. 13–15. Tomar, Portugal (2016)
6. Kim, M., Rabelo, J., Goebel, R.: BM25 and transformer-based legal information extraction and entailment. In: Proceedings of the COLIEE Workshop in ICAIL (2021)
7. May, P.: Machine Translated Multilingual STS Benchmark Dataset (2021)
8. Nguyen, H.T., Vuong, H.Y.T., Nguyen, P.M., Dang, B.T., Bui, Q.M., Vu, S.T., Nguyen, C.M., Tran, V., Satoh, K., Nguyen, M.L.: JNLP team: Deep learning for legal processing in COLIEE 2020 (2020). arXiv:2011.08071
9. OpenAI: GPT-4 technical report (2023)
10. Raffel, C., Shazeer, N., Roberts, A., Lee, K., Narang, S., Matena, M., Zhou, Y., Li, W., Liu, P.J.: Exploring the limits of transfer learning with a unified text-to-text transformer. J. Mach. Learn. Res. **21**(140), 1–67 (2020)
11. Real, L., Fonseca, E., Oliveira, H.G.: The assin 2 shared task: a quick overview. In: International Conference on Computational Processing of the Portuguese Language, pp. 406–412. Springer, Berlin (2020)
12. Reimers, N., Gurevych, I.: Sentence-BERT: sentence embeddings using siamese BERT-networks. In: Proceedings of the 2019 Conference on Empirical Methods in Natural Language Processing. ACL (2019)
13. Reimers, N., Gurevych, I.. In: Proceedings of the 2020 Conference on Empirical Methods in Natural Language Processing. ACL (2020)

14. Reimers, N., Gurevych, I.: Making monolingual sentence embeddings multilingual using knowledge distillation. In: Proceedings of the 2020 Conference on Empirical Methods in Natural Language Processing. ACL (2020)
15. Robertson, S., Zaragoza, H.: The probabilistic relevance framework: Bm25 and beyond. Found. Trends Inf. Retr. **3**(4), 333–389 (2009). https://doi.org/10.1561/1500000019
16. Souza, F., Nogueira, R., Lotufo, R.: Portuguese named entity recognition using BERT-CRFv (2019). arXiv:1909.10649
17. Souza, F., Nogueira, R., Lotufo, R.: BERTimbau: Pretrained BERT Models for Brazilian Portuguese. In: Cerri, R., Prati, R.C. (eds.) Intelligent Systems, pp. 403–417. Springer International Publishing, Cham (2020)
18. Thakur, N., Reimers, N., Rücklé, A., Srivastava, A., Gurevych, I.: BEIR: A heterogeneous benchmark for zero-shot evaluation of information retrieval models. In: Thirty-fifth Conference on Neural Information Processing Systems Datasets and Benchmarks Track (Round 2) (2021)
19. Touvron, H., Lavril, T., Izacard, G., Martinet, X., Lachaux, M.A., Lacroix, T., Rozière, B., Goyal, N., Hambro, E., Azhar, F., Rodriguez, A., Joulin, A., Grave, E., Lample, G.: LLaMA: Open and efficient foundation language models (2023)
20. Vaswani, A., Shazeer, N., Parmar, N., Uszkoreit, J., Jones, L., Gomez, A.N., Kaiser, L.u., Polosukhin, I.: Attention is all you need. In: Advances in Neural Information Processing Systems. vol. 30. Curran Associates, Inc. (2017)
21. Wang, K., Reimers, N., Gurevych, I.: TSDAE: Using transformer-based sequential denoising auto-encoderfor unsupervised sentence embedding learning. In: Findings of the ACL: EMNLP 2021, pp. 671–688. ACL, Punta Cana, Dominican Republic (2021)
22. Wang, K., Thakur, N., Reimers, N., Gurevych, I.: GPL: Generative pseudo labeling for unsupervised domain adaptation of dense retrieval. In: North American Chapter of the ACL (2021)
23. Zhelezniak, V., Savkov, A., Shen, A., Hammerla, N.: Correlation coefficients and semantic textual similarity. In: Proceedings of the 2019 Conference of the North American Chapter of the ACL: Human Language Technologies, vol 1, pp. 951–962. ACL, Minneapolis, Minnesota (2019)

Artificial Intelligence in Power
and Energy Systems

The AI Act Meets General Purpose AI: The Good, The Bad and The Uncertain

Nídia Andrade Moreira[1]([✉]), Pedro Miguel Freitas[1], and Paulo Novais[2]

[1] Universidade Católica Portuguesa, Católica Research Centre for the Future of the Law, Porto, Portugal
{s-njamoreira,pfreitas}@ucp.pt
[2] Algorithm Centre/LASI, University of Minho, Braga, Portugal

Abstract. The general approach of the Draft of AI Act (December 2022) expanded the scope to explicitly include General Purpose Artificial Intelligence. This paper presents an overview of the new proposals and analyzes their implications. Although the proposed regulation has the merit of regulating an expanding field that can be applied in different domains and on a large scale due to its dynamic context, it has some flaws. It is essential to ascertain whether we are dealing with a general-risk category or a specific category of high-risk. Moreover, we need to clarify the allocation of responsibilities and promote cooperation between different actors. Finally, exemptions to the regulation should be properly balanced to avoid liability gaps.

Keywords: AI Act · General purpose · Artificial intelligence

1 AI Act: The Regulation of GPAI

1.1 Context

In April 2021, the European Commission published the Draft Proposal of AI Act (AIA), aimed at establishing a coordinated European approach to addressing the human and ethical implications of AI.

Throughout the law-making process[1], governments, experts and stakeholders formulated amendment proposals to improve it, highlighting the potential risks and misuse of technology and the need to protect innovation. With recent developments like GPT-4, the so-called "General Purpose Artificial Intelligence" (GPAI) has become a topic of discussion.

The initial Draft (April 2021) did not explicitly reference GPAI, but this did not necessarily exclude it from the scope of the AIA. If a GPAI system entailed a high-risk purpose, it had to comply with the requirements of high-risk AI.

During the Slovenian Presidency (November 2021), a proposal was made to exclude an automatic application of the AIA to the development and use of GPAI. The AIA

---

[1] The procedure 2021/016(COD) can be followed at https://eur-lex.europa.eu/procedure/EN/202 1_106.

would only apply if the GPAI system had an intended purpose within the meaning of the AIA or if it was integrated into an AI system that was subjected to the AIA (article 52a and recital 70a).[2] However, the French Presidency (May 2022) proposed to expand the scope of the AIA to include these systems and explicitly regulate them to promote the safe development of AI.[3] The new proposal adapted the requirements of high-risk AI to GPAI systems, unless the provider of the GPAI excluded any high-risk uses in the documentation accompanying the GPAI.

The French proposal was a major development but, in the meantime, the Czech Presidency made some amendments to the AIA proposal. Specifically, the direct application of the requirements for high-risk AI systems was replaced with the possibility of future implementing acts. Discussions are currently underway based on the General Approach (December 2022) prepared by the Czech Presidency.

In this paper, we analyze how the General approach (December 2022) regulates such systems.

1.2 Definition: Dimensions of Generality

AI models typically exhibit narrow capabilities and are designed or trained for specific tasks (fixed-purpose systems). However, we are now witnessing the emergence of AI systems that lack an intended and specific purpose and can be adapted to different tasks and contexts. These systems can perform tasks that were not foreseen by their creators.

Considering this reality, the latest versions of the AIA proposal explicitly mention "generative AI systems" (article 3(1)), but more importantly, they introduced the concept of "general purpose AI system (article 3 (1b)). The definition of a GPAI refers to an AI system that is intended to "perform generally applicable functions" and may be "used in a plurality of contexts" and be "integrated in plurality of other AI systems". Therefore, the key elements of the GPAI definition seem to include (i) a range of purposes, (ii) the ability to operate in various contexts and (iii) integration into other AI systems, namely high-risk systems. However, are these definitional elements unique to GPAI and are they be cumulative?

The concept of generality in the context of AI itself is complex.[4] Some AI systems, like Stable Diffusion or Midjourney have different and combined *abilities* in image generation (text2img, outpaiting, inpaiting, img2img, img2text). Other AI systems like GPT-4 possess specific ability such as natural language processing and perform a wide range of *tasks* [24], e.g. creating social media content, summarizing text, translating text,

---

[2] Presidency compromise text (Brussels, 29 November 2021)—see recital 70a and title IVA. According to ALLAI [1, pp. 13-14] the Presidency considers that it is impossible for providers to comply with requirements of high-risk because GPAI does not have a "intended purpose" (article 8 (2)). However, as mentioned by ALLAI, it is possible to reasonably foresee its use.

[3] Proposition de Règlement du Parlement européen et du Conseil établissant des règles harmonisées concernant l'intelligence artificielle (législation sur l'intelligence artificielle) et modifiant certains actes législatifs de l'Union—Text de compromis de la présidence (13 May 2022). The final compromise text of French Presidency was released in 15 June 2022.

[4] Gutierrez et al. [17, p. 2] refers to four alternatives: ability, domain, task and output considering that is the task the key to define GPAI.

writing code, and more recently, accepting images as prompts; and can also be employed in various *domains* such as education or law.[5].

The proposed definition is worded in a way that is not sufficiently useful and clear. It remains unclear whether the requisites should be seen as cumulative for an AI system to be classified as a GPAI, or if the characteristic of generality should be dependent on the intentionality behind the AI system.

Recital 12c states that GPAI "are AI systems that are intended by the provider to perform generally applicable functions, such as image/speech recognition, and in a plurality of contexts". Although this definition is clearer in the sense that a GPAI implies the provider's intentionality towards a variety of purposes and contexts, it is not identical to the one found in article 3 (1b), in several ways.

The particularity of GPAI systems is that they can be used for different tasks (multi-purpose systems) in different domains and with different types of input [15, p. 3]. Furthermore, these models can be seen as "Foundation Models" [4], serving as a base for downstream applications or tasks.[6]

According to this, a task-approach [17], along with a taxonomy-based approach should be taken. Even when trained for a specific task, GPAI could perform a wide variety of tasks, some of which were not even intended from the start. The crucial point is that an AI system can serve various purposes depending on the context and can be integrated into different systems. This is possible due to specific characteristics that make them powerful and flexible models, such as their large scale and abstraction capabilities.

Despite their differences from traditional systems, as they can perform a variety of tasks with minimal fine-tuning, the versatility of these models should not be confused with Artificial General Intelligence (AGI).[7] These models "are unable to generalize to completely different data types outside of their training data" [12, p. 17]. Therefore, even though we are witnessing a significant evolution of technology, it is not, however, a major breakthrough.

These AI systems are large-scale models trained on extensive datasets, capable of accepting different types of inputs and possess a high number of parameters. They can also be fine-tuned to perform multiple tasks.[8] They serve as a pre-products that can be tailored to specific purposes or act as adaptable systems, serving as a base model that can be adjusted for different tasks.[9]

---

[5] For example, the genesis.studio developed the GPJ (Practical Guide to Justice) with the support of Microsoft Portugal to be used by the Portuguese Ministry of Justice. Is a chatbot platform based on ChatGPT that answers legal questions in natural language and it aims to explain how to initiate divorce proceeding and bridge the gap between the justice system and citizens ([16]).

[6] See the definition of [1, p. 12]. Recently a new amendment adopted by the European Parliament on 14 June 2023 introduces specific obligations for providers of foundation models—article 28 b.

[7] Madiega [25] considers that they are part of a new wave of AGI technologies.

[8] One popular example is GPT-3 that was trained to predict the next word of a sentence and then has adapted to answer question, translate and other tasks. Launched in March 2023, GPT-4 is more powerful and performs even more complex tasks [30].

[9] See [6]. LLMs can be important in the development of general language systems.

The definition is provided by the AIA is overly inclusive [18, p. 4].[10] Our suggested approach aims to refine the proposed definition by excluding systems that were specifically designed and trained for tasks like speech recognition but can be (i) used for different purposes in various of contexts and (ii) integrated into other AI systems. These systems should not be classified as GPAI since they have a different model structure. The use of the system in different domains or within different AI systems should be a necessary condition, but not sufficient to classify it as a GPAI [18, p. 5]. However, even in this case, we may question how many tasks are necessary to classify an AI system as a GPAI. Should we adopt a quantitative perspective that considers to the level of capabilities or accuracy for tasks [18, p. 5] or should we employ other criteria, such as a taxonomy-based approach? The introduction of specific rules for GPAI requires a clear definition as a starting point.

1.3 Regulation: Challenges and Risks

Despite the numerous benefits of these models,[11] there are potential risks[12] and difficult choices regarding their regulation [25]. Since these models are trained on large datasets, often referred to as big data [9], they face specific challenges related to quality[13] and security throughout the data lifecycle [26, p. 1600]. As Foundation Models, any flaws in the base model and in data governance can have implications for later applications. Consequently, these AI systems can amplify biases and discrimination[14] found in the training data. Therefore, it is crucial to adopt data governance practices that require the use of curation techniques to measure bias,[15] filter and label the data,[16] ensuring that the final model meets quality requirements.[17]

Other risks must be addressed, such as copyright infringement [5], the generation of disinformation at scale [7], criminal misuse [14] and other potential damages that are difficult to enumerate,[18] such as encouraging physical harm or what Kolt [20] coined as "black swans" damages, which are highly consequential risks that are challenging to predict in advance but easy to explain in hindsight.

---

[10] The definition has been shortened in the recent amendment proposed by the European Parliament on 14 June 2023—see Article 3(1d).

[11] For example, an experimental study has shown that ChatGPT can increase productivity and equality between workers [28].

[12] See [40]. Analyzing the risks of GPT-4, see [29].

[13] For this reason, some authors proposed a quality assessment method that attends to big data's characteristics. See the proposal of [8].

[14] See examples in [3].

[15] See [27].

[16] It could include pre-moderation or other techniques that filter data, detect and remove some content. This takes us to another ethical problem associated to the creation of AI related to workers exposed to such sensitive contact—as hate speech, images of sexual violence—for which they are not given extra care and are poorly paid ([32]).

[17] Some bias can be explained not only by the number of inputs or the quality of data but also by the way data is labeled or trained [41].

[18] Other risks come from a climate policy perspective [39].

Privacy concerns should also receive specific attention. Since GPAI models are trained on scraped data from the internet, issues related to transparency and consent arise in data collection and processing.

However, the absence of regulation of GPAI could stifle innovation and competition. As mentioned earlier, these systems can be adapted for downstream tasks. Without regulation, the responsibility of complying with the AI Act falls on the downstream users, which could be "too much of a burden, especially for SME's and micro enterprises" or perhaps even technically impossible [1, p. 14]. In such scenario, the market would be (further) dominated by big tech companies.

Considering that the original developers often possess greater resources and knowledge compared to downstream providers, it is essential to rethink the value chain, responsibilities and cooperation. Otherwise, the non-regulation of GPAI would exempt the creators of the GPAI from responsibility and shift the focus solely to downstream applications [12, p. 23].[19]

2 AIA Draft

2.1 AI Requirements and Obligations

In order to address the specific characteristics of these systems, a new title—"General Purpose AI Systems"—has been added to the AIA draft, which establishes specific requirements for GPAI systems (article 4a—article 4c).

While there are some other articles in the AIA draft that are directly applicable to GPAI systems, such as articles 5, 52, 53 and 69, the core requirements and obligations that these systems must comply with are defined in article 4b. It is presumed that GPAI systems have a high-risk use if they possess such capability unless the provider explicitly excludes all high-risk uses in the instructions or information related to the GPI system.

Therefore, unless the GPAI system is prohibited (article 5) or cannot be used in a high-risk manner or as a component of a high-risk AI system, or if its high-risk uses have been excluded by the provider, it must meet certain requirements (title III, Chap. 2) which will be described in a future implementing act (article 4b (1)).

AIA draft adopts a risk-based approach, which classifies risk based on the "intended purpose" for which the GPAI system was developed. However, this type of approach presents certain difficulties.

One issue is that by focusing on regulating specific uses of AI and disregarding the underlying foundation models, a loophole is created for GPAI systems [34, p. 369]. There can also be a discrepancy between the indicated purpose of an AI system and its actual purpose, as it may be used for different purposes that originally intended. A key characteristic of GPAI models is precisely their lack of a specific intended purpose. Consequently, the risk classification should consider "foreseeable purpose(s)" [13, p. 3, 33, p. 67]. In such cases, the provider of a GPAI should explicitly state those purposes

---

[19] Engler and Renda [12] consider that the division of responsibility should be based on the "cheapest cost avoider". This means that we should analyze which entity is best positioned to identify and mitigate risks at the moment they are most easily identifiable.

during the conformity assessment.[20] Finally, if a GPAI is designed to perform multiple tasks without a specific intended purpose, it could potentially be used for any high-risk application.[21]

As it stands, two options become evident: (i) identify and map all foreseeable uses and only apply the requirements if a high-risk purpose is identified, or (ii) consider that a high-risk purpose could be implicit, leading to the application of requirements to all GPAI systems.

In practice, it is likely that users, rather than providers, will determine the uses of GPAIs. Consequently, it appears that all GPAIs could fall under this category since, as base models, they can be utilized as high-risk AI systems or a components of AI high-risk system. If a GPAI lacks an intended purpose and the provider does not exclude a high-risk usage, then it *may be* employed in high-risk applications. Otherwise, we would be left with an ineffective risk-based approach.

Regarding "Foundational Models", one possible solution is to establish limits from the beginning, considering that they could be utilized for such purposes at any time. However, this approach risks over-regulating GPAI models [19, p. 3], as it would mean applying specific requirements to all GPAI models. To address this, Helberger and Diakopoulos [19] propose a new approach to regulating these models: a general-risk category. This may have been the intention behind the wording of a specific title for the regulation of these models, but its interpretation remains unclear [2].

As previously mentioned, GPAI systems are required to fulfill certain requirements (article 4b (1)) and impose specific obligations on providers (article 4b (2–6)), although not all of these requirements are clearly defined.

For instance, when examining the obligations outlined in Chap. 2, Title II, which will be further specified in future implementing acts based on the "characteristics, technical feasibility, specificities of the AI value chain and market and technological developments", there is a possibility of unforeseen risks that have not been taken into account, often referred to as "black swan" risks.

Given the potential risks associated with GPAI systems, particularly those with significant economic and social impact, it is important to approach the establishment of specific requirements for these systems with caution. The purpose of these requirements should be to act as preventive measures against risks, which should be assessed based on both the potential uses of such systems and the possibilities of misuse. This depends on the fulfilment of a prior obligation of analysis of the misuses. However, it is important to note that we can only reasonably foresee certain risks [15, p. 6] and not all potential risks.

Requirements such as the risk management (article 4b (6), article 9(2)) and ensuring performance, robustness, and cybersecurity (article 15(1)) of these models should be based on reasonably foreseeable risks rather than being overly stringent, as exhaustively addressing all risks may be unviable or impossible. It may be preferable to identify specific sensitive scenarios that require scrutiny. However, certain requirements will likely necessitate ongoing monitoring to keep up with evolving developments.

---

[20] Another problem is who, and when, should label an AI system as high-risk [33, pp. 67–68].

[21] Engler and Renda [12, pp. 20–21] consider that all GPAI systems would trigger these requirements.

Regarding conformity assessment procedures before deploying GPAI systems in the market or putting them into service (article 4b (2–3), article 16 (e)), multi-purpose systems raise some questions. Conducting separate conformity assessments for each possible use could be expensive or even impossible, especially if the creator is unaware of all downstream uses. One possible solution could involve imposing a duty on providers to indicate the foreseen uses of the model at the time of its creation and to distinguish between safe and unsafe uses.[22] Based on this information, providers could then recommend measures to mitigate risks associated with downstream applications in domains they consider safe.

Lastly, it is worth noting that article 4b (2) does not explicitly mention all the obligations outlined in article 16, omitting obligations such as keeping automatically generated logs by an AI (article 16d) or informing the relevant national competent authority in case of adopting corrective actions (article 16h). The reason for these omissions while including other obligations remains unclear.

2.2 Key Elements: Value Chain and Cooperation

One of the issues with the draft regulation is the uncertainty surrounding the responsibility for complying with the requirements of a GPAI system. If a provider makes significant modifications to a high-risk system, they should be subject to obligations (article 3(23), article 23a (1c)) while the upstream provider would not have these obligations (article 23 a (3)).

According to Engler and Renda [12, p. 18], GPAI models typically require retraining and fine-tuning, which qualifies as a substantial modification. This leads to differing responsibilities. Kolt [20, p. 33] expresses concern about the allocation of responsibilities in the new Draft, as it assigns responsibilities to entities with fewer resources and ability to mitigate risks, while exempting organizations with greater resources and expertise— the creators. Big tech suppliers play a crucial role in this context, as they possess technical control and better resources to understand, modify and test the models [10, p. 10].

Policymakers should differentiate between the various entities involved in order to establish different obligations. Hacker et al. [18] suggests that four entities—developers (providers), deployers (users or providers), users (professional or non-professional) and recipients—should have different responsibilities. Some requirements apply universally to all AI systems and must be met from the beginning of the lifecycle, while others depend on the specific use of AI. In the former case, the requirements should be imposed on developers—e.g., developers should comply with non-discrimination laws and data governance. In the latter cases, the requirements should be tailored to those who deploy and use such models—e.g. risk management should be the responsibility of deployers, taking into account the specific use.

The contractual relationship between the provider and user is a crucial factor in allocating responsibilities. However, it also has the potential to create power imbalances. To promote fairness and cooperation among actors, Helberger and Diakopoulos [19,

---

[22] Similar to [12, p. 27]. They propose the adoption of a code of conduct created by the initial providers.

p. 5] suggest adopting mechanisms for regulatory scrutiny of contractual terms[23]. While this may be a suitable solution, there should be a greater balance in the distribution of obligations, fostering an environment of cooperation throughout the lifecycle of these systems. Users also have obligations in this regard and must publicly declare their use of such tools for professional purposes.

Understanding the lifecycle of these systems is essential in clarifying the responsibilities of the different actors based on the various components of the process, the actors involved in the value chain, the level of control (including downstream provider access)[24] and technological capabilities to "ensure a fair sharing of responsibilities along the AI value chain" (recital 12c). However, the new regulation may potentially exempt everyone from responsibility, as it excludes this obligation for small and medium-sized enterprises (article 55a (3)).

Companies with advanced technology can easily make technological adjustments to comply with AIA requirements and, in fact, some requirements—e.g., transparency—need to be observed from the early stages of development [18, p. 9].

The level of technical knowledge about the model will also be relevant: It is different (i) when downstream providers have limited access to the AI system without knowledge of the technical details, compared to (ii) having total access to the model and technical documentation. In the former case, continuous cooperation between the provider and downstream developer is required, expanding the responsibility of the upstream provider to control access and prevent misuse. In the latter case, the prevention of misuse should be addressed through contractual stipulations in advance.

This could lead us to another discussion about the release and research access of the models that has been ongoing[25]. If the models were not released, the risk would be better contained, but with public access, there is a better understanding of the risks, while it allows for algorithms' auditing by third parties [22]. Structured access [36] or the existence of a review board ([22] are solutions that deserve some thought.

Regulators also need to give special thought to open-source models. It is true that public access can improve innovation and promote cross-examination of the source code which can be valuable towards ethical AI [11][26], but on the other hand, it makes risk control incredibly difficult [37, p. 4] and creates more opportunities for malicious uses and cyberattacks.

The responsibility of providers could be different according to the release procedure and option for the AI. Limited access potentially blocks or diminishes high-risk or out-of-scope uses, although there are loopholes, as mentioned by Solaiman [37, p. 5], because users can share access with unauthorized users. These can be seen a kind of know-your-customer approach. In this case, the developers can limit who will use their models and define how they can be used, confirming this periodically.

---

[23] That seems to be the intention with the proposed article 28a of the draft regulation adopted by the European Parliament on 14 June 2023.

[24] This is more complex because there will be different relations between providers and different levels of control of the system according to the strategy adopted to distribute the GPAI [21].

[25] For example, see [31, 35, 38].

[26] Otherwise, we could have a concentrated power of organizations [37, p. 3].

Considering the downstream use of the GPAI on high-risk systems, the *cooperation* between providers was considered a key element of regulation. Article 4b (5) determine that providers should provide "necessary information to other providers intending to put into service or place such systems on the Union market as high-risk AI systems or as a component of high-risk AI systems" for the latter to meet the requirements.

This legal basis of cooperation encourages cooperation between providers, especially if a GPAI will be used for a specific high-risk purpose. The Commission should adopt an implementing Act to define what is "necessary information". At least, the provider should be obligated to provide information—but also instruction—about the safety of the system.

This cooperation is essential because we are faced with a paradigm shift in relations among providers and users that is characterized by the *interdependence* between upstream and downstream providers.

Trade secrets or IP rights must be protected, which has led some authors to propose the adoption of protective measures such as nondisclosure agreements or access to the information under certain conditions [18, p. 10]. Protective measures are essential to encourage cooperation.

However, this obligation occurs only at an initial stage—"to put into service or place such systems on the Union market". Nevertheless, this obligation should not be limited to that moment but should also be extended to allow for continuous cooperation and monitoring of the system to mitigate its risks [12, p. 26]. Therefore, this obligation must be complemented by the requirement for periodic and regular mandatory assessment on the risks of the system, including potential new uses.

2.3 Exemptions

The obligations established on article 4b are not applied if the provider "has explicitly **excluded** all high-risk uses in the instructions of use or information accompanying" (article 4c (1)). However, if providers consider that there may be misuse, the requirements established on article 4b apply (article 4c (2)). If the providers are aware—whether detected or informed—of any misuse, they should adopt measures to prevent further misuse (article 4c (3)).

It is difficult for providers to rely on the exception stated on article 4c (1), at least in good faith. Unless a provider is technically able to exclude high-risk use, the myriad of uses of a GPAI system means that it *may be* used for high-risk purposes [18, p. 5], and thus the obligations are applicable (article 4c (2)).

The "notice-and-action mechanism" aligns with the post-monitoring of obligation (Title VIII, Chap. 1). Periodical risk monitoring assessments must be mandatory—similar to systemic risk monitoring approach outlined in article 34 of the Digital Services Act [19, p. 4]. Additionally, other *ex post* measures should be considered, such as technical measures—*e.g.*, providers could disable access to certain users through APIs [12, p. 21] (although not applicable in the case of open-source).

Additionally, according to article 55a (3), these requirements and obligations do not apply to micro, small and medium-sized enterprises. However, this raises the question: if the objective of the AIA is to regulate technology that could have high impact, should SMEs be excluded from its scope? If SMEs wish to create GPAI systems, shouldn't they follow the same set of requirements and obligations, at least to some extent? The argument that compliance with the AIA's requirements and obligations might prove to be burdensome for SMEs, but a solution could be found either in government support to the companies with fewer resources or by establishing a simplified set of requirements and obligations.

3 Conclusions

GPAI in an expanding branch of AI. The development of GPAI systems is a prominent trend that needs to be regulated, taking into account their features and the complexity of the value chain. These increasingly powerful systems are multi-purpose and can be applied to tasks they were not initially trained for.

As mentioned, we can identify the potential risks and adopt some strategies to mitigate them. However, not all risks and harms can be anticipated from the beginning since it can be challenging or even impossible to predict all the uses. Therefore, the regulations should encompass the entire lifecycle of AI.

In case of a high-risk use, the requirements should align with those specified in Title III. The final model intended for high-risk purposes should have specific requirements regardless of the AI system used, but these requirements may need to be adapted through implementing acts. Other GPAI systems, that do not have a specific high-risk purpose but may adopt one, should have certain requirements and obligations based on their specific characteristics—a specific-risk approach.

However, the distinction between providers/developers and users/deployers does not neatly apply to these systems. In fact, there can be intermediate entities who adapt or fine-tune the model. As a result, the relationship between actors is more complex, as is the lifecycle of these systems.

Damages can arise during the entire lifecycle of AI, from the upstream development to concrete application. There has to be a balanced distribution of responsibilities, ensuring a fair and clear allocation. Some issues may arise from the very beginning, at the source of value chain. Therefore, at the very least, a fundamental rights assessment should be required, taking into consideration vulnerable groups, potential misuses and the need for upstream providers to address problems discovered downstream.

The AI Act may slow down the development of AI [23] but will not impede innovation. Instead of merely balancing innovation and trustworthiness or fearing new developments, the focus should be on the type of AI that we desire.

Regulation will govern the future of increasingly important systems. However, to avoid stifling innovation and to encourage cooperation, regulations should be proportionate and tailored to the nature of the sector and the stage of technological development. In this regard, regulators may seek the involvement of technology experts and companies operating in these emerging sectors to help develop more precise and suitable regulations. Therefore, a collaborative environment among different actors—companies, regulator, and other stakeholders—will foster responsible innovation and ensure a safe and ethical development of new technologies.

Acknowlegments. The work of Nídia Andrade Moreira has been supported by FCT—Fundação para a Ciência e Tecnologia within the Grant 2021.07986.BD and the Project UIDB/04859/2020.

The work of Paulo Novais has been supported by FCT—Fundação para a Ciência e Tecnologia within the R&D Units Project Scope: UIDB/00319/2020.

References

1. ALLAI. AIA in-depth. Objective, scope, definition. Articles 1–4 & Annex I. (2022)
2. Bertuzzi, L.: AI Act: EU Parliament's crunch time on high-risl categorization, prohibited practices. (2023). https://www.euractiv.com/section/artificial-intelligence/news/ai-act-eu-parliaments-crunch-time-on-high-risk-categorisation-prohibited-practices/. Last accessed 23 April 2023
3. Biddle, S.: The internet's new favorite AI proposes torturing Iranians and surveilling mosques, The Intercept. (2022). https://theintercept.com/2022/12/08/openai-chatgpt-ai-bias-ethics/. Last accessed 02 April 2023
4. Bommasani et al.: On the opportunities and risks of foundation models. (2022). https://arxiv.org/abs/2108.07258
5. Brittain, B.: Lawsuits accuse AI content creators of misusing copyrighted work. Reuters. (2023). https://www.reuters.com/legal/transactional/lawsuits-accuse-ai-content-creators-misusing-copyrighted-work-2023-01-17/. Last accessed 02 April 2023
6. Brown, T., et al.: A. Language models are few-shot learners. Adv. Neural Inf. Process. Syst., **33**,1877–1901 (2020)
7. Buchanan, B., et al.: Lies and automation. How language models could change disinformation. (2021)
8. Cai, L., Zhu, Y.: The challenges of data quality and data quality assessment in the big data era. Data Sci. J. **14**(2), 1 (2015). https://doi.org/10.5334/dsj-2015-002
9. Dhirani, L.L., et al.: Ethical dilemmas and privacy issues in emerging technologies: a review. Sensors **23**(3), 1151 (2023). https://doi.org/10.3390/s23031151
10. Edwards, L.: Regulating AI in Europe: four problems and four solutions. Expert Opinion. Ada Lovelace Institute, (2022)
11. Engler, A.: How open-source software shapes AI policy. Report from The Brookings Institution's Artificial Intelligence and Emerging Technology. (2021)
12. Engler, A.C., Renda, A.: CEPS in-depth analysis. Reconciling the AI value chain with the EU's artificial intelligence Act. (2022)
13. European Consumer Voice in Standardization (ANEC). ANEC comments the European Commission proposal for an Artificial Intelligence Act. Position Paper. (2021)
14. Europol. ChatGPT. The impact of large language models on law enforcement. (2023)
15. Future of Life Institute. General Purpose AI and the AI Act. (2022)
16. Genesis.studio.: GPJ—A implementação do chatGPT para o Ministério da Justiça pelo genesis.stiduo. (2023). https://genesis.studio/gpj-a-implementacao-do-chatgpt-para-o-ministerio-da-justica-pela-genesis-studio/. Last accessed 02 April 2023
17. Gutierrez, C.I., et al.: A proposal for a definition of general purpose artificial intelligence systems. (2022)
18. Hacker, P., Engel, A., Mauer, M.: Regulating ChatGPT and other large generative AI models. Working Paper (version April 5, 2023). Avaliable at https://arxiv.org/abs/2302.02337
19. Helberger, N., Diakopoulos, N.: ChatGPT and the AI Act. Internet Policy Rev., **12** (1), (2023)
20. Kolt, N.: Algorithmic black swans. Washington University Law Review, vol. 101, Forthcoming. (2023). Available at SSRN: https://ssrn.com/abstract=4370566
21. Küspert , S., Moës, N., Dunlop, C.: Ada Lovelace Institute Blog The value chain of general-purpose AI. (2023)

22. Liang, P., Bommasani, R., Creel, K., Reich, R.: The time is now to develop community norms for the release of foundation models. Stanford University Human-Centered Intelligence, (2022)
23. Liebl, A., Klein, T.: AI act impact survey. Exploring the impact of the AI Act on Startups in Europe. (2022)
24. Lim, R, Wu, M., Miller, L.: Customizing GPT-3 for your application. OpenAI. (2021). https://openai.com/blog/customizing-gpt-3. Last accessed 02 April 2023
25. Madiega, T.: General-purpose artificial intelligence. Digital issues in focus at a glance. European Parliamentary Research Service, (2023)
26. Moura, J., Serrão, C.: Security and privacy issues of big data. In: I. Management Association (ed.) Cloud security: concepts, methodologies, tools, and applications, pp. 1598–1630. IGI Global, (2019). https://doi.org/10.4018/978-1-5225-8176-5.ch080
27. Nadeem, M., Bethke, A., Reddy, S.: StereoSet: Measuring stereotypical bias in pretrained language models. arXiv preprint arXiv:2004.09456. (2020)
28. Noy, S., Zhang, W.: Experimental evidence on the productivity effects of generative artificial intelligence. (2023)
29. OpenAI.GPT-4 System Card (2023). https://cdn.openai.com/papers/gpt-4-system-card.pdf
30. OpenAI. GPT-4 Technical Report (2023). https://arxiv.org/pdf/2303.08774.pdf
31. Ovadya, A., Whittlestone, J.: Reducing malicious use of synthetic media research: Considerations and potential release practices for machine learning. arXiv preprint arXiv:1907.11274. (2019)
32. Perrigo, B.: OpenAI used kenyan workers on less than $2 per hour to make ChatGPT less toxic, TIME (2023). https://time.com/6247678/openai-chatgpt-kenya-workers/. Last accessed 02 April 2023
33. Raposo, V.L.: The European draft regulation on artificial intelligence: houston, we have a problem. In: Marreiros, G., Martins, et al.. (eds.) Progress in artificial intelligence. EPIA 2022. Lecture Notes in Computer Science, vol 13566. Springer, Cham (2022)
34. Ruschemeier, H.: AI as a challenge for legal regulation—the scope of application of the artificial intelligence act proposal. Era Forum. **23**, 361–376 (2023)
35. Sastry, G.: Beyond "release" versus "not release". (2021). https://crfm.stanford.edu/commentary/2021/10/18/sastry.html. Last accessed 03 April 2023
36. Shevlane, T.: Structured access: An emerging paradigm for safe AI deployment. In: Justin B. Bullock and others (eds.) The Oxford Handbook of AI Governance. (2022)
37. Solaiman, I.: The gradient of generative AI release: Methods and considerations. (2023)
38. Staff, P.: Managing the risks of AI research: Six recommendations for responsible publication. (2021)
39. Taddeo, M., Tsamados, A., Cowls, J., Floridi, L.: Artificial intelligence and the climate emergency: Opportunities, challenges, and recommendations. One Earth **4**(6), 776–779 (2021)
40. Weidinger, L. et al.: Ethical and social risks of harm from language models. (2021)
41. Zhao, Z., et al.: Calibrate before use: Improving few-shot performance of language models. In: Proceedings of the 38th international conference on machine learning, PMLR, vol 139, pp. 12697–12706. (2021)

Rule-Based System for Intelligent Energy Management in Buildings

Aria Jozi, Tiago Pinto(✉), Luis Gomes, Goreti Marreiros, and Zita Vale

School of Engineering, GECAD–Research Group on Intelligent Engineering and Computing for Advanced Innovation and Development, Polytechnic of Porto, Porto, Portugal
tcp@isep.ipp.pt

Abstract. The widespread of distributed renewable energy is leading to an increased need for advanced energy management solutions in buildings. The variability of generation needs to be balanced by consumer flexibility, which needs to be accomplished by keeping the consumption cost as low as possible, while guaranteeing consumer comfort. This paper proposes a rule-based system with the aim of generating recommendations for actions regarding the energy management of different energy consumption devices, namely lights and air conditioning. The proposed set of rules considers the forecasted values of building generation, consumption, user presence in different rooms and energy prices. In this way, building energy management systems are endowed with increased adaptability and reliability considering the lowering of energy costs and maintenance of user comfort. Results, using real data from an office building, demonstrate the appropriateness of the proposed model in generating recommendations that are in line with current context.

Keywords: Building energy management · Consumer comfort · Intelligent energy systems · Rule-based systems

1 Introduction

Buildings account for a substantial part of the energy consumption, and it is where people spend most of their time, whether for housing, working or leisure. Due to the relationship between productivity and comfort at work, the operation costs of an office building are directly linked to the workers' income [1]. In this sense, energy consumption and the conditions of environmental comfort are, in most cases, in conflict with each other. Smart building is, therefore, a pivotal technology to contribute to improving social wellbeing and economic growth while at the same time, reduce fossil fuels dependence and the emissions footprint [2].

To attain those goals, smart buildings require not only adequate hardware but also efficient computational tools [3]. Artificial intelligence can play a significant role in this sense by introducing learning capabilities and real-time consumption control [4]. Some recent studies advocate the use of advanced learning techniques, such as case-based reasoning (CBR) to predict patterns and energy consumption in smart buildings [5, 6]. In [7]

N. Moniz et al. (Eds.): EPIA 2023, LNAI 14116, pp. 169–181, 2023.
https://doi.org/10.1007/978-3-031-49011-8_14

a novel Case-Based Reasoning (CBR) application for intelligent management of energy resources in residential buildings has been proposed. Satisfactory results are obtained without compromising the comfort of the users. The work in [8] develops a practical data mining approach using the data from power consuming appliance of an office to learn the occupant "passive" behavior. The consumption of heating, ventilation, and air conditioning is studied. Results capture diversified individual behavior in using office appliances. In [9], authors propose an innovative method to manage the appliances on the house during a demand response event. The main contribution of this work is to include time constraints in resources management, and the context evaluation to ensure the required comfort levels. The study in [10], presents an agent-based home energy management approach, using ontologies to enable semantic communications between heterogeneous multi-agent entities. In [11] an intelligent decision support model using rulesets has been proposed for a typical building energy management system. These works show that energy system in the building can be complex, depending on the types of building and of energy consumers [12]. Additionally, the variety of consumption devices requires the consideration of many different factors to have a clear and trustable recognition analysis of the consumption behavior on the building. Moreover, the limitation of the available data made it difficult for this kind of systems to create a suitable adaptation of the consumption profile which considers all the important aspects of the market and corresponds to all of the needs and comforts of the users [13].

Consequently, this work proposes a rule-based model that generates recommendations regarding the consumption of different devices, based on different types of information collected from the target building. In this way, the actions to be performed by an intelligent building energy management system can be adapted to control the usage of energy consuming appliances according to the demand and generation variations, the user comfort, and the variation of market prices [14].

After this introductory section, Sect. 2 describes the proposed solution, and Sect. 3 presents the achieved results. Finally, Sect. 4 finalizes the paper with the most relevant conclusions.

2 Proposed Model

This paper presents a set of statistical rules that have been created to make recommendations about the energy consumption appliances of a building. These rulesets are integrated with an intelligent energy management system for a building which considers the comforts and habits of the residents as well as the energy consumption cost of the building [14]. This system acts as a recommender system to comply with the comforts of the residents with the minimum consumption cost. In this way, a set of data preparation and data mining techniques is used to reach the necessary estimation values. The predicted data is then sent to the proposed rulesets to achieve the final recommendations. Figure 1 presents a general perspective of this sequence.

In order to achieve the desired recommendations, the necessary data is received, cleaned, aggregated and finally used for the required forecasting processes (generation, consumption, presence in each room, electricity market prices). These forecasts are then used by the rulesets that manage the air conditioning devices and lights of a building.

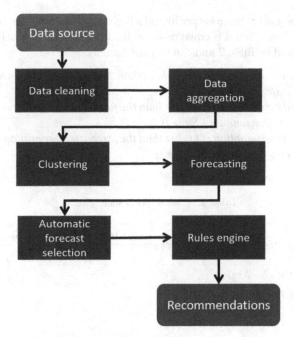

Fig. 1. General process of the recommendations

2.1 Power Consumption State Ruleset

The power consumption state of the building is a relative variable that represents the feasibility of the building to consume more energy. This variable is corresponding to the estimated consumption and generation of the building during the next period and the current electricity price. When this value is higher, it means that at the moment an additional consumption has a higher cost. Table 1 presents the input variables of this ruleset.

Table 1. Input variables for power consumption state ruleset

Variable	Description
Consumption forecast (CF)	Forecasted power consumption in the building during the next time period
Generation forecast (GF)	Forecasted power generation in the building during the next time period
Current price (CP)	Current electricity market price received from
Average price (AvgP)	Daily average electricity market price received from

The electricity market price is considered a high price when it is more than the daily average price and low when it is equal or lower than the average price. The rules of this ruleset are presented in Table 2 and can be explained as:

- *If the forecasted generation is higher than the forecasted consumption, then Consumption State is 1.*
- *If the forecasted consumption is higher than the forecasted generation and the current price is low, then Consumption State is 2.*
- *If the forecasted consumption is higher than the forecasted generation and the current price is high, then Consumption State is 3.*

Table 2. Consumption state ruleset

Conditions	Consumption state (CS)
(GC > FC)	1
(GC < = FC) & (CP < = AvgP)	2
(GC < = FC) & (CP > AvgP)	3

Based on the created rules the consumption state of the building is selected at each moment. This value will be used in the other rulesets to calculate the comfort radius in the case of any device.

2.2 Air Conditioning System Ruleset

For the air conditioning (AC) ruleset the objective is to recommend the state of the AC (ON or OFF) for the next period. The system first needs to predict the activity in the rooms and the ideal temperature for the users during the upcoming period. These values are predicted by the previous phases of the system, using the historical data of the room. Table 3 presents the list of the input variable for this ruleset.

The first step is to calculate the Temperature Comfort Interval (TCI). This interval presents the temperature values that the system recommends as the ideal temperature. This interval is based on the predicted ideal temperature, Consumption State of the building and TCR value, which is considered as 1 °C. When the cost of additional consumption in the building is high, the TCI must be a larger interval. So, the possibility of recommending to turning on the AC will increase. Equation (1) calculates the TCI.

$$TCI = [FT - (TCR * CS), FT + (TCR * CS)] \tag{1}$$

Figure 2 shows the TCI for different values for Consumption State.

After detecting the Temperature Comfort Interval, the system uses the following rules to make the recommendation.

- *If the forecasted activity is NO, then the AC state should be "OFF".*
- *If the forecasted activity is YES and the current temperature is in temperature comfort interval, then the AC state should be "OFF".*

Table 3. List of input variables for AC ruleset

Variable	Description
Consumption state (CS)	The power consumption state of the building calculated by Consumption State ruleset
Forecasted activity (Act)	The forecasted activity in the room for the next time interval. It is a YES or NO value
Forecasted ideal temperature (FT)	The forecasted ideal temperature for the users in the next period
Current temperature (CT)	The current temperature of the room
Temperature comfort basis rate (TCR)	Basis rate at which the temperature comfort interval will be varied
Temperature comfort interval (TCI)	The Temperature value interval that the system recognizes as the comfort temperature for the users

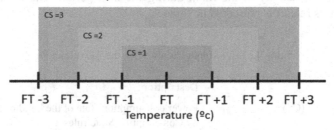

Fig. 2. Temperature comfort Interval in case of every consumption state

- *If the forecasted activity is YES and the current temperature is NOT in temperature comfort Interval, then the AC state should be "ON".*

Figure 3 presents the decision tree that represents these rules.

Based on these rules the system only recommends turning on the AC when the current temperature of the room is not in the TCI. In the end, the final recommended AC state, Ideal Temperature (FT), Maximum and Minimum value of TCI will be inserted into the Result DB and available to be activated.

2.3   Brightness Ruleset

As same as the AC ruleset, the objective of the brightness ruleset is to recommend the state of the lights in the building or rooms. For this ruleset, it has been considered that the intensity of the lights in the target building is controllable, and the residents are able to select the intensity of the light between 0 and 100%. Therefore, the recommendations for the intensity of the lights will recommend one of possible four states: OFF, REDUCE, KEEP and INCREASE. Before executing this ruleset there are a set of variables that must be generated by the forecasting component of the system such as estimated ideal

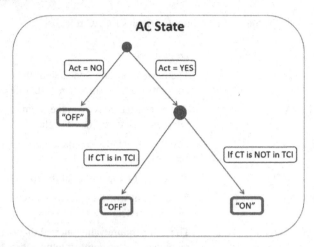

Fig. 3. AC ruleset decision tree

brightness and the activity of the room during the next period. The list of all input variables for this ruleset is presented in Table 4.

Table 4. List of input variables for the AC ruleset

Variable	Description
Consumption State (CS)	Power consumption state of the building calculated by Consumption State ruleset
Forecasted Activity (Act)	Forecasted activity in the room for the next time interval. It is a YES or NO value
Forecasted ideal Brightness (FB)	Forecasted ideal brightness in the room during next time period
Current Brightness (CB)	Current brightness in the room
Brightness Comfort basis Rate (BCR)	Basis rate at which the brightness comfort interval will be varied
Brightness Comfort Interval (BCI)	Brightness percentage interval that the system recognizes as the comfort percentage for the users

The Brightness Comfort Interval (BCI) calculation in this ruleset uses the same approach as the AC ruleset to calculate the minimum value. However, when considering the maximum value, the ideal forecasted brightness is always considered. This occurs because, if the current brightness is higher than the ideal brightness and even if the generation of the building is more than its consumption and the power consumption cost of the building is zero, there is no reason to consume energy to have this higher brightness; so the light intensity of the room should be reduced. Consumption State (CS) of the building is used to calculate the minimum value of this interval as well as the

Brightness Comfort Rate (BCR) which is considered as 5%. BCI calculation formula is as presented in (2).

$$BCI = [FB - (BCR * CS), FB]$$ (2)

The possible BCIs for different consumption states is shown in Fig. 4.

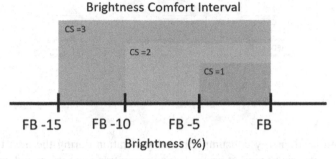

Brightness Comfort Interval

Fig. 4. Brightness comfort interval in case of every consumption state

The following step is to use the calculated BCI to run the rules and find the best state for the Lights. The following rules have been created for this purpose.

- *If the forecasted activity is NO, then the state of the lights should be "OFF".*
- *If the forecasted activity is YES and the current brightness value is higher than the maximum value of Brightness Comfort Interval, then the state of the lights should be "REDUCE".*
- *If the forecasted activity is YES and the current brightness value is the Brightness Comfort Interval, then the state of the lights should be "KEEP".*
- *If the forecasted activity is YES and the current brightness value is lower than the minimum value of Brightness Comfort Interval, then the state of the lights should be "INCREASE".*

Figure 5 presents the decision tree that leads to these rules.

3   Rulesets Evaluation

In this section, the generated recommendations by the system are discussed. These recommendations are created based on three rules sets: Consumption state, Air conditioning system and Brightness ruleset. The three following sections present the recommended actions by these rulesets and the rationale behind them. All used data regards an office building, being focused on a specific office. Details on the used data and on the system in which these rulesets have been incorporated can be found in [14].

3.1   Consumption State Ruleset

The Consumption State ruleset has been created to indicate a number between 1, 2 or 3 which presents the state of the energy consumption in the building. This value is

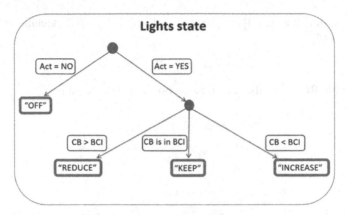

Fig. 5. Brightness ruleset decision tree

relative to estimated energy consumption and generation during the next time period and the current electricity market price. The consumption state value and consumption cost of the building are directly related, a higher consumption state value means a higher consumption cost for the building. To evaluate the results of this rule set Fig. 6 presents the obtained consumption state values by this ruleset as well as the electricity market price during 11/6/2019.

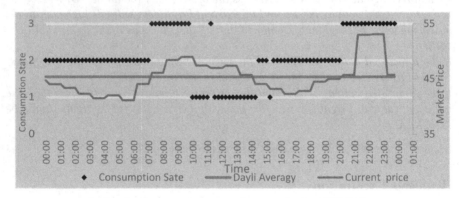

Fig. 6. Consumption state ruleset results for 11/6/2019

During the initial hours of the day as the market price is lower than the daily average, the CS is 2. Form the 7:00 to 14:00 the market price is above the average and the CS should be 3. But in another hand from 10:00 to 14:00 the estimated generation is higher than the estimated consumption and that is the reason why the CS is 1 during these hours. For the rest of the day the estimated consumption is always higher than the estimated generation, so the CS is 2 while the price is less than the average and 3 when its higher.

3.2   Brightness Ruleset Case Study

The objective of the Brightness ruleset is to recommend the state of the lights for the next period which in this case study is next 15 min. The state of the lights should be selected between four options: OFF, REDUCE, KEEP and INCREASE. To evaluate the performance of this ruleset, Fig. 7 presents the recorded recommendations for lights during 24 h of 11/6/2019, registered in the database of the system.

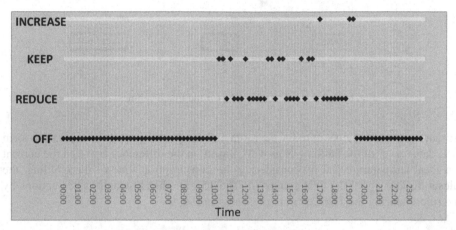

Fig. 7. Brightness ruleset results for 11/6/2019

As can be seen in the presented results, the recommendations during the night until 10:15 are all "OFF" because the system predicts no activity for these hours, which is correct. As it is an office room usually everyone come to work between 10:00 and 10:30 and that is the reason that from 10:15 the system recommends turning on the lights. The commands KEEP, REDUCE and INCREASE are recommended when the lights are on or should be turned on. During the working hours, the system mostly recommends reducing the lights because the ideal forecasted brightness is less than the current brightness. As these recommendations are not being activated in the room, the situation stays the same for the next periods. If after the first REDUCE command the lights had been reduced, the next recommendations would be KEEP.

For illustrative purposes, let's take a look at one specific moment in time, namely time 14:00. In this case, the current brightness is 62.9%, being lower than the predicted ideal brightness, which is of 61.99%. Even though the consumption state is 1 and the generation of the building is more than its consumption, the system recommends to reduce the intensity of the lights to cut the unnecessary extra consumption. Figure 8 presents the lights state decision tree for this case.

3.3   Air Conditioning System Ruleset Case Study

The goal of this ruleset is to recommend the state of the AC system of the room which can be selected between two options: "OFF" and "ON". For this objective, the system

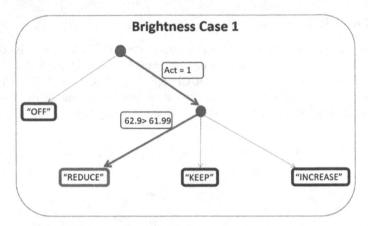

Fig. 8. lights state decision tree for the first brightness case

estimates the ideal temperature for the room and receives the current temperature form SQL data server of the building N as well. Based on the difference between the current and ideal temperature and by considering the consumption state of the building, the ruleset decides about the final command. The 15 min ahead recommended actions by this ruleset during the 11/6/2019 are presented in Fig. 9.

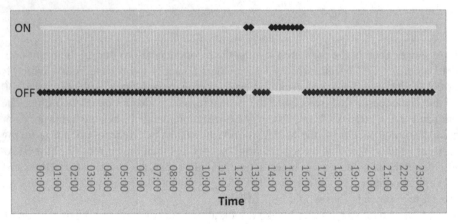

Fig. 9. AC ruleset results for 11/6/2019

During the night, the system prediction for activity in the room is zero activity, and the recommendation for AC state is always OFF when there is no activity in the room. As this is an office room, the activity hours in this room are usually from 10:00 to 19:00. During these hours the system calculates the difference between the ideal and current temperature, and if this difference is more than 1*consumption state value, the system recommendation will be "ON". Otherwise, it will be "OFF".

Figure 10 presents the AC state decision tree for the specific case of time 11:15. IN this case the current temperature is 24.7 °C, and the ideal predicted temperature is

22.64 °C. The difference between these two values is 2.06. The consumption state for this period is 3, which means that the consumption of the building is more than its generation and the electricity market price is high. So, the usage of the AC system has a high cost at this moment. In such a situation, the system only recommends using the AC, if the difference between the current and ideal temperature is more than 3. In this case, as this difference is 2.06, the recommendation for AC state is "OFF".

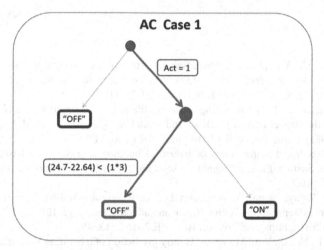

Fig. 10. AC state decision tree for case 1

4 Conclusions

Energy management systems for different types of building are becoming one of the most relevant topics in power and energy systems. However, only a few studies consider taking advantage of intelligent techniques to control the consumption of the building in order to meet the comfort and demand of the building users. This work proposed an intelligent rule-based system that enables buildings energy management systems to adapt the functionality of the electrical appliances of the building according to the comforts and habits of the users while considering the consumption cost of every action.

The presented results demonstrate that the designed rulesets can create rational recommendations based on the forecasted values by the system and current state of the consumption. According to the presented case studies and analyses, the system has achieved its goal. The implemented system is able to recognize the comfort and habits of the residents of the building and it is able to act according to their comfort within acceptable margins. Based on this recognized comfort, the system generates recommendations that consider the cost of the possible actions and recommends the best and affordable actions for the upcoming period.

As future work, the contextualization capabilities of the rule-based system will be improved, by adding additional adaptation capabilities by identifying different contextual situations (e.g. seasonality, different combinations of users present in the same room. Moreover, the adaptability of the system regarding upcoming situations will be improved, considering the continuous adaptation to the predicted presence of users in the upcoming time periods.

Acknowledgments. The authors acknowledge the work facilities and equipment provided by GECAD research center (UIDB/00760/2020) to the project team.

References

1. Soares, N., et al.: A review on current advances in the energy and environmental performance of buildings towards a more sustainable built environment. Renew. Sustain. Energy Rev. **77**, 845–860 (2017). https://doi.org/10.1016/j.rser.2017.04.027
2. Saad, M.M., Eicker, U.: Investigating the reliability of building energy models: Comparative analysis of the impact of data pipelines and model complexities. J. Build. Engineering. **71**, 106511 (2023). https://doi.org/10.1016/j.jobe.2023.106511
3. Zhao, H.: Intelligent management of industrial building energy saving based on artificial intelligence. Sustain. Energy Technol. Assess. **56**, 103087 (2023). https://doi.org/10.1016/j.seta.2023.103087
4. Manic, M., Wijayasekara, D., Amarasinghe, K., Rodriguez-Andina, J.J.: Building energy management systems: the age of intelligent and adaptive buildings. IEEE Ind. Electron. Mag. **10**, 25–39 (2016). https://doi.org/10.1109/MIE.2015.2513749
5. Platon, R., Dehkordi, V.R., Martel, J.: Hourly prediction of a building's electricity consumption using case-based reasoning, artificial neural networks and principal component analysis. Energy Build. **92**, 10–18 (2015). https://doi.org/10.1016/j.enbuild.2015.01.047
6. Wang, Z., Srinivasan, R.S.: A review of artificial intelligence based building energy use prediction: Contrasting the capabilities of single and ensemble prediction models. Renew. Sustain. Energy Rev. **75**, 796–808 (2017). https://doi.org/10.1016/j.rser.2016.10.079
7. Corchado, J.M., Abrishambaf, O., Vale, Z., Fernandes, F., Pinto, T., Faia, R.: Case based reasoning with expert system and swarm intelligence to determine energy reduction in buildings energy management. Energy Build. **155**, 269–281 (2017). https://doi.org/10.1016/j.enbuild.2017.09.020
8. Zhao, J., Lasternas, B., Lam, K.P., Yun, R., Loftness, V.: Occupant behavior and schedule modeling for building energy simulation through office appliance power consumption data mining. Energy Build. **82**, 341–355 (2014). https://doi.org/10.1016/j.enbuild.2014.07.033
9. Fernandes, F., Morais, H., Vale, Z., Ramos, C.: Dynamic load management in a smart home to participate in demand response events. Energy Build. **82**, 592–606 (2014). https://doi.org/10.1016/j.enbuild.2014.07.067
10. Santos, G., Femandes, F., Pinto, T., Silva, M., Abrishambaf, O., Morais, H., Vale, Z.: House management system with real and virtual resources: Energy efficiency in residential microgrid. In: 2016 Global information infrastructure and networking symposium, GIIS 2016. (2017). https://doi.org/10.1109/GIIS.2016.7814943
11. Doukas, H., Patlitzianas, K.D., Iatropoulos, K., Psarras, J.: Intelligent building energy management system using rule sets. Build. Environ. **42**, 3562–3569 (2007). https://doi.org/10.1016/j.buildenv.2006.10.024
12. Jamil, M., Mittal, S.: Building energy management system: a review. In: 2017 14th IEEE India council international conference, INDICON 2017. (2017). https://doi.org/10.1109/INDICON.2017.8488004

13. Zhao, H.X., Magoulès, F.: A review on the prediction of building energy consumption. Renew. Sustain. Energy Rev. **16**, 3586–3592 (2012). https://doi.org/10.1016/j.rser.2012.02.049

14. Jozi, A., Pinto, T., Vale, Z.: Contextual learning for energy forecasting in buildings. Int. J. Electr. Power & Energy Syst. **136**, 107707 (2022). https://doi.org/10.1016/j.ijepes.2021.107707

Production Scheduling for Total Energy Cost and Machine Longevity Optimization Through a Genetic Algorithm

Bruno Mota[1,2] , Daniel Ramos[1,2] , Pedro Faria[1,2(✉)] , and Carlos Ramos[1,2]

[1] GECAD—Research Group on Intelligent Engineering and Computing for Advanced Innovation and Development, Rua Dr. António Bernardino de Almeida 431, 4200-072 Porto, Portugal
pnf@isep.ipp.pt

[2] Polytechnic of Porto, Rua Dr. António Bernardino de Almeida 431, 4200-072 Porto, Portugal

Abstract. With the remnants of a COVID-19 pandemic still crippling the European economy, and the Russo-Ukrainian war propagating this crisis even further, it has become more than crucial to invest in renewable energy resources to mitigate energy dependencies. As a result, these crises have lowered the competitiveness of European manufacturers when compared to the rest of the world. Nevertheless, machine longevity is also essential to consider in manufacturing environments, since maintenance costs due to poor load management can lead to considerable additional monetary costs in the long term. The premise of the present paper is to propose a production scheduling algorithm that focuses on optimizing the total energy costs and machine longevity in a flexible job shop manufacturing layout. To achieve this, a Genetic Algorithm is employed to shift tasks in order to reduce load during peak demand times, utilize locally generated energy to its potential, minimize single-machine task overload, and consider imposed constraints in the production schedule. To validate the proposed methodology, a case study from the literature that uses real-production data is explored and compared to the present paper's solution. Results show that the proposed methodology was capable of reducing single-machine task overload, that is, improving machine longevity, by 87.8%, while only increasing the energy costs, as a consequence, by 12.8%.

Keywords: Energy cost · Job shop · Machine longevity · Production scheduling optimization · Renewable energy resources

1 Introduction

The European economy is still suffering supply and energy price instability as a result of the COVID-19 epidemic and, more recently, the Russo-Ukrainian war, primarily in the manufacturing sector [1, 2]. As a result, many businesses have faced large rises in energy costs, which translates to higher production expenses [3]. These monetary expenditures consequently result in more expensive products, lowering the competitiveness of European manufacturing enterprises in the global market [4]. To address this issue, member states have begun to partake in Renewable Energy Resources (RER)s generation, by utilizing, for example, locally generated solar and wind energy, since member states that had a higher percentage of RER witnessed smaller energy price increases during the COVID-19 pandemic [1]. Additionally, RERs can substitute fossil fuels, contributing significantly to climate change mitigation [5]. These considerations have prompted the manufacturing sector to invest in more energy-efficient manufacturing systems, with the goal of not only reducing energy consumption in production lines, but also focusing on the most important component that keeps businesses running, monetary cost savings. These systems often employ load shifting, which focuses on shifting tasks (i.e., load) from peak demand to off-peak times in order to reduce total peak energy demand, thereby influencing the load curve and cutting energy costs while boosting dependability [6].

Nonetheless, the manufacturing sector is also struggling with other issues other than high retailer energy prices. An important challenge that manufacturers must also face is machine degradation, which can greatly impact the number of necessary maintenance activities on a machine. Adding to the fact that maintenance expenses can run anywhere from 15% to an astounding 70% of the cost of manufacturing a product, it is essential to improve machine longevity [7]. Intelligent production scheduling systems can enhance machine longevity through preventive maintenance by balancing production while taking equipment failure rates into account and single-machine task overload [8]. Accordingly, load shifting is essential for optimizing not only energy usage in manufacturing environments, through volatile retailer energy prices and locally generated RERs usage, but also to optimize machine longevity, in order to reduce the number of necessary maintenance activities to minimize additional monetary expenses in the long term.

2 Related Works

For load shifting energy cost and/or machine longevity optimization, there is a wide range of artificial intelligence algorithms that can be employed, such as Particle Swarm Optimization (PSO), Grey Wolf Optimizer (GWO) [9], Sub-gradient Descent (SD) [10], Reinforcement Learning (RL) [11], and the most popular, Genetic Algorithms (GA)s [12, 13]. Accordingly, a GA was chosen to be implemented as the solver in the present paper's proposed methodology. In addition, GAs are a well-studied metaheuristic search-based optimization algorithm that provides good solutions primarily in extensive and challenging search spaces, such as in the current problem.

With regards to works that have similar objectives to the present paper's, the work in [9] proposes an energy management system for household appliances that aims to minimize the total energy costs, by shifting appliances to lower electricity retailer price times, while also respecting imposed constraints. To achieve this, it implements and explores two swarm intelligence algorithms: a PSO and a GWO. Reference [10] also focuses on reducing energy costs, but in a manufacturing environment, by using a Primal-dual SD algorithm for load shifting. Complementing the previous work, it not only takes into account peak demand periods, which typically have high retailer electricity prices but also utilizes RERs to further reduce dependency on retailer energy and minimize energy costs. The work proposed in [12] utilizes a GA to schedule tasks in a flexible job shop manufacturing environment. It considers a multi-objective function to optimize the total cost, task completion time, and penalties for completing tasks ahead of time. Moreover, sequential, resource, cost and other constraints are taken into account in the problem formulation. For preventive maintenance and production scheduling, an RL algorithm using the Markov decision process is proposed in [11]. It is employed for multi-state single-machine production systems that consider degradation. The main objectives are to minimize processing and maintenance costs, as well as maximize completion rewards. Also tackling preventive maintenance, the work proposed in [13] focuses on a preventive maintenance scheduling system that uses a GA to generate maintenance schedules that lower machine life-cycle expenses and prevent impending failures. It explores numerous failure mechanisms and categorizes them into two types: deteriorated, indicating some degradation; and functional failure, indicating approaching failure.

While the works cited above include some features that help in optimizing energy costs and machine longevity, none of them incorporate both of these issues to the extent of the present paper's methodology. For instance, the work in [9] while it focuses on energy cost optimization and load constraints, it does not take into account any machine longevity/degradation optimization in the problem formulation. Furthermore, it is applied to household appliances, a much more simplified problem when compared to heavy manufacturing load scheduling problems. In addition, for reducing energy costs, it only considers retailer electricity prices, as opposed to the present paper which also utilizes RER, such as Photovoltaic (PV) panels, to further reduce these costs. Also, while the proposed work in [10] complements to some degree the previously mentioned work, by including RER and being employed in a manufacturing environment, its drawbacks are not considering possible constraints and no machine longevity optimization. The work in [12] is one of the few works in the literature that tackle production scheduling in the complex flexible job shop layout, the same layout considered in the present methodology. Nevertheless, it does not integrate any type of machine longevity optimization. Finally, the works [11] and [13] both integrate machine longevity optimization through preventive maintenance. However, these works fail to consider the many features that the previously cited works contemplate, such as volatile retailer energy prices, RER usage, and constraints. Accordingly, the premise of the present paper is to optimize both energy costs and machine longevity, in a flexible job shop layout, while at the same time considering factors that further optimize these objectives, such as intelligent use of volatile retailer energy prices and locally generated energy (i.e., RERs), and acknowledge that there are constraints that might need to be imposed during the manufacturing process.

3   Proposed Methodology

The proposed methodology aims to optimize total energy costs and machine longevity in manufacturing production lines that follow a flexible job shop layout. This is achieved by utilizing a GA to schedule tasks, for requested products to manufacture, through load shifting. To reduce the total energy costs the proposed scheduler considers the intelligent use of volatile retailer energy prices and locally generated energy (e.g., solar and wind energy) to shift tasks to lower energy price times and higher local generation times. Optimization of machine longevity is done by minimizing single-machine task overload, by way of balancing tasks between the different machines available for manufacturing. These two objectives, that is, total energy cost and machine longevity, are balanced intelligently by the scheduler according to weights stipulated by the user.

There are considerations in the problem formulation regarding time and energy units that allows for greater input flexibility in the proposed methodology:

- **Time Frame**—represents a specific interval of time, for example, 30 s, 30 min, or 1 h. It is defined by the user and needs to be consistent in the input data;
- **Energy Unit**—portrays a unit of energy per time frame, for instance, Wh/time frame, kWh/time frame, MWh/time frame. Also defined by the user and constant throughout the input.

In essence, for example, when considering a time frame of 30 min for the scheduler and defining that task α has a duration of 3 time frames, with the corresponding energy consumption 20Wh, 10Wh, and 30Wh, respectively for each mentioned time frame, it means that in the first 30 min task α consumes 20W, the next 30 min 10W, and the final 30 min 30W.

The domain model of the proposed methodology is composed of six concepts:

- **Request**—depicts the commission of products to be manufactured;
- **Product**—portrays an item that can be manufactured, has a task completion list;
- **Machine**—represents manufacturing equipment capable of processing products;
- **Task**—describes an activity done by a machine to process a product;
- **Energy Source**—designates energy either obtained from retailers or local generation;
- **Constraints**—defines production or time rules imposed on the scheduler that need to be followed. The present paper proposes the following constraints: order between tasks (i.e., task β then task α), incompatible simultaneous execution between tasks (i.e., task α and task β cannot be in the same time frames), deadlines for requested products (i.e., all tasks of a given requested product must be completed by a stipulated deadline), and non-schedulable time frames (i.e., time frames that are skipped when scheduling, commonly used in working day transitions).

4 Genetic Algorithm Implementation

The implementation of the proposed GA for total energy cost and machine longevity optimization follows the conventional procedures, that is, the initial population, crossover, mutation and selection procedures, as portrayed in Fig. 1. It is worth mentioning that the implemented GA does not make use of any available GA library, since there are no libraries that allowed to implement the desired features into the scheduler, for instance, the non-schedulable time frames constraint.

4.1 Initial Population Procedure

The initial population is the first procedure executed by the GA, with the aim of creating a semi-random group of unique and valid (i.e., comply with all constraints) schedules (i.e., GA individuals), also known as a GA population, to initialize the GA in its subsequent procedures (i.e., crossover, mutation, and selection). Four fundamental steps are followed in this procedure:

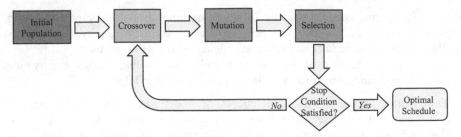

Fig. 1. Flowchart of the genetic algorithm for total energy cost and machine longevity optimization

1. Creation of a random GA population, with a size defined by the user;
2. Removal of duplicated individuals in the GA population;
3. Repair of individuals constraints in the GA population, if not possible, the individual is discarded;
4. Repeat steps 1, 2, and 3 until there is a unique valid GA population with the user stipulated size.

The final result of the initial population procedure is a GA population composed of unique and valid individuals, each representing a possible production schedule. To describe individuals, a matrix approach is used, where rows depict the machine's production plan and columns a specific time frame, as shown in Fig. 2.

Machine	Time Frame									
	1	2	3	4	5	6	7	8	9	10
M_1	Task_A							Task_E		
M_2		Task_D						Task_F		
M_3										
M_4			Task_B							
M_5							Task_C			

Fig. 2. Example of an individual of the Genetic Algorithm for total energy cost and machine longevity optimization.

4.2 Crossover Procedure

After obtaining the initial population, a genetic generation begins, which is composed of the procedures crossover, mutation, and selection. The initial population is only used in the first genetic generation, subsequent generations use the GA population obtained in the previous generation.

In the first genetic generation procedure, the crossover, two individuals in the GA population are paired randomly with each other in order to be applied with a crossover procedure, which aims to breed the chromosomes of two individuals. From two individuals (i.e., crossover parents) two possible resulting individuals (i.e., crossover children) can be obtained, depending on which parent the crossover begins with. A crossover procedure applied to two parents in order to obtain two of the children takes the following steps:

1. Creation of a task list ordered by decreasing task processing time, and increasing machine compatibility, if two tasks have equal processing time;
2. Assignment of tasks to the child, following the obtained ordered task list, according to the parents' task position, starting with one of the parents. For instance, from parents 1 and 2 if starting with parent 1 then the assignment goes task α from parent 1, task β from parent 2, task γ from parent 3, and so forth;

   - For unsuccessful assignments, the parent alternates;
   - Even if unsuccessful when alternating parents, assignment is done semi-randomly to not hinder future assignments.

3. Discard the obtained child on the condition that it is an invalid individual;
4. Repeat steps 2 and 3, one more time, but with the assignment starting with the other parent.

An approach for using an order task list instead of more conventional crossover approaches, such as single- or two-point crossover, or uniform crossover, was chosen to reduce the likelihood of resulting children not complying with constraints or impossible crossovers due to the nature of the individual being a matrix.

4.3 Mutation Procedure

The second procedure in a genetic generation focuses on introducing diversity into the GA population, by mutating individuals obtained through the crossover procedure. All individuals have a likelihood to mutate, hence not all individuals are bound to be mutated. To successfully mutate an individual, the GA considers the following steps for each individual:

1. Identify if the individual can be mutated, by randomly picking a number and comparing it to the defined likelihood of mutation by the user;
2. Switch two tasks' positions in the individual;
3. Discard the mutated individual if it does not comply with imposed constraints or the mutation is impossible (e.g., one of the tasks being swapped is bigger than the other and cannot fit in the swapped position);
4. Repeat steps 2 and 3 until there is a valid mutated individual.

4.4 Selection Procedure

The last procedure of a genetic generation has the goal of selecting the individuals that inherit the following genetic generation. Two populations are considered for the selection: the original population of the genetic generation (i.e., old, crossover and mutation were not applied) and the processed population (i.e., new, crossover and mutation were applied). In the genetic generation, selection is the most complex procedure, as it follows a number of steps in order to select the individuals that inherit:

1. Combine both original and processed populations;
2. Removal of duplicated individuals in the combined population;
3. Evaluate individuals' fitness based on the Fitness Score (*FS*) equation (i.e., Eq. (7));
4. Select the individuals with the best *FS* (i.e., elite selection);
5. Select the remaining individuals, that is, defined GA population size minus elite size, based on non-elite tournaments (i.e., non-elite selection), where individuals are randomly paired and compete using their *FS*;

   • The likelihood of winning is higher for individuals that have a better *FS*;
   • While with low probability, it is still possible that an individual with worse *FS* wins versus an individual with better *FS*.

6. Merge the elite selection and non-elite selection individuals to create the GA population that will inherit to the following genetic generation.

To obtain the *FS* of each individual, seven equations are formulated: time frame energy consumption, time frame retailer energy, total energy cost, machine task identifier, machine task occupation rate, machine occupancy rate standard deviation, and the fitness score equation.

The Time Frame Energy Consumption (*TFEC*), represented by $TFEC_{Demand(t)}$ and Eq. (1), gives the energy consumed in a specific time frame t.

$$TFEC_{Demand(t)} = \sum_{m=1}^{M} E_{Demand(t,m)} \tag{1}$$

Variable t depicts a specific time frame, m a machine index, M the total number of machines, and $E_{Demand(t,m)}$ the energy consumed in machine m during time frame t.

Subsequently, the Time Frame Retailer Energy (*TFRE*), depicted by $TFRE_{Demand(t)}$ and Eq. (2), allows obtaining the retailer energy to pay in a specific time frame t.

$$TFRE_{Demand(t)} = \begin{cases} 0, if E_{Generation(t)} \geq TFEC_{Demand(t)} \\ \left(TFEC_{Demand(t)} - E_{Generation(t)}\right) \\ \times E_{Retailer\ Price(t)} \end{cases} \tag{2}$$

Variable $E_{Generation(t)}$ portrays available locally generated energy (e.g., solar and wind energy) in time frame t, and $E_{Retailer\ Price(t)}$ the retailer's energy price in time frame t.

Finally, to calculate the total energy costs of an individual it is used the Total Energy Cost (*TEC*) equation, as shown by Eq. (3).

$$TEC = \sum_{t=1}^{T} TFRE_{Demand(t)} \tag{3}$$

Variable T represents the time window of the schedule, defined by the user.

Regarding single-machine task overload, it is first used the Machine Task Identifier (*MTI*), described by $MTI_{Scheduled(t,m)}$ and Eq. (4), which identifies if machine m in time frame t has a task scheduled.

$$MTI_{Scheduled(t,m)} = \begin{cases} 1, if\ task\ scheduled \\ 0, if\ empty\ space \end{cases} \tag{4}$$

Afterward, the Machine Task Occupation Rate (*MTOR*), represented by $MTOR_{Schedule(m)}$ and Eq. (5), obtains the occupation rate of tasks to empty spaces in a given machine m.

$$MTOR_{Schedule(m)} = \frac{\sum_{t=1}^{T} MTI_{Scheduled(t,m)}}{T} \qquad (5)$$

Lastly, the Machine Occupancy Rate Standard Deviation (*MORSD*) of an individual is obtained through Eq. (6), using the population standard deviation.

$$MORSD = \sqrt{\frac{\sum_{m=1}^{M} \left(MTOR_{Schedule(m)} - \left(\frac{\sum_{m=1}^{M} MTOR_{Schedule(m)}}{M} \right) \right)^2}{M}} \qquad (6)$$

With total energy cost and machine occupancy rate standard deviation (i.e., *TEC* and *MORSD*, respectively) calculated, the fitness score (i.e., *FS*) of an individual in the GA is given using the multi-objective Eq. (7).

$$FS = TEC_{Norm} \times W_{TEC} + MORSD_{Norm} \times W_{MORSD} \qquad (7)$$

Variable TEC_{Norm} describes the normalized *TEC* value, W_{TEC} the optimization weight for the *TEC* objective, $MORSD_{Norm}$ the normalized *MORSD* value, and W_{MORSD} the optimization weight for the *MORSD* objective. Normalization of *TEC* and *MORSD* values is done using a Min-Max approach. Furthermore, the sum of W_{TEC} and W_{MORSD} is always 1, with the weights having a value between 0 and 1, inclusive. It is worth noting that, the objective function is the minimization of Eq. (7), thus individuals with lower *FS* have better overall fitness in the problem at hand.

When the selection procedure ends, a new genetic generation begins with the individuals that inherited from the current generation. However, if at least one stop condition (i.e., GA execution time, number of genetic generations, and *FS* stagnation) is satisfied then there is no new genetic generation, and the GA extracts the best individual found, that is, the optimal schedule obtained by the GA.

5 Case Study

The proposed methodology is validated using a case study from the literature, from the work in [14], that uses real-production data. In the case study from the cited work, a total energy cost optimization scenario, available in [15], is considered as the baseline scenario to validate the present paper methodology in optimizing energy costs as well as machine longevity by minimizing task overload in single machines. Validation focuses on incorporating machine longevity optimization, by balancing tasks between machines, in the cited total energy cost scenario [15], from the work [14], and evaluating the effectiveness of the proposed methodology in balancing the energy costs and machine longevity objectives while also taking into account the energy costs.

The case study describes a working week of a manufacturing textile business, which is composed of Monday through Saturday, with 7:00 being the standard starting working hours and 23:00 the corresponding closing hours. As such, when decomposing the problem at hand with a concept of 5-min time frames, each day is decomposed into 192 time frames, hence a total of 1152 time frames are considered in the case study, when taking into account the six working days. It is worth noting that, while the case study from the literature corresponds only to a working week of six days, the present methodology could be applied to longer periods of time, for instance, a month, if need be, with the drawback that it could require longer scheduler execution times.

Regarding production data, which is available in [15], there are three unique machines that have distinct task compatibilities, MAQ118, MAQ119, and MAQ120, which are described in-depth in the above-mentioned dataset. Therefore, the representation of a GA individual matrix has a dimension of 3×1152, that is, 3 rows portraying the machines' production plan and 1152 describing the total number of time frames in the time window of the schedule. Furthermore, a heavy load of tasks is considered for scheduling in the case study, with 132 units of 14 unique products being requested, which, when taking into account that products can have multiple tasks associated, the schedule amounts to 275 tasks to be scheduled in a flexible job shop layout.

For energy retailer prices, the case study uses the MIBEL (Iberian Electricity Market) [16] prices from the 7th to the 12th of January 2019. Also, for PV generation, it is considered the energy obtained from a 3kW peak PV installation in Portugal, from the 6th to the 11th of June 2020.

In the case study, four constraints, equivalent to the present paper constraints, are imposed:

- **Order between tasks**—tasks "Harden [2]" precede tasks "Harden [1.5]";
- **Incompatible simultaneous execution between tasks**—tasks "Harden [2]" and tasks "Sublimation" cannot be scheduled at the same time;
- **Deadlines for requested products**—A request for product "Elastic w/ inscr" needs to be done by 23:00 on Friday;
- **Non-schedulable time frames**—The time frames that represent working day transitions, that is, from 23:00 of the current day to 7:00 of the next day, are not to be considered for scheduling.

For comparison in the following results and discussion section, the scenario in the literature for only total energy cost optimization [15] achieved a total energy cost of 36.42 EUR, without any deliberation for task balancing between machines.

6   Results and Discussion

The present paper's scenario replicates the literature scenario considering only total energy cost optimization, with the exception of also taking into account task balancing between tasks, to not only minimize energy costs but also minimize single-machine task overload which leads to machine degradation. It focuses on demonstrating how the proposed scheduler is able to balance tasks between machines while also reducing overall costs. For the total energy cost and machine longevity optimization scenario, it was considered an optimization weight of 0.5, that is, 50% weight, for both the total energy costs and machine occupancy deviation objectives (i.e., metric to evaluate overload on single machines). Moreover, the GA was executed for 2 h, the same as in the literature scenario. In addition, it was executed in a computer with an AMD® Ryzen 7 3700X (4.05 GHz) processor, 32 GB of RAM, and Windows 10 Home version 21H1. The complete data is available at [17].

The machine occupation rates without the machine occupancy deviation optimization (i.e., from the baseline scenario) and with such optimization (i.e., from the present scenario) are presented in Fig. 3. As a result, without the machine occupancy deviation optimization, there is a machine occupancy rate standard deviation of around 0.0997% while with the optimization it achieves 0.0122%, a decrease of 87.8%.

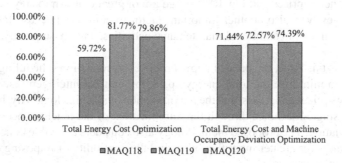

Fig. 3. Machine occupation rates per machine without and with the occupancy optimization.

On the other hand, the total energy cost went up by 12.8%, from 36.42 EUR to 41.07 EUR. This clearly demonstrates that the proposed scheduler is able to improve machine longevity, by reducing overload and usage of single machines, while also balancing it with the total energy cost, by not allowing a drastic increase in the overall costs. The total energy cost and machine occupancy rate deviation of the best individual of each genetic generation, for this scenario, are represented in Fig. 4. It shows an average performance regarding the total energy cost evolution since it follows a decreasing logarithmic function for the first 1000 generations, but it also shows how the scheduler is able to intelligently balance these objectives, by decreasing or increasing the total energy costs and machine occupancy rate deviation.

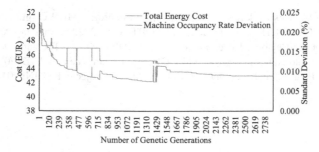

Fig. 4. Total energy cost and machine occupancy deviation per generation of the Genetic Algorithm for the total energy cost and machine occupancy deviation optimization scenario.

It is worth mentioning that, to the knowledge of the authors there are no technologies that tackle the same type of problem (i.e., energy costs and machine longevity through overload optimization) that could be compared to the present work.

7   Conclusions

High retailer energy prices due to the COVID-19 pandemic and the Russo-Ukrainian war have greatly hindered European manufacturing businesses' competitiveness. This has led many experts in investing in RER to reduce the need to resort to retailer energy prices. While high energy prices and low RER usage are of great concern to stay competitive, machine longevity is also another important factor to consider, because fast machine degradation can lead to additional maintenance activities, and consequently, additional expenses.

To address this issue, the present paper proposes a production scheduling algorithm using a GA to minimize the total energy costs, through the intelligent use of volatile retailer energy prices and RERs, and the maximization of machine longevity, by reducing overload on single-machines through the minimization of the machine occupancy rate standard deviation. The proposed methodology also considers a flexible concept of time and energy units for greater input flexibility and the possibility of imposing constraints on the production schedule.

The proposed methodology is validated using a case study from the literature that uses real-production data and a baseline scenario, from the mentioned case study, is used as a comparison. In the case study, 275 tasks are to be scheduled in 3 machines, within a working week, from Monday to Saturday, 7:00 through 23:00 each day. The obtained results demonstrate that the proposed scheduler is able to reduce single-machine overload by up to 87.8%, and at the same time maintain reasonable levels of energy costs by increasing them only up to 12.8% of the original energy cost.

In future work, maintenance scheduling will be considered along with machine degradation to further improve longevity in machines. Furthermore, an operation cost parameter limiter will be incorporated to limit the impact on operational costs, to better control the scheduler. In addition, a more in-depth analysis will also be considered with the Cost-Benefit-Analysis (CBA) and Net Present Value (NPV), to possibly incorporate CBA and NPV knowledge into the fitness function to improve optimization efforts.

Acknowledgments. This work has received funding from project MUWO (grant agreement No 771066), through COMPETE program, under the PORTUGAL 2020 Partnership Agreement, and through the European Regional Development Fund (ERDF/FEDER). The authors acknowledge the work facilities and equipment provided by GECAD research center (UIDB/00760/2020) to the project team. Pedro Faria has Support from FCT through project CEECIND/01423/2021.

References

1. Halbrügge, S., Schott, P., Weibelzahl, M., Buhl, H.U., Fridgen, G., Schöpf, M.: How did the German and other European electricity systems react to the COVID-19 pandemic? Appl. Energy **285**, 116370 (2021). https://doi.org/10.1016/j.apenergy.2020.116370
2. Cui, L., Yue, S., Nghiem, X.-H., Duan, M.: Exploring the risk and economic vulnerability of global energy supply chain interruption in the context of Russo-Ukrainian war. Resour. Policy **81**, 103373 (2023). https://doi.org/10.1016/j.resourpol.2023.103373
3. Siksnelyte-Butkiene, I.: Combating Energy Poverty in the Face of the COVID-19 Pandemic and the Global Economic Uncertainty. Energies (Basel) 15, 3649 (2022). https://doi.org/10.3390/en15103649
4. Serrano González, J., Álvarez Alonso, C.: Industrial electricity prices in Spain: a discussion in the context of the European internal energy market. Energy Policy **148**, 111930 (2021). https://doi.org/10.1016/j.enpol.2020.111930
5. Abrishambaf, O., Lezama, F., Faria, P., Vale, Z.: Towards transactive energy systems: an analysis on current trends. Energy Strat. Rev. **26**, 100418 (2019). https://doi.org/10.1016/j.esr.2019.100418
6. Jabir, H.J., Teh, J., Ishak, D., Abunima, H.: Impacts of demand-side management on electrical power systems: a review. Energies 11, 1050. 11, 1050 (2018). https://doi.org/10.3390/EN11051050
7. Thomas, D.S.: The costs and benefits of advanced maintenance in manufacturing. National Institute of Standards and Technology 1–45 (2018). https://doi.org/10.6028/nist.ams.100-18
8. Belyi, D., Popova, E., Morton, D.P., Damien, P.: Bayesian failure-rate modeling and preventive maintenance optimization. Eur. J. Oper. Res. **262**, 1085–1093 (2017). https://doi.org/10.1016/j.ejor.2017.04.019
9. Tavares, I., Almeida, J., Soares, J., Ramos, S., Vale, Z., Foroozandeh, Z.: Optimizing energy consumption of household appliances using PSO and GWO. Lecture Notes in Computer Science (including subseries Lecture Notes in Artificial Intelligence and Lecture Notes in Bioinformatics). 12981 LNAI, 137–150 (2021). https://doi.org/10.1007/978-3-030-86230-5_11/COVER
10. Cui, W., Li, L., Lu, Z.: Energy-efficient scheduling for sustainable manufacturing systems with renewable energy resources. Nav. Res. Logist. **66**, 154–173 (2019). https://doi.org/10.1002/nav.21830
11. Yang, H., Li, W., Wang, B.: Joint optimization of preventive maintenance and production scheduling for multi-state production systems based on reinforcement learning. Reliab. Eng. Syst. Saf. **214**, 107713 (2021). https://doi.org/10.1016/j.ress.2021.107713
12. Wang, Y., Fu, L., Su, Y., Yang, Q., Wu, L.: Genetic algorithm in flexible work shop scheduling based on multi-objective optimization. J. Interdis. Math. **21**, 1249–1254 (2018). https://doi.org/10.1080/09720502.2018.1495398
13. Duan, C., Deng, C., Gong, Q., Wang, Y.: Optimal failure mode-based preventive maintenance scheduling for a complex mechanical device. Int. J. Adv. Manuf. Technol. **95**, 2717–2728 (2018). https://doi.org/10.1007/s00170-017-1419-2
14. Mota, B., Gomes, L., Faria, P., Ramos, C., Vale, Z., Correia, R.: Production line optimization to minimize energy cost and participate in demand response events. Energies (Basel) 14, 462 (2021). https://doi.org/10.3390/en14020462
15. Mota, B., Gomes, L., Faria, P., Ramos, C., Vale, Z.: Production line dataset for task scheduling and energy optimization – Schedule Optimization. (2020). https://doi.org/10.5281/ZENODO.4106746
16. Mibel—Mercado Ibérico de Electricidade, https://www.mibel.com/, last accessed 2022/01/23

17. Mota, B.: Joint optimization of production and maintenance for cost-effective manufacturing and demand response participation dataset—total cost and machine occupancy deviation optimization. (2022). https://doi.org/10.5281/ZENODO.7055580

A Novel Federated Learning Approach to Enable Distributed and Collaborative Genetic Programming

Bruno Ribeiro⬤, Luis Gomes(✉)⬤, and Zita Vale⬤

GECAD Research Group On Intelligent Engineering and Computing for Advanced Innovation and Development, LASI—Intelligent Systems Associate Laboratory, Polytechnic of Porto, R. Dr. António Bernardino de Almeida, 431, 4200-072 Porto, Portugal
lfg@isep.ipp.pt

Abstract. The combination of genetic programming with federated learning could solve the computational distribution while promoting a collaborative learning environment. This paper proposes a federated learning configuration that enables the use of genetic programming for its global model. In addition, this paper also proposes a new aggregation algorithm that enables the collaborative evolution of genetic programming individuals in federated learning. The case study uses flexible genetic programming, an existing and successful algorithm for image classification, integrated into a federated learning framework. The results show that the use of genetic programming with federated learning achieved a classification error rate of 1.67%, better than the scenario without federated learning, that had an error rate of 3.33%, considering a configuration with three clients with different datasets each.

Keywords: Genetic programming · Federated learning · Evolutionary computation · Collaborative learning · Image classification · Computer vision · MNIST

1 Introduction

Computer Vision (CV) is an Artificial Intelligence (AI) subdomain, where the idea is to extract relevant knowledge from two dimensional images [1]. This subdomain is one of the most discussed topics in AI and is well-valued, being projected that its market will reach USD 51.3 billion by 2026 [2]. The most used techniques in this field are deep neural networks. These techniques can have great precision in image classification tasks being the main advantage of the automatic detection of the most important features in an image, without human supervision [3]. However, two challenges must be approached. One is the knowledge needed to create the right architecture for the task at hand. The other is the need of large amounts of data to train. In the literature, Genetic Programming (GP) is starting to gain some relevance in this field given that overcomes these two challenges while achieving good precisions [4].

N. Moniz et al. (Eds.): EPIA 2023, LNAI 14116, pp. 195–206, 2023.
https://doi.org/10.1007/978-3-031-49011-8_16

GP is an Evolutionary Computation (EC) technique used to develop programs automatically. It was created around 1980 [5] and has been adapted throughout the years for different applications [6], but more recently has been used for feature learning and image classification [4]. Several works shown that this technique is very promising and can achieve high-quality solutions. The only problem that is related to this technique is shared by almost every technique in the EC domain, which is the computation costs needed to get good-quality solutions [4]. One way to overcome this issue is by using distributed computation to allow the workload to be shared among several devices. In that regard, Federated Learning (FL) is the appropriate solution to solve the computation distribution problem, while protecting personal data, and allowing more users to collaboratively train a model to a common problem.

The fundamental idea of FL is that instead of the data being shared among the users, like in traditional machine learning, the users share a global model and train it together in a distributed manner. This allows the users to have a generalized model that can predict not only based on the user's specific data but based on a wider range of information [7]. Typically, the FL systems focus a lot on deep learning models, however, little research has been done on adapting other types of models [8, 9].

This paper proposes a novel solution that integrates GP algorithms in an FL environment while allowing collaborative improvement through the evolution process without sharing private data. To allow the collaborative evolution, two different aggregation algorithms are proposed, one for aggregating the fitness values of the individuals, and the other to aggregate the results of the evaluation phase. The solution was tested and compared with the standalone solution of the GP algorithm.

This paper is structured into seven sections. The Sect. 1 is the current section, introduction, and describes an overview of the topics explored in this paper. The Sects. 2 and 3 are titled, respectively, Genetic Programming and Federated Learning and describe the related works of the respective methodologies. The Sect. 4 is the Methodology where the solution proposed in this paper is described. The Sect. 5 is the Case Study section where the details of the case study are described. In the Sect. 6, Results and Discussion, the results of the case study will be shown and analyzed and the comparison between the standalone GP and the GP in the FL system are compared and discussed. Finally, the Sect. 7 will summarize the main conclusions of this work and describe future work.

2 Genetic Programming

GP is an evolutionary algorithm used to evolve computer programs automatically [10]. There are plenty of ways to represent a program. The most used and well-known is in a tree format. To construct these programs, normally its used simple mathematic operations like addition, multiplication, maximization, and numerical terminals. When applying GP to an image classification problem, this type of operations are not ideal. The way to adapt GP to image classification is by changing the functions set and the terminals set [4]. The functions are represented by the internal nodes of the tree and the variables of the program, called terminals in GP, are the leaves of the tree. The functions used in image classification are related to image processing functions, like image filtering, feature extraction, and pooling functions [11]. The way GP does the classification is by using a proper classifier in the root of the tree, so after all the image processing the classifier can train and classify the data instances based on the output of the image processing functions.

More recently the GP algorithms have been achieving great results in the domain of CV. A GP algorithm for image classification with a new program representation that learns features and evolves ensembles classifiers is proposed in [12]. In [13], it is proposed a new flexible program structure for the GP algorithm for feature learning, named Flexible Genetic Programming (FGP). In [14], it is proposed a GP approach for image classification with a different program representation, new functions, and terminals, and a new mutation operator. However, no application of image classification GP algorithms has been studied in an FL setting.

3   Federated Learning

FL is a recent machine learning architecture that appeared with the purpose of protecting the privacy of personal data while still training machine learning models on that data [7]. Instead of the clients sending the data to a central server so it can build the model based on the data [15, 16], the server initializes the model and sends it to the clients. The clients train the model locally using their data [8]. After training, the clients send the updates of the model to the server and the server must aggregate them and update the global model with those new updates. Then the server sends back the updated model to the clients and a new iteration begins. This machine learning architecture has great applicability for knowledge distributed problems like in energy systems [17–19] and in the medical domain [20, 21].

In the literature, there are a lot of implementations of evolutionary algorithms in a federated learning setup. However, these implementations are normally related to the optimization of some FL internal algorithm, client selection, or optimizing the global model [22], which is normally a deep neural network. However, in [23], it is proposed the use of a GP algorithm as a global model in an FL configuration, enabling a combination of GP and FL with a new aggregation algorithm based on the federated averaging (FedAvg) aggregation algorithm.

Another area of research that can be related to this field is distributed evolutionary computation, where the idea is to distribute computation power to minimize the execution time of such solutions [24]. For example, in [25], where a parallel distributed GP was introduced, in [26], where a distributed and parallel evolutionary algorithm to solve a large number of equations was applied, and in [27] where an hybrid parallel implementation of the ant colony optimization and genetic algorithm was proposed.

Despite existing indirectly related works, none of them describes a solution that integrates the evolutionary computation algorithm as the global model of the FL system with the application and aggregation algorithms proposed by the current paper.

4   Methodology

In this paper, the proposed solution is a combination of a preexisting GP algorithm for image classification and an FL system (Fig. 1). Instead of the global model of the FL system being a deep learning model, it is used a GP algorithm. Additionally, two aggregation algorithms are proposed and described to enable the integration and proper evolution of the solutions throughout the execution of the federation.

Because there are already a lot of different implementations and adaptations of the GP algorithm for image classification, and many of them with good results, it was used the Flexible Genetic Programming (FGP) [13]. This implementation was chosen because of its good results and the code being available, allowing it to be explored in detail. FGP offers a new solution to solve image classification problems. The name derives from the flexible program structure that the FGP has. The structure of each individual's program is divided into four layers: the filtering layer, the pooling layer, the feature extraction layer, and the concatenation layer. The classification is made at the end of the individual by using a min–max function that feeds a support vectors machine algorithm. The fitness function of the FGP algorithm calculates the classification error rate of the individual. For more details on how the algorithm works please read its authors' work [13].

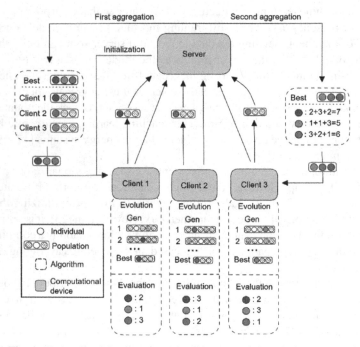

Fig. 1. Example of the process and architecture of the solution proposed

The architecture of the proposed solution is based on a traditional in FL infrastructure. The solution follows a centralized architecture, where the server is responsible for synchronizing the whole operation. The whole operation is divided into five different steps: the initialization phase, the evolution phase, the first aggregation phase, the evaluation phase, and, finally, the second aggregation phase. In this operation, a round is started in the evolution phase and ends in the evaluation aggregation phase. The number of rounds can be defined by the federation. The initialization phase is used to create the first population to be used in the federation. It can either be the server creating or the clients and can either be partially created, fully created, or non-existent. After the creation of the first population (empty in the case of non-existent), a set of clients are selected and the initial population is sent to them.

The evolution phase then starts with the clients executing the GP algorithm, in this case the FGP, using the initial population sent by the server. The fitness of the individuals is calculated using the FGP fitness function and the dataset they have for training the model. To maintain the best individuals produced during the generations a Hall of Fame (HoF) is used. The HoF is a simple mechanism that compares individuals against each other's and orders them from the best to the worst. The size of the HoF can be pre-defined. After each client reaches the maximum number of generations, they send the HoF to the server. The reason why the clients send the HoF instead of one individual is that the best local individual may not be the best global individual.

The first aggregation phase starts after the server receives all the HoF from the clients. Here is where a new aggregation algorithm is applied. This new algorithm allows the FL system to integrate GP algorithms. What it does is create a global HoF where every individual will be tested to filter the best individuals from the whole federation. The comparison made will consider only the local fitness of each client. After filtering the best individuals, the server will send the new HoF to the clients for them to start the next phase.

The next phase is the evaluation phase, and the main objective is to evaluate the individuals of the global HoF on the client side. The clients will receive the global HoF and they will test them against their test dataset, which is separate from the training dataset. After evaluating all the individuals, the client sends back the HoF but with the client's evaluation results. The server, after receiving the clients' HoF's with the updated fitness a new phase starts.

In the second aggregation phase, another novel aggregation algorithm was built, but this time for the evaluation results. To calculate the global fitness of an individual the mean was calculated for each individual considering the fitness of each client. This approach allows the individuals to be properly evaluated considering the data from the federation instead of only their origin clients. After the calculation of the mean, a new HoF is created with the newly updated individuals. Then the new HoF is sent to the clients and a new round begins. To develop this solution, it was used Distributed Evolutionary Algorithms in Python (DEAP) [28], scikit-image [29], SciPy [30] and Flower [31]. DEAP was used by the FGP algorithm, which was integrated into the FL system. The scikit-image and SciPy were used in the image processing functions. The Flower framework was used to implement the FL system.

5 Case Study

The main idea of this case study is to test the performance of the GP algorithm in an FL environment by testing two characteristics, the impact of the number of clients of the federation on the precision of the model and how the sizes of the train and test datasets in each client can influence the performance of the model. To see if the performance is coherent with different problems, two different datasets were used.

The datasets used are MNIST and an MNIST variation. MNIST is a widely used dataset, especially to benchmark CV algorithms. The dataset is composed of images in a grayscale of handwritten digits, from 0 to 9. The size of the images is 28 × 28 pixels. The number of instances inside the training dataset is 12,000 and in the test dataset is 60,000. The MNIST variation, named MNIST-ROT, is identical to the original with just a little twist. The difference is that the images were rotated using a random degree. Because the number of instances of these datasets is very large only a part was used in the execution of the case study, as will be described later.

As is possible to see in Table 1, for each dataset three scenarios were made. One where there are three clients and the number of instances in the training dataset for each client is 120 and in the test dataset is 600. In the next scenario, the number of instances present in each dataset is the same, but the number of clients was increased to five. Lastly, in the third scenario, the number of clients is five but the number of instances in the training dataset is 1,000, and in the test dataset 2,000. The data is divided into different batches for each client, so each client has different data. One extra scenario was run parallel to scenario one, with the same configurations but without the aggregation algorithms, to test if the aggregation is benefiting the overall performance of the GP or not.

Table 1. Scenarios' description used in the case study

	Scenario 1	Scenario 2	Scenario 3
Client	3	5	5
Train set size	120	120	1000
Test set size	600	600	2000

The size of the population, the number of generations, the number of rounds, and the size of the HoF were kept the same throughout the scenarios. Regarding the number of rounds, the idea was to follow the same practice used in the GP community, by doing 30 runs when benchmarking an algorithm. One way to integrate this in an FL system is by doing 30 rounds. The difference is that after each round the top 10 best individuals of the federation are preserved and used in the beginning of the next round by each client as part of the new population. To be possible to achieve a precision close to the one registered in [13] regarding the same datasets, some GP hyper parameters used in [13] were adopted.

In this case study no initial global population is initialized to encourage the variety of individuals produced in the federation. So, for each scenario, the FL process goes like this: initially the server selects all the clients available. The clients then start to evolve the populations for 10 generations. The population has 100 individuals. To train each individual, a training batch of size 120 is used. After the 10 generations, each client will send their HoF to the server. The HoF contains the top 10 best local individuals. The server will then aggregate every HoF into a single global HoF of the same size. After the aggregation, the server will ask the clients to evaluate the global HoF. The clients will evaluate individually the global HoF by using the training dataset and then the test dataset to test the accuracy of the individual. After that, the results are sent to the server.

Then the aggregation of the evaluations starts on the server side. The round then ends, and the process repeats from the client selection phase, and it stops after 30 rounds.

6 Discussion and Results

To further analyze the impact of the federated configuration on the performance of the FGP algorithm, it is necessary to compare it to the results gathered in [13], where FL was not used. Nonetheless, it should be mentioned that the proposed work used a small dataset (i.e., of 15,000 records, representing 25% of the complete dataset) and that this dataset was distributed differently among multiple FL clients depending on the scenario (Table 1). Table 2 has the data comparing the results which are divided into two columns, one per dataset. Each dataset column is also divided into two sub-columns, named Global and Local. The Global column shows the error rate of the best global individual, after averaging the errors of the global HoF on the server side. The second column (Local) refers to the individual with the lower error rate found individually on the client's side. In the FGP row, there is only one result per dataset.

Table 2. Description of the classification error rate (%) from this case study, globally and locally, and from the original FGP paper

	MNIST (%)		MNIST-ROT (%)	
	Global	Local	Global	Local
Scenario 1	11.94	1.67	49.00	38.33
Scenario 2	14.63	0.83	49.67	10.00
Scenario 3	3.79	1.70	27.14	21.30
FGP original paper	1.18		7.37	

Regarding the Global results, in scenario one the results are good in the MNIST dataset reaching an 11.94% error rate, but in the MNIST-ROT the error rate is very high reaching 49%. In scenario two, the errors were slightly bigger than the first one reaching the MNIST dataset with an error rate of 14.63%, and in MNIST-ROT an error rate of 49.67%. Scenario three results were better. In the MNIST dataset the result was 3.79%, and in the MNIST-ROT was 27.14%.

Regarding the Local results, in the MNIST dataset, the results were very close to the FGP original paper. In scenario one the error rate was 1.67%. In scenario two the error rate is better than the FGP reaching a rate of 0.83%. In scenario three the error rate is also close, reaching a rate of 1.7%. In the MNIST-ROT dataset in the first scenario, the error rate is distant from the FGP, reaching an error rate of 38.33%. However, in scenario two the error rate was almost as good as the FGP, reaching a rate of 10%. And in the third scenario, the result was 1.7% in the MNIST dataset, and 21.3% in the MNIST-ROT. FGP had a classification error rate of 1.18% in the MNIST dataset and 7.37% in the MNIST-ROT.

In this comparison is it possible to see that the results from the experiment were very close to the original FGP (where the full dataset was used), and in some cases surpassing its performance, even though FL are known to decrease the precision of the model. Depending on the configurations of the system and using the aggregation algorithms proposed in this paper, the results can be close or even better for the clients than running the GP algorithm on their own. This is verified by analyzing the results from scenario one and the extra scenario, where the clients run the algorithms alone. In scenario one the result was 1.67%, almost twice as better as the extra scenario (3.33%) where no FL was used.

The difference between scenarios one and two shows that the number of clients can decrease the precision of the model in a global perspective. However, the local performance can improve with twice the precision in the case of MNIST and almost four times in the MNIST-ROT. This happens especially if the dataset used to train and test the individuals are smaller. If the training and test dataset is increased, as done in scenario three, even with more clients, the global error is decreased by 10% in MNIST and 20% in MNITS-ROT, and locally the error increases slightly. The reason the MNIST results are better than the MNIST-ROT is that it is more difficult to find a good solution using the MNIST-ROT.

One important aspect to analyze is the evolution of the classification error rate of the best global individuals between scenarios in every round. In Fig. 2, it is possible to see that evolution (a). The green lines represent the MNIST dataset, and the blue lines the MNIST-ROT. The green and blue dot lines are the results from scenario one, the dashed lines are from scenario two, and the solid lines from scenario three. The red ones are the baseline of the best FGP in the MNIST dataset (solid line) and the MNIST-ROT (dashed line). Almost in every scenario the evolution seems to be constant after some rounds showing that 30 rounds are enough to achieve a good result.

In Fig. 2 (a) it is possible to see and analyze the distance in the results of each scenario. From this perspective, it is possible to see that the number of clients and the number of data present in the client's dataset can influence the precision of the models. By only increasing the number of clients it is possible to see a difference in precision in the MNIST dataset. Scenario one, which has only three clients, has better global results than scenario two, which has five clients. In the MNIST-ROT the precision of the first and second scenarios are not much different. That can be related to the complexity of the MNIST-ROT dataset which would need more time for the evolutions to start to see a big difference. If the size of the datasets is increased in every client it is possible to see that the global precision of the models increases significantly. This difference is more prominent in the MNIST-ROT dataset which is possible to see a decrease of 20% in the global error rate. In the MNIST dataset, the same behaviors can be seen but the difference is not so significant.

Regarding the approximation of the scenario results with the FGP results, scenario three stands out. In the MNIST dataset, the result is very close to the result of FGP. This shows that even if the best global individual precision is not so great compared with the FGP, the individual can maintain a successful rate of classification while enabling the generalization of the model. In the MNIST-ROT dataset, the result is a bit far from the

FGP results. This however could be solved by increasing the dataset size used by the clients and letting the evolutions run for more rounds.

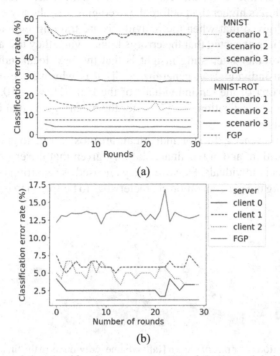

(a)

(b)

Fig. 2. a Evolution of the classification error rate (%) of the best global individuals in each scenario and each dataset, as well as the FGP best error rate; **b** Evolution of the classification error rate (%) of the best local and global individuals in each round of scenario 1

To analyze better the relationship between the local and the global individuals from scenario one, the graph presented on the right side of Fig. 2 was made (b). The lines represent the evolution of the best global (green) and the best locals (each blue representing different clients) throughout the rounds.

As it is possible to see in Fig. 2(b), and in Table 2, the clients locally have better individuals when compared to the global ones. Is expected that the local individuals have the worst results when testing in generalized data. This gives because the individuals are trained with local data, so the more generalized and more varied data a client has locally the better global individuals it will produce. What is also interesting is that the clients can reuse the best global individuals from the past round to create better individuals based on the more generalized ones. That is why the results of local individuals can achieve results almost as good and, in some cases, even better than the standalone approach. Another curious event in this graph is that the server error rate seems to vary oppositely to the error rate of the client 0. This is probably to the fact that the individuals created were more proficient locally to the client 0 than when compared to the global data.

Another important factor to be discussed is the difference that the aggregation algorithm has on the HoF individuals. Figure 3 is a demonstration of the ten individuals of the global HoF before (blue bar) and after (orange bar) the averaging in scenario two, in the first round of the execution. The dataset used in this case is MNIST.

In Fig. 3, it is possible to see that for each individual the error rate after the mean aggregation algorithm is higher than before the averaging. As already explained, that is what was expected given that when the individuals are training individually, they use their own data. So, it is expected that the error is higher when they test against the other clients' datasets. Another interesting insight is that the best local individuals are not necessarily the best individuals at generalizing. That is why we see the difference in Fig. 3 where the worst of the ten individuals of the HoF (I1, with 10.83% before the mean) is the best at generalization (20.57% after the mean), given that it has the lowest error after the averaging.

Despite these differences, the HoF individuals are mostly used to guide the evolution process of the algorithm, and not as final solutions, given that the error is much higher compared to the local individuals. However, they are used as a starting point for the next generations, enabling the generalization characteristics to be spread to better individuals.

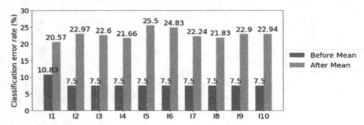

Fig. 3. The classification error rate of the ten Hall of Fame individuals in the first round of Scenario 2 using MNIST, before and after the mean operation in the evaluations aggregation

7 Conclusion

The solution proposed in this paper is a new solution to integrate genetic programming algorithms in the collaborative environment of federated learning. Two aggregation algorithms were proposed to help the evolution process of the algorithm to be guided through their generalization capacity. The evolution aggregation algorithm aggregates the best individuals of the current round, and the evaluation aggregation algorithm aggregates the results of the best individuals against all the clients to see which was the best at generalizing the model.

The proposed case study tested the federated learning capacity and benefits when integrating with genetic programming. The results were interesting and have shown that this methodology enables the clients to have better models locally and with better generalization capacity. Another advantage of this approach is the privacy and security of the data that is provided by the federated learning. Further work can be done to explore more alternatives to the aggregation algorithms. Overall, it is possible to see that genetic programming has great potential when applied to federated learning.

Acknowledgements. This article is a result of the project RETINA (NORTE-01-0145-FEDER-000062), supported by Norte Portugal Regional Operational Programme (NORTE 2020), under the PORTUGAL 2020 Partnership Agreement, through the European Regional Development Fund (ERDF). The authors acknowledge the work facilities and equipment provided by GECAD research center (UIDB/00760/2020) to the project team.

References

1. Szeliski, R.: Computer Vision. Springer International Publishing, Cham (2022)
2. Markets and Markets: Ai in Computer Vision Market, https://www.marketsandmarkets.com/ Market-Reports/ai-in-computer-vision-market-141658064.html
3. O'Mahony, N., Campbell, S., Carvalho, A., Harapanahalli, S., Hernandez, G.V., Krpalkova, L., Riordan, D., Walsh, J.: Deep learning vs. traditional computer vision. In: CVC 2019: Advances in Computer Vision, pp. 128–144 (2020)
4. Khan, A., Qureshi, A.S., Wahab, N., Hussain, M., Hamza, M.Y.: A recent survey on the applications of genetic programming in image processing. Comput. Intell. **37**, 1745 (2021)
5. Smith, S.: A Learning System Based on Genetic Adaptive Algorithms. University of Pittsburgh (1980)
6. Ahvanooey, M., Li, Q., Wu, M., Wang, S.: A survey of genetic programming and its applications. KSII Trans. Internet Inf. Syst. **13** (2019)
7. Jin, Y., Zhu, H., Xu, J., Chen, Y.: Federated Learning. Springer Nature Singapore, Singapore (2023)
8. Wen, J., Zhang, Z., Lan, Y., Cui, Z., Cai, J., Zhang, W.: A survey on federated learning: challenges and applications. Int. J. Mach. Learn. Cybern. (2022)
9. Banabilah, S., Aloqaily, M., Alsayed, E., Malik, N., Jararweh, Y.: Federated learning review: Fundamentals enabling technologies, and future applications. Inf. Process Manag. **59**, 103061 (2022)
10. Doerr, B., Neumann, F.: Theory of Evolutionary Computation. Springer International Publishing, Cham (2020)
11. Bi, Y., Xue, B., Zhang, M.: Genetic Programming for Image Classification, vol. 24. Springer International Publishing, Cham (2021)
12. Bi, Y., Xue, B., Zhang, M.: Genetic programming with a new representation to automatically learn features and evolve ensembles for image classification. IEEE Trans. Cybern. **51**, 1769 (2021)
13. Bi, Y., Xue, B., Zhang, M.: Genetic programming with image-related operators and a flexible program structure for feature learning in image classification. IEEE Trans. Evol. Comput. **25**, 87 (2021)
14. Fan, Q., Bi, Y., Xue, B., Zhang, M.: Genetic programming for feature extraction and construction in image classification. Appl. Soft Comput. **118**, 108509 (2022)
15. Pereira, H., Gomes, L., Vale, Z.: Peer-to-peer energy trading optimization in energy communities using multi-agent deep reinforcement learning. Energy Inform. **5**, 44 (2022)
16. Mota, B., Pinto, T., Vale, Z., Ramos, C.: Deep learning in intelligent power and energy systems. In: Intelligent Data Mining and Analysis in Power and Energy Systems, pp. 45–67. Wiley (2022)
17. Teixeira, N., Barreto, R., Gomes, L., Faria, P., Vale, Z.: A trustworthy building energy management system to enable direct IoT devices' participation in demand response programs. MDPI Electron. **11**, 897 (2022)
18. Ramos, D., Khorram, M., Faria, P., Vale, Z.: Load forecasting in an office building with different data structure and learning parameters. Forecasting **3**, 242 (2021)

19. Pinto, T., Gomes, L., Faria, P., Vale, Z., Teixeira, N., Ramos, D.: Intelligent simulation and emulation platform for energy management in buildings and microgrids. Mach. Learn. Smart Environ./Cities, 167–181 (2022)
20. Pu, L.: Fairness of the distribution of public medical and health resources. Front Public Health **9** (2021)
21. Tong, J., et al.: Distributed learning for heterogeneous clinical data with application to integrating COVID-19 data across 230 sites. NPJ Digit. Med. **5**, 76 (2022)
22. Zhu H., Jin, Y.: Multi-Objective Evolutionary Federated Learning (2018)
23. Dong, J., Zhong, J., Chen, W.-N., Zhang, J.: An efficient federated genetic programming framework for symbolic regression. IEEE Trans. Emerg. Top Comput. Intell. **1** (2022)
24. Gong, Y.-J., et al.: Distributed evolutionary algorithms and their models: A survey of the state-of-the-art. Appl. Soft Comput. **34**, 286 (2015)
25. Poli, R.: Parallel Distributed Genetic Programming, in Conference: New Ideas in Optimization (1999)
26. Jahan, M., Hashem, M.M.A., Shahriar, G.A.: Distributed evolutionary computation: A new technique for solving large number of equations. Int. J. Parallel Distrib. Syst. (2013)
27. Abdoun, O., Moumen, Y., Abdoun, F.: Parallel evolutionary computation to solve combinatorial optimization problem. In: 2017 International Conference on Electrical and Information Technologies (ICEIT), IEEE, pp. 1–6 (2017)
28. Fortin, F., Rainville, F., Gardner, M., Parizeau, M., Gagné, C.: DEAP: Evolutionary algorithms made easy. J. Mach. Learn. Res. **13**, 2171 (2012)
29. van der Walt, S., et al.: Scikit-image: Image processing in python. PeerJ **2**, e453 (2014)
30. Virtanen, P., et al.: SciPy 1.0: Fundamental algorithms for scientific computing in python, Nat. Methods **17**, 261 (2020)
31. Beutel, D.J., et al.: Flower: A Friendly Federated Learning Research Framework, (2020)

Artificial Intelligence in Medicine

A Scoping Review of Energy Load Disaggregation

Balázs András Tolnai[(✉)] ⓘ, Zheng Maⓘ, and Bo Nørregaard Jørgensenⓘ

SDU Center for Energy Informatics, The Maersk Mc-Kinney Moller Institute, University of
Southern Denmark, 5230 Odense, Denmark
bat@mmmi.sdu.dk

Abstract. Energy load disaggregation can contribute to balancing power grids by enhancing the effectiveness of demand-side management and promoting electricity-saving behavior through increased consumer awareness. However, the field currently lacks a comprehensive overview. To address this gap, this paper conducts a scoping review of load disaggregation domains, data types, and methods, by assessing 72 full-text journal articles. The findings reveal that domestic electricity consumption is the most researched area, while others, such as industrial load disaggregation, are rarely discussed. The majority of research uses relatively low-frequency data, sampled between 1 and 60 s. A wide variety of methods are used, and artificial neural networks are the most common, followed by optimization strategies, Hidden Markov Models, and Graph Signal Processing approaches.

Keywords: Energy load disaggregation · Scoping review · Load disaggregation methods · Data and data source

1 Introduction

The increasing electricity demand coupled with the uneven production of renewable energy sources and imbalanced electricity consumption puts immense pressure on the existing power grids [1]. Demand-side management and load shifting can address these issues by redistributing electricity consumption away from peak periods, thus creating a more balanced consumption curve or aligning consumption peaks with electricity generation peaks [2, 3]. Accurate knowledge of individual appliance consumption at specific times can help identify shiftable loads, enabling more precise demand-side management. Load disaggregation can also promote electricity-saving behaviors among individuals by raising awareness of their consumption patterns [1, 2].

Load monitoring, or load disaggregation, involves measuring the electricity consumption of individual consumers. Intrusive Load Monitoring (ILM) is a traditional method that requires submetering appliances, necessitating a measurement device for each monitored consumer [4]. This approach results in high hardware requirements, which can be expensive and logistically challenging to deploy. In contrast, Non-Intrusive Load Monitoring (NILM) was first introduced by [5]. NILM calculates the consumption of individual appliances by using the electricity measurements already available at aggregation points, such as electricity meters.

N. Moniz et al. (Eds.): EPIA 2023, LNAI 14116, pp. 209–221, 2023.
https://doi.org/10.1007/978-3-031-49011-8_17

However, the field of energy load disaggregation still lacks a comprehensive overview of the various domains, datasets, and methodologies employed in the research. Without a comprehensive overview, it becomes challenging for researchers and practitioners to identify knowledge gaps, potential areas for innovation, and best practices for effective load disaggregation [6]. Therefore, this paper aims to present an in-depth review of load disaggregation literature using a scoping review method, providing a systematic analysis of the current state of the field, and identifying challenges, and opportunities for future research and development.

The paper is organized as follows: First, the methodology section presents the scoping review process including the search strategy and inclusion and exclusion criteria; the results section provides an overview of the key findings from the reviewed literature, highlighting the domains, datasets, and methods used in energy load disaggregation research. Subsequently, the discussion section delves into the implications of these findings, addressing the challenges, limitations, and opportunities within the field, as well as offering recommendations for future research directions. Finally, the conclusion section summarizes the main contributions of the paper and emphasizes its relevance to the ongoing development of load disaggregation research and applications.

2 Methodology

This paper employs the scoping review methodology introduced in [7] which involve a systematic literature search to identify and analyse the relevant articles on load disaggregation. The first step in the literature search process was to apply the search string "load disaggregation" in the Web of Science database. The reason for choosing the Web of Science as the primary source for this search was due to its comprehensive coverage of high-quality, peer-reviewed research articles from various disciplines, including energy and engineering fields. No filtering was applied based on publication date. The initial search resulted in 131 articles with the search string appearing in their titles. The reason for focusing on titles was to ensure that the selected articles had a strong and direct focus on load disaggregation as a primary research topic, which is essential for the scope of this review.

To further refine the search and ensure that the articles matched the paper's scope, the search string "energy OR electricity OR heat" was applied to the abstracts of the 131 identified articles. This step was necessary to confirm that the selected articles addressed load disaggregation in the context of energy, electricity, or heat. This filtering process resulted in 122 relevant articles for further analysis.

To ensure the quality of the literature analysis, only peer-reviewed journal articles were considered for the review. A full-text search was conducted, and full texts for 72 out of the 122 relevant articles were retrieved. The 72 full-text articles were thoroughly reviewed, and relevant data, such as authors, publication year, research methods, main findings, and key contributions, were extracted.

3 Results

The scoping review results of load disaggregation research can be divided into the applied domains, data and data sources, as well as the various methods employed.

3.1 Applied Domains

As illustrated in Fig. 1, residential homes and households represent the most common domain, with 54 out of the 72 investigated articles focusing on disaggregating the load for these types of consumers. Other domains explored include commercial buildings (4 articles), electric vehicles (3 articles), and industrial parks (2 articles). Three articles examined the disaggregation of larger, bulk supply points for multiple buildings.

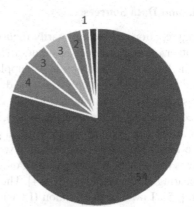

- ■ Residental Buildings
- ■ commercial buildings
- ■ electric vehicles
- ■ larger suply points
- ■ Industrial parks
- ■ commercial and residental buildings
- ■ residential and industrial buildings

Fig. 1. The investigated domains in the literature

Households are the predominant research domain in load disaggregation. Most studies in this area aim to disaggregate major, easily metered household appliances, such as washing machines, dishwashers, kettles, microwaves, and ovens [8–15]. Four articles [2, 16–18] specifically focused on identifying heating and cooling-related loads and separating them from the rest. Two articles aimed to disaggregate household electricity load while incorporating electricity generated by solar panels [19, 20]. Another study sought to predict battery failures by adding battery simulations to the load profile and detecting anomalous battery behaviour through load disaggregation [21].

In the commercial sector, two studies examined the measurement of typical office devices like lamps, computers, and coffee machines [22]. One of them [23] used disaggregation to identify individuals' departure and arrival times. An article [24] disaggregated the lighting load profile using only ambient lighting information measured by light sensors and knowledge of the light bulb numbers and energy uptake, while [25] employed NILM to disaggregate various cooling loads from an aggregate cooling load already separated from the overall electricity consumption.

Research in the industrial sector primarily focused on disaggregating the consumption of different industrial tools. Disaggregation of various tools in [26] was used to enhance a demand response scheduling algorithm's performance. Similarly, [27] employed load disaggregation to assist demand-side management.

Three studies concentrated on electric vehicle charging. In [28] a framework was developed for disaggregating the total energy of plug-in electric vehicles at the feeder head level. A different article [29] modelled the electricity consumption of charging stations, using similarities between the created models to better understand the future requirements of similar charging stations. Article [30] disaggregated feeder head-level consumption into separate smart meter readings, encompassing both industrial and residential buildings. An article [4] used bulk supply point measurements to disaggregate them into several categories, such as switch mode power supply, different induction motors, lighting, rectifiers, and resistive load, while [8] also considered plug-in electric vehicles at the feeder head level.

3.2 Data and Data Sources

Load disaggregation research primarily focuses on electricity loads, occasionally incorporating other information such as outdoor temperature and solar radiation. One article [27] also includes gas consumption as supplementary information for electricity load disaggregation. Multiple publicly available datasets are commonly used in the literature, as demonstrated by the distribution in Fig. 2. The most popular dataset is the REDD (Reference Energy Disaggregation Data Set), used in 16 standalone articles and an additional 16 articles in conjunction with other datasets. The UK-DALE (UK Domestic Appliance-Level Electricity) dataset is the second most popular, used three times alone and 11 times with other datasets. The AMPds (Almanac of Minutely Power dataset) ranks third, appearing in seven articles [31–34]. The least popular datasets—LIFTED, GreenD [35], Eco [35], Low Carbon London (LCL) [36], and Rainforest Automation Energy Dataset (RAE) [37]—each appeared only once in the reviewed articles. Furthermore, multiple studies used non-public datasets.

Residential buildings. The most commonly used dataset for residential household research is the REDD dataset, featured in 29 articles, e.g., [21, 38–45], followed by the UK-DALE dataset, used in 12 articles, e.g., [39, 46–48]. The least used datasets, such as LIFTED, appeared in only one article [49]. Meanwhile, most residential load disaggregation research is conducted on relatively low-frequency data, as seen in 37 articles. For example, [50] tested their model on data sampled at 15, 30, and 60-s intervals, while [51] used data sampled at 6 and 60-s intervals. Six articles use data between 1 and 15 min [16, 52, 53], five use frequencies higher than 1 s [49, 54], two work with hourly data [2, 55], and one with 30-min sampling rate [17].

The REDD dataset, publicly available and comprising metering data from real US residential houses, monitors central, aggregate consumption at a high frequency of 15 kHz, while individual appliances are monitored at lower frequencies of 0.5 or 1 Hz [56]. The UK-DALE dataset, collected from UK domestic houses, records central consumption at a high frequency of 16 kHz (downsampled from 433 MHz) and appliance-level consumption at a lower frequency of 1/6 Hz, including up to 54 appliances per house [15].

Regarding frequency, most research (42 articles, such as [50] and [21]) is based on a range of 1 min to 1 s. Six articles work with 1–15 min, three with a 30-min sampling rate, and seven with an hourly sampling rate. An additional seven articles utilize high-frequency data [57–59], ranging from 60 measurements per second up to 44.1 kHz. This information is depicted in Fig. 3.

Commercial buildings. Research on commercial office buildings typically relies on non-public datasets. One study [23] utilized data from a preliminary study conducted in an office space owned by the University of Nebraska. Another study focusing on heating and cooling loads in an office environment collected data from a large Chinese office (32,000 m^2) with hot summers and cold winters [25].

In terms of sampling rates for commercial buildings, three articles use 1 s to 1-min rates, though only one employs NILM [23]. The other two utilize hourly sampling rates [25, 60]. Industrial research is predominantly based on private datasets, with articles [26, 27] using data collected from Iranian industrial zones.

The WHITED dataset [61], employed by [62, 63], includes both industrial and residential appliances with high measurement frequency (44.1 kHz), while [26, 27] use real industrial data applying hourly sampling rates.

Electric vehicles. There are limited datasets involving electric vehicles. The EA Technology company conducted the My Electric Avenue project in 2017 to understand the impact of electric vehicles on local electricity grids. The project released a dataset used by article [28]. Another British study, the Low-Carbon-London project, also released electric vehicle charging data, utilized by article [36].

The three articles in this domain used varying sampling rates. For residential plug-in electric vehicle load disaggregation, the article employed hourly data [28], while [36] used a 30-min sampling rate in their research. In article [28], which focuses on feeder head-level electric vehicle load disaggregation, the electric vehicle data was combined with zonal load data released by Independent System Operators in New England. Duke Energy provided a dataset for [30], collected in North Carolina.

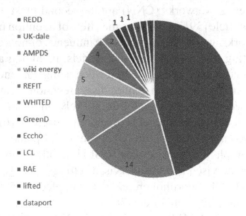

Fig. 2. The distribution of the public datasets used

3.3 Related Methods

Numerous methods and approaches exist for NILM, which can be primarily classified into supervised and unsupervised learning algorithms [2]. Supervised learning algorithms rely on labeled data for training, which can be difficult to obtain as it necessitates intrusive load monitoring techniques. Consequently, several studies focus on unsupervised models that do not require a learning phase, although manual tuning is necessary [64].

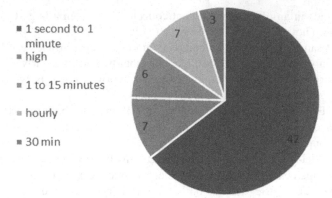

Fig. 3. Data frequency distribution

Many NILM methods are event or state-based, making the feature extraction and event detection phases crucial for these algorithms. As illustrated in Fig. 4, neural network-based solutions are the most prevalent due to the wide variety of models available. Long Short-Term Memory (LSTM) models are popular as they can capture the temporal features of the data. For example, [46] employs a multiple-output LSTM model, while [65] applies a deep composite LSTM network to address the disaggregation problem. Convolutional Neural Networks (CNN) are the second most common neural network in the literature. Article [39] investigates the effect of attention mechanisms on both CNN and LSTM networks, while [25] explores the influence of non-electric data on load disaggregation by testing three neural network models, including a sequence-to-point and sequence-to-sequence version of CNN, and a denoising autoencoder.

The second most common approach defines disaggregation as an optimization problem. Optimization-based methods generally do not rely on events [66]. Several optimization algorithms exist, such as integer programming used by [67, 68], an improved version of the Prey-Predator Optimization Algorithm in [50], and particle swarm optimization in [62, 69]. Graph Signal Processing (GSP) is another popular method and can be employed in both supervised and unsupervised settings, e.g., [70–72]. For instance [16] apply a supervised GSP algorithm on real data sampled at 15-min intervals, while Ming-Yue Zhai also uses GSP in an article [36].

Hidden Markov Models (HMM), often factorial HMMs, are frequently used either independently or in conjunction with other methods. Typically employed in a non-event-based manner, HMMs can also be utilized based on events to address issues related to other HMM algorithms, as demonstrated in [49]. Wen Fan [54] uses FHMM to model appliance states and an optimization method to solve the disaggregation problem. Less common methods include probability-based approaches, such as Gaussian Mixture Models in [64], or Linear Discriminant Classifier Group in [73].

Applied Domains. In the residential domain, the distribution of models aligns with the overall results. The four most common model types are neural networks, optimization and HMM-based models, graph signal processing, while less popular methods include Gaussian mixture models and classifier chains [74].

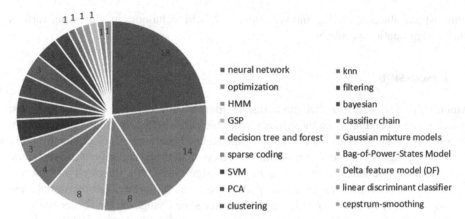

Fig. 4. The distribution of methods used for Load disaggregation

For office buildings, three studies utilize NILM. One study employs random forest and Fourier transform for feature extraction [25]. Article [60] works with both residential and commercial buildings using a mask-based deep neural network to disaggregate flexible, primarily heating and cooling-related, electricity loads [75]. In the third article, Hamed Nabizadeh Rafsanjani develops a disaggregation framework that uses the DBSCAN clustering method to identify electricity load events caused by the same person.

Both research articles conducted on industrial parks employ optimization frameworks. Article [26] utilizes an algorithm called OLDA (Optimization-Based Load Disaggregation Algorithm) developed in [39]. Another article creates an optimization model that leverages industry-specific features alongside electricity load for improved disaggregation results [27].

Articles working with electric vehicles employ various methods. A Kalman filter-based method is used in [28], which disaggregates feeder head-level residential electric vehicle load. Another study that attempts to identify the number of electric vehicles at a charging station employs matching pursuits, a sparse approximation algorithm [36].

Data and Data Sources. The most researched sampling frequency ranges between 1 s and 1 min. These studies employ a wide variety of methods, with neural networks being the most common. For example, some articles explore the use of attention mechanisms to improve disaggregation models [39, 51, 76]. The second most popular approaches are HMM-based [77, 78] and GSP-based models [36, 43]. Less commonly used methods include filtering techniques, such as particle filtering in article [79], and decision trees [47].

Optimization frameworks are the most utilized methods for data with frequencies between 1 and 15 min, such as linear optimization used by [67]. Other less common methods include neural networks [52] and clustering [18]. For very low-frequency data, sampled at 30 min or an hour, most studies employ neural networks [17] or optimization [26]. Less frequently used are GPS [55] and sparse coding [36]. For high-frequency data, optimization [62] and HMM-based methods [49] are the most common. Overall, the diverse range of methods employed across different domains and data frequencies demonstrates the adaptability and versatility of NILM techniques in addressing various load disaggregation problems.

4   Discussion

Among the five main applied domains, residential households represent the most researched area and have the most freely available datasets, leading to the development of new models specifically for residential data. Related challenges include the difficulty of gathering high-frequency data and the limited computational capacity of smart meters, which restricts the integration of disaggregation algorithms [80]. Research on bulk and feeder head level data is less common, partly due to the limited availability of data and the impossibility of detecting individual appliance state changes at the feeder head.

The challenge related to commercial buildings is mainly the low availability of data [81, 82]. Office buildings typically have numerous appliances, which would be expensive to individually submeter [83]. A significant portion of consumption comes from lighting, which is more difficult to submeter than plug-in devices [84].

The main challenge in research on industrial data faces challenges such as industrial secrecy, which limits the availability of public datasets, and the difficulty of generalizing between different industrial consumers due to variations in industrial processes [85]. Submetering all devices to collect disaggregation data is also challenging.

Electric vehicle research faces challenges due to the diverse electricity load that electric vehicles produce, as well as the added complexity introduced by Vehicle-to-Grid (V2G) capable vehicles feeding electricity back into the grid [86, 87].

Regarding data and data sources, studies most commonly use data with a frequency range of 1 s to 1 min, which is still considered low-frequency data and does not permit the extraction of transient features. Consequently, steady-state features are used for load classification, which can be more challenging to distinguish.

High-frequency data allows for the extraction of transient states, which are easier to classify than steady states. However, obtaining and processing high-frequency data is more difficult and expensive due to the need for specialized equipment and increased computational resources.

Working with lower sampling rate data complicates the extraction of even steady-state transitions, making disaggregation particularly difficult for appliances with short operation times and low power consumption. To address this issue, complementary information is often employed, such as outside temperature for heating and cooling loads or occupant behavior for residential loads.

Various methods are used for load disaggregation, with the primary categories being unsupervised and supervised learning. Supervised learning algorithms can be accurate but require large amounts of data, which can be difficult to acquire. Unsupervised algorithms are often less accurate and cannot identify specific appliances without prior knowledge. Neural networks, optimization GSP, and HMMs are among the popular methods employed. However, each method has its limitations, such as computational complexity, sensitivity to noise, inability to handle unknown devices, and the need for high-frequency data.

Considering the multiple obstacles in collecting high-frequency data, future research should focus on low-frequency disaggregation. The development of computationally inexpensive yet accurate algorithms is essential, especially for residential domains, to achieve smart meter integrable solutions.

Exploring lightweight state-of-the-art deep learning approaches, such as knowledge distillation, and investigating the potential of federated learning to overcome privacy and secrecy issues could lead to models with better generalization capabilities. Moreover, expanding research into fields other than domestic loads and exploring disaggregation of other energy carriers, such as gas or district heating, can open up new opportunities for energy management and efficiency.

5 Conclusion

This paper presents a comprehensive review of energy load disaggregation, offering an overview of the field by examining the domains of research, datasets employed, and methodologies utilized. The most extensively investigated area in the reviewed literature involves the disaggregation of the electricity load in residential homes, with a focus on individual appliances. Industrial load disaggregation and the disaggregation of electricity at bulk supply points remain the least explored topics.

The majority of studies investigate sampling frequencies between 1 s and 1 min, while 1 to 15-min and 30-min sampling rates receive less attention. In terms of methods, deep neural network models are the most widely used due to their versatility, followed by optimization-based approaches, Hidden Markov Model (HMM) based techniques, and graph signal processing. Less commonly explored methods include Gaussian mixture models, filtering, and delta feature models.

This paper's scope is limited to the publications identified by the utilized search string, which may exclude relevant studies. Future research should employ search strings with broader coverage, such as "non-intrusive load monitoring." As this is a literature review paper, the recommendations provided require further investigation and validation through empirical research.

Future research should prioritize the reduction of computational requirements for load disaggregation, as current methods often entail high computational costs. Efforts should also be made to improve the accuracy of frameworks working with very low-frequency data, thereby easing data collection requirements and increasing the accessibility of such models. Additionally, currently under-researched areas, such as industrial load disaggregation, warrant further exploration.

Acknowledgements. This paper is part of the project "Data-dreven smarte bygninger: data sandkasse og konkurrence" (Journalnummer: 64021-6025) by EUDP (Energy Technology Development and Demonstration Program), Denmark.

References

1. Ma, Z., J∅rgensen, B.N.: Energy flexibility of the commercial greenhouse growers: The potential and benefits of participating in the electricity market. In: 2018 IEEE Power & Energy Society Innovative Smart Grid Technologies Conference (ISGT) (2018)
2. Massidda, L., Marrocu, M.: A bayesian approach to unsupervised, non-intrusive load disaggregation. Sensors **22**(12) (2022)
3. Værbak, M., et al.: Agent-based modelling of demand-side flexibility adoption in reservoir pumping. In: 2019 IEEE Sciences and Humanities International Research Conference (SHIRCON) (2019)
4. Xu, Y.Z., Milanovic, J.V.: Artificial-intelligence-based methodology for load disaggregation at bulk supply point. IEEE Trans. Power Syst. **30**(2), 795–803 (2015)
5. Hart, G.W.: Nonintrusive appliance load monitoring. Proc. IEEE **80**(12), 1870–1891 (1992)
6. Howard, D.A., Ma, Z., Jørgensen, B.N.: Evaluation of industrial energy flexibility potential: A scoping review (2021)
7. Ma, Z.G.: Scoping review in one week: A cookbook for beginners to conduct scoping reviews and write review papers with simple steps (2022). Amazon.com
8. Chalmers, C., et al.: Detecting activities of daily living and routine behaviours in dementia patients living alone using smart meter load disaggregation. IEEE Trans. Emerg. Top. Comput. **10**(1), 157–169 (2022)
9. Zhou, G., et al.: Sequence-to-sequence load disaggregation using multiscale residual neural network. IEEE Trans. Instrum. Meas. **70** (2021)
10. Zeinal-Kheiri, S., Shotorbani, A.M., Mohammadi-Ivatloo, B.: Residential load disaggregation considering state transitions. IEEE Trans. Industr. Inf. **16**(2), 743–753 (2020)
11. Massidda, L., Marrocu, M., Manca, S.: Non-intrusive load disaggregation by convolutional neural network and multilabel classification. Appl. Sci.-Basel **10**(4) (2020)
12. Yuan, Q.B., et al.: A fusion load disaggregation method based on clustering algorithm and support vector regression optimization for low sampling data. Future Internet **11**(2) (2019)
13. Xia, M., et al.: Dilated residual attention network for load disaggregation. Neural Comput. Appl. **31**(12), 8931–8953 (2019)
14. Xia, M., et al.: Non-intrusive load disaggregation based on deep dilated residual network. Electr. Power Syst. Res. **170**, 277–285 (2019)
15. Marceau, M.L., Zmeureanu, R.: Nonintrusive load disaggregation computer program to estimate the energy consumption of major end uses in residential buildings. Energy Convers. Manage. **41**(13), 1389–1403 (2000)
16. Green, C., Garimella, S.: Analysis of supervised graph signal processing-based load disaggregation for residential demand-side management. Electr. Power Syst. Res. **208** (2022)
17. Zou, M. Z., et al.: Heating and lighting load disaggregation using frequency components and convolutional bidirectional long short-term memory method. Energies **14**(16) (2021)
18. Deb, C., et al.: Automated load disaggregation for residences with electrical resistance heating. Energy Build. **182**, 61–74 (2019)
19. Sun, J.X., et al.: Power load disaggregation of households with solar panels based on an improved long short-term memory network. J. Electr. Eng. & Technol. **15**(5), 2401–2413 (2020)
20. Liu, Y., et al.: A robust non-intrusive load disaggregation method with roof-top photovoltaics. Electr. Power Syst. Res. **208** (2022)
21. Wang, W., et al.: Bats: An appliance safety hazards factors detection algorithm with an improved nonintrusive load disaggregation method. Energies **14**(12) (2021)
22. Doherty, B., Trenbath, K.: Device-level plug load disaggregation in a zero energy office building and opportunities for energy savings. Energy Build. **204** (2019)

23. Rafsanjani, H.N., et al.: A load-disaggregation framework to sense personalized energy-use information in commercial buildings. Energy Build. **207** (2020)
24. Jazizadeh, F., et al.: Spatiotemporal lighting load disaggregation using light intensity signal. Energy Build. **69**, 572–583 (2014)
25. Xiao, Z.W., et al.: Cooling load disaggregation using a NILM method based on random forest for smart buildings. Sustain. Cities Soc. **74** (2021)
26. Oskouei, M.Z., et al.: Optimal scheduling of demand response aggregators in industrial parks based on load disaggregation algorithm. IEEE Syst. J. **16**(1), 945–953 (2022)
27. Tavakoli, S., Khalilpour, K.: A practical load disaggregation approach for monitoring industrial users demand with limited data availability. Energies **14**(16) (2021)
28. Ebrahimi, M., Rastegar, M., Arefi, M.M.: Real-time estimation frameworks for feeder-level load disaggregation and PEVs' charging behavior characteristics extraction. IEEE Trans. Industr. Inf. **18**(7), 4715–4724 (2022)
29. Liu, Q., et al.: A sensory similarities approach to load disaggregation of charging stations in internet of electric vehicles. IEEE Sens. J. **21**(14), 15895–15903 (2021)
30. Wang, J.Y., et al.: A data-driven pivot-point-based time-series feeder load disaggregation method. IEEE Trans. Smart Grid **11**(6), 5396–5406 (2020)
31. Wang, H.J., et al.: An optimal load disaggregation method based on power consumption pattern for low sampling data. Sustainability **11**(1) (2019)
32. Wang, H.J., Yang, W.R.: An iterative load disaggregation approach based on appliance consumption pattern. Appl. Sci.-Basel **8**(4) (2018)
33. Kong, W.C., et al.: An extensible approach for non-intrusive load disaggregation with smart meter data. IEEE Trans. Smart Grid **9**(4), 3362–3372 (2018)
34. Bhotto, M.Z.A., Makonin, S., Bajic, I.V.: Load disaggregation based on aided linear integer programming. IEEE Trans. Circuits Syst. Ii-Express Briefs **64**(7), 792–796 (2017)
35. Pochacker, M., Egarter, D., Elmenreich, W.: Proficiency of power values for load disaggregation. IEEE Trans. Instrum. Meas. **65**(1), 46–55 (2016)
36. Wang, S.Y., et al.: Electric vehicle load disaggregation based on limited activation matching pursuits. Innov. Solut. Energy Transit. **158**, 2611–2616 (2019)
37. Lemes, D.A.M., et al.: Load disaggregation based on time window for HEMS application. Ieee Access **9**, 70746–70757 (2021)
38. Qi, B., Liu, L.Y., Wu, X.: Low-rate nonintrusive load disaggregation for resident load based on graph signal processing. IEEJ Trans. Electr. Electron. Eng. **13**(12), 1833–1834 (2018)
39. Liu, Q., et al.: Improving wireless indoor non-intrusive load disaggregation using attention-based deep learning networks. Phys. Commun **51** (2022)
40. Aiad, M., Lee, P.H.: Non-intrusive load disaggregation with adaptive estimations of devices main power effects and two-way interactions. Energy Build. **130**, 131–139 (2016)
41. Wong, Y.F., Drummond, T., Sekercioglu, Y.A.: Real-time load disaggregation algorithm using particle-based distribution truncation with state occupancy model. Electron. Lett. **50**(9), 697–698 (2014)
42. Feng, R.H., et al.: Nonintrusive load disaggregation for residential users based on alternating optimization and downsampling. IEEE Trans. Instrum. Meas. **70** (2021)
43. Moradzadeh, A., et al.: Improving residential load disaggregation for sustainable development of energy via principal component analysis. Sustainability **12**(8) (2020)
44. Yang, C.C., Soh, C.S., Yap, V.V.: A systematic approach in load disaggregation utilizing a multi-stage classification algorithm for consumer electrical appliances classification. Front. Energy **13**(2), 386–398 (2019)
45. Zhang, L.L., et al.: Assessment metrics for unsupervised non-intrusive load disaggregation learning algorithms. Pract. Appl. Intell. Syst., Iske **2014**(279), 197–206 (2013)
46. Fang, Y.F., et al.: Non-intrusive load disaggregation based on a feature reused long short-term memory multiple output network. Buildings **12**(7) (2022)

47. Abbas, M.Z., et al.: An adaptive-neuro fuzzy inference system based-hybrid technique for performing load disaggregation for residential customers. Sci. Rep. **12**(1) (2022)
48. Alkhulaifi, A., Aljohani, A.J.: Investigation of deep learning-based techniques for load disaggregation, low-frequency approach. Int. J. Adv. Comput. Sci. Appl. **11**(1), 701–706 (2020)
49. Yan, L., et al.: EFHMM: Event-based factorial hidden markov model for real-time load disaggregation. IEEE Trans. Smart Grid **13**(5), 3844–3847 (2022)
50. Xia, D., Ba, S.S., Ahmadpour, A.: Non-intrusive load disaggregation of smart home appliances using the IPPO algorithm and FHM model. Sustain. Cities Soc. **67** (2021)
51. Weng, L.G., et al.: Non-intrusive load disaggregation based on a multi-scale attention residual network. Appl. Sci.-Basel **10**(24) (2020)
52. Gois, J., Pereira, L., Nunes, N.: A data-centric analysis of the impact of non-electric data on the performance of load disaggregation algorithms. Sensors **22**(18) (2022)
53. Eskander, M.M., Silva, C.A.: A complementary unsupervised load disaggregation method for residential loads at very low sampling rate data. Sustain. Energy Technol. Assess. **43** (2021)
54. Fan, W., et al.: Multi-objective non-intrusive load disaggregation based on appliances characteristics in smart homes. Energy Rep. **7**, 4445–4459 (2021)
55. Zhao, B.C., et al.: Non-intrusive load disaggregation solutions for very low-rate smart meter data. Appl. Energy **268** (2020)
56. Kolter, J.: And M, p. 25. A Public Data Set for Energy Disaggregation Research. Artif. Intell, Johnson, REDD (2011)
57. Kong, S., et al.: Home appliance load disaggregation using cepstrum-smoothing-based method. IEEE Trans. Consum. Electron. **61**(1), 24–30 (2015)
58. de Souza, W.A., et al.: Load disaggregation using microscopic power features and pattern recognition. Energies **12**(14) (2019)
59. Quek, Y.T., Woo, W.L., Logenthiran, T.: Load disaggregation using one-directional convolutional stacked long short-term memory recurrent neural network. IEEE Syst. J. **14**(1), 1395–1404 (2020)
60. Song, J., Lee, Y., Hwang, E.: Time-frequency mask estimation based on deep neural network for flexible load disaggregation in buildings. IEEE Trans. Smart Grid **12**(4), 3242–3251 (2021)
61. Kahl, M., et al.: WHITED—A Worldwide Household and Industry Transient Energy Data Set (2016)
62. Liu, H., et al.: An improved non-intrusive load disaggregation algorithm and its application. Sustain. Cities Soc. **53** (2020)
63. Chui, K.T., et al.: Handling data heterogeneity in electricity load disaggregation via optimized complete ensemble empirical mode decomposition and wavelet packet transform. Sensors **21**(9) (2021)
64. Qureshi, M., Ghiaus, C., Ahmad, N.: A blind event-based learning algorithm for non-intrusive load disaggregation. Int. J. Electr. Power & Energy Syst. **129** (2021)
65. Xia, M., et al.: Non-intrusive load disaggregation based on composite deep long short-term memory network. Expert. Syst. Appl. **160** (2020)
66. Qi, B., Liu, L.Y., Wu, X.: Low-rate non-intrusive load disaggregation with graph shift quadratic form constraint. Appl. Sci.-Basel **8**(4) (2018)
67. Dash, S., Sodhi, R., Sodhi, B.: An appliance load disaggregation scheme using automatic state detection enabled enhanced integer programming. IEEE Trans. Industr. Inf. **17**(2), 1176–1185 (2021)
68. Lima, D.A., M.Z.C. Oliveira, Zuluaga, E.O.: Non-intrusive load disaggregation model for residential consumers with Fourier series and optimization method applied to White tariff modality in Brazil. Electr. Power Syst. Res. **184** (2020)
69. Guo, Y., et al.: Research on non-intrusive load disaggregation method based on multi-model combination. Electr. Power Syst. Res.. **200** (2021)

70. Zhai, M.-Y.: A new graph learning-based signal processing approach for non-intrusive load disaggregation with active power measurements. Neural Comput. Appl. **32**(10), 5495–5504 (2019). https://doi.org/10.1007/s00521-019-04623-w
71. He, K.H., Stankovic, V., Stankovic, L.: Building a graph signal processing model using dynamic time warping for load disaggregation. Sensors **20**(22) (2020)
72. He, K.H., et al.: Non-intrusive load disaggregation using graph signal processing. IEEE Trans. Smart Grid **9**(3), 1739–1747 (2018)
73. Yu, J.Y., et al.: Non-intrusive load disaggregation by linear classifier group considering multi-feature integration. Appl. Sci.-Basel **9**(17) (2019)
74. Sahrane, S., Adnane, M., Haddadi, M.: Multi-label load disaggregation in presence of non-targeted loads. Electr. Power Syst. Res. **199** (2021)
75. Vanting, N.B., Ma, Z., Jørgensen, B.N.: A scoping review of deep neural networks for electric load forecasting. Energy Inform. **4**(2), 49 (2021)
76. Piccialli, V., Sudoso, A.M.: Improving non-intrusive load disaggregation through an attention-based deep neural network. Energies **14**(4) (2021)
77. Kwak, Y., Hwang, J., Lee, T.: Load disaggregation via pattern recognition: A feasibility study of a novel method in residential building. Energies **11**(4) (2018)
78. Aiad, M., Lee, P.H.: Unsupervised approach for load disaggregation with devices interactions. Energy Build. **116**, 96–103 (2016)
79. Egarter, D., Bhuvana, V.P., Elmenreich, W.: PALDi: Online load disaggregation via particle filtering. IEEE Trans. Instrum. Meas. **64**(2), 467–477 (2015)
80. Chahine, K., et al.: Electric load disaggregation in smart metering using a novel feature extraction method and supervised classification. Impact Integr. Clean Energy Futur. Mediterr. Environ. **6**, 627–632 (2011)
81. Ma, Z., Jørgensen, B.N.: A discussion of building automation and stakeholder engagement for the readiness of energy flexible buildings. Energy Inform. **1**(1), 54 (2018)
82. Ma, Z., et al.: An overview of digitalization for the building-to-grid ecosystem. Energy Inform. **4**(2), 36 (2021)
83. Ma, Z.: Survey data on university students' experience of energy control, indoor comfort, and energy flexibility in campus buildings. Energy Inform. **5**(4), 50 (2022)
84. Howard, D.A., et al.: Greenhouse industry 4.0—digital twin technology for commercial greenhouses. Energy Inform. **4**(S2) (2021)
85. Howard, D.A., Ma, Z., Jørgensen, B.N.: Digital Twin Framework for Energy Efficient Greenhouse Industry 4.0. in Ambient Intelligence—Software and Applications. Springer International Publishing, Cham (2021)
86. Ma, Z., Christensen, K., Jorgensen, B.N.: Business ecosystem architecture development: A case study of electric vehicle home charging. Energy Inform. **4**, 37 (2021)
87. Ma, Z., et al.: Ecosystem-driven business opportunity identification method and web-based tool with a case study of the electric vehicle home charging energy ecosystem in Denmark. Energy Inform. **5**(4), 54 (2022)

Deep Learning Survival Model to Predict Atrial Fibrillation From ECGs and EHR Data

Giovanni Baj[1(✉)], Arjuna Scagnetto[2], Luca Bortolussi[1], and Giulia Barbati[3]

[1] Department of Mathematics and Geosciences, University of Trieste, Trieste, Italy
giovanni.baj@phd.units.it, lbortolussi@units.it
[2] Cardiovascular Department, Azienda Sanitaria Universitaria Giuliano Isontina
(ASUGI), Trieste, Italy
arjuna.scagnetto@asugi.sanita.fvg.it
[3] Biostatistics Unit, Department of Medical Sciences, University of Trieste, Trieste,
Italy
gbarbati@units.it

Abstract. Atrial fibrillation (AF) is frequently asymptomatic and at the same time a relevant risk factor for stroke and heart failure. Thus, the identification of patients at high risk of future development of AF from rapid and low-cost exams such as the electrocardiogram (ECG) is of great interest. In this work we trained a deep learning model to predict the risk to develop AF from ECG signals and electronic health records (EHR) data, integrating time-to-event in the model and accounting for death as a competing risk. We showed that our model outperforms the CHARGE-AF clinical risk score and we verified that training the model with both ECGs and EHR data led to better performances with respect to training on single modalities. Models were evaluated both in terms of discrimination and calibration.

Keywords: Atrial fibrillation · Deep learning · Survival analysis

1 Introduction

Atrial fibrillation (AF) is a common arrhythmia and represents a relevant risk factor for several important adverse outcomes, including stroke and heart failure [26]. Unfortunately, AF is frequently asymptomatic and thus often unrecognized and untreated. Identifying patients at high risk of future development of AF is of great interest, mainly because cardiac rhythm monitoring may identify individuals with unrecognized AF, thereby enabling the prevention of fatal outcomes [19]. In particular, the development of tools to predict AF from routine and low-cost exams such as the electrocardiogram (ECG) would be an important step toward targeting patients at risk.

Recent work has highlighted the potential for deep learning (DL) methods to predict AF from 12-lead ECGs [3,7,8,14,21]. However, most of these works [7,8,21] approached the AF prediction as a binary classification task: the ECG signal is used to predict the probability that a patient without AF history will develop AF within a certain time window, without including information about the time-to-event or censoring. Khurshid et al. [14] were the first to explicitly incorporate the time until the AF event and missingness due to right censoring in their model, which is important for accurate estimates of absolute risk. To do so, they used the method proposed by Gensheimer and Narasimhan [10], a discrete-time survival model designed for neural networks.

An aspect that was not considered in Khurshid et al.'s work [14] was the presence of competing risks. In the case of AF, death is the primary competing risk, and it should be taken into account when developing a survival prediction model [4]. A method that combines deep learning, survival analysis, and the possibility of handling competing risks is DeepHit [17]. Similarly to [10], DeepHit is a discrete-time survival method designed for neural networks, with the difference that it parameterizes the probability mass function (PMF) of the survival distribution instead of the discrete hazard rate.

Combining information from the raw 12-lead ECG signal with electronic health records (EHR) data may also improve predictive performance. In this regard, Biton et al. [7] trained a random forest classifier to predict the 5-year risk of AF development using features obtained from different modalities, namely demographics, clinical information, and features extracted from the ECG. The authors showed that the integration of all data sources led to better performance compared to using individual modalities.

The main goal of this work was the development of a survival model to predict new-onset AF from ECGs and EHR data, taking into account death as a competing risk. This was achieved by combining the DeepHit method with a multi-modal deep neural network (DNN) able to process both ECG signals and tabular data. As a comparison, we trained other two survival models with the DeepHit approach, but on the single data modalities. To have a further benchmark, we also trained models with the same architectures but in a binary classification setting: in this case, the model predicts the probability that a patient will develop AF within a time window of 5 years. We then compared the predictive accuracy of our model with CHARGE-AF score [2], an AF risk scoring system well-known in clinical literature.

2 Materials and Methods

2.1 Data

The dataset used for this study comprises all standard 10-second, 12-lead ECGs acquired at the Cardiovascular Department of Azienda Sanitaria Universitaria Giuliano Isontina (ASUGI) in Trieste, between February 2, 2007, and December 31, 2022. Since AF is very rarely encountered in young subjects, we extracted only ECGs of patients aged >30. ECGs were recorded using the Mortara^{TM} devices ELI230 and ELI250 at a frequency of 1 kHz and then resampled at 500Hz for computational reasons. By linking the ECG exams with the

EHR of the regional epidemiological repository of Friuli Venezia Giulia region (Italy), we could access demographics, clinical information and drug prescription/consumption of patients at the exam date.

To identify the AF events, we combined information from four different sources, including reports from emergency access or cardiological visits, discharge codes for hospitalizations, and ECG reports. We defined the first AF diagnosis found in any of these sources as the first AF event for each patient. We excluded patients who had experienced AF prior to 2007 or who had undergone pacemaker implantation, Implantable Cardiac Defibrillator (ICD) placement, or Cardiac Resynchronization Therapy (CRT) treatment. Additionally, we did not include in our analysis subjects with an AF diagnosis at the time of their first ECG exam or those with missing AF-event dates.

In the survival setting, we extracted all available ECGs of the patients without any AF event in the observation period, while for patients that developed AF, we used only the ECGs recorded before the first AF event. We then associated each ECG with a label indicating the type of event the patient underwent (censoring, AF, or death), and the time to the event. In the binary classification setting, we included by design only censored cases with a minimum follow-up of 5 years. In this case, ECGs were labelled 1 if the corresponding patient developed AF within 5 years, and 0 otherwise.

For each ECG, we extracted from the EHR a set of 62 features. These included demographics, diagnosis and drug consumption of the patients at the exam date. Furthermore, we decided to include also the wave morphology's features automatically extracted from the ECG signal by the Mortara devices: onset and offset of P and T waves and of the QRS complex, the PR and corrected QT intervals, P, T, QRS axis and the cardiac frequency.

2.2   Model Development

Regarding the data modality given as input to the model, we considered three different approaches for the AF prediction: ECG signals, tabular data and the integration of both modalities. For each data modality, we trained a model both in a survival and in a binary setting. Thus, a total of 6 models were trained for this study.

Survival Models In order to build the survival models we used the DeepHit method, which is designed to deal with right-censored survival data and the presence of competing risks. DeepHit employs a network architecture (sketched in Fig. 1) that consists of a single shared sub-network and a number of cause-specific sub-networks (in our case 2, corresponding to AF and death events). The shared sub-network is an encoder that learns a deep latent representation of the input data, and its structure depends on the data modality considered. In the case of ECG signals alone, the encoder's architecture is a convolutional neural network (CNN), while for tabular data is a fully-connected network (FCN). The integration of both data modalities is obtained by combining the CNN and the

FCN with a joint fusion strategy [12], as depicted in Fig. 1: each network processes the corresponding data modality and the learned feature representations are joined in a common layer. After the encoder, the latent features are used by each cause-specific sub-network to predict the discrete probability distribution of the corresponding event. Finally, the output layer of the whole network is obtained concatenating the outputs of the cause-specif sub-networks and normalized so that it can be interpreted as the joint probability distribution of the two competing events. More precisely, normalization is done with a single softmax layer that is designed to allow for survival past the maximum follow-up (as described in [16]).

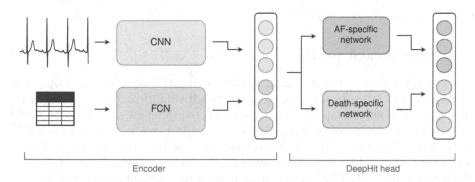

Fig. 1. Schema of the deep multi-modal network for survival analysis. For the single-modality networks, only one between the CNN and the FCN constitutes the encoder, while in the classification setting the DeepHit head is substituted by the binary-classification head.

Binary Models As regards the binary prediction task, the networks adopted have the same encoder architectures described above. The difference is that the encoder is now followed by an FCN composed of one hidden layer of $2n_{lf}$ units (where n_{lf} is the number of latent features extracted by the encoder) and an output layer of two units normalized with a softmax function.

Network Architectures The CNN's architecture is the one used by Scagnetto et al. [23], originally proposed by Goodfellow et al. [11] for the identification of AF in single lead ECGs. The network consists of 13 blocks, each of which includes a 1D convolution, batch normalization. A max-pooling layer is present in blocks 1, 6 and 11. After the convolutional blocks, a global average pooling layer is used to obtain the features that are then used to make a prediction. The FCN is a multi-layer perceptron with two hidden layers made of $2n$ and n units, where n is the number of tabular features (62 in this study). The cause-specific sub-networks for the DeepHit method are fully-connected networks composed of one hidden layer of 10 units, followed by an output layer with a number of neurons equal to the number of discrete time intervals. In all networks the activation function used is ReLU and dropout is adopted for regularization.

CHARGE-AF Score CHARGE-AF (Cohorts for Aging Research and Genomic Epidemiology—Atrial Fibrillation) is a well-validated clinical risk score for the development of AF [2]. The score was derived by estimating a Cox proportional hazards model, trained with the variables age, race, height, weight, systolic and diastolic blood pressure, current smoking, use of antihypertensive medication, diabetes, history of myocardial infarction and heart failure. 5-year AF risk estimates for CHARGE-AF were computed using the equation $1 - 0.9718412736^{\exp(af\_score - 12.58156)}$ where af_score is the individual's CHARGE-AF score obtained as a linear combination of the risk factors [2].

2.3   Experimental Setting

The dataset was split into training, validation and test sets, with a proportion of respectively 7:1:2. In the case of patients with multiple ECGs, we ensured that there was no overlap of patients between the different sets. We also made sure that the fraction of positive samples in each set was as similar as possible to the overall fraction (10%). The validation set was used to evaluate the model during training and to apply early stopping to avoid overfitting. Before feeding them to the network, ECG signals were filtered to remove baseline wander and high-frequency noise with a zero phase second-order infinite impulse response bandpass filter, in the band 0.67–100 Hz [15]. Then, ECGs were also normalized subtracting from each channel its mean and dividing it by its standard deviation. For tabular data, we used a Min-max scaler to normalize each feature between 0 and 1.

Since the DeepHit method requires time to be discrete, we had to perform a discretization of the time scale. More precisely, we made an equidistant grid with 50 grid points and we then expressed the time to event of each ECG in this discrete time scale, following the procedure proposed in [16].

Both the survival and the binary classification models were trained via AdamW optimizer, with a batch size of 128 and a learning rate of 10^{-3}. The loss function maximized was the DeepHit loss for the survival model and the binary cross-entropy loss for the binary classifier.

2.4   Evaluation Metrics

For the survival models, we inspected their discriminative performance computing the area under the time-dependent receiver operating characteristic curve (AUC), with the cumulative/dynamic definition [13]. To account for potential biases, AUC was calculated taking into account the presence of a competing risk event (death) and using inverse probability of censoring weights. To assess calibration, we computed the Integrated Calibration Index (ICI) for competing-risk survival models, as proposed by Austin et al. [5]. ICI is based upon a graphical assessment of calibration: a calibration curve is obtained regressing the cumulative incidence function of the cause-specific outcome of interest on the predicted outcome risk with a Fine-Gray sub-distribution hazard model, and then ICI is computed as the average prediction error weighted by the empirical risk distribution. For the binary classification models, we computed AUC and ICI defined for a binary outcome [6]. Since binary models estimate the risk to develop AF within 5 years, we focused on the predicted 5-year risk also in the survival setting.

Standard errors and corresponding 95% confidence intervals (CI) were estimated using 100-iteration bootstrapping, for both the metrics considered.

3   Results

The final dataset included a total of 350 701 recordings from 128 030 unique patients. See Table 1 for a descriptive snapshot of the population. The median and interquartile age for the recordings was 66 [54–75], while the percentage of males was 50.3%. From Table 1 we can also notice that the sample of patients that developed AF was significantly older and with a higher rate of comorbidities with respect to the sample that did not develop AF. The overall median follow-up time was 6.45 years, while it was 4.26 years restricting to individuals that developed AF. In the binary classification setting, we excluded by design censored cases with a follow-up shorter than 5 years, reducing to 226 529 signals for 95 823 unique patients.

In Table 2 we report 5-year AUC and ICI values (and corresponding 95% CI) for the six trained models. The first thing that we can notice is that the survival model trained combining ECG and EHR data shows good performance, with an AUC of 0.845 and an ICI of 0.010. To visually inspect the model's output, we plot in Fig. 2 the observed cumulative incidence function for the AF event, stratified by the 5-year risk predicted by the model. Looking at the figure, it is possible to see that the incidence curves differ significantly, and in particular that patients with higher predicted risk are associated to higher AF incidence at 5 years.

As regards the comparison with the other approaches, we can notice from Table 2 that, from a discrimination point of view, the survival and binary classification models behave in a very similar way, while the most influential factor on discrimination is the data modality used to train the model. In particular, the best-performing models in terms of AUCs are the ones that integrate ECG information and clinical tabular data, with AUCs of 0.845 and 0.842 for the survival and the binary models, respectively. The use of ECG signals alone leads to models with an AUC of approximately 0.82, while the weakest discrimination is obtained when only tabular data are used to train the algorithm (AUC around 0.81). Moving to calibration, we can see that all the models are well calibrated in general, with the maximum ICI value of 0.024 obtained for the binary model trained with tabular data alone. The second worst calibrated model is again the one trained only with tabular data, but in the survival setting, with ICI equal to 0.017. For the rest of the models, the calibration performance is similar.

Table 1. Descriptive features of the dataset. For all binary variables we report the percentage of 1s.

| | Overall | Grouped by AF | |
		0	1
n	351 701	315 348	36 353
Age, median [Q1,Q3]	66 [54, 75]	65 [52, 75]	74 [68, 80]
Gender (males)	50.3	49.9	54.2
Ischemic disease	23.2	22.1	32.8
AMI	14.3	13.8	18.9
TIA/Stroke	4.9	4.5	8.3
COPD	23.9	23.4	28.4
Diabetes	45.2	44.4	51.8
Chronic heart failure	8.7	7.6	17.9
Chronic kidney disease	14.6	13.5	24.3
Anticoagulants	8.2	7.7	13.0
Antihypertensive	56.6	54.1	78.4
Calcium blockers	18.8	17.5	29.9
Antiarrhythmics	2.7	2.1	8.0
Beta-blockers	30.7	28.9	46.2
Diuretics	12.4	11.6	19.8

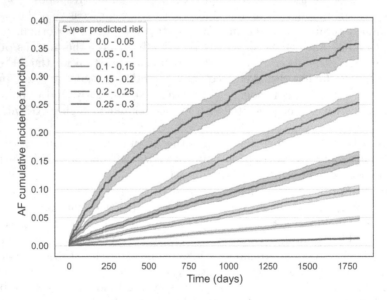

Fig. 2. Observed cumulative incidence function for the AF event, stratified by the 5-year AF risk predicted by the DeepHit model trained with both ECGs and EHR data. Cumulative incidence is estimated with the Aalen-Johansen estimator. Shaded areas around curves indicate 95% confidence intervals.

Table 2. Models performance for atrial fibrillation prediction in test sets

Model	5-year AUC	5-year ICI
DeepHit (ECG + tabular)	0.845 (0.839, 0.851)	0.010 (0.008, 0.011)
DeepHit (ECG)	0.820 (0.812, 0.826)	0.005 (0.004, 0.007)
DeepHit (tabular)	0.810 (0.804, 0.816)	0.017 (0.015, 0.019)
Binary (ECG + tabular)	0.842 (0.835, 0.849)	0.006 (0.004, 0.009)
Binary (ECG)	0.821 (0.814, 0.827)	0.013 (0.010, 0.016)
Binary (tabular)	0.812 (0.806, 0.819)	0.024 (0.021, 0.027)

We compared the survival model trained with both ECGs and tabular data to the CHARGE-AF clinical score, as reported in Table 3. For this comparison, we restricted to the subset of the test set for which we had no missing values in the predictors of CHARGE-AF. CHARGE-AF demonstrated moderate discrimination and calibration, with AUC and ICI of 0.744 and 0.036, respectively. In the same sample, the DeepHit model showed consistently better performance both in terms of discrimination (AUC of 0.811) and calibration (ICI 0.009). Notice that DeepHit discriminative performances decreased significantly when compared to the results on the entire test set (Table 2). This may probably be related to different sample characteristics, since, for example, the CHARGE-AF sample is characterized by a higher risk to develop AF (the fraction of ECGs associated with a future AF event is approximately 12% in the CHARGE-AF sample, against the 10% of the entire dataset).

Table 3. Comparison between model performance and CHARGE-AF clinical score, on the subset of patients that do not have missing values in CHARGE-AF predictors.

Model	5-year AUC	5-year ICI
DeepHit (ECG + tabular)	0.811 (0.800, 0.824)	0.009 (0.007, 0.013)
CHARGE-AF	0.744 (0.735, 0.754)	0.036 (0.032, 0.043)

4   Discussion

In this study, we developed a deep learning model for the prediction of incident AF using 12-lead ECG signals and EHR data, explicitly incorporating in the model time to the event and censoring information. The prediction of AF is a critical medical task due to its high prevalence in the elderly population and the importance of an early diagnosis that could prevent stroke or other fatal outcomes.

The model was trained on roughly 240 000 ECGs and it showed good performance on the test set, both in terms of discrimination (AUC 0.845) and calibration (ICI 0.010). When compared to the models trained on single-modality data (ECG or EHR), the complete model showed better discriminative performance and a similar calibration. Taking into account that the higher the model complexity is the lower calibration is expected, this is a very interesting result. Moreover, it confirms the intuitive idea that the fusion of data from multiple modalities can improve the model's predictive power, probably due to the fact that each modality contains complementary information that the model smartly integrates for the prediction. We also compared our model to the CHARGE-AF risk score. What we have found is that our model consistently outperforms CHARGE-AF in terms of discrimination and calibration.

Our results seem to indicate that, given the data modality used for training, survival and binary approaches lead to a similar predictive performance. However, there is more than one reason why it should be preferred to work in a survival setting. First of all, the use of a survival model makes it possible to leverage information about all patients. Indeed, in the binary classification task, censored patients with a follow-up shorter than the study time window should be discarded by design. Conversely, when training a survival model all censored individuals can be used, and they contribute to the loss function only at time bins occurring before censoring. We expect this aspect to be relevant in particular in case of smaller sample sizes. Second, a survival model gives the possibility to predict risk at different time distances, while a binary classification model could consider only a fixed time window at a time. Last, but not least, the survival setting that we used takes into account also the survival time of the competing event, and in general long-term cohort studies this aspect is quite relevant (for increasing incidence of the competing event). To the best of our knowledge, our model is the first deep learning model, in the context of AF prediction from ECGs, to account for competing risks. This aspect is fundamental since failing to consider competing events during model development can lead to an overestimation of the predicted risk [1,25]. In our cohort, the percentage of patients with death events was approximately 17%, and thus we decided to account for it in our model.

The prediction of AF from ECG signals has been investigated by recent literature. Raghunath et al. [21] developed a deep-learning model to predict incident AF using >1 million 12-lead ECGs, demonstrating good discrimination at 1 year (AUC of 0.83, 95% CI 0.83-0.84). The authors also showed that including age and sex in their model slightly improved discrimination (AUC 0.85, 95% CI 0.84-0.85). Although the sample size and the time-frame prediction period considered were clearly different from ours, the performance is comparable with our findings (Table 2). However, no measures of calibration were reported in the study, a fundamental metric for clinical risk prediction models [24]. Khurshid et al. [14] trained a CNN to infer 5-year incident AF risk using 12-lead ECGs, and were the first to explicitly incorporate survival time and censoring in this context. An aspect that authors did not account for was death as a competing risk, given the low death rates within the time window of interest (4.6% in the internal test set). In our cohort, the death rate at 5 years was much higher (12.2%) and could not be ignored. The authors obtained the best predictive performance (AUC 0.838 [95% CI, 0.807 to 0.869], ICI 0.012) fitting a proportional hazard model composed of the 5-year risk predicted by the CNN and the CHARGE-AF risk score. They also assessed model performance on 2 external test sets, an aspect which is lacking in our study. A recent study that combined information derived from the raw 12-lead ECG with clinical information to predict AF development is the one by Biton et al. [7]. In their work, authors trained a random forest classifier using EHR variables, ECG-engineered features and features extracted from the ECG with a previously trained deep learning network. They obtained a very accurate model, with an AUC of 0.909 (0.903, 0.914), indicating the great potential of integrating data from different sources. However, it should be noticed that their data-fusion approach is different from ours, since in our case the latent feature representation learning is not separated from the prediction model, since the two data modalities are processed by the same network. This should make it possible to learn better feature representations for the different modalities [12]. Compared to our study, Biton et al. worked with a much larger sample size (more than 1 M recordings) and with a considerably smaller mean follow-up (1.25 years, against 6.45 years in our study population). Since we expect that the distance to the event plays an important role in the prediction of AF development, this is a detail that should not be ignored. Model calibration was not assessed in this study and time to event was not integrated in the model.

Our study has some limitations. First of all, we could not validate our results in an external validation cohort, which represents a critical step in the development of machine learning models in medicine to assess the generalizability of the prediction algorithm [22]. Second, we did not perform any explainability analysis of our model. Indeed, it would be of interest to understand which parts of the ECG and which clinical features have the greatest influence on model-predicted risk estimates. This is an aspect that we would like to explore in future works. Another aspect where there is room for improvement is the way we integrate data from different sources. Indeed, the choice we made is straightforward and maybe it is not the best one to learn a joint embedding space of the two data modalities. In this regard, we expect that self-supervised learning, the machine learning paradigm in which unlabeled data are processed to obtain useful latent representations that can improve downstream learning tasks [9], could help. Recent findings have shown that self-supervised representation learning can significantly enhance model performance when applied to both ECG signals [18, 20] and tabular data [27]. Thus, we would like to explore this technique in a multi-modal setting [28].

5   Conclusion

We are the first to develop a survival deep learning model for AF prediction that accounts for death as a competing risk. We showed that integrating data from different modalities (ECG signals and EHR tabular data) improved model performance with respect to models trained on single modalities, in line with previous findings.

References

1. Abdel-Qadir, H., Fang, J., Lee, D.S., Tu, J.V., Amir, E., Austin, P.C., Anderson, G.M.: Importance of considering competing risks in time-to-event analyses: application to stroke risk in a retrospective cohort study of elderly patients with atrial fibrillation. Circ.: Cardiovasc. Qual. Outcomes **11**(7), e004580 (2018)
2. Alonso, A., Krijthe, B.P., Aspelund, T., Stepas, K.A., Pencina, M.J., Moser, C.B., et al.: Simple risk model predicts incidence of atrial fibrillation in a racially and geographically diverse population: the charge-af consortium. J. Am. Heart Assoc. **2**(2), e000102 (2013)
3. Attia, Z.I., Noseworthy, P.A., Lopez-Jimenez, F., Asirvatham, S.J., Deshmukh, A.J., Gersh, B.J., et al.: An artificial intelligence-enabled ecg algorithm for the identification of patients with atrial fibrillation during sinus rhythm: a retrospective analysis of outcome prediction. Lancet **394**(10201), 861–867 (2019)
4. Austin, P.C., Lee, D.S., Fine, J.P.: Introduction to the analysis of survival data in the presence of competing risks. Circulation **133**(6), 601–609 (2016)
5. Austin, P.C., Putter, H., Giardiello, D., van Klaveren, D.: Graphical calibration curves and the integrated calibration index (ici) for competing risk models. Diagn. Progn. Res. **6**(1), 2 (2022)
6. Austin, P.C., Steyerberg, E.W.: The integrated calibration index (ici) and related metrics for quantifying the calibration of logistic regression models. Stat. Med. **38**(21), 4051–4065 (2019)
7. Biton, S., Gendelman, S., Ribeiro, A.H., Miana, G., Moreira, C., Ribeiro, A.L.P., Behar, J.A.: Atrial fibrillation risk prediction from the 12-lead electrocardiogram using digital biomarkers and deep representation learning. Eur. Hear. J.-Digit. Health **2**(4), 576–585 (2021)
8. Christopoulos, G., Graff-Radford, J., Lopez, C.L., Yao, X., Attia, Z.I., Rabinstein, A.A., et al.: Artificial intelligence-electrocardiography to predict incident atrial fibrillation: A population-based study. Circ.: Arrhythmia Electrophysiol. **13**(12), e009355 (2020)
9. Ericsson, L., Gouk, H., Loy, C.C., Hospedales, T.M.: Self-supervised representation learning: introduction, advances, and challenges. IEEE Signal Process. Mag. **39**(3), 42–62 (2022)
10. Gensheimer, M.F., Narasimhan, B.: A scalable discrete-time survival model for neural networks. Peer J. **7**, e6257 (2019)
11. Goodfellow, S.D., Goodwin, A., Greer, R., Laussen, P.C., Mazwi, M., Eytan, D.: Towards understanding ecg rhythm classification using convolutional neural networks and attention mappings. In: Machine Learning for Healthcare Conference, pp. 83–101. PMLR (2018)
12. Huang, S.C., Pareek, A., Seyyedi, S., Banerjee, I., Lungren, M.P.: Fusion of medical imaging and electronic health records using deep learning: a systematic review and implementation guidelines. NPJ Digit. Med. **3**(1), 136 (2020)
13. Kamarudin, A.N., Cox, T., Kolamunnage-Dona, R.: Time-dependent roc curve analysis in medical research: current methods and applications. BMC Med. Res. Methodol. **17**(1), 1–19 (2017)

14. Khurshid, S., Friedman, S., Reeder, C., Di Achille, P., Diamant, N., Singh, P., et al.: Ecg-based deep learning and clinical risk factors to predict atrial fibrillation. Circulation **145**(2), 122–133 (2022)
15. Kligfield, P., Gettes, L.S., Bailey, J.J., Childers, R., Deal, B.J., Hancock, E.W., et al.: Recommendations for the standardization and interpretation of the electrocardiogram: part i: the electrocardiogram and its technology: a scientific statement from the american heart association electrocardiography and arrhythmias committee, council on clinical cardiology; the american college of cardiology foundation; and the heart rhythm society endorsed by the international society for computerized electrocardiology. Circulation **115**(10), 1306–1324 (2007)
16. Kvamme, H., Borgan, Ø.: Continuous and discrete-time survival prediction with neural networks. Lifetime Data Anal. **27**, 710–736 (2021)
17. Lee, C., Zame, W., Yoon, J., Van Der Schaar, M.: Deephit: A deep learning approach to survival analysis with competing risks. In: Proceedings of the AAAI Conference on Artificial Intelligence, vol. 32 (2018)
18. Liu, H., Zhao, Z., She, Q.: Self-supervised ecg pre-training. Biomed. Signal Process. Control **70**, 103010 (2021)
19. McBride, R., et al.: Stroke prevention in atrial fibrillation study. final results. Circulation (New York, NY) **84**(2), 527–539 (1991)
20. Mehari, T., Strodthoff, N.: Self-supervised representation learning from 12-lead ecg data. Comput. Biol. Med. **141**, 105114 (2022)
21. Raghunath, S., Pfeifer, J.M., Ulloa-Cerna, A.E., Nemani, A., Carbonati, T., Jing, L., et al.: Deep neural networks can predict new-onset atrial fibrillation from the 12-lead ecg and help identify those at risk of atrial fibrillation-related stroke. Circulation **143**(13), 1287–1298 (2021)
22. Rose, S.: Machine learning for prediction in electronic health data. JAMA Netw. Open **1**(4), e181404–e181404 (2018)
23. Scagnetto, A., Barbati, G., Gandin, I., Cappelletto, C., Baj, G., Cazzaniga, A., et al.: Deep artificial neural network for prediction of atrial fibrillation through the analysis of 12-leads standard ecg (2022). arXiv:2202.05676
24. Van Calster, B., McLernon, D.J., Van Smeden, M., Wynants, L., Steyerberg, E.W.: Calibration: the achilles heel of predictive analytics. BMC Med. **17**(1), 1–7 (2019)
25. Van Geloven, N., Giardiello, D., Bonneville, E.F., Teece, L., Ramspek, C.L., Van Smeden, M., et al.: Validation of prediction models in the presence of competing risks: a guide through modern methods. bmj **377** (2022)
26. Wolf, P.A., Dawber, T.R., Thomas, H.E., Kannel, W.B.: Epidemiologic assessment of chronic atrial fibrillation and risk of stroke: the fiamingham study. Neurology **28**(10), 973–973 (1978)
27. Yoon, J., Zhang, Y., Jordon, J., van der Schaar, M.: Vime: extending the success of self-and semi-supervised learning to tabular domain. Adv. Neural. Inf. Process. Syst. **33**, 11033–11043 (2020)
28. Zong, Y., Mac Aodha, O., Hospedales, T.: Self-supervised multimodal learning: a survey (2023). arXiv:2304.01008

Generalization Ability in Medical Image Analysis with Small-Scale Imbalanced Datasets: Insights from Neural Network Learning

Tetiana Biloborodova[1]([✉]) [iD], Bríd Brosnan[2] [iD], Inna Skarga-Bandurova[2] [iD], and Daniel J. Strauss[1] [iD]

[1] Systems Neuroscience and Neurotechnology Unit, Neurocenter, Faculty of Medicine, Saarland University and School of Engineering, htw saar, Saarbrücken, Germany
tetiana.biloborodova@htwsaar.de
[2] Oxford Brookes University, Oxford, UK

Abstract. Within the medical image analysis domain, the lack of extensive and well-balanced datasets has posed a significant challenge to traditional machine learning approaches, resulting in poor generalization ability of the models. In light of this, we propose a novel approach to evaluate the efficacy of neural network learning on small imbalanced datasets. The proposed methodology uncovers the relationships between model generalization ability, neural network properties, model complexity, and dataset resizing. This research highlights several key findings: (1) data augmentation techniques effectively enhance the generalization ability of neural network models; (2) a neural network model with a minimal number of each layer type can achieve superior generalization ability; (3) regularization layers prove to be a crucial factor in achieving higher generalization ability; (4) the number of epochs is not a determining factor in enhancing generalization ability; (5) complexity measures exhibit no significant correlation with generalization ability in the described scenarios. The findings from this study offer a practical roadmap for model selection, architecture search, and evaluation of the methods' effectiveness in medical image analysis.

Keywords: Generalization Ability · Convolution Neural Network · Medical Image Analysis

1 Introduction

Convolutional neural networks (CNNs) have demonstrated remarkable success in image analysis tasks, due to the availability of large-scale, representative datasets [1]. In particular, CNNs have proven to be a powerful approach for medical image classification and disease identification [2–4]. However, such models rely heavily on the availability of training data to establish generalization ability, which is crucial for accurate classification and identification of new data [5, 6]. Regrettably, reduced training data size inevitably leads to diminished generalization ability, consequently hindering the model's

N. Moniz et al. (Eds.): EPIA 2023, LNAI 14116, pp. 234–246, 2023.
https://doi.org/10.1007/978-3-031-49011-8_19

ability to predict new, unseen data with precision [7]. To counter this issue, contemporary techniques have primarily focused on preventing neural network overfitting by using early stopping and learning rate adjustments. While these measures effectively mitigate overfitting, they do not enhance the generalization ability of the model when trained on small datasets.

In the field of medical image analysis, small-scale sample sizes are a pervasive issue due to difficulties in acquiring sufficient images, thereby making it impossible to use traditional techniques. This problem is especially relevant for histological image analysis, including cervix histological image analysis. Moreover, there is no universal approach to influence model's ability to generalize well. Additionally, rare events in medical image analysis cause class imbalance, which can also affect model generalization ability. Moreover, one of the issues with neural networks is the observation that highly over-parameterized neural networks, i.e., networks with high complexity, can risk misclassification of new data [8]. A recent study [8] identified the neural network architecture, optimization, and generalization ability as crucial research directions for analyzing overall neural network model error. However, lack of generalization, and associated overfitting, still remain a major challenge when training large neural networks, or training on very small amounts of data. Many approaches are taken to avoid overfitting in the presence of an imbalanced dataset [7], when acquiring more training data is not possible: re-acquiring some data from the existing dataset through processing, producing some new data based on the distribution of the existing data set, reducing hypothesis complexity, and using weights for majority and minority classes. Typically, generalization ability under small imbalanced image datasets can be handled by dataset resizing, and configuration of network architecture properties. Dataset resizing approaches increase the number of dataset samples and adjust the class imbalance ratio to achieve a balanced distribution between classes. Notably, data augmentation has been identified in [9] as a crucial method for improving generalization ability, particularly in small datasets. Additionally, oversampling methods, which utilize feature augmentation [10], have been shown to effectively mitigate issues related to class imbalance.

Configuration of network architecture properties can help tune the network to improve the learning process. At architecture level, functional solutions such as dropout regularization [11], batch normalization [12], and activation function [13] as well as their combination [14] can be used to improve model generalization ability and mitigate overfitting. Furthermore, the generalization ability of CNNs can be affected by various factors, including the number of training iterations, the specific network properties, and the resulting complexity of the neural network architecture [15]. Model complexity evaluation can provide insights into understanding approaches to improve model performance and generalization ability [16]. Model complexity may depend on the properties of the trained neural network model, optimization approaches, and data [17–19]. Approaches to measuring model complexity are classified [18] into the following categories: PAC-Bayes based approaches [20], VC-dimension based approaches [21], and norm-based bounds [22]. As proposed in [21], the VC-dimension serves as a measure for evaluating model complexity, providing a precise bound with minimal assumptions [23], thus making it applicable in a wide range of cases. A recent paper [24] noted that while PAC-Bayes-based approaches may demonstrate some correlation between PAC-Bayes and generalization error, they are not always reliable and can fail. While a relationship between complexity measures and generalization ability has been considered [18, 24, 25], further research is needed to fully understand the intricacies and mechanisms that govern this connection. For instance, some complexity measures can capture false correlations that do not reflect causal relationships with generalization.

The primary objective of this study is to identify patterns that reveal how model generalization ability and performance on unseen data are influenced by neural network properties, model complexity, and dataset resizing approaches. This work sheds new light on the problem of generalization ability and overfitting under small imbalanced datasets by making the following key contribution. We propose a strategy to assess appropriate neural network learning by assessing generalization error, neural network complexity and model accuracy. The strategy can aid understanding of how to change the network behaviour to yield improved classification accuracy when the model is trained on a small imbalanced dataset.

The paper is organised as follows. In Sect. 2, the methodology for generalisation ability and model complexity assesment is presented. Section 3 describes and discusses experiment results. Section 4 provides the conclusions.

2 Methods

Consider an image dataset as a set $\{(x_1, y_1),(x_2, y_2),\ldots,(x_n, y_n)\} \in \mathbf{R}$, where (x_i, y_i) is the pair of the inputs and outputs of the i-th sample. The neural network classification task is to learn y_i with a function F that approximates the unknown underlying mapping function from x_i to y_i based on a samples $\{(x_1, y_1),(x_2, y_2),\ldots,(x_n, y_n)\}$, i.e. $f: \mathbf{R}^{input} \rightarrow \mathbf{R}$ is a neural network with a certain architecture, that is used to classify the label y of an image x on a new data, unseen in training, given by (1).

$$f(x_{1,\ldots,n}) = a\left(\sum_{i=1}^{n} x_i, w_i - b\right) = a(\langle x, w \rangle - b),   \tag{1}$$

where w_i is weights $w_1,\ldots, w_l \in \mathbf{R}$, b is a bias $\in \mathbf{R}$, and a is an activation function such as $a: \mathbf{R} \rightarrow \mathbf{R}$.

2.1 Definition of Neural Network Architecture Components

The number of layers L, and the activation functions a are considered key elements of neural network design. During the learning process, these two components compute the weight matrices $(W_l)_{l=1}^{L}$ and biases $(b_l)_{l=1}^{L}$ for each neural network layer. The learning process consists of learning the affine-linear functions based on weight matrices and biases (2).

$$T_l x = W_l x + b_l.   \tag{2}$$

Therefore, a neural network model is defined as $F: \mathbf{R}^{input} \rightarrow \mathbf{R}^{output}$, given by (3).

$$F(x) = T_L a(T_{L-1} a(\ldots a(T_1(x)))), x \in \mathbf{R}^{input}.   \tag{3}$$

2.2 Generalization Ability

The learning process includes splitting the dataset $(x_i, y_i)_{i=1}^{\tilde{m}}$ into training subset $(x_i, y_i)_{i=1}^{m}$ and test (i.e. unseen data) subset $(x_i, y_i)_{i=m+1}^{\tilde{m}}$. Model generalization ability is evaluated on the test subset by analyzing $F_{(W_l, b_l)_l}(x_i) \approx y_i$, for all $i = m + 1, ..., \tilde{m}$.

The goal of investigating model generalization is to find the model F, which is able to generalize on new unseen data. For classification purposes, generalization problems can be expressed in terms of the empirical risk minimization [8].

Model generalization ability can be defined considering the risk R_G of a function f: $\mathbf{R}^{\text{input}} \to \mathbf{R}$ following the assumption that there exists a function g: $\mathbf{R}^{\text{input}} \to \mathbf{R}$ such that the train subset $((x_i, y_i)_{i=1}^{m}$ is of the form $(x_i, g(x_i))_{i=1}^{m}$, where $x_i \in [0, 1]^{\text{input}}$ for all $i = 1, ..., m$.

$R_G(F)$ is estimated by the generalization error between the trained model and optimal function g by (4) [26].

$$R_G = R(F) - \hat{R}(F), \tag{4}$$

where $\hat{R}(F)$ is empirical risk, i.e., training error obtained by model training, and $R(F)$ is actual risk, i.e., test error obtained with a model on the test subset.

2.3 Model Complexity

The proposed measures to assess model complexity are VC-dimension and PAC-Bayes based measure. According to [18, 27], given a neural network F, with a number of layers L, layer index i, and a number of convolutional filters c_i at layer i with a kernel size $k_i \times k_i$, the effective complexity measure C_{VCD} of neural network F based on VC-dimension can be defined as (5).

$$C_{VCD}(F) = \sum_{i}^{L} k_i^2 c_{i-1}(c_i + 1). \tag{5}$$

According to [18, 19] based on PAC-Bayes magnitude flatness given a neural network F with a number of weights w, the complexity measure C_{PAC} is calculated by adding Gaussian perturbations to the weights of a trained model. The magnitude-aware σ' is chosen to be the largest number such that $\mathbb{E}_{\mathbf{u}}[\hat{R}(F_{\mathbf{w+u}}) \leq 0.1]$ where $u_i \sim \mathcal{N}(0, \sigma'^2 |w_i|^2 + \epsilon^2)$ and ϵ set to 10^{-3} (6).

$$C_{PAC}(F) = \frac{1}{\sigma'^2}. \tag{6}$$

The correlations between VC-Dimension complexity and generalization error, PAC-Bayes magnitude flatness and generalization error are calculated to find a pattern with generalization ability.

3 Results and Discussion

Data. The experiment was conducted on the CHI [28] and MTCHI [29, 30] datasets. Both datasets were modified to align with the research objectives. The joint dataset included 46 slide images, out of which 15 images were diagnosed as normal, 5 were assigned to CIN1, 14 to CIN2, and 12 to CIN3 grade. All images were prepared by extracting stratified squamous epithelium (SSE) and creating 244 SSE patches including 105 Normal, 20 CIN 1, 73 CIN 2, and 46 CIN 3. The patches were resized to 200 × 200 pixels and the combined images were shuffled and split into training and test datasets at an 80:20 ratio. The validation dataset included 18 patches.

Software setup and model properties. The software implementation was carried out using Tensorflow and Keras. Candidate CNN architectures were selected, based on previous research: N1 is CNN from scratch, N2 [31], N3 [32], N4 [33], N5 [34], N6 [35].

Cross-entropy served as a loss metric, and accuracy as a performance metric. All models were trained with an Adam optimizer with a learning rate of 0.001. Activation functions were ReLU and softmax. Early stopping was not used, because of the requirement to obtain and trace generalization error.

The details of the neural network properties and hyperparameters, used in this research, are shown in Table 1. The characteristics include the number of convolution layers, type and number of pooling layers, type, number and rate of regularization layers (rate can be different at each regularization layer or the same at all regularization layers), and number of dense layers.

Table 1. Neural networks properties.

CNN	Layers			
	Convolution layers		Core layers	
	2D convolution, number of layers	Pooling layer, number of layers	Regularization layer, number of layers, layers rate	Dense layer, number of layers
N1	3	Max pooling 2D, 2	Dropout, 2, (0.25; 0.5)	2
N2	4	Max pooling 2D, 2	Dropout, 3, (0.01)	2
N3	4	Max pooling 2D, 3	Dropout, 4, (0.25)	3
N4	5	Max pooling 2D, 5	Dropout, 1, (0.5)	3
N5	3	Max pooling 2D, 3	–	2
N6	3	Max pooling 2D, 2	–	2

The approaches used to increase initial data amount are data augmentation and feature oversampling. Data augmentation methods are rescaling, zooming, rotation, brightness mode modification, and horizontal flipping. The following augmentation parameters were set for training data: rescale, zoom, rotation, brightness range, horizontal flip, and rescale for test dataset. Synthetic Minority Oversampling Technique (SMOTE) is used for features oversampling, where the number of generated samples is defined by majority class.

Classification training scenarios. The following scenarios were used for the defined CNN architectures:

(S1): The models were trained for 100 epochs.

(S2): The models were trained for 100 epochs. Augmentation was used.

(S3): The models were trained for 500 epochs. Augmentation was used.

(S4): The models were trained for 100 epochs. Data oversampling for non-majority classes was used.

CNNs complexity assessment. The complexity measure is computed using the implementation [25]. The following average model complexity of studied neural network properties were obtained (see Table 2). The Kendall correlation coefficient was used to calculate correlations between the model complexity and generalization error.

Table 2. Complexity measures and correlation with generalization error.

CNN	$C_{VCD}(F)$	Correlation $C_{VCD}(F)$ and R_G	$C_{PAC}(F)$	Correlation $C_{PAC}(F)$ and R_G
N1	366.132	0.632	530.201	0.738
N2	366.132	0	1058.859	−0.359
N3	513.293	−0.632	0.041	−0.632
N4	390.593	−0.632	1310.724	−0.632
N5	183.242	0.316	1323.706	0.316
N6	259.249	−0.316	1323.706	−0.316

No common significant correlations between model complexities and generalization errors were identified for C_{VCD}, and C_{PAC}. Significant correlation was identified for the N1 model complexity and generalization error for the VC-Dimension and PAC-Bayes magnitude flatness measures. However, the same VC-Dimension complexity for N2 shows zero correlation with generalization error.

Generalization error and model accuracy evaluation. Model performance evaluation using accuracy metric is shown in Fig. 1. The results were obtained on unseen test data.

(S1) model shows very low accuracy. Accuracy on unseen data ranged from 32.1% for N6 to 53.48% for N3. Accuracy less than 50% is considered a random choice.

(S2) test accuracy ranged from 48.16% for N4 to 72.84% for N5.

(S3) test accuracy ranged from 56.88% for N4 to 78.99% for N6.

(S4) test accuracy ranged from 43.47% for N2 to 59.63% for N6.

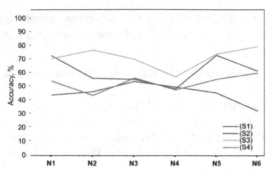

Fig. 1. Neural network models accuracy according to scenarios.

The highest accuracy was obtained for scenario (S3): image augmentation and training for 500 epochs, with neural network architecture N6: 3 convolution layers, 2 pooling layers, and 2 dense layers. Generalization error is calculated based on training and test errors (see Table 3).

Table 3. Loss on train and test phase, generalization error.

Scenario	Phase	N1	R_G	N2	R_G	N3	R_G	N4	R_G	N5	R_G	N6	R_G
(S1)	train	0.26	4.72	0.13	6.79	0.22	3.38	0.45	3.78	0.12	7.5	0.38	10.34
	test	4.98		6.92		3.60		4.23		7.62		10.72	
(S2)	train	0.64	0.16	0.72	0.74	0.66	0.45	0.7	0.97	0.41	0.39	0.45	1.02
	test	0.8		1.46		1.11		1.67		0.8		1.47	
(S3)	train	0.3	1.09	0.2	0.78	0.23	1.8	0.9	0.68	0.11	1.4	0.15	0.9
	test	1.39		0.98		2.03		1.58		1.51		1.05	
(S4)	train	0.17	3.35	0.19	5.57	0.13	3.05	0.42	4.45	0.06	2.54	0.05	1.88
	test	3.52		5.76		3.18		4.87		2.6		1.93	

Scenario (S1) indicated high test loss and high generalization error for all models. Test loss ranged from 3.6 for N3 to 10.72 for N6. Generalization error ranged from 3.38 for N3 to 10.24 for N6. (S2) test loss ranged from 0.8 for N1, N5 to 1.67 for N4. Generalization error ranged from 0.16 for N1 to 1.02 for N6. (S3) test loss ranged from 0.98 for N2 to 2.03 for N3. Generalization error ranged from 0.68 for N4 to 1.8 for N3. (S4) indicated high test loss and high generalization error for all models except for N6. Test loss ranged from 1.93 for N6 to 5.76 for N2. Generalization error ranged from 1.88 for N6 to 5.57 for N2. The lowest generalization error was obtained for 4 models using (S2), and the other two models had lowest errors using (S3). The minimal generalization error was obtained with scenario (S2) which included image augmentation and training for 100 epochs, and neural network with architecture N1: 3 convolution layers, 2 pooling layers, 2 dropout layers with different rate, and 2 dense layers.

CNNs generalization error according to the 4 scenarios is presented in Fig. 2.

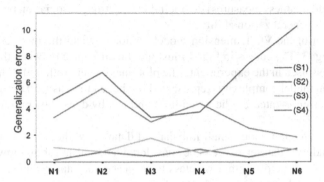

Fig. 2. CNNs generalization error according to scenarios

Higher generalization errors are obtained at (S1) scenario without dataset resizing and at (S4) scenario with data oversampling. Generalization errors obtained at scenarios (S2) and (S3) show that data augmentation helps to improve model generalization ability. The comparison of model performance, generalization error according to scenario and model complexity for all scenarios is shown in Table 4.

Table 4. Scenarios with max accuracy and min generalization error.

Scenario	Model performance			Generalization ability		
	Max Accuracy	CNN	Model complexity $C_{VCD}(F)$	Min R_G	CNN	Model complexity $C_{VCD}(F)$
(S1)	53.48	N3	513.294	3.38	N3	513.294
(S2)	72.84	N5	183.242	**0.16**	**N1**	366.132
(S3)	**78.99**	**N6**	259.249	0.68	N4	394.718
(S4)	59.63	N6	259.2492	1.88	N6	259.249

The worst results were obtained with scenario (S1) when the learning model tries to find patterns under small dataset samples. (S1) shows the lowest accuracy, which can be considered a random choice, and the highest generalization ability. The results of scenario (S4) are better than (S1), but also close to it. (S4) highest accuracy is only 59.63%, and generalization error is higher than in (S2) and (S3). Scenarios (S2) and (S3) show higher accuracy for N5 and N6 and higher generalization ability for N1 and N4. N5 and N6 do not have regularization layers. N1 has 2 dropout layers, and N4 - 1 dropout layer, which is less than in N2 and N3. The higher number of training epochs in S3 helps to improve classification result.

This research has not identified significant patterns between model complexities, accuracy and generalization errors when a model is trained on small size imbalanced dataset. The minimal N1 generalization error, and the significant correlation identified for N1 model complexity and generalization error (applying VC-Dimension and PAC-Bayes magnitude flatness measures) do not indicate a strong association between model complexity and generalization ability.

Comparison of the VC-Dimension model complexity and the number of layers is provided in Fig. 3. The curves in Fig. 3 illustrate the difference between the number of layers for CNNs used in the experiment. The plot lines closely follow the changes in the VC-Dimension model complexity (represented by the red line) as well as the number of pooling layers (represented by the green line) and nearby dense layers (represented by the yellow line).

Image classification under small imbalanced datasets, without applying additional techniques to address dataset size, can be considered random, and shows low generalization ability. SMOTE helps to improve classification accuracy and reduce generalization error, but the model accuracy can be too low and may be considered random. Augmentation improves accuracy and reduces generalization error. Increasing the number of training epochs improves classification accuracy while maintaining generalization ability.

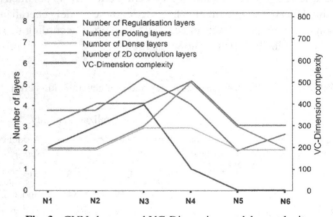

Fig. 3. CNNs layers and VC-Dimension model complexity

Model validation. To assess generalization ability, the higher accuracy and lower generalization error models were validated on new data. The validation subset consisting of 18 images, had not been used during model training and testing. Accuracy, sensitivity and F1-score were computed based on confusion matrices for model N1 trained with scenario (S2), and model N6 trained with scenario (S3) (see Table 5).

Model N1, which had been trained with scenario (S2), and had shown the lowest generalization error, (i.e., highest generalization ability), indicated the higher model quality criteria on the validation subset. Model N6, which had been trained with scenario (S3), and had shown the highest accuracy, did not generalize well on new data. Therefore, the trained model with lower generalization error and lower accuracy shows higher generalization ability on new data than the trained model with higher accuracy and

Table 5. Model validation result.

Metrics	N1 trained with scenario (S2)	N6 trained with scenario (S3)
Accuracy, %	94.00	83.00
Sensitivity, %	91.50	80.25
Precision, %	95.75	79.00
F1-score, %	94.00	79.62

higher generalization error. According to obtained generalization errors, the results reveal that the trained model improved the performance over these four metrics: accuracy, sensitivity, precision, F1-score. Therefore, the realized model improves generalization ability and reduces misclassification risk.

Findings indicate accuracy may be misleading in some cases as a generalization ability measure. Moreover, generalization error is a more accurate criterion to assess generalization ability of neural network trained under small-scaled imbalanced image datasets. The results of complexity measures, and the number of layers comparison, demonstrate the effect of the number of Pooling and Dense layers on VC-dimension. This can be used for ranking tuning parameters, according to their ability to control VC-dimension for research on the relationship between VC-Dimension and the effect of noisy data.

4   Conclusion

This study proposed a strategy to assess neural network learning with small imbalanced datasets, focusing on generalization error, neural network complexity, and model accuracy. The strategy helps to find patterns between the model generalization ability and neural network properties, model complexity, and dataset resizing approaches. We outline and report on experiments studying how well the criteria can find patterns of generalization ability. However, the results are currently limited to one histology images dataset, and it would be interesting to extend these results to other datasets. Furthermore, this paper does not address the pre-trained models for image classification.

Although the optimal combination of neural network properties and dataset resizing approaches for capturing the generalization ability of neural networks remains elusive, this study has identified several promising approaches. Specifically, we have found that certain combinations of expected neural network properties and dataset resizing techniques are capable of capturing a significant proportion of the generalization ability of neural networks. The key insights gained from the proposed strategy include:

- Scenarios with data augmentation help to improve generalization ability;
- CNN model with minimal number of each layer type (convolution, pooling, regularization, dense) can achieve higher generalization ability;
- Regularization layer such as Dropout helps to achieve higher generalization ability;
- The number of epochs is not a key criterion for higher generalization ability;

- The results of the models' complexity measures and generalization ability did not demonstrate a significant correlation between complexity measures (VC-Dimension, PAC-Bayes magnitude flatness measures) and generalization ability when the model is trained on a small-size dataset.

These insights offer valuable contributions to the model selection, architecture search, and assessment of the methods effectiveness for medical image analysis, and we anticipate that they will inspire further research and advancements in this domain.

Acknowledgements. This research is supported by funds from the Alexander von Humboldt Foundation.

References

1. Shorten, C., Khoshgoftaar, T.M.: A survey on image data augmentation for deep learning. J. Big Data **6**(1), 1–48 (2019)
2. Banik, D., Bhattacharjee, D.: Mitigating data imbalance issues in medical image analysis. In: Data Preprocessing, Active Learning, and Cost Perceptive Approaches for Resolving Data Imbalance, pp. 66–89. IGI Global (2021)
3. Sheremet, A., Kondratenko, Y., Sidenko, I., Kondratenko, G.: Diagnosis of lung disease based on medical images using artificial neural networks. In: 2021 IEEE 3rd Ukraine Conference on Electrical and Computer Engineering (UKRCON), pp. 561–565. IEEE (2021)
4. Liu, X., et al.: Segmentation and identification of spectral and statistical textures for computer medical diagnostics in dermatology. Math. Biosci. Eng. J. **19**(7), 6923–6939 (2022)
5. Komura, D., Ishikawa, S.: Machine learning methods for histopathological image analysis. Comput. Struct. Biotechnol. J. **16**, 34–42 (2018)
6. Flotho, P., et al.: Multimodal data acquisition at SARS-CoV-2 drive through screening centers: Setup description and experiences in Saarland. Germany. J. Biophotonics **14**(8), e202000512 (2021)
7. Ying, X.: An overview of overfitting and its solutions. In: Journal of Physics: Conference Series, vol. 1168, p. 022022. IOP Publishing (2019)
8. Kutyniok, G.: The mathematics of artificial intelligence. arXiv preprint. arXiv:2203.08890 (2022)
9. Buiu, C., Dănăilă, V.R., Răduță, C.N.: MobileNetV2 ensemble for cervical precancerous lesions classification. Processes **8**(5), 595 (2020)
10. Yijing, L., Haixiang, G., Xiao, L., Yanan, L., Jinling, L.: Adapted ensemble classification algorithm based on multiple classifier system and feature selection for classifying multi-class imbalanced data. Knowl.-Based Syst., **94**, 88–104 (2016)
11. Qian, L., Hu, L., Zhao, L., Wang, T., Jiang, R.: Sequence-dropout block for reducing overfitting problem in image classification. IEEE Access **8**, 62830–62840 (2020)
12. Sun, Y., Zheng, W. and Ren, Z.: Application of convolutional neural network in image processing. In: Application of Intelligent Systems in Multi-modal Information Analytics: The 4th International Conference on Multi-modal Information Analytics (ICMMIA 2022), 2, pp. 375–383. Cham: Springer International Publishing (2022)
13. Shridhar, K., Lee, J., Hayashi, H., Mehta, P., Iwana, B.K., Kang, S., Uchida, S., Ahmed, S., Dengel, A.: Probact: A probabilistic activation function for deep neural networks. arXiv preprint. arXiv:1905.10761 (2019)

14. Thanapol, P., Lavangnananda, K., Bouvry, P., Pinel, F. and Leprévost, F.: Reducing overfitting and improving generalization in training convolutional neural network (CNN) under limited sample sizes in image recognition. In: 2020–5th International Conference on Information Technology (InCIT), pp. 300–305. IEEE (2020)
15. Yu, H.: Network complexity analysis of multilayer feedforward artificial neural networks. In: Applications of Neural Networks in High Assurance Systems, pp. 41–55. Springer, Berlin, Heidelberg (2010)
16. Allen-Zhu, Z., Li, Y. and Liang, Y.: Learning and generalization in overparameterized neural networks, going beyond two layers. In: Proceedings of the 33rd International Conference on Neural Information Processing Systems, pp. 6158–6169 (2019)
17. Hu, X., Chu, L., Pei, J., Liu, W., Bian, J.: Model complexity of deep learning: a survey. Knowl. Inf. Syst. **63**, 2585–2619 (2021)
18. Jiang, Y., Neyshabur, B., Mobahi, H., Krishnan, D., Bengio, S.: Fantastic generalization measures and where to find them. In: 8th International Conference on Learning Representations, ICLR 2020 (2020)
19. Dziugaite, G.K., Drouin, A., Neal, B., Rajkumar, N., Caballero, E., Wang, L., Mitliagkas, I., Roy, D.M.: In search of robust measures of generalization. In: Annual Conference on Neural Information Processing Systems 2020, NeurIPS 2020 (2020)
20. McAllester, D.A.: PAC-Bayesian model averaging. In: Proceedings of the Twelfth Annual Conference on Computational Learning Theory, pp. 164–170 (1999)
21. Vapnik, V.N., Chervonenkis, A.Y.: On the uniform convergence of relative frequencies of events to their probabilities. In: Measures of Complexity: Festschrift for Alexey Chervonenkis, pp.11–30 (2015)
22. Neyshabur, B., Li, Z., Bhojanapalli, S., LeCun, Y., Srebro, N.: Towards understanding the role of over-parametrization in generalization of neural networks. arXiv preprint. arXiv:1805.12076 (2018)
23. Valle-Pérez, G., Louis, A.A.: Generalization bounds for deep learning. arXiv preprint. arXiv: 2012.04115 (2020)
24. Vakanski, A., Xian, M.: Evaluation of complexity measures for deep learning generalization in medical image analysis. In: 2021 IEEE 31st International Workshop on Machine Learning for Signal Processing (MLSP), pp. 1–6 (2021)
25. Jaegerman, J., Damouni, K., Hosseini, M.S., Plataniotis, K.N.: In search of probeable generalization measures. In: 2021 20th IEEE International Conference on Machine Learning and Applications, December, pp. 1106–1111. IEEE. (2021)
26. Michel, B., Nouy, A.: Learning with tree tensor networks: complexity estimates and model selection. Bernoulli **28**(2), 910–936 (2022)
27. Bartlett, P.L., Harvey, N., Liaw, C., Mehrabian, A.: Nearly-tight VC-dimension and pseudo-dimension bounds for piecewise linear neural networks. J. Mach. Learn. Res. **20**(63), 1–17 (2019)
28. Biloborodova, T., Lomakin, S., Skarga-Bandurova, I., Krytska, Y.: Region of interest identification in the cervical digital histology images. In: EPIA Conference on Artificial Intelligence, pp. 133–145. Springer, Cham (2022)
29. Meng, Z., Zhao, Z., Li, B., Su, F., Guo, L.: A Cervical histopathology dataset for computer aided diagnosis of precancerous lesions. IEEE Trans. Med. Imag. **40**(6), 1531–1541 (2021)
30. Meng, Z., Zhao, Z., Li, B., Su, F., Guo, L., Wang, H.: Triple up-sampling segmentation network with distribution consistency loss for pathological diagnosis of cervical precancerous lesions. IEEE J. Biomed. Health Inf. **25**(7), 2673–2685 (2020)
31. Kunakornvong, P., Asriny, D.M.: Apple image classification using convolutional neural network. In: 34th International Technology Conference Circuits/Systems, Computing Communication (2019)

32. AlMubarak, H.A., et al.: A hybrid deep learning and handcrafted feature approach for cervical cancer digital histology image classification. Int. J. Healthc. Inf. Syst. Inform. **14**(2), 66–87 (2019)

33. Sornapudi, S., et al.: Automated cervical digitized histology whole-slide image analysis toolbox. J. Pathol. Inform. **12**, 26 (2021)

34. TensorFlow Tutorial Image Classification. https://www.tensorflow.org/tutorials/images/classi fication. Last Accessed 16 March 2023

35. Simple CNN on CIFAR10 dataset. https://tensorflow.rstudio.com/examples/cifar10_cnn. html. Last Accessed 16 March 2023

Multi-omics Data Integration and Network Inference for Biomarker Discovery in Glioma

Roberta Coletti[1](✉) 🆔 and Marta B. Lopes[1,2,3] 🆔

[1] Center for Mathematics and Applications (NOVA Math), NOVA School of science
and Technology (NOVA SST), Caparica, Portugal
{roberta.coletti,marta.lopes}@fct.unl.pt
[2] Department of Mathematics, NOVA SST, Caparica, Portugal
[3] UNIDEMI, Department of Mechanical and Industrial Engineering, NOVA SST,
Caparica, Portugal

Abstract. Glioma is a family of brain tumors with three main types
exhibiting different progressions, which lack effective therapeutic options
and specific molecular biomarkers. In this work, we propose a pipeline
for multi-omics integrated analysis aimed at identifying features that
could impact the development of different gliomas, assigned according
to the latest classification guidelines. We estimate networks of genes and
proteins based on human data, via the graphical lasso, as a network-
based step towards variable selection. The estimated glioma networks
were compared to disclose molecular relations that can be important for
the development of a certain tumor type. Our outcomes were validated
both mathematically, and through principal component analysis to determine if the selected subset of variables carries enough biological information to distinguish the three glioma types in a reduced dimensional
subspace. The results highlight an overall agreement in variable selection across the two omics. Features exclusively selected by each glioma
type appear as more representative of the pathological condition, making them suitable as potential diagnostic biomarkers. The comparison
between glioma-type networks and with known protein-protein interactions reveals the presence of molecular relations that could be associated
to a pathological condition. The 59 features identified by our analysis
will be further considered to extend our work by integrating targeted
biological evaluation.

Keywords: Network inference · Glioma · Transcriptomics ·
Proteomics · Network distance · Principal component analysis

1 Introduction

Glioma is a group of highly heterogeneous brain tumors arising from glial cells.
The main types of glioma are glioblastoma (GBM), astrocytoma, and oligodendroglioma, the latter two also historically designated by lower-grade glioma

N. Moniz et al. (Eds.): EPIA 2023, LNAI 14116, pp. 247–259, 2023.
https://doi.org/10.1007/978-3-031-49011-8_20

(LGG). Since these glioma types present distinct molecular and histological features, they may require different treatment approaches [17].

In recent years, the increasing molecular understanding of glioma improved the procedure for type classification, leading to the 2021 guidelines from the World Health Organization (2021-WHO) [7]. These guidelines are constantly updated and revised according to newest discoveries arising from different types of molecular information (commonly designated as *omics*). Recent advances in technologies for data retrieval have led to the generation of large amounts of multi-omics data, which can be used to identify potential biomarkers for early detection and diagnosis, and for assisting clinical decision. However, the analysis of this huge amount of information requires the use of techniques, such as regularization models, to reduce the dimensionality of omics data to an interpretable set of relevant molecular features. Another challenge when analysing omics data concerns the underlying intra- and inter-omics relations between the molecular entities. For instance, gene expression (transcriptomics) and protein expression (proteomics) are clearly connected. Genes interact between them, while influencing protein expression and the way in which proteins interplay. However, these relationships are complex, as changes in gene expression levels do not always translate to changes in protein expression levels [15]. To explore the unknown underlying mechanisms involved in a given disease, network estimation techniques are usually employed, as molecular entities can be considered nodes of a graph, while edges approximate their relations [4]. Moreover, coupling network inference with regularization methods can be used to discover these relations while reducing data dimension [10]. Indeed, estimating sparse adjacency matrices induces a network-based variable selection, as nodes that are not linked to the others might be neglected.

In the context of glioma, the three types would be described by different networks, therefore evaluating how much they differ is important to detect relevant relations, peculiar of each glioma type. Different metrics for network distance are defined in literature, either focused on nodes and edges [12]. The Frobenius norm is one of the most popular way to evaluate distances comparing edges. However, it does not take into account the graph topology, which can be a noteworthy limitation for biological networks. A valid alternative is to use a measure that consider the general structure of the graphs, as is the DeltaCon distance [6], which evaluate similarity matrices taking into account all the possible paths connecting two nodes.

In this work, we explored the molecular networks behind glioma heterogeneity at the transcriptomics and proteomics levels. Differently from previous bioinformatic studies on glioma, the presented analysis considers recently updated datasets [9], where the observations have been reclassified following the 2021 WHO classification guidelines, increasing the potential impact of our multi-omics methodology in the glioma-type specific biomarker discovery. The goal of this study was to infer gene and protein networks describing each glioma type, through graphical lasso, a widely known method for undirected graph estimation [3]. The analysis of these networks, as well as the comparison between them and known protein-protein interaction (PPI) networks was used to detect variables of potential interest. Moreover, principal component analysis was performed to investigate the ability of the set of selected variables to characterize the different glioma types, and then if they could be good candidate as diagnostic biomarkers.

The paper is organized as follows: in Materials and Methods section we provide an overview of the methods used for our analysis, we described the multi-omics dataset, the analysis pipeline developed and the validation performed. In the Results and Discussion sections the outcomes of our analysis are presented and discussed in light of their potential biological application and impact.

2 Materials and Methods

2.1 Graphical Lasso

Let $\mathbb{G}$ be a graph with $X = (X_1, ..., X_p)$ nodes with multivariate normal distribution. The graphical lasso [3] (glasso), estimates the precision matrix Θ, by solving a Gaussian log-likelihood maximization problem with a lasso penalty:

$$\arg\max_{\Theta}\{\log(\det\Theta) - tr(S\Theta) - \rho||\Theta||_1\}, \tag{1}$$

where S is the empirical covariance matrix and where $tr(\cdot)$ is the trace operator. The presence of regularization term $\rho||\Theta||_1$ induces sparsity into the solution, which degree depends on the value of the parameter ρ (the higher it is, the more the matrix Θ will be sparse). The precision matrix Θ is a good estimation of the undirected graph with nodes $X = (X_1, ..., X_p)$: if $\theta_{i,j} = 0$ the two variables X_i and X_j can be considered conditionally independent given the others X_k, $k = 1, ..., n$, $k \neq i, j$.

2.2 Network Distance

Let $\mathbb{G}_1$ and $\mathbb{G}_2$ be two graphs represented by A_1 and A_2, $N \times N$ adjacency matrices.

The Frobenius distance between them is computed by

$$d_F(A_1, A_2) = ||A_1 - A_2||_F = \sqrt{\sum_{i,j}^{N}(a_{i,j}^1 - a_{i,j}^2)^2}. \tag{2}$$

This measure provides a value of the distance between the two graphs $\mathbb{G}_1$ and $\mathbb{G}_2$ based on how much the edges differ. In a weighted graph, it depends on edge weights, so it can be properly employed if the elements of the adjacency matrices are comparable in terms of order of magnitude.

Another way to evaluate the distance between $\mathbb{G}_1$ and $\mathbb{G}_2$ is through the DeltaCon method, which quantifies the similarity of the two graphs based on their structure. The idea of this method is considering all the possible paths connecting two nodes to compute the affinity between them through the personalized Random Walks with Restarts theory [6]. Specifically, given an adjacency matrix A, the affinity of each pair nodes is provided by $S = (I + \varepsilon D - \varepsilon A)$, where D is the degree diagonal matrix (having the degree of each node in the diagonal), and $\varepsilon > 0$ is a small constant. Then, DeltaCon method uses the root Euclidean distance to compute the distance between the two affinity matrices:

$$d_{DC}(S_1, S_2) = \sqrt{\sum_{i,j}^{N} (\sqrt{s_{i,j}^1} - \sqrt{s_{i,j}^2})^2}, \tag{3}$$

where $s_{i,j}^1$ and $s_{i,j}^2$ are the elements in row i and column j of S_1 and S_2, affinity matrices of the graphs $\mathbb{G}_1$ and $\mathbb{G}_2$.

2.3 Data Description

We considered gene and protein expression data from the TCGA-LGG and TCGA-GBM projects [1,8,14] downloaded from the firebrowse.org. Transcriptomics and proteomics datasets comprise different numbers of samples and variables. In this work, we considered only common samples and matching variables (i.e., genes in the trascriptomics dataset coding for the proteins available in the proteomics dataset). To assess the graphical lasso hypothesis, the variables were normalized through the `huge.npn` R function (**huge** package [18]), and only normally distributed variables according to the Jarque-Bera test [5] were taken into account. The samples were grouped based of the corresponding glioma-type. The diagnostic labels provided by TCGA were updated based on 2021 WHO guidelines, as described in Mendonça et al. [9].

Finally, we obtained our reference datasets comprising of 114 genes and 172 protein expression variables, for 465 samples (206 astrocytoma, 143 oligodendroglioma and 116 GBM).

2.4 Pipeline and Implementation

Figure 1 shows a schematic representation of the pipeline implemented. For each omics layer, glasso algorithm was independently applied to every glioma-type dataset by `huge.glasso`, R function from **huge** R package [18]. The regularization parameter ρ was tested between different values ($\{0.5, 0.6, 0.65, 0.7\}$). This choice influences the network sparsity, which consequently affects the number of connected variables in each case. Since we limited our analysis to the connected nodes, we set the value $\rho = 0.65$, which led to a 50%-variable reduction (i.e., a total of 80 genes and 94 proteins selected by the three glioma-type datasets).

The estimated networks were then explored from different perspectives. For each omics, the network-based variables selection was analyzed to identify features that have been commonly or exclusively selected by the different glioma-types (*variable-selection* analysis in Fig. 1). Then, a comparison across the two omics was performed, in order to detect gene-protein pairs which, despite being independently selected from transcriptomics and proteomics layers, are in agreement (i.e., the gene and the corresponding protein have been selected for the same glioma type). Next, we focused our analysis on proteomics, in order to be able to compare the estimated networks for each glioma type with the STRING

PPI network [11] (*protein-network* analysis in Fig. 1). We computed the Frobenius (**nd.edd** R function) and the DeltaCon[1]

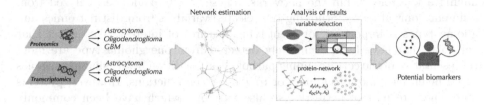

Fig. 1. Analysis scheme. Multi-omics datasets (proteomics and transcriptomics) are preprocessed and updated to group samples according to the WHO-2021 classification. Networks describing different glioma condition from different layers are estimated through glasso. The results are analyzed by cross-comparing the features selected, as well as the protein-network structure in different glioma types or with the STRING PPI network. The features identified from our analysis are listed as potential biomarkers.

2.5   Network Validation

The network-based variable selection performed through glasso has been mathematically validated by comparing the value of $O = \log(\det \Theta) - tr(S\Theta)$ (first term in Eq. (1)) computed by the optimal set of selected variables, with the one obtained by 1000 random datasets of the same dimension. The idea is estimating a non-sparse precision matrix by imposing $\rho = 0$ (Eq. (1)) on a reference dataset composed by, on one side, the variables which have been selected by glasso ($\hat{O}$), and, on the other side, the other random subsets (O_r). If the solution of (1) is optimal, we should always obtain $\hat{O} > O_r$.

Principal Component Analysis was also used to determine if the variables selected are able to maintain, or improve, the 2D representation of omics data in terms of glioma type distinction. For both omics layers, we performed PCA for (i) the complete original datasets, (ii) the set of selected variables, and (iii) the set of variables exclusively selected for each glioma type.

Additionally, the proteomics estimated network for every glioma type were compared with the STRING network, to identify the presence of distinct PPIs that could be representative of the pathological condition.

3   Results

The datasets we are considering for our analysis have more than 100 variables. In this setting, considering networks fully connected has two limitations. On one hand, computation issues might arise, since the number of variables is similar

---

[1] DeltaCon distance was computed by a modified version of the **delta_con** R function (package **rdsg**) [6].

to the number of samples. On the other hand, biological interpretation of large networks is non trivial, and variable reduction might help.

With glasso, we discard weak edges, by focusing the analysis on the variables having a key role within the networks. These results could be analyzed from different point of views. Studying the selected variables from distinct omics and glioma types is important for identifying features of interest. We expect that variables that have been exclusively detected from one glioma type are more representative of the corresponding pathological condition, while shared variables could be either related to glioma or to general cell functions. However, proteins and genes are part of networks, so also variables which have been commonly selected by all the glioma types could interact in different ways, and then can help in characterising the disease, making essential a network analysis of the shared variables.

3.1   Variable Selection

A total of 80 genes and 94 proteins were selected by glasso. Figure 2 shows the Venn diagrams representing the variables selected from each glioma type, with many features shared by the three. Astrocytoma and oligodendroglioma have more common variables compared to GBM, by considering both transcriptomics and proteomics layers. Few variables were exclusively selected by a single glioma type.

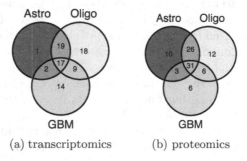

(a) transcriptomics   (b) proteomics

Fig. 2. Venn diagrams with the number of selected features from **a** the transcriptomics and **b** the proteomics datasets, for each glioma type. Astro: astrocytoma; Oligo: oligo-dendroglioma; GBM: glioblastoma.

We remark that this network-based variable selection was independently performed for the two omics, as well as between the different glioma-types. Features selected in agreement from both transcriptomics and proteomics (i.e., both gene and corresponding protein have been selected), and that stood out from the same glioma type could be extremely important for the corresponding disease condition. For this reason, we performed a cross-comparison between the two omics layers. Overall, a total of 57 genes selected based on transcriptomics encode 66 proteins identified from proteomics. Table 1 resumes the complete results, to further investigate which glioma type led to the selection of these paired features. Rows and columns represent, respectively, the results coming from transcriptomics and proteomics layer. Each cell reports the number of gene-protein pairs selected for the corresponding glioma types. For instance, the second row reports that, among the genes exclusively selected for oligodendroglioma (based on transcriptomics), one gene encodes a protein which has been selected for astrocytoma, two genes encode proteins exclusively identified for GBM, while seven and four genes encode proteins selected for all the glioma types and for both LGG, respectively. In this example, the complete agreement gene-protein is not achieved, since the diagonal cell does not report a number. Diagonal cells, which are colored in grey, always refer to results that are completely in agreement between omics. Partial agreements (light grey cells) could also be variables of interest. For instance, from the last row, we discover that two genes which are expected to be important for LGG encode proteins which have been exclusively identified for astrocytoma, suggesting that the impact of these genes on proteomics layer could be different between astrocytoma and oligodendroglioma.

Table 1. Cross-comparison of variable selection between the two omics. Cells contain the number of paired features selected by both transcriptomics and proteomics layers. Gray cells highlight the complete agreements, while light gray cells emphasize partial agreements between the selected gene-protein pairs. Results from transcriptomics are represented in blue (rows), and from proteomics are in green (columns). Astro: astrocytoma; Oligo: oligodendroglioma; GBM: glioblastoma.

		Proteomics				
	Glioma types	Astro	Oligo	GBM	Shared all	Shared LGG
	Astro	–	1	–	–	–
	Oligo	1	–	2	7	4
Transcriptomics	GBM	–	2	2	3	2
	Shared all	1	1	–	5	4
	Shared LGG	2	3	2	5	8

Although the importance of agreement between the results from different omics, also features identified for one glioma type from a single omics might be important from biological perspective. From the transcriptomics layer, seven genes were identified for oligodendroglioma, while four for GBM. From the proteomics, five genes were selected for astrocytoma and five for oligodendroglioma. All gene-protein pairs corresponding to the highlighted cells of Table 1, as well as the exclusive features from a single layer, were included in the list of potential biomarkers, for a total of 56 features.

3.2   Protein Networks

Besides the study of the selected variables, to detect biomarkers it could be crucial to investigate how the estimated networks differ from each other and against the corresponding network in non-disease scenario available from the literature. To this end, we focused on proteomics layer to evaluate how much the estimated networks are different from known PPI of the selected proteins based on STRING. Distance in terms of edges and overall network structures were evaluated by Frobenius and DeltaCon measures, respectively. We considered two different cases of study: the complete networks (case 1), and the subnetworks composed by the shared proteins (case 2). Table 2 reports the values of the distances obtained in each case. These values are affected by the number of nodes, therefore the networks were confronted case by case. STRING network distances were only evaluated through the DeltaCon method, since their edge weights cannot be compared with the one provided by glasso.

Considering the complete networks (case 1), the distance between the different glioma-type graphs confirms that astrocytoma and oligodendroglioma are more similar than GBM by both edges and structure of the estimated protein relations. Considering the STRING PPI network with the same nodes, distances increased more than 50% in all cases, and astrocytoma stood out as the glioma type with the most different network structure. These results are confirmed if we consider as nodes only the features that were commonly selected by the three glioma types. Interestingly, despite in this case the compared graphs have the same nodes, the values of both distances highlight a structural difference between the three types.

Table 2. Frobenius and DeltaCon distances between glioma-type networks and known PPI from STRING. (case 1) the complete network is considered. (case 2) only the subset of shared nodes between the three glioma types is considered. Astro: astrocytoma; Oligo: oligodendroglioma; GBM: glioblastoma.

	Frobenius			DeltaCon			
case 1		Astro	Oligo		Astro	Oligo	GBM
	GBM	0.45	0.46	GBM	0.46	0.46	–
	Oligo	0.33	–	Oligo	0.36	–	–
				STRING	0.74	0.72	0.73
case 2		Astro	Oligo		Astro	Oligo	GBM
	GBM	0.27	0.31	GBM	0.26	0.24	–
	Oligo	0.19	–	Oligo	0.16	–	–
				STRING	0.39	0.37	0.33

Detecting the major differences in these networks enables the identification of proteins that interact in distinct ways in each glioma scenario. To assess this, we visually compared the shared-protein networks (Fig. 3). We focused the analysis on the isolated nodes of the STRING network, which in glioma networks appear connected with other proteins (in Fig. 3a, b, c these nodes are highlighted in yellow). As an example, we observe the relation involving RBM15, which in our estimated network is always linked to ATM. Furthermore, in STRING (Fig. 3d) ATM is directly linked to XRCC5, relation also observable in astrocytoma and oligodendroglioma networks (Fig. 3a, b). Conversely, in GBM (Fig. 3c), the relation between ATM and XRCC5 is mediated by RBM15, suggesting that this protein could have a different role in this glioma type, and making these three variables potential novel biomarkers candidates.

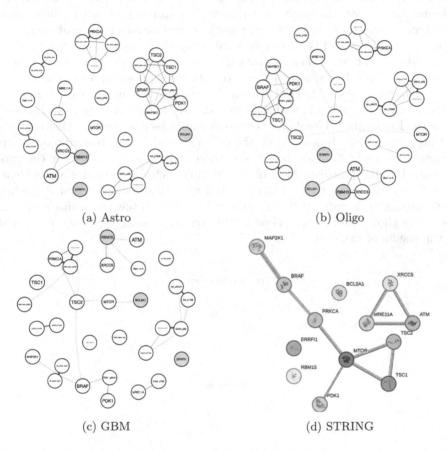

(a) Astro

(b) Oligo

(c) GBM

(d) STRING

Fig. 3. Shared protein networks estimated through glasso. Nodes are in common among the three glioma types. Yellow nodes highlight STRING isolated proteins. Astro: astrocytoma (**a**); Oligo: oligodendroglioma (**b**); GBM: glioblastoma (**c**).

3.3   Validation Outcomes

For each glioma type, both transcriptomics and proteomics set of variables selected were mathematically validated by comparing the value of $O = \log(\det \Theta) - tr(S\Theta)$, for non-sparse Θ estimated for the set of selected variables ($\hat{O}$), and for 1000 random datasets of the same dimension (O_r). The values of the best random set randomly identified, as well as the average and median values were evaluated. In all cases $\hat{O} \gg O_r$, confirming the proposed selection as good choice.

PCA results are shown in Fig. 4. Rows contain transcriptomics and proteomics results, while columns distinguish the three case of study, namely PCA obtained for (i) the complete datasets, (ii) the sets of selected variables, and (iii) the sets of the variables exclusively selected for each glioma type. By looking (i)-column, we discover the ability of the complete starting dataset in distinguish the three glioma types in a 2D linear projection. Conversely to proteomics (in which we can only see LGG cases assembled together), by transcriptomics data we are able to obtain a visual separation of the three types, despite low variance percentages. Indeed, in this representation, the cases appear spread in all the 2D plane, especially for GBM. The performed variable selection ((ii)-row) maintains the same cases distribution, with a slight increase of the percentages of explained variance. Favourably, the subset of exclusive variables ((iii)-row) further improve the previous results. Indeed, while the overall variability in trascriptomics was maintained, the LGG class spread is reduced along the first PC. For the proteomics data the positive effects of considering exclusive variables are evident, since they consistently reduced the variability of GBM along the first PC, while LGG variability is reduced in the second PC, making the visual distinction of these two glioma groups very clear in this representation, especially compared to the results of cases (i) and (ii).

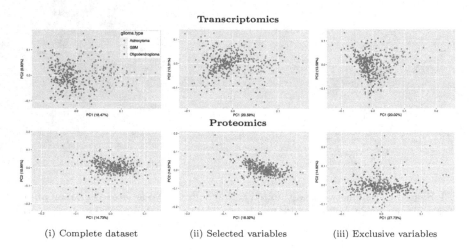

Fig. 4. PCA performed by considering different datasets: (i) all the variables (ii) variables selected by glasso, and (iii) only exclusively selected variables. The legend is reported on the first chart. Red, blue and green points are associated to astrocytoma, oligodendroglioma and glioblastoma, respectively. On the two axis there are the percentages of variance of each principal component.

4   Discussion

In this work, we propose network inference as a general tool to detect new potential biomarkers arising from transcriptomics and proteomics layers. This multi-omics study considers TCGA dataset updated according to the latest WHO glioma classification guidelines released in 2021, with the aim to support the revision of the glioma diagnostic process, and, consequently, a more accurate therapy design. Using the graphical lasso method, we estimated the undirected relations between graph nodes representing genes and proteins, by simultaneously performing network-based variable selection. These estimates have been mathematically validated by comparing the optimal solution with 1000 randomly selected variable subsets. We also performed a validation through PCA, to assess if the selected features were able to distinguish the glioma classes in a 2D subspace projection. PCA showed that glioma-type exclusive variables improve the distinction of different glioma types, especially in terms of LGG versus GBM, suggesting the exclusive variables as potential diagnostic biomarkers.

Results from the two omics were compared to find pairs of features (gene and the corresponding protein) which are selected in agreement across different omics. Interestingly, our results shown a high percentage of agreement between transcriptomics and proteomics, with more than 70% of pairs of gene-protein features independently selected. Although not all of them figured out as important for the same glioma type, this analysis led to the identification of a subset of 35 potential biomarkers, for each omics. Moreover, the analysis of the exclusive variables performed in each omics revealed other 21 possible candidates.

Focusing on the estimated proteomics networks, we evaluated distances between the three glioma types, and known PPI obtained from STRING, to detect differences in feature relations that could be associated with a specific pathological condition. By looking at the features selected by all the glioma types, we were able to identify interesting relations, e.g. the ones between ATM, RBM15 and XRCC5 (Fig. 3). In particular, we noticed that both astrocytoma and oligodendroglioma networks present a direct relation between these proteins, while GBM misses the edge connecting ATM with XRCC5. On the other hand, the PPI from STRING revealed a known relation between ATM and XRCC5, while there are no edges connecting RBM15. Interestingly, a literature research revealed that the protein expression of ATM is known to be lower in glioma than normal cells [13]. Moreover, both XRCC5 (a.k.a. Ku80) and ATM expressions are associated to the sensitiveness to radiotherapy of glioma and GBM, respectively [13,16]. However, there are no glioma-related information about RBM15 protein, whose expression is used as a biomarker for pancreatic adenocarcinoma [2,19]. Hence, the biological literature seems to support the potentiality of biological evaluation of the role of this protein, and its relation with ATM and XRCC5, in glioma.

Overall, this work allowed for the identification of a total of 59 potentially relevant features, for different glioma types. Our next goal is to validate our findings through biological experiments. To this purpose, supported by a comprehensive literature review, we plan to reduce the list of the 59 features to the ones never studied in glioma, yet having a role in cancer-related processes. The impact on prognosis of the selected features will be explored through survival analysis, and a ranked list will be formulated to prioritize molecular candidates for biological tests. A biological investigation of the role of these features is essential to discover their impact in the different glioma type progression and development.

Acknowledgment. These results are based on data from the TCGA Research Network: https://www.cancer.gov/tcga.

This work is part of the MONET project PTDC/CCI-BIO/4180/2020, supported by FCT, with references CEECINST/00042/2021, UIDB/00297/2020, UIDP/00297/2020 (NOVA Math), UIDB/00667/2020 and UIDP/00667/2020 (UNIDEMI).

References

1. Brennan, C., et al.: The somatic genomic landscape of glioblastoma. Cell **155**, 462–477 (2013). https://doi.org/10.1016/j.cell.2013.09.034
2. Dong, H., et al.: Proliferation, migration and invasion of pancreatic cancer cell lines. Cancers **15** (2023). https://doi.org/10.3390/cancers15041084
3. Friedman, J., Hastie, T., Tibshirani, R.: Sparse inverse covariance estimation with the graphical lasso. Biostatistics **9**, 432–441 (2008). https://doi.org/10.1093/biostatistics/kxm045
4. Hawe, J.S., Theis, F.J., Heinig, M.: Inferring interaction networks from multi-omics data. Front. Genet. **10** (2019). https://doi.org/10.3389/fgene.2019.00535
5. Jarque, C.M.: Jarque-bera test. Int. Encycl. Stat. Sci. (2011)
6. Koutra, D., et al.: Deltacon: Principled massive-graph similarity function with attribution. ACM Trans. Knowl. Discov. Data **10** (2016). https://doi.org/10.1145/2824443
7. Louis, D.N., et al.: The 2021 WHO classification of tumors of the central nervous system: a summary. Neuro-Oncology **23**, 1231–1251 (2021). https://doi.org/10.1093/neuonc/noab106
8. McLendon, R., et al.: Comprehensive genomic characterization defines human glioblastoma genes and core pathways. Nature **455**, 1061–1068 (2008). https://doi.org/10.1038/nature07385
9. Mendonça, M.L., et al.: Updating TCGA glioma classification through integration of molecular profiling data following the 2016 and 2021 WHO guidelines. bioRxiv p. 2023.02.19.529134 (2023). https://doi.org/10.1101/2023.02.19.529134
10. Qiao, L., Zhang, L., Chen, S., Shen, D.: Data-driven graph construction and graph learning: a review. Neurocomputing **312**, 336–351 (2018). https://doi.org/10.1016/j.neucom.2018.05.084
11. Szklarczyk, D., Franceschini, A., Wyder, S., Forslund, K., et al.: String v10: protein-protein interaction networks, integrated over the tree of life. Nucleic Acids Res. **43**, D447–D452 (2014)
12. Tantardini, M., Ieva, F., Tajoli, L., Piccardi, C.: Comparing methods for comparing networks. Sci. Rep. **9**, 17557 (2019). https://doi.org/10.1038/s41598-019-53708-y
13. Tribius, S., Pidel, A., Casper, D.: Atm protein expression correlates with radioresistance in primary glioblastoma cells in culture. Int. J. Radiat. Oncol. Biol. Phys. **50**, 511–523 (2001). https://doi.org/10.1016/S0360-3016(01)01489-4

14. TCGA, Network: Comprehensive, integrative genomic analysis of diffuse lower-grade gliomas. N. Engl. J. Med. **372**, 2481–2498 (2015). https://doi.org/10.1056/NEJMoa1402121
15. Wang, D.: Discrepancy between mrna and protein abundance: Insight from information retrieval process in computers. Comput. Biol. Chem. **32**, 462–468 (2008). https://doi.org/10.1016/j.compbiolchem.2008.07.014
16. Yang, J., Qianxue, C.: Expression of ku proteins in glioma and their association with radiotherapy sensitivity and prognosis. Acta Med. Mediterr. Int. Sci. J. Clin. Med. **4**, 1065 (2018). https://doi.org/10.19193/0393-6384_2018_4_163
17. Yang, K., et al.: Glioma targeted therapy: insight into future of molecular approaches. Mol. Cancer **21**, 39 (2022). https://doi.org/10.1186/s12943-022-01513-z
18. Zhao, T., et al.: The huge package for high-dimensional undirected graph estimation in r. J. Mach. Learn. Res.: JMLR **13**, 1059–1062 (2012). https://doi.org/10.1093/nar/gku1003
19. Zhao, Z., Ju, Q., Ji, J., Li, Y., Zhao, Y.: N6-methyladenosine methylation regulator rbm15 is a potential prognostic biomarker and promotes cell proliferation in pancreatic adenocarcinoma. Front. Mol. Biosci. **9** (2022)

Better Medical Efficiency by Means of Hospital Bed Management Optimization—A Comparison of Artificial Intelligence Techniques

Afonso Lobo[1]([✉]), Agostinho Barbosa[2], Tiago Guimarães[1], João Lopes[1], Hugo Peixoto[1], and Manuel Filipe Santos[1]

[1] Centro ALGORITMI, University of Minho, 4800-058 Guimarães, Portugal
wolf.afonso@gmail.com, a83946@alunos.uminho.pt, {tsg, mfs}@dsi.uminho.pt, lopesit@outlook.pt, hpeixoto@di.uminho.pt
[2] Centro Hospitalar do Tâmega e Sousa, 4564-007 Penafiel, Portugal
a.barbosa@chts.min-saude.pt

Abstract. The combination of the phenomenon of overcrowding with inefficient management of resources is a major obstacle to the good performance of hospital units and consequently the degradation of the medical service provided. This paper provides an analysis to understand the correlation between poor bed allocation and hospital performance. The lack of an efficient resource planning among the various medical specialties can negatively impact the quality of service. Four different techniques were compared to realize which is better suited for optimizing the allocation of beds in Hospital units. Hill Climbing and the Genetic Algorithm stood out the others, the latter presenting greater consistency and a shorter computation time. When tested with real data from Centro Hospitalar do Tâmega e Sousa, attained a total of 0 wrongly allocated patients against 92 when compared with former methods. This translates into better patient service, reduced waiting time and staff workload, which means increased performance in all adjacent medical issues.

Keywords: Artificial Intelligence · Modern Optimization · Hospital Bed Management · Medical Efficiency

1 Introduction

Nowadays, more and more data regarding hospitals and all the surrounding area in the health sector are becoming available to us. This means an increasingly facilitated use of artificial intelligence techniques to seek a significant improvement in the efficiency of these services, from component optimization to efficient management of resources in the hospital units, contributing in a significant way to monetary cost reduction [1].

The approach performed in this type of problem is called prescriptive analysis. It is an analysis with the purpose of responding to real decisions regarding the planning of resources in the hospital units as well as the allocation of certain medications depending on the context, always aiming to reach the best possible solution [2]. This study is centered on the development and comparison of Machine Learning Optimization Algorithms (MLOA), for intelligent and efficient management of beds in the different specialties of a hospital, corresponding in the best possible way to the needs of the hospital as a whole.

The application of these algorithms is becoming more and more relevant as we are witnessing a global aging of the population which causes the flow of patients to be greater and the pressure on health services to increase. The result of this pressure, without proper planning, is an inefficient management and organization of hospital units, falling short of their needs and an increase in operating costs [3].

Adopting optimization algorithms to answer these questions and obtain the best possible planning has been one of the best answers to this type of problem, representing an increase in performance in service delivery and operation of hospital units [4].

In the realization of this project as followed the approaches of Design Science Research.

2 Background

2.1 Resources Planning in Hospital Settings

A good planning of resources in health care units to guarantee an adequate response and performance to their needs is becoming increasingly difficult and therefore it becomes more pertinent to find ways to obtain a better use and optimization of resources through successful planning and management.

The main obstacle to a good organization and management of resources in a hospital is due to the current phenomenon of overcrowding coupled with an inefficient management of resources, increasingly accentuating the underutilization of them, i.e. the flow of patients is too high for the response that hospitals can give, reducing the response capacity and consequent overcrowding [5].

According to a study conducted at the University of California, the main reasons for this Overcrowding are concentrated in the high volume of patients, the complexity of related medical issues, delays in the provision of services and mainly in the poor management and allocation of beds in hospitals being this factor considered as the one that represents more weight for the problem in question [6].

The inadequate allocation of beds is due, besides the lack of available beds, to an inefficient management of resources which causes a negative differential between the needs presented and the response capacity. This means that even in scenarios where the resources can meet the needs, occurs a suboptimal use of them resulting in loss of performance, causing delays and cancellation of admissions and surgeries, early transfers of patients and accumulation of costs [7].

To this end, it is important to find a form or model of organization based on two main variables: the occupancy of beds and the forecasting of patient flow, in order to obtain an efficient management of resources that allows the proper functioning of hospital institutions being able to provide adequate care to their patients to ensure a response capacity appropriate to the needs [5, 6].

2.2   Related Work

The planning and management of resources in hospital units represent a need and a pertinent concern in our days. We are therefore witnessing a systematic attempt to find the best possible solution that allows us to respond effectively to the problem of overcrowding using more efficient management of means. There are several studies proposing solutions and showing important characteristics to be considered to achieve the desired success.

One way to promote efficient resource management in hospitals is the use of the Markov model. The Markov model, or strategy, is a mathematical queuing model intending to predict and improve the waiting time of patients for service. This approach was the target of a study published in Healthcare Engineering, where the focus was optimizing a model in order to obtain greater efficiency in bed allocation. This model was based on several indicators such as the average number of patients, bed utilization rate, patient stop rate, and patient average waiting time. Simulations and several experiments conducted with this model showed a significant improvement in resource allocation and overall patient satisfaction [8].

It was made in 2022 a study with the intent of predicting patient Length Of Stay (LOS) through machine learning models and input data regarding medical records and demographic information of patients in the internal medicine specialty of a hospital in Portugal. The authors followed two scenarios: one that predicts the LOS at the time of admission; and another that updates the prediction during the hospitalization process. They compared four machine learning algorithms: decision tree, random forest, k-nearest neighbors and gradient boosting. They found that gradient boosting performs the best, achieving an accuracy of about 96%. They also found that including data about the patient's health electronic record, such as exams, lab results, medications and surgeries, improves the predictive capacity of the model. They concluded that their model can help health professionals plan and manage hospital resources more efficiently and improve the quality of care for patients [9].

In 2020, In Brazil in Minas Gerais the use of optimization algorithms, more specifically a genetic algorithm, was also the target of study to improve the allocation of beds in hospitals in the region, proving, despite an increase of 13% in operating costs, a reduction up to 1/30 of the refusal patient rate [10].

Following the application of MLOA, more specifically the genetic algorithm, a study was conducted at Tous Hospital in Tehra based on patient flow data, a study aimed at optimizing the use of human resources in the hospital in question. The objective was to find a solution that represented the minimum optimal number of staff required to meet the needs of the hospital, thus leading to a reduction in waste, operating costs and an increase in the efficiency and effectiveness of the service provided, through a better distribution of staff hours. In the application of this algorithm, the fitness function, a constituent function of the algorithm, whose purpose is to attribute a certain score to a certain solution to the problem, took into consideration parameters such as the employee's salary, the number of patients seen on average per employee and the available work shifts. It was then, after 500 generations, found a solution for staff hourly allocation in which only 69 employees were needed compared to the 108 actives in function daily in the hospital, to give the same or better response to the needs presented [11].

When it comes to comparing optimization algorithms with each other, a study was conducted at the Fukuoka Institute in Japan, to evaluate the performance of algorithms such as Hill Climbing, Simulated Annealing and Genetic Algorithm for optimal allocation of routers in order to promote better coverage and connection conditions to Local Area Networks. From this study resulted an advantage of Hill Climbing and Simulated Annealing, showing to reach the desired results faster [12].

Following the performance comparison between the algorithms, a study was conducted in order to understand the behavior of the Hill Climbing and Genetic algorithms for digital predistortion model sizing. From this study it was concluded that the genetic algorithm is dependent on the input parameters, and that the larger the population size, the better the results, which also means a proportional increase in execution time. The Hill Climbing algorithm, on the other hand, does not depend on the input parameters and can present itself with a shorter execution time due to the increase in the population size of the genetic algorithm. As for the performance comparison regarding the quality of the solution obtained, the genetic algorithm reached the optimal solution more often, while the hill climbing also presented local optimal solutions, i.e., solutions close to the best possible solution, but not being so [13].

In the big picture we can observe several different ways to try to achieve a more efficient management of resources in hospitals. In most of the studies regarding the allocation of beds and resources in hospital units, factors such as the Length Of Stay (LOS) and the Occupation Rate are highlighted. The application of MLOA to solve this type of problems has been studied and its behavior is also observed, not only in allocation problems related to the Hospital industry but also in the application of several types of contexts.

In this study the focus will be on the application of four different machine learning optimization algorithms with the objective of obtaining an optimal solution for the distribution of beds by the different specialties of the hospital, avoiding overcrowding. They will then be compared and concluded which one presents the greatest impact and significant improvement in the matter of medical issues.

3 Materials and Methods

3.1 Methodologies

The document was developed according to the Design Science Research methodology, a methodology with the objective of creating a framework to help solve and investigate problems. In this framework artifacts that generate new knowledge are generated and analyzed. This methodology is composed of six distinct phases: Problem Identification and Motivation (1), Defining the Objectives for the solution (2), Design and Development (3), Demonstration (4), Evaluation (5) and Communication (6) [14].

3.2 Tools and Algorithms

The development of this project was all based on the Python language and its respective libraries (NumPy, Pandas, Matplotlib, Math, DateTime). The development platform was Google's Colab. The algorithms used are Machine Learning Optimization

Algorithms, highlighting, Random Search, Hill Climbing, Simulated Annealing, and Genetic/Evolutionary Algorithm.

3.3 Data Sets

The datasets used are related to patient flow at the Centro Hospitalar do Tâmega e Sousa (CHTS) and its respective specialties, for a period corresponding to 4 years. This dataset contained information such as, admissions, discharges, respective days and times, number of specialty beds, which patients were allocated to each specialty and which patients were the responsible of each specialty, and also contained information about which days the patient was hospitalized in service, in a particular specialty.

4 Experiments

The following section describes the experiments in all their phases.

4.1 Problem Formulation

The aim is to improve the misallocation of patients in different specialties due to poor management and planning of resources, specifically beds. The inefficiency on management leads to an underutilization of resources and a consequent increase in overcrowding. The proposed challenge was to obtain an optimal solution for planning and distributing beds in the different specialties of the hospital, considering:

- Max_bed—The total number of beds in a hospital;
- Specialties—All the 36 specialties in the hospital;
- Beds_needed—Number of beds needed on a certain day for each specialty;
- Bed_available—Number of beds available/empty in each specialty.

It is important to mention that the model solution for this problem would always have to comply with two restrictions:

1. The sum of beds to be allocated in each specialty on a given day, by the applied algorithm, should never exceed the maximum limit of available beds to be used;
2. The maximum number of beds to be allocated to a given specialty should never exceed the number of needs presented, thus avoiding the underuse of resources.

4.2 Data Provided

The dataset provided for the study corresponded to the flow of patients in the CHTS over a period of 4 years (2019–2022) and it had an initial dimension of 708492 rows × 15 columns. Table 1 shows the various sources provided and a brief description of them.

It was possible to obtain daily information about admissions, discharges, patient transfers, and the days on which they were under admission for each specialty. It was also possible to determine that the maximum number of beds available in the hospital was 551 beds.

Table 1. Data Sources

Data Sources	Description
Admissions	Data regarding the admission of patients to the Hospital, their specialties, dates, and times
Discharges	Data identical to those of patient's admission to the hospital, but referring to the discharges
Allocation	Data regarding the specialty where a certain patient was allocated
Specialties	A data set that contained all the information regarding the hospital's specialties
Beds	Real data regarding the number of beds existing in the hospital, in each specialty, and about the type of bed in question

4.3 Data Preparation

In the data preparation phase for later use in the optimization models, all data with construction errors or Null or NaN values were first identified. Next, relevant data for the analysis of bed allocation, repeated or redundant attributes were identified. To a better impact understanding and problem-solving, an important transformation was performed distinguishing two classes of inpatients:

- Physical patients—patients physically admitted to the service responsible for their treatment;
- Responsible patients—patients who are physically hospitalized in services other than those that treat them.

These two classes correspond to correct and incorrect bed distribution, respectively. A correct bed allocation matching the daily needs of each specialty would maximize physical patients and minimize responsible ones. After these changes the dataset was transformed into a time series, moving the date attribute to index and divided into 36 different sub-datasets each corresponding to a specific specialty. Is then possible, for a given day, to know the flow of patients, what the status of the occupation of beds is and how many supplementary beds are necessary to supply the real needs of the specialty.

4.4 Domain and Fitness Function

Before applying MLOA algorithms, it is necessary to define: (i) the solution space of the problem; (ii) how solutions will be represented; (iii) how to define the constraints; and (iv) how to evaluate the efficiency of the presented solutions. It is therefore imperative to define the problem domain and the objective function. The problem domain defines how the solution set will be represented given the problem constraints. The domain corresponds to the minimum and maximum number of beds available in each specialty so that the solution is always possible in the space of the problem since it doesn't exceed the maximum number of beds needed for the day.

In order to optimize the algorithms' performance and decrease the probability of underutilization of resources, a "dynamic domain" was created depending on the day in question. Contrary to what is usually understood as a fixed variable in the problem, in this problem the domain may vary according to the daily needs of the different specialties of the hospital. In other words, for each day, the domain could vary between 0 and the number of patients under the responsibility of each specialty. The solution was represented in an array of 1 dimension, with 36 elements, each corresponding to an integer number of beds to allocate in a given specialty for the day in question. The fitness function or objective function has as its main objective to evaluate a set of solutions. This function assigns a certain score to the solution to be evaluated taking into a account a set of conditions specific to the context of the problem.

```
    1.    Fitness Function Pseudo Code
score = 0
solution = solution input
max_bed = 551
If sum(solution) > max beds then
    score = -100
For each specialty in solution do
  If beds_needed == beds in solution  and beds available == 0
then
     score += 2
  Else if beds_needed == beds in solution  and beds available >
0 then
            score += 1
  Else if beds_needed not equal to beds in solution:
          score -= |beds_in_solution - beds_needed| * 0.1
End If
End For
Return satisfaction
```

The goal is to minimize or maximize the score. Presented in Pseudocode 1, the fitness function tries to maximize the number of correct bed assignments knowing the daily Speciality while minimizing the number of empty on unused beds. This leads to maximizing the number of patients correctly assigned to a bed, i.e. maximizing physical patients to rather than responsible patients.

4.5 Optimization Techniques

For optimizing the allocation of beds to patients, four different Optimization Algorithms were compared in order to understand which one would represent a better performance. The configuration of the algorithms was adapted to take the date in one of the parameters, since it is an input variable in the fitness function and essential to define the daily domain of the problem. The algorithms that were considered in this study are presented below.

- Random Search (RS)

A method based on the random search for solutions during a certain number of rounds. Note that the greater the number of rounds the more likely it is that a better solution will emerge, increasing in the same way the computation time [15].

```
  2.    RS Pseudo Code
round = 0
best_score = 0
best solution TO NULL
While round < rounds
  solution = random solution between the domain values
  score = fitness function(date, solution)
  If score > best_score then
      best_score = satisfaction
      best solution = solution
  End If
  round ++
End While
Return best solution
```

- Hill Climbing (HC)

Hill Climbing is a local search algorithm, based on increments and decrements of the generated solutions, called "neighbors", starting with an initial random or previously provided solution within the domain. In its execution, each generated neighbor is analyzed and evaluated through the fitness function as to its quality, and if one of the neighbors generated in the iteration presents a better result, it becomes the current solution. The algorithm continues until there is no possibility of improvement in the solutions. This algorithm tends to find local optimal solutions.

```
  3.    HC Pseudo Code
Generate an initial solution s0,
s = s0
score = fitness(date, s)
While termination criteria not met do
      neighbor_sol = Gen_Neighbor(s, domain)
      neighbor_score = fitness(date, neighbor_sol)
      If neighbor_score > score then
          s = neighbor_sol
          score = neighbor_score
      End If
  End While
Return s
```

- Simulated Annealing (SA)

Simulated Annealing is a thermodynamic analogous method inspired by the metal cooling process. This algorithm consists in a sequence of iterations where a progressive decrease of temperature occurs, initializing it in a high value where each change is accepted, being this acceptance probability smaller and smaller as the temperature decreases according to a cooling rate. The search method is identical to the HC algorithm based on the transformation of solutions through increments to the previous solution, the big difference is that through the acceptance or not of the solutions this approach avoids getting stuck with local min or max.

```
4.    SA Pseudo Code
Generate an initial solution s0,
s = s0
score0 = fitness(date, s)
While temperature  > 0.1 do
     s1 = Generate(s0, domain)
     score1 = fitness(date, s1)
     If Accept(score0, score1, temperature) then
       score0 = score1
       s0 = s1
     End If
     temperature = temperature * cooling
End While
Return s0
```

- Genetic Algorithm (GA)

The Genetic Algorithm is based on Charles Darwin's theory of evolution. It acts on a set of possible solutions called individuals of a population. The algorithm starts with an initial population and transformations are performed on each of the individuals through mutation or crossover, whose decision is based on a previously defined probability. The best individuals are chosen according to an elitism number to generate the new population. The algorithm ends when the desired number of populations/generations is reached and the best individual from the last population is reached. It should be noted that, according to several studies such as the one carried out at the University of Neuchâtel in Switzerland, it was found that these algorithms show better results with larger populations than with increasing the max number of generations [16].

```
5.    GA Pseudo Code
Initialize population
elite = elistism  * Population-Size
For i in range number_generations
     fitness(date, individual) for each individual in popula-
tion
     Select the elite with the best result
     Insert elite into new_population
     While new population-size < Population-Size
       IF probability of mutation
         Mutate elite individual - > new individual
       ELSE
           Crossover elite indivduals -> new individual
       Insert individual into new population
     End While
End For
Return last generation best indvidual
```

4.6 Evaluation

In order to evaluate the performance of each model, 10 runs of each one were performed. For each were saved the score obtained and the computation time required. For the experiment all the models were executed with data based on the date of May 5, 2021, taking into account that the domain corresponds to a variable that would change day after day, depending on real needs of the hospital. No difference was perceived in the success rate whether considering 1 or 50 days. Table 2 presents the metrics used for evaluating the techniques as well as a brief description.

Table 2. Metrics

Metric	Description
Score	Mean of all the scores obtained in the 10 Executions
Run Time	Mean of the execution times
STD	Standard Deviation of the scores obtained

In a perfect scenario, the allocation of beds corresponds to the daily needs of these specialties and the number of unused beds tends to 0. The maximum score obtained would be 2 points for each one of the 36 specialties, i.e. 2×36, meaning a maximum score of 72 points. It is necessary to take into account that for this score to be reached the hospital is not in a state of over/under capacity. All the beds would be occupied and allocated to the specialties correctly, which is not observed in about 99% of the occurrences. The STD of the run time was not recorded since it was insignificant differences among runs for the same algorithm, what could be the result of the computational conditions in the development environment.

5   Results and Discussion

5.1   Algorithm Settings

To run the algorithms considered in this study it was necessary to define their initial input parameters except for HC. In the Table 3 are presented the values used for the implementation of each technique.

The number_generations defined for GA were obtained through several runs until the stabilization of the fitness function as represented in Fig. 1.

5.2   Results

The performance of each one of the algorithms has been recorded considering a total of 10 runs as presented in Table 4.

From these results we can see that both Hill Climbing and Genetic Algorithm stand out positively in terms of performance. In a fair comparison, we can say that the HC, despite obtaining the best average scores, also registers a higher standard deviation. This means that in a larger set of runs, the average can be changed by the variance of the solutions presented. GA, on the other hand, has almost the same average score, with a difference of 1 point and a significantly lower standard deviation, promoting greater

Table 3. Algorithms' Parameters

Model	Paramteres
Random Search	*Rounds - >10000*
Hill Climbing	None
Simulated Annealing	*Cooling Rate - >0.95* *Temperature - >10000000000*
Genetic Algortihm	*Population-size - >400* *Number_Generations - >25* *Probability of Mutation - >0.2* *Elitism - >0.2*

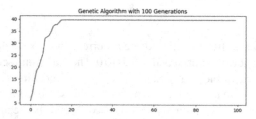

Fig. 1. GA 100 Generations

Table 4. Results

Model	MS	STD	ART
Random Search	13.78	1.86	10 min
Hill Climbing	43.2	2.97	14 min
Simulated Annealing	−11.9	7.52	Less then 1 min
Genetic Algorithm	42.2	1.88	6 min

consistency of results in the long term and greater reliability. Regarding computing time, GA presents less than half of HC.

On the negative side, Simulated Annealing does not present a single feasible solution, however, this fact is due to the parameters chosen in its implementation. More specifically the initial temperature used, which despite being high, is a parameter that should be changed depending on the scenario. In order to make a fair comparison with the other algorithms, it would have to be found out what is the optimal value to use for this parameter, which is a very complex task. The Random Search did not observe any surprises in its behavior as the solutions are generated through random probabilities.

Figures 2, 3, 4 and 5 represent the results obtained for the 10 executions done for each algorithm. At the time of the execution, there was a case of overcrowding with 53 more patients than beds to be made available. This combined with the wrong allocation of

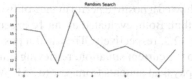

Fig. 2. Random Search Execution

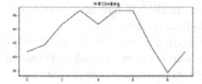

Fig. 3. HillClimbing Execution

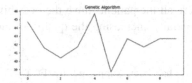

Fig. 4. Genetic Algorithm Execution

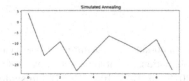

Fig. 5. Simulated Annealing Execution

beds led to the registration of about 92 patients allocated to the wrong specialties. When we compare the results presented by HC and GA, despite complying with the present bed limitations did not require wrong allocation of patients. The number of physical patients was maximized from 459 to 551 and the responsible class was minimized from 92 patients to 0.

6 Conclusions

In this study, the focus was on performing a comparison through four different optimization algorithms and understanding which one would give the best response in bed allocation problems. At the same time promote hospital units the opportunity to improve their medical service provided, enjoying efficient management of their resources and thus combating the current overcrowding verified in health systems.

The study carried out showed a positive performance of two algorithms: Hill Climbing and the Genetic Algorithm. Both, evaluated along 10 executions, obtained identical average scores of 43.2 and 42.2, respectively. They had a positive impact on bed management when compared to the current situation, retrieving minus 92 wrong allocations and increasing the class of physical patients from 459 to 551. When it comes to standard deviation, GA stands out, with a value of 1.88 compared to the value of 2.97 obtained by HC, thus more consistent. For the execution time, the difference becomes significant once GA presents less than half of HC. It is therefore concluded from this study that the best algorithm to be used in the allocation of beds to promote increased efficiency and performance of hospitals to their patients is GA.

For future studies, it is advised a deeper study on algorithms dependent on the optimization of input parameters, as is the case of GA and especially Simulated Annealing, which with the input variables optimization can present very good results.

Implementing the algorithms tested in this study, mainly the GA, can lead to a resource waste decrease by allowing hospital units the opportunity to face overcrowding and being capable of matching their daily needs. This leads to a much better bed management and planning, where all the patients have the possibility of being allocated to their right unit / hospital specialty, increasing the quality of medical services provided to patients.

Acknowledgments. This work has been supported by FCT—Fundação para a Ciência e Tecnologia within the R&D Units Project Scope: UIDB/00319/2020.

References

1. Tekieh, M.H., Raahemi, B.: Importance of data mining in healthcare: A survey. In: Proceedings of the 2015 IEEE/ACM International Conference on Advances in Social Networks Analysis and Mining, ASONAM 2015, pp. 1057–1062 (2015). https://doi.org/10.1145/2808797.280 9367
2. Ogundele, I., Popoola, O., ... O.O.-I.J. of, 2018, undefined: A review on data mining in healthcare. academia.edu
3. Rashwan, W., Abo-Hamad, W., Operational, A.A.-E.J. of, 2015, undefined: A system dynamics view of the acute bed blockage problem in the Irish healthcare system. Elsevier
4. Saghafian, S., Austin, G., Healthcare, S.T.-I.T., on, 2015, undefined: Operations research/management contributions to emergency department patient flow optimization: review and research prospects. Taylor & Francis **5**, 101–123 (2015). https://doi.org/10.1080/19488300.2015.1017676
5. Erenler, A.K., et al.: Reasons for overcrowding in the emergency department: experiences and suggestions of an education and research hospital. Turk J. Emerg. Med. **14**, 59–63 (2014). https://doi.org/10.5505/1304.7361.2014.48802
6. Richards, J.R., Navarro, M.L., Derlet, R.W.: Survey of directors of emergency departments in California on overcrowding. West. J. Med. **172**, 385 (2000). https://doi.org/10.1136/EWJM.172.6.385
7. Ravaghi, H., Alidoost, S., Mannion, R., Bélorgeot, V.D.: Models and methods for determining the optimal number of beds in hospitals and regions: a systematic scoping review. BMC Health Serv. Res. **20** (2020). https://doi.org/10.1186/S12913-020-5023-Z

8. Wu, J., Chen, B., Wu, D., Wang, J., Peng, X., Xu, X.: Optimization of Markov queuing model in hospital bed resource allocation. J. Healthc. Eng. (2020). https://doi.org/10.1155/2020/663 0885

9. Peixoto, D., Faria, M., Macedo, R., Peixoto, H., Lopes, J., Barbosa, A., Santos, M.F.: Determining internal medicine length of stay by means of predictive analytics. EPIA 2022, Lecture Notes in Computer Science, Subseries Lecture Notes in Artificial Intelligence (2022)

10. e Oliveira, B.R.P., de Vasconcelos, J.A., Almeida, J.F.F., Pinto, L.R.: A Simulation-Optimisation approach for hospital beds allocation. Int. J. Med. Inform. **141** (2020). https://doi.org/10.1016/J.IJMEDINF.2020.104174

11. Apornak, A., Raissi, S., Keramati, A., Khalili-Damghani, K.: Human resources optimization in hospital emergency using the genetic algorithm approach. Int. J. Healthc. Manag. **14**, 1441–1448 (2021). https://doi.org/10.1080/20479700.2020.1763236

12. Sakamoto, S., Kulla, E., Oda, T., Ikeda, M., Barolli, L., Xhafa, F.: A comparison study of hill climbing, simulated annealing and genetic algorithm for node placement problem in WMNs. J. High Speed Netw. **20**, 55–66 (2014). https://doi.org/10.3233/JHS-140487

13. Wang, S., Hussein, M.A., Baudoin, G., Venard, O., Gotthans, T.: Comparison of hill-climbing and genetic algorithms for digital predistortion models sizing. In: 2016 IEEE International Conference on Electronics, Circuits and Systems, ICECS 2016. pp. 289–292. Institute of Electrical and Electronics Engineers Inc. (2017)

14. Peffers, K., Tuunanen, T., … M.R.-J. of, 2007, undefined: A design science research methodology for information systems research. Taylor & Francis **24**, 45–77 (2007). https://doi.org/10.2753/MIS0742-1222240302

15. Bergstra, J., Ca, J.B., Ca, Y.B.: Random search for hyper-parameter optimization Yoshua Bengio. J. Mach. Learn. Res. **13**, 281–305 (2012). https://doi.org/10.5555/2188385.2188395

16. Vrajitoru, D.: Large population or many generations for genetic algorithms? Implications in information retrieval

AI-Based Medical Scribe to Support Clinical Consultations: A Proposed System Architecture

Larissa Montenegro[1] (ID), Luis M. Gomes[2] (ID), and José M. Machado[1]([✉]) (ID)

[1] Centro ALGORITMI/LASI, University of Minho, Braga, Portugal
larissa.montenegro@algoritmi.uminho.pt, jmac@di.uminho.pt
[2] Centro ALGORITMI/LASI, University of Azores, Ponta, Delgada, Portugal
luis.mp.gomes@uac.pt

Abstract. AI applications in hospital frameworks can improve patient-care quality and efficient workflows and assist in digital transformation. By designing Smart Hospital infrastructures, creating an efficient framework enables patient information exchange between hospitals, point of care, and remote patient monitoring. Deep learning (DL) solutions play important roles in these infrastructures' digital transformation process and architectural design. Literature review shows that DL solutions based on Automatic Speech Recognition (ASR) and Natural Language Processing (NLP) are rising concerning clinical data digitalisation, population health management, and improving patient care. Nevertheless, one of the literature's shortcomings highlights the limited research using these solutions in real-world medical environments. As part of smart hospitals, smart medical scribes have been presented in several studies as a promising solution. However, just a few studies have tested it in real settings. Moreover, it was limited to non-existent studies on non-English systems, even yet to be found similar studies for European Portuguese. The proposed study evaluates NLP-based solutions in real-life Portuguese clinical settings focused on patient care for Smart Healthcare applications.

Keywords: Digital transformation · Smart healthcare · Natural language processing · Automatic speech recognition

1 Introduction

The COVID-19 pandemic highlighted the need for and accelerated the digital transformation process in hospitals. Smart healthcare systems can bring solutions in the acquisition and process of population data both health related data (e.g., patient symptoms across locations) and non-health-related data (e.g., population movement, infrastructure use) to foresee potential disease outbreaks, reduce administrative burden and consequently reduce workforce burnout. According to a survey presented in 2020, in Europe was estimated that a physician's working time was split approximately equally between treating patients and administrative tasks, such as Electronic Health Record (EHR). Meanwhile, medical assistants spend 65% of their time on patient care and 35% on telephone queries and transcriptions. At the same time, however, it has been predicted that with AI technologies, doctors could spend 17% more of their time with patients, as the administrative burden of time-consuming tasks would be reduced [18].

By implementing AI applications in hospital information systems, they can improve patient-care quality and efficient workflows and assist in digital transformation. The goal is to create Smart Hospital infrastructures, creating an efficient framework that enables the exchange of patient information between hospitals, point of care, and remote patient monitoring. Machine Learning solutions play important roles in this digital transformation process and the architectural design of hospital information systems. The digitization of medical care means that hospitals can increasingly collect large amounts of data managed through large information systems. With its ability to process large data sets, machine learning technology is ideally suited to analyse medical data and provide efficient algorithms. For example, neural networks have been used effectively in complex decision-making in strategic management, specifically in strategic planning and decision-making, to evaluate performance [15].

Within the European Union, municipalities are trying to use technology to create more efficient and environmentally friendly cities by developing Smart Cities [8,14]. A smart city's purpose is to optimize its governmental functions and services, thereby driving economic growth while improving the quality of life of its citizens. The structure of a smart city framework includes Information and Communication Technologies (ICT) and data management networks, such as the Internet of Things (IoT), Big Data and Cloud Computing Technologies [20]. It is pointless for the government to invest in infrastructure, such as intelligent sensors, without using suitable data analysis and monitoring applications. Thereby, there must be synchrony between the government, the citizens, and the IoT technology implemented [9].

Machine Learning solutions play important roles in this digital transformation process and the architectural design of these infrastructures. Deep Learning-powered solutions, such as digital medical scribe, would help reduce the administrative burden on doctors and medical assistants by performing tasks such as transcription, extracting medical information, and assisting doctors with general administrative tasks. Nevertheless, one of the literature's shortcomings highlights the limited research using these solutions in real-world medical environments. Automatisation of clinical documentation by solutions such as smart medical scribes as part of smart hospitals has been presented in several studies as a promising solution. However, just a few studies have tested it in real settings. Moreover, it was limited to non-existent studies on non-English systems, even yet to be found similar studies for European Portuguese. The proposed study aims to evaluate the current state of the art of digital medical scribe architectures based on deep learning algorithms. This research is part of developing an AI-based digital medical scribe for the European Portuguese language.

This paper is sectioned as follows, starting with the introduction. This section will be followed by a literature review of the current status of studies related to medical scribing, ASR and NLP. The third section includes an evaluation of the needs and problems of digital transformation and how neural network models would benefit in solving these problems. In addition, current deep learning models that are part of a medical digital scribe architecture model will be evaluated. And finally, we present the conclusions and outline future work.

2   Literature Review

In this section we present the current status of a digital medical scribe, the methods used in its development, and the implementation in clinical practice. The need to implement digital medical scribes based on AI techniques, such as automatic speech recognition (ASR) and natural language processing (NLP), has been evaluated. Additionally, we include studies on the current state of the digital medical scribes, ASR and NLP.

2.1   Digital Medical Scribe

The development of digital scribes has increased in recent years, as evidenced in recent literature. Showing continued growth and interest. There is a growth in academic research and private companies with digital scribe development, such as Microsoft, Google, EMR.AI, Suki, Robin Healthcare, DeepScribe, Tenor.ai, Saykara, Sopris Health, Carevoice, Notable, and Kiroku. These applications on the market have a common architectural basis based on recording/acquiring conversational audio, converting audio to text, extracting information from text, and producing documentation [13]. Van Buchen et al. [21] reviewed the current status of the digital scribe for a medical practice to develop and evaluate the implementation of a digital scribe in medical consultations in the Netherlands. The researchers contacted some private companies developing digital scribes about technical documentation through the research phases but failed to access the documentation. Meanwhile, Coiera et al. [5] developed a framework to understand with literature the capabilities found in digital scribes and the future trajectory of its evolution. The researchers pointed out challenges to its success, such as engagement in the medical community to adjust to new workflows and focus on the quality and safety of clinical-patient interactions. It was concluded that implementing digital scribes in medical consultation EHR workflow would offer benefits such as decision support for diagnostics, prognosis and therapeutic tasks. A literature review on digital scribes, voice-to-text conversation and information extraction was presented by Ghatnekar et al. [7]. Their literature review, which includes fifteen articles, led them to conclude that the digital scribe is a solution to the weak interaction with the EHR. Additionally, it pointed to the risks such as automatisation bias and risks to data privacy.

Wang et al. [22] developed a digital scribe to automate medical documentation in English. The generated documentation was centred on patient communication. The researchers focus on two elements: summarising the conversation by recapping information from the provider and confirming accurate understanding from the patient, and signposting, which involves providers using transition questions and statements to guide the conversation. Their results showed that it was 2.7 times faster than typing and dictation. During the medical examination, the digital scribe was 2.17 times faster than typing and around 3.12 times faster than dictation. It was observed that the providers required minimal training to use the digital scribe. Li et al. [12] presented a study evaluating the use of digital scribe systems in a user-centred simulated medical consultation. Their study aimed to comprehend the physicians' interaction with the digital scribe, specifically strengths, limitations and workflow. The researchers evaluate the digital scribe with three scenarios:

(1) the digital scribe generates a summary without needing to receive edits.
(2) a medical resident edits the summary generated per the digital scribe, and
(3) a medical resident does the whole process without the intervention of the digital scribe. The physician then evaluates the final report. Their results have shown that the digital scribe had the lower evaluation score of the three scenarios, Although the physician was open to using the digital scribe. The researchers still were optimistic about the implementation of the system.

However, it is important to keep the user experience through the development phases of the prototype. Among the feedback, the language is a limitation, and it needs to be considered to change the consultation workflow and address ethical concerns about privacy content.

From the literature obtained on a digital scribe, information was not obtained on non-English systems. The question remains about the status of commercial systems in other languages remains open. In addition, up-to-date current published research has not been found that is undertaking the development of a similar prototype for European Portuguese.

2.2 Automatic Speech Recognition and Natural Language Processing Algorithms

Meripo et al. [11] proposed an end-to-end approach for ASR error detection using audio-transcript entailment. The research aims to improve transcription errors in doctor-patient conversations. The model showed a classification error rate of 26.2% on all transcription errors and 23% on medical errors. Mani et al. [10] presented a study for error correction of ASR by machine learning translation method. They compared the performance of two ASR systems, the Google ASR and the open-source ASPIRE model. The machine learning model for error correction was a sequence-to-sequence model, and it was trained with a doctor-patient conversation dataset. Overall, it was observed a 7% improvement in word error rate. Hagen et al. [17] presented research that describes a method for extracting clinically relevant information from a medical conversation from Google Is. The method is based on Recurrent Neural Network Transducer (RNN-T) for long audio form. The model performed a 20% WER on the ASR task.

A review by Bahja [2] described that NLP applications in healthcare on the rising were related to clinical data, value-based care, population health management, empowering health literacy, and improving patient healthcare provider interaction.

Sheikhalishahi et al. [16] provide a comprehensive overview of the development of NLP methods applied to clinical notes related to chronic disease. The state of the art of information extraction methods is rule-based learning; however, in recent years, there has been an increase in studies based on machine learning algorithms, such as CRFs, and SVMs. The authors report that SVMs were the most commonly used algorithm in predicting heart disease extracted from medical records and progressive EHR notes to identify diabetes and categorization breast radiology reports. Naïve Bayes was the second most reported implemented for classifying smoking status, extracting information from EHR records to identify multiple sclerosis, and classifying EHR records for obesity and cancer. CRF and Random Forests have also been implemented for similar tasks but were the least implemented. In the case of deep learning, the authors reported only three studies where neural networks were implemented in EHR to identify study candidates and derive clinical narratives. CNN was reported for disease risk assessment.

Van Buchem et al. [21] presented a literature review describing neural network-based models for medical information extraction. Among the models described, they mention models based on Attention-based neural networks, which consider the sequence of words and have an attention layer, which acts as a filter that passes only relevant information from the input to the next layer of the model. The models described are sequence2sequence, span-attribute tagging model and pointer generator network. Another technique implemented has been word embedding, which is implemented to represent words in numerical form; among the techniques are ELmo and BERT.

3   System Architecture

Recent studies show that EHR-related clinical documentation burden is associated with burn-out and increased cognitive load in physicians and their assistants, to loss of information and extra administrative work that reduces the quality of patient care [1,21]. One solution has been the integration of medical scribes in medical practices responsible for transcribing information into EHR from conversations between doctors and patients, which has shown advantages in improving doctor productivity and doctor and patient satisfaction. Although a medical scribe reduces the administrative burden on doctors, they increase clinics' costs and shift the administrative burden to other medical staff [13,21].

An AI-powered medical digital scribe is a system capable of capturing the conversation between the physician and the patient and generating documentation related to the consultation. The system would perform the tasks of a medical scribe with the difference that it would reduce costs, the administrative burden on medical staff and the need to divide care between computer and patient while maintaining visual interaction between patient and doctor, potentially increasing productivity and improving quality of care. A digital medical scribe that generates conversational notes of consultations should be composed of three parts: (1) recording the doctor-patient conversation, (2) converting and transcribing audio to text, and (3) extracting information from the text and summarising the information. The AI-powered system architecture implements automatic speech recognition (ASR) and natural speech processing (NLP) modules [13,21].

The initial challenge in developing a digital medical scribe is the high-quality recording of the doctor-patient conversation. A high-quality recording would minimise errors in the pipeline architecture between modules and the final result. In addition to audio quality, there is the quality and clarity of the doctor-patient conversation. Spontaneous conversations increase the error vulnerability of ASR models, as these conversations include non-lexical filler words, as well as interruptions and overlapping speech between speakers. Another challenge is the quality of the comprehension of the ASR transcript. This issue would include, for example, the structure of the conversation and the order and subject matter of the primary and non-primary content of the conversation. This type of problem could influence the quality of content that could be included in the EHR summary. Another restriction to be evaluated is the variability, accessibility and accuracy of existing Speech-to-Text APIs of the European Portuguese language. A further consideration is the extraction of information from transcripts of patient-physician conversations. As such, it can face heterogeneity of medical language processing tools which could lead to inaccuracies and terminological mismatches. On the other hand, the summarised content to be extracted from the conversation must be defined while maintaining consistency. Consideration should also be given to including changes in the physician's workflow within the consultation, e.g., vocalising the observations to be included in the summary either during or after the consultation, in case the physician does not wish to share them with the patient. Finally, determine which implications bring the implementation between existing EHR providers and the digital medical scribe. Ethically, the NLP system should not be allowed to produce an EHR without human intervention at some point, i.e., verification of the report content by the physician [13].

Specifically, the main objective is to implement an ASR and NLP-based system in a clinical setting focused on patient-physician interaction, see Fig. 1. The system should transcribe conversations in European Portuguese and extract relevant knowledge. The system shall comprehend (i) automatic speech recognition in European Portuguese, (ii) knowledge extraction, and (iii) consultation summary. The system must go through several phases of evaluating its reliability before being implemented in a real-life setting. For this purpose, different points will be evaluated within the doctors' workflow, taking into account security and patient privacy as essential aspects. The system will be carried out through

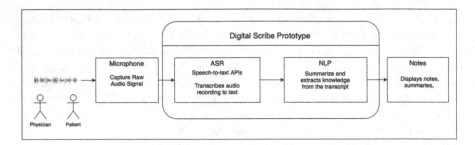

Fig. 1. Digital medical scribe prototype

different phases of research where its sustainability, technical validity, clinical validity, clinical usability, clinical utility, and safety will be evaluated.

In order to implement ASR APIs in our system, it is necessary to understand their technical operation. The ASR includes knowledge and research in computer science, linguistics and computer engineering. It is aimed at converting spoken words into text and vice-versa. The state-of-the-art architecture of a standard ASR system that uses the stochastic HMM-based approach is presented in Fig. 2.

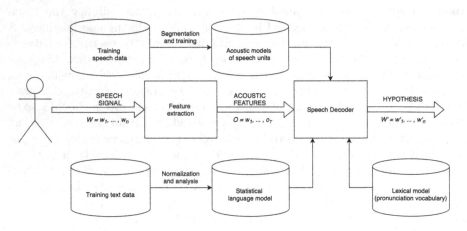

Fig. 2. State-of-the-art automatic speech recognition system and its components [3]

This system works in two modes: model training and speech decoding. The architecture comprises three main components: acoustical (acoustic-phonetic) modelling, lexical modelling, which is pronunciation lexicon/vocabulary, and language modelling. Besacier et al. [3] describe the state-of-art ASR architecture as follow: the training process aims to improve models for speech acoustics, language and recognition lexicon. The acoustical modelling allows representing the audio signals to discriminate asses of basic speech units and consider speech variability concerning the speakers, channel, and environment. Then, vectors of speech signal features are extracted from the acoustical signal for dimensional reduction and probabilistic modelling. Any ASR system integrates a speech decoder, which performs speech input processing and converts audio speech signals into a sequence of orthographic words.

The traditional machine learning algorithm approach was Hidden Markov Models (HMMs), which model speech signals by modelling the probability distribution of speech features as a sequence of hidden states [4, 19]. Gaussian Mixture Models (GMMs) is another method used to model the probability distribution of speech features. This method in combination with HMMs is used to improve the accuracy of ASR systems. Other algorithmic models that have gained attention in the area of ASR are Recurrent Neural Networks (RNNs), which is implemented to model sequences of speech signals. Deep Learning Long Short-Term Memory (LSTM) has been implemented through a method called Connectionist Temporal Classification (CTC), which outperforms HMM. This method was implemented by Google in 2015, which improved the performance of Google Voice by 49%. Additionally, Deep Neural Networks (DNNs) have been implemented to model the acoustic characteristics of speech signals. These types of models have the advantage that through their many deep layers of neurons a better representation of complex information characteristics is possible. DNNs models showed an important result by decreasing the Word Error Rate by 30% for IBM and Google systems. Convolutional Neural Networks (CNN) used in conjunction with RNN algorithms improve the accuracy of speech signal feature extraction [19]. Unfortunately, most end-to-end ASR systems are not easily reproduced since they require vast amounts of data. Some widely used contemporary end-to-end approaches are: connectionist temporal classification (CTC), attention encoder-decoder (AED) and RNN Transducer (RNNT). The outcomes transcription from the ASR module goes into the NLP module for knowledge extraction and summarisation.

For the correct development of the digital medical scribe prototype, the stakeholders directly interacting with the system will be defined. Stakeholders, persons, or groups must have an interest that influences the project workflow and outcome. It is important to consider the stakeholders and include their interests and perspective during the different phases of prototype development. At this stage, stakeholders were identified and categorized into primary and secondary stakeholders. Table 3 shows an initial analysis of the stakeholders. Primary stakeholders are actively working within the project and the developed tools, thus being highly influenced by both the project and the secondary stakeholders, who work and make decisions based on the feedback provided by the primary stakeholders. Within this context, the stakeholder was identified as follows:
Primary Stakeholder

- Patient: accepts/rejects treatment options that impact the selection of applicable medical devices and treatment tools.
- Physician: primary user of the medical devices and tools and main point of medical decision making.

Stakeholder	Interests
Primary Stakeholders	
Patient	Quality treatment & care
	Feeling of comfort to the exposed treatment and related tools
	Physician's attention on the
Doctor	More time dedicated to patients / Higher patient focus
	Lower administrative workload to avoid overworking and burn-out
	Improved inter-team communication
Secondary Stakeholders	
Medical Staff	More time dedicated to patients
	Improved inter-team communication
Hospital	High reputation for patient centricity
	Efficient use of available resources including staff time and their focus on patient care
	Improved bureaucratic workflows

Fig. 3. Stakeholder evaluation

Secondary Stakeholder

– Medical Staff: secondary user of the medical devices and tools and work with outputs generated by primary stakeholders (e.g., consultation transcriptions).
– Hospital: oversees and accepts/rejects applicable medical devices in their installations

Additional stakeholders may apply at later stages but have yet to be applicable for the prototype development phase. During the prototype development phase, experiences and evaluations of similar studies will be included, especially feedback to improve the prototype, as is the case of the study presented by Wang et al. [22]. Additionally, in the case of Portugal, stakeholder interviews will be conducted to know the level of interest and how open they are to this prototype and to include it as part of their work routine. Other groups may be added during the development of the project.

4   Conclusion and Further Work

One of the major challenges and risks in developing and implementing the ASR-NLP-based system inside interaction between patient-physician is the authorization of the use of data, i.e., audio record, transcription of the conversation, and summary from the patient and physician's point of view. The major concern regarding using the data is to comply with the General Data Protection Regulation (GDPR). Therefore it will be vital to guarantee anonymity and data protection and maintain the privacy of data acquired and produced within the medical consultation. This study aims to produce knowledge that contributes to the current research on implementing artificial intelligence-based technologies in smart cities, specifically in health care-identifying key points that help close a little the gap to achieve feasible solutions in Smart Healthcare.

The digital medical scribe system should be expected to meet the requirements to perform its function in an interoperable environment to ensure consistency with existing systems. One of the expected outcomes is to acquire the clinical knowledge extracted from a medical conversation between doctor and patient in the form of a summary, facilitating the administrative workflow, digital transformation and improving the quality of care and innovations for the patient.

The main drawback of the digital medical scribe with DP algorithms is that they require considerable training data and hours to achieve state-of-the-art performances. There are more Speech-to-Text APIs for ASR offers in the market for English than in other languages due to limited access to publicly available datasets in the language.

In future steps, the implementation of the described prototype will be evaluated in a real-life setting. This step includes observing and evaluating the results when used in a hospital on the island of Azores and the north of Portugal. Intermediately before the final implementation of the AI-Based Medical Scribe, trials will be performed that will include end-user feedback to improve the integration and usability process within medical environments. Speech-to-Text APIs WER performance for medical conversations will be evaluated in English and European Portuguese. Fareez et al. [6] presented a dataset that covers a series of medical conversations in Objective Structured Clinical Examinations (OSCE) format. The dataset is focused on respiratory cases in audio format and transcriptions. The dataset is aimed to be used for speech-to-text errors and training NLP models to extract symptoms, among others. Although the dataset is in English, if necessary, a similar study could be recreated for the Portuguese language to reduce errors in medical conversations.

It should also be evaluated what kind of content summaries generated by the NLP system are relevant for physicians. Additionally, what kind of algorithms have better accuracy in a medical context, especially with the European Portuguese language? Moreover, structured knowledge extraction from the transcriptions needs to be defined and evaluated from the medical conversations and how the information (systems, personal data, medications) can be implemented into the EHRs System. As part of an application within the context of smart cities, this solution is also expected to be a further step towards a digital transformation within healthcare facilities, including developing mobile and web applications.

Overall, future research would extensively evaluate ASR and NLP NN-based models in medical conversation and summarization. Comparison between models' performance in European Portuguese. Moreover, technical and clinical validity and usability, and investigating the clinical utility of digital scribes in smart healthcare.

Acknowledgements. This work has been supported by "FCT-Fundação para a Ciência e Tecnologia" within the R&D Units Project Scope: UIDB/00319/2020. The authors declare no conflict of interest.

References

1. Avendano, J.P., Gallagher, D.O., Hawes, J.D., Boyle, J., Glasser, L., Aryee, J., Katt, B.M.: Interfacing with the electronic health record (EHR): a comparative review of modes of documentation. Cureus (2022). https://doi.org/10.7759/cureus.26330
2. Bahja, M.: Natural language processing applications in business. In: Wu, R.M., Mircea, M. (eds.) E-Business, chap. 4. IntechOpen, Rijeka (2020). https://doi.org/10.5772/intechopen.92203
3. Besacier, L., Barnard, E., Karpov, A., Schultz, T.: Automatic speech recognition for under-resourced languages: a survey. Speech Commun. **56**, 85–100 (2014). https://doi.org/10.1016/j.specom.2013.07.008
4. Carvalho, C., Abad, A.: TRIBUS: an end-to-end automatic speech recognition system for european portuguese. In: IberSPEECH 2021. ISCA (2021). https://doi.org/10.21437/iberspeech.2021-40
5. Coiera, E., Kocaballi, B., Halamka, J., Laranjo, L.: The digital scribe. NPJ Digit. Med. **1**(1) (2018). https://doi.org/10.1038/s41746-018-0066-9
6. Fareez, F., Parikh, T., Wavell, C., Shahab, S., Chevalier, M., Good, S., Blasi, I.D., Rhouma, R., McMahon, C., Lam, J.P., Lo, T., Smith, C.W.: A dataset of simulated patient-physician medical interviews with a focus on respiratory cases. Sci Data **9**(1) (2022). https://doi.org/10.1038/s41597-022-01423-1
7. Ghatnekar, S., Faletsky, A., Nambudiri, V.E.: Digital scribe utility and barriers to implementation in clinical practice: a scoping review. Health Technol. **11**(4), 803–809 (2021). https://doi.org/10.1007/s12553-021-00568-0
8. https://research-and-innovation.ec.europa.eu/funding/funding-opportunities/funding-programmes-and-open-calls/horizon-europe/eu-missions-horizon-europe/climate-neutral-and-smart-cities_en
9. Kirimtat, A., Krejcar, O., Kertesz, A., Tasgetiren, M.F.: Future trends and current state of smart city concepts: a survey. IEEE Access **8**, 86448–86467 (2020). https://doi.org/10.1109/ACCESS.2020.2992441
10. Mani, A., Palaskar, S., Konam, S.: Towards understanding ASR error correction for medical conversations. In: Proceedings of the first workshop on natural language processing for medical conversations. association for computational linguistics (2020). https://doi.org/10.18653/v1/2020.nlpmc-1.2
11. Meripo, N.V., Konam, S.: ASR error detection via audio-transcript entailment (2022). arxiv:2207.10849
12. Proceedings of the 2021 CHI conference on human factors in computing systems (2021). https://doi.org/10.1145/3411764
13. Quiroz, J.C., Laranjo, L., Kocaballi, A.B., Berkovsky, S., Rezazadegan, D., Coiera, E.: Challenges of developing a digital scribe to reduce clinical documentation burden. NPJ Digit. Med. **2**(1) (2019). https://doi.org/10.1038/s41746-019-0190-1
14. Smart cities: Digital solutions for a more livable future. https://www.mckinsey.com/business-functions/operations/our-insights/smart-cities-digital-solutions-for-a-more-livable-future. Accessed 30 Apr. 2022

15. Shahid, N., Rappon, T., Berta, W.: Applications of artificial neural networks in health care organizational decision-making: a scoping review. Plos One **14**(2), 1–22 (2019). https://doi.org/10.1371/journal.pone.0212356

16. Sheikhalishahi, S., Miotto, R., Dudley, J.T., Lavelli, A., Rinaldi, F., Osmani, V.: Natural language processing of clinical notes on chronic diseases: systematic review. JMIR Med. Inform. **7**(2), e12239 (2019). https://doi.org/10.2196/12239

17. Soltau, H., Wang, M., Shafran, I., Shafey, L.E.: Understanding medical conversations: rich transcription, confidence scores & information extraction. In: Interspeech 2021. ISCA (2021). https://doi.org/10.21437/interspeech.2021-691

18. Stewart, C.: Time AI could save in healthcare administration Europe 2020 (2022). https://www.statista.com/statistics/1202254/time-ai-could-save-in-healthcare-administration-europe/

19. Trabelsi, A., Warichet, S., Aajaoun, Y., Soussilane, S.: Evaluation of the efficiency of state-of-the-art speech recognition engines. Procedia Comput. Sci. **207**, 2242–2252 (2022). https://doi.org/10.1016/j.procs.2022.09.534

20. Ullah, Z., Al-Turjman, F., Mostarda, L., Gagliardi, R.: Applications of artificial intelligence and machine learning in smart cities. Comput. Commun. **154**, 313–323 (2020). https://www.sciencedirect.com/science/article/pii/S0140366419320821

21. van Buchem, M.M., Boosman, H., Bauer, M.P., Kant, I.M.J., Cammel, S.A., Steyerberg, E.W.: The digital scribe in clinical practice: a scoping review and research agenda. NPJ Digit. Med. **4**(1) (2021). https://doi.org/10.1038/s41746-021-00432-5

22. Wang, J., Lavender, M., Hoque, E., Brophy, P., Kautz, H.: A patient-centered digital scribe for automatic medical documentation. JAMIA Open **4**(1) (2021). https://doi.org/10.1093/jamiaopen/ooab003

Combining Neighbor Models to Improve Predictions of Age of Onset of ATTRv Carriers

Maria Pedroto[1,2]([✉])[ID], Alípio Jorge[1,3][ID], João Mendes-Moreira[1,2][ID], and Teresa Coelho[4]

[1] Laboratory of Artificial Intelligence and Decision Support (LIAAD), Porto, Portugal
amjorge@up.pt, jmoreira@up.pt
[2] Department of Informatics Engineering, Faculty of Engineering, University of, Porto, Portugal
maria.j.pedroto@inesctec.pt
[3] Department of Computer Science, Faculty of Sciences, University of Porto, Porto, Portugal
[4] Unidade Corino de Andrade, Centro Hospitalar Universitário de Santo António, R. D. Manuel II, Pavilhão 2 (ex-Cicap), 4050-345 Porto, Portugal
tcoelho@netcabo.pt

Abstract. Transthyretin (TTR)-related familial amyloid polyneuropathy (ATTRv) is a life-threatening autosomal dominant disease and the age of onset represents the moment when first symptoms are felt. Accurately predicting the age of onset for a given patient is relevant for risk assessment and treatment management. In this work, we evaluate the impact of combining prediction models obtained from neighboring time windows on prediction error. We propose Symmetric (Sym) and Asymmetric (Asym) models which represent two different averaging approaches. These are incorporated with a weighting mechanism as to create Symmetric (Sym), Symmetric-weighted (Sym-w), Asymmetric (Asym), and Asymmetric-weighted (Asym-w). These four ensemble models are then compared to the original approach which is focused on individual regression base learners namely: Baseline (BL), Decision Tree (DT), Elastic Net (EN), Lasso (LA), Linear Regression (LR), Random Forest (RF), Ridge (RI), Support Vector Regressor (SV) and XGBoost (XG). Our results show that by aggregating predictions from neighbor models the average mean absolute error obtained by each base learner decreases. Overall, the best results are achieved by regression-based ensemble tree models as base learners.

Keywords: Additive ensemble · Age of onset prediction · Regression ensemble

---

Supported by Centro Hospitalar Universitário de Santo António.

N. Moniz et al. (Eds.): EPIA 2023, LNAI 14116, pp. 286–297, 2023.
https://doi.org/10.1007/978-3-031-49011-8_23

1   Introduction

In this work, we focus on the medical problem of predicting the age of onset of Familial Amyloid Polyneuropathy (ATTRv Amyloidosis) patients. The age of onset is the moment when a patient starts to feel symptoms of a disease. Its accurate prediction can impact a patient's life while laying the path to improve medical operational scheduling and budgeting actions. Amyloid transthyretin (ATTR) amyloidosis is a progressive and systemic disease divided into either hereditary (ATTRv) or sporadic (ATTRwt) [4]. Until 30 years ago thought to be restricted to Portugal, Sweden and Japan, currently it is known to have a greater impact and be widely dispersed [1].

Previously, in [13], we predicted the age of onset of ATTRv patients by taking into account a patient's age and the current clinical and genealogical data, while in [14] we studied the effect of combining different feature sets that differ accordingly to the level of genealogical relation. For that, the proposed approach builds a bag of models, each of which is specialized in one specific age. For the training phase, each recorded patient is unfolded in a number of age-centered replicas, one for each different age. In this case, for a patient and a set of different age scenarios, our approach delivers the evolution of starting to feel symptoms. These results correspond to the different age scenarios requested. Overall, our results dramatically improved a known clinical baseline, clearly justifying the use of a machine learning-based approach, as opposed to current medical prediction practice. Now we exploit the effect of aggregating the predictions of models from neighboring ages. Our objective is to develop a model that blends information from neighboring age base learners, thus improving the prediction of the future age of onset for an asymptomatic patient. Here, we focus on homogeneous ensembles, thus aggregating only base estimators that share the same learning algorithm.

Our research questions are: (Q1) can we improve the predictive results by combining different age-neighbor models; (Q2) what is the impact of incorporating a weighting strategy to these bags of predictions; and (Q3) how can we combine our sets of base learner prediction results. Of note that, regarding the last research question, we deem it important to study combination strategies focused in the prediction phase, so as to work towards combining base learners developed in geographically distinct clinical reference centers. By this we mean that it is important to develop ways to combine multiple models created in different locations so as to improve the general accuracy of predictions, without compromising the privacy and security of patients' personal information. This way our work ensures that patient data remains confidential thus agreeing with guidelines for data protection.

The rest of this work is organized as follows: (i) in Sect. 2 we introduce ensemble learning and review related medical works; (ii) in Sect. 3 we present our base and ensemble approaches; in Sect. 4 we present current results, and discuss major findings; (iii) in Sect. 5 we elaborate as to our main conclusions and plan future work directions.

2   Background

2.1   Ensemble Learning

Regression models forecast a value given a feature vector. Traditional algorithms to obtain regression models are: Linear Regression (LR) [19], Decision Tree Regressor (DT) [5], Elastic Net (EN) [10], Lasso (LA) [20], Ridge (RI) [3], and Support Vector Regressor (SV) [18]. There are also approaches for ensemble learning, namely Random Forest (RF) [6] and Extreme Gradient Boost (XG) [8,9]. These are focused in bagging and boosting the results. Overall, all the regression algorithms have different responses when working with data sets that contain outliers, are unbalanced, and/or contain missing information.

Ensemble methods represent generalization approaches that combine traditional methods created with the joint purpose of predicting a specific outcome [12]. The strategies often consist of leveraging statistical concepts, such as mean or median functions, or concatenating sequential results. This can be done in stages. In the first stage, i.e. model construction, we can build different models with different training subsets or different algorithms. In the second stage, i.e. model selection, the aim is to reduce the number of models to combine. The third stage, which corresponds to the integration phase, combines the results of the chosen models. Our focus in this work will be on this third phase.

Overall the results obtained with ensemble models reduce the generalization error of individual learners. Standard strategies correspond to **bagging**, **boosting** and **stacking** models. While bagging corresponds to the aggregation of multiple models trained and instantiated in parallel and boosting instantiates a new model sequentially to the previous one, stacking corresponds to combining a set of different estimators (first-layer) using a meta-model that depending on the type of model combines them in order to maximize the robustness of the final model. Although prediction frameworks already supply implementations of specific ensemble algorithms such as RF and XG we are interested in considering these as base learners and further agregate the results.

2.2   Related Work

Overall, in the onset prediction problem, the accurate prediction of diabetes is essential, as the number of patients increases rapidly. In [21] authors concatenate the results from Logistic Regression, K Nearest Neighbors, Random Forest, and Soft Voting to answer whether a patient has a risk of developing diabetes in the near future or not. In [15] authors develop a baseline ensemble model that stacks a set of machine learning algorithms to predict if a person has diabetes. Authors report having obtained a 10% increase in accuracy when comparing the ensemble with the best single algorithm. In [17] authors present an ensemble-based framework that uses XGBoost, Random Forest, Support Vector Machine, Neural Network, and Decision Trees to predict diabetes status among patients while reporting accuracy of 95%. In [2] authors utilized Multiple Linear Regression, Artificial Neural Network and Random Forest to model and predict the age at onset of Type 1 Diabetes in children in Saudi Arabia. The best results were achieved with the Random Forest with a mean absolute error of 0.11 years.

Although diabetes is an important area of application, other diseases have shown promising results with the combination of different predictors. In [16] authors use prospective survey data and ensemble machine learning, namely super learning, to develop algorithms predicting adult onset internalizing disorders. From the set of internalizing disorders, the authors focused on anxiety disorder, panic disorder, social phobia, depression, and mania. In this case, authors focused on: logistic regression, least absolute shrinkage, and selection operator (LASSO), penalized (logistic) regression, random forests, Bayesian main-terms logistic regression, generalized additive modeling, adaptive splines, k-nearest neighbors, linear support vector machines, and linear discriminant analysis. Although authors acknowledge the superiority of combining the results, they refer that the magnitude of the differences was relatively small in some of their experiments.

In [7] authors present a framework based on an ensemble approach to deliver explainable personalized risk prediction models for dementia. They report that while the best source model achieves a geometric accuracy of 87%, specificity of 99%, and sensitivity of 76%, their target model achieves better performance across several metrics, with an increase in geometric accuracy of 16.9%, specificity of 2.7%, and sensitivity of 19.1%, among others.

Overall, it is noticeable the improvement of using ensemble approaches for onset prediction on a wide range of diseases, as opposed to single algorithm-based approaches. In most cases, authors rely on classification approaches and not regression methods. The comparison of a large poll of single algorithms is an important step, seeing that these respond differently accordingly to specific data conditions. In our work, we focus on the regression setting and explore the aggregation of models built for neighboring ages.

3   Single Learning Approach and Combination Strategies

3.1   Prediction Problem and Single Learning Approach

As stated, in this work, we are focused on predicting the age of onset of ATTRv patients. So, for a given patient X known to be a carrier of the ATTRv mutation, at a given moment in time T, we want to estimate the variable Y that represents the age when symptoms will manifest (onset).

Our base predictive models are obtained from one baseline (BL) and several state-of-the-art regression methods, namely: a Decision Tree (DT) model chosen by its interpretability; an Elastic Net (EN), Lasso (LA), and Ridge (RI) approach due to temporal relations in the chosen features; a Linear Regression (LR) for its simplicity; a Random Forest (RF) for its results when working with problematic data sets, i.e. noisy, irregular and outlier prone data; Support Vector Regression Machine (SV) for allowing to model non-linear relationships between variables; and finally XGBoost (XG) for its efficient boosting approach.

Our BL was implemented following the current medical practice [11] regarding the predicted age of onset of symptomatic patients. In this case and assuming a linear trend between the age of onset of a patient and that of his/her transmitting ancestor these rules state that:

- if (father and son) → target = parent(ageonset)—6.06;
- if (father and daughter) → target = parent(ageonset)—1.23;
- if (mother and son) → target = parent(ageonset)—10.43;
- if (mother and daughter) → target = parent(ageonset)—7.43.

3.2   Data and Evaluation Strategy

Our data was supplied by Centro Hospitalar Universitário de Santo António at two different time moments. These were: (i) before 2018 with this subset of data being used for training and validating individual algorithms; (ii) after 2018 with this subset being used for subsequent testing regarding the original and ensemble scenarios. For the set of features please check [13,14]. Each patient record is constituted by sets of demographic, genealogical and clinical features.

Training Phase In the training phase, we took the information from all the patients diagnosed previously to 2018 and unfolded each of them into a set of age-specific projections. For each age and patient, we gather the data up to the year when the patient reached that age until the patient becomes symptomatic. Each of these patient-age projections becomes one training example described by clinical as well as genealogical features. The value of the respective age of onset is the target value. We consider ages from 22 to 64 with a step of 3 years (22, 25, 28, ..., 64).

After feature construction, we run a training pipeline that for each training example imputes missing data with a 5-nearest neighbor approach. It also performs algorithm hyper-parameter tuning using 5-fold-cross-validation. For each age and learning algorithm, we finally obtain a prediction model from the respective age-specific patient projections.

Testing Phase In the testing phase, and to evaluate our prediction pipeline, we took patients diagnosed after 2018 and, after performing the same pre-processing activities as in the training data, predicted their age of onset for each model individually. This phase includes the ensemble combination strategies, defined next. So, by taking the data obtained previously to 2018 and for each current symptomatic patient we considered the information known at the time at which they were 22, 25, 28, 31, 34, 37, 40, 43, 46, 49, 52, 55, 58, 61, and 64 years-old (as long as they were still asymptomatic), and instantiate an individual model. This means that for each age group we have a single experiment with each of the 9 different algorithms (i.e. BL, DT, EN, LA, LR, RF, RI, SV and XG). Later in the validation phase we took patients diagnosed after 2018 and predicted their age of onset for each algorithm individually.

3.3   Combination Strategies

In this work, we study the effect of combining different models to obtain a new, stable, less variance-prone, generic model. In this case, we concatenate models that share the same algorithm, while focusing on neighboring age instances.

So, considering a patient x with an age a (Eq. 1), for whom we want to make an age of onset prediction, we have two aggregation scenarios. In the first scenario, we combine the results of an age-based model with the models from the two previous time frames, namely $age - 3$ and $age - 6$ ages. This corresponds to the **asymmetric scenario** with a set of predictions (Eq. 4) that averaged (Eq. 6) generate an ensemble result. When combined with a γ weight vector (Eq. 2) they generate a weighted set of results (Eq. 8).

Alternatively, we combine the current age model's prediction with the predictions for age $age - 3$ and at age $age + 3$. In this case the set of results (Eq. 5) are later combined with a weight feature vector (Eq. 3) to generate a weighted (Eq. 9) or simple ensemble (Eq. 7). This corresponds to the **symmetric scenario**.

$$y_b = model(x, a) \tag{1}$$

$$\gamma_{asym} = (0.14, 0.29, 0.57) \tag{2}$$

$$\gamma_{sym} = (0.25, 0.5, 0.25) \tag{3}$$

$$\overrightarrow{y}_{asym}(x, a) = (y_b(x, a - 6), y_b(x, a - 3), y_b(x, a)) \tag{4}$$

$$\overrightarrow{y}_{sym}(x, a) = (y_b(x, a - 3), y_b(x, a), y_b(x, a + 3)) \tag{5}$$

$$asym(x, a) = mean\,\overrightarrow{y}_{asym}(x, a)) \tag{6}$$

$$sym(x, a) = mean(\overrightarrow{y}_{sym}(x, a)) \tag{7}$$

$$asym_w(x, a) = \frac{1}{3}\overrightarrow{y}_{sym}(x, a) \cdot \gamma_{asym} \tag{8}$$

$$sym_w(x, a) = \frac{1}{3}\overrightarrow{y}_{sym}(x, a) \cdot \gamma_{sym} \tag{9}$$

Weighting Mechanism To obtain the weighting vectors referenced in Eqs. 2 and 3 we took into consideration a generic weight formula presented in algorithm *WeightingPredictions*. This method takes as input a set of time points. By time points we refer, for example, to the sym_w by a vector with references t − 3, t, t + 3. From lines 1–3 we generate the vector of weights, while from lines 5–7 we scale this vector in order for its *sum* to be equal to one.

As an example, to generate the weights for sym_w as presented in Eq. 3 the input must be [−1, 0, +1]. For the $asym_w$ the same function generates the results in Eq. 2 with the input [−2, −1, 0]. In these experiments we did not have into account the age gap difference.

Algorithm 1 Weighting Predictions
    Input *agevec*
    Output *weightvec*
1: **for** i in agevec **do**
2:    $w[i] = 0.5^{abs(i)}$
3: **end for**
4: $total = sum(weightvec)$
5: **for** i in range(len(agevec)) **do**
6:    $w[i] = w[i]/total$
7: **end for**

3.4   Evaluation

Both with traditional and ensemble modeling strategies we measure performance by averaging a set of prediction results regarding a specific error metric. In this work, we will use the mean absolute error (Eq. 10) which is expressed in the same unit as the target variable and for which larger errors have the same impact as smaller ones. Other metrics, such as mean squared error (MSE) and root mean squared error (RMSE), are focused on evaluating the error when there is the need to differentiate between larger and smaller errors. In this case, for this medical problem, we do not see it as a requirement and are interested in the greater interpretability of absolute errors.

$$MAE = \frac{1}{V} \sum_{i=1}^{V} |x_i - y_i| \tag{10}$$

4   Results and Discussion

As is, for each tuple (age, algorithm) we have a set of five macro-level prediction results: (i) original prediction results where these are given by a BL, DT, EN, LA, LR, RF, RI, SV, XG model (Eq. 1); (ii) asymmetric prediction results; (iii) symmetric prediction results; (iv) asymmetric-w prediction results; (v) and symmetric-w prediction results. To clarify, the original results correspond to the single learning approach results explained in Sect. 3.1 while the symmetric, asymmetric-w and symmetric-w correspond to the combination strategies referenced in Sect. 3.3. The overall experimental setup and the different testing combination strategies are schematically referenced in Fig. 1.

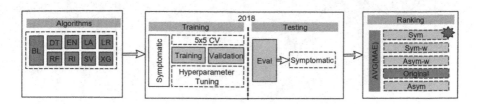

Fig. 1. Conceptual models for the aggregation scenarios

After each aggregation, we implemented a clipping operation that transforms invalid results, namely those where the prediction result is smaller than the corresponding age, into a valid one. The operator changes the predicted result to two years from the current age a.

To analyze each scenario we compared the average MAE of the original approach with the asymmetric and symmetric scenarios (Table 1). An analysis of these results shows that: (i) we have a clear improvement of the predictive results by combining different prediction moments, namely by considering the symmetric scenario, both with and without the weighting mechanism; (ii) in the asymmetric scenario there is a predictive improvement when adding the weighting mechanism, i.e. when adding a vector of weights [0.14, 0.29, 0.57], for the bag of current and neighbor predictions; and, (iii) in the symmetric scenario there isn't a predictive improvement when adding the weighting mechanism, i.e. the results of $(Sym >> Sym - w)$ when adding a vector of weights [0.25, 0.5, 0.25].

In Fig. 2 we show the average error of the BL and the top MAE performers, which correspond to DT, SV and XG. Here it is noticeable that: (i) the machine learning approach improves prediction results when compared with the medical baseline; (ii) there is some interpolation between the original and the symmetric results with the original results being quite irregular over very close ages; (iii) when combining the predictions we encounter a smoothing effect over the different age models; (iv) late onset age models (models for ages greater than 50 years) there the smoothing effect is accompanied with an overall improvement in the results for DT and XG, while in the SV it is clear that this does not happen due to the very large peaks in ages around 55 and 58 years. Of note that these results are impacted by the **original** individual results of each model. This fact leaves us thinking what could the effect be to combine models not only over the ages but also over the algorithms since some models work better with heterogeneous datasets.

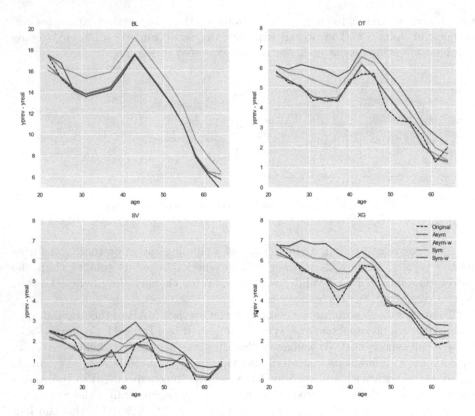

Fig. 2. Results of the prediction error over the different ages for BL and the three best ML methods—DT, SV and XG—for the test data. Each graph contains the results for the original and each of the different combination strategies (Asym, Asym-w, Sym, Sym-w)

Table 1. Average MAE for each pair (algorithm, scenario). With a grey background, we have the approaches that beat the original or base learners.

	Original	Asym	Asym-w	Sym	Sym-w
BL	14.39	14.60	15.65	14.30	14.30
DT	5.64	6.13	5.85	5.34	5.38
EN	7.43	8.15	7.87	7.26	7.30
LA	8.68	9.23	8.96	8.54	8.58
LR	7.30	7.93	7.69	7.07	7.10
RF	6.01	6.62	6.29	5.77	5.81
RI	7.33	8.02	7.76	7.15	7.17
SV	3.29	3.31	3.25	3.14	3.16
XG	5.91	6.56	6.22	5.68	5.72

5 Conclusions and Future Work

In this work, we focused on predicting the age of onset of ATTRv Amyloidosis patients. We transformed a predictive approach first introduced in [13,14], in order to determine if single algorithm results would outperform different combination scenarios (Q3). In this case, we experimented with two different aggregation scenarios. One is symmetric, centered on the age of the patient. The other is asymmetric with the age of the patient at the right. We also took these scenarios and further enhanced them using a weighting mechanism.

Regarding our research questions we have seen that (Q3) we could indeed take different aggregation approaches and achieve different prediction results. Here, if on the one hand, we were able to improve the predictive accuracy of an aggregation scenario when compared to the single stand-alone algorithms (Q1), we also were able to improve upon these results by adding a weighting factor in the asymmetric case. For reference purposes, in the asymmetric case, we weren't able to improve the original single-algorithm runs (Q2). The most noticeable fact of these sets of results comes from the smoothing effect that the different combination strategies have when compared with the SV results. This, we believe, can help non-data experts grasp the overall results of the machine learning prediction based approach when compared with the BL results.

In the future, we plan to study the effect of different algorithm-wise ensemble aggregations as well as to study different optimization strategies for our weighting mechanism, i.e. by making it dependable on the difference between the considered ages. This way we plan to focus on creating new neighboring approaches, as well as improve the current symmetric and asymmetric scenarios. Of note that the success of an ensemble approach depends on its capacity of melting various predictors, each of them optimized to focus on different but complementary sets of data. This is quite different than improving the overall prediction results of individual predictors, which is achieved by, for example, optimizing hyper parameters.

Acknowledgements This work is financed by National Funds through the Portuguese funding agency, FCT—Fundação para a Ciência e a Tecnologia, within project LA/P/0063/2020.

Data Availability Statement Patient data is not publicly available due to restrictions e.g. "containing information that could compromise research participant privacy/consent".

Ethics Statement The study was approved by the ethical and institutional review boards at Centro Hospitalar Universitário de Santo António, Porto, Portugal, prior to subject enrollment. All methods were performed in accordance with the relevant guidelines and regulations.

References

1. Adams, D., Koike, H., Slama, M., Coelho, T.: Hereditary transthyretin amyloidosis: a model of medical progress for a fatal disease (2019). https://doi.org/10.1038/s41582-019-0210-4
2. Alazwari, A., Abdollahian, M., Tafakori, L., Johnstone, A., Alshumrani, R.A., Alhelal, M.T., Alsaheel, A.Y., Almoosa, E.S., Alkhaldi, A.R.: Predicting age at onset of type 1 diabetes in children using regression, artificial neural network and random forest: a case study in Saudi Arabia. Plos One **17**(2 February) (2022). https://doi.org/10.1371/journal.pone.0264118
3. Alldredge, J.R., Gilb, N.S.: Ridge regression: an annotated bibliography. Int. Stat. Rev./Revue Internationale de Statistique **44**(3), 355–360 (1976). http://www.jstor.org/stable/1402352
4. Ando, Y., Adams, D., Benson, M.D., Berk, J.L., Planté-Bordeneuve, V., Coelho, T., Conceição, I., Ericzon, B.G., Obici, L., Rapezzi, C., Sekijima, Y., Ueda, M., Palladini, G., Merlini, G.: Guidelines and new directions in the therapy and monitoring of ATTRv amyloidosis. Amyloid **29**(3), 143–155 (2022). https://doi.org/10.1080/13506129.2022.2052838
5. Breiman, L., Friedman, J.H., Olshen, R.A., Stone, C.J.: Classification and Regression Trees (1983)
6. Breiman, L.: Random Forests. Tech. rep. (2001)
7. Danso, S.O., Zeng, Z., Muniz-Terrera, G., Ritchie, C.W.: Developing an explainable machine learning-based personalised dementia risk prediction model: a transfer learning approach with ensemble learning algorithms. Front. Big Data **4** (2021). https://doi.org/10.3389/fdata.2021.613047
8. Friedman, J.H.: Greedy function approximation: a gradient boosting machine. Ann. Stat. **29**(5), 1189–1232 (2001). https://doi.org/10.1214/aos/1013203451
9. Friedman, J.H.: Stochastic gradient boosting. Comput. Stat. Data Anal. **38**(4), 367–378 (2002). https://doi.org/10.1016/S0167-9473(01)00065-2. https://www.sciencedirect.com/science/article/pii/S0167947301000652
10. Hastie, T., Tibshirani, R., Friedman, J.: The Elements of Statistical Learning: data Mining, Inference, and Prediction, 2nd edn (Springer Series in Statistics). Springer, New York (2009). https://doi.org/10.1007/978-0-387-84858-7. https://web.stanford.edu/~hastie/ElemStatLearn/
11. Lemos, C., Coelho, T., Alves-Ferreira, M., Martins-Da-Silva, A., Sequeiros, J., Mendonça, D., Sousa, A.: Overcoming artefact: anticipation in 284 Portuguese kindreds with familial amyloid polyneuropathy (FAP) ATTRV30M. J. Neurol. Neurosurg. Psychiat. (2014). https://doi.org/10.1136/jnnp-2013-305383. https://www.ncbi.nlm.nih.gov/pubmed/24046394
12. Mendes-Moreira, J., Soares, C., Jorge, A.M., Sousa, J.F.D.: Ensemble approaches for regression. ACM Comput. Surv. (2012). https://doi.org/10.1145/2379776.2379786
13. Pedroto, M., Jorge, A., Mendes-Moreira, J., Coelho, T.: Predicting age of onset in TTR-FAP patients with genealogical features. In: Hollmén, J., McGregor, C., Soda, P., Kane, B. (eds.) 31st IEEE International Symposium on Computer-Based Medical Systems, CBMS 2018, Karlstad, Sweden, pp. 199–204. IEEE Computer Society (2018). https://doi.org/10.1109/CBMS.2018.00042
14. Pedroto, M., Jorge, A., Mendes-Moreira, J., Coelho, T.: Impact of genealogical features in transthyretin familial amyloid polyneuropathy age of onset prediction. In: Florentino, F.R., Saberi, M., Mohamad, Rocha, M., De Paz Juan, F., González

Pascual (eds.) 12th International Conference on Practical Applications of Computational Biology and Bioinformatics, pp. 35–42. Springer International Publishing (2019)

15. R, S., M, S., Hasan, M.K., Saeed, R.A., Alsuhibany, S.A., Abdel-Khalek, S.: An empirical model to predict the diabetic positive using stacked ensemble approach. Front. Pub. Health **9**, 792124 (2021). https://doi.org/10.3389/fpubh.2021.792124

16. Rosellini, A.J., Liu, S., Anderson, G.N., Sbi, S., Tung, E.S., Knyazhanskaya, E.: Developing algorithms to predict adult onset internalizing disorders: an ensemble learning approach. J. Psychiat. Res. **121**, 189–196 (2020). https://doi.org/10.1016/j.jpsychires.2019.12.006

17. Singh, A., Dhillon, A., Kumar, N., Hossain, M.S., Muhammad, G., Kumar, M.: eDiaPredict: an ensemble-based framework for diabetes prediction. ACM Trans. Multimed. Comput. Commun. Appl. **17**(2s) (2021). https://doi.org/10.1145/3415155

18. Smola, A.J., Sc, B.: A Tutorial on Support Vector Regression*. Stat. Comput. **14**(3), 199–222 (2004). https://alex.smola.org/papers/2004/SmoSch04.pdf

19. Stanton, J.M.: Galton, pearson, and the peas: a brief history of linear regression for statistics instructors. J. Stat. Educ. **9**(3) (2001). https://doi.org/10.1080/10691898.2001.11910537

20. Tibshirani, R.: Regression Shrinkage and selection via the Lasso. J. R. Stat. Soc. (1996)

21. Warsi, G., Saini, S., Khatri, K.: Ensemble learning on diabetes data set and early diabetes prediction. In: International Conference on Computing, Power and Communication Technologies (2019)

Unravelling Heterogeneity: A Hybrid Machine Learning Approach to Predict Post-discharge Complications in Cardiothoracic Surgery

Bruno Ribeiro[1] , Isabel Curioso[1], Ricardo Santos[1,2(✉)],
Federico Guede-Fernández[3,5], Pedro Coelho[4,5], Jorge Santos[4,5],
José Fragata[4,5], Ana Londral[3,5], and Inês Sousa[1]

[1] Associação Fraunhofer Portugal Research, Porto, Portugal
[2] LIBPhys-UNL, NOVA School of Science and Technology, Caparica, Portugal
ricardo.santos@fraunhofer.pt
[3] Value for Health CoLAB, Lisboa, Portugal
[4] Hospital de Santa Marta, Centro Hospitalar Universitário Lisboa Central, Lisbon, Portugal
[5] Comprehensive Health Research Center, NOVA Medical School, Lisbon, Portugal

Abstract. Predicting post-discharge complications in cardiothoracic surgery is of utmost importance to improve clinical outcomes. Machine Learning (ML) techniques have been successfully applied in similar tasks, aiming at short time windows and in specific surgical conditions. However, as the target horizon is extended and the impact of unpredictable external factors rises, the complexity of the task increases, and traditional predictive models struggle to reproduce good performances. This study presents a two-step hybrid learning methodology to address this problem. Building up from identifying unique sub-groups of patients with shared characteristics, we then train individual supervised classification models for each sub-group, aiming at improved prediction accuracy and a more granular understanding of each decision. Our results show that specific sub-groups demonstrate substantially better performance when compared to the baseline model without sub-divisions, while others do not benefit from specialised models. Strategies such as the one presented may catalyse the success of applied ML solutions by contributing to a better understanding of their behaviour in different regions of the data space, leading to an informed decision-making process.

Keywords: Machine learning · Clustering · Cardiothoracic surgery · Unsupervised learning · Supervised learning

1 Background

Cardiothoracic surgery is a clinical procedure aimed at the heart or the lungs, with great relevance in patient care. Nevertheless, post-surgery complications following these interventions are rather common, leading to readmission rates

N. Moniz et al. (Eds.): EPIA 2023, LNAI 14116, pp. 298–310, 2023.
https://doi.org/10.1007/978-3-031-49011-8_24

of 13–17% in the first month [17,23], and 30% in the first year [6,9]. These occurrences increase the burden on healthcare institutions and, more drastically, have a negative impact on long-term survival rates [24].

Models to predict these incidents can enable informed re-evaluations, adapted recovery plans, and better resource allocation, leading to economic savings and lower readmission and mortality rates. The EuroSCORE [21] and the STS risk scores [25] are the most impactful tools for cardiothoracic surgery outcome prediction. These have been validated and applied in multiple clinical and geographic contexts, with reported Areas Under the Receiver Operating Characteristic curve (AUROC) consistently situated between 70 and 80% in predicting mortality up to 30 days following surgery [27]. This success extends to the prediction of short-term post-surgery complications [28,29]. Even so, some studies exposed the inaptitude of these tools in certain surgical contexts, typically reflected in overestimations of risk [18,26]. Several methods based on Machine Learning (ML) techniques have outperformed the traditional scores in predicting postoperative outcomes such as mortality [1,2,10], or specific complications [3,20,30]. Most research focuses on events occurring up to 30 days following intervention, but longer horizons have been proven relevant too, as the rates of adverse events remain high throughout the 90-day time window [12,15]. Besides, as most works consider target horizons starting immediately after surgery, they do not properly reflect the additional challenges of predicting post-discharge outcomes, where external factors can have a significant impact. Another tendency in the literature is the development of context-specific models to estimate risk for a single type of surgery or to predict a unique outcome. While successful, the applicability of these solutions is limited to those specific tasks. On the other hand, evidence shows that trying to predict different adverse events simultaneously adds to the complexity of the task. Mortazavi et al. [20] reported AUROC scores up to 83% for respiratory failure and infection prediction, but when the target considered different types of adverse events, the results dropped to 66%.

Unsupervised ML strategies can provide useful insights into multiple healthcare problems, such as the identification of multimorbidity patterns [11], patient stratification [13], and even disease prediction [16]. Furthermore, these have the potential to mitigate issues commonly encountered in medical datasets, such as missing data [8] and severe data imbalance [7]. In this study, an ML approach is proposed that leverages both unsupervised learning (UL) and supervised learning (SL) strategies to tackle the challenges of predicting cardiothoracic surgery complications up to 90 days following discharge. This method involves a clustering strategy to establish patient or surgery profiles a priori, followed by specialized predictive classification tasks for each profile. In this way, it leverages the advantages of context-specific methods, while maintaining compatibility with a wide range of scenarios. Beyond aiming at higher performances, the methodology proposed can enable a proper understanding of each data profile and an accordingly personalized decision-making strategy.

2 Dataset

A retrospective clinical database was leveraged referring to all surgical procedures performed in the Cardiothoracic Surgery Department of a Portuguese hospital from 2008 to 2021. The data follows the European Association for Cardio-
Thoracic Surgery (EACTS) Adult Cardiac Database [14] guidelines, and include
105 variables describing patients' demography, pre-surgical state, the procedure's
specifications and post-surgery information such as the length of stay in each
ward and in-hospital complications. These were used as features. All data was
anonymized and processed after the study protocol was approved by the hospital's ethical committee (INV 303) and following the Declaration of Helsinki.

Post-discharge outcomes were registered by the clinical team through phone
calls. Light (e.g., superficial wound infection, arrhythmia, fibrillation) to severe
(e.g., readmission, stroke, sudden death) complications were documented. Severe
complications were combined into a single positive class. Patients who died in
the hospital or did not answer the calls were excluded.

For evaluation, two test sets were partitioned from the dataset. Regarding
the samples referring to the time window from 2008 to 2019, 30% of data was
randomly sampled to create Test A, while the remaining was utilized as the
Train set. To assess the performance of the models over time, all data from 2020
to 2021 was included in Test B. One patient may be subject to multiple surgeries
across time, and one surgery might involve multiple procedures. Therefore, to
avoid data leakage, we ensured that all the samples referring to the same patient
were included in the same set. Table 1 summarizes the distribution of patients,
surgeries and procedures (samples), in each set. The prevalence of positive samples, averaging 7.5% complications per set, exposes a severe class imbalance.

Table 1. Summary of the train, test A, test B and complete sets. A sample corresponds
to one medical procedure performed within a surgery.

	Train (2008–19)	Test A (2008–19)	Test B (2020–21)	Total
No. Patients	3 531	1 514	980	6 025
No. Surgeries	3 693	1 564	1 014	6 271
No. Samples	3 976	1 673	1 099	6 748
No. Positives	290 (7.3%)	128 (7.7%)	88 (8.0%)	506 (7.5%)

3 Methodology

The methodology includes a two-steps hybrid learning approach. It involves the
application of UL techniques to extract data profiles from the training dataset,
which are then leveraged to train specialized models through SL methods. This
chapter describes the processes involved in each of these stages.

3.1   Unsupervised Learning Strategy

The first stage aimed to identify subsets of patients with similar characteristics. With this purpose in mind, a standard unsupervised dimension reduction was performed, followed by a clustering approach for pattern recognition.

The Uniform Manifold Approximation and Projection (UMAP) [19] technique was first applied to training data to perform a non-linear dimension reduction. The selected number of components for the dimension-reduced space was 3 to ensure interpretable representations. The remaining parameters of the UMAP algorithm were set to their default values. The resultant embeddings were then used to cluster the data samples using the Hierarchical Density-Based Spatial Clustering of Applications with Noise (HDBSCAN) [5] algorithm. Different combinations of parameters were tested following the authors' recommendations. The best combination was considered the one that produced clusters that were most aligned with the distinguishable regions in the three-dimensional UMAP space, upon visual inspection.

The dimension reduction followed by clustering was performed once (EXP1) using all the available variables, and a second time (EXP2) after all surgery-specific variables were removed (e.g. the valve intervened is registered only in the context of valve surgery). Since these variables are expected to have a strong impact on the creation of clusters, the second experiment was conducted in an attempt to uncover other hidden and less obvious relationships or patterns.

Finally, to identify the most relevant characteristics of the generated clusters, it was deemed interesting to build an interpretable multi-class classifier to discriminate between samples from different clusters. Therefore, a Random Forest (RF) classifier was trained in this task, from which the Gini features' importance [4] values were retrieved. In addition, the mean values of every feature were calculated and compared between clusters, as well as the distributions of samples and labels.

3.2   Supervised Learning Strategy

The second stage involved training specific models for post-discharge complications prediction upon each of the generated clusters. The training process included a thorough optimisation strategy, schematised in Fig. 1, to ensure that each model would be most adapted to its cluster's characteristics.

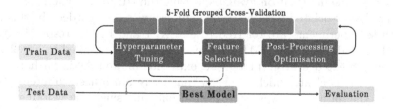

Fig. 1. Machine learning pipeline implemented in the supervised learning phase.

Six different classifiers were tested per cluster. These consisted of a Decision Tree (DT), an RF, a Light Gradient Boosting Machine (LGBM), a Multi-Layer Perceptron (MLP), a Support Vector Machine (SVM), and a Naive-Bayes classifier (NB). Each of them went through hyperparameter tuning, feature selection, and post-processing, sequentially. A 5-fold group cross-validation strategy was adopted, to ensure that data from the same patient was not used for training and validation simultaneously. The optimization metric adopted was the AUROC.

The hyperparameter tuning process was conducted through a grid search. As for the feature selection strategy, it consisted, at first, of establishing an importance ranking through permutation [4]. This ranking was then used as a reference for a forward sequential feature selection process [22], where the best next best feature was added to the training set in each new iteration. The optimal set of features was found through an early stopping strategy, which considered the iteration with the highest AUROC value, provided that the following five iterations held no improvements. A weighting strategy was adopted to tackle the severe class imbalance in the data.

Since multiple procedures can occur in one surgery but each intervention must have a single output associated, a post-processing step is incorporated, consisting of joining the outputs of different procedures from the same surgery. The optimisation of this process consists of identifying the best fusion strategy. Fusion through the maximum, minimum and mean value of the probabilistic outcomes was tested, and the best method was considered the one that, once again, produced the highest AUROC in the majority of the cross-validation folds.

This pipeline was implemented for all the clusters generated with and without surgery-specific information. Additionally, it was also used to train a baseline model with all the data available, without any previous stratification.

4   Results

This chapter presents the main results attained at the two main stages involving (i) the creation of clusters from UMAP representations and (ii) the development of specialized classification models for post-discharge complication prediction.

4.1   Clustering

Two experiments were conducted to test the hybrid learning strategy. The first considered all the information available during the UL task, while in the second every variable associated with a specific surgery was disregarded. In this document, these experiments are referred to as EXP1 and EXP2, respectively. The obtained three-dimensional UMAP representations are depicted in Fig. 2.

In the presented scatter plots, the existence of well-distinguishable high-density regions is clear, which suggests that there are indeed different profiles present in the data. This was an expected outcome since the working dataset contains data regarding different types of surgeries, where a positive label was associated with a broad range of severe complications. In fact, the removal of

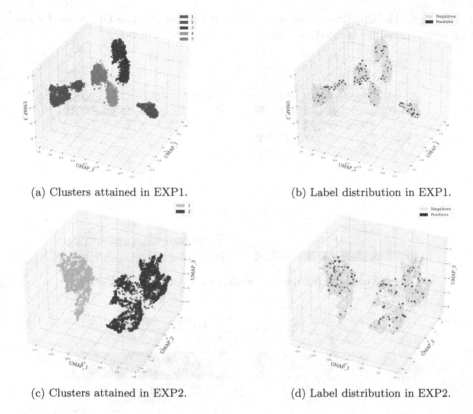

(a) Clusters attained in EXP1.

(b) Label distribution in EXP1.

(c) Clusters attained in EXP2.

(d) Label distribution in EXP2.

Fig. 2. Training data samples represented upon UMAP's three-dimensional space. The upper row refers to EXP1, while the lower row represents EXP2. In the left figures, each colour represents a unique cluster. Grey samples were considered noise and therefore were disregarded.

surgery information between experiments had a great impact on the number of distinct clusters created, reflected in a drop from five to only two clearly separable regions. Nevertheless, the existence of those two regions dictates that the patterns identified go beyond surgical-related divisions.

On another note, positive cases are prevalent across all clusters, excluding the possibility that the divisions could directly contribute to a distinction between classes. Even so, some of the distributions suggest that this division may still be beneficial for the classification task, as some clusters reveal singular patterns that can possibly be disguised when applying a standard full-set approach. For instance, in Fig. 2d, the positive samples of Cluster 1 seem to present a tendency towards the positive values of the third dimension (UMAP-3), which is not verified in the second group of samples, on the right.

Figure 3 denotes the specific characteristics of the clusters generated in EXP1 and EXP2. The variables presented correspond to the four most relevant ones, according to the importance rankings established during the UL phase by the multi-class classifier trained to identify the different clusters.

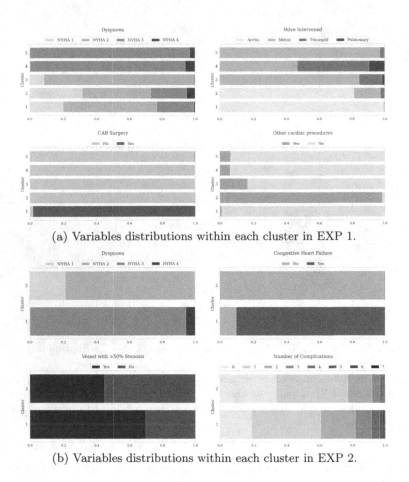

(a) Variables distributions within each cluster in EXP 1.

(b) Variables distributions within each cluster in EXP 2.

Fig. 3. Variable distributions per cluster, observed for the four most relevant features to distinguish between clusters, in each experiment.

As expected, most clusters formed in EXP1 relate to surgery-specific information, e.g., Cluster 1 includes the vast majority of patients who only underwent coronary artery bypass (CAB) graft surgery, Cluster 2 mainly includes patients undergoing cardiac procedures other than CAB and valve surgeries, and the remaining clusters contain predominantly patients that underwent valve surgery. These last three present differences in terms of the dyspnoea New York Heart Association (NHYA) classification, and the specifications of the valve surgery. As for EXP2, the division between patients in each cluster seems to be more related to cardiac history, risk factors and surgical complications. It is noticeable that, in both experiments, the dyspnoea classification presents distinctive traits. In fact, it seems that patients are being grouped according to dyspnoea severity, as higher NHYA classifications tend to appear together.

4.2   Classification

To evaluate the impact of the hybrid learning approach proposed, it was compared to a standard pipeline in predicting complications up to 90 days following discharge. Table 2 presents results for the individual models per cluster, and for merged solutions with inputs from all cluster-specific models, both considering (W) and ignoring weights reflecting the distribution of samples across clusters.

Table 2. Results achieved in predicting any type of severe complication happening up to 90 days following discharge. Results are presented in terms of AUROC.

Approach	Cluster	Model	Performance (AUROC)		
			CV (2008–19)	Test A (2008–19)	Test B (2020/21)
Standard	**Original**	**LGBM**	**70.74 ± 2.02**	**69.24**	**66.35**
EXP1	Cluster 1	MLP	71.25 ± 9.61	61.11	60.45
	Cluster 2	RF	77.81 ± 9.28	60.85	69.61
	Cluster 3	LGBM	74.6 ± 10.35	58.1	52.29
	Cluster 4	**NB**	**81.43 ± 7.07**	**76.38**	**69.56**
	Cluster 5	**MLP**	**82.21 ± 5.4**	**71.67**	**67.98**
	Merged	–	77.46 ± 8.34	65.62	63.98
	Merged (W)	–	76.32 ± 8.7	64.35	62.27
EXP2	**Cluster 1**	**RF**	**73.78 ± 6.82**	**68.43**	**74.32**
	Cluster 2	RF	69.61 ± 4.12	67.13	57.72
	Merged	–	71.7 ± 5.47	67.78	66.02
	Merged (W)	–	71.36 ± 5.25	67.67	64.67

The results of the merged solutions suggest that the divisions performed did not positively impact the original classification task when the data were considered as a whole. On the contrary, the values of AUROC attained in these conditions were lower than those of the standard approach in both experimental cases, especially when the density of samples in each cluster was considered.

Another conclusion one can derive is that no single algorithm consistently outperforms all others in the predictive task. Instead, four different types of algorithms achieved the best results across the experiments. However, when the data space was divided into a higher number of clusters (EXP1), non-tree-based algorithms emerged as superior for specific clusters, which was not the case in the remaining contexts. In fact, the MLP and NB models produced the best results in EXP1. These particular algorithms seemed to benefit from the preliminary segregation of the data space, unlike tree-based algorithms which are more likely to reach a similar segregation on their own.

Looking at the cluster-specific results, there is a high variability between clusters, which points towards different degrees of complexity in different regions. On the other hand, the cross-validation results achieved by cluster-specific models were tendentiously higher, and denote broader standard deviation ranges. Still, this tendency was not verified against the test sets in most cases, exposing a trend towards overfitting.

Another observable pattern relates to a performance drop of most models when tested against Test B, referring to the most recently acquired data samples from the working dataset. The results in this dataset were inferior to the ones achieved in Test A in ten out of the twelve cases presented, which suggests the presence of temporal drift in the data.

Despite this, the results attained in specific clusters are worth noting. Cluster 1 of EXP2 achieved the highest performance in Test B, with an AUROC of 74.32%, while also presenting one of the highest results in Test A. As for the clusters constructed in EXP1, Clusters 4 and 5 hold the best overall performances of all developed models. Looking back at Fig. 3, these clusters are associated with patients with high severity of dyspnoea (NHYA classifications of 3 and 4). This is consistent with the results attained in EXP2, where the best performance was registered for Cluster 1, containing data on patients with the same categories of NHYA classification. Moreover, patients within this cluster present a tendency to suffer from a higher number of in-hospital complications following surgery, and the great majority of them suffer from congestive heart failure. These results suggest that data from healthier patients are harder to model when compared to data regarding patients with degraded health status. This tendency seems to be more clear in patients undergoing valve surgery, as denoted by the higher performances achieved in Clusters 4 and 5 of EXP1.

5   Discussion

The results presented in this study provide valuable insights into the potential of hybrid learning approaches in the early prediction of post-discharge complications in patients undergoing cardiothoracic surgery.

Through the application of UL techniques, it became clear that different profiles can be distinguished in data collected in the context of cardiothoracic surgery procedures. Besides the type of surgery, information such as the dyspnea category, diagnosis of congestive heart failure, or number of surgical complications, appear relevant to the different groups' unique identities.

Separately studying specific data profiles can uncover distinct patterns useful for the classification task, which might be hidden when the available data is considered whole. Although the scatter plots from Fig. 2 do not present clear class-specific patterns, the good results attained by some cluster-specific models suggest that this might have happened in some cases. Even so, when combining the results from all clusters and comparing them to those attained through a standard approach, both experiments produced worse results. This might have happened due to the reduced dimension of the dataset. When the number of data samples is limited, further dividing the data into smaller groups has a cost, as less information is available for training. In imbalanced datasets, this effect can be aggravated, as examples from the minority class are scarce. This phenomenon might be the culprit behind the apparent tendency to overfit in cluster-specific models, as models could be learning specific traits of the few positive examples.

Against the complete test sets, the best performing model was the one trained through a standard SL approach, achieving AUROC values of 69.25% and 66.35% for Test A and Test B, respectively. These values align with some studies from the literature, although several works report higher performance (usually from 70 to 80%) for predicting adverse events in shorter time horizons. Considering longer time windows following discharge for the predictive task is essential, as it might help establish an adequate recovery plan in advance and even re-adjust the allocation of resources, ultimately contributing towards reduced readmission rates by improving personalised patient care.

While the proposed mixed-learning approach could not beat the standard strategy for the whole dataset, the groups resulting from the UL phase should be further investigated, as they might be helpful. In fact, subsequent cluster analysis revealed that models trained and tested on data from patients in a poorer physiological state performed better. This insight could be taken into consideration, along with the specific characteristics of each cluster, in the decision-making process. For instance, one could create a rejection criterion, according to which healthier patients would not be evaluated through the predictive model. An alternative approach would be incorporating these insights in the assessment of the uncertainty associated with each prediction. The existence of data drift should also be investigated, and different countermeasures should be tested. These strategies can be targeted in future work. Furthermore, the proposed methodology should be tested in other contexts, preferably on larger datasets, to unlock its potential truly.

6   Conclusion

In this study, we proposed an alternative approach for predicting post-discharge complications in patients undergoing cardiothoracic surgery, based on a hybrid learning architecture. The results attained showcase the potential of this methodology in capturing context-specific patterns, while still being compatible with different types of surgeries, patient profiles, and outcomes.

Despite not being able to outperform the standard SL strategy when considering the whole working dataset, the proposed method provided interesting results regarding the generated data profiles during the UL stage. Particularly, we found that models trained on data from patients in a poorer physiological state performed better. The insights gathered could be valuable to guide decision-making processes and improve personalized patient care, reduce readmission rates, and support better outcomes following cardiothoracic surgery.

Acknowledgements. This work was conducted under the project "CardioFollow.AI: An intelligent system to improve patients' safety and remote surveillance in follow-up for cardiothoracic surgery", supported by national funds through 'FCT—Portuguese Foundation for Science and Technology, I.P.', with the reference DSAIPA/AI/0094/2020.

References

1. Allyn, J., Allou, N., Augustin, P., Philip, I., Martinet, O., Belghiti, M., Provenchère, S., Montravers, P., Ferdynus, C.: A comparison of a machine learning model with Euroscore II in predicting mortality after elective cardiac surgery: a decision curve analysis. Plos One **12** (2017)
2. Benedetto, U., Dimagli, A., Sinha, S., Cocomello, L., Gibbison, B., Caputo, M., Gaunt, T.R., Lyon, M., Holmes, C.C., Angelini, G.D.: Machine learning improves mortality risk prediction after cardiac surgery: systematic review and meta-analysis. J. Thorac. Cardiovasc. Surg. **163**(6) (2020)
3. Bertsimas, D., Zhuo, D., Dunn, J., Levine, J., Zuccarelli, E., Smyrnakis, N., Tobota, Z., Maruszewski, B., Fragata, J., Sarris, G.E.: Adverse outcomes prediction for congenital heart surgery: a machine learning approach. World J. Pediatric Congenit. Heart Surg. **12**, 453–460 (2021)
4. Breiman, L.: Random forests. Mach. Learn. **45**, 5–32 (2001)
5. Campello, R.J., Moulavi, D., Sander, J.: Density-based clustering based on hierarchical density estimates. In: Advances in Knowledge Discovery and Data Mining: 17th Pacific-Asia Conference, PAKDD 2013, Gold Coast, Australia, Proceedings, Part II 17, pp. 160–172. Springer (2013)
6. Caruso, E., Zadra, A.R.: The trade-off between costs and outcome after cardiac surgery. evidence from an Italian administrative registry. Health Policy **124**(12), 1345–1353 (2020)
7. Cerqueira, V., Torgo, L., Branco, P., Bellinger, C.: Automated imbalanced classification via layered learning. Mach. Learn. 1–22 (2022)
8. Curioso, I., Santos, R., Ribeiro, B., Carreiro, A., Coelho, P., Fragata, J., Gamboa, H.: Addressing the curse of missing data in clinical contexts: a novel approach to correlation-based imputation. J. King Saud Univ.-Comput. Inf. Sci. **35**(6), 101562 (2023)
9. Efthymiou, C.A., O'regan, D.J.: Postdischarge complications: what exactly happens when the patient goes home? Interact. Cardiovasc. Thorac. Surg. **12**(2), 130–134 (2011)
10. Fan, Y., Dong, J., Wu, Y., Shen, M., Zhu, S., He, X., Jiang, S., Shao, J., Song, C.: Development of machine learning models for mortality risk prediction after cardiac surgery. Cardiovasc. Diagnos. Therapy **12**(1), 12–23 (2022)
11. Fränti, P., Sieranoja, S., Wikström, K., Laatikainen, T.: Clustering diagnoses from 58 million patient visits in Finland between 2015 and 2018. JMIR Med. Inform. **10**(5), e35422 (2022)
12. Fry, D.E., Pine, M.B., Nedza, S.M., Locke, B.D.G., Reband, B.A.M., Ba, Pine, G.: Inpatient and 90-day postdischarge outcomes in cardiac surgery. Am. J. Manag. Care **4** (2016)
13. Gordon, M.M., Moser, A.M., Rubin, E.: Unsupervised analysis of classical biomedical markers: robustness and medical relevance of patient clustering using bioinformatics tools. Plos One **7** (2012)

14. Head, S.J., Howell, N.J., Osnabrugge, R.L., Bridgewater, B., Keogh, B.E., Kinsman, R., Walton, P., Gummert, J.F., Pagano, D., Kappetein, A.P.: The European association for cardio-thoracic surgery (EACTS) database: an introduction. Eur. J. Cardiothorac. Surg. 44(3), e175–e180 (2013)
15. Jawitz, O.K., Gulack, B.C., Brennan, J.M., Thibault, D.P., Wang, A., O'Brien, S.M., Schroder, J.N., Gaca, J.G., Smith, P.K.: Association of postoperative complications and outcomes following coronary artery bypass grafting. Am. Heart J. 222, 220–228 (2020)
16. Kaushik, K., Kapoor, D., Varadharajan, V., Nallusamy, R.: Disease management: clustering-based disease prediction. Int. J. Collabor. Enter. 4(1–2), 69–82 (2014)
17. Khoury, H., Ragalie, W.S., Sanaiha, Y., Boutros, H., Rudasill, S.E., Shemin, R.J., Benharash, P.: Readmission following surgical aortic valve replacement in the United States. Ann. Thorac. Surg. 110(3), 849–855 (2020)
18. Kortlandt, F.A., van 't Klooster, C.C., Bakker, A., Swaans, M.J., Kelder, J.C., de Kroon, T.L., Rensing, B.J., Eefting, F.D., van der Heyden, J.A., Post, M.C.: The predictive value of conventional surgical risk scores for periprocedural mortality in percutaneous mitral valve repair. Netherlands Heart J. 24, 475–480 (2016)
19. McInnes, L., Healy, J., Saul, N., Grossberger, L.: Umap: uniform manifold approximation and projection. J. Open Sour. Softw. 3(29), 861 (2018)
20. Mortazavi, B., Desai, N.R., Zhang, J., Coppi, A., Warner, F., Krumholz, H.M., Negahban, S.N.: Prediction of adverse events in patients undergoing major cardiovascular procedures. IEEE J. Biomed. Health Inform. 21, 1719–1729 (2017)
21. Nashef, S.A.M., Roques, F., Sharples, L.D., Nilsson, J., Smith, C., Goldstone, A.R., Lockowandt, U.: Euroscore II. Eur. J. Cardiothorac. Surg.: Official J. Eur. Assoc. Cardio-thorac. Surg. 41(4), 734–44 (2012)
22. Pudil, P., Novovicová, J., Kittler, J.: Floating search methods in feature selection. Pattern Recognit. Lett. 15, 1119–1125 (1994)
23. Sanchez, C.E., Hermiller, J.B., Pinto, D.S., Chetcuti, S.J., Arshi, A., Forrest, J.K., Huang, J., Yakubov, S.J.: Predictors and risk calculator of early unplanned hospital readmission following contemporary self-expanding transcatheter aortic valve replacement from the STS/ACC TVT-registry. Cardiovasc. Revascularization Med.: Incl. Mol. Interv. 21(3), 263–270 (2020)
24. Seese, L.M., Sultan, I.S., Gleason, T.G., Navid, F., Wang, Y., Thoma, F.W., Kilic, A.: The impact of major postoperative complications on long-term survival after cardiac surgery. Ann. Thorac. Surg. 110(1), 128–135 (2019)
25. Shahian, D.M., Jacobs, J.P., Badhwar, V., Kurlansky, P.A., Furnary, A.P., Cleveland, J.C., Lobdell, K.W., Vassileva, C.M., von Ballmoos, M.C.W., Thourani, V.H., Rankin, J.S., Edgerton, J.R., D'Agostino, R.S., Desai, N.D., Feng, L., He, X., O'Brien, S.M.: The society of thoracic surgeons 2018 adult cardiac surgery risk models: Part 1-background, design considerations, and model development. Ann. Thorac. Surg. 105(5), 1411–1418 (2018)
26. Silaschi, M., Conradi, L., Seiffert, M., Schnabel, R.B., Schön, G., Blankenberg, S., Reichenspurner, H.C., Diemert, P., Treede, H.: Predicting risk in transcatheter aortic valve implantation: comparative analysis of Euroscore II and established risk stratification tools. Thorac. Cardiovasc. Surg. 63, 472–478 (2014)
27. Sinha, S., Dimagli, A., Dixon, L., Gaudino, M.F., Caputo, M., Vohra, H.A., Angelini, G.D., Benedetto, U.: Systematic review and meta-analysis of mortality risk prediction models in adult cardiac surgery. Interact. Cardiovasc. Thorac. Surg. 33, 673–686 (2021)

28. Wang, C., Jin, L., Qiao, F., Xue, Q., Zhang, X., Han, L.: Performance of the society of thoracic surgeons 2008 cardiac risk models for major postoperative complications after heart valve surgery in a Chinese population: a multicenter study. Heart Surg. Forum **21**(4), E281–E285 (2018)
29. Wang, T.K.M., Choi, D.H.M., Haydock, D.A., Gamble, G.D., Stewart, R.A., Ruygrok, P.N.: Comparison of risk scores for prediction of complications following aortic valve replacement. Heart Lung Circul. **24**(6), 595–601 (2015)
30. Zhong, Z., Yuan, X., Liu, S., Yang, Y., Liu, F.: Machine learning prediction models for prognosis of critically ill patients after open-heart surgery. Sci. Rep. **11** (2021)

Leveraging TFR-BERT for ICD Diagnoses Ranking

Ana Silva[1,2(✉)] [iD], Pedro Chaves[2] [iD], Sara Rijo[2] [iD], João Boné[2] [iD],
Tiago Oliveira[1] [iD], and Paulo Novais[1] [iD]

[1] ALGORITMI Research Centre/LASI, University of Minho, Braga, Portugal
[2] Select Data, Anaheim, CA 92807, USA
ana.paula.silva@algoritmi.uminho.pt
pedro.chaves@selectdatalabs.com

Abstract. This work describes applying a transformer-based ranking solution to the specific problem of ordering ICD diagnoses codes. Taking advantage of the TFR-BERT framework and adapting it to the biomedical context using pre-trained and publicly available language representation models, namely BioBERT, BlueBERT and ClinicalBERT (Bio + Discharge Summary BERT Model), we demonstrate the effectiveness of such a framework and the strengths of using pre-trained models adapted to the biomedical domain. We showcase this by using a benchmark dataset in the healthcare field—MIMIC-III—showing how it was possible to learn how to sequence the main or primary diagnoses and the order in which the secondary diagnoses are presented. A window-based approach and a summary approach (using only the sentences with diagnoses) were also tested in an attempt to circumvent the maximum sequence length limitation of BERT-based models. BioBERT demonstrated superior performance in all approaches, achieving the best results in the summary approach.

Keywords: Learning-to-rank · Ranking diagnoses · Biomedical language models

1 Introduction

The International Classification of Diseases (ICD) is a comprehensive system of codes widely used to describe and categorize Electronic Health Records (EHR) [23]. This classification is done not only for quality control but also reimbursement purposes, with the set of codes selected by the clinician and/or clinical coder describing each clinical visit or episode. The coding process is typically time consuming, with the selection of the appropriate and sufficiently specific codes taking an average of 20 min [6]. Furthermore, the coding process needs not only to reflect the appropriate codes for the record but also to sort them appropriately—selecting a principal or primary diagnosis and the order in which the secondary diagnoses are coded.

N. Moniz et al. (Eds.): EPIA 2023, LNAI 14116, pp. 311–322, 2023.
https://doi.org/10.1007/978-3-031-49011-8_25

Machine learning and artificial intelligence methods, particularly in the realm of Natural Language Processing (NLP) can contribute to the efficiency and accuracy of this process, by automating information extraction from the unstructured data (text) present in the EHRs.

In this paper, we focus on the particular problem of ICD code sequencing or ranking, by leveraging a transformer-based learning-to-rank framework (TFR-BERT) and tweaking it to the biomedical context using publicly available pre-trained language representation models fine-tuned to the biomedical domain. We demonstrate how such a framework can be effectively used to rank diagnosis codes and could thus be subsequently used as a downstream task in typical NLP pipelines to sort the extracted data (i.e., diagnoses) by their relevance.

Moreover, we briefly explore how the structure of the documents themselves might affect the behavior of this framework.

Clinical Importance By introducing a relevance dimension into the information extraction process, we believe that such an approach can further facilitate the coding procedure, contributing to reduction in human effort and hopefully more precise information. The improvement of the quality of coding information can then not only increase the potential for reimbursement for providers but also contribute to more precise clinical histories, impacting the quality of care given to the patients.

Theoretical Significance While some previous approaches have already framed the sorting of ICD codes as a ranking problem, we take it a step further and demonstrate the feasibility of using transformer-based models in such scenarios, and how using fine-tuned versions of said models brings on improvements over generic language models.

Furthermore, more than helping the clinical coder order the detected or listed diagnoses in the record, this approach can also be used in existing NLP pipelines, by sorting the results from Named Entity Recognition (NER) models—hence going a step further in automating clinical coding.

2   Related Work

The majority of applications from machine learning to clinical coding have focused on trying to directly predict the ICD codes associated with a given record. These predictions can come from the processing of the unstructured text or tabular data (or a combination of both), outputting one or more diagnoses as predictions.

A recent systematic review of automated ICD coding [12] has found that deep learning approaches are seeing an uptake and tend to overcome traditional machine learning algorithms. However, all of the papers reviewed tried to tackle the problem through a classification approach.

Furthermore, recent papers in the field also apply contextualized pre-trained models (i.e., BERT-based). Pascual et al. [16] and Wang et al. [24] are good examples of such work, though focused again on trying to directly predict the ICD codes.

Other than pure classification approaches, information extraction pipelines based on NLP techniques have also seen a sharp rise in use. At the core of these techniques lies Named Entity Recognition (NER), which can be used to automatically extract entities of interest (i.e., diagnoses) from clinical text. These clinical entities can subsequently be normalized against normalized vocabularies through semantic similarity techniques, thus yielding the corresponding ICD code [14]. Nonetheless the ICD codes produced by such approaches lack a quality of relevance or order among them.

Works such as [13] have already explored a ranking perspective to the problem of automated ICD coding—though in the context of multi-label classification. They applied a learning-to-rank model to a candidate list of possible ICD codes output from a previous classification task, as well as an enriched list of candidate codes using the NER output from MetaMap [3]. Furthermore, the features explored by the authors are mostly based on code co-occurrences; thus, not leveraging the rich representations brought on by more sophisticated language models not available at the time of the research.

3 Methodology

In the following section, we describe our methodology for the task of ICD code ranking. We start by providing an overview of our approach and then we move on to a more detailed description of the components of our system.

3.1 Overview

Our approach consists of two main components: a transformer-based learning-to-rank system (TFR-BERT) and fine-tuned language representation models (BioBERT [15], BlueBERT [18] and ClinicalBERT [1]).

The learning-to-rank system is based on the TFR-BERT framework proposed by [8], and it is used to rank the ICD codes associated with an EHR. The input to the system is a list of concatenated pairs of unstructured EHR text (query) and associated ICD code description (document). The output of the system is a score for each ICD code, which is used to rank the codes according to their relevance. Figure 1 shows an example of a ranking problem (input and output) in JSON format for better understanding.

Fine-tuned language representation models were used to obtain more accurate representations of the concatenated text inputs. In this work we used three variants of BERT [7], which are then used to train the learning-to-rank system.

3.2 Learning-to-Rank System

Our approach to learning-to-rank was implemented using the Tensorflow Ranking library (TFR) [17], an open-source library that provides a learning-to-rank functionality for ranking problems in Tensorflow. The goal was to sort

{"rankingProblems": [
    {"queryText": discharge note ,
     "documents": [
       {"relevance": 10,
         "docText": description of primary diagnosis},
       {"relevance": 9,
          "docText": description of secondary diagnosis},
         ...]
    },
    ...
}

{"rankingProblemsOutput": [
    {"queryText": discharge note ,
     "documents": [
       {"relevance": int,
         "docText": description of primary diagnosis,
         "score": 15.606854},

       {"relevance": int,
          "docText": description of secondary diagnosis,
          "score": 9.696366},
         ...]
    },
    ...
}

(a) Input example.   (b) Output example.

Fig. 1. Example of a ranking problem (JSON format).

an unordered list of inputs in the best order of relevance, which has applications in several domains, from search to question answering systems.

To represent inputs to these models, Examples Lists With Context (ELWC) are needed, where a context (also known as query) is a single tf. Example and the list to order (also known as a list of documents) is a list of tf.Examples. The embeddings extracted from this input then go through a scoring function and the losses (which can be pointwise, pairwise or listwise) drive parameter updates.

In this paper we show how this approach can be adapted to the problem of diagnosis ranking with good results, and furthermore explore how tweaking the architecture to leverage pre-trained models from the relevant domain can further improve it.

3.3   Fine-Tuned Language Representation Model

BERT is a pre-trained language representation model that revolutionized Natural Language Processing (NLP). It is based on the Transformer architecture and was pre-trained on general domain corpora (English Wikipedia and BooksCorpus) [7]. To incorporate recent advancements of contextually pre-trained BERT models, we further integrated BioBERT [15], BlueBERT [18] and ClinicalBERT (Bio + Discharge Summary BERT Model) [1], so we could compare the performance against the original BERT model. Theoretically, incorporating domain specific knowledge should improve the task at hands.

All models apart from the base BERT[1] are pre-trained in biomedical domain corpora—while BioBERT[2] integrates PubMed abstracts and PMC full-text articles, BlueBERT[3] integrates PubMed abstracts and MIMIC-III clinical notes,

---

[1] BERT-Base-Cased checkpoint can be downloaded from: https://github.com/google-research/bert.

[2] BioBERT-Base v1.1, based on BERT-base-Cased (same vocabulary), checkpoint can be downloaded from: https://github.com/dmis\discretionary-lab/biobert.

[3] BlueBERT-Base-Uncased, PubMed+MIMIC-III checkpoint can be downloaded from: https://github.com/ncbi\discretionary-nlp/bluebert; or from Hugging Face Hub: https://huggingface.co/bionlp/bluebert_pubmed_mimic_uncased_L\discretionary-12_H\discretionary-768_A\discretionary-12.

and ClinicalBERT[4] was trained on all discharge summaries from MIMIC-III. All these models are also open-source and can be used freely.

Note that due to the nature of the data, many abbreviations are expected to be present and in order to preserve their relevance in a clinical context, cased checkpoints were used. The exception was BlueBERT, since it is not available in a cased version—and as such the data was lowercased first.

4   Experiments and Results

In this section we present the experiments and results of our approach. We start by introducing the dataset used in our experiments and then we move on to the details of our experiments and the results obtained.

4.1   Dataset

The benchmark for healthcare datasets is the Medical Information Mart for Intensive Care (MIMIC) dataset, a large freely available database comprised of unidentified health-related data associated with over forty thousand patients. We used discharge notes from the MIMIC-III [11] database, as version IV notes were not yet available. This version contains information from patients hospitalized in intensive care units at Beth Israel Deaconess Medical Center between 2001 and 2012.

The used subset contained information from discharge reports with the category "discharge summary". Notes with errors were eliminated, as well as those with a description of "addendum". For episodes that had more than one discharge report associated with it, only the last one was considered. Records were filtered to contain up to 10 ICD codes and those with only one ICD code were removed, as there was no need for ranking. Cases with up to 10 ICD codes were removed if the sequence was not complete. From this selection a subset of 25531 cases was obtained, where 70% were reserved for training, 15% for testing and the remaining 15% for evaluation.

Figure 2 shows the distribution of the number of ICD codes per record after the data selection.

4.2   Training Parameters

All training runs used the same hyperparameters, with a learning rate of 5e-6, a maximum sequence length of 512 tokens (the maximum allowed value), and a list size of 10 (maximum number of documents/diagnoses in each ranking problem). Note that increasing the list size value is directly related to memory consumption, which in some cases can also decrease learning performance. The batch size was

---

[4] ClinicalBERT (Bio + Discharge Summary BERT model) checkpoint can be down-loaded from: https://github.com/EmilyAlsentzer/clinicalBERT; or from Hugging Face Hub: https://huggingface.co/emilyalsentzer/Bio_Discharge_Summary_BERT.

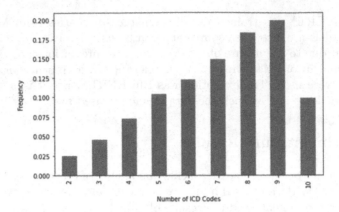

Fig. 2. Distribution of the number of ICD codes per record.

set to 1, in order to fit in the available GPU. Given the listwise nature of the problem [5], the loss function used was the smooth approximation to Normalized Discounted Cumulative Gain (ApproxNDCGLoss), originally proposed by [20]. Normalized Discounted Cumulative Gain (NDCG) is a popular ranking metric that will be described in more detail afterward.

The prediction was given by the scoring function, where diagnoses (documents) with higher scores being more relevant [5].

4.3   Metrics

For the experiments with the learning-to-rank system, we used the TFR-BERT framework described in Sect. 3. We trained the system on the training set and evaluated its performance on the validation and test sets.

We measured the performance of the system using the NDCG, at cutoffs 1, 5 and 10 (overall NDCG) [10,22].

We also used the Spearman's rank correlation coefficient (r_s), commonly referred as Spearman's rho, which is widely used to assess the monotonic relationship between two variables, and results in a score of 1 if the relative positions of the observations are similar [19].

4.4   Additional Approaches

A fundamental limitation of BERT based models is the maximum sequence length it can deal with—specifically it can only consume a maximum of 512 tokens from the text, truncating everything afterwards. This limitation comes from an inherent property in the Attention mechanism, which scales quadratically with the input sequence length.

Figure 3 represents the distribution of token lengths for our training dataset. The average length of 1193 tokens is more than double the maximum sequence length for BERT.

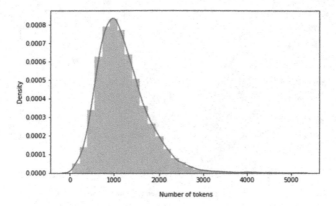

Fig. 3. Distribution of the number of tokens per record (full text).

Windowed Training Approach Given the possibility of losing information in examples longer than this limit, a simple workaround was implemented to explore this hypothesis: we have tweaked the training procedure so that each example is broken down into 3 examples, each representing 512 tokens from the beginning, middle and end of the text.

During inference time, the same approach was taken by predicting the ICD ranking based on each of the 3 segments of the text.

Similar approaches have already been explored by authors such as [2] though with mixed results.

Summarization Training Approach Another potential solution explored was to summarize the discharge notes so as to use only the sentences that had diagnoses. Consequently, we used a custom trained pipeline for diagnose detection (NER), where only sentences with at least 1 diagnosis found were saved. This allowed us to significantly reduce text sizes, as seen Fig. 4.

5   Results

The results presented below reflect the average metrics obtained for the test dataset. We will compare each of the checkpoints with each other, since there's no benchmark to refer to.

5.1   Overall ICD Code Ranking

Table 1 presents the scores on the test set for both NDCG, at cutoffs 1, 5 and 10 (overall NDCG), and Spearman's rank correlation coefficient for each of the models.

Despite the difference between the metrics not being very large, BioBERT achieved the best overall NDCG (NDCG@10) and for the remaining cutoffs. The best r_s was achieved by the ClinicalBERT model.

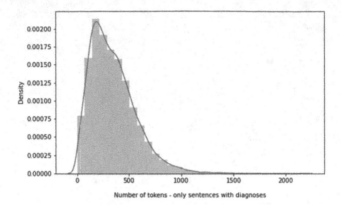

Fig. 4. Distribution of the number of tokens per record (only sentences with diagnoses).

Table 1. Model results—truncated to 512 tokens.

Model	NDCG@1	NDCG@5	NDCG@10	rs
BERT	0.793	0.883	0.907	0.703
BioBERT	**0.825**	**0.895**	**0.918**	0.723
BlueBERT	0.761	0.877	0.900	0.722
ClinicalBERT	0.780	0.882	0.905	**0.727**

5.2   Windowed Training Approach

Table 2 shows the results obtained by the windowed approach.

Table 2. Model results (windowed approach).

Model	Segment	NDCG@1	NDCG@5	NDCG@10	rs
BERT	1	0.787	0.882	0.906	0.707
	2	0.723	0.854	0.883	0.676
	3	0.751	0.866	0.892	0.690
BioBERT	1	**0.817**	**0.891**	**0.916**	0.719
	2	0.756	0.863	0.893	0.681
	3	0.779	0.878	0.903	0.707
BlueBERT	1	0.760	0.878	0.900	**0.721**
	2	0.730	0.864	0.889	0.709
	3	0.736	0.867	0.891	0.708
ClinicalBERT	1	0.736	0.868	0.892	0.716
	2	0.718	0.860	0.885	0.711
	3	0.732	0.867	0.890	0.709

Table 3. Model results (only sentences with diagnoses).

Model	NDCG@1	NDCG@5	NDCG@10	rs
BERT	0.795	0.883	0.908	0.715
BioBERT	**0.823**	**0.896**	**0.919**	**0.732**
BlueBERT	0.763	0.875	0.899	0.712
ClinicalBERT	0.753	0.873	0.896	0.716

While the results for the initial segment are compatible with the previous truncated approach, the values of both NDCG and Spearman's Coefficient drop in the subsequent segments, as can be seen in Table 2. This in turn causes the averages to drop, rendering the overall approach less efficient. Note that the metric values for the first segment are not exactly the same because the training step number is a relation between the number of epochs and the size of the training dataset. In this case, there was almost three times more training data but the number of epochs remained unchanged.

5.3   Summarization Training Approach

Table 3 shows the results obtained from the models trained with summarized data.

All metrics indicated reflect that best model would be BioBERT.

6   Discussion

The work presented in this paper can be summarized around two points: (1) Presenting the feasibility of using ranking based approaches in computer-assisted coding settings; (2) Increased understanding of the workings and applicability of TFR-BERT to specific contexts.

Regarding the first point, it seems clear that the ranking approach implemented in TFR-BERT can effectively learn how to rank ICD codes as they relate to a given EHR text, which is effectively demonstrated for the first time.

The dataset used in this work contained the coded diagnoses associated with the clinical text—however, we suggest that in order to fully leverage this approach to facilitate the coding procedure, such a ranking module could act as the final stage of a complete NLP pipeline, leveraging the results returned by an upstream NER task.

Since the entities found by an NER model can be considerably variable, one should pass it through a resolver/normalizer—thus attributing it an ICD code—before feeding it to the ranking module. This would increase the value of the pipeline's output by providing the coder not only with a list of ICD codes that were found in the document but also how relevant their relationship to each other, effectively guiding the coders' attention to the most relevant information within that list. Moreover, by following a NER-based approach, the typical pitfalls present in classification approaches can be avoided. The wide adoption of existing packages such as spaCy [9] and SparkNLP [14] in the healthcare space greatly facilitates the creation of these pipelines, making it easy to integrate NER and resolver tasks with a final ranking step.

Regarding the second point, we have shown how switching from general language models to context specific models can immediately bring gains in terms of model performance. More specifically, by leveraging a pre-trained model which integrates the same corpus as the corpus we are using in the ranking task—BioBERT—we see an improvement in the ability of the TFR-BERT model to learn how to rank the ICD codes from the discharge notes.

Finally, when considering the results of the windowed approach, we can see that it actually underperforms when compared to the simpler truncated version. We hypothesize that this might be due to the typical structure of the discharge notes, where the majority of the clinical information is immediately summarized and presented. That in turn renders the subsequent segments less informative in predicting the ICD codes relevance and thus a simple average decreases the scores for both metrics.

7   Conclusion and Future Work

This work proposes a new approach to the specific problem of ICD code sequencing by adapting an existing, powerful, learning-to-rank framework.

Leveraging the TFR-BERT framework and adapting it to the biomedical context using publicly available pre-trained language representation models (tuned for the biomedical domain), it was demonstrated how the use of such a structure can be effectively used to help sequence the main or primary diagnoses and the order in which the secondary diagnoses are coded.

The BERT model proved to be quite robust, however the best model in the various approaches turned out to be a domain specific one, BioBERT.

We also try to overcome the fundamental limitation of BERT-based models, namely the maximum sequence length with which it can deal with, by exploring a windowed approach, but the results performed poorly when compared to the simpler truncated version. This may be due to the typical structure of discharge notes, where most of the clinical information is the summary compilation of the patient's stay in the hospital. The summarized version showed great potential, achieving the best results for NDCG@5, NDCG@10/overall and Spearman's rho.

Other limitations found throughout the experiments are related to the resources needed to train the models. For example, as the list size increases, so does the memory problems and resource usage. As such, we need to effectively exclude records for which more than 10 ICD codes were used.

Future work should also focus on further exploring the hypothesis that the informational structure of the discharges influences the performance of a windowed approach. This can be pursued by either carefully manipulating or selecting documents so that relevant clinical information is present in different zones of the text. In a similar line, exploring the performance of Transformer-based models apt for longer documents, such as Longformer [4], could prove useful in scenarios where standard and relevant information is spread throughout longer documents.

Finally, we believe that the next logical step in effectively bringing this approach to a practical realm will require integrating it into more complete NLP pipelines to make use of previously identified ICD codes in the document and as such that feasibility needs to be demonstrated. We also consider this approach equally useful and important to contribute to the automation of the mapping of clinical cases to an argumentation framework [21], by allowing to infer what are the most relevant—and eventually the primary—diagnoses in a given case.

Acknowledgment. We would like to express our appreciation to Select Data, Inc. for supporting this research and publication. The work of Paulo Novais has been supported by FCT—Fundação para a Ciência e Tecnologia within the R&D Units Project Scope: UIDB/00319/2020.

References

1. Alsentzer, E., Murphy, J., Boag, W., Weng, W.H., Jindi, D., Naumann, T., McDermott, M.: Publicly available clinical BERT embeddings. In: Proceedings of the 2nd Clinical Natural Language Processing Workshop. pp. 72–78. Association for Computational Linguistics, Minneapolis, Minnesota, USA (2019). https://doi.org/10.18653/v1/W19-1909
2. Amin, S., Neumann, G., Dunfield, K.A., Vechkaeva, A., Chapman, K.A., Wixted, M.K.: Mlt-dfki at clef ehealth 2019: Multi-label classification of icd-10 codes with bert. In: Conference and Labs of the Evaluation Forum (2019)
3. Aronson, A.R.: Effective mapping of biomedical text to the umls metathesaurus: the metamap program. In: Proceedings of the AMIA Symposium, p. 17. American Medical Informatics Association (2001)
4. Beltagy, I., Peters, M.E., Cohan, A.: Longformer: The long-document transformer (2020). arXiv:2004.05150
5. Bruch, S., Zoghi, M., Bendersky, M., Najork, M.: Revisiting approximate metric optimization in the age of deep neural networks. In: Proceedings of the 42nd International ACM SIGIR Conference on Research and Development in Information Retrieval, pp. 1241–1244. SIGIR'19. Association for Computing Machinery, New York, NY, USA (2019). https://doi.org/10.1145/3331184.3331347
6. Carla Smith, S.B., Dooling, J.A.: Measuring and benchmarking coding productivity: a decade of Ahima leadership (2015)
7. Devlin, J., Chang, M.W., Lee, K., Toutanova, K.: Bert: pre-training of deep bidirectional transformers for language understanding (2019)
8. Han, S., Wang, X., Bendersky, M., Najork, M.: Learning-to-rank with BERT in TF-ranking (2020). arXiv:2004.08476
9. Honnibal, M., Montani, I.: spaCy 2: Natural language understanding with Bloom embeddings, convolutional neural networks and incremental parsing (2017), to appear
10. Järvelin, K., Kekäläinen, J.: Cumulated gain-based evaluation of IR techniques. ACM Trans. Inf. Syst. (TOIS) **20**(4), 422–446 (2002)

11. Johnson, A.E., Pollard, T.J., Shen, L., Lehman, L.W.H., Feng, M., Ghassemi, M., Moody, B., Szolovits, P., Anthony Celi, L., Mark, R.G.: MIMIC-III, a freely accessible critical care database. Sci. Data **3**(1), 1–9 (2016)
12. Kaur, R., Ginige, J.A., Obst, O.: A systematic literature review of automated ICD coding and classification systems using discharge summaries (2021)
13. Kavuluru, R., Rios, A., Lu, Y.: An empirical evaluation of supervised learning approaches in assigning diagnosis codes to electronic medical records. Artif. Intell. Med. **65** (2015). https://doi.org/10.1016/j.artmed.2015.04.007
14. Kocaman, V., Talby, D.: Spark NLP: natural language understanding at scale. Softw. Impacts 100058 (2021). https://doi.org/10.1016/j.simpa.2021.100058
15. Lee, J., Yoon, W., Kim, S., Kim, D., Kim, S., So, C.H., Kang, J.: Biobert: a pre-trained biomedical language representation model for biomedical text mining. Bioinformatics (2019). https://doi.org/10.1093/bioinformatics/btz682
16. Pascual, D., Luck, S., Wattenhofer, R.: Towards BERT-based automatic ICD coding: limitations and opportunities. In: Workshop on Biomedical Natural Language Processing (2021)
17. Pasumarthi, R.K., Bruch, S., Wang, X., Li, C., Bendersky, M., Najork, M., Pfeifer, J., Golbandi, N., Anil, R., Wolf, S.: TF-ranking: Scalable tensorflow library for learning-to-rank. In: Proceedings of the 25th ACM SIGKDD International Conference on Knowledge Discovery & Data Mining, pp. 2970–2978 (2019)
18. Peng, Y., Yan, S., Lu, Z.: Transfer learning in biomedical natural language processing: An evaluation of bert and elmo on ten benchmarking datasets. In: Proceedings of the 2019 Workshop on Biomedical Natural Language Processing (BioNLP 2019), pp. 58–65 (2019)
19. Pirie, W.: Spearman Rank Correlation Coefficient. Wiley (2006). https://doi.org/10.1002/0471667196.ess2499.pub2
20. Qin, T., Liu, T.Y., Li, H.: A general approximation framework for direct optimization of information retrieval measures. Inf. Retr. **13**, 375–397 (2010). https://doi.org/10.1007/s10791-009-9124-x
21. Silva, A., Silva, A., Oliveira, T., Novais, P.: Mapping a clinical case description to an argumentation framework: a preliminary assessment. In: Intelligent Data Engineering and Automated Learning-IDEAL 2020: 21st International Conference, Guimaraes, Portugal, Proceedings, Part I, vol. 21, pp. 338–349. Springer (2020)
22. Wang, Y., Wang, L., Li, Y., He, D., Liu, T.Y.: A theoretical analysis of NDCG type ranking measures. In: Conference on Learning Theory, pp. 25–54. PMLR (2013)
23. WHO: ICD-10: international statistical classification of diseases and related health problems: tenth revision (2004)
24. Zhang, Z., Liu, J., Razavian, N.: BERT-XML: Large scale automated ICD coding using BERT pretraining. In: Proceedings of the 3rd Clinical Natural Language Processing Workshop, pp. 24–34. Association for Computational Linguistics (2020). https://doi.org/10.18653/v1/2020.clinicalnlp-1.3

Artificial Intelligence and IoT
in Agriculture

Evaluating the Causal Role of Environmental Data in Shellfish Biotoxin Contamination on the Portuguese Coast

Ana Rita Baião[1] , Carolina Peixoto[1] , Marta B. Lopes[2,3] ,
Pedro Reis Costa[4] , Alexandra M. Carvalho[5,6] , and Susana Vinga[1(✉)]

[1] INESC-ID, Instituto Superior Técnico, Universidade de Lisboa, 1000-029 Lisbon,
Portugal
susanavinga@tecnico.ulisboa.pt
[2] Center for Mathematics and Applications (NOVA Math), Department
of Mathematics, NOVA FCT, 2829-516 Caparica, Portugal
[3] UNIDEMI, Department of Mechanical and Industrial Engineering, NOVA FCT,
2829-516 Caparica, Portugal
[4] IPMA—Instituto Português do Mar e da Atmosfera, 1495-006, Lisbon, Portugal
[5] Instituto de Telecomunicações, Av. Rovisco Pais 1, 1049-001 Lisbon, Portugal
[6] Instituto Superior Técnico, Av Rovisco Pais 1, 1049-001 Lisbon, Portugal

Abstract. Shellfish accumulation of marine biotoxins at levels unsafe
for human consumption may severely impact their harvesting and farming, which has been grown worldwide in response to the growing demand
for nutritious food and protein sources. In Southern European countries,
diarrhetic shellfish poisoning (DSP) toxins are the most abundant and
frequent toxins derived from algal blooms, affecting shellfish production
yearly. Therefore, it is essential to understand the natural phenomenon
of DSP toxins accumulation in shellfish and the meteorological and biological parameters that may regulate and influence its occurrence. In this
work, we studied the relationship between the time series of several meteorological and biological variables and the time series of the concentration
of DSP toxins in mussels on the Portuguese coast, using the Pearson's
correlation coefficient, time series regression modeling, Granger causality,
and dynamic Bayesian networks using the MAESTRO tool. The results
show that, for the models tested, the mean sea surface and air temperature time series with a one, two, or three-week lag can be valuable
candidate predictors for forecasting the DSP concentration in mussels.
Overall, this proof-of-concept study emphasizes the importance of statistical learning methodologies for analyzing time series environmental
data and illustrates the importance of several variables in predicting DSP
biotoxins concentration, which can help the shellfish production sector
mitigate the negative impacts of DSP biotoxins accumulation.

Keywords: Shellfish contamination · Harmful algal blooms · Time
series regression modeling · Dynamic Bayesian Networks

© The Author(s), under exclusive license to Springer Nature Switzerland AG 2023
N. Moniz et al. (Eds.): EPIA 2023, LNAI 14116, pp. 325–337, 2023.
https://doi.org/10.1007/978-3-031-49011-8_26

1   Introduction

Shellfish farming is a significant sector of aquaculture production worldwide and a sustainable solution with economic and environmental benefits to the growing demand for healthy food and protein sources to feed an increasing world population [1]. Shellfish are filter-feeding organisms that grow from the phytoplankton available in the water. However, among the thousands of phytoplankton species, a few may produce toxic compounds that can accumulate and contaminate shellfish [1,2]. The most common poisoning biotoxins are known by the symptoms they cause, namely diarrhetic shellfish poisoning (DSP), amnesic shellfish poisoning (ASP), and paralytic shellfish poisoning (PSP) [2,3].

Over the past years, harmful algal blooms (HAB) events have been increasing, resulting in severe consequences to the environment, human health, and shellfish safety. Several coastal countries conduct monitoring programs of the shellfish-producing areas to safeguard public health and minimize the acute intoxication risk [3]. A series of EU regulations specify the hygiene rules for live bivalve molluscs before being placed on the market. These include the biotoxins safety limits that shellfish cannot exceed; otherwise, harvesting and farming are temporarily and precautionary closed. These limits are 160 µg OA (okadaic acid) eq. kg^{-1} for DSP, 20 mg DA (domoic acid) eq. kg^{-1} for ASP, and 800 µg STX (saxitoxins) eq. kg^{-1} for PSP [4].

Therefore, it is crucial to develop strategies that allow predicting shellfish contamination to anticipate and mitigate the negative impacts of the sudden closure of shellfish harvesting areas. Several strategies have been developed to forecast HAB events and shellfish contamination based on machine-learning models, such as autoregressive models [5], neural networks [6–8], random forest models [9], and bayesian networks (BNs) [10].

HAB events and biotoxins shellfish contamination are influenced and regulated by atmospheric, oceanographic, and biological factors, which can be interpreted as natural predictors of biotoxins concentration and consequently of HAB events [3]. Hence the interest in studying how the relationship between the different variables and how they contribute to HAB onset and development, influencing the biotoxins concentration level in shellfish and the closures of the shellfish production areas.

Here, we present an analysis of multivariate time series (MTS) of several meteorological and biological variables (temperature, wind, precipitation, chlorophyll) to study the relationship between these available MTS with the DSP toxins concentration time series and, consequently, to try to understand the variables that can be useful in shellfish contamination forecasting. We used the Pearson correlation and the time series regression model to study linear relationships. Moreover, we used the Granger causality test for a causality analysis. Finally, dynamic Bayesian networks were modeled. The present study uses data from the Portuguese coast (https://www.ipma.pt/), but the proposed framework is directly applicable to other countries and shellfish production areas.

2   Methods

2.1   Data Sources and Preparation

All the work presented here is based on data obtained from different sources collected from 2015 to 2020 for 44 shellfish production areas (coastal and estuarine-lagoon zones) in Portugal. The concentrations of DSP, ASP, and PSP toxins for different species of bivalve molluscs were monitored by the Portuguese Institute of Sea and Atmosphere (IPMA) and made available through the website monthly report (https://www.ipma.pt/). These data are complemented with environmental and meteorological data, daily collected by IPMA, including mean air temperature, mean wind intensity, and precipitation. On the other hand, mean sea surface temperature (SST) and chlorophyll-a (chl-a) concentration data along the Portuguese coast are also available from the Copernicus Marine Environment Monitoring Service (CMEMS) website (https://marine.copernicus.eu/).

This study focused on studying the relationship between the abovementioned environmental and meteorological conditions and the concentrations of diarrhetic shellfish poison (DSP) toxins in mussels *Mytilus galloprovincialis*. DSP biotoxins are the most common on the Portuguese coast, with more frequency on values above the regulatory limit. Mussels are widely used as an indicator species for this toxin type because they have high filtration rates and have the capacity to represent the amount of toxins available in the environment once a HAB event initiates. The data was obtained from a sampling location at Ria de Aveiro (RIAV1), a critical shellfish production area, regarding both the frequency and intensity of shellfish contamination.

With all these data, a MTS was created with a weekly frequency index from 2015/01/01 to 2020/12/31 (312 weeks in total), where the weekly record value corresponds to the moving average of the seven days around the new index date in the center. The variables of the MTS are shown in Table 1.

Table 1. Variables description of the MTS created. IQR is the interquartile range and SD is the standard deviation.

Variable	Unit	Mean	IQR	SD
DSP toxins concentration	μg OA equiv. kg^{-1}	277.00	405.50	235.17
Mean air temperature	°C	15.78	6.16	3.79
Mean wind speed	m s^{-1}	2.89	0.73	1.05
Mean of accumulated precipitation	mm	2.41	1.79	5.62
Temperature amplitude	°C	7.58	3.63	2.98
Mean sea surface temperature	K	288.80	3.40	1.81
Mean of chlorophyll-a concentration	mg m^{-3}	3.51	2.55	2.40

2.2   Time Series Modelling

Time Series Regression Models The linear model applied in the time series context assumes that some output or dependent time series, x_t, for $t = 1, \ldots, n$, is expressed as a linear combination of inputs or independent series, $z_{t1}, z_{t2}, \ldots, z_{tq}$ [12]:

$$x_t = \beta_1 z_{t1} + \beta_2 z_{t2} + \ldots + \beta_q z_{tq} + w_t, \tag{1}$$

where $\beta_1, \ldots, \beta_q$ are the regression coefficients and w_t is a random error or noise of independent and identically distributed normal variables with mean zero and variance σ^2. The coefficients β in the linear combinations can be estimated by the least squares method, providing a method for modeling x_t in terms of the inputs by minimizing the error sum of squares [11,12]:

$$\sum_{t=1}^{n} w_t^2 = \sum_{t=1}^{n} (x_t - \beta_1 z_{t1} - \beta_2 z_{t2} - \ldots - \beta_q z_{tq})^2. \tag{2}$$

It is also possible to express x_t as a linear combination of previous values $x_{t-1}, x_{t-2}, \ldots, x_{t-p}$ of the currently observed series. Furthermore, the outputs x_t may also depend on lagged values of another series that can influence [12].

Granger Causality Test The Granger causality test is a statistical hypothesis test widely used in economics and econometrics to investigate dependence relations between time series [13]. Instead of only studying the linear correlations between time series, the Granger causality test aims to test causality by determining the ability to predict or forecast the future values of a time series using prior values of another time series [13,14]. To perform a test for Granger causality, the **grangertest** function in R statistical software was used.

Dynamic Bayesian Networks A BN is defined as a directed acyclic graph (DAG) and an associated joint probability distribution (JPD). A BN model with N nodes can be represented as a triple $\mathbf{B} = (\mathbf{X}, \text{G}, \Theta)$, where $\mathbf{X} = \{X_1, \ldots, X_n\}$ is an n-dimensional finite random vector, G stands for a DAG with N nodes, and Θ stands for the JPD of the BN model [15].

A BN defines a unique JPD given by the product, over all the nodes of the graph, of a conditional probability distribution for each node conditioned on its parents. Assuming $Pa(X_i)$ is the parent set node of X_i in G, the conditional probability distribution of X_i is denoted by $P(X_i|Pa(X_i))$ [15,16].

For a BN, the JPD of $P(X_1, \ldots, X_N)$ is given by:

$$P(X_1, ..X_N) = \prod_{X_i \in \{X_1, \ldots X_N\}} P(X_i|Pa(X_i)). \tag{3}$$

Dynamic Bayesian Networks (DBNs) are an extension of BNs to represent the evolution in time of a system by introducing relevant temporal dependencies that capture the dynamic behaviors of domain variables between representations of the static network at different time slices [17,18].

The transition model from the previous time slice to the current time slice for a DBN can be expressed as:

$$P(X_t|X_{t-1}) = \prod_{i=1}^{N} P(X_t^i|Pa(X_t^i)), \tag{4}$$

where X_t^i is the ith node at time t and $Pa(X_t^i)$ is the parent nodes of X_t^i in G. The JPD for a DBN for $t = 1$ to $t = T$ (T time slices) is defined as:

$$P(X_{1:T}) = \prod_{t=1}^{T}\prod_{i=1}^{N} P(X_t^i|Pa(X_t^i)). \tag{5}$$

Unlike conventional BNs, DBNs are more appropriate for monitoring and forecasting the future probability of a node based on current observation, which makes it convenient for dynamic analysis. In fact, DBNs are capable of representing the state of all variables at any time with respect to BN, being allowed not only intra-slice connections, which are the connections within the time slices but also inter-slice connections, which are connections between variables from different slices [17].

The MAESTRO web tool (https://vascocandeias.github.io/maestro/) was used to obtain and model the DBN [19–21]. The MTS CSV file must be discretised and prepared to train a DBN model using MAESTRO. The DSP toxins concentration time series (TS) was discretized in two levels: 1 if the concentration is above the legal safety limit (160 µg/kg) or 0 if it is below. The rainfall TS was also discretized in two levels: 1 if there was precipitation or 0 if there was not. The TS was discretized in two levels for the remaining variables: L if the value is below the mean or H if it is above. The scoring function used to train the DBNs was the minimum description length (MDL), for different time lags.

3   Results and Discussion

3.1   Correlation Analysis

Firstly, the Pearson correlation coefficient was used to study the relationship between the concentration of DSP toxins and the other variables of interest [22]. Different time lags were used to study the correlation between the current value of DSP toxins concentration in a time step and the values of the other variables in the previous weeks. The results are shown in Table 2.

The variables found significantly positively correlated with DSP toxins concentration were the mean temperature, mean SST, and chl-a concentration (Table 2). The highest Pearson correlation values were obtained for mean temperature and SST variables for the one-week lag, which indicates that the values of these variables are associated with the concentration of DSP toxins of the next week and, consequently, may be used to anticipate HAB events.

3.2 Causality Analysis

Correlation by itself does not imply causality (a cause-and-effect relationship). Hence, the Granger causality test for different time lags was used to provide a more stringent criterion for causality than simply observing a high correlation with some delay.

In agreement with the results obtained for the correlations, the mean air temperature and SST were the variables found significant for the Granger test (Table 3), which means that the time series of these variables are helpful in forecasting the DSP toxins concentration time series for time lags less than or equal to three weeks. After a lag of 5 weeks, only mean temperature shows any effect on the DSP toxins concentration.

Table 2. Pearson correlation coefficient between the concentration of DSP toxins concentration and the variables studied for different time lags. * corresponds to significant correlations (p-value<0.05).

Lag	Temperature	Wind intesity	Rainfall	Amplitude	SST	Chl-a
0	0.369*	0.029	−0.060	−0.041	0.415*	0.291*
1	0.480*	0.123	−0.041	−0.005	0.459*	0.233*
2	0.444*	0.098	−0.015	−0.033	0.432*	0.201*
3	0.414*	0.116*	−0.031	−0.016	0.385*	0.203
4	0.386*	0.086	−0.020	−0.002	0.344*	0.174*
5	0.404*	0.068	−0.052	0.051	0.312*	0.160*
6	0.364*	0.086	−0.077	0.048	0.264*	0.135*
7	0.310*	0.082	−0.022	0.053	0.225*	0.072
8	0.307*	0.103	−0.069	0.035	0.182*	0.098
9	0.286*	0.104	−0.070	−0.012	0.141*	0.112
10	0.243*	0.090	−0.078	−0.031	0.104	0.070

Table 3. Granger causality test p-values for all the variables with different time lags. * corresponds to significant correlations (p-value<0.05).

Lag	Temperature	Wind intesity	Rainfall	Amplitude	SST	Chl-a
1	5.299×10^{-6}*	0.10228	0.42591	0.75670	0.00952*	0.35629
2	2.019×10^{-5}*	0.29785	0.62695	0.65230	0.04478*	0.65192
3	8.126×10^{-5}*	0.39066	0.67244	0.82353	0.02622*	0.67551
4	0.00022*	0.49599	0.81791	0.91941	0.06185	0.76524
5	0.00015*	0.64648	0.72347	0.60070	0.09991	0.86043
6	0.00036*	0.60034	0.71055	0.70795	0.07943	0.93001
7	0.00041*	0.72799	0.51572	0.74259	0.13310	0.71755
8	0.00027*	0.70621	0.44094	0.79251	0.21137	0.40316
9	0.00056*	0.77001	0.53472	0.59109	0.29538	0.44575
10	0.00108*	0.86088	0.61113	0.62014	0.38949	0.30781

3.3 Time Series Regression Models

A time series regression model using least square estimation was also performed to study the linear combinations relationships between the different variables and the DSP toxin concentration. The results for different time lags are shown in Table 4. The best regression model was obtained using one-week lagged variables compared to the DSP toxin concentration ($R^2 = 0.263$). In agreement with the results obtained in the previous sections, the variables that contribute significantly to the regression model were the mean SST ($\beta_{sst} = 0.264$), the mean air temperature ($\beta_{temperature} = 0.234$), the mean wind intensity ($\beta_{wind} = 0.154$), and the chl-a concentration ($\beta_{chl\text{-}a} = 0.114$). The true values of DSP toxins concentration and the fitted values for the one-week lag model are compared in Fig. 1. The prediction of the occurrence or non-occurrence of a HAB event (concentration of DSP toxins above the safety limit defined) using the linear regression model for a one-week lag was corrected for 213 (68.5%) weeks, of which 126 weeks correspond to the occurrence of a HAB event and 87 weeks correspond to a DSP toxins concentration value below 160 μg OA equiv. kg^{-1}.

When the time lag is increased, the R^2 of the model decreases substantially, and only mean air temperature or SST (for lag 9 and 10) are found significant.

The results obtained in the previous sections show that the mean SST and air temperature are the variables with the highest predictive power in relation to the DSP toxins concentration variable for a lag of one or two weeks. The time series of these variables (Fig. 2) show concordance between the variations of DSP toxins concentration through time and the variations of the mean SST and air temperature.

Table 4. R^2, and coefficient values β of the variables for the time series regression models for different lags. * corresponds to variables with p-values<0.05.

Lag	R^2	Temperature	Wind intensity	Rainfall	Amplitude	SST	Chl-a
0	0.249	0.038	0.138*	−0.016	−0.021	0.419*	0.144*
1	**0.263**	0.234*	0.154*	0.029	0.039	0.264*	0.114*
2	0.219	0.210*	0.108	0.051	0.005	0.257*	0.099
3	0.189	0.222*	0.135*	0.021	0.021	0.197*	0.103
4	0.150	0.258*	0.092	0.037	0.032	0.129	0.080
5	0.159	0.406*	0.075	0.011	0.083	−0.022	0.046
6	0.131	0.397*	0.102	−0.041	0.076	−0.063	0.023
7	0.093	0.342*	0.092	0.014	0.108	−0.037	−0.025
8	0.102	0.424*	0.106	−0.059	0.064	−0.165	0.003
9	0.099	0.456*	0.079	−0.079	−0.006	−0.248*	0.038
10	0.077	0.431*	0.062	−0.103	−0.033	−0.262*	0.006

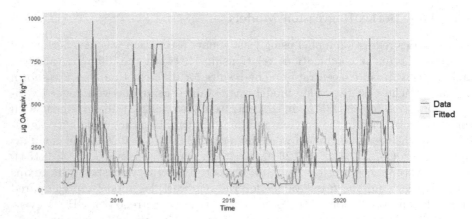

Fig. 1. Time plot of the measured DSP toxins concentration and the predicted DSP toxins concentration for the linear regression model with a one-week lag. The black line indicates the safety limit for DSP toxins concentration.

3.4   Dynamic Bayesian Network

As shown in the previous section (Table 4), the R^2 values obtained for the linear regression models were relatively low ($R^2 = 0.263$). Thus, DBNs were used to study and capture non-linear relationships between the variables using the MAESTRO tool.

Firstly, DBNs were applied for all the variables for the six different years (2015–2020), with different time lags. The network that showed more relationships between the variables was the one referring to the year 2015. In fact, observing Table 5, 2015 is the year with the least missing values for the variables under study and, therefore, with the least imputed values, which may explain the

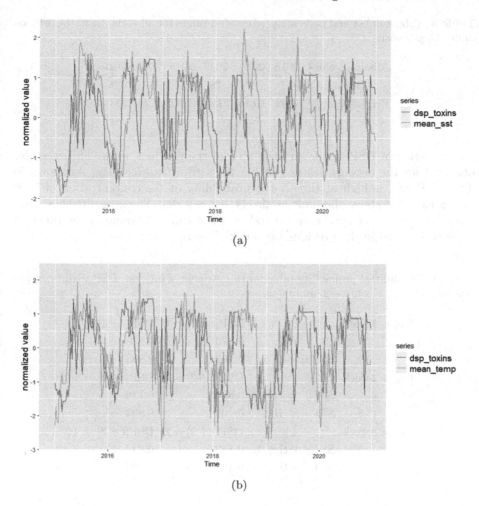

Fig. 2. Time plots of DSP toxins concentration and **a** sea surface temperature or **b** mean air temperature. The data were normalized using the logarithm of 2 of the scaled data.

better performance of the models given the higher power. For this reason, we will analyze the DBNs for the 2015 year to minimize the impact of the imputation methods used, whose impact can be further addressed in the future.

Using MAESTRO, the DBNs learned for one and two-week lags for all the variables are shown in Fig. 3a and b, respectively. The results obtained in Fig. 3a and Table 6 show that the probability of DSP toxins concentration being higher than the legal limit in time $t+1$ when SST was low in time t, was 0.130. On the other hand, if SST is high in time t, the probability of DSP concentration being above the limit is 0.893, which again shows a positive relationship between the

Table 5. Total number and percentage of missing values for all variables in the original datasets, per year.

Missing Values	2015	2016	2017	2018	2019	2020
Total	11	37	78	27	30	73
Percentage (%)	3.02	10.16	21.43	7.42	8.24	20.05

concentration of DSP toxins and the SST of the previous week. This was also observed for the network learned in Fig. 3b with a two-week lag. As shown in Table 6, if SST is high at time t, the probability of the concentration of DSP biotoxins being above the limit at time $t + 2$ is 0.893. These results show that the concentration of DSP may depend on the mean SST value in the previous week $(t - 1)$ and in the previous two weeks $(t - 2)$.

Table 6. Conditional probability table for the variable of interest, DSP toxins concentration, for week $t + 1$, $t + 2$, and $t + 3$.

Lag = 1 week		$DSP[t + 1] = 0$	$DSP[t + 1] = 1$
	$SST[t] = L$	0.870	0.130
	$SST[t] = H$	0.107	0.893
Lag = 2 week		$DSP[t + 2] = 0$	$DSP[t + 2] = 1$
	$SST[t] = L$	0.864	0.136
	$SST[t] = H$	0.107	0.893
Lag = 3 week		$DSP[t + 3] = 0$	$DSP[t + 3] = 1$
	$SST[t + 1] = L$	0.857	0.143
	$SST[t + 1] = H$	0.107	0.893

A DBN was also learned for a three-week lag. However, the probability of the concentration of DSP toxins being high or low at week $t + 3$ does not depend on the SST value at week t, depending only on the SST value at week $t + 1$ (Table 6). These results agree with those obtained using the DBN with one and two-week lags since there is only a relation between the concentration of DSP toxin and the mean SST considering the SST values of the previous week or the previous two weeks.

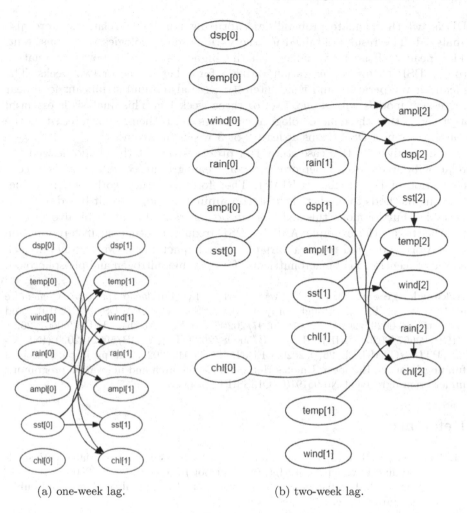

(a) one-week lag.   (b) two-week lag.

Fig. 3. DBNs learned by MAESTRO, for all the variables, for 2015, considering two different lags.

4   Conclusion

HAB are a natural phenomenon influenced by several meteorological and biological factors that cause sudden closures to the shellfish Portuguese production areas, leading to severe economic losses. Thus, it is crucial to study the relationship between meteorological and biological variables with the biotoxins level in shellfish to support the production sector in mitigating the negative impacts of HAB.

Here, we studied the linear relationships between the concentration of DSP toxins and several variables for different time lags using Pearson's correlation coefficient and time series regression models. The Granger causality test and

DBNs, which calculate probabilities capturing non-linear relations, were also analyzed. The results obtained for the various methodologies were consistent. The mean SST is the variable with the highest predictive power in relation to the DSP toxins concentration variable for a lag of one or two weeks. The mean air temperature and wind intensity were also found significant for linear regression models with a one, two, or three-week lag. This analysis is essential as it shows that these meteorological variables can be helpful for forecasting the concentration of DSP toxins at least 2 or 3 weeks in advance.

The analysis of this case study is a proof-of-concept that hypothesized the relation between several meteorological or oceanographic conditions and the concentration of DSP toxins in RIAV1. Therefore, as future work, new machine-learning methods to predict shellfish contamination can be built based on these variables. Furthermore, this analysis can be generalized to other bivalve species, to other toxins (for example, ASP and PSP toxins), to other shellfish production areas worldwide, and to other variables that impact the seawater column, such as the concentration of macronutrients (for example, nitrogen and phosphorous).

Acknowledgment. This work was funded by Fundação para a Ciência e a Tecnologia (FCT) through project MATISSE (DSAIPA/DS/0026/2019), and also UIDB/00297/2020, UIDP/00297/2020 (NOVA Math), UIDB/00667/2020, UIDP/00667/2020 (UNIDEMI), UIDB/50008/2020 (IT), UIDB/50021/2020 (INESC-ID), PTDC/CTM-REF/2679/2020, CEECINST/00042/2021. This project has received funding from the European Union's Horizon 2020 research and innovation programme under grant agreement No 951970 - OLISSIPO project.

References

1. Chinabut, S., Somsiri, T., Limsuwan, C., Lewis, S.: Problems associated with shell-fish farming. Rev. Sci. Tech. (Int. Off. Epizoot.) **25**(2), 627–635 (2006)
2. Grattan, L.M., Holobaugh, S., Morris, J.G., Jr.: Harmful algal blooms and public health. Harmful Algae **57**, 2–8 (2016)
3. Zohdi, E., Abbaspour, M.: Harmful algal blooms (red tide): a review of causes, impacts and approaches to monitoring and prediction. Int. J. Environ. Sci. Technol. **16**, 1789–1806 (2019)
4. Commission, E.: Commission regulation (EC) No 853/2004 of the European parliament and of the council of 29 April 2004 laying down specific hygiene rules for on the hygiene of foodstuffs. Off. J. Eur. Union L **139**, 55–205 (2004)
5. Lui, G.C., Li, W.K., Leung, K.M., Lee, J.H., Jayawardena, A.W.: Modelling algal blooms using vector autoregressive model with exogenous variables and long memory filter. Ecol. Model. **200**(1–2), 130–138 (2007)
6. Lee, S., Lee, D.: Improved prediction of harmful algal blooms in four Major South Korea's Rivers using deep learning models. Int. J. Environ. Res. Public Health **15**(7), 1322 (2018)
7. Cruz, R.C., Costa, P.R., Krippahl, L., Lopes, M.B.: Forecasting biotoxin contamination in mussels across production areas of the Portuguese coast with Artificial Neural Networks. Knowl.-Based Syst. **257**, 109895 (2022)

8. Grasso, I., Archer, S.D., Burnell, C., Tupper, B., Rauschenberg, C., Kanwit, K., Record, N.R.: The hunt for red tides: deep learning algorithm forecasts shellfish toxicity at site scales in coastal Maine. Ecosphere **10**(12), e02960 (2019)
9. Harley, J.R., Lanphier, K., Kennedy, E., Whitehead, C., Bidlack, A.: Random forest classification to determine environmental drivers and forecast paralytic shellfish toxins in Southeast Alaska with high temporal resolution. Harmful Algae **99**, 101918 (2020)
10. Wang, X., Bouzembrak, Y., Marvin, H.J., Clarke, D., Butler, F.: Bayesian Networks modeling of diarrhetic shellfish poisoning in Mytilus edulis harvested in Bantry Bay, Ireland. Harmful algae **112**, 102171 (2022)
11. Hyndman, R.J., Athanasopoulos, G.: Forecasting: Principles and Practice, 2nd edn. OTexts: Melbourne, Australia. OTexts.com/fpp2 (2018)
12. Shumway, R.H., Stoffer, D.S., Stoffer, D.S.: Time Series Analysis and Its Applications, vol. 3. Springer, New York (2000)
13. Diks, C., Panchenko, V.: A new statistic and practical guidelines for nonparametric Granger causality testing. J. Econ. Dyn. Control **30**(9–10), 1647–1669 (2006)
14. Granger, C.W.: Investigating causal relations by econometric models and cross-spectral methods. Econ.: J. Econ. Soc. 424–438 (1969)
15. Carvalho, A.M.: Scoring functions for learning Bayesian networks INESC-ID Tecnical Report 54/2009 Apr 2009 (2009)
16. Ben-Gal, I. (2008). Bayesian networks. In: Encyclopedia of Statistics in Quality and Reliability, vol.1
17. Murphy, K.P.: Dynamic Bayesian Networks: Representation, Inference and Learning. University of California, Berkeley (2002)
18. Mihajlovic, V., Petkovic, M.: Dynamic bayesian networks: a state of the art. University of Twente Document Repository (2001)
19. Monteiro, J.L., Vinga, S., Carvalho, A.M.: Polynomial-time algorithm for learning optimal tree-augmented dynamic Bayesian networks. In: UAI, pp. 622–631 (2015)
20. Candeias, V.: Cloud-based web application for multivariate time series analysis. MSc Thesis, Instituto Superior Técnico, Universidade de Lisboa (2021)
21. Serras, J.L., Vinga, S., Carvalho, A.M.: Outlier detection for multivariate time series using dynamic Bayesian networks. Appl. Sci. **11**(4), 1955 (2021)
22. Patrício, A., Lopes, M.B., Costa, P.R., Costa, R.S., Henriques, R., Vinga, S.: Time-lagged correlation analysis of shellfish toxicity reveals predictive links to adjacent areas, species, and environmental conditions. Toxins **14**(10), 679 (2022)

Sound-Based Anomalies Detection
in Agricultural Robotics Application

André Rodrigues Baltazar[1,2](✉) iD, Filipe Neves dos Santos[1] iD,
Salviano Pinto Soares[2,4] iD, António Paulo Moreira[1,3] iD,
and José Boaventura Cunha[1,2] iD

[1] CRIIS-Centre for Robotics in Industry and Intelligent Systems, INESC
TEC-Institute for Systems and Computer Engineering, Technology and Science,
4200-465 Porto, Portugal
[2] ECT-School of Science and Technology, UTAD-University of Trás-os-Montes and
Alto Douro, 5000-801 Vila Real, Portugal
andre.r.baltazar@inesctec.pt
[3] FEUP-Faculty of Engineering, University of Porto, 4200-465 Porto, Portugal
[4] IEETA—Institute of Electronics and Informatics Engineering of Aveiro, UA
Campus, 3810-193 Aveiro, Portugal

Abstract. Agricultural robots are exposed to adverse conditions reducing the components' lifetime. To reduce the number of inspection, repair and maintenance activities, we propose using audio-based systems to diagnose and detect anomalies in these robots. Audio-based systems are non-destructive/intrusive solutions. Besides, it provides a significant amount of data to diagnose problems and for a wiser scheduler for preventive activities. So, in this work, we installed two microphones in an agricultural robot with a mowing tool. Real audio data was collected with the robotic mowing tool operating in several conditions and stages. Besides, a Sound-based Anomalies Detector (SAD) is proposed and tested with this dataset. The SAD considers a short-time Fourier transform (STFT) computation stage connected to a Support Vector Machine (SVM) classifier. The results with the collected dataset showed an F1 score between 95% and 100% in detecting anomalies in a mowing robot operation.

Keywords: Anomalies Detection · Mowing · Sound-based · STFT

1 Introduction

Environmental sound recognition (ESR) is a problem that has been receiving increasing attention in recent years, and there are different challenges to environmental sound classification [4].

Acoustic Emission (AE) systems for operation monitoring, namely in agricultural robotics applications, have two main advantages: it is a non-destructive technique and involves a minimum machine change for installation [9].

N. Moniz et al. (Eds.): EPIA 2023, LNAI 14116, pp. 338–350, 2023.
https://doi.org/10.1007/978-3-031-49011-8_27

Nowadays, a single-channel microphone is available in all tablets, mobile phones, augmented reality helmets and headsets. The audio signals captured by the microphone can be processed in real-time with relatively lower computational cost [2].

All these factors have meant that in recent years there have been many audio-based works, especially in predictive maintenance [6] and anomaly detection [14] in industrial environments.

The work [14] proposed an acoustic-based anomaly detection system to detect anomalies in machine motion sounds. It records acoustic signals from machines and uses STFT to convert them into spectrogram images. These images are further classified using Convolutional Neural Network (CNN) to detect anomalies in a manufacturing environment.

The approach [15] incorporates IoT devices, neural networks and sound analysis to avoid accidental carrier bearings damage on an assembly conveyor. The resulting system could predict failures that would eventually require an unexpected production stoppage.

In the same year [12] presented a ground robot to inspect conveyor structures. The robot has a sensor set for belt conveyor inspection to collect visual, thermal, acoustic and vibration data. They recorded noises emitted by healthy and damaged bearings based on experienced inspectors that can distinguish them. Then the Fast Fourier Transform (FFT) signal was extracted from the raw record and used in a Random Forest algorithm, obtaining a 95% accuracy score.

In some situations, detecting malfunctions is essential, but this means putting the equipment into an operation state that could be detrimental. For example, in the case of a conveyor belt, it is necessary to detect the need to replace bearings. Ideally, this should be done before the bearings destroy themselves and cause other damage to adjacent components.

In this situation, carrying out a sound-based collection where the bearings are damaged would be necessary, which involves purposely causing damage to these components. In order to avoid this, there are techniques used to create malfunction signals in an alternative way without them having to be collected directly from the machine.

The subsequent four works presented are based on a widespread method: an Autoencoder. An Autoencoder is a semi-supervised learning method commonly used in image reconstruction and denoising [16].

The first work [20] developed a framework to detect anomalies in industrial arms using internal sound sensors. It is based on an Autoencoder that uses standard state signals of the robots, and abnormal states are found from high reconstruction errors. The microphones were attached to stethoscopes, which were then attached to the robot joints. It used STFT to extract the features from the sounds to create spectrogram images.

The second work [9] used a CNN architecture based on a variational Autoencoder to differentiate the abnormal regimes from normal ones in a tribometer. With that, it was possible to train the Machine Learning (ML) algorithms only with the sound data from a microphone related to the regular regime. As a result, these algorithms could detect when a sound associated with an abnormal regime arrives.

The third work [2] developed a real-time Acoustic Anomaly Detection (AAD) system using Autoencoder models in industrial environments.

The fourth work [19] proposed an anomaly detection method based on a deep Autoencoder model. In addition to data from a microphone, it uses data provided by cameras and a force-torque sensor. The system aims to detect the object slip of mobile manipulation robots. The results showed that the performance is better when using multimodal sensors compared to using single sensors independently.

Another solution when you do not have enough fault or error samples is to use data augmentation. Becker et al. proposed a method to detect acoustic cues and errors in a Fused Deposition Modeling printer. It used time stretching, pitch shifting and amplifying to obtain data augmentation. From all the data (augmented and non-augmented), spectrograms were extracted and used these features as input for a Long Short-Term Memory (LSTM) neural network model [3]. Another work used sound measurements to monitor the movements of a 3D printer [18].

In another application area, an anomaly detection algorithm was developed with force, sound and kinematic signals collected from an assistive robot performing different tasks [10].

Although much of the existing work concerns anomaly detection, navigation systems for autonomous agricultural vehicles have also been based on sound-based positioning systems. This approach was applied in outdoor environments [17], and in a greenhouse [7].

All the works mentioned show the feasibility of machine learning methods for environmental sound recognition. In Table 1 is presented a summary of the most relevant works related to anomaly detection. All these works are applied in industrial environments.

In the context of robotics development for agriculture, many solutions would also benefit from a monitoring and anomaly detection system inspired by the works presented in this section. These technologies are implemented to be used daily, often autonomously, and the need for unexpected maintenance can bring different consequences for the farmer.

Thus, in this work, we started with a modular robotic platform with an implement used to cut grass and implemented a system capable of monitoring and detecting anomalies in the operation of this robot.

The remainder of this paper is structured as follows: Sect. 2 introduces the robotic platform used and the modifications needed to perform this work. Section 3 describes the materials and methods for audio data collecting, preprocessing, training and evaluation. Finally, Sect. 4 presents the SVM results using six different descriptors. This is followed by some conclusions and suggestions for future work in Sect. 5.

Table 1. Anomaly detection sound-based approaches comparison.

Work	Application	Signal Preprocessing	Anomaly Detection
[14]	Anomaly detection system to protec smart manufacturing environments	STFT	CNN
[20]	Detecting anomalies in an industrial robot arm system	STFT	Autoencoder
[9]	Identifying normal and abnormal regimes in tribological applications	Downsample of the data from 102.4 kHz to 20 kHz and application of a Butterworth low pass filter of 20 kHz	CNN architecture based on a variational Autoencoder
[3]	Detecting flaws and errors in a Fused Deposition Modeling printer	STFT	LSTM
[2]	Anomaly detection system to detect and interfere with abnormal events in industrial environments	STFT	Autoencoder
[19]	Multimodal anomaly detection for object slip perception of mobile manipulation robots	Mel Frequency Cepstral Coefficients	Autoencoder
[6]	Predictive maintenance in industrial environments	Data augmentation by changing the pitch or by performing audio time stretching	Autoencoder
[12]	Bearing fault detection using sound in outdoor industrial inspection	STFT	Random Forest

2   System Design

This work was developed using a modular and precision terrestrial robot, Modular-E. This robot can operate autonomously on rugged terrain with steep slopes and under the most diverse ground conditions.

A modular agricultural robot can have different implements attached to its structure. This application uses a Mowing Intelligent Tool (MowIT), which is responsible for maintaining the vegetation cover in vineyards and orchards, e.g.

Modular-E and MowIT (Fig. 1) were developed from scratch by INESC TEC.

MowIT is based on a single 3kW electric motor but has three distinct cutting axes using a belt system. It is possible to apply different cutting tools compatible with a brush cutter on these axes. At this point, two cutting tools are used: trimmer lines and blades (Fig. 2).

The microphones used in this work were placed close to the electric motor.

3   Materials and Methods

This section presents how the audio data was acquired and the experimental setup used. Next, the pre-processing and dataset generation are exposed, and finally, the developed classifier and the metrics to evaluate its performance are presented.

Fig. 1. Robotic platform used, composed by a modular terrestrial robot, Modular-E and a Mowing Intelligent Tool (MowIT).

Fig. 2. Different cutting tools used in the Mowing Intelligent Tool (MowIT): blades (**left**) and trimmer lines (**right**).

3.1   Data Acquisition

Two different microphones were used to collect the sound samples, recording the audio with just one single channel, with a sampling rate of 44100 Hz and 16 bits of resolution. The data provided by an inertial measurement unit (IMU) was also recorded since that was already integrated into the MowIT.

With this experimental setup integrated into the robotic platform, two different data collections were performed in different open-air environments with grass to cut.

In each collection, eight different sample sets were made, five with the machine cutting using a trimmer line and the other three using the blades. Various combinations were used in each set, and tools were or were not placed on each of the three cutting axes of the MowIT. For each group, the acquisitions were designated from 0 to 7.

Each folder of the first collection is a combination containing two audio files, one for each microphone used, the IMU data and a photograph of the lower part of the MowIT to understand the configuration used.

In the second collection, to improve the variety of data, three distinct subsets were performed for combination: the first with the MowIT turned on but not cutting grass and the next two cutting grass.

In samples 4 and 7, there is one audio where the MowIT cuts but stops due to motor stress. In sample 6, the initial recording without cutting grass was not made, and only the two recordings were made cutting grass.

Considering the proposed objectives for this work, the IMU data and the audio records with the blades will not be deemed. In other words, just the audios where the MowIT is cutting with the trimmer line are considered.

3.2   Pre-processing and Dataset Generation

STFT is used to analyse the frequency and phase content of multiple signal sections over time. The data to be transformed is divided into multiple parts, and then there is an iterative process where each of these parts is multiplied by a window function to obtain the Discrete Fourier transform using STFT [5,8,13]. The complex result is added to a matrix that stores each point in time and frequency.

In this work, it was used two different window functions: a Boxcar and a Hamming window. The size of the window determines both the temporal precision and spectral resolution. If the time window is narrow, it results in a few data points with few frequencies. As the time window gets longer, the frequency content increases, increasing the frequency resolution. However, the temporal precision will decrease because it integrates activity over extended periods.

This way, the window size was defined as equal to the number of samples in one second (44100), resulting in a length of one second to avoid aliasing. Then, it was iteratively reduced until it affected the system's performance. It also used a 90% overlap between the multiple parts in which the signal is divided.

Each column of the resulting STFT matrix contains the values for a specific frequency, depending on the window size, at a particular time. The first step is calculating the absolute value (magnitude) for every point (the phase value was not used). Each column of the matrix is an array corresponding to a time interval. Each position of this array contains the absolute value of a given frequency range.

For example, we obtain an array with size 22051 for a one-second window size, obtaining an interval of 1 Hz between each position. By applying the STFT to a ten-second signal with a window size equivalent to one second and an overlap of 90% we can extract about one hundred arrays of 22051 positions each from this signal.

All of these arrays are stored as a single sample.

To decrease the size of each sample, it was calculated the magnitude means for sequential 200 array values, inspired in [12]. This results in a decrease in the number of points per sample 200 times. Taking the previous example from the original 22051 positions results in an array with a size of 110. In this way, for each analysed audio, are created two different groups of data containing multiple samples.

Each sample generated in this pre-processing phase will then be assigned a class according to the problem. The sound-based system developed in this work has two main components: monitoring and anomalies detection.

Regarding monitoring, the system should be able to perceive whether or not MowIT is cutting grass when it is working. As for the anomalies detection, it should also be able to detect if it is missing a trimmer line in any of the three cutting axes.

For this purpose, one type of dataset was created for each main component referred to. In the monitoring, we have two different classes: "Cutting" (C) and "Not Cutting" (NC). If the sample resulted from an audio where MowIT was cutting grass, it is labelled as C; conversely, if it is the result of an audio where it is not cutting grass, it is labelled as NC.

In anomalies detection, there are four different classes: "Cutting with three trimmer lines" (CW3), "Cutting with less than three trimmer lines" (CWL3), "Not cutting with three trimmer lines" (NCW3) and "Not cutting with less than three trimmer lines" (NCWL3).

For each class was created a different folder, and inside it are the raw data and the compute means resulting from the STFT, one for each window function used. The dataset is publicly accessible at [1].

3.3 Data Training and Evaluation

We propose an approach called Sound-based Anomalies Detector (SAD). For this approach, six descriptors (Table 2) were designed and tested. These descriptors were reached by combining two main variables: the array size containing the audio pre-processing result and the window function used in the STFT computation. Regarding the array size, the first option, STFT, is to use the results from the absolute values for every point that resulted from the STFT. The second option, STFT Average, considers the amplitude means for sequential 200-band sections.

A third option was created based on the Principal Component Analysis (PCA) method in computing the principal components of the STFT Average data and using them as a descriptor. In this way, the Boxcar and Hamming window is used with each of these three methods (STFT, STFT Average and STFT PCA).

The first step is to read the data created in the pre-processing phase according to the descriptor. Each descriptor was used as the input for the SVM classifier (version 1.1.2 from scikit-learn[11]).

Since the dataset is not perfectly balanced, the F1 score was used to validate the SAD performance instead of the accuracy. The F1 score (Eq. 3) is the first harmonic mean between Recall (Eq. 1) and Precision (Eq. 2). We also represent the confusion matrix for a better understanding of the results.

$$Recall = \frac{TP}{AllGroundTruths} \tag{1}$$

$$Precision = \frac{TP}{AllDetections} \tag{2}$$

Table 2. Different descriptors identification according to the combination of the array size (STFT, STFT Average or STFT PCA) and the window function (Boxcar or Hamming).

Descriptor	STFT	STFT Average	STFT PCA	Boxcar	Hamming
1	X			X	
2	X				X
3		X		X	
4		X			X
5			X	X	
6			X		X

$$F1Score = 2 \times \frac{Precision \times Recall}{Precision + Recall} \tag{3}$$

In Fig. 3 are presented the different components of the SAD system: the sound acquisition with the microphone; the pre-processing phase, applying the STFT to the signals recorded; dataset construction with the resulting STFT data and calculation of the STFT Average and STFT PCA; use of an SVM classifier; and validation of the system in anomaly detection.

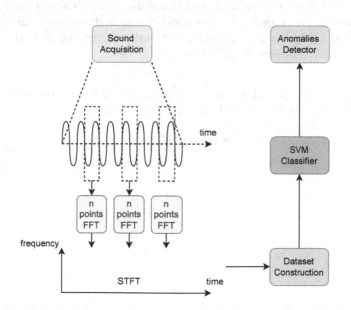

Fig. 3. Sound-based Anomalies Detector (SAD) system architecture.

4   Results and Discussion

The SAD approach's performance in perceiving if the MowIT is cutting grass and if there is some trimmer line missing was evaluated. This evaluation is divided into two parts: monitoring and anomaly detection.

All six descriptors were considered in each part (Table 2). To train the SVM, 80% of the data was used, and the remaining 20% was used to validate and test its performance.

Before performing the tests with the six descriptors, choosing the ideal size for the window function to be used in the STFT computation was necessary. For this purpose, descriptor three was used with the data from the audio files in which MowIT is cutting grass and those not cutting grass.

Several iterative tests were performed where the window size was divided by two at each iteration, starting at one second. The behaviour was measured with the F1 score metric. With this, it was noted that the system performance starts to be affected for a size of 125 ms. The value used in the consequent tests was set to 250 ms, corresponding to the previous iteration.

In the PCA, it is necessary to choose the number of components. Therefore, a similar procedure was adopted to achieve a value as low as possible without affecting the SAD performance. This experiment resulted in the definition of the number of components as equal to five.

With these variables defined, the procedure was repeated in all six tests. Since the distinction between train and test data is made using a random mask, the F1 score was averaged over two trials for each descriptor. All the results were recorded (Table 3). For example, in the descriptor six case, the resulting confusion matrix is presented in Table 4.

Table 3. SVM results using different combinations of STFT Raw Data, STFT Average or STFT PCA and the Boxcar or Hamming window function.

Descriptor	F1 Score
1	1.0
2	1.0
3	0.999
4	0.999
5	0.979
6	0.974

The results obtained show that any descriptor gives outstanding results. Although the F1 score is maximum in the first two descriptors, these are not likely to be used due to the high time it takes to obtain these results. Both window functions are suitable for this application, getting very similar results.

Table 4. Confusion matrix for descriptor 6 with STFT PCA and Hamming window.

Predicted Value True Value	NC	C
NC	0.963946	0.036053
C	0.017210	0.982789

It followed a similar procedure to assess the ability to detect anomalies. In this case, the objective is to assign one of the four classes to each sample: CW3, CWL3, NCW3, and NCWL3.

In the same way, six different tests were performed, and the respective results were recorded (Table 5). Table 6 is the confusion matrix for descriptor three, using STFT Average and Boxcar window.

Table 5. SVM results using different combinations of STFT Raw Data, STFT Average or STFT PCA and the Boxcar or Hamming window function.

Descriptor	F1 Score
1	1.000
2	0.999
3	0.985
4	0.982
5	0.960
6	0.949

Table 6. Confusion matrix for descriptor 3 with STFT Average and Boxcar window.

Predicted Value True Value	CW3	CWL3	NCW3	NCWL3
CW3	0.941463	0.043902	0.014634	0
CWL3	0.003720	0.996279	0	0
NCW3	0	0	1	0
NCWL3	0	0.016513	0	0.983486

The results remained highly promising even with the increase in the number of classes and, consequently, in the system's complexity. In this case, using the Boxcar window gives slightly better results than the Hamming window but nothing relevant. Using the STFT Average or the STFT PCA are two distinct ways of significantly reducing the data size and with a residual effect on the system's performance.

The results show that using sound analysis in this problem is a good approach mainly due to the difference in the frequency range of the sounds relative to the different classes present.

5   Conclusion

In this work, we developed a sound-based system. This system was integrated into a robotic platform capable of operating autonomously on rugged terrain with steep slopes and under the most diverse ground conditions.

We presented an SVM classifier that monitors the MowIT operation and can detect anomalies, namely when some trimmer line is missing in some cutting axes. The dataset used to test the performance of this system was made public.

The tests conducted with the SAD system proved that the solution has considerable potential to increase the safety and efficiency of the agricultural robot's operation.

Nevertheless, some aspects for future work were identified:

- Balance the number of samples between classes.
- Collect data in different open-air environments, to observe the influence of the surrounding environment.
- Validate the system in a real-time application, i.e. during a mowing operation, the system can detect anomalies in real-time and react accordingly.

Acknowledgment. André Rogrigues Baltazar thanks the FCT-Foundation for Science and Technology, Portugal for the Ph.D. Grant 2021.04859.BD. This project has received funding from the European Union's Horizon 2020 research and innovation programme under grant agreement No 101000554. Disclaimer: The sole responsibility for the content on this publication lies with the authors. It does not necessarily reflect the opinion of the European Research Executive Agency (REA) or the European Commission (EC). The REA or the EC are not responsible for any use that may be made of the information contained therein.

References

1. Baltazar, A.: Dataset for Sound-based Anomalies Detection in Agricultural Robotics Application (Oct2022) https://doi.org/10.5281/zenodo.7194547, https://doi.org/10.5281/zenodo.7194547
2. Bayram, B., Duman, T.B., Ince, G.: Real time detection of acoustic anomalies in industrial processes using sequential autoencoders. Expert Syst. **38**. https://doi.org/10.1111/exsy.12564
3. Becker, P., Roth, C., Roennau, A., Dillmann, R.: Acoustic anomaly detection in additive manufacturing with long short-term memory neural networks (2020). https://doi.org/10.1109/ICIEA49774.2020.9102002

4. Chachada, S., Kuo, C.C.J.: Environmental sound recognition: a survey. In: 2013 Asia-Pacific Signal and Information Processing Association Annual Summit and Conference, pp. 1–9 (2013). https://doi.org/10.1109/APSIPA.2013.6694338
5. Gribonval, R.: Linear Time-Frequency Analysis I: Fourier-Type Representations, pp. 61–91 (2010). https://doi.org/10.1002/9780470611203.ch3
6. Henze, D., Gorishti, K., Bruegge, B., Simen, J.P.: Audioforesight: a process model for audio predictive maintenance in industrial environments. In: 2019 18th IEEE International Conference On Machine Learning And Applications (ICMLA), pp. 352–357 (2019). https://doi.org/10.1109/ICMLA.2019.00066
7. Huang, Z., Shiigi, T., Tsay, L.W.J., Nakanishi, H., Suzuki, T., Ogawa, Y., Naoshi, K.: A sound-based positioning system with centimeter accuracy for mobile robots in a greenhouse using frequency shift compensation. Comput. Electron. Agric. **187**, 106235 (2021) https://doi.org/10.1016/j.compag.2021.106235, https://www.sciencedirect.com/science/article/pii/S0168169921002520
8. Oppenheim, A.V., Schafer, R.W.: Discrete-Time Signal Processing, 3rd edn. Prentice Hall Press, USA (2009)
9. Pandiyan, V., Prost, J., Vorlaufer, G., Varga, M., Wasmer, K.: Identification of abnormal tribological regimes using a microphone and semi-supervised machine-learning algorithm **10**, 583–596 (2021). https://doi.org/10.1007/s40544-021-0518-0
10. Park, D., Kim, H., Kemp, C.C.: Multimodal anomaly detection for assistive robots. Auton. Robots **43**(3), 611–629 (2019). https://doi.org/10.1007/s10514-018-9733-6, https://doi.org/10.1007/s10514-018-9733-6
11. Pedregosa, F., Varoquaux, G., Gramfort, A., Michel, V., Thirion, B., Grisel, O., Blondel, M., Prettenhofer, P., Weiss, R., Dubourg, V., Vanderplas, J., Passos, A., Cournapeau, D., Brucher, M., Perrot, M., Duchesnay, E.: Scikit-learn: machine learning in Python. J. Mach. Learn. Res. **12**, 2825–2830 (2011)
12. Rocha, F., Garcia, G., Pereira, R., Faria, H., Silva, T., Andrade, R., Barbosa, E., Santos, A., da Cruz, E., Andrade, W., Serrantola, W., Moura, L., Azpúrua, H., Franca, A., Pessin, G., Freitas, G., Costa, R., Lizarralde, F.: Rosi: A robotic system for harsh outdoor industrial inspection—system design and applications. J. Intell. Robot. Syst. **103** (2021). https://doi.org/10.1007/s10846-021-01459-2
13. Scipy: scipy.signal.stft - SciPy v1.9.1 Manual, https://docs.scipy.org/doc/scipy/reference/generated/scipy.signal.stft.html. Accessed 03 Oct 2021
14. Seo, C.B., Lee, G., Lee, Y., Seo, S.H.: Echo-guard: acoustic-based anomaly detection system for smart manufacturing environments. In: Kim, H. (ed.) Information Security Applications, pp. 64–75. Springer International Publishing, Cham (2021)
15. Tanuska, P., Spendla, L., Kebisek, M., Duriš, R., Strémy, M.: Smart anomaly detection and prediction for assembly process maintenance in compliance with industry 4.0. Sensors **21**, 2376 (2021). https://doi.org/10.3390/s21072376
16. Vincent, P., Larochelle, H., Bengio, Y., Manzagol, P.A.: Extracting and Composing Robust Features with Denoising Autoencoders, pp. 1096–1103. ICML '08, Association for Computing Machinery, New York, NY, USA (2008). https://doi.org/10.1145/1390156.1390294, https://doi.org/10.1145/1390156.1390294
17. Widodo, S., Shiigi, T., Hayashi, N., Kikuchi, H., Yanagida, K., Nakatsuchi, Y., Ogawa, Y., Kondo, N.: Moving object localization using sound-based positioning system with doppler shift compensation. Robotics **2**(2), 36–53 (2013) https://doi.org/10.3390/robotics2020036, https://www.mdpi.com/2218-6581/2/2/36
18. Wüstrich, L., Schröder, L., Pahl, M.O.: Cyber-physical anomaly detection for ICS. In: 2021 IFIP/IEEE International Symposium on Integrated Network Management (IM), pp. 950–955 (2021)

19. Yoo, Y., Lee, C.Y., Zhang, B.T.: Multimodal anomaly detection based on deep auto-encoder for object slip perception of mobile manipulation robots. In: 2021 IEEE International Conference on Robotics and Automation (ICRA), pp. 11443–11449 (2021). https://doi.org/10.1109/ICRA48506.2021.9561586
20. Yun, H., Kim, H., Jeong, Y., Jun, M.: Autoencoder-based anomaly detection of industrial robot arm using stethoscope based internal sound sensor. J. Intell. Manuf. 1–18 (2021). https://doi.org/10.1007/s10845-021-01862-4

Can the Segmentation Improve the Grape Varieties' Identification Through Images Acquired On-Field?

Gabriel A. Carneiro[1,2]([✉]) [ID], Ana Texeira[1,2] [ID], Raul Morais[1,3] [ID],
Joaquim J. Sousa[1,2] [ID], and António Cunha[1,2] [ID]

[1] University of Trás-os-Montes e Alto Douro, 5000-801 Vila Real, Portugal
[2] INESC Technology and Science (INESC-TEC), 4200-465 Porto, Portugal
gabrielc@utad.pt
[3] Centre for the Research and Technology of Agro-Environmental and Biological Sciences, University of Trás-os-Montes e Alto Douro, 5000-801 Vila Real, Portugal

Abstract. Grape varieties play an important role in wine's production chain, its identification is crucial for controlling and regulating the production. Nowadays, two techniques are widely used, ampelography and molecular analysis. However, there are problems with both of them. In this scenario, Deep Learning classifiers emerged as a tool to automatically classify grape varieties. A problem with the classification of on-field acquired images is that there is a lot of information unrelated to the target classification. In this study, the use of segmentation before classification to remove such unrelated information was analyzed. We used two grape varieties identification datasets to fine-tune a pre-trained EfficientNetV2S. Our results showed that segmentation can slightly improve classification performance if only unrelated information is removed.

Keywords: Precision agriculture · Precision viticulture · Grape variety identification · Deep learning · Convolutional neural networks

1 Introduction

Grape varieties play an important role in the wine's production chain, directly influencing its authenticity and singularity. Thus the identification of grape varieties is important in the control and regulating the production, as well as quality assurance. Nowadays, two techniques are widely employed: ampelography and molecular markers analysis, however, there are problems in applying both. Ampelography consists of the visual analysis of phenotypic markers of the plants, therefore it is subjective, time-consuming and error-prone, since the expertise of the professional who is doing it. Otherwise, the molecular analysis is expansive, in terms of costs and time, and part of it relies on ampelography.

N. Moniz et al. (Eds.): EPIA 2023, LNAI 14116, pp. 351–363, 2023.
https://doi.org/10.1007/978-3-031-49011-8_28

Deep Learning (DL) classifiers emerged as a tool to automatically classify grape varieties. Several studies can be found in the literature with the aim of identifying grape varieties through DL-classifiers and leaf images acquired in a controlled environment [1,7] or on-field [3,4,8,10]. In the context of regulating wine production, automatic approaches that use images acquired on-field deliver faster results since no background or specific acquisition devices are needed. Conversely, these images can be composed of a lot of unrelated information, e.g. soil, sky, wire, etc., thus, making the classification more challenging [17].

In our first experiment [3], we identified through Explainable Artificial Intelligence methods, namely Grad-CAM [13] and LIME [11], that the classifier considered unrelated parts of the images to make decisions, then using a rough segmentation as a preprocessing tool [5] we were able to classify successfully the varieties, improving the regions that were looked to make decisions, however, at the cost of decreasing the classifier's performance in 2%.

Similarly, Pereira et al. [10] used a segmentation process, described in [9], aiming to remove unrelated information before grape varieties identification, using region growing based on a colour model and threshold to classify the pixels belonging to grapevine leaves. Other segmentation studies based on classic feature extraction can be found in [2,6,14].

Another challenge linked with the use of images acquired on-field is that they can be composed of different leaf parts. This can be handled by automatically blurring these parts during the acquisition step, for example, using DSLR cameras. However, handheld devices and cameras, e.g. smartphones, tablets, can not blur them properly. This scenario can increase the classifier's performance, acting as a type of data augmentation, or, can insert uncertainty in the classification, since only a small part of these leaves are there.

In this study we present an evaluation of the use of segmentation as a tool to choose the used region before the classification, erasing parts of the image, including secondary leaves. The U-Net [12] segmentation model was used to segment the main region of the image, and the EfficientNetV2S [16] was applied to classify them. Three datasets were used in our evaluation, one for segmentation and two for classification. We shall highlight that different from [3], in this study, the images were accurately annotated, and a dataset made using acquired using different acquisition devices was used.

2   Methods

The proposed method can be divided into five main steps: data collection and preparation, experiments design, data segmentation, data classification and evaluation.

2.1   Data Collection and Preparation

Two main datasets were used in our study: DS12 and DS14. The segmentation dataset was extracted from DS14. The DS12 was obtained using a Canon EOS 600D camera, equipped with a 50mm/1.4 lens, and 18 megapixels resolution, and composed of 12 different varieties allowed in the Douro region in Portugal.

The varieties and a sample for each of them can be seen in Fig. 1. The images were acquired during an entire growing season, between May and September of 2017, so that leaves with different growing states, illumination, and poses are represented within the dataset. The objective was to capture a centred-leaf image. In the end, the images were cropped into squares, normalized to 300 × 300 pixels, and split among training, validation and test subsets. The number of samples per class and per subset can be seen in Table 1.

Fig. 1. Grapevine images of twelve different grape varieties acquired in a natural and complex environment. Legend: Codega (CD), Rabigato (RG), Malvasia Fina (MF), Tinta Amarela (TA), Malvasia Preta (MP), Tinta Barroca (TB), Malvasia Rei (MR), Tinta Roriz (TR), Moscatel Galego (MG), Tinto Cao (TC), Mourisco Tinto (MT), and Touriga Nacional (TN). *Source* [3].

On the other hand, the DS14 was acquired in the years 2021 and 2022 using Apple iPhone 11, Apple iPhone 12, Microsoft Surface Go 2, Samsung Galaxy S7, and Samsung Galaxy Tab S6 in the Casa de Mateus Fundation's farm (41° 17' 49" N 7° 42' 44" O 41° 17' 49" N 7° 42' 44" O). The images were captured in square format, between 20 and 40cm of distance, focusing on a leaf, however, in most of the samples parts of secondary leaves can be seen. The number of samples and an example for each class are exhibited in Fig. 2.

The images varied in terms of the day they were taken, the lighting conditions, the growth stages of the plants, and the background noise. Thereby, they were divided into three groups: train, test and validation, and resized to 300 × 300 pixels. The number of images per class can be seen in Table 2 (original fields). In addition, a shrunken version was also generated in aiming to make this dataset similar to DS12 in terms of the number of images (see Sect. 2.2 for more details).

Table 1. DS12's number of samples per class and subsets.

Class	Train	Validation	Test
CD	60	6	6
MF	55	5	6
MP	55	5	6
MR	57	6	6
MG	51	5	6
MT	56	6	6
RG	53	5	6
TA	56	6	6
TB	58	6	6
TR	62	6	6
TC	55	6	6
TN	57	6	6
Total	675	68	72

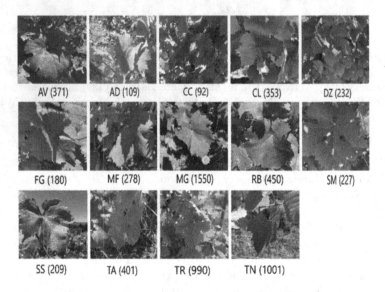

Fig. 2. Grapevine images of twelve different grape varieties acquired in a natural and complex environment. The varieties Alveralhão (AV), Arinto do Douro (AD), Cercial (CC), Códega do Larinho (CL), Donzelinho (DZ), Folgasão (FG), Malvasia Fina, Moscatel Galego, Rabigato, Samarrinho (SM), Sousão (SS), Tinta Amarela, Tinta Roriz, and Touriga Nacional are present in the dataset.

Table 2. DS14's number of samples per class and per subset for the original and shrunken version.

Class	Train		Validation		Test	
	Original	Shrunken	*Original*	Shrunken	*Original*	*Shrunken*
AV	255	46	57	10	59	11
AD	78	62	15	13	16	12
CC	65	60	13	12	14	13
CL	247	53	60	12	46	14
DZ	154	54	44	13	34	13
FG	132	58	22	14	26	12
MF	142	61	34	12	36	14
MG	1028	51	229	11	239	12
RG	311	46	60	9	66	10
SM	155	53	33	13	39	10
SS	151	56	21	13	37	11
TA	227	58	45	12	61	7
TR	692	44	143	9	131	9
TN	717	49	143	11	139	10
Total	4354	751	919	164	943	158

The plurality of acquisition devices makes our dataset more suitable for practical applications, since different devices can use different post-process techniques, have different quality and thus, can capture different leaf details. For comparison purposes, one can see in Fig. 3 images from the MG variety acquired with different devices.

Fig. 3. Samples of MG acquired using different devices. DSLR refer Cannon EOS 600D.

Finally, the DS14 was used to generate the segmentation dataset, which we will refer to as DSEG in the remainder of the text. In the first step, the MobileNetV3S pre-trained on ImageNet was used to extract features from all the DS14's images. Then, the K-Means was used to group the images of the same class in 22 clusters. Later, we selected the image closer to each cluster, calculating the Euclidian distance for each image and its assigned cluster. This approach allowed the selection of different types of images, increasing the dataset samples' diversity. Following, the 22 images were annotated to semantic segmentation so that only the biggest leaf was kept as leaf class, and the remaining regions were assigned to the background class. The tool labelstudio was used. In the end, the DSEG contained 308 images, split into training (216), validation (46) and test (46) subsets. An example of 3 samples and their masks can be observed in Fig. 4.

Fig. 4. Samples of the DSEG. In the first line the images, and their masks in the second line.

2.2   Experiments Design

One segmentation and eight classification experiments were conducted, their names, types, employed datasets and their characteristics (augmented, segmented, or shrunken) can be seen in Table 3.

The segmentation experiment aimed to train the best DL-based segmentation architecture to choose the region of interest for the classification of each image. We applied data augmentation for the DSEG, applying flip, rotations, crops, brightness changes and blur for the images.

The classification experiments aimed to verify if the removal of the background improved the classification in three factors: different datasets, data unbalance influence, and data augmentation employment.

The differences between the DS12 and DS14 are huge. The datasets were acquired in different places, with different acquisition regularity, and with different acquisition devices (in terms of number and type). There is a huge unbalance within the DS14. The MG class is represented by more than 1000 images, otherwise, CC is represented with less than 100 images. In addition, there was no

Table 3. Experiments description

Name	Type	Dataset	Segmented	Augmented	Shrunken
SEXP1	Segmentation	DSEG	–	Yes	No
CEXP1	Classification	DS12	No	Yes	No
CEXP2	Classification	DS12	Yes	Yes	No
CEXP3	Classification	DS14	No	Yes	No
CEXP4	Classification	DS14	Yes	Yes	No
CEXP5	Classification	DS14	No	Yes	Yes
CEXP6	Classification	DS14	Yes	Yes	Yes
CEXP7	Classification	DS14	No	No	No
CEXP8	Classification	DS14	Yes	No	No

human preprocessing after the image acquisition in the DS14, so the images were only normalized.

Considering these factors, we modified the original datasets in two ways: applying data augmentation in both and shrinking DS14 (the number of samples can be seen in Table 2). We applied static modifications (rotation, flips and zoom) in the images as data augmentation, generating 5 new samples per sample within each dataset. There was a difference between the segmented datasets and the original datasets in this case. The newly generated images were padded with the nearest neighbour algorithm, if padding was necessary, while the segmented images were padded by a constant value of 0.

The shrunk of the dataset was made due to two factors: dataset balance and segmentation failure. First, we applied the same technique employed to select the images to DSEG, however, we chose 92 images per class (the number of samples of the more underrepresented class, CC). However, we also noticed that in rare cases the segmentation model returned very small masks to the images and we only used the image if more than 20% of the masks was classified as region of interest. The number of images per sample and class after shrinking the DS14 can be seen in Table 2. This configuration turned the DS14 more similar to the DS12 in terms of data balance.

Thus, the experiments CEXP1, CEXP2, CEXP3 and CEXP4's results were used to compare the background removal in 2 very different datasets; while data unbalance influence could be verified by comparing CEXP3, CEXP4, CEXP5 and CEXP6 performance; finally, the data augmentation impact could be asserted by comparing CEXP3, CEXP4, CEXP7 and CEXP8's results.

2.3   Data Segmentation

This step aimed to remove unrelated information for the classification, e.g. sky, soil, and select a region of interest for the classification, only the central leaf could be kept in the image.

The U-Net [12] architecture was trained to segment the images. The model was chosen due to its wide application in the literature in tasks in which high accuracy is needed and the inference time is not a constraint. The U-Net explores the concept of U-shaped architecture, being composed of two parts a contractor part and an expansive path. We used the architecture EfficientNetB3 [15] as the contractor part of the model.

The training was made in two phases, in the first the contractor was frozen and only the expansive path was trained. In the second, the entire model was trained. We used an input size of 288 × 288 pixels. Both phases shared the Adam as an optimizer, the loss is composed of the sum between Dice and Focal Loss, Sigmoid as output activation function, 100 as the number of epochs of training, and a reducer of learning rate of 10% with the patience of 10 epochs. The learning was 1E-3 for the first phase and 5E-4 for the second. The metric Intersection-Over-the-Union (IoU) was used to evaluate the model.

2.4   Data Classification and Evaluation

The EfficientNetV2S, pre-trained on ImageNet, was employed as a feature extractor and the classifier was composed of two Fully Connected layers of 512 neurons, connected by Dropout of 20% and with ReLU as activation. The output was represented by a Fully Connected Layer with the number of classes as its number of neurons, with SoftMax as activation. The input of 224 × 224 was chosen for the classification. Since our objective was to verify the impact of the segmentation as a pre-processing tool, this size allowed faster training of the models.

The model was trained in two phases, as specified for the Segmentation Model in Sect. 2.3. Both parts shared the SGD as an optimizer, the Cross-Entropy loss, 100 as the number of epochs of training with an early stop with patience of 7 epochs, and a step-decay in 5 epochs as a learning rate scheduler. In the first phase, a learning rate of 1E-2 was used, while in the second we opted for 1E-3. The models were evaluated using the metric F1 Score.

3   Results and Discussion

3.1   Segmentation Experiment

The segmentation model achieved 0.78 of IoU. Examples of the segmentation can be seen in Fig. 5. The model can separate the central leaf of remaining information, such as secondary leaves, wire, sun, sky in both datasets. However, in the DS14, there were a few cases where the model was not able to separate a central leaf (see Sect. 2.2). In the DS12 no case of segmentation failure happened. We hypothesize that two factors contributed to this situation, the first is that the camera's ability to blur the background turned easier the segmentation of DS12, besides of plurality found in DS14 in terms of acquisition. In this scenario, the images with segmentation failure were not removed from the data, and thus, can be seen as an insertion of uncertainty in the classification through noise.

Fig. 5. Examples of segmentation for the DS14 (3 left) and DS12 (2 right)

3.2 Classification Experiments

The overall performance, measured in F1 Score, for all experiments, can be seen in Tables 4 and 5. The segmentation improved the classification achieved by the model in the DS12 (see Table 4), however, in DS14 (see Table 5), the use of segmentation led the model to a worse classification in all the configurations.

Table 4. Results of classification for the DS12-based experiments.

Classe	CEXP1	CEXP2
CD	**0.91**	0.83
MF	0.73	**0.91**
MP	**0.83**	0.73
MR	**1.00**	0.77
MG	**1.00**	0.92
MT	**1.00**	0.91
RG	0.67	**0.91**
TA	0.83	**1.00**
TB	**0.92**	0.62
TR	0.86	**1.00**
TC	0.91	**1.00**
TN	0.83	**0.92**
Total	0.87	**0.88**

Using the trained U-Net to segment images and erasing parts of the image considered as background improved the classification of the DS12 in 0.01. The smaller performance difference was 0.08 (CD) while the biggest was 0.23 (MR)

Table 5. Results of classification for the DS14-based experiments

Class	CEXP3	CEXP4	CEXP5	CEXP6	CEXP7	CEXP8
AV	**0.92**	0.87	**0.69**	0.70	**0.88**	0.81
AD	**0.65**	0.65	**0.75**	0.64	**0.65**	0.55
CC	**0.93**	0.61	**0.73**	0.62	**0.67**	0.63
CL	**0.74**	0.63	**0.48**	0.48	**0.50**	0.43
DZ	**0.53**	0.44	**0.35**	0.19	**0.52**	0.52
FG	**0.64**	0.45	0.39	**0.44**	0.31	**0.34**
MF	0.62	**0.64**	0.32	**0.46**	0.52	**0.48**
MG	**0.93**	0.84	**0.63**	0.56	**0.90**	0.78
RG	**0.88**	0.78	**0.59**	0.33	**0.78**	0.49
SM	**0.50**	0.41	**0.29**	0.19	**0.36**	0.29
SS	**0.87**	0.75	**0.86**	0.71	**0.85**	0.72
TA	**0.87**	0.76	**0.62**	0.33	**0.80**	0.60
TR	**0.95**	0.83	**0.67**	0.67	**0.91**	0.75
TN	**0.96**	0.85	**0.63**	0.70	**0.91**	0.80
Total	0.78	0.68	0.57	0.50	0.68	0.58

in the classes. Thus, despite the similar average, there is a huge difference in the classification of the classes with the application of the segmentation. Otherwise, in the DS14 the application of the segmentation hardly decreased the performance in all configurations (see Table 5). The dataset without segmentation (CEXP3) over-performed the one with (CEXP4) in all the classes, except MF. We hypothesize that the ability of the camera to blur makes the secondary leaves almost do not contribute to the classification in DS12, while in the DS14 they carry relevant information, also used by the model in the classification. Thus, the secondary leaves can act as carriers of information to the classification in the DS14. Moreover, the use of segmentation introduces uncertainty in the classification, which may have contributed to the decline in the model's performance.

The data augmentation contributed to an increase in the performance of the model in 0.10, in both non-masked (CEXP3 vs CEXP7) and non-masked (CEXP4 vs CEXP8) datasets, keeping the difference between them. Shrinking the DS14, trying to decrease the data unbalance, did not change the difference in performance between masked DS14 and DS14 datasets, it was kept at least 0.07 (CEXP5 vs CEXP6). Thus, the data augmentation and unbalance of data did not have a relation with the worse performance achieved using the masked dataset. The achieved results indicate that the richness of information in the removed features and the uncertainty inserted by the segmentation led the model to misclassify more images.

Therefore, the segmentation could improve the performance of DS12, however, in DS14, there was a decrease. In DS14 secondary leaves carry useful information for classification using Convolutional Neural Networks, and thus, erasing them decreases the available information for the classification. In conclusion, segmentation can improve the classification performance if only unrelated information is removed and secondary leaves can also contribute to the identification of grape varieties in images acquired, enriching the classifier with useful information.

4   Conclusion

The identification of grape varieties is important in controlling and regulating the wine's production. In this paper, we presented an analysis of the use of segmentation as a preprocessing tool for the identification of grape varieties through images leaf-centered acquired on-field and through Deep Learning. Our results showed that depending on the acquisition device, the performance can be improved If unrated information is removed from the images. However, in cases where secondary leaves are not blurred, they carry additional information for grape variety identification and must be kept.

For future work, a deep analysis of explanations obtained with Explainable Artificial Intelligence, and the use of masks for conducting the learning, instead of removing information from the image can be explored.

Acknowledgments. This work was supported by the project "DATI-Digital Agriculture Technologies for Irrigation efficiency", PRIMA-Partnership for Research and Innovation in the Mediterranean Area, (Research and Innovation activities), financed by the states participating in the PRIMA partnership and by the European Union through Horizon 2020 and by National Funds through the Portuguese funding agency, FCT - Fundação para a Ciência e a Tecnologia, within project LA/P/0063/2020.

References

1. Adão, T., Pinho, T.M., Ferreira, A., Sousa, A., Pádua, L., Sousa, J., Sousa, J.J., Peres, E., Morais, R.: Digital Ampelographer: a CNN based preliminary approach. In: Moura Oliveira, P., Novais, P., Reis, L.P. (eds.) Progress in Artificial Intelligence, pp. 258–271. Springer International Publishing, Cham (2019)
2. Adeel, A., Khan, M.A., Sharif, M., Azam, F., Shah, J.H., Umer, T., Wan, S.: Diagnosis and Recognition of Grape Leaf Diseases: An Automated System Based on a Novel Saliency Approach and Canonical Correlation Analysis Based Multiple Features Fusion, vol. 24, p. 100349. Elsevier. https://doi.org/10.1016/j.suscom.2019.08.002

3. Carneiro, G., Padua, L., Sousa, J.J., Peres, E., Morais, R., Cunha, A.: Grapevine Variety Identification Through Grapevine Leaf Images Acquired in Natural Environment, pp. 7055–7058. Institute of Electrical and Electronics Engineers (IEEE). https://doi.org/10.1109/IGARSS47720.2021.9555141

4. Carneiro, G.A., Pádua, L., Peres, E., Morais, R., Sousa, J.J., Cunha, A.: Grapevine varieties identification using vision transformers. In: IGARSS 2022–2022 IEEE International Geoscience and Remote Sensing Symposium, pp. 5866–5869 (2022). https://doi.org/10.1109/IGARSS46834.2022.9883286

5. Carneiro, G.A., Pádua, L., Peres, E., Morais, R., Sousa, J.J., Cunha, A.: Segmentation as a preprocessing tool for automatic grapevine classification. In: IGARSS 2022–2022 IEEE International Geoscience and Remote Sensing Symposium, pp. 6053–6056. https://doi.org/10.1109/IGARSS46834.2022.9884946, ISSN: 2153-7003

6. Kirti, K., Rajpal, N., Yadav, J.: Black measles disease identification in grape plant (vitis vinifera) using deep learning. In: Proceedings - IEEE 2021 International Conference on Computing, Communication, and Intelligent Systems, ICCCIS 2021, pp. 97–101. Institute of Electrical and Electronics Engineers Inc. https://doi.org/10.1109/ICCCIS51004.2021.9397205

7. Koklu, M., Unlersen, M.F., Ozkan, I.A., Aslan, M.F., Sabanci, K.: A CNN-SVM Study Based on Selected Deep Features for Grapevine Leaves Classification, vol. 188, p. 110425. Elsevier. https://doi.org/10.1016/J.MEASUREMENT.2021.110425

8. Nasiri, A., Taheri-Garavand, A., Fanourakis, D., Zhang, Y.D., Nikoloudakis, N.: Automated grapevine cultivar identification via leaf imaging and deep convolutional neural networks: a proof-of-concept study employing primary Iranian varieties 10(8). https://doi.org/10.3390/plants10081628, https://pubmed.ncbi.nlm.nih.gov/34451673/, publisher: Plants (Basel)

9. Pereira, C.S., Morais, R., Reis, M.J.C.S.: Pixel-based leaf segmentation from natural vineyard images using color model and threshold techniques. In: Campilho, A., Karray, F., ter Haar Romeny, B. (eds.) Image Analysis and Recognition, pp. 96–106. Springer International Publishing, Cham (2018)

10. Pereira, C.S., Morais, R., Reis, M.J.C.S.: Deep learning techniques for grape plant species identification in natural images 19(22), 4850. https://doi.org/10.3390/s19224850, /pmc/articles/PMC6891615/, publisher: Multidisciplinary Digital Publishing Institute (MDPI)

11. Ribeiro, M.T., Singh, S., Guestrin, C.: "Why should i trust you?": explaining the predictions of any classifier. In: Proceedings of the ACM SIGKDD International Conference on Knowledge Discovery and Data Mining, vol. 13–17, pp. 97–101. Association for Computing Machinery. 10.18653/v1/n16-3020. https://arxiv.org/abs/1602.04938v3

12. Ronneberger, O., Fischer, P., Brox, T.: U-net: convolutional networks for biomedical image segmentation. http://arxiv.org/abs/1505.04597

13. Selvaraju, R.R., Cogswell, M., Das, A., Vedantam, R., Parikh, D., Batra, D.: Grad-CAM: visual explanations from deep networks via gradient-based localization 128(2), 336–359; Springer. https://doi.org/10.1007/s11263-019-01228-7, http://arxiv.org/abs/1610.02391

14. Shantkumari, M., Uma, S.V.: Grape leaf segmentation for disease identification through adaptive snake algorithm model 80(6), 8861–8879; Springer. https://doi.org/10.1007/s11042-020-09853-y, https://link.springer.com/article/10.1007/s11042-020-09853-y

15. Tan, M., Le, Q.V.: EfficientNet: Rethinking Model Scaling for Convolutional Neural Networks 2019-June, pp. 10691–10700. International Machine Learning Society (IMLS) ISBN: 9781510886988, https://arxiv.org/abs/1905.11946v5

16. Tan, M., Le, Q.V.: EfficientNetV2: smaller models and faster training. 10.48550/arXiv.2104.00298, http://arxiv.org/abs/2104.00298

17. Xiong, Y., Liang, L., Wang, L., She, J., Wu, M.: Identification of cash crop diseases using automatic image segmentation algorithm and deep learning with expanded dataset **177**, 105712. https://doi.org/10.1016/j.compag.2020.105712, Elsevier

Enhancing Pest Detection Models Through Improved Annotations

Dinis Costa[1]([✉])[ID], Catarina Silva[1][ID], Joana Costa[1,2][ID],
and Bernardete Ribeiro[1][ID]

[1] CISUC, Department of Informatics Engineering, Coimbra, Portugal
ddcosta@student.dei.uc.pt, {catarina,joanamc,bribeiro}@dei.uc.pt
[2] Polytechnic Institute of Leiria, School of Technology and Management, Leiria,
Portugal

Abstract. AI-based pest detection is gaining popularity in data-centric
scenarios, providing farmers with excellent performance and decision
support for pest control. However, these approaches often face challenges that require complex architectures. Alternatively, data-centric
approaches aim to enhance the quality of training data. In this study,
we present an approach that is particularly relevant when dealing with
low data. Our proposed approach improves annotation quality without
requiring additional manpower. We trained a model with data of inferior
annotation quality and utilized its predictions to generate new annotations of higher quality. Results from our study demonstrate that, using
a small dataset of 200 images with low resolution and variable lighting
conditions, our model can improve the mean average precision (mAP)
score by 1.1 points.

Keywords: Agriculture 4.0 · Machine Learning · Data-Centric ·
Object Detection · Smart Farming

1 Introduction

Pest detection is critical for farmers and agricultural industries worldwide, as
pests can cause significant damage to crops and reduce yields, leading to economic losses. With the advancement of technology, AI-based pest detection has
emerged as a more efficient and accurate solution to these problems. In recent
years, pest detection has become more efficient, thanks to advances in AI technology. Machine learning algorithms, such as Convolutional Neural Networks
(CNNs), have been shown to outperform traditional computer vision techniques
in detecting pests in crops [2].

While there exist annotated datasets on which deep learning models can be
trained or fine-tuned to recognize a broad range of pests with high accuracy,
their performance may suffer when it comes to novel or previously unseen pests
with a limited number of training examples or poorly annotated data.

N. Moniz et al. (Eds.): EPIA 2023, LNAI 14116, pp. 364–375, 2023.
https://doi.org/10.1007/978-3-031-49011-8_29

The quality and quantity of data are in fact an important requirement for AI models to excel, since state-of-the-art models rely on labeled data for training. The labeling process being a human-driven activity is prone to error, even when performed by experts, which can result to incorrect learning by the models and consequently poor performance on tests [8]. Additionally, it can also be time and manpower consuming, since it may be a difficult and ambiguous task. There exist several approaches to tackle such challenges, e.g., Active Learning (AL) techniques, which aims to reduce the amount of data needed for training a model [3,11], one-shot learning, and improving annotations [8].

Our work focuses on a smart farming scenario where the goal is to detect the whitefly pest in natural environments. Specifically, we aim to detect the pest directly on plant leaves using low-resolution images captured under varying lighting conditions.

Whiteflies are one of the most destructive pests, causing significant losses in greenhouse crops [9]. Early detection is crucial to prevent their spread in plantations. However, training a model to accurately detect whiteflies poses a challenge due to the lack of available data. To address this issue, we created a new dataset, which motivated a data-centric approach to training our model.

The aim of this research is to explore methods for enhancing model performance through improved annotations. Object detection models are typically evaluated using the mean Average Precision (mAP) metric, which can be adversely affected if the bounding boxes of the objects to be detected are not accurately positioned and sized. Such inaccuracies can lead to incorrect learning by the model, thereby reducing its effectiveness.

The rest of the paper is organized as follows. Section 2 describes background and related work. In Sect. 3 the methodology is detailed, including dataset creation, annotation improvement strategy, and architecture selection. Section 4 presents and discusses the results and Sect. 5 delineates conclusions and future lines of research.

2   Background and Related Work

The main goal of this global study is to develop a system that can detect pests in plants, providing farmers with a reliable tool that can contribute to improving crop yields. To achieve this goal, the data used for the system must be of high quality to provide the best information for the models to learn from. The resulting tool must also be user-friendly and provide prompt feedback to farmers. As part of this study, this research aims to explore the impact of the data quality on the model's performance.

In this section we will introduce the object detection models, with a focus on the You Only Look Once (YOLO) models. Then, data-centric AI is introduced with recent advancements on improving annotations.

2.1 Object Detection Models

Object detection models can be classified as either "one-phase" or "two-phase", depending on the processing stages involved. The YOLO family processes the images at once, making it a "one-phase" model.

According to [2], the Faster-RCNN, YOLOv4, and YOLOv5 models were compared in the task of detecting the whitefly pest in yellow sticky traps. The study found that the YOLOv5 models performed better than the other models, with a mean Average Precision (mAP) of 89.7%. Based on this research, we decided to explore the YOLOv5 model, since we are able to utilize transfer learning from their model.

The YOLOv5 model was built by Ultralytics[1] and its architecture can be divided into three parts [5] as shown in Fig. 1:

- **Backbone:** The model backbone is composed of CNN architectures and is responsible for extracting features from the input images.
- **Neck:** The model neck processes the features from the model backbone and provides context to the model head.
- **Head:** The model head receives the output of the model neck and provides the final output, which predicts the locations of the objects (bounding box coordinates), the class of each detected object, and the model's confidence in its prediction.

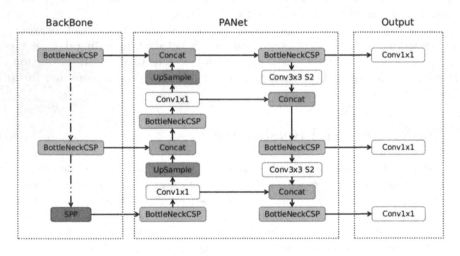

Fig. 1. Overview of YOLOv5 [5]

Recently, YOLOv8 was introduced by Ultralytics, based on the YOLOv5 architecture and is considered to be the state-of-the-art YOLO model [4].

---

[1] https://ultralytics.com/.

Object detection models use annotated data for training, where the annotation is given by bounding boxes of the objects in each image and their corresponding class (label). A bounding box is a box that encapsulates the object and is composed of its coordinates in the image.

To evaluate these models, the mAP metric is used, which is calculated by averaging the Area under the Curve (AuC) of the Precision-Recall (PR) curve over all classes.

To calculate precision and recall, object detection models rely on the Intersection over Union (IoU), which is a metric that computes the overlap between the bounding box predicted by the model and the ground truth bounding box (the annotated one), as shown in Fig. 2. A prediction by the model is considered to be a True Positive (TP) if $IoU >= 0.5$ and a False Positive (FP) otherwise, assuming an IoU threshold of 0.5.

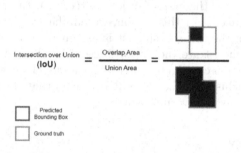

Fig. 2. Intersection over Union Calculation

Understanding the IoU provides insight into the importance of annotation quality, specifically the quality of the bounding boxes. A small error in the position or size of a bounding box can be enough to change a TP to FP and consequently affect the mAP.

2.2   Data-Centric AI—Improving Annotations

Many researchers focus on advancing model design to achieve optimal performance and reduce the resources and time required for training [13,16]. In contrast, the Data-Centric AI approach prioritizes enhancing data quality rather than improving model design.

Several studies have highlighted the issue of label noise in object detection and classification models, which can result from incorrect or missing labels. For instance, in [8], the authors re-annotated the labels of 80k images from the Microsoft Common Object in Context (MS COCO) dataset [7] and 5k images from the Google Open Images dataset [6]. To minimize ambiguity, they established guidelines for the re-annotation process. Subsequently, they trained a set of models to investigate how the quality of the annotations in each dataset split affects the model's performance. Specifically, they trained models using all possible combinations of the splits, including the original dataset and the re-annotated dataset. The results showed that the new annotation negatively affected the mAP for the MS COCO dataset. On the other hand, the re-annotation process improved the mAP for the OpenImages dataset.

Alternatively, other researches focused on studying the label location and the impact on mode's performance [1,14]. In [1] a method for correcting the label location on aerial and satellite imagery was applied, achieving substantial improvements. In contrast, in [14] noise was added to label locations, resulting in substantial decrease on the performance.

Errors in test sets are numerous and widespread [10]. There is a major importance of quality in the test sets, since most of the ML models are evaluated based on the performance achieved on those sets. A better model is one that outperforms another in the test set. If the test set has errors in the labels or in the location of the labels (in the case of object detection), the final judgment of a model could be mistaken. For this reason, we emphasize the importance of the annotation quality of the test set, since it is assumed to reflect the real world.

These studies demonstrate the importance of labeling quality. Noise in the labels or in their location can significantly affect a model's performance and may lead to incorrect conclusions. Therefore, it is crucial that the labeling process is carefully designed to avoid any ambiguities.

3   Methodology

The main goal of this research is enhance pest detection models by adopting a data-centric approach to study the performance impact on object detection models when trained with datasets with different annotation qualities.

(a) Dataset image before   (b) Dataset image after labeling
            labeling

Fig. 3. Labeling Process

3.1   Dataset Creation

We built a dataset of low resolution images containing whitefly-infested tomato leaves. Figure 3 shows the same image before and after the annotation process.

The images were captured under different light exposures. Whiteflies are very small (1–3 mm in length [12]), making the labeling process difficult, as the pests can be hard to detect under those conditions.

For the labeling process 200 images were selected and the contained whiteflies were annotated using *labelImg*.[2]

The labeling process is often ambiguous, as the visibility of the whiteflies can vary depending on their size and position within the image. Furthermore, the focus of the lens can also affect their visibility, with those near the borders being less visible and potentially out of focus. Initially, the labeling process involved annotating all the white points on each image since they were assumed to be whiteflies, even if they were not. However, when the annotations were reviewed by a different person, some of the points were not immediately recognizable as whiteflies. Additionally, some whiteflies could be mistaken for water drops. Figure 4 presents an example of this situation. As a result, a review of the annotation process was necessary to ensure accurate labeling. The dataset with the first annotations is referred as *Original Dataset*.

 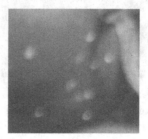

(a) White dots wrongly assumed to be whiteflies

(b) **Whiteflies that could be mistaken as water drops**

Fig. 4. *Original Dataset* Annotations

3.2   Architecture Selection

Due to time and computational power limitations, only one model architecture was defined to be explored. With this in mind, a benchmark experiment was conducted using the the *Original Dataset* for training and testing the following models architectures:

---

[2] Open-source online tool: https://github.com/heartexlabs/labelImg.

- YOLOv5:
  - Nano;
  - Small;
  - Large;
  - XLarge.

- YOLOv8:
  - Nano;
  - Small;
  - Large;
  - XLarge.

The YOLOv5 Small (YOLOv5s) offered the best trade-off between time and performance, achieving 74.7% mAP in 1143 s. On the other hand, the best YOLOv8 architecture was the Medium version, which achieved 68.5% mAP in 2160 s. Therefore, we conducted further experiments using YOLOv5s.

3.3 Improving Annotations Quality

With the preliminary experiments, it was found that the YOLOv5s model can accurately predict the location of whiteflies in the images, significantly optimizing the bounding boxes from the *Original Dataset*, as shown in Fig. 5. We used this model to predict all the object's locations, and with the predicted locations, we created the *Improved Dataset*.

(a) **Whiteflies with noisy bounding** box locations from *Original Dataset*

(b) **Whiteflies annotations from** *Improved Dataset* with bounding box locations predicted by an YOLOv5s model trained with the *Original Dataset*

Fig. 5. *Original Dataset* Annotations Versus *Improved Dataset* Annotations

The goal of creating an object detection model is usually to perform a real-world task. For this purpose, and as mentioned before, it is assumed that the model that performs better on the test set will perform better in real-world tasks. For this reason, it is highly relevant to have a test set that is representative of real-world scenarios. The labeling process is hard and time-consuming, and its requirements increase as the attention to details increases. The Human-In-The-Loop is an area that aims to integrate human knowledge and experience to improve ML accuracy [15]. In this research, we adopt this approach to enhance the test set by readjusting the annotations of a random sample of 40 images from the *Improved Dataset*. The selected images will be used for testing. This approach reduces the labeling process requirements by leveraging the predictions provided by a CV model and, simultaneously, helping the model have the best data for evaluation.

To ensure minimal ambiguity while readjusting the annotations for the 40 selected images, a human expert was involved in the process, following explicit guidelines. The guidelines employed were as follows:

- **"V" shape**: Objects with a "V" shape are annotated as whiteflies due to the shape of their wings.
- **Triangular shape**: Whiteflies can also have triangular shapes due to their wings, consequently objects with a triangular shape are annotated as white-flies
- **Focused sharp white forms**: Objects with sharp white forms are annotated as whiteflies.
- **Shaky or unfocused white forms**: Objects with white forms that are shaky or unfocused are not annotated as whiteflies due to the uncertainty caused by the image quality.

4   Results and Discussion

The goal of the research is to study the impact of different annotation qualities on the performance of a model trained on two datasets: the *Original Dataset* and the *Improved Dataset*. The evaluation is conducted on the same test set, assumed to have perfect annotations. To achieve this goal, 30 runs are conducted, with two models trained in each run using the same images but different annotations from the two datasets. This approach provides diversity in the data used in each run, as the train and validation sets are randomly split for each run.

In Table 1, the obtained results are displayed. The average mAP is 1.1 mAP points higher when using the *Improved Dataset*. As anticipated, improved annotations provide an advantage in model performance. Conversely, training with the *Original Dataset* is marginally faster, by 2.49 s.

Table 1. Results Obtained - The average **mAP (%)** and **time (s)** are presented with standard deviation in parentheses over 30 runs.

Dataset	mAP (%)	Time (s)	Best mAP (%)	Fastest Time (s)
Original Dataset	90.44 (0.70)	**758.20 (5.76)**	91.7	**736.28**
Improved Dataset	**91.54 (0.66)**	760.69(3.62)	**93.1**	753.88

To validate our conclusions, we conducted statistical tests. In order to select the appropriate test, we assessed the normality of the mAP and time results for the 30 paired values. We used the *Shapiro-Wilk* test for normality assessment. Only the data for training time from the *Original Dataset* failed to reject the null hypothesis with a *p-value* of 0.05, indicating that the rest of the data is not normally distributed.

In order to draw a conclusion from the test, we employed the *Wilcoxon* test, whose null hypothesis states that the difference between the pairings has a symmetric distribution around zero. For the mAP pairings, the null hypothesis was not rejected with a *p-value* of 0.05, suggesting that there is no significant difference between the values, and therefore, the *Improved Dataset* did not significantly improve the mAP results.

Regarding the training time, the *Wilcoxon* test results rejected the null hypothesis with a *p-value* of 0.05, indicating that there are significant differences between the values, and therefore, training with the *Original Dataset* is faster.

The above results contradicted our intuition and initial findings. However, the statistical test results are based on all 30 runs. By analyzing the results of the best model trained with both datasets, it is possible to argue that there is an advantage in training with the *Improved Dataset*.

If we analyze both confusion matrices of the best models produced with each dataset (Fig. 6), it becomes clear that the model trained with the *Improved Dataset* is better in terms of correctly detecting whiteflies due to its lower number of FN. On the other hand, the same model has the highest number of FP, meaning that it has a higher tendency to detect whiteflies where they are not. Due to the nature of this task and knowing the dataset, and the subjectivity of identifying whiteflies in images with variable light exposures, different points of focus, and the strict guidelines that were followed to annotate the whiteflies on the test set, it is possible that some of the FP are actually TP, as some whiteflies can be hard to identify in the early stages of their life and on shaky images.

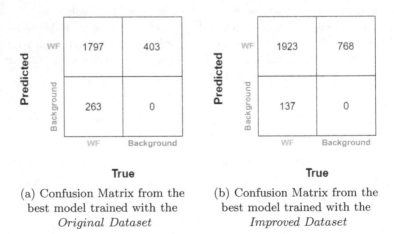

(a) Confusion Matrix from the best model trained with the *Original Dataset*

(b) Confusion Matrix from the best model trained with the *Improved Dataset*

Fig. 6. Comparison of the confusion matrices for the best model trained with different dataset annotations: *Original Dataset* Annotations and *Improved Dataset* Annotations

5   Conclusions and Future Work

The objective of this research was to enhance the model's performance when working with limited amounts of data. To achieve this, we adopted a data-centric approach by improving the quality of the training data. By enhancing the data used to train the model, we aimed to overcome the limitations posed by the lack of data, thereby boosting the model's accuracy in detecting pests.

Adopting a data-centric approach can be particularly useful when working with state-of-the-art model designs, where slight improvements in the quality of the training data can significantly enhance the model's performance. One viable method for enhancing the quality of the data is by improving the annotations, particularly in object detection models. However, improving the data quality can be a time-consuming and expensive process.

In this research, we explored an innovative approach to enhance the data quality without requiring additional manpower. Specifically, we utilized a model trained on a limited dataset with inferior annotation quality to generate predictions, which we then used as annotations of improved quality. This technique enabled us to improve the quality of the training data and enhance the model's accuracy in detecting pests without incurring additional annotation costs.

The results of our study demonstrated that our approach significantly improved the performance of the model, achieving an average increase of 1.1 mAP points. Notably, the best model produced using the dataset with enhanced annotations outperformed the model trained on the original dataset in detecting whiteflies. Moreover, the enhanced model detected more whiteflies than the annotated ones, which suggests that some of the false positives might indeed be true positives that were not annotated due to the strict guidelines and image quality. These findings underscore the potential of our approach to generate high-quality annotations, even when working with limited data and time constraints.

Future work could focus on collecting a dataset of images with superior quality, which would make it easier to identify small pests and improve the performance of the model even further. With a high-quality dataset, our approach to improving data annotation could yield even more promising results, potentially leading to even greater improvements in the accuracy and precision of the model's predictions. These efforts have the potential to not only advance the field of pest detection and control, empowering farmers with more effective tools to monitor and manage their crops, reduce crop losses, and increase yields, but also to be applied to other domains where data scarcity is a challenge.

Acknowledgments. This work was supported by project PEGADA 4.0 (PRR-C05-i03-000099), financed by the PPR - Plano de Recuperação e Resiliência and by national funds through FCT, within the scope of the project CISUC (UID/CEC/00326/2020).

References

1. Bernhard, M., Schubert, M.: Correcting imprecise object locations for training object detectors in remote sensing applications. Remote Sens. **13**(24) (2021). https://doi.org/10.3390/rs13244962, www.mdpi.com/2072-4292/13/24/4962
2. Cardoso, B., Silva, C., Costa, J., Ribeiro, B.: Internet of things meets computer vision to make an intelligent pest monitoring network. Appl. Sci. **12**(18) (2022). https://doi.org/10.3390/app12189397, www.mdpi.com/2076-3417/12/18/9397
3. Costa, D., Silva, C., Costa, J., Ribeiro, B.: Optimizing object detection models via active learning. In: Iberian Conference on Pattern Recognition and Image Analysis: Pattern Recognition and Image Analysis. Springer International Publishing (2023)
4. Jocher, G., Chaurasia, A., Qiu, J.: YOLO by Ultralytics (2023). github.com/ultralytics/ultralytics
5. Jocher, G., Chaurasia, A., Stoken, A., Borovec, J., NanoCode012, Kwon, Y., Michael, K., TaoXie, Fang, J., imyhxy, Lorna, Yifu, Wong, C.V.A., Montes, D., Wang, Z., Fati, C., Nadar, J., Laughing, UnglvKitDe, Sonck, V., tkianai, yxNONG, Skalski, P., Hogan, A., Nair, D., Strobel, M., Jain, M.: ultralytics/yolov5: v7.0 - YOLOv5 SOTA Realtime Instance Segmentation (2022). https://doi.org/10.5281/zenodo.7347926, 10.5281/zenodo.7347926
6. Kuznetsova, A., Rom, H., Alldrin, N., Uijlings, J., Krasin, I., Pont-Tuset, J., Kamali, S., Popov, S., Malloci, M., Kolesnikov, A., Duerig, T., Ferrari, V.: The open images dataset v4. Int. J. Comput. Vis. **128**(7), 1956–1981 (2020). https://doi.org/10.1007/s11263-020-01316-z, 10.1007/2Fs11263-020-01316-z
7. Lin, T.Y., Maire, M., Belongie, S., Hays, J., Perona, P., Ramanan, D., Dollár, P., Zitnick, C.L.: Microsoft coco: common objects in context. In: Fleet, D., Pajdla, T., Schiele, B., Tuytelaars, T. (eds.) Computer Vision - ECCV 2014, pp. 740–755. Springer International Publishing, Cham (2014)
8. Ma, J., Ushiku, Y., Sagara, M.: The effect of improving annotation quality on object detection datasets: a preliminary study. In: 2022 IEEE/CVF Conference on Computer Vision and Pattern Recognition Workshops (CVPRW), pp. 4849–4858 (2022). https://doi.org/10.1109/CVPRW56347.2022.00532
9. Nieuwenhuizen, A., Hemming, J., Suh, H.: Detection and classification of insects on stick-traps in a tomato crop using faster r-cnn (2018). nccv18.nl/program/; the Netherlands Conference on Computer Vision, NCCV18; Conference date: 26-09-2018 Through 27-09-2018
10. Northcutt, C.G., Athalye, A., Mueller, J.: Pervasive label errors in test sets destabilize machine learning benchmarks (2021)
11. Ren, P., Xiao, Y., Chang, X., Huang, P.Y., Li, Z., Gupta, B.B., Chen, X., Wang, X.: A survey of deep active learning (2021)
12. Sani, I., Ismail, S.I., Abdullah, S., Jalinas, J., Jamian, S., Saad, N.: A review of the biology and control of whitefly, bemisia tabaci (hemiptera: Aleyrodidae), with special reference to biological control using entomopathogenic fungi. Insects **11**(9) (2020). https://doi.org/10.3390/insects11090619, www.mdpi.com/2075-4450/11/9/619
13. Terven, J., Cordova-Esparza, D.M.: A comprehensive review of yolo: from yolov1 to yolov8 and beyond (2023)
14. Wang, S., Gao, J., Li, B., Hu, W.: Narrowing the gap: improved detector training with noisy location annotations. Trans. Img. Proc. **31**, 6369–6380 (2022). https://doi.org/10.1109/TIP.2022.3211468

15. Wu, X., Xiao, L., Sun, Y., Zhang, J., Ma, T., He, L.: A survey of human-in-the-loop for machine learning. Futur. Gener. Comput. Syst. **135**, 364–381 (2022) https://doi.org/10.1016/j.future.2022.05.014, www.sciencedirect.com/science/article/pii/S0167739X22001790
16. Zha, D., Bhat, Z.P., Lai, K.H., Yang, F., Jiang, Z., Zhong, S., Hu, X.: Data-centric artificial intelligence: a survey (2023)

Deep Learning-Based Tree Stem Segmentation for Robotic Eucalyptus Selective Thinning Operations

Daniel Queirós da Silva[1,2](✉) [ID], Tiago Ferreira Rodrigues[3] [ID],
Armando Jorge Sousa[2,3] [ID], Filipe Neves dos Santos[2] [ID], and Vítor Filipe[1,2] [ID]

[1] University of Trás-os-Montes and Alto Douro (UTAD), Vila Real, Portugal
[2] INESC Technology and Science (INESC TEC), Porto, Portugal
daniqsilva1997@gmail.com
[3] Faculty of Engineering, University of Porto (FEUP), Porto, Portugal

Abstract. Selective thinning is a crucial operation to reduce forest ignitable material, to control the eucalyptus species and maximise its profitability. The selection and removal of less vigorous stems allows the remaining stems to grow healthier and without competition for water, sunlight and nutrients. This operation is traditionally performed by a human operator and is time-intensive. This work simplifies selective thinning by removing the stem selection part from the human operator's side using a computer vision algorithm. For this, two distinct datasets of eucalyptus stems (with and without foliage) were built and manually annotated, and three Deep Learning object detectors (YOLOv5, YOLOv7 and YOLOv8) were tested on real context images to perform instance segmentation. YOLOv8 was the best at this task, achieving an Average Precision of 74% and 66% on non-leafy and leafy test datasets, respectively. A computer vision algorithm for automatic stem selection was developed based on the YOLOv8 segmentation output. The algorithm managed to get a Precision above 97% and a 81% Recall. The findings of this work can have a positive impact in future developments for automatising selective thinning in forested contexts.

Keywords: Computer vision · Deep learning · Forestry · Instance segmentation · Selective thinning

1 Introduction

Forests cover 31% of the global land area, generate around 86 million green jobs and more than half of world gross domestic product depends on forest services, according to Food and Agriculture Organisation (FAO) [10]. In recent years, worldwide forests have been suffering from wildfires. Forestry operations such as, afforestation, reforestation, cleaning, thinning and harvesting are important not only to protect, reducing the risk of the occurrence of wildfires, but also to improve the profitability of the forest stands.

N. Moniz et al. (Eds.): EPIA 2023, LNAI 14116, pp. 376–387, 2023.
https://doi.org/10.1007/978-3-031-49011-8_30

The main inhabitant forest species in Portugal is eucalyptus (*Eucalyptus globulus*). According to a study carried out in 2015,[1] this species represents 26% of the Portuguese forest area. Normally, in each planting spot, several eucalyptus stems grow, having to compete with each other for nutrients, water and sunlight. These aspects can have a negative impact to the trees health and durability. Therefore, to control this species and maximise its profitability, an operation called selective thinning is performed. This operation consists of selecting and cutting non-dominant trees based on their vigor and disposition on the land, leaving only the trees' shoots [11]. This operation (selection and cut) is performed by an human operator and is time-intensive. Since artificial perception have been developing recently in the forestry area [8], a perception solution capable of performing automatic selection would be beneficial.

In forestry, the automation of selective thinning is an underdevelopment topic. The most significant works that were found were about: simulation of thinning and harvesting operations using algorithms based of tree's physical parameters [21], utilisation of a decision support system working on stand data to help select the stems to remain [23,24], requirements formulation for the design of a robotic system for selective cleaning [22], and application of a multi-criteria simulated annealing meta-heuristic considering forest stand variables [14]. Despite some advances in terms of decision support systems and meta-heuristics, the online acquisition and process of forest stand data is needed. This is the area where robotics combined with advanced perception systems can play an important role [24]. Within this field, some works assessed tree trunks detection and/or segmentation in forest environments using Deep Learning (DL) and cameras [6,7,9,12,15] and/or Light Detection And Ranging (LiDAR) technology [13,20,26] but without any applicability in the specific task of selective thinning. Therefore, in this work we trained three DL-based instance segmentation models in two distinct datasets and we developed an artificial perception system based on computer vision capable of selecting Eucalyptus stems automatically.

The remaining of this article is structured as follows: Sect. 2 formulates the dataset acquisition, annotation and augmentation, the training and test of the DL models to perform Eucalyptus stem segmentation, and defines the algorithm for automatic stem selection. Section 3 presents the segmentation results in each dataset and the results of the automatic stem selection, and Sect. 4 ends this article by stating some conclusions and drawing future work.

2   Materials and Methods

This section presents details about the data acquisition, annotation and augmentation methodologies, about the training and testing processes of the DL models, and also about the automatic stem selection algorithm.

---

[1] https://florestas.pt/conhecer/as-especies-florestais-mais-comuns-da-floresta-portuguesa.

2.1 Data Acquisition

In this work, several videos footage were acquired with an handheld OAK-D[2] in two Portuguese forest areas containing only eucalyptus trees: Melres (41°06′21.1″ N, 8°24′59.0″ W) and Sobrado (41°13′29.6″ N, 8°26′28.4″ W). In Melres the trees had few to no foliage, while in Sobrado there was much more foliage occluding the tree stems. In both areas, the trees were at the stage right before selective thinning.

The images were extracted from the recorded videos and, after being selected, two distinct datasets were built: one called Less Foliage (LF) composed by images from Melres and other named More Foliage (MF) composed by images from Sobrado. LF's dataset ended up with a total of 113 original images and MF's with 95. These two datasets will provide insight regarding the consequences of having partial occlusion by foliage on the DL models performance during tree stems segmentation task. The differences of having less or more foliage, causing stem occlusion, can be observed in Fig. 1. In all images, the tree stems are vertical and some have a minimal inclination.

(a) Eucalyptus stems with less foliage.   (b) Eucalyptus stems with more foliage.

Fig. 1. Examples of images with: **a** low level of foliage and **b** with high level of foliage.

2.2 Data Annotation and Augmentation

The two datasets were both manually annotated using Computer Vision Annotation Tool (CVAT)[3] and both were split in train, validation and test sets with the following split ratios were 50%, 25% and 25%, respectively. These ratios were carefully chosen to produce a balanced distribution that enables efficient model training, fine-tuning, and unbiased evaluation. This division enables the model to learn from a substantial amount of data, optimise its performance based on validation results, and accurately assess its generalisation abilities on unseen test data [1]. Table 1 shows the image split by set in each dataset and also the image resolution of each dataset.

---

[2] https://store.opencv.ai/products/oak-d.
[3] www.cvat.ai.

Table 1. Datasets split into train, validation and test sets

Dataset	Image resolution	Number of images		
		Train	Validation	Test
LF	712 × 400	57 + 1136	28	28
MF	1280 × 720	48 + 965	23	24

Then, the training set of each dataset went through the augmentation operations presented in Table 2 and, in the end, the LF's train set contained 1193 images and MF's 1013. The validation and test sets were left with original images.

Table 2. Augmentation operations applied to the datasets

Operation	Value	Description
Scale	1.3×	Scaling the image
Noise	0–5%	Add salt and pepper noise
Rotation	−15% to +15%	Rotate the image
Flip horizontal	–	Flip the image horizontally
Grayscale	–	Apply grayscale
Hue	−25° to 25°	Change hue levels
Saturation	−30 to +30%	Change saturation levels
Brightness	−25 to +25%	Change image brightness
Exposure	−25 to +25%	Change image exposure
Blur	0–6.25%	Blur the image

2.3   Training and Testing of Deep Learning Models

The DL models selected to perform tree stems segmentation were YOLOv5 Small [17], YOLOv7 [25] and YOLOv8 Small [18] since these are state-of-the-art DL-based object detection and segmentation models. The models were trained during 50 epochs, with a 16 batch size, with a 640×640 default input size and following a transfer learning approach. The training environment was Google Colaboratory[4] with a Tesla T4 Graphics Processing Unit (GPU).

The models were tested on the test set and considering a confidence threshold of 1% and an Intersection over Union (IoU) threshold of 60%. The confidence threshold was kept low to consider the majority of detections. The IoU metric is defined in 1 and it measures the overlapping area between a ground-truth mask ($Mask_{GT}$) and a detected mask ($Mask_{DET}$). This metric is useful to assess whether

---

[4] https://colab.research.google.com.

a detection is considered valid or not, if it lies above or under a threshold, respectively. Besides, the evaluation of the models was performed using four metrics: Precision (P), Recall (R), Average Precision (AP) at an IoU of 50% (AP@50) and over an IoU range between 50% and 95% with steps of 5% (AP@50:95). Precision and Recall combine True Positives (TP), False Positives (FP) and False Negatives (FN) as defined in 2 and 3.

$$IoU = \frac{area(Mask_{GT} \cap Mask_{DET})}{area(Mask_{GT} \cup Mask_{DET})} \tag{1}$$

$$P = \frac{TP}{TP + FP} \tag{2}$$

$$R = \frac{TP}{TP + FN} \tag{3}$$

The Average Precision (AP) is a metric that summarises the Precision×Recall curve shape by computing the average of the maximum Precision values at each Recall level, and at the same time performs interpolation through all the points as it is shown in 4 and 5:

$$AP = \sum_{N}(R_{N+1} - R_N)P_{interp}(R_{N+1}) \tag{4}$$

with

$$P_{interp}(R_{N+1}) = \max_{\tilde{R}:\tilde{R} \geq R_{n+1}} P(\tilde{R}) \tag{5}$$

where $P(\tilde{R})$ is the Precision measured at Recall $\tilde{R}$.

2.4   Automatic Stem Selection Algorithm

The algorithm to perform automatic stem selection was developed to work with coloured monocular images and depth images, and is based of the morphological aspects of pre-segmented stems.

The algorithm starts with the segmentation masks outputted from the DL-based stem segmentation model and then, it calculates the three-dimensional position of each stem, its area (in pixels) and the angle of the its best fitting line relatively to the vertical axis (90°). Considering the 3D information, the stems were grouped in clusters (using the XY data). Afterwards, in each cluster, the two larger stems (the ones with biggest area) and the two less inclined—presenting at most a 30° inclination-, while keeping a minimum distance between each other, are selected. The number of stems chosen to remain was two, since it is the mean term regarding the quantity normally considered, which can vary between one to three stems [11]. Besides, the stems inclination was considered to effectively select the most vigorous ones. The algorithm was tested was evaluated using Precision, Recall, and processing time.

The algorithm was developed to consider and evaluate every segmented stem, in order to solve cases where more than one group of eucalyptus stems appear, such as the one shown in Fig. 2. So, besides testing the algorithm on each test dataset, we gathered a mixed dataset (containing images with less and more foliage all together) in a different forest environment, and aligned coloured and depth images were acquired using OAK-D's stereoscopic vision. With these two types of images, obtaining the 3D information of every stem became possible, as well as the application of a hierarchical spatial clustering technique to group the stems.

Fig. 2. Example of an image containing eucalyptus stems where some groups are located in the background and between some stems of the main (front) group.

One of the key aspects of the algorithm is about taking into consideration the proximity of the stems between each other. A usual practice while performing manual stem selection is about leaving enough space between the selected eucalyptus stems to avoid them to compete with each other for sunlight [11]. These cases, where the second largest stem was selected although is very close to the largest one, were considered as False Positives, and the non-selected and more separated stems were considered False Negatives. These cases were simplified by using of depth information (and further 3D information) provided by the OAK-D sensor.

3 Results

The segmentation results on LF and MF test datasets are presented in Table 3. In both datasets YOLOv8 was the best model in all metrics except Precision in the LF dataset.

The results presented in Table 3 reveal a performance improvement for the LF dataset compared to the MF dataset. This can be attributed to the higher level of occlusion in the MF dataset caused by the greater amount of foliage.

Table 3. Segmentation results on the two test datasets.

Dataset	Model	P	R	AP@50	AP@50:95
	YOLOv5 Small	0.756	0.466	0.599	0.286
LF$_{Test}$	YOLOv7	0.783	0.523	0.648	0.331
	YOLOv8 Small	0.705	0.681	0.748	0.383
	YOLOv5 Small	0.640	0.553	0.579	0.188
MF$_{Test}$	YOLOv7	0.685	0.556	0.618	0.231
	YOLOv8 Small	0.751	0.611	0.660	0.288

The dense foliage makes it challenging for the algorithm to visually detect the eucalyptus stems, resulting in lower instance segmentation accuracy.

In this article, promising results were found, being YOLOv8 the best model for eucalyptus stem segmentation [18], achieving an mAP of 74.8% and 66% for LF and MF datasets, respectively. Besides, this article presents a unique approach to instance segmentation for standing eucalyptus stems before selective thinning, as there are no previous articles on this specific topic. However, there are some articles about similar tasks. In [15], the authors demonstrate that supervised end-to-end deep learning can successfully detect trees in forested environments using different backbones, with a model based on Cascade Mask R-CNN [4] achieving the best performance at 87.2% mAP. In [12], the objective was to perform instance segmentation for autonomous log grasping in forestry operations. The authors concluded that Mask2Former [5] with Swin-B [19] backbone achieved the best performance at 57.53% mAP. Both of these works are related to this article by the forest domain, however they differ in some aspects: the size of the dataset, as our dataset is much smaller; and our dataset was acquired strictly before selective thinning, therefore more challenging visual conditions were expected with more occlusions and unexpected lighting scenarios.

Regarding the automatic stem selection algorithm, the segmentation masks that were considered as input were the ones outputted from YOLOv8, since it was the best model at segmenting eucalyptus stems. The results are shown in Table 4, where it can be seen that again the results are better for the dataset with low level of foliage (LF). This was expected since the existence of more foliage makes it harder for the algorithm to select the best stems due to the occlusions. In addition, the algorithm processing is faster for the LF dataset because of the lower image resolution in this dataset (the images are almost two times smaller).

Table 4. Automatic stem selection results on the two test datasets and on the mixed dataset.

Depth info	Dataset	P	R	Processing time (s)
No	LF$_{Test}$	0.910	0.586	0.113 ± 0.019
	MF$_{Test}$	0.875	0.472	0.181 ± 0.029
Yes	Mixed	0.974	0.810	0.859 ± 0.411

The addition of depth information (with the mixed dataset) contributed to a performance enhancement of the algorithm, as it managed to attain a Precision above 97% (at least, 6% more than without depth) and a Recall of 81% (at least, 21% more than without depth). However, in terms of processing time, depth-aware computation added on average more than 0.6 s. Figure 3 helps visualising the main steps of the algorithm, where the first row are the segmented stems

Fig. 3. Visualisation of the main steps of algorithm: clustering the segmented stems using depth information, and stem selection based of stem area, inclination and inter-stem distance.

provided by YOLOv8, the second row are the clustered stems and the third row represent the selected stems to keep. The algorithm presented promising results, however its ability to reliably select eucalyptus stems can be impacted by some factors. The quality of input images, which can include blurriness, low resolution, and noise can compromise its performance. Furthermore, the significant variances in appearance among the stems, such as colour, texture, form, and size, represent issues that must be addressed for enhanced identification and selection. Furthermore, the adverse environmental conditions inherent in forest environment, such as uneven illumination, dense shadows, and visual obstructions, can further hinder precise stem detection. Lastly, the use of depth images from stereo vision may introduce limitations due to factors like calibration inaccuracies, occlusions, and stereo matching issues, impacting the selection of eucalyptus stems.

4   Conclusions

This work aimed to investigate the ability of YOLO-based instance segmentation models to detect eucalyptus stems, and to use such detections to perform automatic stem selection based on morphological characteristics (stem vigour and inclination). To achieve this objective, two datasets were created—one with 1013 images featuring a higher level of foliage and the other with 1193 images having a lower level of foliage. The results indicated that among the three models evaluated, YOLOv8 was the best performer with an Average Precision of 74.8% for the LF dataset and 66% for the MF dataset. Although all the models showed good performance, we suspect that the results can be improved with the addition of more original images to the datasets.

An automatic stem selection algorithm was also developed that utilises the segmentation masks generated by YOLOv8 and outputs the selected stems presenting more area (in pixels) and less inclination, in each cluster. The algorithm was tested on the test sets and also on a mixed dataset (composed of coloured and depth images). On the test datasets, the algorithm achieved a Precision and Recall above 87% and 47%, respectively, while, on the mixed dataset, the Precision and Recall were higher (above 97% and 81%, respectively), due to the availability of depth information.

This study contributed to the knowledge domain by training and testing three state-of-the-art object detection models (YOLOv5, YOLOv7 and YOLOv8) in the context of eucalyptus stem detection and segmentation. Besides, a novel stem selection algorithm was developed that is capable of performing automatic selection with outstanding precision. At the time of writing this paper, no studies were found about the domain of eucalyptus selective thinning, so it is expected that the findings of this study will provide useful insights for the development of more effective and efficient algorithms to automatise eucalyptus stem selection.

Our computer vision system, besides being able to automate the identification of selectable eucalyptus stems, saving operators valuable time and effort, its integration with existing equipment can streamline thinning operations, maximising productivity and resource utilisation while minimising operational costs.

The system can be integrated in a forest machine or robotic platform to monitor and track throughout the selective thinning process in forestry operations. This way the selected eucalyptus stems are tracked in real-time, including their precise locations and status. This level of insight enables forest managers to effectively manage their inventory, plan subsequent operations, and conduct detailed analysis. The utilisation of this type of information can result in: data-driven decision making, optimisation of resource allocation, and improvement of forest management practices. Although current solutions in the field of forestry robotics are more focused on helping and increasing the efficiency of human operators, the other type of integration and the most futuristic one is about setting up the system on platforms equipped with mechanic arms capable of operating autonomously in this type of context.

Future work includes increasing the size of the datasets to improve models accuracy. Furthermore, benchmarking the models with other real-time methods such as, YOLACT [2,3], would be beneficial since these kind of models are essential for applications where real-time operation is a constraint. Additionally, it would be informative to compare these with non-real-time models such as, the Region-based Convolutional Neural Networks (R-CNN) family [4,16] and Mask2Former [5]. Lastly, we intend to further develop the automatic stem selection system to consider also LiDAR technology, as a way of enhancing its performance, specially when the lighting conditions are rough or when the eucalyptus stems are more distant from the camera.

Acknowledgment. This work is financed by National Funds through the Portuguese funding agency, FCT—Fundação para a Ciência e a Tecnologia, within project LA/P/0063/2020. This work is also financed by the ERDF-European Regional Development Fund, through the Operational Programme for Competitiveness and Internationalisation-COMPETE 2020 Programme under the Portugal 2020 Partnership Agreement, within project SMARTCUT, with reference POCI-01-0247-FEDER-048183. Daniel Queirós da Silva thanks the FCT-Foundation for Science and Technology, Portugal for the Ph.D. Grant UI/BD/152564/2022.

References

1. Bishop, C.M.: Pattern Recognition and Machine Learning. Springer, Berlin, Heidelberg (2006)
2. Bolya, D., Zhou, C., Xiao, F., Lee, Y.J.: Yolact: real-time instance segmentation. In: ICCV (2019)
3. Bolya, D., Zhou, C., Xiao, F., Lee, Y.J.: Yolact++ better real-time instance segmentation. IEEE Trans. Pattern Anal. Mach. Intell. **44**(2), 1108–1121 (2022). https://doi.org/10.1109/TPAMI.2020.3014297
4. Cai, Z., Vasconcelos, N.: Cascade R-CNN: high quality object detection and instance segmentation. IEEE Trans. Pattern Anal. Mach. Intell. **43**(5), 1483–1498 (2021). https://doi.org/10.1109/TPAMI.2019.2956516
5. Cheng, B., Misra, I., Schwing, A.G., Kirillov, A., Girdhar, R.: Masked-attention mask transformer for universal image segmentation. In: 2022 IEEE/CVF Conference on Computer Vision and Pattern Recognition (CVPR), pp. 1280–1289 (2022). https://doi.org/10.1109/CVPR52688.2022.00135

6. da Silva, D.Q., dos Santos, F.N., Filipe, V., Sousa, A.J.: Tree trunks cross-platform detection using deep learning strategies for forestry operations. In: Tardioli, D., Matellán, V., Heredia, G., Silva, M.F., Marques, L. (eds.) ROBOT2022: fifth Iberian Robotics Conference, pp. 40–52. Springer International Publishing, Cham (2023). https://doi.org/10.1007/978-3-031-21065-5_4

7. da Silva, D.Q., dos Santos, F.N., Filipe, V., Sousa, A.J., Oliveira, P.M.: Edge AI-based tree trunk detection for forestry monitoring robotics. Robotics 11(6) (2022). https://doi.org/10.3390/robotics11060136

8. da Silva, D.Q., dos Santos, F.N., Sousa, A.J., Filipe, V., Boaventura-Cunha, J.: Unimodal and multimodal perception for forest management: review and dataset. Computation 9(12) (2021). https://doi.org/10.3390/computation9120127

9. da Silva, D.Q., dos Santos, F.N., Sousa, A.J., Filipe, V.: Visible and thermal image-based trunk detection with deep learning for forestry mobile robotics. J. Imaging 7(9) (2021). https://doi.org/10.3390/jimaging7090176

10. FAO: The State of the World's Forests 2022, p. 28. FAO, Rome (2022)

11. Ferreira, D., Morais, S.: Seleção de varas - Manual técnico de apoio á gestão de talhadias (2022)

12. Fortin, J.M., Gamache, O., Grondin, V., Pomerleau, F., Giguère, P.: Instance segmentation for autonomous log grasping in forestry operations. In: 2022 IEEE/RSJ International Conference on Intelligent Robots and Systems (IROS), pp. 6064–6071 (2022). https://doi.org/10.1109/IROS47612.2022.9982286

13. Fritz, A., Kattenborn, T., Koch, B.: UAV-based photogrammetric point clouds— Tree stem mapping in open stands in comparison to terrestrial laser scanner point clouds. In: The International Archives of the Photogrammetry, Remote Sensing and Spatial Information Sciences XL-1/W2(September), pp. 141–146 (2013). https://doi.org/10.5194/isprsarchives-xl-1-w2-141-2013

14. Gomide, L., Mello, J., Acerbi Júnior, F., Scolforo, J.: Automated selective thinning via multicriteria maetaheuristic procedure. Scientia Forestalis/Forest Sci. 42, 299–306 (2014)

15. Grondin, V., Fortin, J.M., Pomerleau, F., Giguère, P.: Tree detection and diameter estimation based on deep learning. Forest.: Int. J. Forest Res. (2022)

16. He, K., Gkioxari, G., Dollár, P., Girshick, R.: Mask R-CNN. In: Proceedings of the International Conference on Computer Vision (ICCV) (2017)

17. Jocher, G.: YOLOv5 by Ultralytics (2020). https://doi.org/10.5281/zenodo.3908559

18. Jocher, G., Chaurasia, A., Qiu, J.: YOLO by Ultralytics (2023)

19. Liu, Z., Lin, Y., Cao, Y., Hu, H., Wei, Y., Zhang, Z., Lin, S., Guo, B.: Swin transformer: hierarchical vision transformer using shifted windows. In: Proceedings of the IEEE/CVF International Conference on Computer Vision (ICCV) (2021)

20. Mokroš, M., Mikita, T., Singh, A., Tomaštík, J., Chudá, J., Wężyk, P., Kuželka, K., Surový, P., Klimánek, M., Zięba-Kulawik, K., Bobrowski, R., Liang, X.: Novel low-cost mobile mapping systems for forest inventories as terrestrial laser scanning alternatives. Int. J. Appl. Earth Observ. Geoinf. 104 (2021). https://doi.org/10.1016/j.jag.2021.102512

21. Söderbergh, I., Ledermann, T.: Algorithms for simulating thinning and harvesting in five European individual-tree growth simulators: a review. Comput. Electron. Agric. 39(2), 115–140 (2003). https://doi.org/10.1016/S0168-1699(03)00022-X

22. Vestlund, K., Hellström, T.: Requirements and system design for a robot performing selective cleaning in young forest stands. J. Terrramech. 43(4), 505–525 (2006). https://doi.org/10.1016/j.jterra.2005.07.001

23. Vestlund, K., Nordfjell, T., Eliasson, L.: Comparison of human and computer-based selective cleaning. Silva Fennica Monogr. **39**(4), 509–523 (2005). https://doi.org/10.14214/sf.363
24. Vestlund, K., Nordfjell, T., Eliasson, L., Karlsson, A.: A decision support system for selective cleaning. Silva Fennica **40**(2), 271–289 (2006). https://doi.org/10.14214/sf.343
25. Wang, C.Y., Bochkovskiy, A., Liao, H.Y.M.: YOLOv7: Trainable bag-of-freebies sets new state-of-the-art for real-time object detectors (2022). arXiv:2207.02696
26. Zhen, Z., Quackenbush, L.J., Zhang, L.: Trends in automatic individual tree crown detection and delineation-evolution of LiDAR data. Remote Sens. **8**(4), 1–26 (2016). https://doi.org/10.3390/rs8040333

Segmentation as a Pre-processing for Automatic Grape Moths Detection

Ana Cláudia Teixeira[1,2]([⊠]) [iD], Gabriel A. Carneiro[1,2] [iD], Raul Morais[1,3] [iD], Joaquim J. Sousa[1,2] [iD], and António Cunha[1,2] [iD]

[1] Engineering Department, School of Science and Technology, UTAD-University of Trás-os-Montes e Alto Douro, 5000-801 Vila Real, Portugal
[2] Institute for Systems and Computer Engineering, Technology and Science (INESC-TEC), 4200-465 Porto, Portugal
anaclaudia13ct@gmail.com
[3] Centre for the Research and Technology of Agro-Environmental and Biological Sciences, University of Trás-os-Montes e Alto Douro, 5000-801 Vila Real, Portugal

Abstract. Grape moths are a significant pest in vineyards, causing damage and losses in wine production. Pheromone traps are used to monitor grape moth populations and determine their developmental status to make informed decisions regarding pest control. Smart pest monitoring systems that employ sensors, cameras, and artificial intelligence algorithms are becoming increasingly popular due to their ability to streamline the monitoring process. In this study, we investigate the effectiveness of using segmentation as a pre-processing step to improve the detection of grape moths in trap images using deep learning models. We train two segmentation models, the U-Net architecture with ResNet18 and InceptionV3 backbonesl, and utilize the segmented and non-segmented images in the YOLOv5s and YOLOv8s detectors to evaluate the impact of segmentation on detection. Our results show that segmentation pre-processing can significantly improve detection by 3% for YOLOv5 and 1.2% for YOLOv8. These findings highlight the potential of segmentation pre-processing for enhancing insect detection in smart pest monitoring systems, paving the way for further exploration of different training methods.

Keywords: Insect detection · Image segmentation · Smart pest monitoring · Deep learning

1 Introduction

Grape moth is a vine pest that causes significant damage and losses in wine production. It undergoes several stages of morphological development throughout the year, including the egg, caterpillar, pupa, and adult. Adult females lay eggs inside the grapes, which hatch and the caterpillar begins to feed on the grapes, causing them to become deformed and unsaleable [1]. To determine the

© The Author(s), under exclusive license to Springer Nature Switzerland AG 2023
N. Moniz et al. (Eds.): EPIA 2023, LNAI 14116, pp. 388–398, 2023.
https://doi.org/10.1007/978-3-031-49011-8_31

beginning of the morphological cycle of the grape moth, pheromone traps are installed to attract adult moths. This tool allows monitoring the development status of grape moth populations and subsequent decision-making to keep the pest under control, minimize the application of pesticides and reduce significant damage to the crop [3,11].

Smart pest monitoring systems employ a variety of technologies such as sensors, cameras, and artificial intelligence algorithms to identify pests and provide real-time data for pest monitoring and detection. The smart monitoring system regularly collects information from each trap, photographing, detecting, and counting the insects captured inside [2]. The use of smart traps is an option that aims to simplify and streamline the monitoring process, replacing the traditional process in which the task is performed by specialists who need to regularly visit the traps, which can be a difficult, time-consuming, error-prone process, and delay decision-making [10].

The research community has been developing several Deep Learning (DL) applications to detect insects of various species, such as black pine pests [12], whitefly and thrips [5], and riptortus pedestris [6]. Recognizing insects using DL methods is a challenging task that can be tackled by considering the characteristics of the dataset. The primary challenge is related to the quality of the dataset images, which may not accurately represent insects due to poor visibility. Traps placed in outdoor environments are susceptible to various obstacles, including larger insects, shadows, and excessive brightness, making it challenging to identify small insects composed of only a few pixels [10].

Experiments previously conducted by our team demonstrated successful detection of the grape moth, achieving an average precision (AP) of 90.9% with the YOLOv5s model [9]. Some of the images used in the previous experiments conducted by the team showed that the predictions made by the model extended beyond the boundaries of the trap and into the background, showing some false positives, as evidenced by the illustration in Fig. 1. To address this issue, one possible solution is to perform trap segmentation as a pre-processing step before the detection task. The main research question that was formulated is:

Can improve the detection task for a grape moth when performed segmentation as a preprocessing step using DL models?

To answer this question, the study proposes evaluating the detection task after removing background regions from trap images using DL models. Two DL-based methods, the U-Net architecture with two different backbones, ResNet18 and InceptionV3, were trained to automatically perform segmentation. Then, utilized both segmented and non-segmented images in the YOLOv5s and the latest version, YOLOv8s, to determine the impact of trap segmentation in detection.

2 Methodology

The methodology employed in this study is comprised of three distinct steps: dataset preparation, segmentation, and detection. During the dataset preparation step, the dataset was organized and prepared for both segmentation and

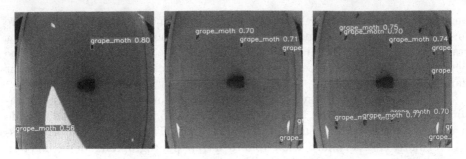

Fig. 1. Examples of three images with detections in the background outside the trap. These images were predicted by the YOLOv5s model in a previous study [9].

detection tasks. In the segmentation step, two models were trained: U-Net with ResNet18 (Seg-R) and U-Net with InceptionV3 (Seg-I). Both models were evaluated with Intersection over Union (IoU) and F1-score metrics. In the detection step, two YOLOv5s and YOLOv8s detectors were trained, with each model being trained through four separate experiments—two with non-segmented data (v5-NSD and v8- NSD) and two with segmented data (v5-SD and v8-SD). Ultimately, the performance of all four models was evaluated through the calculation of the AP. All experiments are summarised in Table 1.

Table 1. Description of all experiments implemented.

Experiment	Task	Dataset	Model
Seg-R	Segmentation	100 images	U-Net with ResNet18
Seg-I	Segmentation	100 images	U-Net with InceptionV3
v5-NSD	Detection	Non-segmented data (448 images)	YOLOv5s
v5-SD	Detection	Segmented data (448 images)	YOLOv5s
v8-NSD	Detection	Non-segmented data (448 images)	YOLOv8s
v8-SD	Detection	Segmented data (448 images)	YOLOv8s

2.1   Dataset and Data Preparation

The dataset was collected between 2021 and 2022 using a pheromone trap installed in a vineyard at the University of Trás-os-Montes and Alto Douro, as shown in the Fig. 2. It comprises 446 images with a resolution of 640 × 640 pixels. For the segmentation task, 100 representative images were selected from the dataset and divided into three sets for training (70), validation (15), and testing (15). The Label Studio tool was employed to annotate all the images with a mask. The remaining images in the dataset (346) were not used in the segmentation model. The segmentation was predicted by the model (Seg-R or

Seg-I) with the highest IoU and F1-score value. In the detection task, the complete dataset was utilized and split into training (321), validation (84), and test (41) subsets. All images in the dataset have annotations of the grape moth in YOLO format, accounting for 13,117 grape moth instances.

Fig. 2. Example of pheromone trap installed in a vineyard at the University of Trás-os-Montes and Alto Douro.

2.2 Segmentation Task

The segmentation experiments aimed to enhance insect detection results by eliminating non-trap areas. Since the non-trap region is the outer edge of the trap, the U-Net architecture was chosen. U-Net is a successful image segmentation technique that can segment based on small data [8]. In Seg-R, ResNet18 was used as the backbone for the U-Net architecture due to its fast convergence, good performance, and only 18 layers. In Seg-I, the U-Net with InceptionV3 backbone was used to improve gradient flow and combat gradient fading problems, and it has 48 layers. Both backbones were initialized with pre-trained weights on ImageNet.

Data augmentation methods like horizontal flips, perspective rotations, brightness manipulations, image blurring and sharpening, and random cuts were used to create new training data from the samples already available. The focus loss and dice loss were added together. While the focal loss concentrated on improving the most challenging prediction, the dice loss supplied information about the loss both globally and locally. The Adam optimizer was used to train the models over 150 iterations, with a learning rate that was set at 0.001, and the batch size was set at 12. The IoU and F1-score were utilized as the evaluation metrics for both experiments.

2.3 Detection Task

The initial YOLO version underwent additional development following its release in 2016, however, several iterations continue to be produced to enhance detection performance and lower computing costs. YOLO solves the detection problem by instantly predicting object categories and object placements from regression, as opposed to the two-stage technique of first identifying regions of interest and then classifying them [7]. This study was included in YOLOv5s and the latest version YOLOv8s.

YOLOv5 is that it uses a simpler, more effective architecture than previous versions, maintaining high precision while using a simpler, more efficient design. Use the CSPDarknet-53 as the foundation and apply dynamic dimensioning and multiscale forecasting in addition to these cutting-edge methods. The spatial pyramid group is incorporated in this version, which enhances the flow of low-level resources and increases the accuracy of item localization, particularly for smaller objects. The classification loss and regression loss functions employed by YOLOv5 are binary cross-entropy and complete IoU, respectively [13].

YOLOv8 architecture has undergone several changes. Overall, paying great attention to its design and training regimen, YOLOv8 has been meticulously created and enhanced. As a consequence, a very successful object detection model has been produced. These include many adjustments to the backbone that introduce and replacement of new convolutions. The other YOLO versions used anchor boxes, which were problematic since they might not have adequately reflected the distribution of custom datasets. Instead, YOLOv8 predicts an object's center directly, lowering the number of box predictions and accelerating the non-maximum suppression post-processing stage. Varifocal and complete IoU are the two loss types used by YOLOv8 [4].

Four experiments were carried out using the segmented and unsegmented datasets, with YOLOv5 (v5-SD and v5-NSD) and with YOLOv8 (v8-SD and v8-NSD). The datasets were divided in same way, and there were 150 training epochs with a batch size of 16 for both training and validation in every experiment. The models' performance was assessed using AP metric. AP computes the area under the precision-recall curve. Precision and recall are calculated for each threshold value. Precision is the percentage of true positives, i.e. correct detections. Recall is a percentage of predicted positive instances (true positives) to the total number of positive instances (true positives and false negatives).

3   Results and Discussion

3.1   Segmentation Task

The results of segmentation experiments are summarised in Table 2. The best result achieved using backbone InceptionV3, experiment Seg-I, obtaining the highest value of IoU and F1-score. Comparing the metrics of the two experiments, it was verified that both had a high performance and the differences between them are not significant. However, this result was expected since InceptionV3 is a deeper convolutional neural network, with more layers, and improves the feature extraction that allows it to capture features at multiple scales and resolutions, which can be particularly useful for tasks such as segmentation.

Table 2. Results of segmentation experiments.

Experiment	IoU (%)	F1-score (%)
Seg-R	97.61	98.79
Seg-I	**98.32**	**99.16**

Four examples of correct and incorrect segmentations for each experiment on test set images are illustrated in Fig. 3. Overall, we can see that image (a) yielded correct predictions for both experiments. The Seg-R experiment failed to segment the full background for images (b) and (d), while it correctly segmented image (c). The Seg-I experiment correctly predicted image (b); presented segmentation errors in image (c) when segmenting parts of the trap, despite not having impact on the detection task, as the segmented locations do not contain insects; a and image (d) was not fully segmented, still containing small background details.

After identifying the experiment that yielded the best performance in the segmentation task, we needed to generate segmentations for the remaining dataset, which consisted of 346 images that were not used in this task. To accomplish this, we utilized the weights from the Seg-I experiment to predict their segmentation. As a result, we were able to obtain segmentations for all of the images in the dataset.

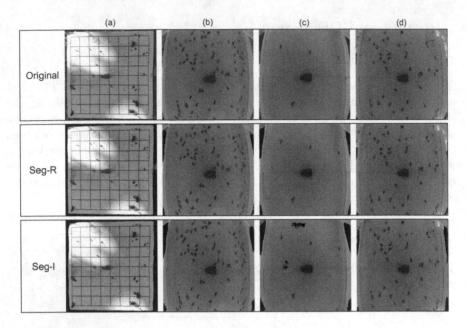

Fig. 3. Four examples of segmented images by each segmentation experiment.

3.2 Detection Task

Table 3 summarises the results of the detection experiments. The AP metric obtained was 90.9%, 93.9%, 93.6% and 94.8%, for experiments v5-NSD, v5-SD, v8-NSD and v8-SD, respectively.

Table 3. Results of segmentation experiments.

Experiment	N⁰ of parameters	AP (%)
v5-NSD	7,200,000	90.9
v5-SD	7,200,000	93.9
v8-NSD	11,200,000	93.6
v8-SD	11,200,000	**94.8**

The best performance was achieved by YOLOv8 with thread preprocessing (v8-SD). The two experiments that used the dataset in which the segmentation preprocessing was performed showed a significant improvement in the AP value, in the case of YOLOv5 it improved by 3% and in the case of YOLOv8 it improved by 1.2%.

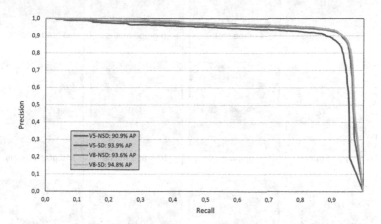

Fig. 4. Comparisons of precision-recall curves between v5-NSD, v5-SD, v8-NSD and v8-SD experiments.

Figure 4 shows the graph of the recall-precision curve used to calculate the AP value. A comparison of the PR curves revealed that the detection accuracy of the v8-SD experiment was greater than that of all experiments under the same recall conditions. The v5-NSD stands out for its lower value than the other models, and the rest are very close to the curve of the v8-SD. Comparing between YOLO versions, YOLOv8 was expected to have the superior result since it is the latest architecture and is designed for better detections of smaller objects with higher accuracy.

Figure 5 shows the prediction results of each model for three sample images. Image (a) contains 4 moths, image (b) 10 moths, and image (c) 58 moths. The v5-NSD experiment failed to predict the two images, detecting 2 insects outside the trap, and when applied to the segmented dataset (v5-SD), this error did not occur, correctly predicting the two images. In the v8-NSD experiment, an out-of-trap detection was detected and later, when applied to the segmented data, it was not verified. Another previously identified issue is the tendency for detection models to fail when traps have dozens of insects. In this case, with the image (c) containing 58 grape moths, it is possible to verify that only the v8-SD experiment was correct in the number of insects. Therefore, in addition to improving the metric result, this trend was also verified in the predictions in the test set, both in detections outside the trap and in detections in traps with dozens of insects.

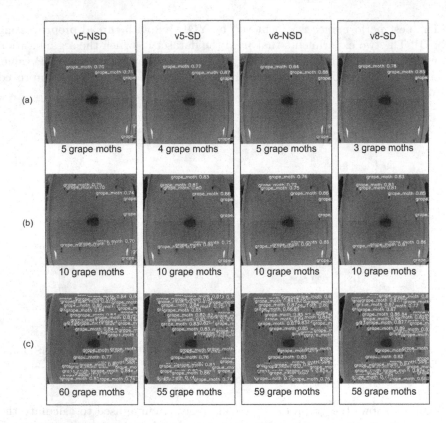

Fig. 5. Illustration of the predictions made by different experiments for three sample image. In each image, the number of detected grape moths is indicated, the bounding box with the location of the insect and the label with the degree of confidence.

Considering the main research question of this work, it is possible to answer that yes, segmentation helped to improve detection results with YOLOv5 and YOLOv8. In our case, in some images, the outer background of the trap is not highly representable in the image, but even so it manages to improve the detection task. Therefore, pre-processing with a segmentation can be a fundamental task to improve the performance of detectors.

4   Conclusion

In conclusion, the evaluation of the detection task after pre-processing with segmentation of trap resulted in significant improvements in the detection accuracy. Two experiments were conducted to identify the best-performing segmentation method, with the U-Net using the InceptionV3 backbone achieving the highest IoU of 98.32% and F1-score of 99.16%. Next, four experiments were carried out using YOLOv5s and YOLOv8s detectors with both segmented and non-segmented datasets. The results showed that the use of segmentation pre-processing improved the detection accuracy by 3% for YOLOv5 and 1.2% for YOLOv8. The study highlights the potential of segmentation pre-processing for enhancing insect detection and paves the way for further exploration of different training methods. The next step is to develop a field application using the most suitable experiment to maximize the benefits of segmentation pre-processing for insect detection.

Acknowledgments. This work was supported by the project "DATI-Digital Agriculture Technologies for Irrigation efficiency", PRIMA-Partnership for Research and Innovation in the Mediterranean Area, (Research and Innovation activities), financed by the states participating in the PRIMA partnership and by the European Union through Horizon 2020. This work was also financed by National Funds through the Portuguese funding agency, FCT-Fundação para a Ciência e a Tecnologia, within project LA/P/0063/2020.

References

1. Altimira, F., Vitta, N., Tapia, E.: Integrated pest management of Lobesia botrana with Microorganism in Vineyards: an alternative for clean grapes production (2021). https://doi.org/10.5772/intechopen.99153
2. Chen, C.J., Huang, Y.Y., Li, Y.S., Chang, C.Y., Huang, Y.M.: An AIoT based smart agricultural system for pests detection. IEEE Access **8**, 180750–180761 (2020). https://doi.org/10.1109/ACCESS.2020.3024891
3. Duso, C., Pozzebon, A., Lorenzon, M., Fornasiero, D., Tirello, P., Simoni, S., Bagnoli, B.: The impact of microbial and botanical insecticides on grape berry moths and their effects on secondary pests and beneficials. Agronomy **12**(1) (2022). https://doi.org/10.3390/agronomy12010217, https://www.mdpi.com/2073-4395/12/1/217
4. Jocher, G., Chaurasia, A., Qiu, J.: YOLO by Ultralytics (2023). https://github.com/ultralytics/ultralytics
5. Li, W., Wang, D., Li, M., Gao, Y., Wu, J., Yang, X.: Field detection of tiny pests from sticky trap images using deep learning in agricultural greenhouse. Comput. Electron. Agric. **183**, 106048 (2021). https://doi.org/10.1016/j.compag.2021.106048
6. Park, Y.H., Choi, S., Kwon, Y.J., Kwon, S.W., Kang, Y., Jun, T.H.: Detection of soybean insect pest and a forecasting platform using deep learning with unmanned ground vehicles. Agronomy **13**, 477 (2023). https://doi.org/10.3390/agronomy13020477
7. Redmon, J., Divvala, S., Girshick, R., Farhadi, A.: You only look once: unified, real-time object detection (2016)
8. Ronneberger, O., Fischer, P., Brox, T.: U-net: convolutional networks for biomedical image segmentation (2015)
9. Teixeira, A.C., Morais, R., Sousa, J.J., Peres, E., Cunha, A.: A deep learning approach for automatic counting of bedbugs and grape moth. Procedia Comput. Sci. **219**, 145–152 (2023). https://doi.org/10.1016/j.procs.2023.01.275
10. Teixeira, A.C., Ribeiro, J., Morais, R., Sousa, J.J., Cunha, A.: A systematic review on automatic insect detection using deep learning. Agriculture **13**(3) (2023).

https://doi.org/10.3390/agriculture13030713, https://www.mdpi.com/2077-0472/13/3/713

11. Ünlü, L., Akdemir, B., Ögür, E., Şahin, : Remote monitoring of European grapevine moth, Lobesia Botrana (Lepidoptera: Tortricidae) population using camera-based pheromone traps in vineyards. Turkish J. Agric. Food Sci. Technol. **7**(4), 652–657 (2019). https://doi.org/10.24925/turjaf.v7i4.652-657.2382, http://www.agrifoodscience.com/index.php/TURJAF/article/view/2382

12. Yun, W., Kumar, J.P., Lee, S., Kim, D.S., Cho, B.K.: Deep learning-based system development for black pine BAST scale detection. Sci. Rep. **12** (2022). https://doi.org/10.1038/s41598-021-04432-z

13. Zhu, L., Geng, X., Li, Z., Liu, C.: Improving yolov5 with attention mechanism for detecting boulders from planetary images. Remote Sens. **13**(18) (2021). https://doi.org/10.3390/rs13183776, https://www.mdpi.com/2072-4292/13/18/3776

Artificial Intelligence in Transportation Systems

Safety, Stability, and Efficiency
of Taxi Rides

Martin Aleksandrov[1]($\boxtimes$) and Tobias Labarta[2]

[1] Freie Universität Berlin, Berlin, Germany
martin.aleksandrov@fu-berlin.de
[2] Technische Universität Berlin, Berlin, Germany
labarta@campus.tu-berlin.de

Abstract. We propose a *novel* approach for limiting possible sexual harassment during taxi rides, where penalizing harassing drivers and matching them to passengers play key roles. In this paper, we focus on the matching part. In particular, we propose a *novel* two-sided market model, with drivers on one side and passengers on another side, where drivers have (1) *safety* preferences, (2) *profit* preferences, and (3) *gender* preferences, for passengers, and passengers have (1) *safety* preferences, (2) *delay* preferences, and (3) *gender* preferences, for drivers. Given these three-layer preferences, we study increasing the safety and stability in matchings, thus possibly reducing the chance of sexual harassment. In addition, we combine safety and stability with maximizing total profit or minimizing total delay. We design a number of algorithms throughout the paper and measure their safety, stability, and efficiency.

Keywords: Social choice · Multi-layer preferences · Taxi dispatching

1 Introduction

Sexual harassment could occur at various places during our daily routine: at home, on the way to work, at work, and on the way home: see e.g. a study by the US Center for Disease Control and Prevention (CDC) [1]. Fighting sexual harassment in public transport is particularly challenging because sexual harassment there is often committed by strangers whose personal information we may never be able to collect for further processing in court. For example, one Statista study[1] from 2016 shows that 18+-year-old women across France are often subject to the following sexual harassment types at public transport: out of 6227 respondents, 83% go for "whistling", 87% go for "invasive presence", 36% go for "intrusive question", 36% go for "insult, threat", 41% go for "sexual exhibition", 40% go for "sexual assault", 1% goes for "rape", and 4% go for "other". By these statistics, it follows that some of these victims have experienced multiple sexual harassment types either during different rides or during the same ride, possibly even by the same perpetrators.

---

[1] https://www.statista.com/statistics/1118528/types-bullying-women-transport-public-france/.

© The Author(s), under exclusive license to Springer Nature Switzerland AG 2023
N. Moniz et al. (Eds.): EPIA 2023, LNAI 14116, pp. 401–412, 2023.
https://doi.org/10.1007/978-3-031-49011-8_32

Victims of public transport sexual harassment may therefore prefer private transportation such as taxi services over the perceived threat of taking a metro or a bus. Although taxis are considered safer, there has been an increasing number of sexual harassment cases in them as well [4]. This is especially concerning because taxis might be the only option for women from underrepresented groups such as those with disabilities and those from various cultural minorities. But, in cases where this option can no longer be considered safe, women from such groups might feel less socially included, which in turn could harm their status in society. This could apply to women with low incomes, who already face restrictions in single-sex ride-sharing services, where they cannot share a trip with male passengers [2]. But, *how can we reduce sexual harassment in taxis?*.

Without having a reliable way of tracking harassment behavior, we cannot even hope to have a reliable way of fighting such behavior. Hence, tracking harassment behavior is necessary for fighting it. Currently, the existing approach for fighting harassment works as follows: (1) match drivers and passengers; (2) collect harassment claims; (3) issue fines to drivers. We depict it on the left side of Fig. 1. The drawback of this approach is that taxi companies remain unaware of and, therefore, cannot track the harassment behavior of their drivers. In response, we propose the following novel approach for tracking harassment behavior: (1) collect sexual harassment claims, (2) penalize harassing drivers, and (3) match drivers and passengers. We depict it on the right side of Fig. 1.

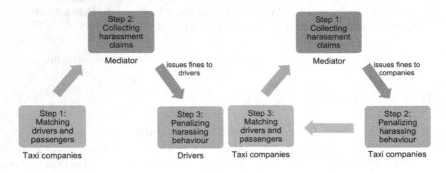

Fig. 1. Two approaches for fighting sexual harassment during taxi rides: (left) the existing approach; (right) the proposed approach.

1.1   Step 1: Collecting Harassment Claims

We propose to involve an independent governance body that can serve as a mediator between passengers and drivers. For example, the Taxi and Limousine Commission (TLC) in New York opened an Office of Inclusion, where passengers can submit sexual harassment claims after rides requested via an app, over the phone, or from the street. Such a body could thus regularly (e.g. every month) be sending to taxi companies **anonymous** feedback about how many claims were submitted against each of their drivers, without revealing any passenger data, preventing leakages of it to drivers.

1.2   Step 2: Penalizing Harassing Drivers

We propose the following novel **disciplinary** mechanism: the mediator (e.g. TLC) could issue fines to taxi companies, based on claims from the last feedback cycle (e.g. last month), thus motivating companies to design local prevention mechanisms; then, companies could detain the permits of harassing drivers and ask them to attend mandatory subsidized workshops before receiving their permits back. Companies could thus deploy a disciplinary approach for educating staff about basic principles for preventing sexual harassment during rides in their local areas, such as avoiding cheesy language, explaining victim perspectives, and increasing cultural awareness.

1.3   Step 3: Matching Drivers and Passengers

Most cases of sexual harassment are done by male drivers to female passengers [4]. This is possible partly because companies do *not* elicit from passengers their preferences over the gender of their potential matching driver. We propose to elicit such preferences during bookings. Also, we let passengers submit to dispatchers the times they can depart from their pickup locations, allowing dispatchers to compute the *delays* of drivers for picking up passengers. Furthermore, based on past rides, some passengers and drivers might have made, say through familiarity, *safe* rides and, for future matches, prefer such rides. We propose to elicit the permit numbers of familiar drivers during bookings. In this paper, we thus propose a two-phase matching method for **reducing possibly the chance of submitting sexual harassment claims to the mediator, by firstly maximizing the level of safety (Phase 1) and secondly optimizing the stability over the gender types (Phase 2).**

2   Related Work

Taxi dispatching relates to the seminal work of Karp et al. [8]. Since then, there are various extensions of this work. Mehta [11] presents a thorough survey of such works. Unlike us, the vast majority of these works consider one layer of preferences. For example, Zhao et al. [13] studied stable matchings under distance preferences of passengers over drivers and identical profit preferences of drivers over passengers. Also, Lesmana et al. [10] investigated efficient and fair matchings under delay preferences of passengers over drivers. Indeed, multi-layer matchings received significantly less attention in the research literature. One exception is the work of Chen et al. [3] who looked at a model where agents have multiple preference lists. Thus, they studied one notion of two-layer stability and showed that matchings that satisfy two-layer stability may not exist. We extend this work by running extensive simulations to confirm how close to two-layer stability we might get in practice. Furthermore, we are not aware of any prior work that focuses on integrating a theoretical two-sided market model with three-layer preferences into a practical approach for reducing possible sexual harassment in taxis.

3   Our Novel Model

We let t denote a point in time. We consider n drivers from $D = \{d_1, \ldots, d_n\}$ that are available at time t. We also consider m passengers from $P = \{p_1, \ldots, p_m\}$ whose requests for rides have not been serviced by time t. As our model is a two-sided market model, we refer to the parameter $\max\{n, m\}$ as *market size*. Pick driver $d_i \in D$. In practice, drivers service requests one after another. Thus, as in [13], we aim at matching $\min\{n, m\}$ drivers, each servicing exactly one request. We suppose that they have a depot location l_{d_i}. This might be a central or current location. Pick passenger $p_j \in P$. We let p_j have a pickup location l_{p_i}. This might be a public or private location.

3.1   Preferences Layers

Layer 1: Safety Preferences: Based on familiarities (e.g. location experiences, driver-passenger friendships), we let passengers and drivers submit incomplete safety preference lists. For passengers, we encode these as a complete safety relation $S_1 = (s_{1ji})_{m \times n}$, where $s_{1ji} = 1$ if p_j feels safe to be serviced by d_i, and else $s_{1ji} = 0$, indicating that it is unknown to the central planner whether p_j feels safe to be serviced by d_i. Similarly, for drivers, we encode these as a complete safety relation $S_2 = (s_{2ij})_{n \times m}$, where $s_{2ij} = 1$ if d_i feels safe to service the area of location l_{p_j}, and else $s_{2ij} = 0$, indicating that it is unknown to the central planner whether d_i feels safe to service the area of location l_{p_j}. We thus let $\Sigma = (\sigma_{ji})_{m \times n}$ denote the *joint safety* relation, where $\sigma_{ji} = 1$ if $s_{1ji} = 1$ and $s_{2ij} = 1$ hold, and else $\sigma_{ji} = 0$. We thus let passengers and drivers prefer rides that are safe for both of them to rides that feel unsafe for any of them.

Layer 2: Profit-delay Preferences: We suppose that each d_i derives a *profit* $\pi_{ij} > 0$ from servicing passenger p_j. The profit π_{ij} might also indicate how profitable p_j is for the business if serviced by d_i. For example, π_{ij} could be the charge for the ride minus the fuel cost. We let $\Pi = (\pi_{ij})_{n \times m}$. At the We suppose that t_{ij} denotes the estimated time of arrival (ETA) of d_i for picking up p_j at l_{p_j} from l_{d_i}. We let t_{ij} be computed with respect to (WRT) time t when we want to match drivers and passengers. That is, we suppose that $t_{ij} \geq t$ holds. We next suppose that p_j knows the time τ_j after which they have to depart from l_{p_j}. As p_j is not serviced by time t, we let $\tau_j \geq t$ hold. If p_j is not picked up by τ_j then they experience a *delay*, defined as follows: $\delta_{ji} = 0$ if p_j is matched to d_i and $t_{ij} \leq \tau_j$; $\delta_{ji} = (t_{ij} - \tau_j) > 0$ if p_j is matched to d_i and $t_{ij} > \tau_j$; $\delta_{ji} = 0$ if p_j is matched to d_k for some $k \neq i$. When booking a ride, p_j may not have knowledge of the location of d_i, which means that it is not possible for them to calculate t_{ij}. For this reason, we assume that p_j submits τ_j to a central planner who can calculate each t_{ij} and each δ_{ji}. We let $\Delta = (\delta_{ji})_{m \times n}$.

Layer 3: Gender Preferences: Let us assume that the central planner has access to the gender of their drivers. We let $\mathcal{G} = \{g_f = \text{female}, g_m = \text{male}, g_d = \text{diverse}\}$ contains the gender types. We let each p_j have a gender ranking that they submit to the central planner. For example, p_j may prefer ($\succ$) female drivers to male drivers and male drivers to diverse drivers. In this case, their gender ranking is $g_f \succ g_m \succ g_d$. We suppose that rankings may contain ties. For example, p_j may be indifferent ($\sim$) between male drivers and diverse drivers. In this case, their gender ranking is $g_f \succ g_m \sim g_d$. We also suppose that this ranking may be incomplete. For example, p_j may submit that they prefer female drivers. In this case, their gender ranking is g_f. We suppose that the central planner can complete (arbitrarily) incomplete rankings by appending the missing gender types and assuming passengers are indifferent among them. For example, they can complete g_f to $g_f \succ g_m \sim g_d$. By using the gender ranking for each p_j, we can calculate a complete ordinal ranking over the drivers, $\phi_j := d_{i_1} \circ \ldots \circ d_{i_n}$ with $\circ \{\succ, \sim, \succeq\}$ and where $(i_1, \ldots, i_n)$ is a permutation of $(1, \ldots, n)$, which for g_i of d_i and g_h of d_h is defined as follows: $d_i \succ d_h$ iff $g_i \succ g_h$; $d_i \sim d_h$ iff $g_i \sim g_h$; $d_i \succeq d_h$ iff $g_i \succ g_h$ or $g_i \sim g_h$. Additionally, we let each d_i have a gender ranking that the central planner could use to calculate similarly a complete ordinal ranking over the passengers, $\chi_i := p_{j_1} \circ \ldots \circ p_{j_m}$ with $\circ \{\succ, \sim, \succeq\}$ and where $(j_1, \ldots, j_m)$ is a permutation of $(1, \ldots, m)$, but we assume that they do not know this gender ranking as, otherwise, they would have had to elicit the gender data from passengers, which may discourage them from participation.

3.2   Matchings

Eligibility graphs: We consider a bipartite graph $G = (V_P, V_D, E)$, where the sets of passenger and driver vertices are V_P and V_D, respectively, and the *eligibility* relation between them is $E \subseteq V_P \times V_D$. For example, when going to the airport, d_i may not be eligible for servicing p_j in case p_j has many luggage items that cannot fit in the vehicle trunk of d_i. Thus, for each $(p_j, d_i) \notin E$, we set $\pi_{ij} = 0$ and $\delta_{ji} = K >> \max_{(p_g, d_h) \in E} \delta_{gh}$.

Matchings: We write $M = \{(p_{j_1}, d_{i_1}), \ldots, (p_{j_{\min\{n,m\}}}, d_{i_{\min\{n,m\}}})\}$ for a *matching* in G, where $j_1, \ldots, j_{\min\{n,m\}}$ are different indices among $1, \ldots, m$ and $i_1, \ldots, i_{\min\{n,m\}}$ are different indices among $1, \ldots, n$.

Jointly safe matchings: The overall joint safety level in M is $TS(M) = \sum_{(p_j, d_i) \in M \cap E} \sigma_{ji}$. We say that matching M is *jointly safe* if, for any other M', $TS(M) \geq TS(M')$ holds.

Blocking pairs: We let l denote the number of the preference layer in our model. That is, $l \in \{1, 2, 3\}$. We say that (p_j, d_i), which is in E but not in M, is a *blocking pair* for M on layer l iff p_j and d_i prefer each other to their current matches in M, say d_h and p_g, respectively: for $l = 1$, this means $\sigma_{ji} > \sigma_{gi}$ and $\sigma_{ji} > \sigma_{jh}$; for $l = 2$, this means $\pi_{ij} > \pi_{ig}$ and $\delta_{ji} < \delta_{jh}$; for $l = 3$, this means $d_i \succ d_h$ WRT ϕ_j and $p_j \succ p_g$ WRT χ_i.

Stable matchings: We say that matching M is *stable on layer l* iff, for each (p_j, d_i), that is in E but not in M, (p_j, d_i) is not a blocking pair for M on layer l. We say that matching M is *stable* iff, for each layer l, M is stable on l.

Efficient matchings: The total profit in M is $TP(M) = \sum_{(p_j, d_i) \in M \cap E} \pi_{ij}$. We say that matching M is *profit-efficient* if, for any other M', $TP(M) \geq TP(M')$ holds. The total delay in M is $TD(M) = \sum_{(p_j, d_i) \in M \cap E} \delta_{ji}$. We say that matching M is *delay-efficient* if, for any other M', $TD(M) \leq TD(M')$ holds.

4 Phase 1: Computing Jointly Safe Sub-Matchings

We warm up by considering how we might compute jointly safe sub-matchings over G. Many sexual harassment cases occur during rides in unsafe areas which drivers and passengers do not know very well, which increases the chance of victims submitting claims. From this perspective, we believe that focusing on achieving joint safety first is likely to reduce this chance because our notion of it is based on familiarity relations between passengers and drivers and the safety of areas.

4.1 Joint Safety

When computing jointly safe matchings, we need to respect the joint safety relation Σ and the eligibility relation E. For this purpose, we consider another bipartite graph $G_s = (V_P, V_D, E_s)$, where $E_s = \{(p_j, d_i) | (p_j, d_i) \in E, \sigma_{ji} = 1\}$. As it turns out, jointly safe matchings are maximum-cardinality matchings in the graph G_s and, therefore, can be computed in polynomial time.

Theorem 1. *There is an $O(\max\{n, m\}^{5/2})$ time algorithm that returns a jointly safe sub-matching.*

Proof. Given graph G_s, we can use the Hopcroft-Karp algorithm [6] for computing in $O(\max\{n, m\}^{5/2})$ time a maximum cardinality matching M_s over G_s. We argue that the returned matching is jointly safe. Indeed, if it were not, then there would be another M' such that $TS(M') > TP(M_s)$ would hold. Therefore, as each safety coefficient σ_{ji} is either one or zero, it would follow that M' would have a strictly greater cardinality than M_s. But, this would be in conflict with the correctness of the Hopcroft-Karp algorithm.   □

4.2 Joint Safety and Efficiency

If the best safe match provides the worst profit then there is clearly a profit loss. If the best safe match provides the longest delay then there is clearly a delay loss. For this reason, we might wish to compute a profit-efficient or a delay-efficient matching from within the set of jointly safe matchings.

If we insist on achieving both types of efficiency, we may not be able to combine them with joint safety because there are instances where each of the matchings is neither profit-efficient nor delay-efficient. So, profit efficiency, and delay efficiency are not compatible in general. We demonstrate this Example 1.

Example 1. Let us consider $D = \{d_1, d_2\}$ and $P = \{p_1, p_2\}$. Furthermore, let us consider the only two possible matchings $M_1 = \{(p_1, d_1), (p_2, d_2)\}$ and $M_2 = \{(p_1, d_2), (p_2, d_1)\}$. We next define only the preferences on layer two as follows: the profits of driver 1 are $\pi_{11} = 2$ and $\pi_{12} = 1$; the profits of driver 2 are $\pi_{21} = 1$ and $\pi_{22} = 2$; the delays of passenger 1 are $\delta_{11} = 2$ and $\delta_{12} = 1$; the delays of passenger 2 are $\delta_{21} = 1$ and $\delta_{22} = 2$.

We note that M_1 is profit-efficient ($TP(M_1) = 4$) but gives a total delay of 4 ($TD(M_1) = 4$). By comparison, M_2 is delay-efficient ($TD(M_2) = 2$) but gives a total profit of 2 ($TP(M_2) = 2$). Hence, M_1 is not delay-efficient and M_2 is not profit-efficient. This means that neither M_1 nor M_2 satisfies both efficiencies.

By Example 1, it follows that it may not be possible to achieve joint safety, profit efficiency, *and* delay efficiency. Hence, we attempt to combine joint safety with either profit efficiency *or* delay efficiency. Such matchings always exist. To compute one of them, we designed Algorithm 1.

Algorithm 1 Joint safety and efficiency.

1: **Input**: $P, D, E, \Sigma, \Pi, \Delta$
2: **Output**: a matching M_{se} that is jointly safe and efficient
3: **Result**: Joint safety on layer 1 and efficiency on layer 2
4: **procedure** JOINTSAFETY1EFFICIENCY2GENERALCASE
5:     $G_s \leftarrow (V_P, V_D, E_s)$
6:     $M_s \leftarrow$ a jointly safe matching over G_s
7:     $P_s \leftarrow$ the set of passengers matched in M_s
8:     $D_s \leftarrow$ the set of drivers matched in M_s
9:     $H_s \leftarrow (P_s, D_s, E_s)$
10:     $M_{se} \leftarrow$ an efficient matching over H_s ▷ either profit-efficiency *or* delay-efficiency *but* both may not be guaranteed
11:     **return** M_{se}

Theorem 2. *Algorithm 1 can return in $O(\max\{n, m\}^3)$ time a jointly safe and profit-efficient sub-matching, or a jointly safe and delay-efficient sub-matching, from within the set of jointly safe sub-matchings.*

Proof. Given G_s, Algorithm 1 can return, in $O(\max\{n, m\}^{5/2})$ time, a jointly safe sub-matching M_s: see Theorem 1. Next, it determines in $O(\min\{n, m\})$ time the graphs P_s and D_s, and also constructs in $O(\min\{n, m\}^2)$ time the graph H_s. Given H_s, Algorithm 1 can construct two weighted graphs, say W_{1s} and W_{2s}. $W_{1s} = (P_s, D_s, E_s, w_{1s})$ is such that, for each $e = (p_j, d_i) \in E_s$, $w_{1s}(e) = \pi_{ij} > 0$. $W_{2s} = (P_s, D_s, E_s, w_{2s})$ is such that, for each $e = (p_j, d_i) \in E_s$, $w_{2s}(e) = (K - \delta_{ji}) > 0$. It can then use a version [12] of the Hungarian algorithm [9] for computing in $O(\max\{n, m\}^3)$ time a maximum total weight (i.e. the sum of the individual edge weights) matching M_{se} over W_{1s} or W_{2s}. M_{se} is also a maximum cardinality matching over W_{1s} or W_{2s} as, otherwise, there would be another matching over W_{1s} or W_{2s} of strictly greater weight than M_{se} and this would contradict the correctness of the Hungarian method. Hence, M_{se} is also jointly safe over W_{1s} or W_{2s}. Finally, as M_{se} achieves the maximum total weight in W_{1s} or W_{2s}, it satisfies profit efficiency in W_{1s} or delay efficiency in W_{2s}. $\square$

Finally, any jointly safe M_s over G_s is stable on layer one. Otherwise, there would be (p_j, d_i), that is in E but not in M_s, which would block two edges from M_s on layer one, say (p_j, d_h) and (p_g, d_i) because $\sigma_{ji} = 1$ but $\sigma_{jh} = 0$ and $\sigma_{gi} = 0$ would hold. But, then M_s would not be jointly safe over G_s.

5   Phase 2: Computing Stable Sub-Matchings

In Phase 1, we computed safe M_s over $G_s = (V_P, V_D, E_s)$. We let P_s denote the passenger set in M_s and D_s denote the driver set in M_s. For each $(p_j, d_i) \in V_P \times V_D$, that is not matched in Phase 1, it follows by the maximality of M_s in G_s that either $(p_j, d_i) \notin E$ or $\sigma_{ji} = 0$ holds. In this section, we consider another graph $G_e = (V_P \setminus P_s, V_D \setminus D_s, E_e)$, where $E_e = \{(p_j, d_i) | p_j \in V_P \setminus P_s, d_i \in V_D \setminus D_s, (p_j, d_i) \in E\}$. For each $(p_j, d_i) \in E_e$, we note that $\sigma_{ji} = 0$ holds because of $(p_j, d_i) \in E$ and $(p_j, d_i) \notin M_s$. Thus, we focus on preference layers two and three in our model.

If we want to maximize the total profit across matchings over G_e, then we can run the Hungarian algorithm with the underlying profit-weighted graph, as we did for graph H_s in Theorem 2. If we want to minimize the total delay across matchings over G_e, then we can run the Hungarian algorithm with the underlying delay-weighted graph, as we did for graph G_s in Theorem 2. By our running example, it follows that we may not be able to achieve profit efficiency and delay efficiency simultaneously. For these reasons, we investigate achieving stability on layers two and three simultaneously.

Stability often relates to reducing the risk of sexual harassment and its associated chance of submitting claims. For example, as most sexual harassment cases occur from male drivers to female passengers, we expect that female passengers rank female drivers as their top choice and male drivers rank female passengers as their top choice. However, we assumed previously that passengers do not submit their gender during the booking process. From this perspective, we believe that achieving stability with the gender preferences of passengers over drivers would limit the number of female passengers matched to male drivers.

If we consider just layer two or three, stable matching always exists because the corresponding preference relations in our model may contain ties but are complete [7]. But, matchings that are stable on both layers may not exist. This follows by the non-existence result for two-layer stable matchings from [3]. We designed therefore an experimental setup in which we wanted to test how close to two-layer stability we might get in practice. The architecture was MacBook Pro M1 2020, 16GB RAM, 250GB Disk Space, and macOS Ventura 13.0.

Instances   For market size $n \in \{20, 40, 60, 80, 100\}$, we generated 10000 instances of n drivers who are eligible for n passengers. In each instance, there were two layers of preferences, one corresponding to layer two and another to layer three.

For layer two, we sampled uniformly at random each profit π_{ij} from $[1, 100]$, say in €, and each ETA t_{ij} from $[1, 60]$, say in *min*. In half of the instances, we set each departure time τ_j to 0, modeling *impatient* passenger behavior. This captured settings where passengers cannot wait before their departures (e.g. going from the airport to home). In the other half of the instances, we sampled uniformly at random each departure time τ_j from $(0, 30]$, modeling *patient* passenger behavior. This captured settings where passengers can wait before their departures or need some time to move to their pickup locations.

For layer three, we considered three gender types, namely 'male', 'female', and 'diverse', encoded as 0, 1, and 2, respectively. From among these gender types, we thus sampled uniformly at random the gender type of each p_j and each d_i. We also sampled uniformly at random the ranking over these gender types for each p_j and each d_i. By using these rankings, we calculated each ϕ_j and χ_i.

Algorithms We design an *eligibility* version of the Gale-Shapley algorithm [5] that uses strict passenger ordering. Thus, for each unmatched passenger p_j that comes next in the ordering, p_j makes a matching offer to the eligible driver they prefer, among the eligible drivers they have not yet already made an offer to. Each d_i, who has received an offer, evaluates it against their current match if they have one. If an eligible driver is not yet matched, or if they receive an offer from a passenger they prefer (based on their profit preferences or gender preferences which are known just to them) than their currently matched passenger, they accept the new offer and become matched to the new passenger. Otherwise, they reject the new offer. This process is repeated until matching is returned. With preferences on layer two (three), this returns a matching that is stable on layer two (three), but perhaps not stable on layer three (two). Thus, we propose the following extensions:

- RUNGS2COUNT3: (1) run the eligibility version of the Gale-Shapley algorithm on layer two; (2) count how many pairs block the returned sub-matching on layer three, and
- RUNGS3COUNT2: (1) run the eligibility version of the Gale-Shapley algorithm on layer three; (2) count how many pairs block the returned sub-matching on layer two.

5.1 Stability

RUNGS2COUNT3 returns a matching that is stable on layer two but may not be stable on layer three. RUNGS3COUNT2 returns a matching that is stable on layer three but may not be stable on layer two. For these reasons, we quantified the *stability gaps* of RUNGS2COUNT3 and RUNGS3COUNT2 on layers three and two by counting the numbers of pairs from these layers that block their returned matchings, respectively. The baseline is 0. It is achieved when no such blocking pairs exist.

Figure 2 shows our results. The gaps are bounded from above by the number n^2 of edges in the underlying graph. The gaps of RUNGS2COUNT3 on layers two and three are 0 and around 20% of n^2, respectively. This supports its superior efficiency performance but may indicate a greater chance of harassment. The gaps of RUNGS3COUNT2 on layers two and three are around 25% of n^2 and 0, respectively. This may indicate a lower chance of sexual harassment but supports its inferior efficiency performance.

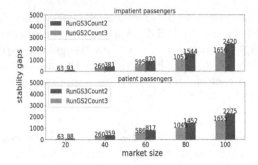

Fig. 2. The stability gaps of RUNGS3COUNT2 and RUNGS2COUNT3.

5.2 Stability and Efficiency

RUNGS3COUNT2 and RUNGS2COUNT3 induce efficiency losses. We used the minimum possible total delay—$\sum_{p_j \in P} \min_{d_i \in D} \delta_{ji}$—as a baseline for delay efficiency. Then, we calculated the *performance ratios for delay efficiency* between this baseline and the total delay of the matchings of RUNGS3COUNT2 and RUNGS2COUNT3. Similarly, we used the maximum possible total profit—$\sum_{d_i \in D} \max_{p_j \in P} \pi_{ij}$—as a baseline for profit efficiency. Then, we calculated the *performance ratios for profit efficiency* between the total profit of the matchings of RUNGS3COUNT2 and RUNGS2COUNT3 and this baseline.

Figure 3 depicts our results across all instances, where the lower-triangle trend traces the average performance of RUNGS3COUNT2 and the upper-triangle trend traces the average performance of RUNGS2COUNT3. The areas around these trends trace their worst and best performances, respectively.

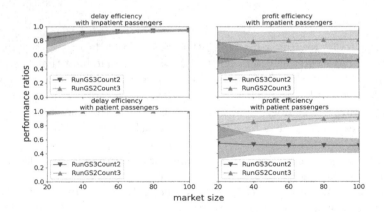

Fig. 3. The minimum, mean, and maximum performance ratios of RUNGS3COUNT2 and RUNGS2COUNT3. All ratios lie in $[0, 1]$.

Regarding delay efficiency, we made two observations (see the left plots in Fig. 3). Firstly, the performance of both algorithms converged steadily to optimality as we increased the market size. For example, with impatient passengers, their minimum performance ratios started from around 0.63 for $n = 20$ and increased to around 0.93 for $n = 100$. This could be because the greater the market size is the greater the expected number of most preferred options is. Secondly, the patience level of passengers mattered significantly as to how quickly the performance of both algorithms converged to optimality. For example, for $n = 20$, their minimum performance ratios started from around 0.63 with impatient passengers and increased to around 0.94 with patient passengers. This might be because the greater the departure time preferences are the lower the pickup delay preferences are.

Regarding profit efficiency, we also made two observations (see the right plots in Fig. 3). Firstly, as we increased the market size, the performance of RuNGS2COUNT3 converged slowly to optimality, and the performance of RuNGS3COUNT2 diverged slowly from optimality. For example, with impatient passengers, the minimum performance ratio of RuNGS2COUNT3 increased from around 0.47 for $n = 20$ to around 0.66 for $n = 100$ and the maximum performance ratio of RuNGS3COUNT2 decreased from around 0.79 for $n = 20$ to around 0.60 for $n = 100$. This is because RuNGS2COUNT3 returns a matching that is stable on layer two whereas RuNGS3COUNT2 is not guaranteed to return such a matching. Secondly, the patience level of passengers mattered significantly as to how steadily the performance of RuNGS2COUNT3 converged to optimality. For example, for $n = 100$, its minimum performance ratio started from around 0.66 with impatient passengers and increased to around 0.85 with patient passengers. This might be because more patient passengers are indifferent among more drivers and, for this reason, such passengers could have picked more profitable drivers.

6   Conclusion and Future Work

We proposed an approach for possibly fighting sexual harassment during taxi rides by maximizing safety and optimizing stability when matching drivers and passengers. Our findings confirm that safe and stable matchings often exist. Thus, we lay down the blueprints for future work. For example, we will look at how we might deploy the disciplinary mechanism in our approach. Also, we will look at how we might generalize other single-layer properties to our setting. Finally, it will be interesting to quantify the probability of sexual harassment in taxi dispatching and derive theoretical bounds on how much achieving safety, stability, or efficiency decreases this probability.

Acknowledgements. Martin Aleksandrov was supported by the DFG Individual Research Grant on "Fairness and Efficiency in Emerging Vehicle Routing Problems" (497791398).

References

1. Breiding, M.J.: Prevalence and characteristics of sexual violence, stalking, and inti-mate partner violence victimization-national intimate partner and sexual violence survey, united states, 2011. Morbidity and mortality weekly report. In: Surveil-lance summaries (Washington, DC: 2002), vol. 63, no. 8, p. 1 (2014). https://ajph.aphapublications.org/doi/10.2105/AJPH.2015.302634
2. Brown, E.: Fare trade: reconciling public safety and gender discrimination in single-sex ridesharing. Yale L. & Pol'y Rev. **35**, 367 (2016). https://www.jstor.org/stable/26601904
3. Chen, J., Niedermeier, R., Skowron, P.: Stable marriage with multi-modal prefer-ences. In: Proceedings of the 2018 ACM Conference on Economics and Computa-tion, pp. 269–286. EC '18, Association for Computing Machinery, New York, NY, USA (2018). https://doi.org/10.1145/3219166.3219168
4. Fileborn, B., Cama, E., Young, A.: Perceptions of safety among taxi and rideshare service patrons: gender, safekeeping and responsibilisation. Int. J. Crime Jus-tice Soc. Democr. **11**(4), 40 (2022). https://www.crimejusticejournal.com/article/view/2085
5. Gale, D., Shapley, L.S.: College admissions and the stability of marriage. Am. Math. Mon. **69**(1), 9–15 (1962). https://www.jstor.org/stable/2312726
6. Hopcroft, J.E., Karp, R.M.: A n5/2 algorithm for maximum matchings in bipartite. In: Proceedings of the 12th Annual Symposium on Switching and Automata The-ory (Swat 1971), pp. 122–125. SWAT '71, IEEE Computer Society, USA (1971). https://doi.org/10.1109/SWAT.1971.1
7. Iwama, K., Manlove, D., Miyazaki, S., Morita, Y.: Stable marriage with incomplete lists and ties. In: Wiedermann, J., van Emde Boas, P., Nielsen, M. (eds.) Automata, Languages and Programming, pp. 443–452. Springer, Berlin Heidelberg, Heidelberg (1999). https://link.springer.com/chapter/10.1007/3-540-48523-6_41
8. Karp, R.M., Vazirani, U.V., Vazirani, V.V.: An optimal algorithm for on-line bipar-tite matching. In: Proceedings of the Twenty-Second Annual ACM Symposium on Theory of Computing, pp. 352–358. STOC '90, Association for Computing Machin-ery, New York, NY, USA (1990). https://doi.org/10.1145/100216.100262
9. Kuhn, H.W.: The Hungarian method for the assignment problem. Naval Res. Logist. Quart. **2**(1–2), 83–97 (1955). https://doi.org/10.1002/nav.3800020109. March
10. Lesmana, N.S., Zhang, X., Bei, X.: Balancing efficiency and fairness in on-demand ridesourcing. In: Wallach, H., Larochelle, H., Beygelzimer, A., d'Alché-Buc, F., Fox, E., Garnett, R. (eds.) Advances in Neural Information Processing Systems. vol. 32, pp. 5309–5319. Curran Associates, Inc. https://proceedings.neurips.cc/paper/2019/hash/3070e6addcd702cb58de5d7897bfdae1-Abstract.html
11. Mehta, A.: Online matching and ad allocation. Found. Trends Theor. Comput. Sci. **8**(4), 265–368 (2013). https://doi.org/10.1561/0400000057
12. Tomizawa, N.: On some techniques useful for solution of transportation network problems. Networks **1**, 173–194 (1971). https://onlinelibrary.wiley.com/doi/abs/10.1002/net.3230010206
13. Zhao, B., Xu, P., Shi, Y., Tong, Y., Zhou, Z., Zeng, Y.: Preference-aware task assignment in on-demand taxi dispatching: an online stable matching approach. In: Proceedings of the AAAI Conference on Artificial Intelligence, vol. 33, pp. 2245–2252 (2019). https://ojs.aaai.org/index.php/AAAI/article/view/4060

Improving Address Matching Using Siamese Transformer Networks

André V. Duarte(✉) and Arlindo L. Oliveira

Instituto Superior Técnico/INESC-ID, Lisbon, Portugal
{andre.v.duarte,arlindo.oliveira}@tecnico.ulisboa.pt

Abstract. Matching addresses is a critical task for companies and post offices involved in the processing and delivery of packages. The ramifications of incorrectly delivering a package to the wrong recipient are numerous, ranging from harm to the company's reputation to economic and environmental costs. This research introduces a deep learning-based model designed to increase the efficiency of address matching for Portuguese addresses. The model comprises two parts: (i) a bi-encoder, which is fine-tuned to create meaningful embeddings of Portuguese postal addresses, utilized to retrieve the top 10 likely matches of the un-normalized target address from a normalized database, and (ii) a cross-encoder, which is fine-tuned to accurately re-rank the 10 addresses obtained by the bi-encoder. The model has been tested on a real-case scenario of Portuguese addresses and exhibits a high degree of accuracy, exceeding 95% at the door level. When utilized with GPU computations, the inference speed is about 4.5 times quicker than other traditional approaches such as BM25. An implementation of this system in a real-world scenario would substantially increase the effectiveness of the distribution process. Such an implementation is currently under investigation.

Keywords: Address matching · Deep learning · Pre-trained transformer models · Siamese neural networks

1 Introduction

Over the past few years, the value of global e-commerce sales has been steadily increasing, leading to a considerable rise in the number of parcels being shipped worldwide every day [15]. The effective delivery of parcels relies on the crucial role played by delivery companies and post offices in connecting senders with recipients. Therefore, it is essential that these companies have efficient methods to ensure successful deliveries of parcels. Although most parcels have accurate address information, there are instances where addresses are written in an unstructured way, leading to incorrect or failed deliveries. The errors may include insufficient information, redundant information, or spelling mistakes, among others.

© The Author(s), under exclusive license to Springer Nature Switzerland AG 2023
N. Moniz et al. (Eds.): EPIA 2023, LNAI 14116, pp. 413–425, 2023.
https://doi.org/10.1007/978-3-031-49011-8_33

While there is no publicly available information on how companies address these issues, some methods involve address normalization, such as converting "Street" to "St.", or parsing the address elements followed by pair-wise matching. However, these techniques are not perfect and frequently require human intervention.

The primary objective of this work is to develop a solution that can enhance the quality of postal and parcel delivery services by reducing the number of misdelivered parcels and minimizing human involvement. Given the recent advancements that transformers have provided in the natural language processing field, we have chosen a fully transformer-based architecture for our solution. We combine a siamese neural network (bi-encoder: retriever) with a DistilBERT [13] model adapted for sentence-pair classification (cross-encoder: reranker). To the best of our knowledge, our work is the first one to use this type of approach to tackle an address-matching task.

2   Background and Related Work

Determining if two addresses refer to the same location can be a challenging task. The most straightforward method for this is to calculate the similarity metrics between the strings that describe each address. The standard algorithm used for this purpose is the edit distance, also known as the Levenshtein distance (LD) [7]. However, the LD fails to provide accurate results, even for simple cases. To address this issue, more sophisticated algorithms have been developed, such as searching for the largest sub-sequences of common words, or tokenizing strings by words and sorting them alphabetically, so that the original word order is not relevant. Nevertheless, the effectiveness of string similarity measures for string matching varies depending on the task, and no single algorithm can be claimed to be superior [11].

A significant challenge associated with traditional string similarity measures is to choose an appropriate threshold that determines when a match is considered correct or not. Santos et al. addressed this issue by proposing a supervised machine learning approach that leverages string similarity values as the model features [14]. This method reduced the need for manual threshold tuning and improved the matching performance against the more traditional approaches.

The methods previously discussed are effective at identifying symbolic similarities between addresses. However, they often struggle to accurately match addresses that share semantic meaning but are written differently. Deep Learning (DL) techniques have brought a new level of flexibility to string matching algorithms by leveraging sentence-level features that capture semantic similarities. As a result, recent studies in address matching have shifted towards DL methods due to their ability to produce superior results [8].

Comber et al. proposed a novel approach [2] that leverages the benefits of both conditional random fields (CRFs) and Word2Vec [9] for address matching. CRFs are employed to parse the address into its main components, and then Word2Vec is used to create an embedding for each parsed field. The similarity between fields is computed using cosine similarity, and a machine learning classifier is then used to determine whether the two addresses match. The author's proposed approach outperformed previous techniques such as CRF + Jaro-Winkler similarity [2].

Lin et al. proposed a novel approach for address matching using the Enhanced Sequential Inference Model (ESIM). The first step is to train a Word2Vec model to transform address records into their corresponding vector representations. Then, the ESIM model is applied, which consists of four main steps. Firstly, the input addresses are encoded using a Bi-LSTM. Then, local inference is performed on the encoded addresses through a decomposable attention mechanism. Next, a new Bi-LSTM layer is applied to extract higher-level representations of the addresses. Finally, a multilayer perceptron (MLP) is used to indicate whether the address pairs are a match. The proposed Word2Vec + ESIM approach outperformed simpler methods, such as Word2Vec + Random Forest, demonstrating its effectiveness for address matching [8].

Another alternative solution that has been proposed to address the issue of address matching is the Attention-Bi-LSTM-CNN (ABLC) network based on contrast learning, which has demonstrated better performance than the ESIM model [1]. The ABLC model combines an attention mechanism, bidirectional long short-term memory (Bi-LSTM), and convolutional neural networks (CNN) to extract features from the addresses.

A distinct methodology that has been proposed for address matching and is also relevant for multiple similarity search tasks involves the use of the best match 25 (BM25) algorithm in conjunction with BERT [5]. The method starts by employing the BM25 algorithm to retrieve the top-10 most probable records from a database for a given query. BERT [3] is then applied to re-rank the retrieved candidates. This approach has demonstrated superior performance when compared to other models, such as Word2Vec + ML Classifiers.

For similarity search tasks, pre-trained deep transformers have proven to be highly effective [3]. There are two main types of transformers that are commonly used: cross-encoders [4,16,17], which use full self-attention to encode the pair, and dual-encoders, which encode the pair separately. Dense Passage Retrieval (DPR) [6] and SBERT [12] are two well-established dual-encoder approaches widely used for similarity search tasks.

3   Data Description and Preparation

3.1   Addresses Structure

This work employed two main types of addresses: (i) normalized addresses—follow a specific structure and adhere to predefined rules and (ii) unnormalized addresses—often unstructured and, therefore, more difficult to interpret. When sending a parcel, the sender usually writes the recipient's address in an unnormalized format. Classifying an address as unnormalized does not necessarily mean that it is incorrect, but rather that it does not fully comply with the standardized structure. A typical normalized Portuguese address comprises several essential elements, including (1) Artery Type—the configuration of the artery; (2) Artery Name; (3) Door ID—the house or apartment number; (4) Accommodation ID—details about the floor and accommodation and (5) ZIP-Code—a 7-digit code followed by a Postal Designation determined by the Post Office (known as CP4-CP3 combination). An example of a portuguese normalized address would be: R Bartolomeu Dias, 4, 9ºDto, 2685-187, Portela LRS.

3.2 Datasets

Normalized Dataset The normalized addresses dataset used in this work was made available by CTT-Correios de Portugal, the national post office company of Portugal. The dataset comprises approximately 430k addresses, which corresponds to roughly 10% of the universe of addresses in Portugal. Although not all addresses are included, the provided data covers the entire country and not just a specific region. As the data was previously curated by CTT, no additional cleaning steps were required.

Dataset for Training the Bi-Encoder The dataset used to train the bi-encoder model consists of pairs of unnormalized-normalized addresses, along with a label indicating whether they match. The unnormalized address data was also obtained from CTT, based on the history of delivered parcels over a 3-month period, which resulted in over 3 million records. However, the data required deduplication and cleaning. The deduplication process consisted in removing exact duplicates, while the cleaning process restructured some records with information in the wrong columns and discarded others that lacked mappings to the normalized database. The resulting cleaned unnormalized addresses file contained approximately 1.1 million valid records.

For training the bi-encoder, 90% of these records were sampled and duplicated to form address pairs with a 1:1 positive-to-negative ratio. The normalized address for the false matching pair is generated from three categories, each with an equal probability of occurrence: easy match (random address), hard match (address with a string similarity metric >0.8), and very hard match (address in the same ZIP-Code). This approach was chosen to increase the number of challenging records in the training dataset.

Test Dataset and Dataset for Training the Cross-Encoder Approximately 120k unnormalized records were not used for training the bi-encoder. From this pool of records, we extracted a random sample of around 60k addresses to build the test dataset used to assess the final model's performance.

The remaining available addresses were used to fine-tune the cross-encoder, with an approximate positive-to-negative ratio of 1:9. Negative samples were generated by querying the bi-encoder with the unnormalized address and retaining the top-9 most probable addresses that did not match with the unnormalized one.

4 Model Implementation

4.1 Proposed Model: Bi-Encoder + Cross-Encoder

Reimers et al. noted that performance-wise, for a sentence similarity task, the cross-encoder achieves a better performance than a bi-encoder [12]. However, using only the cross-encoder for address matching is not feasible. If one wants to search on a normalized database for the address most similar to the unnormalized address that is being paired, all the combinations of (unnormalized, normalized$_i$) must be fed to the cross-encoder, which is computationally demanding. For that reason, a decision was made to not use the cross-encoder by itself for the final solution, but rather a combination of the cross-encoder with the bi-encoder, in order to get the best features of each model. The proposed model is named Bi-Encoder + Cross-Encoder or BI+CE.

Our bi-encoder is a dual-encoder network trained in a siamese way with the purpose of learning how to derive meaningful sentence embeddings that can be compared with others through cosine-similarity.

We use the multilingual DistilBERT [13] as the base transformer due to its ability to maintain a base performance that is comparable to the one of the original multilingual BERT. Moreover, from a deployment perspective, the adoption of a more compact model is generally preferred. In order to generate fixed-length embeddings of the addresses, we apply mean pooling on the DistilBERT output, which is then passed through an MLP with hyperbolic tangent activation. This reduces the dimensionality of the address embeddings to 512. We employ the standard contrastive loss function as our optimization objective.

$$\frac{1}{2}[y \cdot D^2(x_A, x_B) + (1 - y) \cdot \{\text{relu}(\alpha - D(x_A, x_B))\}^2] \tag{1}$$

Here, x_A and x_B represent the embeddings of addresses A and B, respectively, while y is the label indicating whether both addresses are related. The distance metric D between x_A and x_B is calculated as 1—cosine similarity(x_A, x_B). Additionally, the margin α is introduced to ensure that the negative pair is at least separated by a distance equal or greater than that value. The architecture of the bi-encoder considered for fine-tuning on the address data is displayed in Fig. 1.

Regarding the cross-encoder, we adopt an architecture as the one BERT uses for a sentence pair classification task [3]. We also consider the multilingual DistilBERT as the base transformer and we optimize the cross-entropy loss when fine-tuning.

Figure 2 presents the full architecture of the model for the address matching task. There are two main modules in our architecture: (1) the database pre-embedding module and (2) the predicting module.

The database pre-embedding module is not mandatory but, if included, increases the speed of the predicting module significantly. Its goal is to create and store in memory all the embeddings related to the normalized database. Since the database will be static most of the time, it is unnecessary to recompute embeddings every time the model is initialized. The module receives as input each normalized address and computes its corresponding embedding through the bi-encoder. The final outputs are aggregated on a normalized embeddings file. In order to increase the performance speed in the predicting module, an extra step is performed: nine auxiliar databases are created according to the nine possible first digits in a CP4. Each unnormalized address is, therefore, on the predicting stage, compared only with the addresses on the corresponding auxiliar database.

The predicting module is the main part of the BI+CE model. The process of finding the corresponding pair in the normalized database for the target unnormalized address (x_1) is done by: (i) feeding x_1 to the bi-encoder; (ii) comparing the embedding of x_1 (E_1) with the correspondent auxiliar embeddings through cosine-similarity; (iii) returning the k-most similar addresses (in this case k = 10); (iv) feeding the pairs $(x_1, \text{returned}_{address_i})$ to the cross-encoder, which will re-rank them.

The reason behind selecting the top-10 addresses instead of only the most similar is due to the fact that the bi-encoder sometimes misses at assigning the highest probability to the correct address. However, the correct address is usually retrieved in the top-10, hence, the cross-encoder is used. More details on this topic are provided in Sect. 5.

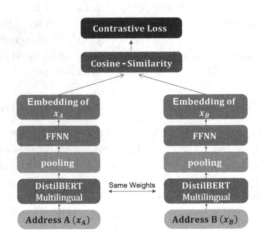

Fig. 1. Bi-encoder architecture considered for fine-tuning on the address data.

4.2   Training Overview

Both the bi-encoder and the cross-encoder are initialized with their pre-trained weights but, in order for their parameters to reach an optimal value for the specific address matching task, the models are fine-tuned. Table 1 displays the combination of the best hyperparameters, chosen for fine-tuning the bi-encoder

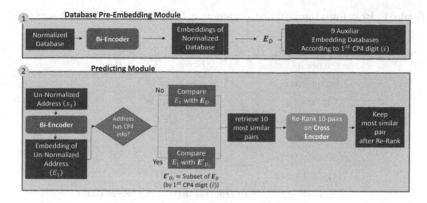

Fig. 2. Architecture of the bi-encoder + cross-encoder model.

and the cross-encoder. They were reached by trial and error using the common good practices to fine-tune this type of models [12].

Regarding the values for the bi-encoder, the variable that is further apart from the usual values is the epoch number. Usually this variable is never higher than 4. However, we decided to select a value of 20. A study was performed on the impact of the epoch number on the fine-tuning performance of models like BERT, and the conclusions were that a larger number of epochs, such as 20, works better [10]. As for the cross-encoder, we explored various epoch values, including 20, in order to keep the hyperparameters similar to the bi-encoder, but determined that 15 yielded the best results.

Both bi-encoder and cross-encoder are fine-tuned using one NVIDIA Tesla V100S (32 GB).[1] Each fine-tuning process takes approximately eight hours to complete and is done using the python package 'sentence-transformers'.[2] The experimental results for the traditional approaches consist of individual runs for each model. However, we conducted multiple runs of both the bi-encoder and the cross-encoder models after obtaining the optimized hyperparameters. To ensure the robustness of our findings, we run each model 5 times and report the results using the ones with the most consistent performance across the runs, as determined by the median outcome accuracy at the door level. Our results demonstrate that fine-tuning remains stable across the runs. We observed a low standard deviation of 0.077 for door level accuracy in the bi-encoder and 0.084 in the cross-encoder.

4.3   Model Evaluation

For comparison purposes, we evaluated several models: (i) the proposed one (BI+CE), (ii) two traditional string matching algorithms, token sort and token

---

[1] Code available at: https://github.com/avduarte333/adress-matching.
[2] https://github.com/UKPLab/sentence-transformers.

Table 1. Best found fine-tuning parameters for bi-encoder and cross-encoder.

Parameter	Bi-encoder	Cross-encoder
Epochs	20	15
Batch Size	16	
Optmizer	AdamW	
Learning Rate	10^{-5}	
Scheduler	Linear	
Warmup Steps	100	
Weight Decay	0.01	
Loss	Contrastive loss margin = 0.5	Cross-entropy
Base Transformer	Multilingual DistilBERT	

set,[3] (iii) a bi-encoder, (iv) a BM25 ranking function combined with a cross-encoder (BM25+CE), based on the approach of Gupta et al. [5], and (v) a Dense Passage Retrieval (DPR) model as introduced by Karpukhin et al. [6], where we used two independent pre-trained multilingual DistilBERTs as base transformers.

The models were evaluated based on two metrics: (1) inference time, which is the number of matches performed by the model in one second, and (2) accuracy, which is the proportion of correctly predicted pairs out of all pairs. Additionally, we analyzed the quality of the top-k retrieval for the approaches (iii), (iv), and (v).

The primary objective of the model is to achieve high accuracy at the door level, as correctly identifying the door is crucial for parcel delivery services. While retrieving the correct artery is important, failure to identify the correct door results in an incorrect mapping. However, misidentifying doors in the same artery should not significantly impact delivery efficiency, as they are typically close in geographic proximity. Thus, the results are reported for both artery and door level accuracy.

In practical applications, it is crucial to minimize the number of misdelivered parcels. To achieve this, we propose imposing a threshold or filter value (cutting value) on the matching probability variable to ensure that only address pairs with high matching probability are accepted as correct, and the remaining pairs are subjected to manual inspection. In all experiments, we used this criterion and selected the optimal filter values by examining the match confidence variable's distribution.

---

[3] https://github.com/seatgeek/fuzzywuzzy.

5   Results and Discussion

5.1   Inference Time

The average number of unnormalized addresses paired per second for each tested model is presented in Table 2. To ensure a fair comparison, we made sure that each model performs roughly the same number of operations when pairing new addresses.

Table 2. Average number of iterations/second for each model (it/s). We run the DL models on GPU. However, instead of batching, we process each address individually, as displayed in Fig. 2, to perform a fairer comparison to the traditional approaches. The best results are highlighted in bold.

	Token Sort	Token Set	BM25+CE	DPR	Bi-encoder	BI+CE
Without CP4 Filter	0.01	0.07	0.09	0.76	**0.91**	0.80
With CP4 Filter	0.96	0.61	0.83	3.64	**5.40**	3.70

As anticipated, the inference speed improves when CP4 filtering is applied, regardless of the approach. Without the CP4 filter, the inference time ranges from 0.07 to 0.91 iterations per second, while with CP4 filter, the inference time ranges from 0.61 to 5.40 iterations per second. However, there is a significant difference in the performance between the traditional string matching algorithms and the ones where dense vectors are utilized (DPR, bi-encoder and BI+CE). This can be attributed to the fact that calculating cosine similarity between an address and the candidate addresses in the normalized database is a faster operation than computing string metrics.

The results presented in Table 2 also reveal that adding a cross-encoder to the model architecture decreases the model's inference speed. This is expected, as the extra layer of complexity introduced by the cross-encoder leads to an increase in computational workload.

5.2   Accuracy Results—Test Dataset

Results—Traditional String Matching Algorithms From Table 3, both results at artery and door level suggest that the token set algorithm performs better than the token sort, since it usually achieves higher accuracies while retaining more addresses (27.09 vs. 17.57% at door level). However, when performing the manual filtering, the great majority of addresses are discarded, and there is no significant improvement in the overall accuracy. Results at artery level are significantly better than the ones at the door level but none of the algorithms achieved results that may be considered promising enough to solve the address matching problem successfully.

Results—Bi-Encoder, DPR and BM25+CE When evaluating the retrieval capabilities of the bi-encoder, DPR and the BM25+CE,[4] one can consider two scenarios: the top-1 retrieval and the top-k. Table 4 displays, for each method, the proportion of instances where the correct normalized address is among the retrieved addresses.

Table 3. Accuracy (%) at artery and door level for the tested approaches as a function of the filter value. The best results are highlighted in bold.

Algorithm	No Filter Artery	No Filter Door	Filter Value	With Filter Artery	With Filter Door	Discarded Addresses
Token Sort	51.09	17.57	0.85	68.40	25.60	92.80
Token Set	64.67	27.09	0.85	69.44	32.20	54.80
BM25 + CE	79.78	63.31	0.95	98.47	84.34	38.03
DPR	95.48	85.91	0.90	99.50	91.50	19.80
Bi-encoder	96.49	95.68	0.99	97.82	97.39	23.37
BI+CE	**97.08**	**95.32**	0.90	**99.71**	**98.35**	**18.08**

Table 4. Proportion of instances (%) where the correct normalized address (door level) is among the retrieved addresses. The best results are highlighted in bold.

	Bi-encoder	DPR (no rerank)	BM25
Top-1	**95.68**	80.92	33.49
Top-10	**99.41**	97.02	72.80

It is evident from Tables 3 and 4 that introducing the dense retrievers, like the bi-encoder or DPR, in the solution enhances the results significantly. Its accuracies both on artery and door level are above 85%, while for BM25 and the traditional methods they never surpass 63.31%.

Table 4 also highlights two major advantages of the bi-encoder in terms of retrieval quality. Firstly, the top-1 retrieval alone is a near-perfect solution, with a door level accuracy of 95.68%. Secondly, the top-10 retrieval gives almost every address a chance of being correctly paired. Our experimental results indicate that while DPR achieves a top-10 accuracy comparable to that of the bi-encoder, its top-1 accuracy falls short by nearly 15% (95.68–80.92%). Regarding BM25, its top-1 accuracy is limited to 33.49 and 72.80% at most when considering top-10 retrieval. Despite being more than double, it still falls short compared to the bi-encoder. Therefore, using the BM25 or DPR as a solution for the problem is not optimal. Nevertheless, it is worth mentioning that the rerankers can leverage the retrieval results of the BM25 and the DPR significantly. When considering

---

[4] Although the model under study is the BM25+CE, when evaluating the retrieval capabilities, the cross-encoder is not used, therefore, for notation simplicity, the model is mentioned as BM25.

the top-1 address before and after the reranking, the door level accuracies shift from 33.49 to 63.31% for BM25 and from 80.92 to 85.91% for DPR (Table 3).

When studying the optimal cutting value for filtering the bi-encoder results, two interesting properties in the distribution of the match confidence variable (Fig. 3a) were identified: (i) distribution strongly skewed and (ii) 77% of the pairs have a matching probability that lies in the [0.99;1.00] interval. Combining these factors, the cutting value chosen was 0.99.

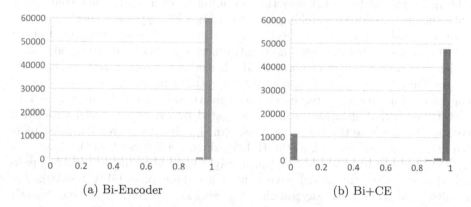

(a) Bi-Encoder   (b) Bi+CE

Fig. 3. Histogram of the matching probability assigned by the bi-encoder model (left) and the BI+CE model (right).

The hypothesis that implementing this filtering technique would result in near-perfect classification was not supported by the data (Table 3). Despite an overall increase in the model's accuracy (95.68–97.39% at door level) and the fact that only 23.37% of records were discarded, there remains room for improvement. Therefore, in light of these findings and the ones from the BM25 and DPR experiments, it was decided to incorporate the cross-encoder into the proposed model.

Results—BI+CE (Proposed model) Contrary to the expectation, the model's overall accuracy at the door level did not improve in comparison to the bi-encoder approach—4.68% of the addresses remain incorrectly classified (Table 3: 100–95.32%). It improved, though, at the artery level, but only slightly (96.49–97.08%). The matching probability distribution is, however, quite different in this scenario (Fig. 3b).

In the bi-encoder experiment, the lowest matching probability assigned by the model was 0.689. In the BI+CE model, the lowest probabilities assigned are really low values (<1%). Figure 3b displays a big gap between the highest probable pairs and the lowest probable ones. There are a few pairs spread across the x-axis scale. However, their proportion is just 2.28% of the total number of addresses. The cutting value chosen for filtering, in this case, is 0.90. Performing this step provided interesting results, namely: the variation of the accuracy on artery and door level is quite positive (from 97.08 to 99.71% on artery and from 95.32 to 98.35% on door) and the number of discarded addresses is lower than the number discarded on the bi-encoder experiment (from 23.37 to 18.08%).

6　Conclusions

The main goal of this work was the development of a model that could solve with success an address matching task, by using a DL approach, specifically pre-trained transformers. The bi-encoder proved to be a fundamental piece in the solution, not only for the speed up it introduces but also for its retrieval quality which can place the correct normalized address in the top-10 retrievals 99.41% of the time. We also found that the cross-encoder increases the robustness of the model's accuracy, at the cost of a negative impact on the inference time. Nevertheless, that drawback can be mitigated by using the model with GPU computations where the inference speed can significantly increase against more traditional approaches such as the BM25 (roughly 4.5 times faster).

In a real application, we would probably assume that the only correct pairs are the ones that the model gave a high matching probability (>0.90). The results in the test dataset suggest that imposing such criteria would significantly reduce the number of misdelivered packages, although a small proportion of the addresses ($\sim18\%$) would still require a manual correction. There are other alternatives, such as disregarding the matching probability variable, which would mitigate the time spent on manual correction. It would, however, introduce some downsides such as a higher error rate on the package delivery.

Acknowledgements. The authors would like to acknowledge the support of Dr. Egídio Moutinho, Drª. Marília Rosado, Dr. Rúben Rocha, Dr. André Esteves, Dr. Paulo Silva, Dr. Gonçalo Ribeiro Enes and Dr. Diogo Freitas Oliveira in the development of this project. We also gratefully acknowledge the financial support provided by Recovery and Resilience Fund towards the Center for Responsible AI project (Ref. C628696807-00454142) and the multiannual financing of the Foundation for Science and Technology (FCT) for INESC-ID (Ref. UIDB/50021/2020).

References

1. Chen, J., Chen, J., She, X., Mao, J., Chen, G.: Deep contrast learning approach for address semantic matching. Appl. Sci. **11**(16), 7608 (2021)
2. Comber, S., Arribas-Bel, D.: Machine learning innovations in address matching: a practical comparison of Word2vec and CRFs. Trans. GIS **23**(2), 334–348 (2019)
3. Devlin, J., Chang, M.W., Lee, K., Toutanova, K.: BERT: Pre-training of Deep Bidirectional Transformers for Language Understanding. In: Proceedings of the 2019 Conference of the North American Chapter of the Association for Computational Linguistics: Human Language Technologies, Volume 1 (Long and Short Papers), pp. 4171–4186. Association for Computational Linguistics (2019)

4. Glass, M., Rossiello, G., Chowdhury, M.F.M., Naik, A., Cai, P., Gliozzo, A.: Re2G: retrieve, rerank, generate. In: Proceedings of the 2022 Conference of the North American Chapter of the Association for Computational Linguistics: Human Language Technologies, pp. 2701–2715. Association for Computational Linguistics, Seattle, United States (2022)
5. Gupta, V., Gupta, M., Garg, J., Garg, N.: Improvement in semantic address matching using natural language processing. In: 2021 2nd International Conference for Emerging Technology (INCET), pp. 1–5 (2021)
6. Karpukhin, V., Oguz, B., Min, S., Lewis, P., Wu, L., Edunov, S., Chen, D., Yih, W.t.: Dense passage retrieval for open-domain question answering. In: Proceedings of the 2020 Conference on Empirical Methods in Natural Language Processing (EMNLP), pp. 6769–6781. Association for Computational Linguistics (2020)
7. Levenshtein, V.I.: Binary codes capable of correcting deletions, insertions, and reversals. Soviet Phys. Doklady **10**(8), 707–710 (1965)
8. Lin, Y., Kang, M., Wu, Y., Du, Q., Liu, T.: A deep learning architecture for semantic address matching. Int. J. Geogr. Inf. Sci. **34**(3), 559–576 (2020)
9. Mikolov, T., Chen, K., Corrado, G., Dean, J.: Efficient estimation of word representations in vector space (2013). arXiv:1301.3781
10. Mosbach, M., Andriushchenko, M., Klakow, D.: On the stability of fine-tuning BERT: misconceptions, explanations, and strong baselines (2020). arXiv:2006.04884
11. Recchia, G., Louwerse, M.: A comparison of string similarity measures for toponym matching. In: COMP 2013—ACM SIGSPATIAL International Workshop on Computational Models of Place, pp. 54–61 (2013)
12. Reimers, N., Gurevych, I.: Sentence-BERT: sentence embeddings using Siamese BERT-networks. In: Proceedings of the 2019 Conference on Empirical Methods in Natural Language Processing. Association for Computational Linguistics (2019)
13. Sanh, V., Debut, L., Chaumond, J., Wolf, T.: DistilBERT, a distilled version of BERT: smaller, faster, cheaper and lighter (2019). arXiv:1910.01108
14. Santos, R., Murrieta-Flores, P., Martins, B.: Learning to combine multiple string similarity metrics for effective toponym matching. Int. J. Digit. Earth **11**(9), 913–938 (2018)
15. Statista.: (2021). https://www.statista.com/chart/10922/parcel-shipping-volume-and-parcel-spend-in-selected-countries/
16. Urbanek, J., Fan, A., Karamcheti, S., Jain, S., Humeau, S., Dinan, E., Rocktäschel, T., Kiela, D., Szlam, A., Weston, J.: Learning to speak and act in a fantasy text adventure game. In: Proceedings of the 2019 Conference on Empirical Methods in Natural Language Processing and the 9th International Joint Conference on Natural Language Processing (EMNLP-IJCNLP), pp. 673–683. Association for Computational Linguistics, Hong Kong, China (2019)
17. Wang, Z., Ng, P., Ma, X., Nallapati, R., Xiang, B.: Multi-passage BERT: a globally normalized BERT model for open-domain question answering (2019)

An Ethical Perspective on Intelligent Transport Systems

António Ribeiro da Costa[1,2](✉) iD, Zafeiris Kokkinogenis[1,2] iD,
and Rosaldo J. F. Rossetti[1,2] iD

[1] Artificial Intelligence and Computer Science Lab (LIACC), Porto, Portugal
{amrpcosta,kokkinogenis,rossetti}@fe.up.pt
[2] Faculty of Engineering, University of Porto, Porto, Portugal

Abstract. Intelligent Transport Systems (ITS) is a fast evolving domain
with an increasingly important role in shaping the future of transport and
a significant impact on a wide range of issues, many of which have ethical
implications. On the other hand, Ethics is essential to ensure that ITS are
safe, fair, accountable, trustworthy, and respectful of privacy. This study
reflects on the ethical concerns around transport system and its impact
on economic, social and environmental dimensions, from the spirit of the
foundational concepts of Ethics to the specific issues raised by intelligent transport, including those enhanced by Artificial Intelligence (AI)
and Machine Learning (ML) systems. The primordial ethical concerns of
transport have, in some extent, been mitigated with the introduction of
the ITS paradigm, but others have arisen as a result of emerging technologies. Ethics is therefore critical in intelligent transport because of its
potential to significantly impact individuals, communities, and society as
a whole, and is an important tool to design more sustainable, equitable,
and fair transport systems.

Keywords: Transport systems · Ethics · Intelligent transport systems

1 Introduction

Transport encompasses a broad range of ethical issues, present in all phases
of the life-cycle of a transport system. Intelligent Transport Systems (ITS) are
advanced applications aimed at improving its efficiency, safety, and sustainability. While it may alleviate some of the core ethical concerns in transport, the
addition of Artificial Intelligence (AI) and Machine Learning (ML) systems may
introduce new implications, becoming important to comprehend the principles
underlying transport systems, as well as their continued ethical assessment and
careful review.

The remainder of the paper is organized as follows. The next Section reviews
the relevant work. Section 3 examines the relevance of transport for ethics, in its
relationship with society and the environment. In Sect. 4, fundamental issues of
transport are analysed in the perspective of the foundations of Ethics. Section 5

N. Moniz et al. (Eds.): EPIA 2023, LNAI 14116, pp. 426–437, 2023.
https://doi.org/10.1007/978-3-031-49011-8_34

focus on the particular ethical concerns raised by ITS, including when enhanced with AI. Finally, the main conclusions and future directions are discussed in Sect. 6.

2 Related Work

The concept of transport refers to the deliberate movement of masses, of any kind, from one place to another [4], providing a mechanism for the exchange of people, goods, and information, travelling over and under the land, over the ocean, and over the sky, to meet the basic needs of society that require mobility and accessibility [13]. A transport system, because of its impact on individual, societal, and environmental well-being, both negative and positive, has great relevance for Ethics, encompassing various ethical considerations related to transport systems, policies, and practices.

Some ethical issues concerning transport are presented by Anciães and Thomopoulos [1], with an approach to the social aspects of transport, including public intervention, accessibility, safety, and environmental effects. As inequalities and equity in mobility stand out as a key research theme, Bert van Wee [33], conducted an ethical analysis to the use of Cost-Benefit Analysis (CBA) for transport policy options, which is based on utilitarian theory, i.e. the conviction that the best decision is the one providing the greatest net benefits to society. In a critical stance of CBA, discussed their relevance for accessibility, the environment, and safety. Other studies address policy making, and the underlying ethical concerns, such as safety [5] and sustainability assessment [31], rainsing questions about individual freedom, privacy, responsibility, fairness and equity.

In the context of ITS, most studies are focused on the technology [9], its advantages and disadvantages, although from this it can be inferred how they address some ethical concerns of transport [20]. Notwithstanding the variety of technology that falls within the scope of ITS, in recent years particular emphasis has been given to AI, with an important role in enabling the development of sophisticated algorithms and ML models used in transport systems, enhancing them with more efficient, effective, and safe solutions. However, this transition step towards smart transport brings a set of challenges inherent to AI, such as the conveyance and processing of massive volumes of data and the proper making of logical judgements [19].

Concerns about the ethical implications of AI and ML, including risks of bias, discrimination, privacy violations, among others, have led to the concept of Trustworthy AI [8,28], introduced in a 2018 report by the High-Level Expert Group on Artificial Intelligence (AI HLEG) [7], appointed by the European Commission, emphasizing the importance of developing systems that are trustworthy, reliable, and safe. These guidelines reflected in other initiatives, such as responsible AI, based on the social topics of fairness, privacy, accountability, ethics, transparency, safety, and security [2]. Users' trust about algorithmic decisions was analyzed with respect to the widely adopted Fairness, Accountability, Transparency, and Explainability (FATE) set [24,25]. Gaur and Sahoo [10], in turn, address these explainable AI concepts in the particular context of ITS. However, the most prominent current line of research about Ethics in ITS is embracing the fields of Autonomous Intelligent Systems [16] and Connected Autonomous Vehicles [6, 22, 23, 26, 34]

In this work, an analysis is made of the individual, social and environmental issues raised by a transport system in the spirit of the core concepts of Ethics, the way they are addressed by ITS, and the new ethical issues arising from AI.

3   The Relevance of Transport for Ethics

Transport, by definition, is a deliberate carrying or conveyance of people, animals or things from one place to another. Throughout the history of civilization, it has played a major role in human development. It allowed people to travel increasingly greater distances, facilitated the exchange of goods and the flow of production surpluses, but also the interchange of cultures. It shaped the geography of the Earth, influencing the creation, implantation and growth of urban, commercial and industrial centres, and strategic trading points and interconnections between the communities that were being formed [21]. At the same time, there was parallel development of transport systems, a wider concept that encompasses the physical infrastructure, the rolling stock, and the support services and communication technologies of the diverse modes of transport. With a considerable effect in shaping the human society, its social, economic, cultural and political impact seems inevitable.

Ethics, for its part, has no easy definition. Commonly, it is understood as a subfield of philosophy concerned with moral values and principles that guide a person's behaviour, which does a systematic reflection on what is moral [29, 32]. In a broader sense, ethics reflects on freedom, responsibility and justice, but particularly on the interaction of human beings with their fellow human beings and with nature, a *human independence* centred on the relationship between the human being and the world, that is a primordial condition in ethical decision-making and objective factual analysis.

From the notions above, it emerges a common denominator: the *human society*. While transport has an effect on the shaping of the human society, Ethics provides a framework for understanding and assessing moral dilemmas and issues that arise in society, as well as guiding decision-making processes.

3.1   Transport Impacts that May Raise Ethical Concerns

The importance of transport systems in society is observed in diverse domains and at several levels and dimensions, influencing from the economic growth and social interaction to the individual mobility and environmental sustainability [15]. Nevertheless, as this has an implicit reshaping of society and its environment, it may raise several ethical concerns, particularly the economic, social, and environmental dimensions, as they are interconnected and often have an impact on each other [11].

Economic, Social and Environmental Impacts. At an *economic* level, transport creates opportunities. It is a mean to connect producers and consumers, to access resources, to link geographic regions, facilitating the movement of goods and people, and the exchange of commodities and services. This promotes economic growth by increasing trade, expanding markets and supporting the creation of new businesses and technologies. However, there is a constant demand for efficiency, to reduce transport costs and to increase travel or delivery speed. Development, construction and operation of infrastructures and transport technologies creates jobs in different sectors of activity. But traffic congestions, accidents, and unforeseen delays, may result in economic losses due to increased travel times and late deliveries, decreased productivity and other factors.

Taking a *social* perspective, transport connects people and communities, promoting cultural exchange and enhancing social inclusion and cohesion [18]. It provides access to employment, health care, education, and other essential services, but also increases the independence of people with reduced mobility, such as the elderly and those with physical disabilities. Nonetheless, there are some negative effects, like the construction of transport infrastructure and facilities that may involve communities displacement, or traffic congestion (in the various transport modes), noise, and pollution, with adverse consequences for well-being and public health.

Another impact of transport, and interrelated with the previous ones, are the *environmental* repercussions, such as air and noise pollution, and greenhouse gases emissions. In addition, there are consequences for land use and biodiversity, with habitat fragmentation and ecosystem disturbance. Indeed, in this relationship between the human being and nature, the effects of transport are mainly negative, which implies special efforts to ensure sustainable development.

Impact by Spacial Organization. Transport impacts could also be seen in terms of spatial organization (cf. [21]), from an individual scope to the global level. On the *individual* sphere it enables independence, social mobility, and access to services, both for business and leisure purposes, helping to strengthen social bonds and build social capital. Despite the increasing in opportunities, it is important to take into account that at this level transport usually represents a substantial expense associated with purchase and maintenance of vehicles, fuel costs, and taxes.

At a *local* level, transport infrastructures and services address the need for mobility of passengers and freight, contributing to economic and social development. A well-designed and well-maintained transport network may influence and attract industry, businesses, and investment to the region. This leads to tax revenue, job creation, and economic activity, shaping the social fabric of cities by determining the way people interact with each other and their surroundings, also contributing to reduce social isolation and increase social cohesion [18]. Environmental consequences of transport infrastructures, however, could adversely impact the quality of life for nearby communities.

Progressing to a macro perspective, at *regional* level the transport system relies on corridors, linking a set of specialized locations, main centres of economic activity, oriented along an axis. It plays an important role in promoting social equity by providing access to opportunities, and supporting the national economy by fostering the movement of people and goods across different regions.

Viewed at a *global* scale, transport supports and shapes economic specialization and productivity through international trade. It is heavily influenced by connectivity, based on gateways and hubs, capable of supporting large passenger and cargo flows, such as maritime and air transport. While facilitating cross-border exchanges and enabling the integration of world markets, they have significant impacts on the global climate, contributing to the loss of biodiversity and natural ecosystems, as well as increased resource consumption and waste production.

With technological progress and the advent of ITS, increasingly complemented by solutions based on AI, the aim is to maximize the positive aspects of those impacts and mitigate the negative consequences.

3.2 From an Ethical Standpoint

When considered from an ethical perspective, those impacts, on other human beings and on nature, are assessed as a consequence of a moral choice or decision, and taking into account the values and principles that are relevant to the situation. Therefore, in the domain of transport, there are a multitude of ethical issues that could arise at different stages of a system lifecycle, from planning to design, implementation, maintenance, and management.

Keeping within the ethical dimensional space mentioned above, at the *economic* level transport raises issues about the distribution of benefits and costs of infrastructure and services across society, and how equitable, sustainable, and socially responsible investments are.

Transport is essential to *social* justice, and a key element for accessibility and mobility. Limiting these properties may condition people's access to education, health care, employment, and other opportunities, or even basic needs.

In *environmental* terms, transport choices can contribute to the degradation of the environment and the depletion of natural resources, from the individual to the global level, and how this will affect the planet and future generations.

Other concerns relate to safety and the balance between benefits and risks associated with transport, which depend on human behaviour at the system user level, but also on decisions regarding the infrastructure, policies and regulation of the transport system.

Ethical issues regarding transport, in particular due to technological developments and emerging technologies, occur in a broader set of dimensions. With the introduction of ITS, then enhanced with AI, some specificities arise such as privacy and data security, the need to protect personal information and prevent the misuse of data. Within the scope of planning and management, issues related to transparency, accountability and decision-making processes may be raised. In the planning phase, there is a need to consider environmental impacts, equity and social responsibility. At implementation, questions related to safety and accessibility may be brought up. On traffic management, there is a need to balance efficiency with safety and equity. Ultimately, addressing ethical issues in transport requires a comprehensive approach that takes into account the full range of impacts and stakeholders involved in transport decision-making.

4 Ethical Theories and Transport

There are several viewpoints to tackle ethical issues and dilemmas (cf. [27]), philosophical frameworks that offer a systematic approach to understanding and assessing moral actions and decisions. More practical in nature, they belong to the branch of Normative Ethics. Each of them emphasizes different points, decision-making styles or decision rules to reach an ethically correct decision, and they are referred to as *ethical theories.* Therefore, the assessment of a particular ethical issue may involve the consideration of several perspectives (or theories), attending to their strengths and weaknesses in dealing with a specific situation.

Furthermore, for an ethical theory to be useful, it must be oriented towards a common set of goals, the ethical principles that can guide ethical decision-making. However, it is important to note that sometimes when considering different ethical theories, those may conflict with one another, so determining the most appropriate theory for a given situation requires careful consideration of relevant factors and circumstances [14].

4.1 Common Ethical Principles

The four main principles of Ethics are beneficence, non-maleficence, autonomy, and justice, the foundations of bioethics [30], but that also can relate with transport systems, by accompanying their lifecycle and being transversal to all sectors involved, whether in technology development, infrastructure design and implementation, public policies and regulations or investment decisions.

The *principle of beneficence* refers to moral obligation to act in the best interest of others and prevent harm. In the transport sector, it concerns promoting the well-being of individuals and communities, while ensuring a balance between benefits and risks. Examples are measures that can contribute to improving independent mobility and accessibility, promoting public health, increasing opportunities and economic development, facilitating social inclusion.

The *principle of non-maleficence* (similar to the previous one) states that there is an obligation not to cause harm to others. It deals with situations in which no choice appears beneficial, and decision-makers have to choose to inflict as little harm as possible and harm the fewest people. In transport, it can be applied by promoting options that minimize social and environmental harm, such as ensuring safety, reduce the carbon footprint, and guaranteeing privacy and data security.

The *principle of autonomy* involves respect for the freedom of choice of the individual, allowing people to make decisions that apply to their own lives. Three conditions are necessary for autonomous action by people with ability to choose: intentionality, understanding, and the absence of controlling influences that constrain their action. This means, for example, offering transport options that promote individual autonomy, allowing the choice of what best fits their needs and preferences; prioritizing user experience through clear information that enables an informed decision; and promoting accessibility and independent mobility.

There are, however, two ways of looking at respect for autonomy. A *paternalistic* viewpoint, in which an authority prioritizes the best interests of a dependant over the wishes of the dependant; and a *libertarian* viewpoint, whereby the wishes of the dependant take priority over its best interests. In the first case we have, for instance, traffic control and regulatory measures, which impose restrictions in the best interest of the users of the transport system (like the use of seatbelts or speed limits); and in the second the set of recommendations disseminated by an infrastructure that the user may or may not follow, even if it is in its best interest.

The *principle of justice* demands an equitable and fair distribution of benefits, risks, costs, and resources. This includes ensuring access to transport, but taking into account economic and social inequalities, implying special attention in the analysis of priorities for investments in infrastructure and policies for the use of the system, in order to ensure that disadvantaged communities have adequate access to opportunities and services, distributing the benefits and costs fairly. It is important to address the differentiated impacts caused by transport, both in terms of social justice and environmental justice.

4.2 Forms of Ethical Theories

Ethical theories are sets of principles that provide a framework for evaluating a moral decision (cf. [17]). The branch of Normative ethics centres on exploring what actions are morally right or wrong and how to behave in various situations. Three major theories are: consequentialism, deontology, and virtue ethics.

Consequentialist theories focuses on the consequences of an act to determine whether the act is moral or immoral. The ultimate goal is to achieve the greatest number of benefits for the greatest number of people. These perspectives give priority to reducing negative consequences and maximising benefits, including through measures to promote sustainable transport and efficient options as well as investment in infrastructure in under-served areas.

Utilitarian theories are a consequentialist ethical approach that focuses on the outcomes of actions. They argue that these should be evaluated on the basis of their ability to promote the greatest amount of happiness or well-being for the greatest number of people. In transport systems, it could mean creating policies and investments in infrastructure to promote accessibility, maximize efficiency, and ensure equity.

Deontological theories focuses on the act, and uses rules to distinguish right from wrong. The morality of an action is assessed on the basis of its adherence to a set of rules or principles. In this approach, transport systems should respect the rights and dignity of individuals, notably by providing accessible and non-discriminatory transport options, and ensure the ability to travel freely, safely and without constrains. It is also within this framework that there is compliance with norms, regulations, and professional codes of conduct.

Virtue Ethics theories focuses on the character traits of the agent (people or organization). A virtuous agent will act morally. This includes the practice of responsible and defensive driving, complying with traffic laws and avoiding reckless behaviour, promoting safety and avoid causing damage to third parties; there is the promotion and adherence to cooperative transport systems and priority is given to the choice of transport modes that enable environmental sustainability.

This section addressed the basic tools of ethical analysis in its articulation with the transport domain, namely ethical theories, more abstract and general, and ethical principles, more specific and focused on practical guidance for decision-making in specific contexts, viewpoints that can offer orientations at both the end-user, developer, and decision-maker levels of a transport system.

5 Ethics for Intelligent Transport Systems

Nowadays, large cities and metropolitan areas already use some form of ITS as part of their traffic management plan. By integrating telecommunications, electronics and information technologies with the transport infrastructure, they contribute to improving the environmental performance, efficiency, safety and security of freight transport and passenger mobility in a way that is often economical, environmentally friendly and unobtrusive, enabling the various users to be better informed and make a safer, more coordinated and 'smarter' use of transport networks [20].

By its definition, this paradigm already tackles several of above-mentioned ethical principles and concerns within the realm of transport, in the individual, social and environmental dimensions. However, due to the evolving relationship between the transport system and individuals and society, other ethical dilemmas are emerging as a result of new developing technologies.

5.1 Novel Ethical Issues

Potentially omnipresent, connected and autonomous, and heavily reliant on data and information processing (collection, storage, use, and transfer), there are concerns related to data protection, among others raised by technology dependence.

ITS acquire vast amounts of data about drivers' behaviours, locations, and travel patterns. It can be used for various purposes, such as improving traffic flow, reducing congestion, and enhancing safety, but it also brought up concerns about *privacy*, data misuse or abuse, or surveillance. In addition, as everything is increasingly connected, assess *cybersecurity* vulnerabilities is critical in the effort to ensure the *safety* and *reliability* of the system, particularly with the deployment of driverless self-aware vehicles capable of making its own choices, and interacting with humans in a mixed traffic environment. Safety issues and the question of *responsibility* arise.

At the social level, it is essential to determine whether the benefits of ITS are *equitably* distributed and do not contribute to gentrification or to the exacerbation of existing social inequalities. Disadvantaged communities may not have access to the latest technology and could be disproportionately affected. Moreover, *inclusive design* is needed, making technologies accessible to all users regardless of their origin, education, condition or socio-economic status. All this can lead to *algorithmic bias*, resulting in unfair outcomes or discriminating against certain groups or populations.

For the individual, there is also a risk of technological dependency for transport as these systems become more prevalent, potentially leading to a loss of skills and knowledge related to traditional modes of transport, and creating vulnerabilities in the event of system failure or compromise.

5.2   Novel Dimensions of Ethical Concern

As technology evolves and presents new dilemmas, the four core principles of Ethics (4.1) may not have enough power to deal with some situations and risk overlapping in tension among themselves (cf. [12]). Therefore, several approaches and tools have been devised to assess the social and ethical impact of emerging technologies [3], notably in the AI domain, with which ITS share many concerns.

In order to stimulate user acceptance, and then to encourage its adoption and use, guidelines for a Trustworthy AI have been created, grounded on four ethical principles in fundamental rights [7]. At least seven requirements—not exhaustive but covering individual, societal and systemic aspects—must be met:

- *Human agency and oversight* advocates that ITS should prioritize human control and decision-making, ensuring that users can understand and intervene in the system's behaviour when necessary. It should be designed to augment. human capabilities rather than replace them.
- *Technical robustness and safety* are crucial in ITS. Rigorous testing and validation processes are essential to minimize risk and ensure the reliability and resilience of the system.
- As for *privacy and data governance*, ITS handles large amounts of data, including personal information. Privacy by design principles should be followed, such as data minimization, anonymization and secure data storage. Clear consent mechanisms are mandatory and users should have control over their data and be informed how it is used.
- *Transparency* is essential to build trust in AI systems. In ITS, there should be an effort for making the system's decision-making processes and criteria, such as route recommendations or traffic forecasts, understandable and explainable.
- About *diversity, non-discrimination and fairness*, ITS should actively address bias and discrimination by ensuring that AI algorithms and data sources do not perpetuate existing biases or discriminate against specific groups, populations or geographical areas.

- ITS should be designed with the aim of contributing to *social and environmental well-being*. This includes promoting efficient transport options, optimizing traffic flow to reduce congestion and emissions, and considering the social impact on different communities.
- In ITS, clear lines of *accountability* must be established. Developers and operators should take responsibility for the behaviour and impact of the system. It is important to set up feedback, complaint handling and redress mechanisms for users affected by system failure or malfunction, as well as to regularly audit and report on system performance.

By following the guidelines and incorporating the seven requirements of trustworthy AI into the design and operation of ITS, it its possible to ensure that these systems are safe, ethical, and serve the best interests of society.

6 Conclusions

This study has traversed a narrowing path about the ethical considerations regarding transport, from fundamental concepts to the concerns raised by intelligent transport, including those enhanced by AI and ML systems.

The impact of a transport system is quite significant, notably in the economic, social, and environmental dimensions. Various ethical theories can be used in the assessment of a specific situation, according to their weaknesses and strengths in dealing with it, based on the four core principles of Ethics: beneficence, nonmalificence, autonomy, and justice.

Ethical issues may arise at each stage of the transport system life-cycle, involving end-users, developers, and decision-makers. In addition, over time, other perspectives have become desirable, notably with the emergence of intelligent transport and, more recently, the addition of AI and ML systems, and novel ethical concerns particularly related to fairness, accountability, transparency, and explainability.

Ethics is crucial in ITS to ensure that its benefits are maximized and harms mitigated. Future work includes expanding this analysis, namely to the specificity of connected autonomous vehicles, with particular attention to decision-making processes and their logical formalization from an ethical standpoint.

Acknowledgments.. This work results from project DynamiCITY: Fostering Dynamic Adaptation of Smart Cities to Cope with Crises and Disruptions [reference NORTE-01-0145-FEDER-000073] supported by Norte Portugal Regional Operational Programme (NORTE 2020), under the PORTUGAL 2020 Partnership Agreement, through the European Regional Development Fund (ERDF). It was financially supported by Base Funding UIDB/00027/2020 of the Artificial Intelligence and Computer Science Laboratory (LIACC), through national funds FCT/MCTES (PIDDAC).

References

1. Anciães, P.R., Thomopoulos, N.: Ethical Issues. In: Garrett, M. (ed.) Encyclopedia of Transportation: social Science and Policy, vol. 2, pp. 534–541. SAGE Publications, Thousand Oaks, California (2014)
2. Barredo Arrieta, A., Díaz-Rodríguez, N., Del Ser, J., Bennetot, A., Tabik, S., Barbado, A., Garcia, S., Gil-Lopez, S., Molina, D., Benjamins, R., Chatila, R., Herrera, F.: Explainable artificial intelligence (XAI): concepts, taxonomies, opportunities and challenges toward responsible AI. Inf. Fusion **58**, 82–115 (2020). https://doi.org/10.1016/j.inffus.2019.12.012. Jun
3. Boldt, J., Orrù, E.: Towards a unified list of ethical principles for emerging technologies. Sustain. Fut. **4**, 100086 (2022). https://doi.org/10.1016/j.sftr.2022.100086. Jan
4. Cooley, C.H.: The theory of transportation. Publ. Am. Econ. Assoc. **9**(3), 13–148 (1894)
5. den Berghe, W.V.: Ethical issues in road safety policy-making. In: Proceedings of 7th Transport Research Arena TRA 2018, Vienna (2018)
6. Dimitrakopoulos, G., Uden, L., Varlamis, I.: User acceptance and ethics of ITS. In: Dimitrakopoulos, G., Uden, L., Varlamis, I. (eds.) The Future of Intelligent Transport Systems, pp. 85–91. Elsevier (2020). https://doi.org/10.1016/B978-0-12-818281-9.00007-3
7. European Commission. Directorate General for Communications Networks, Content and Technology., High Level Expert Group on Artificial Intelligence.: Ethics Guidelines for Trustworthy AI. Publications Office, LU (2019)
8. Floridi, L.: Establishing the rules for building trustworthy AI. Nat. Mach. Intell. **1**(6), 261–262 (2019). https://doi.org/10.1038/s42256-019-0055-y. Jun
9. Garg, T., Kaur, G.: A systematic review on intelligent transport systems. J. Comput. Cogn. Eng. (2022). https://doi.org/10.47852/bonviewJCCE2202245
10. Gaur, L., Sahoo, B.M.: Explainable Artificial Intelligence for Intelligent Transportation Systems: ethics and Applications. Springer International Publishing, Cham (2022). https://doi.org/10.1007/978-3-031-09644-0
11. Geurs, K.T., Boon, W., Van Wee, B.: Social impacts of transport: literature review and the state of the practice of transport appraisal in the Netherlands and the United Kingdom. Transp. Rev. **29**(1), 69–90 (2009). https://doi.org/10.1080/01441640802130490. Jan
12. Hansson, S.O. (ed.): The Ethics of Technology: methods and Approaches. Philosophy, Technology and Society, Rowman & Littlefield International, London (2017)
13. Hoel, L.A., Garber, N.J., Sadek, A.W.: Transportation Infrastructure Engineering: a Multimodal Integration. Thomson Nelson, Toronto (2008)
14. Kizza, J.M.: Ethics and ethical analysis. In: Kizza, J.M. (ed.) Ethical and Social Issues in the Information Age, pp. 29–51. Texts in Computer Science, Springer, London (2013). https://doi.org/10.1007/978-1-4471-4990-3_3
15. Kulash, D.J.: Transportation and society. In: Transportation Planning Handbook, 2nd edn., pp. 4–24. Institute of Transportation Engineers, Washington D.C. (1999)
16. Leikas, J., Koivisto, R., Gotcheva, N.: Ethical framework for designing autonomous intelligent systems. J. Open Innov.: Technol. Mark. Complex. **5**(1), 18 (2019). https://doi.org/10.3390/joitmc5010018. Mar
17. Malomo, A.O., Bernstein, M.: Ethics principles and theories. In: Ammar, A., Bernstein, M. (eds.) Neurosurgical Ethics in Practice: value-based Medicine, pp. 11–21. Springer, Berlin, Heidelberg (2014). https://doi.org/10.1007/978-3-642-54980-9_2

18. Miciukiewicz, K., Vigar, G.: Mobility and social Cohesion in the Splintered City: challenging technocentric transport research and policy-making practices. Urban Stud. **49**(9), 1941–1957 (2012). https://doi.org/10.1177/0042098012444886. Jul
19. Oladimeji, D., Gupta, K., Kose, N.A., Gundogan, K., Ge, L., Liang, F.: Smart transportation: an overview of technologies and applications. Sensors **23**(8), 3880 (2023). https://doi.org/10.3390/s23083880. Jan
20. Parliament, E.: Council of the European Union: Directive 2010/41/EU of the European Parliament and of the Council of 7 July 2010 on the framework for the deployment of Intelligent Transport Systems in the field of road transport and for interfaces with other modes of transport. Off. J. Eur. Union **L207**, 1–13 (2010). Aug
21. Rodrigue, J.P.: The Geography of Transport Systems, 5th edn. Routledge/Taylor & Francis Group, Abingdon, Oxon, New York, NY (2020)
22. Ryan, M.: The future of transportation: ethical, legal, social and economic impacts of self-driving vehicles in the Year 2025. Sci. Eng. Ethics **26**(3), 1185–1208 (2020). https://doi.org/10.1007/s11948-019-00130-2. Jun
23. Santoni de Sio, F.: The European Commission report on ethics of connected and automated vehicles and the future of ethics of transportation. Ethics Inf. Technol. **23**(4), 713–726 (2021). https://doi.org/10.1007/s10676-021-09609-8
24. Shin, D.: User perceptions of algorithmic decisions in the personalized AI system: perceptual evaluation of fairness, accountability, transparency, and explainability. J. Broadcast. Electron. Media **64**(4), 541–565 (2020). https://doi.org/10.1080/08838151.2020.1843357. Oct
25. Shin, D., Park, Y.J.: Role of fairness, accountability, and transparency in algorithmic affordance. Comput. Hum. Behav. **98**, 277–284 (2019). https://doi.org/10.1016/j.chb.2019.04.019. Sep
26. Smith, B.W.: Ethics of artificial intelligence in transport. In: Dubber, M.D., Pasquale, F., Das, S. (eds.) The Oxford Handbook of Ethics of AI, p. 0. Oxford University Press (2020). https://doi.org/10.1093/oxfordhb/9780190067397.013.42
27. Taylor, R.M.: Ethical principles and concepts in medicine. Handb. Clin. Neurol. **118**, 1–9 (2013). https://doi.org/10.1016/B978-0-444-53501-6.00001-9
28. Thiebes, S., Lins, S., Sunyaev, A.: Trustworthy artificial intelligence. Electron. Mark. **31**(2), 447–464 (2021). https://doi.org/10.1007/s12525-020-00441-4. Jun
29. Thiroux, J.P., Krasemann, K.W.: Ethics: theory and Practice, 11th edn. Pearson, Boston (2015)
30. Varkey, B.: Principles of clinical ethics and their application to practice. Med. Princ. Pract. **30**(1), 17–28 (2020). https://doi.org/10.1159/000509119
31. Vassallo, J.M., Bueno, P.C.: Sustainability assessment of transport policies, plans and projects. In: Mouter, N. (ed.) Advances in Transport Policy and Planning, New Methods, Reflections and Application Domains in Transport Appraisal, vol. 7, pp. 9–50. Academic Press (2021). https://doi.org/10.1016/bs.atpp.2020.07.006
32. van de Poel, I., Royakkers, L.M.M.: Ethics, Technology, and Engineering: an Introduction. Wiley-Blackwell, Malden, Mass (2011)
33. van Wee, B.: Transport and Ethics: ethics and the Evaluation of Transport Policies and Projects. Edward Elgar Publishing (2011)
34. Wang, H., Khajepour, A., Cao, D., Liu, T.: Ethical decision making in autonomous vehicles: challenges and research progress. IEEE Intell. Transp. Syst. Mag. **14**(1), 6–17 (2022). Jan

Using CDR Data to Understand Post-pandemic Mobility Patterns

Cláudia Rodrigues[1](✉) [ID], Marco Veloso[2] [ID], Ana Alves[3] [ID], and Carlos Bento[1] [ID]

[1] Department of Informatics Engineering, University of Coimbra, Center for Informatics and Systems of the University of Coimbra, Pinhal de Marrocos, Coimbra 3030-290, Portugal
cbarodrigues@dei.uc.pt, bento@dei.uc.pt
[2] Instituto Politécnico de Coimbra, ESTGOH, Rua General Santos Costa, Oliveira do Hospital, Coimbra 3400-124, Portugal
mveloso@dei.uc.pt
[3] Instituto Politécnico de Coimbra, ISEC, Rua Pedro Nunes—Quinta da Nora, Coimbra 3030-199, Portugal
ana@dei.uc.pt

Abstract. During the COVID-19 pandemic, the measures imposed to slow the spread of the virus had a profound impact on population dynamics around the world, producing unprecedented changes in mobility. Spatial data on human activity, including Call Detail Records (CDRs), have become a valuable source of information for understanding those changes. In this paper we study the population's mobility after the first wave of the pandemic within Portugal, using CDR data. We identify the movements and stops of the citizens, at an antenna level, and compare the results in the first months after the lifting of most of the contingency measures with the same period of the following year, highlighting the advantages of using CDRs to analyze mobility in pandemic contexts. Results based on two mobile phone datasets showed a significant difference in mobility in the two periods.

Keywords: COVID-19 · Mobility · CDR Data · Trajectory analysis · Clustering

1 Introduction

The pandemic dealt an extreme blow to the Portuguese economy. This crisis had and continues to have tremendous impacts on societies both in the short and long term, including lowering physical activities, increasing working from home, and reducing public transportation usage [1]. Public transport was particularly hindered. Most of the changes were related to the number of users, travel distance, mode share, and location during the day [2]. Such changes might result in a revolution in mobility.

Human mobility has become a prominent research field over the last decades, mostly due to the growing need to understand how people move and use urban space [3]. The access to mobile phone datasets offers the possibility to predict and study mobility patterns [4]. This ubiquitous data is often used for location analytics with the aim of characterizing various aspects of human mobility [5]. In particular, CDRs are a type of Global System for Mobiles (GSM) data often collected by mobile operators and used to study human movements and social networks. This data type is generated every time a client interacts with the network, providing knowledge on the sent and received calls and text messages [6]. Moreover, CDRs also give information on the antenna that received/transmitted the communication, enabling the inference of the client's location at an antenna level. By analyzing patterns in CDR data, it is possible to gain insights into how people move and interact in different locations and at different times, which can be useful for a range of applications, including urban planning.

In this paper, we study human mobility patterns within Portugal. The goal is to understand changes that were most probably caused by COVID-19 after the first wave of the pandemic and underline the benefits of using CDRs for this type of analysis. To understand the effects, we compare the dynamics in 2020, respectively in the following months after the lifting of the pandemic contingency measures, with the dynamics in the same period of 2021 (at the time, about 86% of the Portuguese population was fully vaccinated). Instead of using data collected explicitly for the purpose of analyzing mobility, such as Global Positioning System (GPS) data [7,8] or data from surveys [9,10], we use anonymized ubiquitous data collected by a Portuguese leading mobile phone operator. The mobile phone data correspond to CDRs obtained between September and October 2020 and between September and October 2021 and belong to nearly 5 000 individuals that had registered their residence in the district of Coimbra, Portugal.

During the pandemic's first waves, mobile phone data was highly used to track, monitor, and assist in the modeling of the geographical spread of the virus [11,12]. However, there is a gap in the literature regarding understanding the effects of the pandemic in mobility through the analysis of passively generated mobile phone data. In this study, we seek to understand: Has COVID-19 altered the movements and the spatial behavior of the population?

This paper is structured as follows: Sect. 2 presents a brief review of the related work, Sect. 3 gives a presentation of the data and its analysis, including some background of COVID-19 in Portugal, Sect. 4 presents the analysis made on mobility and discusses the results obtained, and Sect. 5 the conclusions.

2   Related Work

Mobile phone data, including CDRs, has been used to sense urban dynamics, helping urban planners and designers to cope with urban growth and endorsing and resolving a variety of social issues [13]. CDRs' temporal density has increased due to the popularity of smartphones in the last decades, however, this data continues to present some challenges, such as spatial and temporal sparseness. As a consequence, the amount of in-depth research conducted into mobility and behavior patterns is low compared to studies using GPS data [14]. Besides the challenges, many researchers and institutions are aware of CDRs' potential in reflecting human mobility and identifying important places [5]. Graells-Garrido et al. [13] used CDRs to identify citizens' meaningful places and to understand land use. CDRs were used to identify home and work locations and recreate the population distribution as well as commuting trips. Also, Rodrigues et al. [6] used CDRs to identify home, work, and second home locations and Ferreira et al. [3] to identify routine locations.

Regarding the analysis of changes in mobility caused by the pandemic, Sevtsuk et al. [7] used GPS data from smartphones to analyze the impact of COVID-19 on trips to urban amenities. The study traces the changes in amenity visits from before the pandemic to after the first wave of the pandemic (January 2019 to December 2020). Their findings suggest even though overall trip volumes remained lower than normal levels throughout the remainder of the year, preferences towards specific cluster attributes mostly returned to expected levels by the end of 2020. Also, Sevtsuk et al. [8] examined changes in mobility between residents of highest and lowest Socio-Economic Index (SEI) during the COVID-19 pandemic, using GPS data. In general, low-SEI groups traveled shorter distances but visited more locations before the pandemic. Contrary, high-SEI residents universally reduced their mobility to a greater extent during the pandemic, highlighting that COVID-19 significantly widened these differences thereby exacerbating "mobility gaps" between low-SEI and high-SEI groups.

Shamshiripour et al. [10] used data from a survey to study how and to what extent people's mobility styles and habitual travel behaviors have changed during the COVID-19 pandemic in Chicago. The analysis showed significant changes in mobility habits, predispositions, and higher-level orientations towards online activities and travel (i.e., long-distance commutes and urban travel mode choice) during and after the COVID-19 pandemic. To point out the changes in mobility, the analysis of Palma et al. [1] shows that after the pandemic the demand for parks increased significantly and that the public transportation sector is therefore expected to face serious monetary problems as a result of the loss of income during the confinement period and decreased demand afterward.

3   Data Exploration

3.1   COVID-19 Statistics

COVID-19 was declared a global pandemic in March 2020. The consequent policy measures to safeguard public health have profoundly altered the normality of Portuguese life. One year after the beginning of the pandemic, the number of deaths had increased, resulting in an excess of 1 925 deaths on average monthly. The Direção Geral de Saúde (DGS - Health Authority in Portugal) [15] reported that between March 2020 and February 2021, there were 11 170 deaths registered: an increase of 21.9% compared to the previous 12 months. The DGS registers point out that, up until September 2020, 75 542 infections and 1 971 deaths were registered. The numbers increased in the following year. In 2021, until September, 1 069 473 infections and 13 446 deaths were registered. The numbers show the effects of lifting the contingency measures in 2021, with the infections augmenting 1 316% and the deaths 582%. Specifically, in the central region (the main area of study), the number of infections increased 2 220% and deaths 1 096%.

In 2020, the negative impact of the COVID-19 pandemic was felt in all modes of transport, with a decrease in the number of passengers transported by rail (-41.7%), underground metro (-47.8%), highway (-42.0%) [16].

3.2 Study Area

Portugal is the area of study, with specific attention to the District of Coimbra. Coimbra is a district from the central region of Portugal with an area of 3 974 km^2 and 408 631 inhabitants [17]. The telecommunication company owns more than 48 000 antennas in Portugal, 2 093 of which are in the district of Coimbra. Figure 1 presents the district and the geographical distribution of antennas/cell towers in the area. It is observable that there are areas of higher density of antennas.

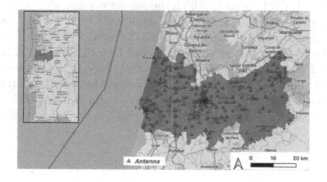

Fig. 1. District of Coimbra and distribution of antennas

To analyze the antennas' distribution, a density-based clustering algorithm, the Density-Based Spatial Clustering of Applications with Noise (DBSCAN), was used to separate areas with high density of antennas from areas of low density. This algorithm can recognize areas of elevated density of events, defining that two points are in the same cluster if the distance between them is below the threshold epsilon (*eps*) [18]. In addition, it is also capable of handling outliers. In this algorithm, it is assumed that all points within a cluster are density reachable and points across different clusters are not. The idea is that the neighborhood of a given radius must contain at least a minimum number of points. For that, two input parameters are required: the maximum physical distance between two samples, for one to be considered a neighbor of the other (*eps*) and the minimum number of points, in the neighborhood, to form a cluster [18]. Two areas of high density of antennas were found, corresponding to urban areas, namely, the two major cities of the district (Coimbra and Figueira da Foz). It was also observed that in areas of high density where the antennas are closest (urban areas), the mean coverage area of the antennas is 2 246 meters and in areas of low density (rural areas), the mean coverage area of the antennas is 4 062 meters.

3.3   Call Detail Records

The data correspond to anonymized CDRs that were generated by nearly 5 000 individuals registered as residents in the city of Coimbra, throughout September and October of 2020 and in the same period of 2021. A CDR contains information about interactions that pass through the telecommunications network. These records are generated in large quantities as a by-product of the billing by mobile operators and typically contain such information fields as the ID of the sender and receiver, the ID of the origin and destination cell tower, the time and date that the event started, and the duration of the communication. It is also usual that some telecommunication companies attach to these datasets information about the user or the location of the cell tower [19].

The datasets used in this analysis contain such information as the ID of the sender, the ID of the cell tower to which the sender was connected when the event started, the time that the event started, and some information about the cell tower. As presented in Fig. 2 most of the CDRs were registered during daytime both in 2020 and 2021. In the September and October of 2020, 221 400 CDRs were generated and in the same months of 2021, 526 033 CDRs were generated by the studied population. Despite that difference, the activity matches in terms of hours: in both periods rise at 7 AM and stay at a high level until 7 PM, before dropping and reaching a low between 1 AM and 5 AM. This study is related to weekday usage.

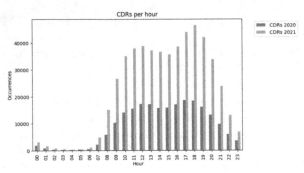

Fig. 2. CDR events registered per hour

4   Mobility Analysis

As mentioned, massive mobility datasets have been fostering a vast scientific production on various applications of mobility analysis, including urban planning and transportation. To capture mobility and study the changes in movement patterns caused by COVID-19, we use a Python library that performs analysis of mobility data: Scikit-mobility. This library has the capacity to load and represent mobility data, both at the individual and the collective level, and clean and pre-process mobility data using techniques, such as trajectory clustering, compression, segmentation, and filtering [20].

To analyze mobility in the two different years and compare the results, we started by creating two data structures for each dataset: a trajectory dataframe and a flow dataframe. In the trajectory dataframe objects are ordered as a sequence of spatio-temporal events and each row represents a point of a trajectory. The trajectory dataframe may contain many trajectories. So, to create these data structures, the CDRs of each user were ordered by time and each CDR was associated with a point in a trajectory. A flow dataframe describes an origin-destination matrix. A row of the dataframe represents a flow of multiple users between two locations. Normally, the territory is discretized, mapping the coordinates to a spatial tessellation that divides the space into a countable number of geometric shapes, called tiles, with no overlaps and no gaps.

Once the data structures were created, we focused our analysis on the processing of the trajectory's dataframe. We started by identifying the individuals' "stops". The stop points are points in a trajectory that can represent meaningful places [20]. So, for each individual, we considered a stop, where more than 20 min were spent [21] within a distance of 2 246 m (average coverage radius of the antennas in urban areas). The coverage of the antennas overlaps most of the time and sometimes situations of load sharing may occur. In some cases of variations in cellular traffic, the closest antenna is not always the one the user connects to. This phenomenon is often called load sharing and consists of the network transferring traffic from overloaded antennas to neighboring ones. So, to prevent errors provoked by this phenomenon, in a radius of 2 246 m, if the cell phone switches between multiple antennas, it is considered that the individual visited only one location.

Considering that the goal is not to study individual but collective patterns, to perform the analysis at a group level we use a clustering algorithm. In this phase, the stops of the individuals in the trajectory dataframe were grouped. Meaning that the stops in the same group/cluster correspond to visits of several individuals to the same location at different times, based on spatial proximity. The clustering algorithm used was DBSCAN. After the processing, the stops that belong to the same cluster have the same label. To handle the varying densities of points in the different datasets, the parameters of the algorithm, the *eps* and minimum number of points, were applied based on the characteristics of the data. The elbow/knee method was used to identify the ideal *eps* parameter. In this process, the selection of the optimal values is made by looking at the distance from a point to its kth neighbor (k-$dist$), resulting in a k-$dist$ plot. All k-$dists$ are computed for all data points for some k. Next, the values of the distances are sorted in ascending order and plotted. In the k-$dist$ plots, the sharp change at the k-$dists$ value, corresponds to a suitable value of the *eps* [22]. So, we measure the distance between the stops of users in each trajectory dataframe and use the optimal distances as parameters. The minimum points parameter was applied based on the average number of stops registered per user in each period.

4.1   Comparison and Discussion

The comparison of the flow dataframes, in Fig. 3, indicates that in 2020 most of the interregional flows were within the central region. In comparison, in 2021 it is observable a higher number of migrations from the center region to the other regions of the country, including the islands. Although in both periods most of the events were registered in Coimbra, there are CDRs registered in antennas all across the country.

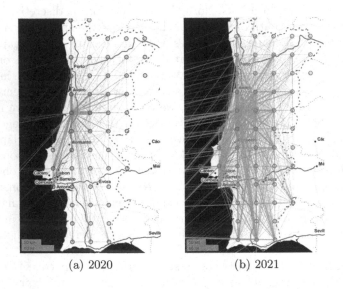

(a) 2020   (b) 2021

Fig. 3. Flow dataframes (origin-destination matrices)

By analyzing the trajectory dataframes it was possible to analyze the characteristics of the individuals' trips. In 2020, the average maximum distance traveled from home by an individual was 44.97 km and, in 2021, 263.03 km. The home location was determined based on the location most visited by an individual during nighttime. Regarding general traveling, the average distance of each trip made in 2020 was 17.45 and 55.08 km in 2021. This confirms the previous analysis, indicating that in the first period, most trips were made in a more restricted area and later, trips began to be to regions further away from home (Coimbra).

After the identification of stop locations, in 2020, 54 009 stops were identified and 147 930 in 2021. In 2020, each individual registered an average of 8.95 stops; in the same period of 2021, the average number of stops increased to 32.12 per user. However, besides the different number of stops in the two years, the quantity of stops is similar in both periods in terms of hours (Fig. 4). Just like in the CDRs, the number of stops is higher during the day and lower during the night.

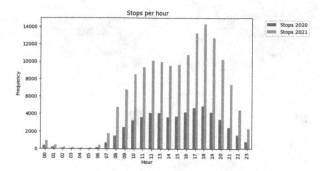

Fig. 4. Stops registered per hour

The heatmaps in Fig. 5 highlight the regions of Portugal where most of the stops were made in 2020 and 2021. These figures exhibit that in 2020 most of the stops were registered in the district of residence (Coimbra) or in the neighboring districts. Contrary, other areas of the country were visited in 2021, with a higher frequency. Nevertheless, in both periods, Coimbra was, with distinction, the most visited district, with more than 40 000 stops registered in 2020 and 100 000 in 2021, an increase of 150%.

After applying the clustering algorithm, 17 clusters were found in 2020 and 281 in 2021. The heatmaps in Fig. 6 present regions where most of the clusters were found. These maps were created based on the weight of the clusters, which means that clusters associated with more visits are highlighted more (have a brighter color). As observed in the first year, most of the locations visited were in Coimbra, with some exceptions, for example, visits to the south of Portugal. In the following year, even with the extreme number of infections and deaths, according to DGS [15], the individuals traveled and visited almost all districts across the country. The same was verified on the Azores and Madeira islands, where it is observable the identification of more clusters in 2021. The data comprehends two months that in Portugal are considered typical months of vacation when it is common for people to travel to other locations, and also months when typically people return to normal routines (school and work). Some districts where the increase in the number of visits is notorious, such as in the south of Portugal or the islands, are considered typical regions for tourism in Portugal.

As observed, more clusters were found in 2021, even though in September and October of 2020 most of the contingency measures were already dropped. The analysis of the results needs to take into consideration that the geo-references in CDRs, correspond to the locations of the antennas to which the phone was connected. Therefore, with this type of data, locations are only known at an antenna level. However, this data benefits from being collected without requiring

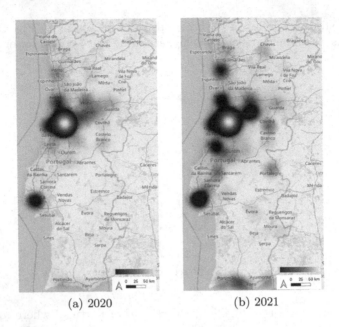

(a) 2020   (b) 2021

Fig. 5. Heatmap of stops

user participation, not intrusive and anonymized, and is available for all groups of the population [6].

5   Conclusions

Due to the pandemic, the routines of the population changed provoking multiple alterations in urban dynamics. Some differences were observed in commuting trips and business travel. With the adoption of remote work, most people started working from home, avoiding commuting. This also had an effect on the locations visited, with long-distance travel restricted, most of the routine locations remained in the neighborhoods, increasing local travel. As mentioned, public transportation also suffered significant changes, not only in the number of passengers (people started preferring to travel isolated) but also in the spatial transportation patterns. This analysis shows the results of a study that aims to analyze collective mobility patterns in the post-pandemic scenario through the analysis of mobile phone data.

Results show that people traveled shorter distances in the following months of the first wave of the pandemic. Most of the trips were made in the district of residence, near home, or to the neighboring districts. It also shows that people communicate less or that the main channel of connection changed over the two periods, most probably because in the first period, people stayed at home and used VOIP (Voice-over-IP) connections. Mobility increased over the second

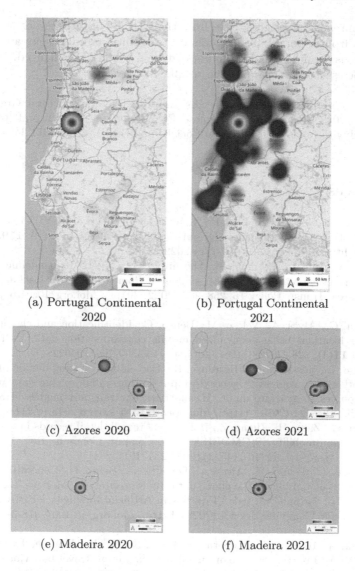

(a) Portugal Continental
2020

(b) Portugal Continental
2021

(c) Azores 2020

(d) Azores 2021

(e) Madeira 2020

(f) Madeira 2021

Fig. 6. Heatmap of clusters

year of the pandemic. The locations visited were more dispersed, with more districts being visited, also increasing the distance of the trips. The visits to the Portuguese islands have increased as well. This study also highlights the benefits of studying mobile phone data to understand changes in mobility caused by pandemic situations. While the observed low number of CDRs-based communications in the first year of the pandemic may raise some concerns about the representativeness of the data, 2020 was an atypical year with events that affected everyone's movements in a similar way, so this indicator may not substantially impact the insights taken from the CDRs. For future work, we will use CDR data from a period ahead to analyze mobility and also compare the routine locations to understand if the population's habits have changed. Moreover, it would be essential to validate the results.

Acknowledgements. This research was supported by the doctoral Grant PRT/ BD/154266/2022 financed by Portuguese Foundation for Science and Technology (FCT), and with funds from European Social Fund (ESF), under MIT Portugal Program.

References

1. de Palma, A., Vosough, S., Liao, F.: An overview of effects of COVID-19 on mobility and lifestyle: 18 months since the outbreak. Transp. Res. Part A **159**, 372–397 (2022). https://doi.org/10.1016/j.tra.2022.03.024
2. Marra, A., Sun, L., Corman, F.: The impact of COVID-19 pandemic on public transport usage and route choice: evidences from a long-term tracking study in urban area. Transp. Policy **16**, 258–268 (2022). https://doi.org/10.1016/j.tra.2022.03.024
3. Ferreira, G., Alves, A., Veloso, M., Bento, C.: Identification and classification of routine locations using anonymized mobile communication data. ISPRS Int. J. Geo-In **11**(4), 228 (2022). https://doi.org/10.3390/ijgi11040228
4. Montero, L., Ros-Roca, X., Herranzc, R., Barcelób, J.: Fusing mobile phone data with other data sources to generate input Fusing mobile phone data with other data sources to generate input OD matrices for transport models. Transp. Res. Procedia 417–424 (2019). https://doi.org/10.1016/j.trpro.2018.12.211
5. Ranjan, G., Zang, H., Zhang, Z., Bolot, J.: Are call detail records biased for sampling human mobility? SIGMOBILE Mob. Comput. Commun. Rev. **16**(3), 33–44 (2012). https://doi.org/10.1145/2412096.2412101
6. Rodrigues, C., Veloso, M., Alves, A., Ferreira, G., Bento, C.: Generating the users geographic map using mobile phone data. In: Marreiros, G., Martins, B., Paiva, A., Ribeiro, B., Sardinha, A. (eds.) Progress in Artificial Intelligence EPIA 2022. Lecture Notes in Computer Science (2022). https://doi.org/10.1007/978-3-031-16474-3_25
7. Sevtsuk, A., Hudson, A., Halpern, D., Basu, R., Ng, K., Jong de, J.: The impact of COVID-19 on trips to urban amenities: examining travel behavior changes in Somerville, MA. PLoS ONE **16**(9) (2021). https://doi.org/10.1371/journal.pone.0252794
8. Sevtsuk, A., Basu, R., Halpern, D., Hudson, A., Ng, K., Jong de, J.: A tale of two Americas: socio-economic mobility gaps within and across American cities before and during the pandemic. Cities 131 (2022). https://doi.org/10.1016/j.cities.2022.104006
9. Manteu, C., Monteiro, N., Sequeira, A.: The short-term impact of the COVID-19 pandemic on Portuguese companies. 03 Occasional Papers 2020 (2020)
10. Shamshiripour, A., Rahimi, E., Shabanpour, R., Mohammadian, A.: How is COVID-19 reshaping activity-travel behavior? Evidence from a comprehensive survey in Chicago. Transp. Res. Interdiscip. Perspect. **7** (2020)

11. Grantz, K., Meredith, H., Cummings, D., Metcalf, C., Grenfell, B., Giles, J., Mehta, M., Solomon, S., Labrique, A., Kishore, N., Buckee, C., Wesolowski, A.: The use of mobile phone data to inform analysis of COVID-19 pandemic epidemiology. Nat. Commun. **11** (2020). https://doi.org/10.1038/s41467-020-18190-5
12. Oliver, N., Lepri, B., Sterly, H., Lambiotte, R., Deletaille, S., Nadai, M., Letouzé, E., Salah, A., Benjamins, R., Cattuto, C., Colizza, V., Cordes, N., Fraiberger, S., Koebe, T., Lehmann, S., Murillo, J., Pentland, A., Pham, P., Pivetta, F., Saramaki, J., Scarpino, S., Tizzoni, M., Verhulst, S., Vinck, P.: Mobile phone data for informing public health actions across the COVID-19 pandemic life cycle. Sci. Adv. **6**(23) (2020). https://doi.org/10.1126/sciadv.abc0764
13. Graells-Garrido, E., Peredo, O., García, J.: Sensing urban patterns with antenna mappings: the case of Santiago, Chile. Sensors **16**(7) (2016). https://doi.org/10.3390/s16071098
14. Kanno, T., Sekimoto, Y., Kanasugi, H., Shibasaki, R.: Real-time passenger location estimation using CDRs and train objects generated from crowdsourced timetables. In: PUbiComp/ISWC'15 Adjunct: Adjunct Proceedings of the 2015 ACM Int. Joint Conf. on Pervasive and Ubiquitous Computing and Proceedings of the 2015 ACM Int. Symposium on Wearable Computers, pp. 1197–1205 (2015)
15. DGS: RELATÓRIO DE SITUAÇÃO. https://covid19.min-saude.pt/relatorio-de-situacao/. Accessed 20 Dec 2022
16. Instituto Nacional de Estatística: Estatísticas dos Transportes e Comunicações. Instituto Nacional de Estatística (2021)
17. City Population. https://www.citypopulation.de/en/portugal/ua/06_coimbra/. Accessed 27 Dec 2022
18. Ester, M., Kriegel, H., Sander, J., Xu, X.: A density-based algorithm for discovering clusters in large spatial databases with noise. In: Proceedings of the Second International Conferences on Knowledge Discovery and Data Mining, pp. 226–231 (1996)
19. Barboza, M., Alencar, R., Cahves, J., Silva, M., Orrico, R., Evsukoff, A.: Identifying human mobility patterns in the Rio de Janeiro metropolitan area using call detail records. Transp. Res. Rec. **2675**(4), 213–221 (2020). https://doi.org/10.1177/0361198120977655
20. Pappalardo, L., Simini, F., Barlacchi, G., Pellungrini, R.: Scikit-mobility: a Python library for the analysis, generation and risk assessment of mobility data. Phys. Soc. (2021)
21. Willberg, E., Järv, O., Väisänen, T., Toivonen, T.: Escaping from cities during the COVID-19 crisis: using mobile phone data to trace mobility in Finland. ISPRS Int. J. Geo-Inf. **10**(2) (2020). https://doi.org/10.3390/ijgi10020103
22. Liu, P., Zhou, D., Wu N.: VDBSCAN: varied density based spatial clustering of applications with noise. In: International Conferences on Service Systems and Service Management, pp. 1–4 (2007). https://doi.org/10.1109/ICSSSM.2007.4280175

Artificial Intelligence in Smart Computing

Using Artificial Intelligence for Trust Management Systems in Fog Computing: A Comprehensive Study

Mohamed Abdel Rahman[1], Ahmed Dahroug[1], and Sherin M. Moussa[2,3]($\boxtimes$) (iD)

[1] College of Computing and Information Technology, Arab Academy for Science, Technology and Maritime Transport, Cairo 11799, Egypt
mrahman@student.aast.edu, adahroug_87@aast.edu
[2] Faculty of Computer and Information Sciences, Ain Shams University, Cairo 11566, Egypt
sherinmoussa@cis.asu.edu.eg, sherin.moussa@ufe.edu.eg
[3] Laboratoire Interdisciplinaire de L'Université Française d'Egypte (UFEID Lab), Université Francaise d'Egypte, Cairo 11837, Egypt

Abstract. Fog computing has recently attracted great attention as an emerging computing paradigm, avoiding the latency concerns of the cloud. However, because of the distributed, decentralized nature of the fog, several security and privacy issues arise when fog nodes interact and exchange data in specific tasks. Fog servers must be trustworthy for delegation since they are close to the end user and can obtain sensitive information. Yet, normal cryptographic solutions cannot be used to control internal attacks, i.e., from a rogue node that has been authenticated to join the network, raising the concern of how to establish a trustworthy communication between the fog nodes. Trust Management Systems (TMS) have been developed to calculate the level of assurance between fog nodes based on their communication behavior to detect the rogue nodes in the network. Password-based, Traditional authentication methods, i.e., biometric-based and certificated-based, do not fit the fog because of its uniqueness architecture, consuming substantially additional processing power and provoking latency. Thus, several research issues remain open for TMS in the fog, including creating trusted execution environments, trust and security during fog orchestration, collusion attack and access control. In this paper, we investigate using artificial intelligence techniques to tackle the main challenges of TMS in fog computing. We conducted a comparative study to evaluate the major TMS in literature and identify their advantages and disadvantages. We then highlight 17 primary insights and recommendations to improve TMS using artificial intelligence to have more efficient TMS in fog computing.

Keywords: Fog/Edge Computing · Trust Management · Internet of Things (IoT) · Artificial Intelligence (AI)

1 Introduction

Fog computing sets a large number of cloud computing resources at the edge of a network instead of creating ad hoc channels for a centralized remote cloud infrastructure [1]. This paradigm provides a superior experience to end-users, improves the Quality of Service (QoS) and decreases service latency [2, 3]. As a new architectural style, fog computing enables a huge range of applications, including artificial intelligence (AI), augmented reality, fifth generation (5G) wireless networks, and Internet of Things (IoT) [4]. Additionally, it is commonly believed that fog computing is more secured than cloud computing, as the data gathered are analyzed and quickly maintained on fog nodes that are nearby to the sources of data, which makes it harder for intruders to have access to user's information and reduces the dependency on Internet connections because of the different and separate security measures at various fog nodes. Compared to a more centralized cloud computing architecture, this reduces the quantity of user data that might be accessible in any particular data breach [1].

However, maintaining security and privacy in fog computing presents a number of issues, wherein the data exchange between user devices and fog nodes could subject to similar risks or among numerous fog nodes [5, 6]. Services based on fog are typically owned by a variety of parties based on: (1) providing extra resources on a nearby private cloud as leasing fog services to local businesses, (2) choosing wireless carriers or Internet service providers for deployment, (3) extending current cloud-based services out to the edge for performance improvement [6]. The trust situation got complicated among fog nodes due to this flexibility. Additionally, although fog users' devices are frequently seen as resourceful in terms of their capabilities, they are still unable to carry out a certain complicated task, such as those necessary in applications of smart transportation, virtual/augmented reality, and image processing [7]. As a result, these tasks are handed over to the fog layer, where the fog nodes collaborate or operate independently to complete these tasks in order to fulfil the overall goal. An adversary can simply launch further attacks by tampering with or stealing user sensitive data since the outsourced data can be transmitted to a rogue fog node. A rogue node is a harmful fog device that entices clients to use it by pretending to be trustworthy. There are several cryptographic-based techniques that can successfully thwart externally attacks, but they are ineffective against inside attacks, when rogue fog nodes currently exist in the system and using real identities. Therefore, to reduce security risk, we turn to trusting "single out" rogue fog nodes. In order to estimate their reliability for handling upcoming jobs based on past behavior, fog nodes are intended to be cooperatively monitored by their neighboring nodes for any indication of divergence from approved behaviors [1].

Artificial intelligence (AI) has recently been widely adopted across several commercial sectors and industries, producing several ground-breaking services and applications that are largely supported by high-performance computing and cloud storage infrastructure. Emerging applications like autonomous systems, IoT, Fog computing and trust management for trust aggregation components, place a great demand on the integration of intelligence into edge devices. To increase energy and spectrum efficiency, increase security, and reduce latency in various applications, it is preferable to process data close to or at the source of data [8]. Trust is the degree of belief to foresee the object's behavior

[9]. Fog is a distributed, decentralized, and open computing architecture, where numerous fog devices participate from different geographical locations. Different independent owners own fog devices, and they can join and quit fog networks dynamically [10]. Access control is a security technique that defines an object's access privileges on another object. Trust management is a distinct approach to identify and interpret relationships, authentication information and security policies that permit direct authorization to do security-critical operations [11]. TMS computes the trust value of a fog node and reflect one fog node's opinion on the trustworthy nature of another fog node. It categorizes network objects into untrusted, trusted, uncertain, and malicious fog node. As stated by fog computing characteristics, fog node trust is asymmetric, subjective, dynamic, may not be transitive and context dependent. Along with security, trust management may help with additional duties such as determining to add new fog nodes and dynamically picking fog nodes with different properties to mask the object's location. It also aids in the transition between fog nodes during computational offloading and former node failure.

In this paper, we provide a comprehensive survey for the main studies that addressed TMS in the fog, investigating the effectiveness and efficiency of these systems with versus without the adoption of AI for trust management in fog computing. Thus, the main contributions of this paper can be formulated as follows:

- Providing a comprehensive review for the applied trust management techniques in the fog.
- Evaluating the adoption of AI in the current TMS in the fog.
- Pointing out the current challenges and future research directions for trust management in the fog.

The rest of the paper is structured as follows. Section 2 overviews the main survey studies that have been conducted for TMS in fog computing. Section 3 presents the main methods considered for trust management in fog computing that do not rely on AI techniques. Section 4 discusses the main studies that adopted AI techniques for trust management in fog computing, whereas Sect. 5 provides a detailed discussion and analysis for the presented studies to evaluate the adoption of AI in TMS on the fog and to deduce the possible future directions for enhancement. Section 6 concludes the study.

2 Related Reviews

Several surveys have been conducted on trust management for IoT and fog computing. Most of these studies either addressed the security concerns of fog and IoT, or just concentrated on IoT security and a single aspect of fog. In this section, we present the main studies that have conducted surveys on trust management for IoT and fog computing. Authors in [9] discussed the three-layer of fog computing architecture, Numerous security and trust open issues in fog computing and the state-of-the-art systems identified. Their research was limited to fog computing architectures. In [12], the main focus was on different trust-related challenges in the fog, such as location-based trust, middleware trust models, service trust, trust-related attacks, as well as recent open challenges, including privacy and security challenges in fog computing, whereas in [13], analyzed the architectures of fog computing to identify the associated possible security and trust challenges. The existing literature was comprehensively reported in a presented taxonomy to categorize trust and security approaches related to fog computing. Another review was presented in [14] that addressed trust solutions for IoT at the fog layer, discussing several points for improving trust at the fog layer and IoT paradigm by proposing a model for trust management.

Authors in [15] presented a systematic review of studies related to fog and edge computing trust management, dividing trust management techniques into three main categories: model/framework, architecture, and algorithm. They compared among the edge and fog computing trust management models based on benefits and drawbacks, significant trust metrics, evaluation techniques and tools and simulation architectures. In [16], the authentication and privacy of fog nodes was overviewed in a comprehensive survey, explaining various security issues, including user access security, access control, hypervisors, and fog devices in fog computing. Various fog level architectures, associated with the threats that exist at this layer were discussed in [17] through a systematic literature review, analyzing statistically and systematically the most common attacks that take place in the IoT-Fog scheme to critically examine the impact of trust on the various security pillars. In [18], the authors analyzed the current state of trust management for IoT, presenting a classification based on the used methods, while in [19], another survey was provided for IoT trust management systems, including stages and capabilities and challenges to assess the design and implementation of IoT trust management issues. However, both reviews were relevant to the IoT scheme only. Table 1 provides a comprehensive summary of the existing surveys considering trust management in fog computing.

Considering the presented studies, it is evident that despite the copious number of surveys that have been introduced in this field, no investigation has been conducted to evaluate the extent of how AI is utilized in TMS to solve trust management issues of IoT in fog computing. Several studies have recently emerged to apply AI in TMS at the fog layer, but there is still no comprehensive study to assess these works from the AI perspective, which would pave the way for many insights and recommendations to consider for better AI utilization in trust management at the fog level.

3   Non-AI Methods for Trust Management in the Fog

Trust management in fog computing is in its early stage. Some works have considered methods based on non-AI techniques to manage trust challenges in the fog. In this section, we discuss the main studies presented in the literature in this category. Authors in [20] proposed a fog-based trust model based on a trust and reputation algorithm to assist IoT devices in establishing safe connections with other trustworthy IoT devices. The trust level of IoT devices is evaluated, monitored, and stored by a fog node and shared with other IoT devices on demand. IoT device trust consists of either indirect or direct trust. Direct trust is determined by direct experience, whereas indirect trust is measured by a weighted aggregate of other IoT devices' direct experience/recommendations. The weight given to each recommendation is determined by the confidence factor. Penalty concepts and Incentive were mentioned to motivate honest behavior, but it wasn't clear

Table 1. A comprehensive summary of surveys for trust management in fog computing.

Ref. #	Published Year	Survey Scope	Num. of Studies included	Coverage Duration
[9]	2022	Trust management in fog computing	7	2019–2021
[12]	2019	Trust management in fog computing	15	2013–2018
[13]	2018	Security and trust issues in fog computing	86	2014–2018
[14]	2020	Fog computing for trust in the IoT	23	2005–2019
[15]	2022	Techniques, trends, and challenges of trust management in fog/edge computing	82	2014–2021
[16]	2021	Privacy, authentication, threats, access control in trust management for fog computing	36	2009–2019
[17]	2021	Architecture, prevalent threats and trust models in fog steered IoT	102	2012–2020
[18]	2022	Trust management for IoT	62	2011–2023
[19]	2020	Various applications of trust management and examined issues in the design and deployment of trust management for IoT	76	2011–2019

how incentives and penalties are incorporated. The main limitation of this model considering only fog nodes when evaluating trust, ignoring the malicious and service behaviors of fog nodes.

In [21], Tidal Trust and other mathematical algorithms were used to propose a secure handoff mechanism, employing a trust manager between the fog layer and IoT layer to rank the fog and IoT nodes and evaluate the trust value. The approach proposed protected against IoT device handoff attacks, identified, and reduced malicious fog nodes, and enhanced system response time, performance, and accuracy. However, it did not compute the trust of IoT, and fog node services based on any random or dynamic parameters, It also did not take into account various forms of threats particular to the fog environment. A fog-based hierarchical trust mechanism framework was introduced in [22] to detect hidden data attacks and only communicating with trustworthy edge nodes using mathematical algorithms to calculate direct trust value and comprehensive trust among nodes. The fog layer acted as a trust buffer between the sensor network layer and cloud layer to detect the wireless sensor network's trust status, monitor their behavior and to perform analysis tasks. However, the framework focused on forwarding delay, route failure rate and the packet loss rate only causing the system to be slow with poor stability because It is unable to efficiently filter out poor recommendations in order to mitigate the effect of rogue nodes.

In [23], a lightweight multidimensional trust evaluation algorithm was proposed to address the difficulty of evaluating edge device trust in a service-oriented IoT environment using mathematical algorithms to calculate indirect trust from multi-source feedback based on double-filtering method. The proposed model enhanced the robustness, adaptability, credibility, and reliability of the IoT edge environment. However, a trust update model was missing, as well as that it needs to improve the aggregating process that increases flexibility. A two-way trust management approach was introduced in [24] that used the Bayes model to assess the trust of fog nodes. Two types of trust were considered: Bayes trust and computed trust, to determine a fog node's final trust. A weighted sum approach is used to evaluate computed trust, considering service score as the trust metrics, degree centrality, reputation, and direct trust. Bayes trust, on the other hand, is determined using the beta probability function. While assessing the node's reputation, a discounting approach was employed to weight recommendations from other nodes. If the service provider's final trust was greater than the predetermined threshold, the connection is started; otherwise, the connection is dropped. Yet, this approach resulted in serious overheads because of the discounting operations on the received recommendations (Table 2). Table 3 gives a summarized overview of the main studies that addressed non-AI techniques for trust management in fog computing.

4   Adopting AI Techniques for Trust Management in the Fog

With the advancements of AI in the fog and IoT domains, current studies show the applicability of AI methods to solve many trust management concerns in fog computing. Trust computation, behavior learning, privacy, and security. In this section, we present the main studies that adopted AI techniques for trust management in fog computing and IoT. In [1], Fuzzy Logic technique was used to carry out a fog computing trust assessment, recommendation approach, management using Quality of Service (QoS), Quality of Security (QoSec) and quality of Protection (QoP) histories to assess the trustworthiness of fog nodes. The method detected malicious fog nodes, decreased attacks, offered a safe and trusted environment to share node's resources and reduced service response time, promoted load-balance, and observed fog efficiency. However, it did not address the energy consumption for nodes to perform such successive processes, and the scalability of the approach was not investigated.

-NoValue-In [25], a two-way trust management system was proposed based on Fuzzy Logic to provide secure fog-to-fog collaboration, allowing a service requester and service provider to assess each other's level of trust. The experiment result showed that the model was accurate, efficient, reliable, and secure; however, the authors did not consider the scalability, energy consumption and mobility of fog nodes and IoT devices and they supposed the fog nodes were static. The system evaluated direct trust based on fuzzy logic, which is a highly computational process. Moreover, Because the whole trust evaluation started at the fog client, causing trust management to be inefficient when running on low-powered fog clients. A trust model based on subjective logic was introduced in [26] to detect a rogue fog node. It took into consideration other nodes' recommendation opinions consisting of uncertainty factor, disbelief, and belief to evaluate the node's trust. The model used consensus and discounting methods to

Table 2. A summarized overview of non-AI trust management techniques in fog computing.

Ref. #	Objective	Methodology used	Dataset Synthetic?	Trust parameters considered?	Evaluation Criteria	Limitations
[20]	Assist IoT devices to interact securely with other honest IoT devices	Trust and Reputation Algorithm	Yes	Direct trust based on direct experience. Indirect trust based on weighted aggregation of other IoT devices	Scalability, Efficiency, Performance protecting from attacks: Bad mouthing, on/off, self-promoting	Did not consider neither rouge nodes, Biasing, nor social relationships
[21]	Assessment of trustworthiness of IoT devices & fog nodes, detecting malicious IoT & fog nodes	Tidal Trust Algorithm	Yes	Trust Value, Trust Factor, Social Impact Theory Optimizer	Scalability, probability, Accuracy, Response time, resource utilization, security	Did not consider different types of malicious activities, low adaptability, heterogeneity, integrity, and scalability
[22]	Resource consumption, monitor trust state of whole network. Detect and recover data attacks and misjudgment nodes	Direct trust algorithm, comprehensive trust among nodes algorithm	Yes	real-time comparison of service parameters. Exception information in wireless sensor networks. Targeted quantitative evaluation of entities	Energy consumption, Reliability detecting hidden data attacks, recovering misjudgment nodes, scalability	Did not consider various attacks, low stability, focused on packet loss rate, route failure rate, forwarding delay only
[23]	Lightweight multidimensional algorithm to evaluate trust in IoT service-oriented environment	Indirect trust calculation algorithm, K-means clustering algorithm	Yes	multidimensional trust evaluation, resisting malicious attacks, computational efficiency, capability trust, direct and indirect trust from feedback	Reliability, adaptability, credibility, Robustness, scalability, accuracy	Low scalability, slow centralized structure, trust calculation is done on edge devices, malicious devices can rebuild their trust at the same rate as a genuine device
[24]	Providing two-way trust management scheme for Fog Computing Paradigm to increase its reliability and efficiency	Bayes model, Trust Computation Algorithm	Yes	Trust metrics, Direct trust, Reputation metric, Degree centrality, Service score	Accuracy, faster convergence, Resilience against trust-based network attacks, computation cost	High overhead because of discounting operations on received recommendations

set weights to other nodes' recommendations then aggregated them. One of the key drawbacks of the subjective logic technique is that it necessitates a large amount of storage for each trust value of the involved entities. Besides, if two entities have no interaction history, their recommendation weight becomes zero resulting in a zero-trust value. The system also lacked experimental attempt to illustrate how the subjective logic-based trust system tackled the damage resulting from rogue fog nodes and their related attacks.

Another model in [27] used subjective logic for a distributed two-way trust management in fog computing. Before availing and supplying computation services, the system allowed the fog server and fog client to assess each other's trust value. A fog server's trust is computed using ownership factors, packet delivery ratio, and latency, whereas a client's trust is calculated using ownership, honesty, and friendship parameters. Consideration of the ownership parameter is significant since it tackles the social relationship between fog devices for trust computation. Anyone may own fog; hence anyone can possess an unlimited number of fog devices. As a result, when one fog node demands service from another fog node, and both are owned by the same individual, the degree of trust between them is the maximum. This trust reflects direct trust, whereas recommendations computed using the subjective logic approach include indirect trust. The combination of both indirect and direct trust is the final trust value is. The challenge of this model is that it resulted in uneven load balancing and overhead, making it insufficient for strict-latency applications where minor latency violations may cause serious damages to users. In [28], a broker-based fuzzy trust evaluation framework was introduced to select a highly trusted fog provider. Broker performed the trust management and mapped service requests by considering the preference order for some trust metrics (feedback, security, and quality of service) selected by the users and the load balancing between the fog providers based on threshold utilization. However, this work considered QoS only to determine the trustworthiness of fog nodes, as well as it did not mention how these trust metrics were aggregated for the final calculation of the trust value. It lacked experiments/simulations that would reflect the benefits of incorporating trust management. It also did not consider the fog node's malicious nature after the IoT request was submitted at the fog node, nor did it mention how the trust value was revised after serving current IoT requests. Authors in [29] used a machine learning random forest regression model to formulate a statistical regression problem based on multi-factor trust parameters to compute trust. They presented TMS for fog-enabled cyber-physical systems and a generic trust credibility model. Simulation result showed that the proposed model discovered data deviations, countered collusion attacks and prevented rogue nodes' improper behavior in both non hostile and hostile environments. However, the model was only based on quality of service and did not consider recommendations and social relationships. Table 3 gives a summary of the main studies that applied AI techniques for trust management in fog computing.

5   Discussion and Insights

Analyzing the main studies that have been introduced in the literature for trust management models on fog computing and IoT, our comparative study classified those models based on their utilization (or none) of AI techniques to address the challenges of trust

Table 3. A summarized overview of AI-based trust management techniques in fog computing.

Ref. #	Objective	AI technique used	Dataset Synthetic?	Trust parameters considered?	Evaluation Criteria	Limitations
[1]	Provide a fog computing trust assessing, management, recommendation approach to evaluate the trust level of fog nodes	Fuzzy Logic	Yes	QoS and QoP history	Scalability, Performance, Security, load balancing, energy consumption, response time,	Low scalability, high energy, assumes that IoT devices are trusted, did not consider social relationships, and requires a central authority
[25]	Enables service provider and service requester to assess each other's level of trust	Fuzzy Logic	Yes	QoS, QoSec, social relationships, self-observation, past reputation, recommendations	Security accuracy, reliability efficiency	Low mobility and scalability, high energy, all fog devices are treated as one network, cannot support IoT devices, which cannot act as fog node
[26]	Provide a system help clients guarantee that a fog node provides the necessary service and ensures that the fog client is sufficiently protected	Subjective Logic	Yes	direct trust, and indirect belief model	Efficiency, trustworthiness, scalability, Performance, energy consumption, computation cost	Low security, requires high storage, model is not intransive and asymmetric means, did not consider social relationships. if there is no interacting history between two entities, its recommendation weight becomes zero leading to zero trust value. Insecure against network attacks. The method requires high storage for storing each trust value of participating entities

(continued)

Table 3. (*continued*)

Ref. #	Objective	AI technique used	Dataset Synthetic?	Trust parameters considered?	Evaluation Criteria	Limitations
[27]	enables a service requester to verify whether a service provider can give reliable and secure services and lets the service provider check the trustworthiness. of the service requester	Subjective Logic	Yes	QoS, social trust metrics, self-observation, recommendations of neighboring nodes	Accuracy, convergent Overhead, load balancing, security Trustworthiness, energy consumption, Resilience against network attacks	Low scalability. High overhead. All fog devices are treated as one network, cannot support IoT devices. In trust calculation, social relationship is restricted to ownership, not considering fog-to-fog collaboration. Only direct trust is considered. It results in overhead and uneven load balancing, making it unsuitable for strict-latency applications where little violation in latency can cause severe damage to users
[28]	identifying a trustworthy fog to fulfill the user requests while taking the users' specific preferences into consideration	Fuzzy Logic	Yes	QoS, QoSec, user feedback, and cost	Availability, Trustworthiness, resource Utilization, cost adaptability, network Resilience, Maintainability overhead	Low adaptability, network resilience and maintainability. High energy Consumption and overhead. Considers only QoS, does not mention how trust metrics are aggregated. Unidirectional. Broker results in complete cessation of the trust evaluation framework. Neither considers the malicious nature of the fog node after the IoT request is submitted at the fog node nor mentions how the trust value is revised after serving current IoT requests

(*continued*)

Table 3. (*continued*)

Ref. #	Objective	AI technique used	Dataset Synthetic?	Trust parameters considered?	Evaluation Criteria	Limitations
[29]	Formulating the trust computation as a statistical regression problem and proposing a generic trust management system for fog-enabled cyber-physical systems	Machine Learning Random Forest Regression Model	Yes	Computing trust values in hostile and in a legitimate/normal environment trust computation is formulated as a statistical regression problem and random forest regression is employed to solve it	Scalability, cost, network cost, accuracy, dependability, Attack resistant., Credibility, Sec	Low scalability. High-cost, energy consumption and overhead. Only based on QoS and does not consider social relationships and recommendations

management in the fog. Based on our assessment, analysis, and evaluation of the afore-mentioned limitations of the existing models, we can deduce a list of insights and recommendations to enhance trust management in fog computing and IoT layers by using AI techniques to:

1. Predict social relationships between fog nodes to avoid false recommendations.
2. Build a model considering energy consumption, network cost and overhead to reduce consuming fog resources and IoT resources.
3. Support system scalability, network resilience and load balancing to increase or decrease in performance and cost in response to changes in system processing demands.
4. Better predict direct/indirect trust to simplify trust computation.
5. Smartly detect and prevent malicious fog nodes and IoT devices from interaction with other nodes and devices in the network.
6. Evaluating IoT devices behavior as done on fog nodes to have correct trust computation.
7. Evaluate trust without a dependent central authority to avoid complete cessation of the trust evaluation framework.
8. Treat each fog node on the network separately to avoid scalability issues.
9. Allow IoT devices have sufficient storage and processing power to act as a fog node to increase network resources and support load balancing.
10. Consider the mobility and the dynamic nature of IoT devices to deal with IoT unique attributes, such as geo-distribution, heterogeneity, mobility, proximity to end users and fugacity.
11. Ensure robust network security and network availability to avoid network threats.
12. Build intransitive and asymmetric model to consider all types of relationships.
13. Build bi-directional trust models to enable service provider and service requester to assess each other's level of trust.
14. Consider other AI techniques instead of Subjective Logic for storage optimization, computation, and performance to minimize the associated overheads.
15. Allow fog to fog, fog to IoT, IoT to fog, and IoT to IoT collaborations to consider all types of collaborations to detect all anomalies.
16. Avoid high latency and bias in trust-based systems to have fair representation of different types of parameters in fog and IoT network for accurate trust result.
17. Build trust models considering several trust properties, such as QoS, social trust and QoSec parameters etc. to have sufficient trust computation.

6 Conclusion

With the advent of fog computing and IoT, trust, and reputation all play important roles in decision making processes of limiting rogue nodes. As a result of the scalable and dynamic nature of IoT, trust management is a challenging issue. In this survey paper, we established a comprehensive review based on two main design perspectives for fog trust and reputation: non-AI techniques and AI-based techniques for trust management in fog computing. In this study, we investigated the impact of using AI techniques for fog trust management compared to the other mathematical non-AI related techniques, in which we deduced many open directions that would be worthy for further research. We proposed 17 recommendations to consider for further research and investigation to improve the trust management capabilities in the fog layer. New AI techniques are eagerly needed, since the fog is widely distributed and needs to interact with several hardware platforms supplied by different vendors. Therefore, security and trust management must be distributed and dynamic. The recommended 17 insights would tackle the limitations currently unresolved in trust management systems in fog computing for secured and trusted computations in the fog.

References

1. Al-Khafajiy, M., et al.: COMITMENT: s fog computing trust management approach. J. Parallel Distrib. Comput. **137**, 1–16 (2020)
2. Abbas, N., Asim, M., Tariq, N., Baker, T., Abbas, S.: A mechanism for securing IoT-enabled applications at the fog layer. J. Sens. Actuator Netw. **8**(1), 16 (2019)
3. Baker, T., Asim, M., MacDermott, Á., Iqbal, F., Kamoun, F., Shah, B., Alfandi, O., Hammoudeh, M.: A secure fog-based platform for SCADA-based IoT critical infrastructure. Softw. - Pract. Exp. (2019)
4. Chiang, M., Zhang, T.: Fog and IoT: An overview of research opportunities. IEEE Internet Things J. **3**(6), 854–864 (2016)
5. Ni, J., Zhang, K., Lin, X., Shen, X.S.: Securing fog computing for Internet of Things applications: challenges and solutions. IEEE Commun. Surv. Tutor. **20**(1), 601–628 (2017)
6. Yi, S., Qin, Z., Li, Q.: Security and privacy issues of fog computing: a survey. In: International Conference on Wireless Algorithms, Systems, and Applications, pp. 685–695. Springer (2015)
7. Aazam, M., Zeadally, S., Harras, K.A.: Offloading in fog computing for IoT: review, enabling technologies, and research opportunities. Future Gener. Comput. Syst. **87**, 278–289 (2018)
8. Zou, Z., et al.: Edge and fog computing enabled AI for IoT-an overview. In: 2019 IEEE International Conference on Artificial Intelligence Circuits and Systems (AICAS). IEEE (2019)
9. Singh, S., Kandpal, M.: A comprehensive survey on trust management in fog computing. In: ICT Analysis and Applications, pp. 87–97 (2022)
10. Guo, J., Chen, R.: A classification of trust computation models for service-oriented internet of things systems. In: 2015 IEEE International Conference on Services Computing. IEEE (2015)
11. Blaze, M., Feigenbaum, J., Lacy, J.: Decentralized trust management. In: Proceedings 1996 IEEE Symposium on Security and Privacy. IEEE (1996)
12. Manvi, S.S., Chandra Gowda, N.: Trust management in fog computing: a survey. In: Applying Integration Techniques and Methods in Distributed Systems and Technologies, pp. 34–48. IGI global (2019)
13. Zhang, P., Zhou, M., Fortino, G.: Security and trust issues in fog computing: a survey. Futur. Gener. Comput. Syst. **88**, 16–27 (2018)
14. Sadique, K.M., Rahmani, R., Johannesson, P.: Fog computing for trust in the Internet of Things (IoT): a systematic literature review. In: 2020 International Conference on Computer Science, Engineering and Applications (ICCSEA). IEEE (2020)
15. Nikravan, M., Haghi Kashani, M.: A review on trust management in fog/edge computing: techniques, trends, and challenges. J. Netw. Comput. Appl. 103402 (2022)
16. Patwary, A.A.-N., et al.: Towards secure fog computing: A survey on trust management, privacy, authentication, threats and access control. Electronics **10**(10), 1171 (2021)

17. Verma, R., Chandra, S.: A systematic survey on fog steered IoT: architecture, prevalent threats and trust models. Int. J. Wirel. Inf. Netw. **28**, 116–133 (2021)
18. Konsta, A.M., Lluch Lafuente, A., Dragoni, N.: Trust Management for Internet of Things: a systematic literature review. arXiv preprint. arXiv:2211.01712 (2022)
19. Sharma, A., et al.: Towards trustworthy Internet of Things: a survey on trust management applications and schemes. Comput. Commun. **160**, 475–493 (2020)
20. Shehada, D., et al.: Fog-based distributed trust and reputation management system for internet of things. J. King Saud Univ.-Comput. Inf. Sci. **34**(10), 8637–8646 (2022)
21. Rathee, G., et al.: A trust computed framework for IoT devices and fog computing environment. Wirel. Netw. **26**, 2339–2351 (2020)
22. Wang, T., et al.: A novel trust mechanism based on fog computing in sensor–cloud system. Future Gener. Comput. Syst. **109**, 573–582 (2020)
23. Gao, Z., et al.: A credible and lightweight multidimensional trust evaluation mechanism for service-oriented IoT edge computing environment. In: 2019 IEEE International Congress on Internet of Things (ICIOT). IEEE (2019)
24. Hamza, M., et al.: A social qualitative trust framework for Fog computing. Comput. Electr. Eng. **102**, 108195 (2022)
25. Ogundoyin, S.O., Adeniyi Kamil, I.: A trust management system for fog computing services. Internet of Things **14**, 100382 (2021)
26. Al Muhtadi, J., et al.: Subjective logic-based trust model for fog computing. Comput. Commun. **178**, 221–233 (2021)
27. Alemneh, E., et al.: A two-way trust management system for fog computing. Future Gener. Comput. Syst. **106**, 206–220 (2020)
28. Rahman, F.H., et al.: Find my trustworthy fogs: a fuzzy-based trust evaluation framework. Future Gener. Comput. Syst. **109**, 562–572 (2020)
29. Junejo, A.K., et al.: Trustee: A trust management system for fog-enabled cyber physical systems. IEEE Trans. Emerg. Topics Comput. **9**(4), 2030–2041 (2019)

Source-Code Generation Using Deep Learning: A Survey

Areeg Ahmed[1]([✉]), Shahira Azab[1], and Yasser Abdelhamid[1,2]

[1] Department of Computer Science, Faculty of Graduate Studies for Statistical Research (FGSSR), Cairo University, Giza, Egypt
Areeg.ahmed@hotmail.com, shahiraazazy@cu.edu.eg
[2] The Egyptian E-Learning University, Giza, Egypt

Abstract. In recent years, the need for writing effective, reusable, and high-quality source code has grown exponentially. Writing source code is an integral part of building any software system; the development phase of the software life-cycle contains code implementation, refactoring, maintenance, and fixing bugs. Software developers implement the desired solution by turning the system requirements into viable software products. For the most part, the implementation phase can be challenging as it requires a certain level of problem-solving skills and the ability to produce high-quality outcomes without decreasing productivity rates or not meeting the business plans and deadlines. Programmers' daily tasks might also include writing large amounts of repetitive boilerplate code, which can be tedious, not to mention the potential bugs that could arise from human errors during the development process. The ability to automatically generate source code will save significant time and effort invested in the software development process by increasing the speed and efficiency of software development teams. In this survey, we review and summarize the recent studies on deep learning approaches used to generate source code in different programming languages such as Java, Python, and SQL (Structured Query Language). We categorize the surveyed work into two groups, Natural Language-based solutions for approaches that use natural text as input and Computer Vision-based solutions which generate code based on images as input.

Keywords: Code generation · Deep learning · Transformers · Machine learning · Natural language · Computer vision

1 Introduction

The concept of generating source code using Genetic Programming has been around for a while [1]. However, recent advancements in Machine Learning (ML) and Deep Learning (DL) have greatly contributed to automated code generation. Deep learning techniques applied in Natural Language Processing (NLP) and Computer Vision (CV) have led to more efficient solutions. Large Language Models (LLMs) and Transformers [2], such as OpenAI's Chat-GPT [3], have been used for tasks like code generation, enabling developers to write and debug programs. To provide insights into this research area, we

N. Moniz et al. (Eds.): EPIA 2023, LNAI 14116, pp. 467–482, 2023.
https://doi.org/10.1007/978-3-031-49011-8_37

conducted a review of recent studies focusing on source code generation using deep learning techniques. Our inclusion criteria required studies published between 2016 and 2023, with a primary focus on deep learning-based source code generation using natural text or images. We excluded studies unrelated to code generation, those using classical machine learning or reinforcement learning, and those generating code in a different programming language from the input. Our search strategy employed relevant keywords and deep learning terminology across multiple databases. We identified 29 experimental studies, with 24 using natural text and 5 using images as inputs for deep learning-based source code generation. Table 1 shows the search results summary. Figures 1 and 2 illustrate the number of categorized papers per publisher and publication year, respectively.

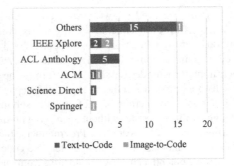

Fig. 1. The number of surveyed papers grouped by publisher. Bars are classified by approach

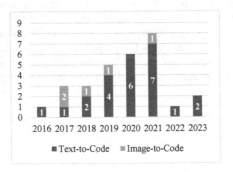

Fig. 2. The number of surveyed papers grouped by year of publication. Bars are classified by approach

1.1 Related Surveys

In our review of existing surveys on source code generation, we found that previous literature reviews and survey papers were often limited to specific approaches or broader programming-related activities. Some focused on natural language features, machine learning methods for source code analysis, or source code generation with natural language descriptions. Others explored code documentation, refactoring, and code translation. Pulido-Prieto and Juarez-Martinez [4] conducted a comprehensive review in 2017, discussing natural language elements in code generation and naturalistic programming concepts. Allamanis et al. [5] focused on probabilistic models for source code analysis in 2018. Jiho Shin and Jaechang Nam [6] presented a survey in 2021, specifically on source code generation with natural language descriptions. Chen Yang et al. [7] conducted a systematic study on code generation, mainly limited to natural language approaches. In 2022, Enrique Dehaerne et al. [8] provided a systematic review of source code generation using machine learning, covering various methods including deep learning and extending to code documentation, refactoring, and translation. Their study identified description-to-code, code-to-description, and code-to-code paradigms. Another review by different authors [9] focused on deep learning methods for source code generation, with an emphasis on the encode-decoder framework. Code comment generation [10, 11] and code review using machine learning [12] were surveyed separately. Broad surveys covering diverse software engineering tasks were presented in [13] and [14]. In contrast, our survey primarily focuses on the work published since 2016 that utilizes deep learning techniques in source code generation, encompassing models that handle natural text and images as inputs. Figure 3 shows an example of generated Python code from Chat-GPT [3] using natural text as input; Fig. 4 is from Sketch2Code [64] tool that utilizes DL to convert images with UI sketches to HTML.

Table 1. Code generation using deep learning search results

Search database	Included	Total search results
Springer	1	12
Science Direct	1	11
ACM digital library	2	8,153
ACL Anthology	5	24,200
IEEE xplore	4	490
Others	16	–

Fig. 3. An example of a Python function that sums two numbers, generated by Chat-GPT

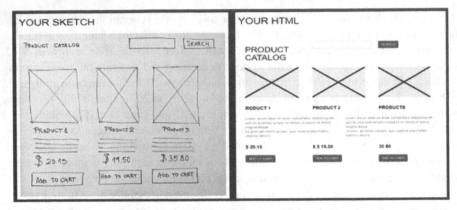

Fig. 4. An example of a hand-written sketch uploaded to Sketch2Code tool and converted to an HTML design

1.2 Survey Organization

The remaining sections of this survey are structured as follows: Section 2.1 presents a compilation of NLP approaches that employ natural language text as input to generate source code, commonly known as Text-to-Code. Section 2.2 provides an overview of the integration of CV techniques in generating source code using images as input, referred to as Image-to-Code. Section 3 offers a comprehensive description of the collected corpora, encompassing relevant characteristics and attributes. Sections 4 and 5 discuss code generation evaluation metrics and draw conclusive remarks, respectively.

2   Surveyed Approaches

Tables 2 and 3 present surveyed papers on text-to-code and image-to-code approaches, respectively, organized chronologically by their publication dates.

2.1   Text-To-Code

Table 2. Text-to-Code surveyed studies summary

Ref	Proposed approach	Results
[15]	A convolutional attentional neural network to extract long-range features and localized patterns in highly structured source code text	The model's best performance metrics are as follows: F1 score of 59.6%, exact match of 33.7%, precision of 74.9%, and recall of 54.2%
[16]	BAYOU [17], a strongly-typed Java-like programming language code generator that uses a Gaussian encoder-decoder RNN	The results showed that BAYOU outperformed or tied to the Gaussian Stochastic Neural Network model

(continued)

Table 2. (*continued*)

Ref	Proposed approach	Results
[18]	An intelligent code completion solution using standard RNN, a tailored attention mechanism and pointer mixture network	The model achieved an accuracy of 81% on the JS dataset and 70.1% on the Python dataset
[19]	A neural semantic parser called TRANX that maps natural language utterances into formal Meaning Representations (MRs) using a transition-based approach	The GEO and ATIS datasets achieved the highest accuracy scores at 88.2% and 86.2%, respectively. The model obtained 72.7% accuracy on the DJANGO dataset and 68.6% exact match accuracy on the WikiSQL dataset without parent feeding. With parent feeding, the accuracy on the DJANGO dataset improved to 73.7%
[22]	An approach that generates code using a network of LSTM and MLP by generating the Abstract Syntax Tree (AST) of the source code instead of using the text	The AST-LSTM and AST-MLP approaches achieved accuracy scores of 90.3% and 90.1%, respectively
[23]	Several LSTM and Transformer-based baseline models are evaluated on the proposed dataset JuICe	The LSTM model obtained the best scores, achieving a BLEU score of 21.66 and 20.92 on the development and testing sets, respectively, and exact match accuracies of 5.57 and 5.71
[24]	PATOIS, a system that uses an encode-decoder architecture to generate code from natural language specifications	The Hearthstone testing set achieved a sentence BLEU score of 0.780, a corpus BLEU score of 0.766, and an exact match of 0.197
[27]	TreeGen, a tree-based neural architecture for code generation consisting of a natural language reader, an AST reader, and a decoder	The model was evaluated on the HearthStone, ATIS, and GEO datasets, with accuracy scores of 25.8% and 33.3% on the HearthStone dataset with plain and structural preprocessing, respectively, and 89.1% and 89.6% accuracy scores on the ATIS and GEO datasets
[28]	A machine learning-based tool called GRT to automate the analysis of a Syntax Guided Synthesis (SyGuS) grammar and synthesis constraints, it consists of two main predictors: the first predictor is trained on a corpus of 124,928 programs generated by CVC4 [29] with their corresponding constraints randomly generated; the second predictor is trained on 30 SyGuS problems (10 human-generated and 20 randomly selected problems)	GRT improved the SyGuS solver's performance in 50% of the benchmarks, reducing total synthesis time from 1304.87 s without GRT to 683.09 s with GRT
[30]	A system for generating source code using the PBE technique and a custom dataset backed by test cases	The best performance was achieved with three layers of neural networks with LeakyReLU and Nadam optimizer

(*continued*)

Table 2. (*continued*)

Ref	Proposed approach	Results
[31]	A method for improving code generation by incorporating external knowledge through pre-training on NL-code pairs obtained from external resources, and fine-tuning on a small manually presented corpus	The proposed method surpassed the previous state-of-the-art model by up to 2.2% absolute, resulting in a BLEU score increase from 30.1 to 32.3. The evaluation encompassed various combinations of the CoNaLa, CoNaLa-Mined, and API Documentation Pairs datasets, with the highest achieved BLEU score being 32.26
[32]	Using BERT and a simple encoding method to generate SQL code from natural language questions	The model's performance was assessed on the WikiSQL dataset, resulting in an accuracy of 83.7% for the logic form and 89.2% for the execution test. The results were slightly enhanced to 84.5% for the logic form and 90.1% for the execution test by employing execution-guided decoding
[33]	A bidirectional LSTM with a tanh activation function and Adam optimizer	The proposed model mostly outperforms the baselines, but ties with uniform-random search in certain cases
[34]	A Relevance Transformer model that uses Transformer-based architectures for code generation, incorporating pseudo-relevance feedback decoding and a copy-generation method	The model outperforms all state-of-the-art models on DJANGO, Hearthstone, and CoNaLa datasets, achieving BLEU scores of 82.3, 74.5, and 22.3, respectively
[35]	A group of deep neural networks models which are Average Stochastic Gradient Descent (ASGD) Weight-Dropped LSTM (AWD-LSTM) [36], Quasi-Recurrent Neural Networks (QRNNs) [37], and Transformer	AWD-LSTM with character tokenization achieved the highest accuracy at 77%, followed by GPT-2 [39] transformer model at 74%, and AWD-QRNN with char tokenization at 73%
[40]	A pre-trained language model is used to enhance the task of automatically completing a function from its signature and human-readable documentation	The proposed model had a higher BLEU score than the char-RNN baseline, achieving 0.22 compared to the baseline's 0.117
[41]	Codex, a GPT language model that generates Python code from doc-strings	The proposed model outperformed GPT-3 [42] and GPT-J [43], solving 28.8% of the problems
[44]	Latent Programmer (LP) method, which predicts a discrete latent code from input/output examples using a two-level beam search to produce a plan and then synthesize the program based on that plan	The LP model achieves BLEU scores of 14, 18.6, and 21.3, respectively, with beam sizes set at 1, 10, and 100, outperforming both LSTM and Transformer RobustFill baseline models in code generation
[46]	REDCODER, a framework that retrieves relevant code or summaries from a database and feeds them into code generation or summarization models	The performance of the REDCODER framework was evaluated using two datasets, CodeXGLUE and Concode. The BLEU scores achieved on CodeXGLUE Java and Python code were 28.98 and 24.43, respectively. Additionally, the Concode dataset achieved a BLEU score of 42.5

(*continued*)

Table 2. (*continued*)

Ref	Proposed approach	Results
[49]	A technique called "deep distilling", which utilizes Essence Neural Networks (ENNs) to learn patterns from data and then compresses it into a brief, functional computer code	The proposed approach outperformed simple deep learning and random forest model baselines on a Python dataset containing input-output pairs of different programming problems
[50]	NSGs, a neuro-symbolic method that generates code using a static-analysis tool, which can compute long-distance dependencies between program variables and statements	The code generated by NSG passed all static checks for 86.41% of the samples, while the highest percentage among the baselines was 67.73%
[51]	COMPCODER, a system for compliable code completion and generation tasks	The evaluation metrics used are Levenshtein Edit Similarity (ES) [52] and Compilation Rate (CR) [53], COMPCODER demonstrates a substantial enhancement in the average compilation rate of the latest version of CodeGPT. In the code completion task, the compilation rate is boosted from 44.18 to 89.18, while in the code generation task, it significantly increases from 70.3 to 96.2
[54]	ExploitGen, a template-augmented model for exploit code generation based on CodeBERT [55]	In terms of BLEU, ROUGE, and Accuracy, the proposed model outperformed all baselines, achieving a score of 91.27%, 75.68%, and 70.93%, respectively, on the Python dataset. For the Assembly dataset, it achieved an 88.70% BLEU score, 74.25% ROUGE, and 66.89% Accuracy
[58]	CODEGEN, a family of large language models with up to 16.1B parameters. CODEGEN is an interactive system that generates subprograms based on natural language specifications from the user	Using the unbiased estimator "pass@k" proposed in [41], CODEGEN-MONO 16.1B, the largest proposed model achieved pass@k of 29.28%, 49.86%, and 75% for k of 1, 10, and 100, respectively, on the HumanEval benchmark

2.2 Image-To-Code

Table 3. Image-to-Code surveyed studies summary

Ref	Proposed approach	Results
[60]	Pix2code, a model that generates code from a single input image using a CNN to map the image to a learned representation and two LSTMs to perform language modelling on the textual description	The model achieved 77% accuracy using greedy and beam search. Greedy search had 22% and 12% error rates for iOS/Android and web-based datasets, respectively. Beam search had higher error rates, except for the web-based dataset with an 11% error rate using beam search 3
[61]	DLPaper2Code, a method that can extract and understand flow diagrams from deep learning research papers and generate executable code in Keras and Caffe	Experiments conducted on the simulated dataset revealed that the proposed framework demonstrated an accuracy of over 93% in extracting the content of flow diagrams
[62]	An attention-based hierarchical code generation model that combines CNN and LSTMs to describe GUI images in greater detail and generate hierarchically structured code consistent with the GUI's layout	The proposed model achieved accuracy rates ranging from 85.1% to 94% across multiple datasets, while the baseline models ranged from 84.4% to 93.3%. Additionally, the proposed model had lower error rates compared to the baseline models
[63]	An automated code generation approach from hand-drawn mock-ups that utilizes computer vision techniques, CNN, and an HTML builder script	The system achieved 96% method accuracy and 73% validation accuracy using the Sketch2Code dataset provided by Microsoft AI lab
[65]	An RNN-based model and a Transformer-based model, which take hand-drawn sketches as input and generate visualization code in DSL	The transformer model exhibited a notable superiority, achieving a structural accuracy of 95%, while the RNN model lagged at 66%

3 Datasets

Code generation methods utilize diverse datasets based on factors such as input-output types, approach, and model characteristics. Text-to-code approaches involve datasets with semantic parsing or natural language-code pairs. Image-to-code techniques rely on datasets with UI images or hand-drawn sketches. These datasets can be manually annotated or automatically extracted from platforms like GitHub or StackOverflow. Code generation datasets encompass various programming languages including Java, Python, SQL, and others. Table 4 provides an overview of the datasets used in the reviewed studies.

Table 4. Code generation datasets

Used In	Dataset
[15]	A collected dataset that consists of parsed source code of top 11 java projects from GitHub
[16]	A collection comprising 150,000 methods that utilized either Android APIs or the Java library, extracted from a selection of Android applications; totaling 1,500 in number, obtained from the online Android drawer repository
[18]	A Python datasets of 150,000 program files in their AST format, divided into 100,000 training samples and 50,000 testing samples
[18]	A JavaScript datasets of 150,000 program files in their AST format, divided into 100,000 training samples and 50,000 testing samples
[19, 27]	GEO (semantic parsing dataset): a dataset comprising 880 questions related to geographical topics in the United States
[19, 27]	ATIS (semantic parsing dataset): a dataset consisting of 5,410 inquiries related to flight information
[19, 34]	DJANGO [20]: 18,805 lines of Python source code obtained from the DJANGO Web framework, each line is accompanied by a natural language description
[19, 32]	WikiSQL [21]: 80,654 examples of NL questions and annotated SQL queries
[22]	A dataset collected from a substantial GitHub repository with 1,274 Python codes
[23]	JuICe: a large corpus consisting of 1.5 million instances obtained from more than 659,000 publicly available Jupyter notebooks on GitHub. The corpus includes a test set of 3,725 instances collected from 13,905 high-quality nbgrader notebooks

(continued)

Table 4. (*continued*)

Used In	Dataset
[24, 27, 34]	Hearthstone [25]: This dataset consists of 665 instances representing cards from the game Hearthstone. Each instance includes a name, description, and important stats. The English description is represented as a long sequence of text, while the corresponding Python code represents the code portion. The average sequence is 400 tokens, with a significant amount of shared boilerplate Python code
[24]	Spider [26]: an annotated dataset created by 11 students from Yale University. It serves as a comprehensive resource for semantic parsing and text-to-SQL tasks; it comprises 10,181 questions and 5,693 complex SQL queries. The queries are executed on a collection of 200 databases, each containing multiple tables; spanning 138 diverse domains
[31, 34]	CoNaLa: a human-annotated dataset, which consists of 2,179 training, 200 development, and 500 test samples. It contains English queries about Python, covering various intents and topics
[31]	CoNaLa-Mined: 600,000 Python code with associated NL, automatically extracted from StackOverflow
[31]	A dataset of 13,000 unique NL-code pairs extracted from Python API documentation, including libraries, built-in types, and functions found in the Python 3.7.5 distribution
[35, 40, 50, 51]	CodeSearchNet [38]: 2 million pairs of comments and code obtained from open-source libraries. Specifically, a comment corresponds to a top-level function or method comment (such as docstrings in Python), while code refers to an entire function or method. The dataset includes code from several programming languages, including Python, JavaScript, Ruby, Go, Java, and PHP
[41]	HumanEval: a collection of 164 programming problems that have been handwritten. Every problem is accompanied by a function signature, a description, a code implementation, and unit tests. On average, there are 7.7 tests per problem
[44]	150,370 triples consisting of function declarations, associated docstrings, and corresponding function bodies [45]. Multiple corpus splits are provided, along with an additional "monolingual" code-only corpus that includes artificially generated docstrings. However, only 111,000 examples from this dataset were used in the study referenced in [44]
[46, 50]	CodeXGLUE [47]: 10 tasks distributed among 14 datasets, along with a platform designed for model evaluation and comparison
[46]	Concode [48]: more than 100,000 instances comprising Java classes gathered from various online code repositories

(*continued*)

Table 4. (*continued*)

Used In	Dataset
[50]	A large Java source-code file that contains 1.57 million method bodies
[50]	The APPS [66]: 10,000 challenging coding problems, averaging 293.2 words. It includes 131,777 test cases and 232,421 human-written ground-truth solutions. The dataset is evenly divided into 5,000 problems for training and 5,000 for testing. The test set rigorously evaluates program functionality with an average of 21.2 test cases per problem
[50, 58]	The Pile [59]: a language modeling dataset that is open source and diverse, consisting of 22 smaller datasets of high quality; combined to create a total size of 825 gigabytes
[54]	EVIL [56]: it comprises exploit code snippets and their corresponding English descriptions, gathered from publicly available databases like exploitdb, shellstorm, public repositories, and programming guidelines. It has two datasets, namely Python and Assembly, with 15,540 and 3,715 examples, respectively
[51]	AdvTest [47]: 51,820 text and Python code pairs. It comes from CodeSearchNet dataset [38] and exists as part of CodeXGLUE dataset
[58]	BIGQUERY: a publicly accessible dataset provided by Google, containing code written in various programming languages and released under open-source licenses
[58]	BIGPYTHON: a vast collection of Python code that was compiled from publicly accessible Python code from GitHub, obtained in October 2021 and released under permissive licenses
[60]	A dataset that comprises synthesized examples containing both GUI screenshots and corresponding source code for UIs on iOS, Android, and Web platforms
[61]	A manually defined grammar was used to generate 216,000 DL model visualizations, while an additional 5,000 research papers were collected from arXiv.org employing the search keyword "deep learning"
[63]	Sketch2Code [64]: a collection of images provided by Microsoft AI lab as part of Sketch2Code solution that utilizes AI to convert hand-drawn user interface designs from images into valid HTML code
[65]	A dataset of images produced by visualization tools using a style transfer technique to create a hand-drawn appearance. It also contains 100 manually created hand-drawn images, along with their corresponding domain-specific language (DSL) code

4 Metrics

Automatic code generation models undergo quantitative or qualitative evaluation. Quantitative assessment employs metrics like accuracy, precision, recall, F1 score, perplexity, and error rates. Accuracy measures correct code generation, precision gauges relevance, recall captures relevant code proportion, and F1 score combines precision and recall. Perplexity reflects code quality, with lower values indicating higher quality. Error rates quantify incorrect code generation frequency. Some studies evaluate code synthesis speed, reduced synthesis time, or compilation rate. [28] measures reduced total synthesis time, [51] measures average compilation rate for code's compilability, [41] measures problem-solving percentage, and [58] employs "pass@k" metric to compare generated code against ground truth snippets. BLEU score [67], exact match accuracy [68], and ROUGE [57] are common quantitative metrics, assessing resemblance, exact matches, and n-gram overlap. Qualitative evaluation involves manual examination, as seen in [50] and [41], assessing capabilities considering complexity and abstraction.

5 Conclusion

This survey thoroughly examined deep learning techniques in code generation, including Text-to-Code and Image-to-Code approaches. It analyzed experiments, datasets, and outcomes, offering a comprehensive understanding of code generation complexities. The paper emphasized the need for diverse performance measures to evaluate code generation models accurately.

References

1. Banzhaf, W.: Artificial Intelligence: Genetic Programming. In: Elsevier eBooks, pp. 789–792 (2001). doi: https://doi.org/10.1016/b0-08-043076-7/00557-x
2. Vaswani, A. et al.: Attention is All you Need. vol. 30, pp. 5998–6008 (2017). [Online]. Available: https://arxiv.org/pdf/1706.03762v5
3. OpenAI: "ChatGPT" GitHub. [Online]. Available: https://github.com/openai/gpt-3. Accessed: Apr. 23, 2023
4. Pulido-Prieto, O., Juárez-Martínez, U.: A survey of naturalistic programming technologies. ACM Comput. Surv. **50**(5), 1–35 (2017). https://doi.org/10.1145/3109481
5. Allamanis, M., Barr, E.T., Devanbu, P., Sutton, C.: A survey of machine learning for big code and naturalness. ACM Comput. Surv. **51**(4), 1–37 (2018). https://doi.org/10.1145/3212695
6. Shin, J., Nam, J.: A survey of automatic code generation from natural language. J. Inf. Process. Syst. **17**(3), 537–555 (2021). https://doi.org/10.3745/JIPS.04.0216
7. Yang, C., Liu, Y., Yin, C.: Recent advances in intelligent source code generation: A survey on natural language based studies. Entropy **23**(9), 1174 (2021). https://doi.org/10.3390/e23091174
8. Dehaerne, E., Dey, B., Halder, S., De Gendt, S., Meert, W.: Code generation using machine learning: A systematic review. IEEE Access **10**, 82434–82455 (2022). https://doi.org/10.1109/access.2022.3196347
9. Le, T.H.M., Chen, H., Babar, M.E.: Deep learning for source code modeling and generation: Models, applications and challenges. arXiv preprint arXiv:2002.05442 (2020). Available at: http://arxiv.org/pdf/2002.05442
10. Zhang, C., et al.: A survey of automatic source code summarization. Symmetry **14**(3), 471 (2022). https://doi.org/10.3390/sym14030471
11. Song, X., Sun, H., Wang, X., Yan, J.-F.: A survey of automatic generation of source code comments: Algorithms and techniques. IEEE Access **7**, 111411–111428 (2019). https://doi.org/10.1109/access.2019.2931579

12. Xiaomeng, W., Tao, Z., Wei, X., Changyu, H.: A survey on source code review using machine learning. In: Proceedings of the 2018 3rd International Conference on Information Systems Engineering (ICISE), Shanghai, China, pp. 56–60 (2018). doi: https://doi.org/10.1109/ICISE. 2018.00018

13. Yang, Y., Xia, X., Lo, D., Grundy, J.: A survey on deep learning for software engineering. ACM Comput. Surv. **54**(10s), 1–73 (2021). https://doi.org/10.1145/3505243

14. Sharma, T. et al.: A Survey on Machine learning techniques for source code analysis. arXiv preprint arXiv:2110.09610 (2021). Available at: https://arxiv.org/abs/2110.09610

15. Allamanis, M., Peng, H., Sutton, C.: A convolutional attention network for extreme summarization of source code. In: Proceedings of the International Conference on Machine Learning (ICML), pp. 2091–2100 (2016). Available at: http://proceedings.mlr.press/v48/allamanis16. pdf

16. Murali, V., Qi, L., Chaudhuri, S., Jermaine, C.: Neural sketch learning for conditional program generation. In: Proceedings of the International Conference on Learning Representations (ICLR) (2018). Available at: https://arxiv.org/pdf/1703.05698

17. Trishullab: "GitHub—trishullab/bayou: System for synthesizing Java API idioms, powered by Neural Sketch Learning." GitHub. Available at: https://github.com/trishullab/bayou

18. Li, J., Wang, Y., Lyu, M.R., King, I.: Code completion with neural attention and pointer networks. In: Proceedings of the 27th International Joint Conference on Artificial Intelligence (IJCAI) (2018). https://doi.org/10.24963/ijcai.2018/578

19. Yin, P., Neubig, G.: TRANX: A Transition-based neural abstract syntax parser for semantic parsing and code generation. In: Proceedings of the 2018 Conference on Empirical Methods in Natural Language Processing (EMNLP) (2018). https://doi.org/10.18653/v1/d18-2002

20. Oda, Y. et al.: Learning to generate pseudo-code from source code using statistical machine translation. In: Proceedings of the 2015 30th IEEE/ACM International Conference on Automated Software Engineering (ASE), Lincoln, NE, USA, pp. 574–584 (2015). doi: https://doi. org/10.1109/ASE.2015.36

21. Zhong, V., Xiong, C.: Seq2SQL: Generating structured queries from natural language using reinforcement learning. arXiv preprint arXiv:1709.00103 (2017). Available at: https://arxiv. org/abs/1709.00103

22. Tiwang, R., Oladunni, T., Xu, W.: A Deep learning model for source code generation. In: Proceedings of the 2019 SoutheastCon, Huntsville, AL, USA, pp. 1–7 (2019). doi: https:// doi.org/10.1109/SoutheastCon42311.2019.9020360

23. Agashe, R., Iyer, S., Zettlemoyer, L.: JuICe: A large scale distantly supervised dataset for open domain context-based code generation. In: Proceedings of the 2019 Conference on Empirical Methods in Natural Language Processing and the 9th International Joint Conference on Natural Language Processing (EMNLP-IJCNLP) (2019). doi: https://doi.org/10.18653/v1/ d19-1546

24. Shin, E., Allamanis, M., Brockschmidt, M., Polozov, A.: Program synthesis and semantic parsing with learned code idioms. In: Neural Information Processing Systems, vol. 32, pp. 10825–10835 (2019). Available at: http://papers.nips.cc/paper/9265-program-synthesis- and-semantic-parsing-with-learned-code-idioms.pdf

25. Ling, W., Wei, S., Yang, Z., Li, J., Huang, F., Zhou, M.: Latent predictor networks for code generation. In: Proceedings of the 54th Annual Meeting of the Association for Computational Linguistics (vol. 1: Long Papers), Berlin, Germany, pp. 599–609 (2016). doi: https://doi.org/ 10.18653/v1/p16-1057

26. Yu, T., et al.: Spider: A large-scale human-labeled dataset for complex and cross-domain semantic parsing and text-to-SQL task. In: Proceedings of the 2018 Conference on Empirical Methods in Natural Language Processing (EMNLP), Brussels, Belgium, pp.3911–3921 (2018).doi:https://doi.org/10.18653/v1/d18-1425

27. Sun, Z., Zhu, Q., Xiong, Y., Sun, Y., Mou, L., Zhang, L.: TreeGen: A tree-based transformer architecture for code generation. In: Proceedings of the AAAI Conference on Artificial Intelligence, vol. 34, no. 05, pp. 8984–8991 (2020). doi: https://doi.org/10.1609/aaai.v34i05.6430

28. Morton, K., Hallahan, W. T., Shum, E., Piskac, R., Santolucito, M.: Grammar filtering for syntax-guided synthesis. In: Proceedings of the AAAI Conference on Artificial Intelligence, vol. 34, no. 02, pp. 1611–1618 (2020). doi: https://doi.org/10.1609/aaai.v34i02.5522

29. Barrett, C. et al.: CVC4. In: Lecture Notes in Computer Science, Springer Science+Business Media, pp. 171–177 (2011). doi: https://doi.org/10.1007/978-3-642-22110-1_14

30. Shim, S., Patil, P., Yadav, R. R., Shinde, A., Devale, V.: DeeperCoder: Code generation using machine learning. In: 10th Annual Computing and Communication Workshop and Conference (CCWC), Las Vegas, NV, USA, pp. 0194–0199 (2020). doi: https://doi.org/10.1109/CCWC47524.2020.9031149

31. Xu, F.K., Jiang, Z., Yin, P., Vasilescu, B., Neubig, G.: Incorporating External Knowledge through Pre-training for Natural Language to Code Generation. (2020). https://doi.org/10.18653/v1/2020.acl-main.538

32. Guo, T., Gao, H.: Content Enhanced BERT-based text-to-SQL generation. (2019). Retrieved from arXiv.org: https://arxiv.org/abs/1910.07179

33. Grouwstra, K.: Type-driven Neural Programming by Example. (2020). Retrieved from arXiv.org: https://arxiv.org/abs/2008.12613

34. Gemmell, C., Rossetto, F., Dalton, J.: Relevance Transformer: Generating Concise Code Snippets with Relevance Feedback. (2020). Retrieved from Cornell University: doi: https://doi.org/10.1145/3397271.3401215

35. Cruz-Benito, J., Vishwakarma, S., Martín-Fernández, F., Faro, I.: Automated source code generation and auto-completion using deep learning: Comparing and discussing current language model-related approaches. AI 2(1), 1–16 (2021). doi: https://doi.org/10.3390/ai2010001

36. Merity, S., Keskar, N.S., Socher, R.: Regularizing and Optimizing LSTM Language Models. arXiv.org (2017). Available at: https://arxiv.org/pdf/1708.02182

37. Bradbury, J., Merity, S., Xiong, C., Socher, R.: Quasi-recurrent neural networks. arXiv.org (2018). Available at: https://arxiv.org/pdf/1611.01576

38. Husain, H., Wu, H.-H., Gazit, T., Allamanis, M., Brockschmidt, M.: CodeSearchNet challenge: Evaluating the state of semantic code search. arXiv.org (2019). Available at: https://arxiv.org/abs/1909.09436

39. Radford, A., Wu, J., Child, R., Luan, D., Amodei, D., Sutskever, I.: Language models are unsupervised multitask learners. (2019) [Online]. Available: https://cdn.openai.com/better-language-models/language_models_are_unsupervised_multitask_learners.pdf

40. Perez, L., Ottens, L., Viswanathan, S.: Automatic code generation using pre-trained language models. (2021) [Online]. Available: https://arxiv.org/abs/2102.10535

41. Chen, M., et al.: Evaluating large language models trained on code. (2021) [Online]. Available: https://arxiv.org/abs/2107.03374

42. Brown, T., et al.: Language models are few-shot learners. In: Advances in Neural Information Processing Systems, vol. 33, pp. 1877–1901 (2020) [Online]. Available: https://proceedings.neurips.cc/paper/2020/file/1457c0d6bfcb4967418bfb8ac142f64a-Paper.pdf

43. Wang, B., Komatsuzaki, A.: GPT-J-6B: A 6 Billion parameter autoregressive language model. (2021) [Online]. Available: https://github.com/kingoflolz/mesh-transformer-jax

44. Hong, J., Dohan, D., Singh, R., Sutton, C., Zaheer, M.: Latent programmer: Discrete latent codes for program synthesis. In Proceedings of the 38th International Conference on Machine Learning (ICML), vol. 139, pp. 4308–4318 (2021) [Online]. Available: http://proceedings.mlr.press/v139/hong21a/hong21a.pdf

45. Wan, Y., et al.: Improving automatic source code summarization via deep reinforcement learning. In: Proceedings of the 33rd ACM/IEEE International Conference on Automated Software Engineering (ASE), pp. 397–407. Montpellier, France (2018). https://doi.org/10.1145/3238147.3238206

46. Parvez, R., Ahmad, W. U., Chakraborty, S., Ray, B., Chang, K.-W.: Retrieval augmented code generation and summarization. In: Findings of the Association for Computational Linguistics: EMNLP 2021, pp. 2950–2961 (2021). https://doi.org/10.18653/v1/2021.findings-emnlp.232

47. Lu, S., et al..: CodeXGLUE: A Machine learning benchmark dataset for code understanding and generation. arXiv preprint arXiv:2102.04664 (2021) [Online]. Available: https://arxiv.org/abs/2102.04664

48. Iyer, S., Konstas, I., Cheung, A., Zettlemoyer, L.: Mapping Language to Code in Programmatic Context. (2018). https://doi.org/10.18653/v1/d18-1192

49. Blazek, P.J., Venkatesh, K., Lin, M. M.: Deep Distilling: Automated code generation using explainable deep learning. arXiv.org (2021) Available: https://arxiv.org/abs/2111.08275

50. Mukherjee, R., Wen, Y., Chaudhari, D., Reps, T.W., Chaudhuri, S., Jermaine, C.: Neural program generation modulo static analysis. arXiv.org (2021) Available: https://arxiv.org/abs/2111.01633

51. Wang, X., et al.: Compilable Neural Code Generation with Compiler Feedback. (2022). https://doi.org/10.18653/v1/2022.findings-acl.2

52. Svyatkovskiy, A., Deng, S.K., Fu, S.-Y., Sundaresan, N.: IntelliCode Compose: Code Generation Using Transformer. (2020). https://doi.org/10.1145/3368089.3417058

53. Kulal, S., et al.: SPoC: Search-based pseudocode to code. **32**, 11883–11894 (2019) [Online]. Available: http://arxiv.org/pdf/1906.04908.pdf

54. Yang, G., Zhou, Y., Chen, X., Zhang, X., Han, T., Chen, T.: ExploitGen: Template-augmented exploit code generation based on CodeBERT. J. Syst. Softw. **197**, 111577 (2023). https://doi.org/10.1016/j.jss.2022.111577

55. Feng, Z., et al.: CodeBERT: A pre-trained model for programming and natural languages (2020). doi: https://doi.org/10.18653/v1/2020.findings-emnlp.139

56. Liguori, P., et al.: EVIL: Exploiting software via natural language. Cornell Univ. (2021). https://doi.org/10.1109/issre52982.2021.00042

57. Lin, C.-Y.: ROUGE: A Package for Automatic Evaluation of Summaries, pp. 74–81 (2004) [Online]. Available: http://anthology.aclweb.org/W/W04/W04-1013.pdf

58. Nijkamp, E., et al.: CodeGen: An open large language model for code with multi-turn program synthesis. arXiv.org (2022). Available: https://arxiv.org/abs/2203.13474

59. Gao, L., et al.: The Pile: An 800GB Dataset of diverse text for language modeling. arXiv.org (2020). Available: https://arxiv.org/abs/2101.00027

60. Beltramelli, T.: pix2code: Generating code from a graphical user interface screenshot. arXiv.org (2017). Available: https://arxiv.org/abs/1705.07962

61. Sethi, A., Sankaran, A., Panwar, N., Khare, S., Mani, S.: DLPaper2Code: Auto-generation of code from deep learning research papers. In: Proceedings of the AAAI Conference on Artificial Intelligence, vol. 32, no. 1, p. 12326 (2017). doi: https://doi.org/10.1609/aaai.v32i1.12326

62. Zhu, Z., Xue, Z., Yuan, Z.: Automatic graphics program generation using attention-based hierarchical decoder. In: Springer eBooks, Springer Nature (2018), pp. 181–196. doi: https://doi.org/10.1007/978-3-030-20876-9_12

63. Asiroglu, B., et al.: Automatic HTML code generation from mock-up images using machine learning techniques. In: Proceed-ings of the 2019 Electrical-Electronics & Biomedical Engineering and Computer Science (EBBT), pp. 1–6 (2019). doi: https://doi.org/10.1109/ebbt.2019.8741736

64. microsoft: ailab/Sketch2Code at master microsoft/ailab. GitHub. Available: https://github.com/microsoft/ailab/tree/master/Sketch2Code/model/images

65. Teng, Z., Fu, Q., White, J., Schmidt, D. C.: Sketch2Vis: Generating data visualizations from hand-drawn sketches with deep learning. In: Proceedings of the 20th IEEE International Conference on Machine Learning and Applications (ICMLA), pp. 438–445 (2021). doi: https://doi.org/10.1109/icmla52953.2021.00141

66. Hendrycks, D., et al.: Measuring coding challenge competence with APPS. In: Proceedings of the Neural Information Processing Systems (NeurIPS) (2021). Available: https://openreview.net/pdf?id=sD93GOzH3i5

67. Papineni, K., Roukos, S., Ward, T. J., Zhu, W.-J.: BLEU. In: Proceedings of the 40th Annual Meeting of the Association for Computational Linguistics (ACL), pp. 311–318 (2002). doi: https://doi.org/10.3115/1073083.1073135

68. Yin, P., Neubig, G.: A syntactic neural model for general-purpose code generation. Cornell Univ. (2017). https://doi.org/10.18653/v1/p17-1041

An IoT-Based Framework for Sustainable Supply Chain Management System

Muhammad Ali[1], Sehrish Munawar Cheema[2], Ivan Miguel Pires[3]([⊠]),
Ammerha Naz[4], Zaheer Aslam[1], Nasir Ayub[1], and Paulo Jorge Coelho[5,6]

[1] Department of Software Engineering, The Superior University Lahore, Lahore, Pakistan
[2] Department of Computer Science, University of Management and Technology, Sialkot,
Pakistan
sehrish.munawar@skt.umt.edu.pk
[3] Instituto de Telecomunicações, Escola Superior de Tecnologia e Gestão de Águeda,
Universidade de Aveiro, Águeda, Portugal
impires@ua.pt
[4] Department of Computer Science, University of Sialkot, Sialkot, Pakistan
[5] Institute for Systems Engineering and Computers at Coimbra (INESC Coimbra), Coimbra,
Portugal
paulo.coelho@ipleiria.pt
[6] Polytechnic of Leiria, Leiria, Portugal

Abstract. The "smart supply chain" is a new way of doing business made possible by smart, sustainable business and IT trends. Sustainable supply chains are a creative movement that uses information technology to improve the quality of operations at their sites so that activities can be changed to meet social and environmental needs. IoT is one of the most critical parts of smart's technological foundation in this way. This paper shows how to set up a sustainable supply chain based on IoT. Based on the IoT's four-stage architecture, this framework was made by looking at the research, surveying general people, and evaluating the opinions of people who work in this field. This way of thinking makes it easy to make good environmental decisions throughout the supply chain. It also shows the direct link between data collection and how it interacts with sectors that are affected by environmental sustainability. Experts in the supply chain have approved this framework, which can help technology-focused industrial organizations adopt the smart supply chain.

Keywords: Internet of things · Supply chain management · Supply chain integration · Sustainability · Smart supply chains · Transparency · Supply chain processes

1 Introduction

Smart systems have been proposed as a strategy to stabilize economic growth in recent years. It increases customer engagement by improving a company's productivity and product quality. This method improves customer-company interactions, and modern

N. Moniz et al. (Eds.): EPIA 2023, LNAI 14116, pp. 483–494, 2023.
https://doi.org/10.1007/978-3-031-49011-8_38

businesses use data to create new issues and opportunities. Due to advancements in information technology, custom software has been introduced in the market [2]. It makes 21st-century businesses will be more productive and efficient. Privacy and commercial data security are also concerns. People engage with enterprises via many technologies and systems. Companies and people in the supply chain may now communicate and share resources because of the Internet and mobile devices [14].

Path analysis can help to find the fastest route between a current location and a desired destination. It uses historical data to construct probabilistic traffic projections for a set of routes to determine the busiest route and enables the choice of a traffic-friendly path [9]. An environmentally friendly Information and communication technologies (ICT) infrastructure includes the Internet of Things since it can make organizations more sustainable.

Moreover, the IoT alters urban and environmental technologies in complex ways. Massive data quantities influence new Internet of Things applications, although IoT is becoming robust for computing and analyzing vast amounts of data [16]. Figure 1 explains the basic supply chain process that includes the Supplier–Producer–Customer as primary product flow and the Customer–Producer–Supplier as primary cash flow.

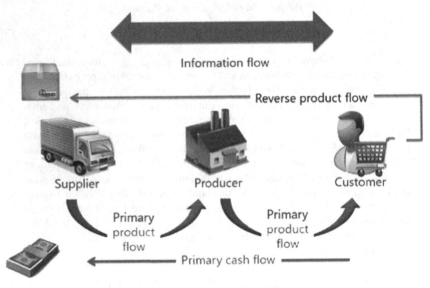

Fig. 1. Basic supply chain architecture

This benefits sensible business and environmental applications in industrialized nations. Because the IoT can analyze plenty of data. The Internet of Things unites digital and physical infrastructures. This allows cutting-edge services and apps to assist in balancing the environment. This shows how the IoT may aid humans [13]. If a system uses minimal power, its sensors, gadgets, apps, and services may flourish on the Internet of Things. The massive amounts of data created in sustainable smart organizations can be challenging to interpret, yet the large amounts of data available in many disciplines are beneficial [4]. Urban planners and IT professionals can help sustain the environment.

Even while research on the Internet of Things and data-related urban planning projects is rising, commercial IoT applications have received less attention than consumer ones [10]. Since this is the case, the most crucial question is how big data processing and the Internet of Things can improve the data landscape of tech-savvy, environmentally conscious organizations [12].

This study aims to show how crucial an Internet of Things supply chain is. This considers all sales and distribution steps. IoT-based creative solutions will improve the environment long term. The framework needs massive data spread by the Internet of Things (IoT). Nature-friendly methods are chosen. An IoT-based supply chain management solution that performs effectively and lasts should have these parts. This method produces the most environmentally friendly supply chain results and can be used to identify areas for improvement because it alters the most critical variables. Researchers could construct analytical frameworks to explore sustainable, intelligent systems using data from building and testing the recommended paradigm.

This paragraph ends the introductory section. The remaining sections are organized as follows: Sect. 2 presents the literature review. The system design is presented in Sect. 3, presenting both the methodology and results. Finally, Sect. 4 presents the discussion and conclusions of this study.

2 Literature Review

In Nozari et al. [11], manufacturers emphasize technology that can increase their yield and lay the groundwork for a sustainable and eco-friendly supply chain. Smart, eco-friendly industry and information technology (IT) developments created the "green smart supply chain concept." Supply chains that are environmentally responsible and sustainable are modifying their business practices to be more closely aligned with the expectations of society and the environment. The study presented here suggests a strategy for establishing an internet-of-things-based green supply chain to accomplish this goal. This framework was established based on the four-stage architecture of the IoT by studying the available research and interviewing and evaluating the expert perspectives of individuals in the field. As a result, good environmental and long-term supply chain decisions are simplified by the authors of [15]. It also highlights the natural relationship between data collecting and the sectors influenced by environmental sustainability. Experts in supply chains have demonstrated that this strategy can assist industrial firms in building a more environmentally friendly supply chain that emphasizes the use of technology.

Alawi et al. [1] investigated whether or not the use of blockchain technology results in improvements in the administration of supply chains. The Fuzzy Analytical Hierarchy Process-based Smart Decision-Making technique is the foundation for this methodology. This way of doing things will serve as the basis for the method. In this approach, the prerequisites for using blockchain technology in supply chain management are given higher importance than previously held in the plan. Traceability should be prioritized while designing applications for supply chain management that use blockchain technology. After that, ensure that your top objectives are keeping yourself safe and maintaining meaningful connections with others. When deciding whether to employ blockchain technology, upper management might consult the plan developed by the department responsible for supply chain management for guidance. This department would be responsible for producing the plan, and this would be helpful in the transfer of payments and goods among the various installations of Blockchain technology that are currently in operation.

In Zhang et al. [18], most businesses utilize supply chain management to ensure their continued profitability and customers' happiness. According to the findings of this study, the challenges associated with supply chain management include inadequate customer service, rising costs, poor risk management, and inefficiency [5]. The handling of cognitive conflicts in supply chains has the potential to boost both supply chain efficiency and customer service (HCCCMF). The HCCCMF reduces expenses and saves time while controlling the supply chains for labor, energy, and raw materials. Behavior analysis is used in supply chain management to improve customer–supplier relationships and service quality. Authors claim that analysis of the policy matrix ensures that reasonable rates are applied, preventing operational concerns. The HCCCMF method that has been developed improves productivity by 94.3% in comparison to other methods, efficiency by 96.5%, performance by 98.4%, accuracy by 97.8%, low trade cost by 15.3%, and reliability by 95.5%.

Al-Rakhami et al. [3] presented that the global food system is estimated to be worth $8 trillion, or 10% of the world's GDP [6]. To achieve food quality across all operations, specific crucial environmental indicators that could drastically affect product quality must be examined and documented often. Using specialized sensors and the Internet, the Industrial Internet of Things (IIoT) may help solve and avoid food-related issues. Its parts constantly monitor, assess, and record food processing. Also, regularly tests product quality. However, even the IIoT has problems, such as data storage and retrieval, which are the initial ones. What would help industry companies share information? Finding multi-owner artifacts is the second hardest. The authors propose ProChain, an Internet of Things-compatible traceability architecture emphasizing provenance. The comprehensive design that considered sensor and provenance data solved these issues. Modeling the entire framework on the Internet-of-Things Device Raspberry PI 3B and comparing the results to those in the cloud tested ProChain's viability to determine which strategy was more accurate. ProChain showed IOTA 2.0 protocol functionalities in the food supply chain. Openness, transparency, and strong security are offered.

In Zekhnini et al. [17], the impact digital tools have had on the management of supply chains is analyzed and evaluated. In addition to that, you will receive an analysis of recent research on supply chain management version 4.0. (SCM 4.0). The most recent study was reexamined, and a quantitative evaluation was conducted. This article looks at the numerous linkages in the supply chain and analyzes how introducing innovative technology affects those links. It serves as a Launchpad for additional research and future applications. The proposed study will shed light on critical parts of the supply chain transformation process, making it useful for academics and practitioners. Various possible lines of research are suggested, all of which might be pursued to gain a deeper comprehension of the long-term trajectory of the topic. Finally, the authors comprehensively reviewed the relevant previous research and presented a novel perspective on SCM 4.0. Currently, there needs to be a more all-encompassing examination of the many supply chain (SC) activities that consider bibliometric analysis, motives, barriers, and the impact of technology.

Mackie and Campbell et al. [8], through their deft use of advertising, businesses, retailers, and designers are pushing customers and the earth to levels of consumption that have never been seen before. This would be detrimental to both people and the natural world. This occurs due to the expansion of the global supply chain utilized by the fashion industry to produce fabric and garments. Many nations are exploited and forced into poverty due to outdated commercial contracts based on their projections of future demand. This occurs when reserves are practically depleted in pursuing new fashions, and customers look for the best deal possible. The so-called "New Emerging Markets" [7] is witnessing a meteoric rise in the net sales of well-established brands such as Adidas. Concerns have been raised over the extent to which this profit is felt across the fashion industry and its impact on the economics of the local communities. What exactly does the term "value" entail when applied to the context of the supply chain? Partnerships, as well as the fostering of deeper connections, the exchange of information, and collaborative efforts can bring about a new perspective and economy in the fashion industry.

The comparative analysis of the state-of-the-art is presented in Table 1, where the different parameters were analyzed.

Table 1. Comparative analysis

Ref	Carbon footprint	Energy consumption	Waste reduction	Operational efficiency
Nozari et al. [11]	High	High	Medium	Medium
Alawi et al. [1]	High	High	Low	Medium
Zhang et al. [18]	High	High	Low	Medium
Al-Rakhami et al. [3]	High	Medium	Low	Low
Zekhnini et al. [17]	High	High	Medium	Medium
Mackie and Campbell et al. [8]	High	High	Low	Medium

Customer satisfaction	Innovation	Risk management	Collaboration	Supply chain transparency
Less	Less	Low	Not Good	Low
Less	Less	Low	Not Good	Low
Less	Less	Low	Good	Low
Less	Less	Medium	Not Good	Low
Less	Less	Low	Not Good	Low
Less	Less	Low	Good	Low

3 System Design

3.1 Research Approach

In this study, qualitative content analysis was chosen as the research approach due to descriptive data depicts a real representation of quantitative data (Taking into consideration its overarching goal, which is to locate, uncover, and provide an explanation of the indicators and aspects that work effectively in the IoT-based smart supply chain procedure). This investigation's findings were derived from reading the pertinent literature and examining and assessing the opinions of field specialists. These individuals were IT and supply chain management industry activists. This study's data was collected through a variety of in-depth interviews. We began by asking, "What are the most distinctive characteristics of a smart supply chain based on the Internet of Things?".

The responses are then utilized to formulate the following set of questions. The following precautions were taken to ensure the accuracy of the data: (1) Notes were gathered during interviews to allow for their verification. Second, experts were granted access to the data and the analysis findings to provide their expert comments. Thirdly, the researchers had specialists review some of the results to ensure they had appropriately interpreted them. Finally, a technique known as "thematic analysis" was employed to examine the interview data. In this study, 15 in-depth interviews were conducted.

Inclusion Criteria: Inclusion criteria for participant selection included active industry involvement, expertise in IoT-based smart supply chain procedures, and significant experience.

Exclusion Criteria: Exclusion criteria ensured the exclusion of participants with limited expertise or insufficient knowledge in the field.

The interview script focused on capturing the distinctive characteristics of an IoT-based smart supply chain. Through thematic analysis of the interview data, recurring patterns and common themes were identified. These themes emerged from the interviewees' responses and provided valuable insights into the effective indicators and aspects of the IoT-based smart supply chain. For example, one interviewee emphasized the importance of enhanced visibility within the supply chain, stating, 'fluctuations are critical for optimizing supply chain operations and reducing disruptions.'

Another recurring theme that emerged from the interviews was the need for collaborative ecosystems and integration. An interviewee expressed, 'Successful implementation of an IoT-based smart supply chain requires seamless integration and close collaboration among stakeholders to enable real-time coordination and information sharing.' These quotations highlight the key findings and illustrate the interviewees' perspectives on the themes identified. By incorporating these actual quotes from the interviews, the analysis is grounded in the interview data, enhancing the credibility and supporting the overall insights of the study.

3.2 Implementation of ICT, IoT, and Big Data in Smart Supply Chain

A supply chain is examined from procurement to distribution to find energy-efficient and environmentally beneficial solutions. However, these examinations showed that sustainable and intelligent supply chains could only be built with big data analytics, IoT, and ICT. It means the smart supply chain is a network of social, physical, and economic infrastructures that sustainably focuses enterprises on important areas such as smart transportation, smart economy, smart environment, smart people, smart management, and smart activities. Figure 2 shows the IoT-based smart supply chain's ICT, IoT, and big data sources.

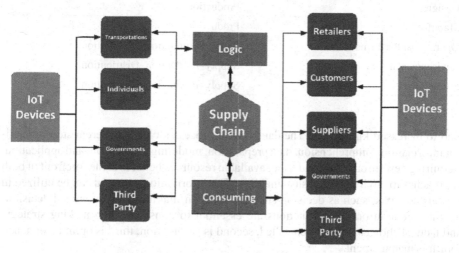

Fig. 2. ICT, IoT, and big data in supply chain

It allows people, processes, and devices to share information and generate massive data. To gain real-time visibility in operations and risk management, big data technology is used in this framework for deeper understanding and for making data-driven decisions. With the help of big data technology, this framework can process an enormous amount of data using big data processing methods (regression, clustering, classification, and other algorithms), techniques (statistical analysis, machine learning, data mining, etc.), to extract insights from enormous datasets quickly. IoT-based sustainable supply chains prioritizing environmentally friendly information and concrete activities have solved environmental sustainability problems caused by ICT inequities. IoT and big data increase the performance of supply chain intelligence and benefit the environment.

3.3 Key Performance Indicators

The most important indicators must be identified to integrate the IoT supply chain into the sustainable supply chain. Table 2 gives examples of KPIs that work for supply chain management firms.

These performance standards and usage of high-quality data enable IoT-based sustainable supply chains system to operate efficiently. Considering this, it is required to gather, store, process, evaluate, integrate into operations, activities, and plans for sustainability (with importance on key indicators) and then communicate the massive volumes of data available across the supply chain. Several procedures, such as selection, preprocessing, modification, exploration, interpretation, and assessment, can all

Table 2. Performance indicators

Performance indicators	Sectors of SCM
Purchasing	Supply
Transportation	Distribution
Design	Production
Manufacturing	Production
Operational Performance	Supply–Production–Distribution
Environmental Management	Supply–Production–Distribution
Storage	Supply–Production–Distribution

lead to increased knowledge. The data mining process includes different steps, including information comprehension, data preparation, modeling, evaluation, and application. Acquiring new information and using available resources better is at the forefront of both approaches to environmental sustainability. The information gathered can be utilized in various contexts, such as decision-support, decision-making, and automated decision-making. Four information functions are essential to consider when making strategic and tactical choices. First is controlled, second is automation, third is optimization, and fourth is management.

3.4 Design

This framework integrates cloud and fog-based Internet of Things technology into a data-intensive "Sustainable smart chain". It is beneficial because it prioritizes sustainability and environmental friendliness. This framework consists of the following components.

Sensor data collection and integration. First, data from different supply chain domains are collected. To collect this data, there is a need to analyze the determinants because every determinant is related to a specific field and influences the overall outcome. Then data from primary and secondary stakeholders. Primary stockholders are retailers, customers, and suppliers, while secondary stakeholders are Governments and third parties. Preliminary stakeholder data is gathered via smart devices, and secondary stakeholder data is collected through observations and transactions. Sensor technologies, computational models, data-driven applications, and data processing systems are all available throughout the supply chain and linked directly to the data sources in the supply chain. Then all this data from the source is stored in a data warehouse.

Data Processing and Decision Support. This component performs data processing with the help of data mining and machine learning techniques. It takes data as input from the data warehouse. It comprises retrieval facilities, information processing platforms, and cloud/fog computing models. Demonstrating the connection between data intake, Internet of Things-based smart analytics, and supply chain position reveals the true nature of that relationship. Based on the performance metrics, it gathers, analyzes, preprocesses, and translates sensor data from different data sources. This is accomplished by utilizing model construction strategies based on data mining and machine learning. As a result, manufacturing units, planning, and other tasks are aided, automated, and made choices with the help of patterns, pattern recognition, and correlations. Using cognitive analysis, we can distill the key points of a framework for a sustainable supply chain that highlights the positive effects of the Internet of Things and large-scale data processing on the environment.

In addition to other types of both real and virtual transactions. The volume and velocity of the data extraction are high. They're unique in their ways, and their geographically dispersed origins further emphasize that fact. Therefore, these data sets are quite large and require expert analysis. The supply chain can easily optimize the environmental sustainability variables that matter most using this information and KPIs. It has advantages in areas like traffic management, fuel monitoring, and optimization, reduced pollution from industrial machinery use, and helps to use energy efficiently. We performed distributed and networked computations on data that had been retrieved and refined. This facilitates the optimization of processes, system performance, and decision-making.

Figure 3 illustrates the sustainable IoT-based SCM framework, representing the supply chain determinants that receives information from the supply chain domain. The information acquired from the supply chain domain and the data science domain are stored in a data warehouse, sending the data for a data processing module that presents the information in the application developed.

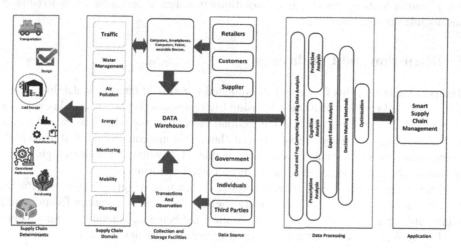

Fig. 3. IoT-based Sustainable supply chain Framework

SSCM Interface. The smart supply chain management interface provides several features to optimize and automate the different processes of smart supply chain management. Its basic features are real-time monitoring, progress tracking, collaboration, and risk management.

Real-Time Monitoring: These features help to monitor different supply chain activities and generate real-time alerts and notifications regarding any issue or milestone.

Collaboration: This feature provides a communication facility to interact with stakeholders like customers, suppliers, or retailers.

Progress Tracking: This feature helps to measure the progress of the supply chain over time by tracking KPIs.

Risk Management: This feature is helpful in the identification and mitigation of the risks like shipping delays or disruption in the shipping of raw materials.

4 Findings

The evaluation of the proposed framework considered key parameters: scalability, maintainability, latency, resource utilization, cost, environmental friendliness, and integration of IoT and big data analytics frameworks. Findings revealed the framework's advantages in scalability and maintainability, enabling efficient handling of large payloads while maintaining acceptable latency levels. However, higher latency rates were observed compared to other systems. Resource utilization was higher, resulting in increased costs. On a positive note, the framework demonstrated environmental friendliness with a low carbon footprint and energy-efficient operations. Integrating IoT and big data analytics frameworks proved crucial in optimizing designs and services for sustainable industries. The framework's multi-layer architecture provided a sustainable solution for IoT-based supply chains. Expert validation confirmed its efficiency and effectiveness, highlighting its superiority. Future research should focus on additional indicators, exploring new paths, and optimizing computational solutions to enhance performance in IoT-based sustainable supply chains.

5 Discussion and Conclusions

The performance of this framework is evaluated in terms of latency, scalability, maintainability, and resource utilization by using high payloads. It has a higher latency rate than others. Moreover, it can bear the payload more than any other system and maintain many connected devices. Even then, its latency is not compromised. It has a high latency rate and is more scalable and maintainable. Meanwhile, it also has a high source utilization than any other system due to its enhanced performance.

Due to high resource utilization, this system's cost is also higher than others. But on the other hand, it is more environmentally friendly due to its low carbon footprint and highly utilizable due to less energy consumption and better collaborations than others.

IoT's effectiveness has attracted smart, sustainable industries. These firms must optimize their information environment by integrating and merging frameworks to improve designs and services for IoT and macro data analytics delivery. IoT and big data research can teach science and industry about the environment. This work investigates, combines, and discusses pertinent data. It helps locate and discuss Big Data applications for environmental sustainability, data processing platforms, and sustainable smart supply chain computing models. This architecture provides a cutting-edge, multi-layer solution for creating a sustainable IoT supply chain. Strong analytics link environmental sustainability statistics to their implications. This framework shows key locations and outlines an IoT-based sustainable supply chain approach. Experts validated the efficiency and usefulness of this framework, and as a result, this framework is much more effective than others due to its multi-layer mechanism. The efficiency and effectiveness of this framework can be enhanced in future research by incorporating more relevant indicators, new paths that correspond to existing indicators, computational solutions, and optimal options.

Acknowledgments. This work is funded by FCT/MEC through national funds and co-funded by FEDER—PT2020 partnership agreement under the project **UIDB/00308/2020**.

This work is funded by FCT/MEC through national funds and co-funded by FEDER—PT2020 partnership agreement under the project **UIDB/50008/2020**.

This article is based upon work from COST Action CA21103—Implementation of Circular Economy in the Built Environment (CircularB). More information on www.cost.eu.

References

1. Alawi, B., Al Mubarak, M.M.S., Hamdan, A.: Blockchain Evaluation Framework for Supply Chain Management: A Decision-Making Approach, pp. 1–15. Taylor & Francis (2022)
2. Aliahmadi, A., Nozari, H., Ghahremani-Nahr, J.: AIoT-based sustainable smart supply chain framework. Int. J. Innov. Manag., Econ. Soc. Sci. **2**, 28–38 (2022)
3. Al-Rakhami, M.S., Al-Mashari, M.: ProChain: Provenance-aware traceability framework for IoT-based supply chain systems. IEEE Access **10**, 3631–3642 (2021)
4. Cheema, S.M., Ali, M., Pires, I.M., Gonçalves, N.J., Naqvi, M.H., Hassan, M.: IoAT enabled smart farming: Urdu language-based solution for low-literate farmers. Agriculture **12**, 1277 (2022)
5. Cheema, S.M., Hannan, A., Pires, I.M.: Smart waste management and classification systems using cutting edge approach. Sustainability **14**, 10226 (2022)
6. Cheema, S.M., Khalid, M., Rehman, A., Sarwar, N.: Plant Irrigation and Recommender System–IoT Based Digital Solution for Home Garden, pp. 513–525. Springer (2018)
7. Hannan, A., Hussain, F., Cheema, S.M., Pires, I.M.: Premises Based Smart Door Chains System Using IoT Cloud, pp 834–846. Springer (2021)
8. Mackie, L., Campbell, D.: Sustainability and the Supply Chain. In: Fashion Marketing in Emerging Economies, vol. I., pp 163–220. Springer (2023)
9. Moosavi, J., Naeni, L.M., Fathollahi-Fard, A.M., Fiore, U.: Blockchain in supply chain management: a review, bibliometric, and network analysis. Environ. Sci. Pollut. Res., 1–15 (2021)
10. Nguyen, T., Duong, Q.H., Van Nguyen, T., Zhu, Y., Zhou, L.: Knowledge mapping of digital twin and physical internet in supply chain management: A systematic literature review. Int. J. Prod. Econ. **244**, 108381 (2022)
11. Nozari, H., Fallah, M., Szmelter-Jarosz, A.: A conceptual framework of green smart IoT-based supply chain management. Int. J. Res. Ind. Eng. **10**, 22–34 (2021)
12. Putro, P.A.W., Purwaningsih, E.K., Sensuse, D.I., Suryono, R.R.: Model and implementation of rice supply chain management: A literature review. Procedia Comput. Sci. **197**, 453–460 (2022)
13. Raja Santhi, A., Muthuswamy, P.: Influence of blockchain technology in manufacturing supply chain and logistics. Logistics **6**, 15 (2022)
14. Rejeb, A., Keogh, J.G., Rejeb, K.: Big data in the food supply chain: A literature review. J. Data, Inf. Manag., 1–15 (2022)
15. Sheikh, J.A., Cheema, S.M., Ali, M., Amjad, Z., Tariq, J.Z., Naz, A.: IoT and AI in precision agriculture: Designing smart system to support illiterate farmers. In: Advances in Artificial Intelligence, Software and Systems Engineering: Proceedings of the AHFE 2020 Virtual Conferences on Software and Systems Engineering, and Artificial Intelligence and Social Computing, July 16–20, 2020, pp. 490–496 (2021). Springer, USA

16. Wang, L., Deng, T., Shen, Z.-J.M., Hu, H., Qi, Y.: Digital twin-driven smart supply chain. Front. Eng. Manag., 1–15 (2022)
17. Zekhnini, K., Cherrafi, A., Bouhaddou, I., Benghabrit, Y., Garza-Reyes, J.A.: Supply chain management 4.0: A literature review and research framework. Benchmarking: Int. J. (2020)
18. Zhang, Y., Montenegro-Marin, C.E., Díaz, V.G.: Holistic cognitive conflict chain management framework in supply chain management. Environ. Impact Assess. Rev. 88, 106564 (2021)

Artificial Intelligence for Industry and Societies

Tool Wear Monitoring Using Multi-sensor Time Series and Machine Learning

Jonathan Dreyer[1,2]($\boxtimes$) (iD), Stefano Carrino[1] (iD), Hatem Ghorbel[1] (iD), and Paul Cotofrei[2] (iD)

[1] Haute Ecole Arc Ingénierie, University of Applied Sciences and Arts Western Switzerland (HES-SO), St. Imier, Switzerland
{jonathan.dreyer,stefano.carrino,hatem.ghorbel}@he-arc.ch
[2] Information Management Institute, University of Neuchatel, Neuchatel, Switzerland
{jonathan.dreyer,paul.cotofrei}@unine.ch

Abstract. In the milling process of micro-machining, the optimization process is one of the keys to reduce production cost. By monitoring the tool wear and detecting when it is no longer acceptable, the machining process can be adjusted more accurately. This research explores four approaches using different machine learning models to predict machining tool wear during the milling process. The study is based on a dataset created with a face milling operation on stainless steel (AISI 303) round material. The machining is divided into a number of stairs and is performed with a 3 mm tungsten carbide. Three different types of sensors are used to measure the wearing process, with acoustic emission, accelerometers and axis currents. The better approach achieved a F1-score of 73% on five classes with an Extra-Trees Classifier.

Keywords: Tool wear monitoring · Milling machining · Multi-sensors time series · Machine learning

1 Introduction

In this article, we explore the possibility of improving machining performance by monitoring and evaluating the tool wear without interrupting the machining process. To be able to perform the tool wear detection, a mix method is used by implementing a state-of-the-art methodology and compare it with other algorithms not used in papers. This can be achieved by measuring in-process with sensors, which help to improve the productivity and the control of the manufacturing [6]. The custom production implies a reduction in the demand for large volumes of production, and the needs of small-sized machine tools satisfy the requirements for micro manufacturing which enables the miniaturization of products and high accuracy [9].

The computer numerical control machining field includes several types of machining such as turning, milling and grinding. The first one is a machining technique where a cutting tool moves longitudinally while the workpiece rotates on itself. The second one is a machining process which uses a rotating cutter

© The Author(s), under exclusive license to Springer Nature Switzerland AG 2023
N. Moniz et al. (Eds.): EPIA 2023, LNAI 14116, pp. 497–510, 2023.
https://doi.org/10.1007/978-3-031-49011-8_39

tool to remove material by moving the cutter tool into a workpiece. The last one is a machining process which uses a circular abrasive wheel to remove material from the surface while creating a smooth surface texture. In this study, we will focus on the milling process with a micro-milling machining.

The low consumption of these micro-machining machine has been possible by scaling down the dimension [22]. This size reduction enables the reduction of the moving masses and a higher dynamic of motion [9]. The high-speed machining (HSM) is of benefit for micro machining and reduces the requirement of cooling during the milling, because a major part of heating is dissipated by chips. The HSM also helps to increase the productivity by speeding up the milling speed and the cutting speed [13].

Actually, the prediction of tool wear in micro milling context with sensors is challenging. To address this problem, we propose various approaches based on several machine learning classification models, including Convolutional Neural Networks (CNN). The machine learning algorithms can enhance the tool wearing detection by analyzing large volumes of datasets and detecting hidden patterns. The objective is to study different machine learning techniques to improve the tool wear detection without interrupting the machining process, by measuring in-process with external sensors.

The rest of the paper is structured as follows. The Sect. 2 is focused on the state of the art of the machining, tool wear sensing & prediction and artificial intelligence models.

The milling process, the necessary materials (e.g. the sensors), and the global methodology in the context of a machine learning approach (from dataset to model evaluation) are detailed in the following section. The Sect. 4 is dedicated to the results for each approach, and, in the final section, the discussion of the results is presented along with the conclusion of the achieved results.

2   State of the Art

The goal of this paper is to study the link between tool wear and the measures recorded by different sensors in the field of micro milling and high-speed milling. We aim to push forward the detection of tool wear and be able to identify the most interesting sensors for tool wear detection.

In the machining field, the wear of tools is due to multiple parameters, such as physical constraints, milling materials, etc. [5]. Tool wear management is one of the keys to optimize the milling process. Physical constraints (e.g. cutting forces, accelerations, vibrations, etc.) can be measured with sensors and used to determine the condition of the tool [6].

2.1   Tool Wear Sensing and Prediction

Adaptive control systems aim at estimating the remaining useful life (RUL) of a tool in order to enable a fine control and optimization of the machining process. The lifetime of a tool can be decomposed into three consecutive stages designated as: break-in, steady-state, and failure [7]. After a relatively short break-in period characterized by a fast wear, the tool will pass into the steady-state in which the wear slowly increases. The last phase of the tool life cycle, failure, is characterized by a rapid deterioration of the tool at the end of which, the tool is no more usable. This degradation can be indirectly observed without stopping the production by using external sensors. This non-destructive method allows estimating the current wear of the tool. It can also be used to detect when the tool is too marked and needs to be replaced [21].

Different sensors can capture various aspects of the milling process and the related physical parameters. These sensors are used to model the behavior of one or multiple physical elements. For instance, the acoustic emission (AE) sensors are indicated as relevant sources of information [14,15]. A drawback of AE sensors is the noisy signal, and the influence of unrelated sounds and vibrations present in a machining environment. Less sensitive to the environment noise than AE, the accelerometers placed on the machine axes can also provide significant results to correlate the tool wear process and estimate the wear [11,23], that allow them to be less sensitive to the environmental noise than AE. Accelerometers provide information about vibration on the axes caused by the interaction between the tool and the material. The physical effort on an axis can be related to the power used by this axis. This power consumption can be measured by the electric current drawn by each motor. The relation between consumption and tool wear has been demonstrated by multiple authors, such as [11,17]. Those various data sources can be used individually or can be merged to create a multivariate dataset as demonstrated by [11,15].

To extract relevant information from data sources and reduce data size, few authors proposed to use features instead of raw data. Authors have demonstrated that spectrograms can be used instead of raw acoustic emission time series [2,4]. The idea behind is to compute features that represents the frequency and his amplitude on a specific period. Statistical features can also be used in place of those computed ones which are less computational cost [11].

2.2 Machine Learning Models

According to the literature, the detection of tool wear can be achieved by several approaches. Machine learning and artificial intelligence methods are widely investigated. Krishnakumar et al. [15,16] used statistical features extracted from vibration signals to train classification models (decision tree, artificial neural network and support vector machine) to predict the stage of the tool wear. Cao et al. has established that features extracted from derived wavelet frames with Convolutional Neural Network (CNN) provide strong results [3].

Modeling tool wear states using deep learning approach was considered by several authors. Dou et al. [7] used a sparse auto-encoder model trained on vibration and force signals, Von Hahn et al. [10] opted for a disentangled-variational-autoencoder, with a temporal convolutional neural network, and Liu et al. [18] proposed a transformer-based neural network and a long-short memory network using temporal features extracted from raw signals.

3 Methodology

3.1 Context

The project focuses on the analysis of a *micro* milling machine, called micro5. The machine has 5-axis with less than 10 Kg of moving masses with high-speed machining (up to 60'000 revolutions/min). The kinematics of the machine combine three linear axes (X-Y-Z) and two rotary axes (B-C). It is corresponding to the type 57 from ISG-kernel.[1] All the data used in this project are produced by sensors integrated into this machine. This dataset is similar to the one introduced in [4] but has some major differences regarding the raw material used for machining and the sensors. The three principal differences are: the shape of the raw material (a cylindrical shape is used here instead of a cubic one), the number of AE sensors (reduced to one) and the use of multiple accelerometers.

Sensors The dataset is composed of signals acquired via three different types of sensors: electric current sensors (one for each axis), accelerometers (placed on different positions inside the machine) and an acoustic emission sensor.

The AE sensor is located inside the milling machine, and positioned close to the raw material where the machining process is performed but not directly glued on the raw material as in [4]. The acoustic sensor is a Vallen VS45-H and the acquisition is realized with an Advantech PCIe

Fig. 1.   C   axis with accelerometers sensors

1840/L. The acquisition sampling is limited to 200 kHz. The sensor is positioned as close as possible that the raw material on the B axis, which allows replacing the raw material without moving the AE sensor.

Multiple accelerometer sensors are located on the spindle axis and the stator of C axis. Two different types of sensors have been used both from *Brüel & Kjær* (triaxial & uniaxial sensor/type 4520 & 4507).

One 3-axis accelerometer sensor is located on the bottom of the spindle (for XYZ axis). Two one-axis accelerometers are located on the top of the spindle (XY axis). On the stator of C axis, three one-axis accelerometers are mounted to measure XYZ axis. All sensors are acquired with National Instruments NI-9234 modules and sampled at 2 kHz. Figures 1 and 2 illustrates sensor placement.

Both acoustic and accelerometers signals are synchronized with an external trigger which is recorded by the acquisition material. For those both data sources, the acquisition frequencies have been chosen by using equipment with a high acquisition frequency and wide bandwidth, in order to retain as much as possible of the information in the signal. The recorded signal is not digitally

Fig. 2. Spindle axis with accelerometers sensors

---

[1] https://www.isg-stuttgart.de/en/.

filtered to keep as much as possible of embedded data. When some of the values are missing, the ongoing milling operation is ignored, as explained in Sect. 3.1.

All axis motors are driven by separated drive and the currents of each are stored during the milling. The acquisition sampling is limited to 1 kHz. For this data source, a digital filter is used to reduce noise from power supply and motor drive. The motor itself also performs as a filter, because it is a large inductive element.

Milling Process The machining process consists in milling the raw material in multiple stairs; to create each stair, the milling path is again divided in several linear passes of identical width to remove the same quantity of material (see Fig. 3). In the following, we will use the term of **experience** for one block of raw material machined where at the beginning the tool is new and at the end the tool breaks or is not more usable. The dataset is composed with a total of six experiences of the same machining path. The cutting technique used for manufacturing experiences parts is conventional milling.

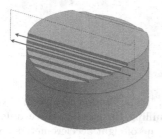

Fig. 3. Multiple linear passes

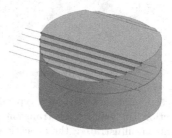

Fig. 4. Different lengths of linear passes

The linear milling path is achieved in three directions of the machine, in X (experiences one and four), in Y (experiences two and three) and in X + Y (experiences five and six). The experience parts are milled from a round bar and are sliced into cylinders. As the shape is a cylinder, the length of the linear passes tangential to the shape is shorter than the length of passes near the center of the raw material (as illustrated in Fig. 4). This means that with this cylindric shape, the distance of the tool out of the material is not uniform and evolve between linear passes.

The tool has a diameter of 3 mm and is made of tungsten carbide. It was replaced at the beginning of each experience. The rotation speed of the spindle and tool was set to 35'000 revolutions per minute (RPM) and was the same for all experiences. The milling of each part was achieved with pressurized air lubrication.

To automatically detect and segment when the tool is milling the raw material, and not just moving without contact, a variable threshold on the intensity of the acoustic signal is used. As first step to dynamically fix the threshold, the signal is filtered using a rolling means. Then, the difference between the maximum value of the signal in the central part of the pass and the maximal value at the beginning and ending of the pass is measured (the machining process design assures that the tool is not touching the material at the beginning and the end of each pass). The mid-point of the difference is used as the threshold to segment each linear pass. In detail, beginning and ending of a pass are defined as the first 2000 values and the 2000 latest values, which is approximately corresponding to 1 ms (see Fig. 5). This procedure is repeated for each linear pass.

In the Fig. 5, three different signals are illustrated: the acoustic emission (gray), one of eight accelerometers (blue) and the spindle electric current (red). The transient phases of a milling pass are indicated in green.

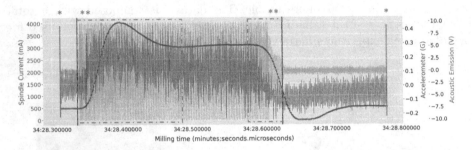

Fig. 5. Signals detected for a typical machining pass. * time window for maximal value detection (in yellow); ** transient phases during milling (in green). Three different signals are illustrated: the acoustic emission (gray), one of eight accelerometers (blue) and the spindle electric current (red).

Objectives of the Study In this article, we focus on the milling process and specifically on the step when the tool removes material. An experience is considered completed, if, at the end of the milling process, a tool is considered as no more usable (broken, burned out, etc.). The main goal is to construct a model able to predict the remaining useful life (RUL) of the tool. In order to apply classification models, the continuous variable RUL must be firstly discretized. We propose to use five states (or labels), denoted by "0" (corresponding to a new tool) to "4" (corresponding to a non-usable tool), to perform a finer tool wear evaluation. We have chosen that at the end of the milling operations, the tool is no longer usable and receives the label "4" (or "worst"). The label "0" (or "the best") corresponds to the first passes when the tool is new. During the milling process, the label of the tool passes from "0" (beginning of the process) to "4" (end of the process). Two different time-related methods are used to distribute the remaining labels. The methods are detailed for each approach in each section below.

Table 1 presents several approaches (or strategies) that we considered and evaluated in this paper. The split between train set and test set follows the k-fold cross-validation methodology [12].

Table 1. Approaches evaluated in this article

Section	Title
3.2.	Initial approach: dataset validation and baseline
3.3.	Focus on machine learning algorithms using statistical features
3.4.	Focus on stationary components of the signals
3.5.	Mixing spectrogram approach and stationary components of the signals

As the dataset contains outliners and peculiar values due to the implicit process variability, the dataset is shuffled multiple times and split into multiple folds in order to mitigate such effects. To evaluate the generalized performance of the classification model we apply a cross-validation methodology using three folds. Therefore, the ratio between training and test set is fixed to 66–33% (train and test respectively). The performance measure used to compare different classification models is the mean of F1-score, returned by the cross-validation process. The F1-score is a measure that balances the precision and recall of a classification model, providing a measure of its overall precision. The processing time of classification is not considered because it is insignificant (few milliseconds).

It is worth to notice that initially in this multi-source/experience dataset, there are some missing data in different experiences. As missing values into one data source can impact the comparison among other data sources, it has been chosen to mitigate this problem by removing those linear passes in all experiences. For instance, if at some point data values are missing for an accelerometer the whole pass is discarded and this is propagated to the other data sources. For the acoustic emission and electric current signals, the same methodology is used. Those removed passes represent around 5.5% of the whole dataset. This technique has been applied to all approaches in Table 1.

3.2 Initial Approach: Dataset Validation and Baseline

This initial approach has the goal to validate the dataset and create a baseline to be used as an initial comparison point among each data sources. The dataset is processed to extract spectrograms from the acoustic emission signal with a length of around 200 ms (39936 values). Only acoustic emission during the milling is used. Depending on the length of the pass one or two spectrograms are extracted from each milling pass. Spectrograms are converted into images and are used to train a CNN. As an image used by the CNN has a fixed size (144 px by 144 px), only the linear passes allowing them to be a multiple of the spectrogram size are used. Too short linear passes are not considered for the creation of the spectrograms. The training of the CNN in this initial approach is repeated 10 times which allows us to stabilize the learning process cross-validation.

In this initial approach, the labeling of the five classes is based on a discrete uniform distribution. In other terms, for each experience, the sequence of all passes is divided in five equal size classes. This methodology will be considered as the baseline performances achieved by analyzing an acoustic emission dataset in the following sections. In addition, we have tried to improve the model performance by forcing the learning process to diagonalize the previous multiclass classification problem, using the implicit class order ("0" > "1" > .. > "4"). This method is also known as *ordinal classification* or *ranking learning* . The idea is more in line with the final objective which is to determine the remaining life of the tool. In this case, the impact of the prediction error is greater if the prediction is further from the truth. For instance, mispredicting the class 0 (the tool is new) for a class 4 (the tool is completely burnt out) should be evaluated considerably worse than mistaking the class 0 with a class 1 (new tool vs tool slightly worn out). As explained by Gaudette and Japkowicz [8], the metrics RMSE (Root-Mean-Square Error) or MSE (Mean Square Error) perform better for this kind of classification.

3.3   Focus on Machine Learning Algorithms Using Statistical Features

This approach, decomposed in two steps, is based on the definition and usage of statistical features to investigate performance of machine learning algorithms using the different data sources. The initial step is, indeed, dedicated to exploring a wide range of machine learning algorithms and statistical features; the second step is devoted to optimizing the most promising algorithms by tweaking hyperparameters of models.

During the exploration phase, multiple classification algorithms with default parameters are compared. In this phase, the *lazypredict* library [19] is used to evaluate a wide variety of algorithms which are based on scikit-learn [20] models.

The features used by algorithms have an important impact on the model's performance. A previous project [4] using the same database provided a reliable performance to determine the level of wear of a tool. Therefore, the choice of the features is made such that to obtain at least a similar performance. In this project, we evaluated the correlation between acoustic emission and the tool wear for a set of features including: mean, std, min, max, first quartile, second quartile, third quartile. All features are extracted from the window provided by the raw signals. The data is divided into three sub-datasets (acoustic emission, accelerometers and currents) and the extraction process generates three separated data sources. Each feature sub-dataset is composed of features of each signal in the data source.

The labeling process used in this approach is also based on five classes, but the label affectation method is different. Instead of equally distributing the sequence of linear passes in the five classes, in this approach we consider that only the actual machining time affect the tool wear (when the tool is not touching the

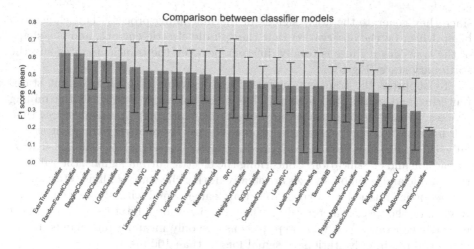

Fig. 6. Result of algorithms comparison using currents as data source

material there is no wear). Practically, the time interval between the beginning and the end of the experience is equally divided in five subintervals, and all passes occurred in a given subinterval receive the same label. This labeling method is more consistent with the tool wear profile (as presented in Sect. 3.2). This approach slightly impacts the label balancing, but it allows conserving an accurate distribution between each class.

Figure 6 presents the performance (90% confidence interval for F1-score) of different classification models using the electric current signals. On other data sources (accelerometers and acoustic emission), algorithms' performances are weaker.

Based on F1-score performance metrics, we selected the two best-performing algorithms for fine-tuning: Extra-Trees classifier and Random Forest classifier. Fine-tuning mostly consisted of hyperparameters optimization. For this second step, the data (in our case the features) used for the training is the same as for the previous step, only the hyperparameters are modified (results are presented below in the Sect. 4).

3.4   Focus on Stationary Components of the Signals

Each linear pass in the material is composed of transient phases (when the tool impacts, enters the material and when the tool gradually leaves the material) and a stationary phase (the tool is completely in the material)—as illustrated in Fig. 5. After machining signal analysis, the transient phase affects the shape of the signals by generating spikes and noise. It was chosen to exclude the transient phases and focus on the stationary components of the signals to improve the prediction performance. Accordingly, the approach presented in this section focuses on the stationary components of the signals for feature extraction. The insight behind this approach is to leave out the transient regimes of each pass since they generate the noisy signals in the machining process. This choice has been driven by the observation that the spindle electric current, and the shape of the transient regimes is totally different between the transient states and the stationary state (Fig. 5).

To suppress the transient signals, the timeframe of both transient states (entering and exiting the material) has been measured during all the milling process. We assessed that the duration of the "entering" transient is less than 150 ms and "exiting" transient is around 50 ms. By removing transient states, only the stationary part of each linear pass of the signal is kept for feature extraction and classification. Concerning the electric current signals, the values of the spindle and nonmoving axes are steady during the stable milling interval. For the acoustic emission, we expect to get a cleaner signal with stable frequencies. Regarding the accelerometer values, the vibration should be steadier as the effort is nearly constant. As a final step, to conserve only meaning full signals, it was chosen to retain only stationary signal longer than 100 ms.

3.5 Mixing Spectrogram Approach and Stationary Components of the Signals

The latest enhancement explored in this article is to use spectrograms and CNN as in [4] by improving the signal pre-processing phase (detailed in the previous sections). In this approach we intend to associate the stationary components of the signals [presented in Sect. 3.4] with the spectrogram. The idea behind this mixed approach is to quantify the impact of transient phase which impacts the acoustic emission.

Using only the stationary components of the signal means that the spectrogram duration will correspond to the new size of the signal which is around half of the length of the original signal. With this approach, the spectrogram representation does not contain the frequencies generated by the transient states of milling, which can pollute spectrograms.

The labeling method used is the same as the one applied in the stationary signals section (labeling on milling duration).

4 Results

The result section is divided into four parts, one for each approach. For all the approaches, the same dataset is used but the data sources and pre-processing change. In each section, the result is detailed with short discussion.

Initial Approach: Dataset Validation and Baseline—The F1-score achieved for this approach is 35% on five classes, which we cannot be used in the field. This result could come from the faulty acoustic data. By modifying the loss function to minimize the diagonal spread (*ordinal classification*), the result is worse with a F1-score decreasing to 25%.

Focus on Machine Learning Algorithms Using Statistical Features—The best result provides by algorithms comparison (Fig. 6) is the *ExtraTreesClassifier* with a F1-score of 62% (ex-aequo with the *RandomForestClassifier*). For other data sources, only the best algorithm score is presented. This score is achieved with the electric current signals. The second data source is the AE with a F1-score of 43%. The F1-score for the latest data source (accelerometers) is 42%. The merged data sources obtain a F1-score of 58%. By optimizing all algorithm parameters described in scikit-learn over 1000 runs with Optuna [1], the F1-score is increased up to 66% on both two top algorithms described below. Optuna is a hyperparameter optimization framework designed to automate the hyperparameter search of machine learning models. It uses efficient algorithms to explore the search space and find optimal configurations, making it an interesting tool for improving model performance.

Focus on Stationary Components of the Signals—In this approach, the same two steps methodology is followed. For the classification of all algorithms, once again the *ExtraTreesClassifier* and the *RandomForestClassifier* reach first with a F1-score of 69% with the electric current signals. For the other data sources, the merged data sources obtain a F1-score of 68%, followed by accelerometers with a F1-score of 49%. Finally, the F1-score of AE data source is 47%. The Optuna optimized F1-score for the best algorithm is then increased to 73%. The confusion matrix resulting from this optimization is shown in Fig. 7.

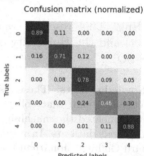

Confusion matrix (normalized)

Fig. 7. Classification performance of ExtraTreesClassifier with Optuna optimization

Mixing Spectrogram Approach and Stationary Components of the Signals—The F1-score of this approach is 38%, and it can be compared to the baseline approach. It can be established that there is no significant difference.

Based on the results presented in the section, it is evident that the spectrogram approaches did not provide satisfying results, while the approaches based on features showed promising results. By optimizing the hyperparameters of the algorithms used in these approaches, the F1-score was increased up to 66 and 73%.

5 Conclusion—Discussion

In this article, we present different approaches to predict machining tool wear in the milling process of micro-machining. This optimization process can significantly improve the milling process and reduce manufacturing costs. The objective of this article is to explore different machine learning techniques to enhance tool wear detection by measuring in-process with three different data sources (acoustic emission, accelerometers and axis currents), without interrupting the machining process.

Between three different data sources, the electrical currents of the machine perform the best. The AE dataset did not provide a reliable result in opposite to other papers. This could be due to an issue during the recording or to a noisy environment. The extra-tree algorithm and random forest algorithm provide the best results and are largely on the top during algorithm comparisons. By optimizing the hyperparameters of the extra-tree algorithm, the model has reached a F1-score of 73% on five classes.

To explain the difficulty to achieve accurate outcomes with the AE dataset, several additional machining would need to be conducted to establish if it is relevance to use this type of data. No filtering of acoustic emission or accelerometer signals has been performed to keep as much as possible of embedded information. A specific study could be interesting to determine the impact on classification performance.

Funding: This research was funded by the CHIST-ERA program (SOON project) and the University of Applied Sciences and Arts Western Switzerland (HES-SO).

Acknowledgments. These results could not have been achieved without the help of the technical team that collected the datasets (instrumented of the machine, design and implemented the machining plan), and the data analysis team that pre-processed and explored datasets. In particular, the authors want to thank Massimo De Santis, Edouard Goffinet, Jonathan Guerne and Célien Donzé.

References

1. Akiba, T., Sano, S., Yanase, T., Ohta, T., Koyama, M.: Optuna: a next-generation hyperparameter optimization framework. In: Proceedings of the 25th ACM SIGKDD International Conference on Knowledge Discovery and Data Mining (2019). https://doi.org/10.1145/3292500.3330701
2. Arslan, M., Kamal, K., Sheikh, M.F., Khan, M.A., Ratlamwala, T.A.H., Hussain, G., Alkahtani, M.: Tool health monitoring using airborne acoustic emission and convolutional neural networks: a deep learning approach. Appl. Sci. **11**(6), 2734 (2021). https://doi.org/10.3390/app11062734
3. Cao, X., Chen, B., Yao, B., Zhuang, S.: An intelligent milling tool wear monitoring methodology based on convolutional neural network with derived wavelet frames coefficient. Appl. Sci. **9**(18), 3912 (2019). https://doi.org/10.3390/app9183912
4. Carrino, S., Guerne, J., Dreyer, J., Ghorbel, H., Schorderet, A., Montavon, R.: Machining quality prediction using acoustic sensors and machine learning. Proceedings **63**(1), 31 (2020). https://doi.org/10.3390/proceedings2020063031
5. Dehen, S., Segebade, E., Gerstenmeyer, M., Zanger, F., Schulze, V.: Milling parameter and tool wear dependent surface quality in micro-milling of brass. Procedia CIRP **87**, 95–100 (2020). https://doi.org/10.1016/j.procir.2020.02.024
6. Dornfeld, D., Lee, Y., Chang, A.: Monitoring of ultraprecision machining processes. Int. J. Adv. Manuf. Technol. **21**(8), 571–578 (2003). https://doi.org/10.1007/s00170-002-1294-2

7. Dou, J., Xu, C., Jiao, S., Li, B., Zhang, J., Xu, X.: An unsupervised online monitoring method for tool wear using a sparse auto-encoder. Int. J. Adv. Manuf. Technol. **106**(5–6), 2493–2507 (2020). https://doi.org/10.1007/s00170-019-04788-7
8. Gaudette, L., Japkowicz, N.: Evaluation methods for ordinal classification. In: Gao, Y., Japkowicz, N. (eds.) Advances in Artificial Intelligence. Lecture Notes in Computer Science, vol. 5549, pp. 207–210. Springer, Berlin Heidelberg, Berlin, Heidelberg (2009). https://doi.org/10.1007/978-3-642-01818-3_25
9. Grimske, S., Kong, N., Röhlig, B., Wulfsberg, J.P.: Square foot manufacturing- a modular and mutable desktop machine tool system. Mech. Based Des. Struct. Mach. **42**(3), 386–397 (2014). https://doi.org/10.1080/15397734.2014.908728
10. Hahn, T.V., Mechefske, C.K.: Self-supervised learning for tool wear monitoring with a disentangled-variational-autoencoder. Int. J. Hydromechatron. **4**(1), 69 (2021). https://doi.org/10.1504/IJHM.2021.114174
11. Harris, K., Triantafyllopoulos, K., Stillman, E., McLeay, T.: A multivariate control chart for autocorrelated tool wear processes. Qual. Reliab. Eng. Int. **32**(6), 2093–2106 (2016). https://doi.org/10.1002/qre.2032
12. Hastie, T., Tibshirani, R., Friedman, J.: The Elements of Statistical Learning. Springer Series in Statistics, Springer, New York, New York, NY (2009). https://doi.org/10.1007/978-0-387-84858-7
13. Jain, A., Bajpai, V.: Introduction to high-speed machining (HSM). In: High Speed Machining, pp. 1–25. Elsevier (2020). https://doi.org/10.1016/B978-0-12-815020-7.00001-1
14. Kishawy, H.A., Hegab, H., Umer, U., Mohany, A.: Application of acoustic emissions in machining processes: analysis and critical review. Int. J. Adv. Manuf. Technol. **98**(5–8), 1391–1407 (2018). https://doi.org/10.1007/s00170-018-2341-y
15. Krishnakumar, P., Rameshkumar, K., Ramachandran, K.I.: Acoustic emission-based tool condition classification in a precision high-speed machining of titanium alloy: a machine learning approach. Int. J. Comput. Intell. Appl. **17**(03), 1850017 (2018). https://doi.org/10.1142/S1469026818500177
16. Krishnakumar, P., Rameshkumar, K., Ramachandran, K.: Tool wear condition prediction using vibration signals in high speed machining (HSM) of titanium (Ti-6Al-4V) alloy. Procedia Comput. Sci. **50**, 270–275 (2015). https://doi.org/10.1016/j.procs.2015.04.049
17. Lauro, C., Brandão, L., Baldo, D., Reis, R., Davim, J.: Monitoring and processing signal applied in machining processes—A review. Measurement **58**, 73–86 (2014). https://doi.org/10.1016/j.measurement.2014.08.035
18. Liu, H., Liu, Z., Jia, W., Lin, X., Zhang, S.: A novel transformer-based neural network model for tool wear estimation. Meas. Sci. Technol. **31**(6), 065106 (2020). https://doi.org/10.1088/1361-6501/ab7282
19. Pandala, S.R.: Lazy predict (2022). https://github.com/shankarpandala/lazypredict
20. Pedregosa, F., Varoquaux, G., Gramfort, A., Michel, V., Thirion, B., Grisel, O., Blondel, M., Prettenhofer, P., Weiss, R., Dubourg, V., Vanderplas, J., Passos, A., Cournapeau, D., Brucher, M., Perrot, M., Duchesnay, E.: Scikit-learn: machine learning in python. J. Mach. Learn. Res. **12**, 2825–2830 (2011)
21. Teti, R., Jemielniak, K., O'Donnell, G., Dornfeld, D.: Advanced monitoring of machining operations. CIRP Ann. **59**(2), 717–739 (2010). https://doi.org/10.1016/j.cirp.2010.05.010
22. Wulfsberg, J.P., Redlich, T., Kohrs, P.: Square foot manufacturing: a new production concept for micro manufacturing. Prod. Eng. Res. Dev. **4**(1), 75–83 (2010). https://doi.org/10.1007/s11740-009-0193-x

23. Yu, J., Liang, S., Tang, D., Liu, H.: A weighted hidden Markov model approach for continuous-state tool wear monitoring and tool life prediction. Int. J. Adv. Manuf. Technol. **91**(1–4), 201–211 (2017). https://doi.org/10.1007/s00170-016-9711-0

Digital Twins: Benefits, Applications and Development Process

Bo Nørregaard Jørgensen⬭, Daniel Anthony Howard⬭,
Christian Skafte Beck Clausen⬭, and Zheng Ma(✉)⬭

SDU Center for Energy Informatics, The Maersk Mc-Kinney Moller Institute, University of
Southern Denmark, Odense, Denmark
zma@mmmi.sdu.dk

Abstract. Digital twin technology has gained considerable traction in recent
years, with diverse applications spanning multiple sectors. However, due to the
inherent complexity and substantial costs associated with constructing digital
twins, systematic development methodologies are essential for fully capitaliz-
ing on their benefits. Therefore, this paper firstly provides an exhaustive synthesis
of related literature, highlighting: (1) ten core advantages of implementing digital
twin technology; (2) five primary domains in which digital twin applications have
been prevalently employed; and (3) ten principal objectives of digital twin applications. Subsequently, we propose a seven-step digital twin application development
process, encompassing: (i) Digital Twin Purposing; (ii) Digital Twin Scoping; (iii)
Physical Twin Modeling; (iv) Calibration and Validation; (v) Application Logic
Development; (vi) External System Integration; and (vii) Deployment and Operation. This structured approach aims to demystify the intrinsic complexity of
twinned systems, ensuring that the deployment of digital twin-based solutions
effectively addresses the target problem while maximizing the derived benefits.

Keywords: Digital twin · Physical twin · Twinning · Applications · Benefit ·
Purpose · Development process

1 Introduction

The concept of a digital twin is not new. The underpinning idea was first introduced in
David Gelernter's book Mirror Worlds in 1991 [1]. However, it is first two decades later,
at a Society of Manufacturing Engineers conference in Troy, Michigan, in 2002, that Dr.
Michael Grieves is credited with first publicly introducing the concept [2]. However, even
though the concept emerged as early as 2002, the first practical definition is considered
to originate from NASA, ten years later, in an attempt to improve the physical-model
simulation of spacecraft, defined it as: "*A Digital Twin is an integrated multi-physics,
multiscale, probabilistic simulation of an as-built vehicle or system that uses the best
available physical models, sensor updates, fleet history, etc., to mirror the life of its
corresponding flying twin* "[3].

Despite its early emergence in the 1990s and subsequent evolution throughout the
2000s, it is essential to understand the fundamental concept of a digital twin and what

© The Author(s), under exclusive license to Springer Nature Switzerland AG 2023
N. Moniz et al. (Eds.): EPIA 2023, LNAI 14116, pp. 511–522, 2023.
https://doi.org/10.1007/978-3-031-49011-8_40

problems it can help to solve before delving into the development of digital twin applications. In recent literature, the digital twin concept has evolved to be generally understood as a digital representation of a real-world object, process, or system [4]. The real-world counterpart of a digital twin is referred to as its physical twin. Examples of physical twins include jet engines, wind turbines, buildings, factories, and cities. The purpose of a digital twin is to serve as an indistinguishable digital representation that accurately reflects its physical twin's observed structure, state, and behavior at a specified fidelity and frequency. Hence, a digital twin simulates the resulting state of the movements, forces, environment-to-system, and system-to-system interactions that the physical twin experience in the physical world.

The development of digital twin applications is generally motivated by the purpose of helping solve problems that are currently underserved by existing technologies. The problems that digital twin applications typically can help to solve involve some level of reflection over a physical twin's past, current, and future states. Such problems typically relate to performance monitoring, process optimization, system maintenance, state estimation, scenario analysis, and similar purposes. Digital twins are, therefore, often used to model, understand, and analyze complex systems where the system's performance, reliability, and safety concerns are critical. In a digital twin application, a physical twin is being observed in the physical world by instrumenting its environment with various sensors that collect data about different operation aspects, such as temperature, pressure, vibration, duration, acceleration, velocity, weight, and more, as illustrated in Fig. 1. This data is then used to update the digital twin's model of the physical twin. The digital twin application can store the collected data for keeping a historical record, use it to reflect upon the current and future state of the physical twin, and intervene in the operation of the physical twin if necessary.

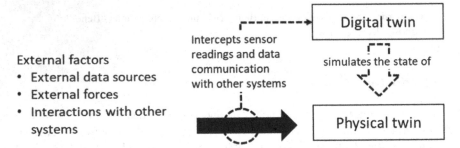

Fig. 1. Conceptual model of the relation between a digital twin and its physical twin.

Due to the intrinsic complexity of the systems being twinned, the twinning process is a costly undertaking requiring significant effort and time. To ensure this effort is worthwhile the benefits of applying a digital twin-based approach to the problem at hand must be properly investigated and understood. Hence, there is a need for establishing systematic development methodologies before the benefits of adopting digital twin-based applications can be fully explored across the different sectors of society.

In this paper, we first review the benefits of digital twins and their applications in different domains, and then we address the unmet challenges of providing a best practice development methodology for digital twin applications [4], by outlining the steps of a development process that have successfully applied across several application domains.

2 Benefits of Digital Twins

Many companies have started to create digital twins for their products, processes, and systems because of the many benefits digital twins are promised to provide. Data collected from existing products and production processes allow digital twins to effectively identify systemic deficiencies, optimize processes, improve quality, and reduce cost. Furthermore, a digital twin can use the same data to lower the environmental footprint and production cost by co-optimizing the design of the following product generation together with its production processes. In the virtual environment provided by digital twins, engineers can effectively simulate real-world conditions, analyze what-if scenarios under any circumstances imaginable, and visualize the outcomes. Hence, digital twins help engineers to analyze and predict a physical twin's performance under different operation conditions. As a result of this, helps engineers to understand the past, view present conditions, and prevent future problems. In short, digital twinning provide improved situation awareness, optimizes decision-making, supports planning, and effective implementation of actions. Based on the statements in the literature, ten primary benefits associated with the implementation of digital twin technology can be summarized:

Efficiency enhancements: Digital twin frameworks can substantially reduce the effort required to perform specific tasks, with up to 50% reduction in certain cases [5]. Moreover, they contribute to a decrease in downtime for manufacturing systems. For instance, employing digital twins for grinding wheels results in a 14.4% increase in energy and resource efficiency, thus promoting sustainable manufacturing processes [6].

Increased adaptability: Digital twins facilitate small size production, catering to individual customer needs and requirements [7]. Furthermore, they enable shorter production cycles through the implementation of smart manufacturing systems, resulting in agile and efficient operations [8].

Superior scheduling and decision-making: The bi-level dynamic scheduling architecture, based on service unit digital twin agents, promotes more effective scheduling practices [9]. By providing real-time monitoring, simulation, and decision-aid systems, digital twins support production operations, predictive maintenance, and strategic planning initiatives [10, 11].

Process optimization and resource management: The integration of digital twin technology within remanufacturing processes leads to optimization and improvements in resource recycling [6, 10]. Additionally, digital twins streamline inventory management within physical internet hubs, enhancing operational efficiency [12].

Autonomous manufacturing capabilities: Digital twin frameworks, such as data– and knowledge-driven models for digital twin manufacturing cells, foster intelligent perception, simulation, understanding, prediction, optimization, and control strategies that support autonomous manufacturing processes [13].

Advanced monitoring and control: Digital twins enable real-time monitoring of maintenance, product quality, resource utilization, and overall efficiency [14]. Consequently, this technology contributes to improved fleet management [15] and smart building management practices [16].

Competitive edge and innovation: The adoption of digital twins equips enterprises with innovative technologies that bolster their market position, enhance product quality, and improve operational efficiency [8, 17].

Sophisticated simulation and training: The use of digital twins in generating realistic simulations for training purposes enriches the learning experience and reduces associated costs, thereby offering a more effective approach to skill development [18].

Secure and reliable data management: The integration of blockchain technology within digital twin systems ensures robust data integrity and security, safeguarding valuable information across various industries [19, 20].

Customized production and sustainable business models: Combining digital twins, blockchain, and additive manufacturing empowers organizations to adopt a customer-centric production paradigm [19]. The utilization of digital twin platform networks enables the development of sustainable business models that encompass economic, social, and environmental benefits [6, 7, 17].

3 Digital Twin Applications

Digital twin technology has experienced rapid adoption across a diverse range of industries, transforming processes and systems with innovative, data-driven solutions. The domains which have popularly applied digital twin technology are manufacturing, energy, buildings, smart cities, logistics and supply chains.

In manufacturing, digital twin technology has been applied across various sub-domains, e.g., equipment design [21], manufacturing resource recommendation [22], personalized production [19], manufacturing processes [23], and additive manufacturing [24]. Digital twins are employed for purposes of monitoring [25], simulation [26], analysis [27], control [28], optimization [21], defect detection [7], automation [29], and continuous improvement [26]. They play a crucial role in Industry 4.0 development, contributing to robustness, resilience, self-adaptation, real-time analysis, and product detection.

In the energy sector, digital twin technology has been applied, e.g., electricity distribution networks [30], planning [31], and consumption management [32], etc. Digital twins have been applied to enhance the efficiency [33], optimization [34] and control [35], facilitate monitoring [32], prediction [36], device health maintenance [30], real-time interaction [31], co-simulation and system performance validation [37].

In the building industry, Digital twin technology provides innovative solutions across various sub-domains. It helps stakeholders make better decisions, improve building performance, and facilitate efficient management of building assets. Applications include building embodied carbon estimation [38], building automation, energy efficiency and occupant comfort [39], and building maintenance [40].

In smart cities, digital twin technology has been applied across various sub-domains, including infrastructure [41], healthcare services [42], urban landscape management

[43], and facility venue management [44]. Each sub-domain leverages digital twins for specific purposes, e.g., monitoring [45], prediction, optimization and control [41], data analysis [42], visualization [43], security [46], and policy development [41], contributing to more efficient, sustainable, and livable urban environments.

Furthermore, digital twin technology has made significant strides in logistics and supply chains, enabling new approaches to monitoring, control, integration, and optimization. These advancements have improved the resilience, efficiency, and sustainability of various sub-domains. Applications include supply chain control [47], production logistics [48], city logistics [45], and supply chain optimization [49].

4 Digital Twin Application Development

A digital twin application is, in essence, a software system that uses real-world data and digital models to predict how a physical twin will perform. To do so, it integrates IoT, Big Data, and AI technologies. IoT and Big Data technologies are used for collecting relevant data about the physical twin's operational environment, and AI technologies are used to analyze the current and predict the future states of the physical twin. The choice of specific technologies depends on the application domain where the digital twin will be used.

A conceptual architectural model of a digital twin application with its constituent elements is shown in Fig. 2. These constituent elements form a recurring architectural pattern that can be observed for the development of digital twin applications across multiple domains.

The development of digital twin applications is a complex and multi-disciplinary effort, involving experts from multiple fields, including engineering, computer science, data science, and domain-specific experts. To support the effective development of digital twin applications the development process has to be divided into a number of steps. The decomposition of the development process into separate steps can be done in different ways and will typically reflect the methodologies of the engineering disciplines taking part in the digital twin development. Based on the authors' observations from several industrial digital twin R&D projects [50, 51], mechanical engineers, data scientists, and software engineers have different perspectives on how to decompose the development of a digital twin. The steps proposed in this paper are based on the authors' practical experience from these R&D projects and are illustrated in Fig. 3.

Digital twin purposing: The first thing to address when starting a digital twin development project is to clearly define the purpose of the digital twin application. What unmet need will the digital twin application fulfill, that cannot simply be fulfilled by using existing technologies. Is a digital twin the right solution; that is, is a digital replica of the physical twin essential to solve the problem at hand. What additional benefits does a digital twin bring that cannot be achieved by existing technologies. How are these benefits assessed and evaluated, and will the expected benefits justify the development cost. First when these concerns have been considered a digital twin development project should be initiated.

Digital twin scoping: The next step is to determine the scope of the digital twin. The scope is defined by the boundary of the real-world object, process, or system being

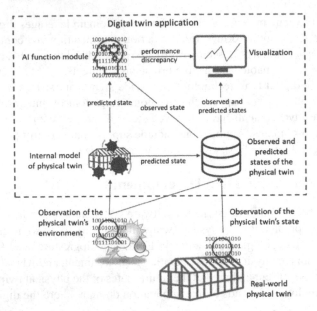

Fig. 2. Example of a digital twin application for continuous energy performance monitoring of a commercial greenhouse.

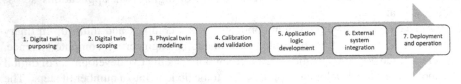

Fig. 3. Steps in the development of digital twin applications.

twinned, and the purpose of developing the digital twin application. Ignoring the importance of correct scoping may lead to undersized or oversized digital twins. That is, the digital twin level of details does not match the required model fidelity for the problem at hand. For instance, if the purpose is to predict the remaining lifetime of a single fan in a building's ventilation system, the scope is defined by the boundary of the mechanic fan and the process parameters affecting the fan's operation conditions. It is therefore not necessary to do detailed twinning of the whole building to meet the purpose of the digital twin application. Due to the natural boundaries of the real-world object, process, or system being twinned, digital twins typically materialize at one of three levels: component, unit, and system. Each of these levels is described in Table 1 based on their general definitions in dictionaries of the English language.

Depending on the application, digital twins can be created as hierarchical architectures that a higher-level digital twin is created by composing digital twins at the lower level, or they can be constructed as monolithic architecture at the respective level.

Table 1. Scope of digital twins.

Component	A component is a constituting functional part or element of a larger whole, especially a part of a machine or vehicle. For example, the fan in a ventilator unit or a joint in a robot arm
Unit	A unit is a single whole part of a system. For example, the ventilator unit in a building's ventilation system or a single robot in a manufacturing production line
System	A system is a group of interacting or interrelated elements that act according to a set of rules to form a unified whole. Hence, a system defines a way of working, organizing, or doing something which follows a fixed plan or set of rules. A system, surrounded and influenced by its environment, is described by its boundaries, structure and purpose and is expressed in its functioning. For example, the ventilation system in a building or a manufacturing production line

Physical twin modeling: This step focuses on creating the digital twin's internal model of the physical twin. The internal model captures the behavior, attributes, and relationships of the physical twin. This model can either be created using a specification-driven or data-driven approach. A specification-driven approach uses relevant design specifications to create a white–or grey-box model of the physical twin, whereas a data-driven approach creates a black-box model based on historical data collected from the physical twin and its environment. White–and grey-box modeling require detailed design specifications of the physical twin, whereas black-box modeling requires big data for the external factors influencing the physical twin and the behavioral response of the physical twin to these external factors. Depending on the application domain such big data can be a large dataset for the production cycles of a product in a manufacturing line, or it can be a large dataset spanning multiple years of data collection, in the case where the behavior of the physical twin depends on external factors such as seasonal weather changes. The latter is for instance the case for digital twins of wind turbines [52], photovoltaic [53], buildings [51], and greenhouses [54–56]. White–and grey-box modeling is typically used when the available data for a physical twin is insufficient to create a black-box model, and black-box modeling is used when the available design specifications are insufficient but there is sufficient data. Deciding on the modeling approach; white box, grey box, or black box, depends on what design specifications and data are and will be available. Making this decision requires identifying the information and data sources, including sensors, control systems, and other sources of information, available for creating the digital twin's internal model of the physical twin. It is the authors' experience that stakeholders often overestimate what design specification and data they have. Hence, the choice of modeling method should not be prematurely decided before the availability of design specifications and data have been properly investigated.

Calibration and validation: The digital twin must be calibrated and validated to ensure that it accurately represents the behavior of the physical twin. Calibration is the process of fine-tuning the digital twin's model parameters to closely match the behavior of the physical twin. It involves adjusting the parameters within the model based on the data collected from the physical twin and its environment. For example, if the digital twin of a greenhouse predicts its energy consumption to be higher than the actual consumption, the model parameters need to be adjusted to better align with the real-world data. This process may require multiple iterations to achieve a satisfactory level of accuracy. After the calibration process, validation is carried out to ensure that the digital twin's model can accurately predict the behavior of the physical twin under various conditions. Validation is done by comparing the digital twin's predictions to independent real-world data that was not used during the calibration process. If the model's predictions closely align with the actual performance of the physical twin, it is considered to be a valid representation of the physical twin.

Application logic development: Developing the logic of a digital twin application requires the creation of an AI function module that encapsulates the application logic required to fulfill its intended purpose. The AI function module leverages the internal digital model of the physical twin, which serves as the foundation for implementing various AI methods. These methods can include statistical analysis, machine learning, deep learning, or agent-based simulation, among others [57]. The selection of an appropriate AI method for implementing the AI function module depends on the specific purpose of the digital twin's development. Different applications may benefit from distinct state-of-the-art methodologies that are best suited to address special challenges and requirements of their use cases. For instance, a digital twin developed for predictive maintenance might employ machine learning algorithms to identify patterns and anomalies in the sensor data, thereby enabling the early detection of potential equipment failures. On the other hand, a digital twin for simulating the effect of electric vehicle charging on the stability of the electricity grid will benefit from agent-based simulation, wherein individual agents represent diverse entities that interact and adapt according to a set of predefined rules. Moreover, it is essential to consider the type and volume of data available for training and validation when selecting an appropriate AI method for the AI function module. While some approaches may require large datasets to deliver accurate predictions, others might be more suitable for scenarios with limited data availability or noisy data. In addition to the AI function module, most digital twin applications include a visualization component that shows relevant information about the physical twin's historical, current, and predicted future state. This visualization component provides actionable insights and supports decision-making.

External system integration: To achieve a successful integration of the digital twin application in its deployment environment, it is important to comply with de jure and de facto standards that can ensure interoperability between the digital twin and existing systems, such as PLC (Programmable Logic Controller), SCADA systems (Supervisory control and data acquisition), IoT and Cloud platforms. These standards facilitate consistent data exchange and communication protocols, enabling the digital twin to access and process real-time data from diverse sources without compatibility issues. Such standards can be industry-specific or based on general-purpose protocols, such as OPC UA (Open Platform Communications Unified Architecture) and MQTT (Message Queuing Telemetry Transport), which are widely employed in the Internet of Things (IoT) domain.

Deployment and operation: Once a digital twin has been created and deployed in an application, it must be continuously monitored and validated to ensure that it remains accurate. Continuous validation is required as the physical twin may change, such as wear and tear, modifications, replacements of components, or updates of its control logic. These alterations can impact the system's performance and behavior, rendering the digital twin's current model of the physical twin potentially outdated. It is therefore necessary to regularly assess the digital twin's accuracy in representing the physical twin, taking into account any changes that have occurred. When discrepancies are identified, the digital twin's model parameters and algorithms must be updated to reflect the new state of the physical twin.

5 Conclusions

The use of digital twins provides promising benefits in many application domains. Digital twins enable better planning, decision-making, and situation awareness by modeling and analyzing the past, present, and future states of physical systems across various industries, such as manufacturing, energy, buildings, smart cities, and logistics. Still, being an emerging technology, its successful adoption requires the development of methodologies that enable best practices of architectural principles and software technological advances to be shared across domains. This paper presented a conceptual architectural model and development process based on the authors' own experience from various industrial R&D projects. Future work will explore the architectural model and development process in greater detail to identify commonalities and variabilities related to the application of digital twins in different domains.

Acknowledgments. The work presented in this paper is part of the Greenhouse Industry 4.0 project, funded by the Danish Energy Agency (EUDP, Project no 64019–0018) and part of the IEA IETS Annex Task XVIII: Digitalization, Artificial Intelligence and Related Technologies for Energy Efficiency and GHG Emissions Reduction in Industry project, funded by EUDP (project number: 134–21010).

References

1. Gelernter, D.: Mirror worlds—or the day software puts the universe in a shoehox. (1991)
2. Grieves, M.W.: Virtually intelligent product systems: digital and physical twins. In: Complex systems engineering: theory and practice, pp. 175–200. American Institute of Aeronautics and Astronautics, Inc (2002)
3. Glaessgen, E., Stargel, D.: The digital twin paradigm for future NASA and US Air Force vehicles. In: 53rd AIAA/ASME/ASCE/AHS/ASC structures, structural dynamics and materials conference 20th AIAA/ASME/AHS adaptive structures conference 2012
4. Semeraro, C., et al.: Digital twin paradigm: A systematic literature review. Comput. Ind. **130**, 103469 (2021)
5. Lehner, D., et al.: AML4DT: A model-driven framework for developing and maintaining digital twins with automation ML. In: 2021 26th IEEE international conference on emerging technologies and factory automation (ETFA). pp. 1–8 (2021)

6. Kannan, K., Arunachalam, N.: A digital twin for grinding wheel: an information sharing platform for sustainable grinding process. J. Manuf. Sci. Eng.-Trans. ASME **141**, 14 (2019)
7. Warke, V., et al.: Sustainable development of smart manufacturing driven by the digital twin framework: a statistical analysis. Sustainability **13**, 49 (2021)
8. Mudassar, R., et al.: Digital twin-based smart manufacturing system for project-based organizations: A conceptual framework. In: Proceedings of international conference on computers and industrial engineering, CIE. Wuhan, China (2019)
9. Zhang, J., et al.: Bi-level dynamic scheduling architecture based on service unit digital twin agents. J. Manuf. Syst. **60**, 59–79 (2021)
10. Lim, K.Y.H., et al.: Digital twin architecture and development trends on manufacturing topologies. In: Intelligent systems reference library, pp. 259–286. Singapore (2021)
11. Süve, M.F., et al.: Predictive maintenance framework for production environments using digital twin. In: Lecture notes in networks and systems. Istanbul, Turkey (2022)
12. Leung, E.K.H., Lee, C.K.H., Ouyang, Z.: From traditional warehouses to Physical Internet hubs: A digital twin-based inbound synchronization framework for PI-order management. Int. J. Prod. Econ., **244**, (2022)
13. Zhang, C., et al.: A data- and knowledge-driven framework for digital twin manufacturing cell. In: 11th CIRP conference on industrial product-service systems. Elsevier, Xian, Peoples R China (2019)
14. Rafsanjani, H.N., Nabizadeh, A.H.: Towards digital architecture, engineering, and construction (AEC) industry through virtual design and construction (VDC) and digital twin. Energy Built Environ., (2021)
15. Renaud, G., Liao, M., Bombardier, Y.: Demonstration of an airframe digital twin framework using a CF-188 full-scale component test. Lect. Notes Mech. Eng., 176–186 (2020)
16. Chevallier, Z., Finance, B., Boulakia, B.C.: A reference architecture for smart building digital twin. In: CEUR workshop proceedings. Nanterre, France (2020)
17. Li, X., et al.: Sustainable business model based on digital twin platform network: the inspiration from Haier's case study in China. Sustainability **12**, 26 (2020)
18. Camacho, F.D., et al.: Validation through a digital twin of a Stewart platform with irregular geometry with 6 DOF for simulation of a transport vehicle. In: 16th IEEE international conference on automation science and engineering (CASE). IEEE, Sangolqui, Ecuador (2020)
19. Guo, D.Q., et al.: A framework for personalized production based on digital twin, blockchain and additive manufacturing in the context of Industry 4.0. In: 16th IEEE international conference on automation science and engineering (CASE). IEEE, Guangdong, Peoples R China (2020)
20. Khan, A., et al.: Toward smart manufacturing using spiral digital twin framework and twinchain. IEEE Trans. Industr. Inf. **18**, 1359–1366 (2022)
21. Mourtzis, D., et al.: Equipment design optimization based on digital twin under the framework of zero-defect manufacturing. In: 2nd international conference on industry 4.0 and smart manufacturing (ISM). Elsevier Science Bv, Rion, Greece (2020)
22. Li, X.X., et al.: Framework for manufacturing-tasks semantic modelling and manufacturing-resource recommendation for digital twin shop-floor. J. Manuf. Syst. **58**, 281–292 (2021)
23. Deac, G.C., et al.: Machine vision inmanufacturing processes and the digital twin ofmanufacturing architectures. In: Annals of DAAAM and proceedings of the international daaam symposium. (2017)
24. Scime, L., Singh, A., Paquit, V.: A scalable digital platform for the use of digital twins in additive manufacturing. Manuf. Lett., (2021)
25. Qamsane, Y., et al.: A unified digital twin framework for real-time monitoring and evaluation of smart manufacturing systems. In: 15th IEEE international conference on automation science and engineering (IEEE CASE). IEEE, USA (2019)

26. Friederich, J., et al.: A framework for data-driven digital twins for smart manufacturing. Comput. Ind., **136**, (2022)
27. Gopalakrishnan, S., Hartman, N.W., Sangid, M.D.: Model-based feature information network (MFIN): A digital twin framework to integrate location-specific material behavior within component design, manufacturing, and performance analysis. Integr. Mater. Manuf. Innov. **9**, 394–409 (2020)
28. Nie, Q.W., et al.: A multi-agent and internet of things framework of digital twin for optimized manufacturing control. Int. J. Comput. Integr. Manuf., 22
29. Göppert, A., et al.: Pipeline for ontology-based modeling and automated deployment of digital twins for planning and control of manufacturing systems. J. Intell. Manuf., (2021)
30. Zhang, G., et al.: An architecture based on digital twins for smart power distribution system. In: 2020 3rd international conference on artificial intelligence and big data (ICAIBD). pp. 29–33 (2020)
31. Niu, W., et al.: Power grid planning framework and application prospects based on digital twin. In: The 10th renewable power generation conference (RPG 2021). pp. 672–677 (2021)
32. Zhang, M., et al.: Equipment energy consumption management in digital twin shop-floor: a framework and potential applications. In: 15th IEEE international conference on networking, sensing and control (ICNSC). IEEE, Beijing, Peoples R China (2018)
33. Aliyu, H.O., et al.: Digital twin framework for holistic and prognostic analysis of the Nigerian electricity supply industry: A proposal. In: 5th IEEE annual international conference on information communications technology and society (ICTAS). IEEE, Minna, Nigeria (2021)
34. Yu, Q., et al.: Research of digital twin in power system optimization-take offshore platform for example. In: IET conference publications. Beijing, China (2020)
35. Wu, J., et al.: Research and design of a digital twin-based enterprise architecture digital control platform for provincial electrical power company. In: 2021 6th international conference on control, robotics and cybernetics (CRC). (2021)
36. Zhang, H., et al.: Hybrid data-physics based digital twin modeling framework for the power system of bobsleigh and tobogganing venue for Beijing winter Olympics. In: 2021 6th international conference on power and renewable energy (ICPRE). (2021)
37. Perabo, F., et al.: Digital twin modelling of ship power and propulsion systems: application of the open simulation platform (OSP). In: IEEE 29th international symposium on industrial electronics (ISIE). IEEE, Trondheim, Norway (2020)
38. Chen, C., et al.: A conceptual framework for estimating building embodied carbon based on digital twin technology and life cycle assessment. Sustainability **13**, (2021)
39. Clausen, A., et al.: A digital twin framework for improving energy efficiency and occupant comfort in public and commercial buildings. Energy Inform., **4**, (2021)
40. Wang, W., et al.: Digital twin-based framework for green building maintenance system. In: 2020 IEEE international conference on industrial engineering and engineering management (IEEM). pp. 1301–1305 (2020)
41. Raes, L., et al.: DUET: A framework for building secure and trusted digital twins of smart cities. IEEE Internet Comput., 1 (2021)
42. Laamarti, F., et al.: An ISO/IEEE 11073 standardized digital twin framework for health and well-being in smart cities. IEEE Access **8**, 105950–105961 (2020)
43. Ruohomaki, T., et al.: Smart city platform enabling digital twin. In: 9th international conference on intelligent systems (IS), pp. 155–161. IEEE, Helsinki, Finland (2018)
44. Meta, I., et al.: The camp nou stadium as a testbed for city physiology: a modular framework for urban digital twins. Complexity, **2021**. (2021)
45. Belfadel, A., et al.: Towards a digital twin framework for adaptive last mile city logistics. In: 2021 6th international conference on smart and sustainable technologies (SpliTech). pp. 1–6 (2021)

46. El Azzaoui, A., et al.: Blockchain-based secure digital twin framework for smart healthy city. Lect. Notes Electr. Eng. **716**, 107–113 (2021)
47. Park, K.T., Son, Y.H., Noh, S.D.: The architectural framework of a cyber physical logistics system for digital-twin-based supply chain control. Int. J. Prod. Res. **59**, 5721–5742 (2021)
48. Pan, Y.H., et al.: Digital twin based real-time production logistics synchronization system in a multi-level computing architecture. J. Manuf. Syst. **58**, 246–260 (2021)
49. Marmolejo-Saucedo, J.A.: Digital twin framework for large-scale optimization problems in supply chains: a case of packing problem. Mob. Netw. & Appl., 17
50. Howard, D.A., et al.: Greenhouse industry 4.0—digital twin technology for commercial greenhouses. Energy Inform., **4**(2), 37 (2021)
51. Clausen, A., et al.: A digital twin framework for improving energy efficiency and occupant comfort in public and commercial buildings. Energy Inform. **4**(2), 40 (2021)
52. Sørensen, J.V., Ma, Z., Jørgensen, B.N.: Potentials of game engines for wind power digital twin development: an investigation of the Unreal Engine. Energy Inform. **5**(4), 39 (2022)
53. Clausen, C.S.B., Ma, Z.G., Jørgensen, B.N.: Can we benefit from game engines to develop digital twins for planning the deployment of photovoltaics? Energy Inform. **5**(4), 42 (2022)
54. Howard, D.A., Ma, Z., Jørgensen, B.N.: Digital twin framework for energy efficient greenhouse industry 4.0. in ambient intelligence—Software and applications. 2021. Springer International Publishing, Cham (2021)
55. Howard, D.A., Ma, Z., Jørgensen, B.N.: A case study of digital twin for greenhouse horticulture production flow. In: 2022 IEEE 2nd international conference on digital twins and parallel intelligence (DTPI). (2022)
56. Howard, D.A., et al.: Data architecture for digital twin of commercial greenhouse production. In: 2020 RIVF international conference on computing and communication technologies (RIVF). (2020)
57. Værbak, M., et al.: Agent-based modelling of demand-side flexibility adoption in reservoir pumping. In: 2019 IEEE sciences and humanities international research conference (SHIRCON). (2019)

Using Deep Learning for Building Stock Classification in Seismic Risk Analysis

Jorge Lopes[1], Feliz Gouveia[1,2], Vítor Silva[1,3], Rui S. Moreira[1,2(✉)],
José M. Torres[1,2], Maria Guerreiro[1], and Luís Paulo Reis[2]

[1] IRIS, University Fernando Pessoa, Porto, Portugal
{jorge.lopes,fribeiro,vsilva,rmoreira,jtorres,mariajoao}@ufp.edu.pt,
vsilva@ua.pt
[2] LIACC, Porto University, Porto, Portugal
lpreis@fe.up.pt
[3] University of Aveiro, Aveiro, Portugal

Abstract. In the last decades most efforts to catalog and characterize the built environment for multi-hazard risk assessment have focused
on the exploration of census data, cadastral datasets, and local surveys.
The first approach is only updated every 10 years and does not provide
building locations, the second type of data is only available for restricted
urban centers, and the third approach requires surveyors with an engineering background, which is cost-prohibitive for large-scale risk studies.
It is thus clear that methods to characterize the built environment for
large-scale risk analysis at the asset level are currently missing, which
hampers the assessment of the impact of natural hazards for the purposes of risk management. Some recent efforts have demonstrated how
deep learning algorithms can be trained to recognize specific architectural and structural features of buildings, which is needed for earthquake risk analysis. In this paper we describe how convolutional neural
networks can be combined with data from OpenStreetMap and Google
Street View to help develop exposure models for multi-hazard risk analysis. This project produced an original comprehensively annotated (15
characteristics) dataset of approximately 5000 images of buildings from
the parish of Alvalade (Lisbon, Portugal). The dataset was used to train
and test different deep learning networks for building exposure models. The best results were obtained with ResNet50V2, InceptionV3 and
DenseNet201, all with accuracies above 82%. These results will support
future developments for assessing exposure models for seismic risk analysis. The novelty of our work consists in the number of characteristics of
the images in the dataset, the number of deep learning models trained
and the number of classes that can be used for building exposure models.

Keywords: Deep Learning · Convolutional Neural Networks ·
Computer Vision · Building Exposure Models · Seismic Risk Analysis

Supported by FCT under grant EXPL/ECI-EGC/1555/2021.

N. Moniz et al. (Eds.): EPIA 2023, LNAI 14116, pp. 523–534, 2023.
https://doi.org/10.1007/978-3-031-49011-8_41

1   Introduction

Due to the increase in the global population, rapid urbanization and climate change, the impact caused by natural hazards has increased considerably. The assessment, and eventual mitigation, of risk due to hazards requires reliable exposure models. Ideally, these models comprise information considering the geographical location, value, occupants and structural characteristics of buildings and infrastructure. In Portugal, the recognition of the importance of exposure models has propelled several efforts at the national and urban scale to characterize the built environment. The national housing census coordinated by the National Statistics Institute collects every 10 years information concerning the number of residential buildings classified according to the main construction material, number of storeys, age of construction and state of conservation.

Exposure data from the housing census has the advantage of having a national coverage, but the spatial resolution renders the data inadequate for the assessment of the impact from localized hazards such as floods or landslides. On the other hand, cadastral data is often collected at the building level, but it is only available for limited areas and neglects vulnerability-related attributes such as the main construction technology or presence of structural deficiencies. This lack of detailed information concerning the built environment prevents the assessment of the potential for damage, economic losses and fatalities, which could support the development of disaster risk management measures. Similarly, this scarcity of data hinders the rapid assessment of the impact shortly after the occurrence of natural or anthropogenic hazards.

For the particular case of Portugal, the evaluation of the impact from natural hazards is based on observations and damage data usually reported weeks or months after the occurrence of the event, thus affecting the strategic allocation of human resources, or the early release of financial aid to support recovery. For the assessment of the impact of natural hazards in the built environment, in addition to an exposure dataset, one hazard model (describing the expected frequency and severity of the hazard intensities in the region of interest) and a set of vulnerability functions (describing the probability of damage or loss conditional on a hazard intensity) are necessary. For the particular case of earthquake hazard, dozens of models have been created in the last decades (e.g., [14,15]), with varying levels of reliability. According to [18], the frequency and size of earthquakes (seismic hazard), the inventory of people and infrastructure (exposure), and the capacity of buildings to handle earthquake loading, can determine the number of people affected as well as the economic losses for a given earthquake (vulnerability). Focusing on the exposure model, which is an overview of all the assets in the region under study, its development is not trivial, particularly in regions like emerging nations where data is not consistently gathered by government organizations. For instance, when examining certain regions, data from local surveys, housing census records, or even cadastral datasets may be used to obtain information on building characteristics (when they exist). But as the area gets bigger, it also gets more expensive and time-consuming to carry out these tasks.

It is thus clear that adopting traditional approaches for the characterization of the built environment for risk assessment is impractical at the national or regional scale. To achieve such a milestone, it is fundamental to rely on recent advancements concerning crowdsourcing, satellite imagery, big data and artificial intelligence. One example of a growing source of building information is the OpenStreetMap (OSM) initiative, an editable map of the world containing information contributed by volunteers. OSM is usually limited to the building footprint and main use, but it has reasonable coverage for most urban centers. Satellite imagery released in the last decade has also achieved a level of spatial resolution that allows identifying exposure attributes, such as the height of buildings and major structures [12]. In this context, the European Joint Research Centre has released a digital elevation model for all European capitals with a high resolution. Finally, the well-known Google Street View (GSV) service allows users to explore and visualize building imagery even in rural areas.

While none of these sources of information alone are sufficient to develop a reliable and comprehensive exposure model, their main features can be combined through an artificial intelligence framework to create digital models of entire regions for the purposes of disaster risk reduction. The work presented in this article consisted of collecting and organizing data, using OSM and GSV, with the aim of training deep learning models to support the seismic risk analysis process (exposure models). Our dataset is comprehensively annotated with 15 building characteristics. We describe how the dataset was built, and then the processing steps to train the models. After training and comparing the algorithms' inference results, the resulting exposure model will be used to estimate the impact of an earthquake scenario, and the obtained results compared with the impact calculated using the ground truth data. We compare the performance of the deep learning models used in the experiments, and propose further organization of the dataset to allow for a more fine-grained analysis of the building stock.

2 Related Work

There has been an increasing interest in using Google Street View imagery and deep learning to perform several studies, including estimating building age [11], detecting building façades with graffiti artwork [13], urban frontage classification [10], visual screening of soft-story buildings [23], classification of building's utility classes [9] and seismic damage prediction [2]. There has also been some recent work concerning the prediction of building characteristics, such as construction material and age, which are of direct concern to our work, and which are presented in the next sections.

2.1 Building Classification

Yu et al. [22] used GSV images and deep learning to identify soft-story buildings at the regional level. They tested four models reaching an accuracy above 80%. The authors discuss the limitations of GSV imagery to detect soft-story buildings, for example the fact that images show only one façade, not revealing if there is a garage's door in the back, and propose solutions to merge classifications from multiple views. Kang et al. [8] proposed to use deep learning to classify façades from GSV images, both at regional and city scale. The authors retrieved, for several cities in Canada and the U.S., the building footprints and their geographic locations from online mapping systems, such as OpenStreetMap. Using the associated coordinates (latitude, longitude), the authors downloaded the corresponding façade images from GSV using an image size and pitch value defined as 512×512 pixels and $10\,°C$, respectively.

Due to the uncontrolled quality of street view images, many of them can not be directly used for the building classification. For example, some of the images are taken inside the building and others have the building façade occluded by vehicles and trees. The authors removed those outliers using the VGG16 model [19] trained on the Places2 dataset [24]. This process resulted in a dataset with 19,658 street view images from eight classes: apartment, church, garage, house, industrial, office building, retail and roof, each with approximately 2500 images, resulting in a balanced dataset.

The authors chose to fine-tune all the convolutional layers of pre-trained CNNs on a large dataset, such as ImageNet. They used AlexNet, VGG16, ResNet18 and ResNet34. Overall, the architecture with the worst classification performance was AlexNet and the best was VGG16 with an F1-Score of 0.53 and 0.58, respectively. They experienced overfitting behavior in both ResNet architectures, possibly due to the large number of parameters.

2.2   Creating Exposure Models

Pelizari [1] created a reference dataset for Santiago (Chile's capital), a city prone to earthquakes, used to train deep convolutional neural networks to predict risk-oriented seismic building structural type (SBST) and to individually estimate the lateral load resisting system (LLRS) material and the height of buildings. In order to categorize building exposure in a standardized manner, the authors used the GEM's GED4ALL taxonomy [4], an adaptation for multi-hazard risk analysis [17]. The goal was to train models to enable the classification of structural features of buildings for large-area seismic risk assessments. The authors obtained the building information and geo-location from the property cadastral data of the chilean Internal Revenue Service and the Ministry of Housing and Urbanism. They used the same process as [8] for downloading the building images and also to remove the outliers, both with minor changes in the parameters' definition.

The authors downloaded 3 GSV images for every building with a size of 640×640 pixels, a field of view of $100\,°C$ and pitch of $15\,°C$; the first image corresponds to the GPS location of the building and the second and third images are $90\,°C$ apart, i.e., right ($+90°$) and left ($-90°$) side views. To remove the images with a non visible or occluded façade, the authors used a VGG16 DCNN trained on the Places365 dataset. The images that remained had 2 of the top 4 predictions in a set of 24 predefined outdoor classes, such as apartment building, beach house, building façade, chalet, church, cottage, courthouse, embassy, fire station, hangar, hospital, hotel, house, hunting lodge, mansion, manufactured home, motel, office building, palace, school-house, shed, skyscraper, synagogue and tower. If an image had less than 2 of the predictions in the set, it was discarded. The cleaned dataset had a total of 204,030 images of building façades that were used to train, using transfer learning, several models such as Inception-ResNetV2 [20], Xception [3] and NASNet-A [26]. The transfer-learned NasNet-A model performed the best overall with accuracy greater than 0.80 and 0.85 for SBST and for LLRS material and height prediction, respectively.

Gonzalez et al. [6] manually annotated and filtered (without using an outlier removal algorithm as the previous authors did) a dataset containing approximately 10,000 GSV images of building façades in the urban area of Medellín (Colombia). Their goal was the same as the Pelizari et al. [1] work, i.e., to predict the building material and the lateral load-resisting system type. They selected five state-of-the-art CNNs that also have shown very good results in ImageNet: VGG16, VGG19, InceptionV3 [21], ResNet50 [7], and Xception [3]. Among the five network architectures ResNet50 showed the best performance because it classified fewer non-ductile buildings as ductile. However, overall, the results were not as good as expected, falling short of the results of the previously mentioned works.

Ghione et al. [5] proposed to develop a cost-effective building exposure model for Oslo. They obtained general information of the buildings, such as their total number with the corresponding coordinates, number of stories, number of housing units, usable and total area, from the public cadastral service of Norway.

The street view images of the façades of the buildings were retrieved using the GSV Static API. The authors also took additional pictures of the façades of the buildings on site. Then, with the help of experts in earthquake engineering, the images were labelled and filtered according to a building typology classification. They did not manually check the quality of the images (for example, whether the facades were occluded by trees, passing vehicles or scaffoldings); instead, during the labelling process, they labelled those images as "other", hoping that it would result in a considerable source of uncertainty for training the models.

Their dataset had a total of 5,074 manually labeled images from fieldwork and from GSV divided into test (20%) and train (80%). For training, and considering the small number of images compared to other approaches, the authors increased the size of the dataset artificially using image augmentation, by applying randomly zooming in by up to 20%, randomly rotating by up to 25 °C and randomly mirroring along the vertical axis. The authors did not apply class-specific weights, i.e., all images were given equal priority which increased the final overall accuracy.

They used several state-of-the-art CNNs pre-trained on the ImageNet database [16], such as Xception, VGG16, VGG19, ResNet50V2, ResNet101V2, ResNet152V2, InceptionV3, InceptionResNetV2, DenseNet121, DenseNet169 and DenseNet201. This last fine-tuned model classified the typology in unseen images with 82.5% accuracy, using only data sources available online: public cadastral data and Google Street View. Without fine tuning, using only the transfer learning method, they reached an accuracy of 76.3%, showing that fine-tuning is greatly beneficial to the overall performance.

3   Materials and Methods

One of the first and most important phases of this work was the data collection and organisation. Our dataset was built using data from the parish of Alvalade (Lisbon, Portugal). Data about the Alvalade parish buildings was retrieved from OpenStreetMap and QGIS, and used to collect the street-level images of the façade of each building from the Google Street View Static API (see Fig. 1). As the number of the collected GSV images was considered insufficient for training, since the deep learning models require large datasets, we also conducted fieldwork to take up to 3 pictures, from different angles, of each building's façade. This latter task was done by 3 civil engineering master students.

Fig. 1. The parish of Alvalade in QGIS.

As a result: (i) a total of 2670 building images were downloaded from GSV and; (ii) 4085 pictures were taken on the field. Of the latter, 366 had black horizontal bands, possibly due to resizing, that were automatically removed. The examples depicted in Fig. 2 show two problems we had to deal with in this raw dataset. On the left, an occluded façade; on the right, an image with black bands. After manual inspection of all images, 5252 remained for further quality control and cleaning.

Quality control of the collected data was performed, during the labelling process, with the help of experienced civil engineers. It was found that, for some buildings, the construction material was hard to identify, and there was a concern to make consensual decisions. A web application was developed to allow experts (civil engineers) to easily add more photos to each building record and to manually annotate the dataset, in particular, it's construction period, construction material, number of stories, number of windows, doors and balconies, roof type, basement, occupation type, and vertical and horizontal irregularities. Compared to the other datasets we mentioned before, our dataset had a comprehensive set of characteristics. The experts also assessed the quality of the GSV images so that we could decide later whether to include them in the dataset or not.

Fig. 2. An unusable image (left) and an image to be improved (rigth).

The last step of the preparation of the dataset used a filtering criterion so that only images showing building façades were left. We cleaned the dataset using a VGG16 model trained on the Places365 dataset to classify our dataset. Places365 is a well known dataset having 365 scene categories/labels [25]. We considered the following subset S of 24 categories to detect a façade from the 365 labels available: `apartment building`, `beach house`, `building facade`, `chalet`, `house`, `church outdoor`, `cottage`, `courthouse`, `embassy`, `fire station`, `hospital`, `hangar outdoor`, `hotel outdoor`, `hunting lodge outdoor`, `mansion`, `manufactured home`, `motel`, `office building`, `palace`, `schoolhouse`, `shed`, `skyscraper`, `tower` and `synagogue outdoor`.

The rule to detect a façade was taken from Pelizari et al. [1]. Given the set C_i, the 4 most likely predicted classes, the label L_i assigned to image i will be given by the rule:

$$L_i = \text{if } (C_i \cap S) \geq 2 \text{ then } facade \text{ else } other \qquad (1)$$

Images not having a `façade` label were discarded. After the cleaning process, the total amount of usable images was 4239. The final dataset is publicly available for download[1]. Although we had several characteristics to choose from, we decided to use only five classes, in those first experiments, combining both construction material and number of floors. These classes were considered to be appropriate, in a first approach, to inform seismic risk analysis: Masonry 1-3, Masonry 4+, Concrete 1-3, Concrete 4-6, Concrete 7+.

---

[1] https://github.com/vsilva028/ML.

We trained all models in a i7 machine, with 64 GB RAM and a recent graphics card (cf. Zotac Gaming GeForce RTX 3090 Trinity OC 24GB GDDR6X). Figure 3 shows the overall pipeline of our work.

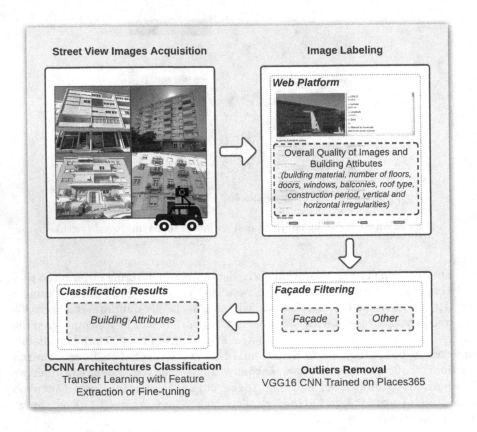

Fig. 3. Overview of the processing pipeline.

The dataset was splitted into train (80%, 2713 images) and test (20%, 678 images) subsets. From the training subset, a validation subset was created (20%, resulting in 848 images). Since the dataset is relatively small, data augmentation was used for training using rotation, vertical and horizontal shifting, random zoom, horizontal flipping and brightness change. We selected some state-of-the-art CNNs that have shown overall good results in the ImageNet challenge, and which were also used in the previously mentioned related works: ResNet50V2, InceptionResNetV2, NASNetLarge, Xception, InceptionV3 and DenseNet201. We used transfer-learning from the Places365 dataset, and fine-tuning procedures. The models were trained with 50 epochs, using an early stopping threshold, and a batch size of 32.

4 Results and Analysis

Without fine-tuning, the best models were ResNet50V2 and DenseNet201 both with an accuracy of 0.772. With fine-tuning, the best performing models were ResNet50V2, with an accuracy of 83,8%, InceptionV3, with an accuracy of 83,4%, and DenseNet201, with an accuracy of 82,3%. Figure 4 shows the validation loss and validation accuracy of ResNet50V2.

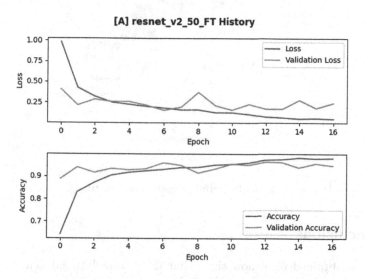

Fig. 4. ResNet50V2 Lost and Accuracy results.

The achieved results match, and some are even better than, the results of the related work referenced earlier.

The model training process stopped at the 50th epoch limit. The confusion matrices showed that some classes were hard to tell apart from others, which also happened when the classification was made by hand, by a trained professional civil engineer. The pairs of classes Masonry 1-3 and Concrete 1-3, and Masonry4+ and Concrete4-6 were more often miss-confused. The number of floors is usually correctly classified. Nevertheless, there is sometimes confusion between Concrete4-6 and Concrete7+, usually due to the difficulty in identifying the ground floor. Figure 5 shows the confusion matrix obtained for ResNet50V2, which reflects these issues. For example, the highest classification errors occurred with misclassifications of Masonry 1-3 as Concrete 1-3 (13.6%), Concrete4-6 as Masonry4+ (13%), Concrete7+ as Concrete4-6 (12%) and Masonry4+ as Concrete4-6 (9.4%). Finally, the best correct classification rate was 89% (for Concrete 1-3) and the worst was 78.5% (for Masonry 1--3), which are, all in all, classification results similar to the ones obtained by trained civil engineers.

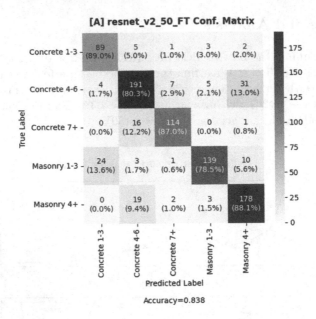

Fig. 5. ResNet50V2 confusion matrix.

5   Conclusions

The results obtained until now show that deep convolutional neural networks can be used with Google Street View imagery to automate the classification of the building stock for exposure modelling. This work provides encouraging results on the use of several existing deep convolutional network models in a small dataset with classes combining both construction material and number of floors.

The overall accuracy of the current experiments was high, and was considered acceptable by experts for risk analysis. The best results were obtained with ResNet50V2 and the associated confusion matrix showed that misclassification of concrete and masonry occurs frequently for the same number of floors. This is expected, as it is also generally difficult for human experts to make such a distinction.

Future work will experiment using additional classes, combining other relevant properties of buildings, to assess the best predicting characteristics. In addition, the trained models will be used in other boroughs of Lisbon, to assess the ability to generalize the overall approach. Further work will also use these results to compare with ground truth data of seismic events.

Acknowledgements. The authors acknowledge the support of Portuguese Science and Technology Foundation (FCT), through grant EXPL/ECI-EGC/1555/2021, project AI4DRR.

This work was financially supported by Base Funding UIDB/00027/2020 of the Artificial Intelligence and Computer Science Laboratory (LIACC), funded by national funds through the FCT/MCTES (PIDDAC).

References

1. Aravena Pelizari, P., Geiß, C., Aguirre, P., Santa María, H., Merino Peña, Y., Taubenböck, H.: Automated building characterization for seismic risk assessment using street-level imagery and deep learning. ISPRS J Photogramm Remote Sens **180**, 370–386 (2021). https://doi.org/10.1016/j.isprsjprs.2021.07.004, https://www.sciencedirect.com/science/article/pii/S0924271621001817
2. Bhatta S, D.J.: Seismic damage prediction of RC buildings using machine learning. Earthquake Eng. Struct. Dyn. 1–24 (2023). https://doi.org/10.1002/eqe.3907
3. Chollet, F.: Xception: Deep learning with depthwise separable convolutions. In: Proceedings of 30th IEEE Conference on Computer Vision and Pattern Recognition. CVPR 2017 (2017)
4. GEMF: Gem global earthquake model foundation website. https://www.globalquakemodel.org. Accessed 01 March 2023
5. Ghione, F., Mæland, S., Meslem, A., Oye, V.: Building stock classification using machine learning: A case study for Oslo, Norway. Front. Earth Sci. **10** (2022). https://doi.org/10.3389/feart.2022.886145
6. Gonzalez, D., Rueda-Plata, D., Acevedo, A.B., Duque, J.C., Ramos-Pollán, R., Betancourt, A., García, S.: Automatic detection of building typology using deep learning methods on street level images. Build. Environ. **177** (2020). https://doi.org/10.1016/j.buildenv.2020.106805
7. He, K., Zhang, X., Ren, S., Sun, J.: Identity mappings in deep residual networks. In: Lecture Notes in Computer Science Including Subseries Lecture Notes in Artificial Intelligence and Lecture Notes in Bioinformatics, vol. 9908 (2016). https://doi.org/10.1007/978-3-319-46493-0_38
8. Kang, J., K"orner, M., Wang, Y., Taubenb"ock, H., Zhu, X.X.: Building instance classification using street view images. ISPRS J. Photogramm. Remote. Sens. **145** (2018). https://doi.org/10.1016/j.isprsjprs.2018.02.006
9. Laupheimer, D., Tutzauer, P., Haala, N., Spicker, M.: Neural networks for the classification of building use from street-view imagery. In: ISPRS Annals of Photogrammetry, Remote Sensing and Spatial Information Sciences IV2, pp. 177–184 (2018). https://doi.org/10.5194/isprs-annals-IV-2-177-2018
10. Law, S., Seresinhe, C.I., Shen, Y., GutierrezRoig, M.: Street-frontage-net: urban image classification using deep convolutional neural networks. Int. J. Geogr. Inf. Sci. **34**(4), 681–707 (2020). https://doi.org/10.1080/13658816.2018.1555832
11. Li, Y., Chen, Y., Rajabifard, A., Khoshelham, K., Aleksandrov, M.: Estimating building age from google street view images using deep learning. In: Melbourne, A. (ed.) Proceedings of 10th International Conference on Geographic Information Science GIScience 2018 (2018)
12. Lovon, H., Silva, V., Vicente, R., Ferreira, T., Costa, A.: Characterization of the masonry building stock in Portugal for earthquake risk assessment. Eng. Struct. (2020)
13. Novack, T., Vorbeck, L., Lorei, H., Zipf, A.: Towards detecting building facades with graffiti artwork based on street view images. ISPRS Int. J. Geo Inf. **9**, 98 (2020). https://doi.org/10.3390/ijgi9020098

14. Pagani, M., Garcia-Pelaez, J., Gee, R., Johnson, K., Silva, V., Simionato, M., Styron, R., Vigano, D., Danciu, L., Monelli, D., Poggi, V., Weatherill, G.: The 2018 version of the global earthquake model: hazard component. Earthq. Spectra (2020)

15. Ritchie, H., Roser, M.: Natural Disasters: Our World in Data. University of Oxford (2014). https://ourworldindata.org/natural-disasters

16. Russakovsky, O., Deng, J., Su, H., Krause, J., Satheesh, S., Ma, S., Huang, Z., Karpathy, A., Khosla, A., Bernstein, M., Berg, A.C., Fei-Fei, L.: Imagenet large scale visual recognition challenge. Int. J. Comput. Vision **115**, 3 (2015). https://doi.org/10.1007/s11263-015-0816-y

17. Silva, V., Crowley, H., Pagani, M., Monelli, D., Pinho, R.: Development of the open quake engine, the global earthquake model's open-source software for seismic risk assessment. Nat. Hazards **72**, 3 (2014). https://doi.org/10.1007/s11069-013-0618-x

18. Silva, V., Crowley, H., Pinho, R., Varum, H.: Seismic risk assessment for mainland Portugal. Bull. Earthq. Eng. **13**(2), 429–457 (2014)

19. Simonyan, K., Zisserman, A.: Very deep convolutional networks for large-scale image recognition. In: International Conference on Learning Representations (2015)

20. Szegedy, C., Ioffe, S., Vanhoucke, V., Alemi, A.A.: Inception-v4, inception-resnet and the impact of residual connections on learning. In: 31st AAAI Conference on Artificial Intelligence, AAAI 2017 (2017). https://doi.org/10.1609/aaai.v31i1.11231

21. Szegedy, C., Vanhoucke, V., Ioffe, S., Shlens, J., Wojna, Z.: Rethinking the inception architecture for computer vision. In: Proceedings of the IEEE Computer Society Conference on Computer Vision and Pattern Recognition (2016)

22. Yu, Q., Wang, C., Cetiner, B., Yu, S., Mckenna, F., Taciroglu, E., Law, K.: Building information modeling and classification by visual learning at a city scale. In: Vancouver, C. (ed.) Proceedings of 33rd Conference on Neural Information Processing Systems (NeurIPS 2019) (2019)

23. Yu, Q., Wang, C., McKenna, F., Yu, S.X., Taciroglu, E., Cetiner, B., Law, K.H.: Rapid visual screening of soft-story buildings from street view images using deep learning classification. Earthq. Eng. Eng. Vib. **19**, 827–838 (2020). https://doi.org/10.1007/s11803-020-0598-2

24. Zhou, B., Lapedriza, A., Torralba, A., Oliva, A.: Places: an image database for deep scene understanding. J. Vis. **17**, 10 (2017). https://doi.org/10.1167/17.10.296

25. Zhou, B., Lapedriza, A., Khosla, A., Oliva, A., Torralba, A.: Places: A 10 million image database for scene recognition. IEEE Trans. Pattern Anal. Mach. Intell. (2017)

26. Zoph, B., Vasudevan, V., Shlens, J., Le, Q.V.: Learning transferable architectures for scalable image recognition. In: Proceedings of the IEEE Computer Society Conference on Computer Vision and Pattern Recognition (2018)

Data Mining Models to Predict Parking Lot Availability

Beatriz Rodrigues[1], Carlos Fernandes[1], José Vieira[1], and Filipe Portela[1,2(✉)]

[1] IOTECH-Innovation On Technology, Trofa, Portugal
cfp@dsi.uminho.pt
[2] Algoritmi Centre, University of Minho, Guimarães, Portugal

Abstract. With the growth of IoT (Internet of Things) technologies, there has been a significant increase in opportunities to enhance various aspects of our daily lives. One such application is the prediction of car park occupancy using car park movement data, which can be further improved by incorporating weather data. This paper focuses on investigating how weather conditions influence car park occupancy prediction and aims to identify the most effective prediction algorithm. To achieve more accurate results, the researchers explored two primary approaches: Classification and Regression. These approaches allow for a comprehensive analysis of the parking scenario, catering to both qualitative and quantitative aspects of predicting car park occupancy. In this study, a total of 24 prediction models, encompassing a wide range of algorithms were induced. These models were designed to consider various details, including parking features, location specifics, time-related factors and crucially, weather conditions. Overall, this study showcased the potential of leveraging IoT technologies, car park movement data, and weather information to predict car park occupancy effectively. By exploring both classification and regression approaches, each yielding accuracy and R2Score values surpassing 85%.

Keywords: Smart Cities · Data Mining · Parking Lot

1 Introduction

The amount of data generated every day is staggering. With the rise of digital technologies and the Internet of Things, we now produce vast amounts of data both in a digital context and in our day-to-day activities. This data both presents a significant challenge for storage and management, and a tremendous opportunity for innovation and problem-solving. In combination with this, due to the fast-paced of the world, efficient urban planning has become crucial, and predicting the occupancy of parking lots has emerged as an essential aspect of this process. According to a study by [1], in Stuttgart, Germany roughly 15% of traffic on busy city streets is caused by drivers searching for a vacant parking spot. Moreover, drivers in dense city districts usually spend from 3.5 min to 15.4 [1] minutes looking for a parking spot, which means spending money and producing pollution, thus affecting the general societal costs.

© The Author(s), under exclusive license to Springer Nature Switzerland AG 2023
N. Moniz et al. (Eds.): EPIA 2023, LNAI 14116, pp. 535–547, 2023.
https://doi.org/10.1007/978-3-031-49011-8_42

Predictive models can assist parking lot managers in making more informed decisions and adjusting parking availability and pricing to meet changing demand patterns. Moreover, parking lot users can also benefit from this information when deciding where to park their vehicle. Predictive scenarios were designed to consider various details such as parking features, location, time, and weather.

This study not only explores the potential impact of weather on predictive models for parking lot occupancy, but also how other features can be incorporated to enhance prediction accuracy. The study compares the performance and outcomes of several predictive model algorithms to achieve this goal. The models created explored two approaches classification with Decision Tree (DT), Naive Bayes (NB) and Support Vector Machines (SVM) and regression with Random Forest (RF). At the end, it allows to determine which algorithm offers the best prediction of parking space availability. To conduct the comparison of the predictive models, a dataset from Lisbon parking lots[1] was utilized. This study is part of the ioCity project and is based on the ioScience patent [2]. By leveraging the directrices of the ioScience patent [2], the solution becomes modular and scalable, meaning that the same model can be easily used with various approaches, scenarios, or different data.

This study is organized into six sections, starting with the Introduction, which lays out the foundation for this study. The second section provides background information on the study, explaining the concept of data mining and presenting related work. The third section describes the materials and methods used in the study, Cross-Industry Standard Process for Data Mining (CRISP-DM) methodology and the technologies and tools used. The fourth section presents all the work developed: business understanding, data understanding, data preparation, modelling, evaluation, and deployment. The remaining two sections report the discussion of the results obtained and the conclusion of the work developed.

2 Background

This section presents some of the main topics of the work, like Smart Cities, Data Mining and ioScience [2].

2.1 Smart Cities

In the past decade, the concept of smart cities has gained significant attention. According to [3], the origin of this attention can be traced back to 2010 when IBM initiated the first smart cities challenge by donating $50 million worth of technology and services to 100 cities. However, due to the diversity of definitions and applications, various indices identify different cities as being smart, based on different criteria. Still according to [3] some cities remain focused on technology, while others rely on a governance model or prioritize citizen wellbeing and engagement. Still, others focus on sustainability. Nevertheless, a broad definition of a smart city is an urban environment where technology enables an efficient relationship between data and its applications, resulting in a responsive, resilient, and healthy environment. The functional aspects of this relationship are

---

[1] https://dados.gov.pt/pt/datasets/ocupacao-de-parques-de-estacionamento-historico/#_.

that a smart city is more immediately responsive, predictive, adaptive, and capable of learning.

Finally, [3] identifies that the outcomes of a smart city include sustainable and healthy lifestyles, economic efficiency, political and social inclusivity through equitable engagement, and the ability for all public and private residents to flourish.

2.2 Data Mining

There are several ways of defining data mining, but before attempting to define this one, and as described by [4], we can emphasize that data mining, also known as "knowledge-discovery in databases" (KDD), has three generic roots [4]: Statistics, Artificial Intelligence and and Database systems (DBS). In another perspective [5] defines data mining as "the study of collecting, cleaning, processing, analyzing, and gaining useful insights from data. A wide variation exists in terms of the problem domains, applications, formulations, and data representations that are encountered in real applications. Therefore, "data mining" is a broad umbrella term that is used to describe these different aspects of data processing."

2.3 Related Work

This work is based on a research and development project—ioCity and ioScience [2]. ioCity is a research project that aims create an intelligent web/mobile application that can integrate and interact with existing systems, predict the occupancy of transportation and parking lots, and suggest the most suitable means of transportation and route. The application utilizes data mining and predictive modelling techniques to analyse data from various sources, such as sensors and traffic patterns, to provide accurate and real-time predictions for transportation and parking occupancy.

By doing so, the ioCity aims to improve urban mobility by reducing traffic congestion, optimizing parking resources, and providing convenient and efficient transportation options for urban residents. ioScience [2] promotes Data Science as a Service (DsaaS), by retrieving information from heterogeneous data sources, processing it, and passing it through an analytical layer, towards a visualisation multi-platform application independent from network connection at all times. This might be applied in any context in which data plays a relevant role, by other means, it is not a closed solution. What is being proposed is a global solution in the area of data science that can be used in whichever business field who might need it.

In the past some other researchers dedicated their time to research this problem like [6–9]. Both [6] and [7] compared different machine learning methods for the prediction of parking space availability, [6] using Santander's parking data set (initiated while working on the H2020 WISE-IoT project) and [7] City of San Francisco, USA and the City of Melbourne, Australia real-time car parking information.

In the case of [8], they proposed efficient unsupervised learning algorithms to predict parking occupancy rates, being that two types of predictions were studied: (a) an offline prediction, and (b) an online prediction.

In [9] study, the main goal is to design an intelligent IoT-based service that can predict, in the next few hours, the parking spaces occupancy of a street, and for that a genetic algorithm was used to optimize predictors parameters.

3 Material and Methods

In this section, an overview is provided of the tools and methodology used on this research, along with a concise description of our research procedures. Our research approach involved conducting a comprehensive search within the scope of the study to identify and select the most relevant papers to review. Then the practical solution was designed and implemented. Design Science Research methodology were used to conduct the research process and CRISP-DM were useful do organize the data mining flow.

3.1 Methods

This project followed Design Science Research (DSR) and CRIPS-DM. DSR process includes six stages: identify problem and motivation, define objectives of a solution, design and development, demonstration, evaluation, and communication [10]. As far as this study is concerned, the first and second stages refer to the introduction, the third and fourth stage to the work, the fifth stage to the discussion and conclusion and the sixth stage to the publication of this study. CRISP-DM, stands for Cross-Industry Standard Process for Data Mining, is a guide for data mining efforts. As a process model, CRISP-DM provides an overview of the data mining life cycle following Business Understanding, Data Understanding, Data Preparation, Modelling and Evaluation [11] and was useful to drive and present the work.

3.2 Technologies and Tools

Here the technologies used in the project are presented, as well as the tools that support them. In Table 1, all the technologies and tools used are presented, as well as the respective justification for the use of each one.

Table 1. Technologies and Tools employed

Technology	Justification	Type
Python	Process data and develop predictive models	Programming
Pandas	Storage data in dataframes and data analysis	Library
Scikit-learn	Provides a range of algorithms for classification, regression, and clustering	Library
imblearn	Handling imbalanced datasets in machine learning by the use of SMOTE	Library

4   Work

The dataset used in this study refers to the period 01/01/2020 to 30/12/2022 and presents 1182275 records/movements (entrances and exits) from ten distinct parks of Lisbon.

4.1   Data Analysis (Data Comprehension)

Table 2 presents a statistical analysis (mean, standard deviation, minimum, quartiles and maximum) of the numeric variables: parking capacity, temperature, precipitation and free spaces.

Table 2. Numerical variable statistics

Variable	Mean	Std	Min	25%	50%	75%	Max
Capacity_max	185.52	94.87	20	118	160	238	650
Precip	0.12	0.96	0	0	0	0	40.75
Temp	17.74	4.92	2.60	14.10	17.50	20.70	39.50
Free_spaces	138.22	96.70	0	65	123	193	614

Figure 1 represents the movements by year and month where, for example, it is possible to see that each year has different behaviours.

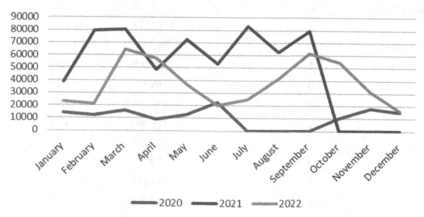

Fig. 1. Movements by Month and Year

Table 3 shows a data distribution (absolute and relative) of the most relevant variables: parishes, parks open day and night, parks with roofs and paid parks. It also presents a distribution of movements by the day of the week (e.g., 0–Monday, 6–Sunday) and the number of activities at the weekend.

Figure 2 presents the data distribution of the classification target (park full or not). A full park is where less than 25% of the lots are available. The target class was defined

Table 3. Categorical variable statistics

Non-Numerical variable		Value	Percentage
Parishes	Santo António	235633	19.93
	Alvalade	118927	10.06
	Lumiar	118891	10.06
	Avenidas Novas	118513	10.02
	Alcântara	118277	10.00
	Santa Maria Maior	118255	10.00
	Belém	118142	9.99
	Misericórdia	118104	9.99
	Areeiro	117533	9.94
Night_day	0	614061	51.94
	1	568214	48.06
Parque_roof	0	473084	40.01
	1	709191	59.99
Parque_paid	0	0	0.00
	1	1182275	100.00
Parque_electric	0	709454	60.01
	1	472821	39.99
Parque_currency	0	0	0.00
	1	1182275	100.00
Parque_ATM	0	592006	50.07
	1	590269	49.93
Day of week	0	168092	14.22
	1	161261	13.64
	2	166080	14.05
	3	171237	14.48
	4	173901	14.71
	5	171916	14.54
	6	169788	14.36
Weekend	0	840571	71.10
	1	341704	28.90

using 25% of availability to avoid wrong predictions with only one free parking lot. It allows the models to prevent flawed assumptions and ensure that if a park has a free place, it effectively has one lot available when the car is nearby. For the regression, the "target" was the number of available lots and ranged from 0 to 614.

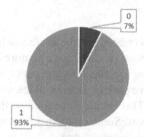

Fig. 2. Target occupancy

As can be observed in Figure 2, the target is biased, so sampling techniques were used in the modelling process.

4.2 Data Preparation

In this data preparation process, information about a parking lot was enriched with location data ('district', 'county', 'parish') through the geoapi.pt[2] api by using the latitude and longitude of the park, as well as relevant information about the parking lot itself ('park_roof', 'park_paid', 'park_electric', 'park_currency', 'park_ATM') through a study of the 10 parks with the most movements. Additionally, due to how weather conditions greatly influence how people travel, weather data ('app_temp', 'precip', 'temp', 'night_day') through the Weatherbit[3] api was incorporated into the dataset based on the date and hour of the movement in the parking lot data, as well as the corresponding latitude and longitude of the park. Finally, the date was parsed into day, month, and year components, and the time was reduced to only the hour.

After incorporating additional data into the dataset, several modifications were made to the existing data. Specifically, the date was disaggregated into day, month, and year, while the time was broken down into hours and minutes. This allowed for the derivation of additional variables such as the day of the week and the week of the year for each record. Moreover, the minute values were grouped into classes (e.g., $1 \rightarrow 0$–15min, $4 \rightarrow 45$–60 min), and the hours were utilized to define different time periods of the day, each one with six hours (e.g., $1 \rightarrow$ Dawn (00:00–05:59), $4 \rightarrow$ Night (18:00–23:59)).

Additionally, the meteorological data was categorized into classes for both temperature (e.g., $1 \rightarrow$ Very cold (below 5 °C), $6 \rightarrow$ Very hot (above 30 °C)) and precipitation (e.g., $1 \rightarrow$ Weak (below 0.5 mm/h), $3 \rightarrow$ Strong (above 4 mm/h)) following Portuguese Institute for Sea and Atmosphere, I. P.[4] (IPMA, IP) criteria.

In the process of forecasting, the Synthetic Minority Oversampling TEchnique (SMOTE) was also employed to address any imbalances within the data.

---

[2] https://geoapi.pt/.

[3] https://www.weatherbit.io/api/historical-weather-api.

[4] https://www.ipma.pt/en/index.html.

4.3 Modelling

Table 4 shows the four scenarios created and the attributes included in each. For example, Scenario A only had details about location, park features and time. In the case of the location, a set of variables can be used because the user can select a specific park, or the system can suggest an alternative park in another place where there is a bus to transport him to the expected location. This option is related to the project goal of combining individual and collective transport. Some other variables were considered (e.g., parking limit, year, and others) but were discarded due to their mutability or inefficiency.

Table 4. Test scenarios

Scenario	Attributes
A	**Location + TIME** ['district', 'county', 'parish', 'park_roof', 'park_paid', 'park_electric', 'park_currency', 'park_ATM', 'hour', 'class_minutes', 'timeofday']
B	**Location + TIME** ['name', 'hour', 'class_minutes', 'timeofday']
C	**Location + TIME + Meteorology** ['name', 'hour', 'class_minutes', 'timeofday', 'class_precip', 'class_temp', 'night_day']
D	**Location + Date + Time + Meteorology** ['name', 'month', 'hour', 'dayofweek', 'weekend', 'weekofyear', 'hour', 'class_minutes', 'timeofday', 'class_precip', 'class_temp', 'night_day']

In addition to the selection of scenarios, a review of classification (Decision Tree (DT), Naive Bayes (NB), Support Vector Machines (SVM) and Neural Networks (ANN)) and regression (Random Forest (RF) and Linear Regressions (LR)) modelling algorithms were carried out, so that the best scenario and classification algorithm could be selected, and the classification and regression algorithms could be compared.

For the classification algorithms some hyper-parameters went through the cross-validation process to define the best values for each model. For the Decision Tree algorithm, the hyper-parameters that went through the cross-validation process were max_depth, min_samples_leaf and criterion. For the Naive Bayes algorithm, the hyper-parameter was var_smoothing. And for the Neural Networks algorithm it was hidden_layer_sizes, activation, and solver.

In the case of the regression algorithm, it used the same classes of classification. However, it discarded the classes (e.g., class_temp, class_precip, class_minutes and timeofday).

In the process of selecting the best prediction model for classification, a total of sixteen models were tested using Ten Folds Cross-Validation with stratification before training. The number of induced models was calculated considering the number of scenarios (s), prediction algorithms (a) and target (t) as follows:

$$M_{s,a,t} = \begin{cases} s = A \dots D \\ a = DT .. ANN \\ t = Occupation \end{cases} \text{Models} = 4 \text{ scenarios} \times 4 \text{ algorithms} \times 1 \text{ target} = 16$$

Regarding the regression algorithms a total of 8 regression models were tested, and this value was calculated in similarity with the previous one as follows:

$$M_{s,a,t} = \begin{cases} s = A \dots D \\ a = RF \\ t = Free\_spaces \end{cases} \text{Models} = 4 \text{ scenarios} \times 2 \text{ algorithms} \times 1 \text{ target} = 8$$

In this first experiment a total of 24 prediction models were induced. It is expected to improve the models and results.

4.4 Evaluation

The results obtained for each scenario using the selected modelling algorithms are as presented in Tables 5 and 6. To select the best classification models, the following minimum threshold was defined, based on the team's scientific experience in several forecasting projects: Accuracy: 80%; Specificity: 80% and Sensitivity: 85%

This limit was defined because the goal is to find available parks (sensitivity), but the number of false positives also should be controlled (accuracy and specificity). F1 scores are used to understand the model behavior better. In Table 5, the best results for the classification scenarios are presented, but the best scenarios for each algorithm are shown below in Table 6.

Table 5. Results obtained from the classification models.

Scenario	Accuracy		Sensitivity		Specificity		F1-Score		Algorithm
	Average	Detour	Average	Detour	Average	Detour	Average	Detour	
A	91.43%	0.99%	91.43%	0.99%	91.43%	0.99%	91.69%	0.10%	DT
B	91.45%	0.94%	91.45%	0.94%	91.45%	0.94%	91.59%	0.04%	DT
C	91.96%	0.71%	91.96%	0.71%	91.95%	0.72%	93.35%	0.35%	DT
D	97.70%	1.08%	97.70%	1.08%	97.70%	1.09%	99.85%	0.02%	DT

Regarding regression, the threshold differs because it depends on several factors, including the range of possible values. For this, based on the team's scientific experience in several forecasting projects, only the R2Score is considered with at least 85%. But metrics like Mean squared error (MSE), Mean absolute error (MAE), Relative absolute error (RAE) were also observed. In Table 7, the best results for the classification scenarios are presented, but the best scenarios for each algorithm are shown below in Table 8.

Regarding the results should be highlighted the following issues:

Table 6. Best scenarios for each classification algorithm.

Algorithm	Accuracy		Sensitivity		Specificity		F1-Score		Scenario
	Average	Detour	Average	Detour	Average	Detour	Average	Detour	
DT	97.70%	1.08%	97.80%	0.99%	97.70%	1.08%	97.70%	1.09%	D
NB	91.00%	0.95%	91.05%	0.91%	91.00%	0.95%	91.00%	0.95%	A
NN	89.62%	1.78%	90.14%	2.01%	89.62%	1.78%	89.59%	1.77%	A

Table 7. Results obtained algorithms for Regression.

Algorithm	MSE	R2Score	MAE	RAE	Scenario
A	1359.73	0.85	18.75	13.56%	RF
B	1359.72	0.85	18.75	13.56%	RF
C	1268.14	0.86	18.06	13.07%	RF
D	285.24	0.97	5.90	4.27%	RF

Table 8. Best Scenarios for each Regression Algorithm.

Algorithm	MSE	R2Score	MAE	RAE	Scenario
RF	285.24	0.97	5.90	4.27%	D
LR	3707.64	0.60	46.49	33.64%	A
DT	349.29	0.96	5.72	4.14%	D

- SVM and ANN did not provide valuable results—the models did not finish their running in an acceptable time;
- Linear Regression model performed poorly, as evidenced by an unsatisfactory residual R2Score.Deployment

The models were included in a rest API and can be consumed by a web/mobile interface. The API receives the user position or park ID, and then the system will find the nearest or specific park and return the best model results. The user can, for example, ask different types of results, like available parks on a date or if a park will be or not be available.

5 Discussion

As can be observed, there is a difference between classification and regression approaches. This strategy lets the system choose the best model/approach for each time/request. This selection will then be configured by using ensembling techniques.

In evaluating the models developed for classification, it has been observed all scenarios achieved good results using decision trees. NB generally achieved worst results.

Several interesting factors emerged from the analysis:

- The algorithms exhibited different behaviours depending on the presence of parking names or parking features. This suggests that the inclusion of such variables can significantly impact the predictive models' performance.
- The models are well-balanced as indicated by the similar values of specificity and sensitivity. This implies that the models have an equal capability of predicting both full and free parking scenarios accurately.
- Meteorological data, when combined with the date, proved to have a positive influence on the models (+7%). This indicates that weather conditions play a significant role in predicting parking occupancy.
- Certain parking features, such as having a roof, were found to have a strong influence on the decision trees. These features often appeared at the top of the decision trees, indicating their importance in determining parking availability.
- The large number of possible combinations of variables limited the ability to run more complex models, such as Support Vector Machines (SVM). This highlights the computational challenges faced when dealing with extensive feature combinations.
- It was observed that some regression algorithms were not well-suited for this specific problem. This suggests that the choice of regression algorithms should be carefully considered based on the nature and characteristics of the parking occupancy prediction problem.

The obtained results in classification, with an accuracy of 97.70%, and regression, with an R2Score of 97%, initially raised concerns and prompted the research team to conduct a thorough analysis. The team carefully examined the data, possible biases, and optimal model fits to validate the accuracy of the results.

Upon closer analysis, it was found that the best results were achieved when all variables—Location, Date, Time, and Meteorology—were combined. The algorithm was able to identify the optimal combinations, further emphasizing the importance of selecting appropriate variables and algorithms for accurate predictions.

These findings demonstrate the intricacies involved in predicting parking availability and highlight the significance of meticulous data analysis and model validation. Despite the initial doubts, the regression models proved to be highly effective in predicting the desired outcomes, achieving impressive results based on the predefined metrics.

This study differs from previous research, presented in the related work, by not only employing multiple prediction algorithms for model comparison but also considering the optimal variables for model runs, like weather data.

6   Conclusion

In conclusion, this study has provided compelling evidence for the effectiveness of integrating weather data in predicting parking lot occupancy, utilizing both classification and regression algorithms. The findings highlight the benefits and limitations of each approach, shedding light on the importance of considering additional data sources.

Including weather data has yielded tangible results, significantly enhancing the accuracy of the predictive models. The classification models achieved a sensitivity of 97.70%, while the regression models achieved an R2Score of 97% with a low MAE. These outcomes demonstrate the valuable insights that weather information brings to parking occupancy prediction.

When comparing the performance of the classification and regression models, the regression models consistently outperformed the classification models, showcasing their superiority in predicting parking lot occupancy. This suggests that regression techniques can lead to more accurate and precise predictions in this domain.

The findings emphasize the significance of incorporating various algorithms and leveraging weather data to develop robust predictive models. By doing so, a comprehensive understanding of the underlying patterns and influential factors in parking lot occupancy can be gained, enabling more informed decision-making and improved efficiency in parking management.

In practical terms, this research advances predictive modelling in parking lot occupancy. The results affirm the value of integrating weather data, demonstrating its impact on enhancing the accuracy and reliability of predictions. In the future, found errors will be solved, new algorithms added, and new variables (e.g., events) explored. Besides, the models will be retrained to avoid possible mistakes.

Acknowledgements. This work has been developed under the scope of the project NORTE-01–0247-FEDER-045397, supported by the Northern Portugal Regional Operational Programme (NORTE 2020), under the Portugal 2020 Partnership Agreement, through the European Regional Development Fund (FEDER).

References

1. Hampshire, R., Shoup, D.: What share of traffic is cruising for parking? J. Transp. Econ. Policy, **52**, (2018)
2. Barros, F., Rodrigues, B., Vieira, J. and Portela, F.:Method to execute offline data analysis. Portugal PT. ID. 116393, IPC: G06F 16/00 (2019.01). IOTECHPIS Innovation on Technology, LDA. (2022)
3. Maheswaran, M., Badidi, E.: Handbook of smart cities: software services and cyber infrastructure. Springer, (2018)
4. Gorunescu, F.: Data mining: Concepts, models and techniques. Springer Science & Business Media, (2011)
5. Aggarwal, C. C.: Data mining: The textbook. Springer, (2015)
6. Awan, F.M., Saleem, Y., Minerva, R., Crespi, N.: A comparative analysis of machine/deep learning models for parking space availability prediction. Sensors **20**(1), 322 (2020). https://doi.org/10.3390/s20010322
7. Badii, C., Nesi, P., Paoli, I.: Predicting available parking slots on critical and regular services by exploiting a range of open data. IEEE Access **6**, 44059–44071 (2018). https://doi.org/10.1109/access.2018.2864157
8. Tamrazian, A., Qian, Z., Rajagopal, R.: Where is my parking spot? Transp. Res. Rec. **2489**(1), 77–85 (2015). https://doi.org/10.3141/2489-09

9. Piccialli, F., Giampaolo, F., Prezioso, E., Crisci, D., Cuomo, S.: Predictive analytics for smart parking: a deep learning approach in forecasting of IoT data. ACM Trans. Internet Technol. **21**(3), 1–21 (2021). https://doi.org/10.1145/3412842
10. Peffers, K., Tuunanen, T., Rothenberger, M.A., Chatterjee, S.: A design science research methodology for information systems research. J. Manag. Inf. Syst. **24**(3), 45–77 (2007). https://doi.org/10.2753/mis0742-1222240302
11. IBM.: IBM SPSS Modeler CRISP-DM Guide. (2021)

Advancements in Synthetic Data Extraction for Industrial Injection Molding

Rottenwalter Georg[✉], Tilly Marcel, Bielenberg Christian,
and Obermeier Katharina

Rosenheim Technical University of Applied Sciences - Hochschulstraße 1, Rosenheim
83024, Germany
{georg.rottenwalter,marcel.tilly,christian.bielenberg}@th-rosenheim.de,
katharina.obermeier@stud.th-rosenheim.de

Abstract. Machine learning has significant potential for optimizing various industrial processes. However, data acquisition remains a major challenge as it is both time-consuming and costly. Synthetic data offers a promising solution to augment insufficient data sets and improve the robustness of machine learning models. In this paper, we investigate the feasibility of incorporating synthetic data into the training process of the injection molding process using an existing Long Short-Term Memory architecture. Our approach is to generate synthetic data by simulating production cycles and incorporating them into the training data set. Through iterative experimentation with different proportions of synthetic data, we attempt to find an optimal balance that maximizes the benefits of synthetic data while preserving the authenticity and relevance of real data. Our results suggest that the inclusion of synthetic data improves the model's ability to handle different scenarios, with potential practical industrial applications to reduce manual labor, machine use, and material waste. This approach provides a valuable alternative for situations where extensive data collection and maintenance has been impractical or costly and thus could contribute to more efficient manufacturing processes in the future.

Keywords: Industry · Injection molding · Synthetic data · Machine learning · Data generation · Time series data

1 Introduction

Machine learning (ML) is used in many industries for quality assurance and production optimization. In future, many production processes and other operations will be optimized by ML models. One of the most prominent challenges to optimizing processes through ML is data collection, which is one of the biggest and most critical bottlenecks. Most of the time dedicated to ML processes from start to finish is typically devoted to data preparation and procurement, encompassing tasks such as data collection, cleaning, analysis, visualization, and feature

N. Moniz et al. (Eds.): EPIA 2023, LNAI 14116, pp. 548–560, 2023.
https://doi.org/10.1007/978-3-031-49011-8_43

engineering [9]. However, since large and high-quality data sets already exist in many areas of the ML world, this is not true for the industry in general. Despite the lack of data, at first glance, data acquisition in the industry should not be a problem, as countless processes can be tracked and recorded in production, which can be used to improve product quality or production optimization. Unfortunately, these processes have to be monitored, stored, and labeled, which is time-consuming and cost-intensive to be able to use the data for ML. This possibility of data acquisition is a double-edged sword since the production cycles only produce the same products or products that are difficult to distinguish. So it is hard to grant greater variance between different states of product quality without being forced to produce broken products. To produce many different qualities would mean a lot of deliberate production waste, many machine hours, a lot of skilled labor time, and wasted materials. Since most companies try to keep the cost-benefit factor of their production chains as high as possible, synthetic data could be used in the future to generate or enrich larger data sets. This would provide cheap and efficient data if large datasets are not existing. For this very purpose, we propose in our paper to enrich and augment too small or insufficient datasets with synthetically generated data. The approach is to build from existing literature by using the simulated operations of production cycles to augment our training dataset for ML. To demonstrate our approach, we have taken an existing Long Short-Term Memory (LSTM) architecture that is designed to classify the quality of an injection molding process and trained it with two data sets. The first data set consisted only of real data and was too small for representative training. A synthetic data set was used as the second data set. In our training, the proportion of total data was then increased with up to 30% synthetic data.

Our goal is to show that it is possible to enhance data from injection molding processes with a certain fraction of synthetically generated data to extend the robustness of the model. With this approach, we want to make the model more adaptable to different scenarios. In this way, we can use simulated production processes to generate production errors as well as normal processes already in the simulated environment, without having to test them on an actual production machine.

2   Related Work

2.1   Synthetic Data Generation

Automatic techniques for generating synthetic datasets with accompanying labels are gaining popularity in ML, owing to their cost-effectiveness and adaptability. This approach offers an efficient alternative to traditional data collection and annotation methods, streamlining the development of ML models [8]. In the field of computer vision, synthetic data can already be generated very successfully via 3D modeling. For example, a purely synthetic data set of 3D models generated from real objects was trained successfully in a Convolutional Neural Network [14]. Another use case for generating synthetic data is text in images. Here, fonts, sizes, and the colors of the text are varied to generate large sets of data [4]. In another method, a synthetic dataset of 2D mechanical designs, called GMCAD, was used to train a deep learning model for Design for Additive Manufacturing [1].

Similar to the data generation methods mentioned above, our approach attempts to generate synthetic data through the simulation of an injection molding process.

2.2   Injection Molding Simulation

The development of a low-cost, desktop-based virtual injection molding system that utilizes virtual reality, finite element analysis, motion simulation, and scientific visualization techniques sought to reduce the number of costly iterations of physical test molding by determining mold structure and process parameters. This system was intended to provide engineers with a comprehensive view of mold structure and assembly while identifying potential defects during the molding process, ultimately improving moldability and product quality [16]. In another study, a 3D simulation of mold filling for high-density polyethylene in injection molding was performed using ANSYS-CFX, as well as injection molding experiments with deliberately short shots at different optimal metering percentages for melt front tracking. The comparison between the simulation and experimental results shows reasonable agreement in terms of the shape of the melt front, with minor variations due to the nature of the injection molding experiments [7]. It is necessary that the inputs and outputs of an injection molding simulation match as closely as possible the actual conditions of a real injection molding machine. By benchmarking injection molding simulations, the importance of matching simulation inputs with actual conditions of real injection molding machines will be discussed. The study examines factors that affect simulation accuracy, such as part geometry, model mesh type, material data, and process settings, as well as validation techniques using transducers and part deflection measurement methods [11].

The preceding approaches are intended to give a small indication of the methods or approaches available in the field of injection molding simulation. Our goal will be to proceed similarly to the studies mentioned above to have our processes recorded by a simulation.

2.3   ML in Injection Molding

The integration of ML techniques in injection molding processes presents opportunities for enhancing optimization and achieving superior performance. For example, Artificial Neural Network (ANN)-based temperature controller design was developed for a plastic injection molding system. For this purpose, an integrator and an ANN were combined. The proposed controller demonstrates improved performance in terms of reduced overshoot and faster transient response compared to an industrial proportional integral derivative regulator [5]. In another project, an ANN-based position controller for an all-electric injection molding machine was presented to improve dynamic positioning characteristics for various components. The ANN was trained with experimental data and back-propagation algorithms to provide accurate control of motor current, position, and velocity, and its efficiency was verified using real-world time series data [13].

Another important approach in the ML injection molding environment is the approach to improve the accuracy of fault detection models in manufacturing processes. There, error rates are typically very low, leading to unbalanced data sets. By using ML and sharing process data between multiple injection molding work systems, model performance can be improved using industry data from approximately two million process cycles [6].

Using similar ML approaches, we are trying to train a neural network to recognize qualities in the injection molding process. Since small and unbalanced data sets are not sufficient to train representative models, we will try to scale up our training data using synthetic data.

3   Methods

Figure 1 shows the system structure of our concept of data generation up to training. The first point *Simulation of products* is responsible for the generation of the synthetic data. In the step *Training enriched data*, the synthetic part of the training sets is determined and trained with a certain part of synthetic data. In the last step, *Training evaluation data* is evaluated and used to compare the model with real data.

- **Simulation of production processes**: This step mainly consists of simulating a real production process on the injection molding machine and storing it in a time series-based file. The data set should store all the values and parameters from the start of the cycle to the end of the cycle.
- **Labeling the simulated product cycles**: In this stage, all collected production cycles are classified and labeled by an already existing classifier. So after this step, each cycle file should have a label with e.g. the production quality.
- **Enrichment of training sets**: To get a reasonable percentage of synthetic data in the real training data, different percentages were tried.
- **Testing and evaluation**: In order to compare the data sets, an LSTM network was trained with the different data, and the accuracy was compared on an independent evaluation dataset.

3.1   Simulation of Production Processes

In the context of generating synthetic data for injection molding processes, a similar approach can be taken as in the previously mentioned research areas such as 3D modeling and text in images. To generate synthetic data sets in a simulated injection molding environment, one can start by collecting real data from actual injection molding processes, which may include process parameters, machine settings, and part geometries.

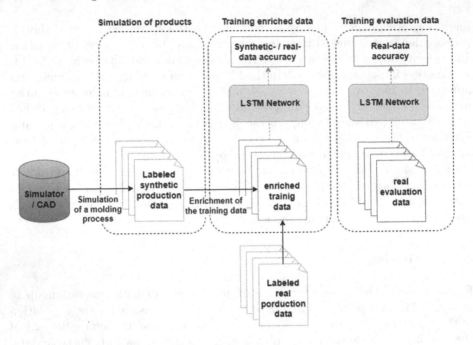

Fig. 1. System design of overall concept.

In our case, a CAD program and a production simulator serve as a virtual environment to generate synthetic data by changing parameters and introducing variability in process settings, part geometries, and material properties. In this way, a simulation model can be developed based on this real data to replicate the injection molding process in CAD and take into account key aspects such as material flow, cooling, and pressure distribution. In order to include all other boundary parameters of this production process, a production simulator, normally used for training purposes, was used to simulate the entire process. The simulator receives setting parameters, such as injection speed, changeover point, holding pressure level, and all common parameters of an injection molding machine. This results in the process parameters such as screw position, residual compound cushion, ejector speed, and many more. The simulator is a clone of the machine control and thus offers the possibility to use all setting parameters of a real machine and generate the production data based on them. All production data are output, but the values are not close to reality, which is why the CAD program mentioned above is used. In order to obtain a complete process as a time series file, the actual process of injecting the plastic was simulated in CAD, and in addition, the operating part and machine process were run on a production simulator.

3.2   Labeling the Simulated Product Cycles

In connection with the generation of synthetic data for injection molding processes, the CAD-based simulation model was extended by integrating a production simulator for generating time series data. This simulator allows us to generate synthetic data that capture the temporal dynamics of the injection molding process and provides valuable information for data-driven modeling and analysis. To obtain accurate labels for the generated time series data, we use our expertise and knowledge of the parameters set in the production simulator, as well as the output quality of the CAD fill study. This manual labeling approach ensures that the synthetic data is appropriately labeled, allowing effective use in ML applications. Alternatively, we could use an already trained simulator to automatically label the data, streamlining the process and increasing the overall efficiency of the data generation pipeline. An important aspect of our synthetic data generation methodology is to intentionally generate a larger percentage of non-compliant or defective products within the simulation. This is done to compensate for the inherent imbalance in real production data, where such cases are generally rare. By generating more diverse and balanced datasets that contain a larger number of non-conforming products, we can improve the performance of ML models, especially in tasks related to defect detection and process optimization.

3.3   Enrichment of Training Sets

To effectively incorporate synthetic data into the training process and improve the performance of ML models, it is critical to determine an appropriate balance between synthetic and real data in the training sets. The goal is to strike a balance between taking advantage of synthetic data and maintaining the authenticity and relevance of real data. Through iterative experimentation with different proportions of synthetic data, the goal is to find an appropriate balance that maximizes the benefits of synthetic data, such as improved model robustness and generalizability, while preserving the essential features of the real production data.

3.4   Testing and Evaluation

In this section, we investigate the impact of different proportions of synthetic data on the overall performance of ML models, specifically using an LSTM network. LSTM networks are an advanced alternative to traditional recurrent neural networks. They have become the first choice for processing time-series data because of their ability to effectively manage long-term dependencies in sequential data such as text, audio, and video [15]. We systematically evaluate different ratios of synthetic to real data in training sets, ranging from minimal inclusion of synthetic data to a significant amount. During this process, the LSTM models are trained and validated with training sets consisting of different mixtures of synthetic and real data. For a comparative analysis, we evaluate the accuracy of

LSTM models trained on semi-synthetic datasets compared to a validation set containing only real data. This approach allows us to measure the effectiveness of including synthetic data in the training process and determine an optimal ratio that maximizes model performance. Insights gained from this analysis help fine-tune the composition of training sets and ultimately contribute to improving the performance of ML models, particularly in tasks related to fault detection and process optimization.

4   Experimental Setup

4.1   Real Training and Validation Data

For our study, a data set of 275 injection molding processes was used as training data. An experienced injection molder evaluated the quality of the parts and recorded the relevant information for each production cycle. To ensure a wide range of processes, we intentionally varied key process parameters such as piston stroke, rounds per minute in odization, injection volume, back pressure, holding pressure, and other relevant factors. Given the inherent time intervals between sensor samples in the data, we chose a data augmentation strategy to improve the training data. The data set had a consistent interval of 10 ms between successive sensor samples within the time series. We enlarged each dataset by quadrupling it and stored each first through the fourth step at 10 ms intervals in separate files. Thus, the expanded data set included a total of 1100 labeled production cycle data points. These are divided into two classes with 56.5% good cycles and 43.5% not good cycles.

As data for the validation process for the trained model, 33% of the real data is taken. This corresponds to 363 data sets, which are shuffled in each training. This evaluation data set is important because it is separate and allows us to independently verify the results from the training and compare them to the data. Thus, the real data is split between 737 training data and 363 validation data.

4.2   Synthetic Data

For the synthetic dataset, 100 synthetic injection molding cycles were generated. These are divided into two classes 60%, not good cycles, and 40% good cycles. The 100 data sets were also quadrupled like the real data to augment them to 400 data sets. As explained in the Methods, the synthetic data were evaluated using the CAD output to assign the correct part quality corresponding to the class in the synthetic data set. Figure 2 illustrates the part qualities that were evaluated using the CAD program. Furthermore, in addition to the illustration, critical quality indicators and optimal parameters in the injection molding process such as material flow, cooling dynamics, and pressure distribution are displayed in the CAD program.

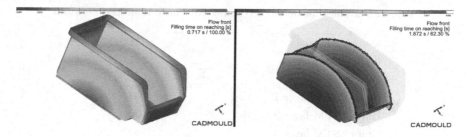

Fig. 2. A pictorial example of the evaluation of a CAD simulated filling study. *The production piece on the left is good, the piece on the right is rated as not good because it is not sufficiently filled.*

4.3   LSTM Training

The LSTM for our neural network, which is designed to process time series data, consists of 34 input neurons that comprise our feature in the injection molding process, one output neuron, and three LSTM layers. After each LSTM layer, a dropout layer is added to avoid overfitting. The first two LSTM layers have the return_sequences attribute set to True so they can maintain their state over multiple time steps. The paper "Sequence to Sequence Learning with Neural Networks" served as the approach for our network [12]. Here, the effectiveness of deep LSTM networks in handling complex tasks was demonstrated, which led us to use a similar architecture. Our LSTM network is designed for classification and follows a unidirectional many-to-one configuration [10]. This configuration allows the network to process a sequence of input data and produce a single output suitable for our classification task. Table 1 provides a detailed overview of the specific settings and variables used in our LSTM network, including layer configurations, activation functions, and other hyperparameters. By carefully selecting and tuning these settings, we aim to create an LSTM network that can provide accurate classification results for our time series data. It's important to note that we did not conduct an extensive comparison with other LSTM architectures for this study. The selected model was the best performer from our initial round of experimentation and seemed promising for our specific task.

The system used for all computation had a 12th Gen Intel Core i9-12900KS 3.40 GHz CPU with 64 GB memory and an NVIDIA GeForce RTX 3090 Ti GPU. As an environment, Tensorflow 2.11.0 and Keras 2.11.0 were used.

5   Results

5.1   Quality of Classification

In the following section, we present the results of our experiments on the classification of component qualities with different proportions of synthetic data. We conducted 7 training sessions with 50 runs each, where the proportion of synthetic data in the training data set ranged from 0% to 30% and was increased in increments of 5%.

Table 1. Variables for network training that have remained constant

Learning rate	0.0001175
Input dimension	34
Output size	1
Units LSTM layer 1	100
Units LSTM layer 2	100
Units LSTM layer 3	100
Dropout rate behind LSTM layer 1 and 2	0.1598
Dropout rate after last LSTM layer	0.279
Optimizer	Adam
Loss	MSE
Batch size	64
Epochs	50

In a subsequent training iteration, the synthetic data was increased in 5% increments within the overall data set. However, the overall size of the data set was kept constant to analyze the effects of a lower ratio of real data to synthetic data.

The goal of these experiments was to analyze the relationship between the inclusion of synthetic data in the training dataset and the performance of our LSTM model in terms of loss and accuracy. For each training session, the maximum and minimum values of loss and accuracy were evaluated and the average values were calculated for each of the 50 runs.

For example, for the test runs without synthetic data, the average validation accuracy was 93,6%, while the training accuracy was 92.8%. When 30% of synthetic data was added to the dataset in the first experimental run, the average validation accuracy dropped slightly to 92.3% and the training accuracy to 85.5%.

A detailed overview of the experimental results, including the different accuracy values and the distribution of synthetic data in the training, can be found in Table 2. Since the percentages are based on the total data set, Table 2 was expanded to include the column *"synthetic fraction training set"* because the training test split reduced the size of the real training set, and thus the percentage of synthetic data in the training had to be adjusted.

In the subsequent training phase, the overall size of the data set was kept constant while the proportion of synthetic data was adjusted. The goal of these experiments was to investigate the effects of adding synthetic variants to a smaller subset of real data. We started with a small subset of the real data and investigated whether the integration of synthetic data could improve performance results. Therefore, we first started the training with a smaller amount of synthetic data and then gradually filled it up with synthetic data until it was equal to the volume of our original real data set used as a benchmark for train-

Table 2. The distribution of the synthetic data added to the training set with the mean results from the validation data, training data, F1 score and AUC-ROC

Added synthetic data				Mean values					
Total set		Training set		Validation		Training		Performance meas.	
%	Count	%	Count	Accuracy	Loss	Accuracy	Loss	F1 score	AUC-ROC
0%	1100	0%	737	0.9363	0.05935	0.9284	0.06972	0.9238	0.9743
5%	1155	7.5%	792	0.9164	0.07419	0.8918	0.09062	0.8979	0.9637
10%	1210	15%	847	0.9221	0.07223	0.8795	0.09691	0.907	0.9673
15%	1265	22.4%	902	0.9007	0.087	0.8464	0.1168	0.8784	0.9542
20%	1320	29.9%	957	0.9165	0.07609	0.8548	0.1089	0.9009	0.9633
25%	1375	37.3%	1012	0.9139	0.07549	0.8515	0.11	0.8945	0.963
30%	1430	44.8%	1067	0.9233	0.07094	0.8523	0.1106	0.908	0.9677

ing. When the training set consisted of 55.2% real data derived from the original dataset and contained no synthetic data, we achieved an average validation accuracy of 82.7% and an average training accuracy of 82%. In contrast, when 44.8% of synthetic data was added to the dataset, the average validation accuracy increased to 83.9%, but the average training accuracy decreased to 75.5%. Table 3 shows these different metrics and represents a marginal deviation from our primary experimental framework.

Analyzing these results, we found that the training accuracy decreased as the proportion of synthetic data increased. The validation accuracy remained relatively stable despite the inclusion of synthetic data. This observation suggests that the inclusion of additional synthetic data in the training process does not significantly affect the overall accuracy of the model, but contributes to its robustness to potential perturbations.

Table 3. The distribution of the real and synthetic data in the training set with the mean results from the validation data, training data, F1 score and AUC-ROC

Training data				Mean values					
Real data		Synthetic data		Real data			Synthetic data		
%	Count	%	Count	Val. acc	Train. acc	F1 score	Val. acc	Train. acc	F1 score
100%	737	0%	0	0.9363	0.9284	0.9238	–	–	–
92.5%	682	7.5%	55	0.919	0.9143	0.9032	0.9144	0.8904	0.8965
85%	627	15%	110	0.906	0.904	0.8855	0.9123	0.8666	0.8941
77.6%	572	22.4%	165	0.8889	0.882	0.8636	0.9059	0.8485	0.887
70.1%	517	29.9%	220	0.8173	0.8201	0.7636	0.8755	0.8076	0.8475
62.7%	462	37.3%	275	0.8491	0.8509	0.8034	0.8576	0.783	0.8182
55.2%	407	44.8%	330	0.8273	0.82	0.7745	0.8397	0.755	0.7922

Figure 3 illustrates the robustness of the model from the first experimental run to perturbations by comparing the validation accuracies and losses for data sets with 0% and 30% synthetic data. It can be observed that the validation accuracy loss graph is relatively similar in both cases, but the training accuracy loss graph shows a larger variation for the dataset with 30% synthetic data than for the dataset with 0% synthetic data. Moreover, the training accuracies and losses decrease more, as shown by the shifted values in the graph.

The robustness of our model from the first experimental run is remarkable given the inherent unpredictability of synthetic data. Despite these challenges, our model showed an small change in the loss and accuracy metrics, as mentioned earlier. This minimal impact was reflected in only negligible changes in the F1 score and the area under the receiver operating characteristic curve (AUC-ROC). Thus, Table 2 shows that the F1 score is 0.9238 for 0% synthetic data and only 0.908 for 30% synthetic data as another example, the ROC-AUC is listed, which is 0.9743 for 0% synthetic data and 0.9677 for 30% synthetic data. This proves that our model maintained not only its robustness but also its predictive capabilities, confirming the usability of synthetic data in data analysis and machine learning tasks.

Table 3 demonstrates that the F1 score is improved with the inclusion of more than 15% synthetic data compared to an absence of synthetic data in our dataset. The results indicate that with a smaller training set, we can slightly enhance validation accuracy, even though the training accuracy is somewhat inferior compared to when the training solely relies on real data. In our second experimental iteration, we illustrate that the high quality of our data enables us to not only strengthen the model with minimal training data but also effectively augment it with data that marginally improves the training, even if just by a single percentage point. Therefore, we observe that the validation accuracy of a modest dataset, when supplemented with synthetic data, surpasses that of a non-augmented dataset.

6   Evaluation

Our study provided us with valuable insights into the use of synthetic data, but we still had two major limitations in our approach.

First, the amount of real-world data available for training was insufficient to create a fully representative dataset. This limitation resulted in the LSTM network achieving an average validation accuracy of about 94% on the real data set, which is a satisfactory result for the beginning, but cannot be generalized due to the small amount of data. Another limitation related to the process of generating synthetic data using CAD simulation. The labeling of the injection molding cycles had to be done manually, as our automated method for this crucial step had not yet been worked out. This manual approach increased the overall time and effort required for data preparation.

Future research should attempt to address these limitations by incorporating larger, more representative real-world datasets and automating the labeling process to generate synthetic data.

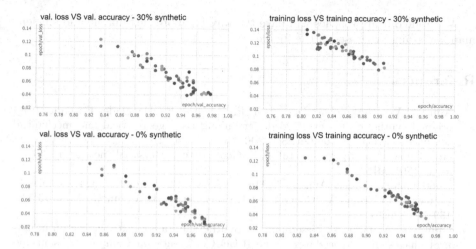

Fig. 3. While the validation accuracies and losses with 30% synthetic data *(top left)* and 0% synthetic data *(bottom left)* remain relatively the same, one can see that the training accuracy loss graph scatters much more for a dataset with 30% synthetic data *(top right)* than to a dataset with 0% *(bottom right)*.

7   Conclusion

We have shown that it is possible to train injection molding processes with a combination of real and synthetic data to improve the robustness of the resulting models. Our results suggest that the inclusion of synthetic data in the training process not only improves the model's ability to handle different scenarios but also offers promising potential for practical industrial applications. By incorporating synthetic data, we can improve the performance and generalization ability of ML models.

Thus, in the next studies, we will try to increase the synthetic fraction in our data as much as possible. In addition, we will try to use Generative Adversarial Networks (GANs) to generate more synthetic data that also take into account the noise and uncertainties of real-world data [2,3]. For a less complex label process to evaluate the production cycles, we will try to train an independent classifier in the future that can label the synthetic data. This will allow us to spend more time augmenting the data and start trying to train a GAN that will generate data without simulation ,which holds the potential to generate more realistic, high-quality synthetic data.

By applying our approach, it may be possible to reduce the need for manual labor, machine usage, and material waste associated with traditional injection molding process optimization. In addition, our method offers a valuable alternative in situations where extensive data collection and maintenance has been impractical or costly. This can be beneficial to any company that does not have the resources to invest in extensive data collection.

We hope our approaches will pave the way for more sustainable and efficient manufacturing processes in the future.

References

1. Almasri, W., Bettebghor, D., Adjed, F., Ababsa, F., Danglade, F.: Gmcad: an original synthetic dataset of 2d designs along their geometrical and mechanical conditions. Procedia Comput. Sci. **200**, 337–347 (2022)
2. Goodfellow, I.: Nips 2016 tutorial: Generative adversarial networks (2016). arXiv:1701.00160
3. Goodfellow, I., Pouget-Abadie, J., Mirza, M., Xu, B., Warde-Farley, D., Ozair, S., Courville, A., Bengio, Y.: Generative adversarial networks. Commun. ACM **63**(11), 139–144 (2020)
4. Gupta, A., Vedaldi, A., Zisserman, A.: Synthetic data for text localisation in natural images. In: Proceedings of the IEEE Conference on Computer Vision and Pattern Recognition, pp. 2315–2324 (2016)
5. Khomenko, M., Veligorskyi, O., Chakirov, R., Vagapov, Y.: An ann-based temperature controller for a plastic injection moulding system. Electronics **8**(11), 1272 (2019)
6. Kozjek, D., Butala, P., et al.: Knowledge elicitation for fault diagnostics in plastic injection moulding: a case for machine-to-machine communication. CIRP Ann. **66**(1), 433–436 (2017)
7. Mukras, S.M., Al-Mufadi, F.A.: Simulation of hdpe mold filling in the injection molding process with comparison to experiments. Arab. J. Sci. Eng. **41**, 1847–1856 (2016)
8. Patki, N., Wedge, R., Veeramachaneni, K.: The synthetic data vault. In: 2016 IEEE International Conference on Data Science and Advanced Analytics (DSAA), pp. 399–410. IEEE (2016)
9. Roh, Y., Heo, G., Whang, S.E.: A survey on data collection for machine learning: a big data-ai integration perspective. IEEE Trans. Knowl. Data Eng. **33**(4), 1328–1347 (2019)
10. Smagulova, K., James, A.P.: A survey on lstm memristive neural network architectures and applications. Eur. Phys. J. Spec. Top. **228**(10), 2313–2324 (2019)
11. Speight, R., Costa, F., Kennedy, P., Friedl, C.: Best practice for benchmarking injection moulding simulation. Plast., Rubber Compos. **37**(2–4), 124–130 (2008)
12. Sutskever, I., Vinyals, O., Le, Q.V.: Sequence to sequence learning with neural networks. Adv. Neural Inf. Process. Syst. **27** (2014)
13. Veligorskyi, O., Chakirov, R., Khomenko, M., Vagapov, Y.: Artificial neural network motor control for full-electric injection moulding machine. In: 2019 IEEE International Conference on Industrial Technology (ICIT), pp. 60–65. IEEE (2019)
14. Wong, M.Z., Kunii, K., Baylis, M., Ong, W.H., Kroupa, P., Koller, S.: Synthetic dataset generation for object-to-model deep learning in industrial applications. Peer J. Comput. Sci. **5**, e222 (2019)
15. Yu, Y., Si, X., Hu, C., Zhang, J.: A review of recurrent neural networks: Lstm cells and network architectures. Neural Comput. **31**(7), 1235–1270 (2019)
16. Zhou, H., Shi, S., Ma, B.: A virtual injection molding system based on numerical simulation. Int. J. Adv. Manuf. Technol. **40**, 297–306 (2009)

Vision Transformers Applied to Indoor Room Classification

Bruno Veiga[1,2], Tiago Pinto[1(✉)] (iD), Rúben Teixeira[2], and Carlos Ramos[1] (iD)

[1] Research Group on Intelligent Engineering and Computing for Advanced Innovation and Development (GECAD), School of Engineering - Polytechnic of Porto (ISEP/IPP), Porto, Portugal
1180712@isep.ipp.pt, bruno.veiga@devscope.net, tcp@isep.ipp.pt, csr@isep.ipp.pt
[2] DevScope, Porto, Portugal
ruben.teixeira@devscope.net

Abstract. Real Estate Agents perform the tedious job of selecting and filtering pictures of houses manually on a daily basis, in order to choose the most suitable ones for their websites and provide a better description of the properties they are selling. However, this process consumes a lot of time, causing delays in the advertisement of homes and reception of proposals. In order to expedite and automate this task, Computer Vision solutions can be employed. Deep Learning, which is a subfield of Machine Learning, has been highly successful in solving image recognition problems, making it a promising solution for this particular context. Therefore, this paper proposes the application of Vision Transformers to indoor room classification. The study compares various image classification architectures, ranging from traditional Convolutional Neural Networks to the latest Vision Transformer architecture. Using a dataset based on well-known scene classification datasets, their performance is analyzed. The results demonstrate that Vision Transformers are one of the most effective architectures for indoor classification, with highly favorable outcomes in automating image recognition and selection in the Real Estate industry.

Keywords: Indoor classification · Computer vision · Deep learning · Vision transformer · Convolutional neural network

1 Introduction

Image Classification is one of the problems treated by Computer Vision [23] and refers to the ability of a machine, when presented with an image, successfully indicating its category [18]. One of the first works in image classification dates back to 1967, with the creation of a face recognition system by Woodrow W. Bledsoe, which used a graphical computer input device named RAND tablet [26].

© The Author(s), under exclusive license to Springer Nature Switzerland AG 2023
N. Moniz et al. (Eds.): EPIA 2023, LNAI 14116, pp. 561–573, 2023.
https://doi.org/10.1007/978-3-031-49011-8_44

After that, several studies appeared basing image processing and classification on low-level image analysis, but this technique presented difficulties in semantically describing scenes [25,27]. The next step was the usage of K-nearest neighbours which was a very predominant technique for this task [27,29], with some papers even pairing it with Bayes Networks [3]. Other classic machine learning algorithms have also been used throughout the years, such as: Random Forest (RF) [4], Support Vector Machine (SVM) [13] or even Decision Tree [16]. More recently, [18] presents an approach that utilizes a 5 step technique: image segmentation, object identification, image feature extraction, image feature selection and classification. For classification, the authors use 4 classifiers: BayesNet, Naive Bayes Updatable, Random Tree and IBk. This aproach presented good results for the Calltech-101 dataset [9] when using the BayesNet classifier, with accuracies above 95%. Despite this, an analysis of the source [9] suggests a recent shift to the usage of Convolutional Neural Networks (CNNs) when training with this dataset, although not many examples are present. This lack of results for the given dataset can also be explained due to the preference of other bigger datasets, that better reflect the quality of these types of models, like ImageNet [6].

Furthermore, the results presented for the ImageNet dataset clearly show that Deep Learning is now the predominant form for classification tasks [21], exhibiting since 2012, an increasing use of CNNs and then more recently, a shift towards Visual Transformers (ViT). The advances in image classification models are relevant for real estate agents, who have to select pictures from homes that need to be sold and present them in their selling platforms. Not only the filtering and selection of images is a time taking task that slows down the process of advertising the houses, it gets increasingly worse when the number of houses increases. In fact, some studies exhibit that the entire uploading procedure is increased by 40 h [5].

For this reason, this paper presents an approach based on Vision Transformers for the task of classifying indoor rooms, in order to avoid leaving these repetitive tasks of manual filtering images for house advertisement to humans, when Computer Vision solutions are perfectly capable of helping with very good performances. Another important contribution provided in this work is the study and comparison between the proposed ViT model and the classic CNNs used for image classification tasks, since, recently, Transformers have proven to be better for state of the art datasets like ImageNet and there is a lack of studies showing how good this new architecture performs for indoor room classification.

Following this first section, Sect. 2 examines related work in this field, delving into techniques, datasets and achieved results. Architectural explanations of ViT and benchmark architectures utilized for comparison are provided in Sect. 3. The explanation of the methodology used for the achieved results is presented in Sect. 4. Case studies' results are presented in Sect. 5, while the conclusions and main contributions of the paper are outlined in Sect. 6.

2   Related Work

In this section, the main results of the research performed to identify similar work in the field is presented, starting with Table 1, where a summary of the most relevant datasets and techniques is presented. After that, a discussion of the most important points brought by these works is presented.

Table 1. Summary of datasets and techniques present in state of art

Paper	Dataset	Technique
Quattoni and Torralba [22]	15620 images and 67 classes	Prototype based model that utilizes local and global information
[8]	Selected images retrieved from Label Me, Google Images and Calltech 101	Generative probabilistic hierarchical model
Nascimento et al. [19]	Scene15, MIT67 and SUN397	Sparse coding setting that utilizes global and local features in a CNN
Wang et al. [31]	5000 images of floor plans crawled from the web	Classification model based on a C4.5 decision tree and YOLOv3
Hayat et al. [10]	MIT-67, Scene-15, Sports-8, Graz-02 and NYU	CNN using a new feature descriptor
Lu et al. [15]	1500 photos taken under very different environment and lighting conditions for 10 different classes	Linear Discriminant Analysis (LDA) and Probability Density Response Maps (PDRM)
Wang et al. [32]	Graph dataset from 224 apartment layouts with 9 room types	Graph Neural networks (GNN) It tries to classify 9 room types and

The work in [12] presents a literature review of the application of computer vision tasks applied to real estate, such as the identification of the architecture style, the elements present, its values, other similar houses and of course, indoor tasks. For indoors, the paper presents, besides classification, reconstruction of 3D images of the spaces and evaluation of the market value based on those indoors. For the specific problem of indoor room classification, the review presents 5 different papers that address it, although the last two only introduce a new dataset, the SUN 397 [33,34] with 108,753 images of 397 categories.

The first one, [22] combines a set of global and local features to help the model. This is defended, because for some indoor spaces, global features will be sufficient to understand the space which is being dealt with, like corridors, while others, like bookshelves make the classification task easier by identifying the existence of books. The dataset is constituted by 15620 images distributed by 67 classes and in order to apply the technique described, the authors utilized a human annotator to segment a set of images with their regions of interest (ROI). These scenes are not labeled, only identified, but the final objective is that these local properties help the model understand what type of room or division is present in an image, since similar objects will likely be in similar divisions. The results are quite heterogeneous for all the classes but that is not totally unexpected since the training was performed with a high number of classes.

The second paper, [8] presents a generative probabilistic hierarchical model, that utilizes the identification of objects present in rooms as intermediate representations to help classify them. Once again, the reason for this approach is that particular scenes will have particular objects that help models predict with bigger conviction levels. Here, a dataset with selected images from Label Me [24], Google Images and Caltech 101 [9] was used. The results were promising, with the authors identifying better performances when compared with Oliva and Torralba Gist approaches [20].

Finally, the third paper, [19] presents a sparse coding setting that utilizes global and local features in a CNN, in order to solve the problem of loosing important local details due to the way weights are adjusted. It shows good results by being able to compete with previous approaches for some datasets, like the MIT67 [22], Scenes15 [2] and SUN 397 [33,34].

The work presented in [31] proposes an approach that aims to facilitate the task of 3D room construction and decoration based on floor plans, by providing a classifier that provides textual information on rooms that are not described, which is required by the 3D models. For that, a door and window detection model is also developed using YOLOv3 to help their classification model based on a C4.5 decision tree perform better. The results were very promising with the classification algorithm having an accuracy of 78.71%.

Reference [10] proposes a CNN that uses a new feature descriptor that deals with the challenge of large-scale spatial layout deformations and scale variations. This is achieved thanks to a new "spatially unstructured" layer that is able to implement robustness against spatial layout deformations and obtains better accuracies than the baseline models, like VGG and GoogLeNet for MIT-67, Scene-15, Sports-8, Graz-02 and NYU datasets.

The work in [15] shows an approach to classify both binary indoor-outdoor images and multi class indoor rooms. This model uses probability density response maps (PDRM) that indicate how likely each region is to be created by a class, extracting features from it and using them to train a Linear Discriminant Analysis (LDA). The model is used for classifying 10 different classes, with a dataset of 1500 photos taken in different conditions, obtaining accuracies of 90.1%.

Paper [32] proposes a new algorithm, SAGE-E that utilizes Graph Neural networks (GNN) to semantic enrich Building Information Modeling (BIM). It uses a graph dataset of 224 different apartment layouts and tries to classify 9 room types and achieves accuracies of 79%. It shows better performances than other algorithms, like decision trees while shortening the training and validation process.

All in all, despite the good results presented by these studies, even in famous research datasets, there is still a gap related to the application and analysis of the performance of Vision Transformers applied to the particular field of indoor room classification. This gap is especially relevant considering the excellent performance Vision Transformers are achieving in other image classification problems.

3   Image Classification Models

3.1   Vision Transformer

In 2020, some work related to the application of Transformers for computer vision tasks started to appear. The article [7] is one of these examples and it presents a Vision Transformer architecture based on the original transformer architecture presented in [30]. Although Transformers are the best architectures for natural language processing, capable of processing over 10B parameters, first tests of this architecture in computer vision did not produce such results. This was due to the fact that Transformers thrive with bigger datasets than the ones that were used at first and when the authors trained these models on datasets with more than 14M images, they were able to obtain state of the art top 1 accuracies of 88.6% for the ImageNet dataset. Figure 1 presents the architecture used by Vision Transformer.

Figure 1 shows that this process starts by dividing the images in several patches of the same size for height and width, each one with several channels. Theses patches are then flatenned and sent to a linear projection where embeddings for each patch will be created, as well as a general embedding representative of the whole image. Position embeddings are also added to help the model understand their original positions.

After that, these patches will be used by the transformer encoder, that consists in several alternating layers of Multi-head Self Attention (MHSA) and Multi Layer Perceptron (MLP) blocks with a normalization applied before each one of them, as well as a residual connection after each block. The MHSA utilizes parallel attention mechanisms to focus on different positions and subspaces, where the attention mechanism relates positions and indicates to one position what to focus on, around it, to help understand its meaning. For example, in a sentence, for a word, the attention mechanism will tell which other words in the sentence are closely related to it, while on images, it will point out the most important parts to classify it.

For this, three vectors are necessary: the Query (Q), Key (K) and Value (V), that are obtained by multiplying the embedding by three trainable weight matrices. Then, the scaled dot-product attention occurs. The dot product between Queries and Keys is calculated, followed by a division of each by the square root of the number of the Key values and an application of a softmax function to get the Value weights that are then multiplied by the Values. In reality, all these operations are done in matrices to increase the speed of processing and the formula can be represented as the Eq. 1 according to [30]:

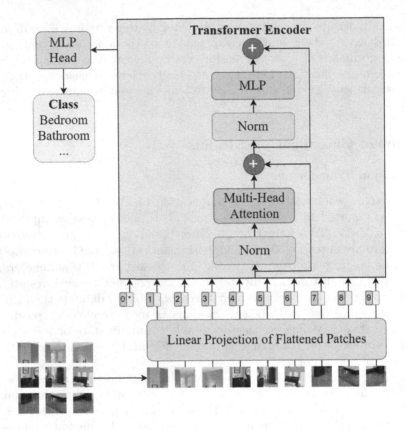

Fig. 1. Vision transformer architecture representation (based on [7])

$$Attention(Q, K, V) = softmax\left(\frac{QK^T}{\sqrt{d_k}}\right)V \qquad (1)$$

where Q, K and V are the Query, Key and Value matrices and d_k is the Key dimension. On the other hand, the MLP consists in two linear layers with a GELU function for non linearity. Finally, a MLP head is added which consists in a simple fully connected layer to classify the outputs of the transformer block in the respective class.

3.2   Benchmark Models

The Benchmark models are composed by classic CNN architectures, selected based on popularity and recent performance.

The Residual Networks or ResNet [11] were for many years the go to model for the problems expressed in this paper and they are still very used because they were the first network that started using the skip connections between layers. This is a type of connection that unites non-sequential layers to avoid the gradient vanishing problem, that deeper networks suffer from, where the gradient tends to reach values of 0 in the initial layers and affect the performance.

EfficientNets [28] are one of the few types of CNNs that recently were still able to rival with Vision Transformers, even though now they are starting to fall even more behind. This type of architecture makes use of the neural architecture search technique to first create a base model and then improves it by scaling hyperparameters, such as the width, depth and resolution using a grid search and a compound coefficient ϕ that represents the available computational resources.

The ConvNeXts [14] are one the most recent CNN architectures created with the purpose of rivaling with Vision Transformers. It establishes itself by trying to apply those properties that have been working really well with the Vision Transformers, more specifically, the Swin-t Transformer. In particular, it incorporates the following changes: compute ratio with 3, 3, 9, 3 blocks, "patchify" stem, fewer activation functions prioritizing the GELU function, normalization layers, down sampling layers and inverted botleneck modules.

4 Methodology

In this section, the datasets and overall methodologies used for creating the case studies are presented. The dataset was created with resource to several research base datasets, like MIT 67 [22], SUN 397 [33, 34], Places 365 [36], Houses Dataset [1] and House Rooms & Streets Image Dataset [17], as well as some web scraping of images.

All these datasets were combined in one, while going for a few pre-processing steps for label treatment and duplication check, as well as a separation in three different sets: train, test and validation. After all this, the final dataset presents the following properties:

- 15 classes: yard, utilityroom, staircase, patio, outsideview, office, livingroom, kitchen, garage, diningroom, corridor, closet, bedroom, bathroom, balcony.
- 4000 images per training class.
- 700 images per testing class.
- 600 images per validation class.

Then, for studying the architectures, three different methodologies that show the layers that are trainable were created:

- **Methodology 1**: Training all the weights available by unfreezing all the pre-trained model layers. This methodology requires low learning rate to avoid overfitting the model, since the first, more general layers are being trained.
- **Methodology 2**: Leaving all the layers of the pre-trained model frozen, acting like a feature extractor in a first instance, and unfreezing all or some of the last blocks of the network when the results are minimally good, retraining, with a low learning rate, the unfrozen layers. This methodology is based on the fact pre-trained weights are usually trained on millions of images and present good performances without retraining.

– **Methodology 3**: Unfreezing only the last blocks of the pre-trained network and train these unfrozen layers from the start. This methodology follows the idea of the previous one, but builds up on the fact that the last layers usually produce more specific features related to the images used in training.

In these methodologies, the objective was creating the best possible model for each one, by tweaking hyperparameters, like the batch size and learning rate, while the resolution of the images was maintained throughout the tests.

The assessed models are those described in Sect. 3, namely the Visual Transformers and the considered benchmark models. The specific versions used for these experiments are as follows:

– **Vision Transformer**: Vision Transformer Base Patch 16.
– **ResNet**: ResNet 152v2 version, due to being the one available with the best pre-trained accuracy.
– **EfficientNet**: EfficientNet V2L version was utilized, since it was the one with the best top-1 accuracy.
– **ConvNeXt**: ConvNeXt Large version was preferred because it was the most balanced in terms of performance and memory.

5   Results

In order to assess the quality of results, Table 2 presents the comparison of the overall results (using the F1-score) of the considered models using the three methodologies described in Sect. 4. Table 3 presents a summarised version of all the results obtained for the best methodology of each architecture. The tables of this section include different colors that highlight the quality of the achieved results, as follows. Red: below 80%, yellow: 80–84%, light green: 85–89%, dark green: 90% or above.

Table 2. F1-score of the different models for the three methodologies

Model	Methodology 1 (%)	Methodology 2 (%)	Methodology 3 (%)
ResNet 152v2	82	81	82
EfficientNet V2L	84	86	86
ConvNeXt Large	87	86	86
ViT B 16	87	86	87

Table 3. F1-score of the best model variation of each architecture

Best model variation	Train accuracy (%)	Validation accuracy (%)	Test accuracy (%)	F1-score (%)
ResNet 152v2	85	86	82	82
EfficientNet V2L	91	88	86	86
ConvNeXt Large	89	90	87	87
ViT B 16	94	90	87	87

From Table 2, one can see that the ViT is the model that achieves the best F1-score among all the tested models. Its performance is very similar to that of ConvNeXt, but the ViT is still able to achieve better results using Methodology 3. From Table 3 it is also visible that, considering only the best model variations and the methodology that achieves the best result for each model, the ViT is able to surpass all the benchmark models regarding training accuracy, while being at least as good as the best benchmark model in terms of validation and test accuracy. Table 4 shows the detail of the F1-score performance that the ViT achieves per classification class. Here, the ViT performs the best for classes bathroom, bedroom, closet, corridor, office and staircase, while presenting the most problems for the class patio. For these classes, ViT is able to achieve F1-scores of at least 90% with at least one of the three methodologies.

ResNet models have all obtained very similar results, with F1-scores of 81% for Methodology 2 and 82% for Methodologies 1 and 3, but some perform better for some classes than the others. For example, Methodology 1 performs the best on the closet, kitchen and living room classes with F1 scores of 87, 80 and 75%, respectively, while Methodology 2 is the best for the balcony, staircase and yard category with F1-scores of 83, 85 and 81%. Methodology 3 has better results for the classes of bedroom, outside view and patio, with respective F1-scores of 87, 83 and 73%.

EfficientNet achieves a general improvement when compared to the ResNet results, with F1-scores of 84, 86 and 86 %, for Methodologies 1, 2 and 3, respectively. Methodology 2 and 3 are the ones with a bigger improvement, where there is only one class with F1-Scores below 80%, the patio, while many others reached the 90% mark, such as the bathroom, bedroom and closet categories. Methodology 1 also improves on the ResNet results by 2%, managing to reach F1-scores of 90% for the classes bathroom, bedroom and corridor.

The ConvNeXt results show that the F1-scores are only improved compared to the other benchmark models when using Methodology 1. The number of classes in Methodology 1 with F1-scores above 90% also increased significantly when compared to ResNet and EfficientNet, with the corridor, office and staircase categories reaching this threshold. Previous problematic classes have also been quite improved with patio still being the only one below 80%, while the categories

Table 4. F1-score for ViT base patch 16 models

Classes	Methodology 1 (%)	Methodology 2 (%)	Methodology 3 (%)
Balcony	86	84	86
Bathroom	92	93	92
Bedroom	94	94	94
Closet	91	91	92
Corridor	92	89	92
Dining room	83	85	84
Garage	89	84	87
Kitchen	82	85	83
Living room	81	82	82
Office	88	90	87
Outside view	86	83	85
Patio	77	77	78
Staircase	91	88	91
Utility room	83	83	83
Yard	84	81	83
overall	**87**	**86**	**87**

kitchen, living room, dining room and yard achieved F1-scores between 83 and 84%. The remaining two methodologies ended with F1-scores of 86%, hence similar to ResNet and EfficientNet.

Overall, the most problematic classes to be classified among all the tested models are related to the living room, kitchen, dining room, patio and yard classifications. Here, the problems are down to the fact these indoor categories such as kitchen, dining room and living room coexist many times with no physical barriers between them, which means that in some of the images, more than one category may be present and the model predicts the one that is not the label. In other cases, some houses do not have a specific dining room and the type of tables that are used for dining, are placed either in the kitchen or the living room, which consequently makes the model predict dining room wrong. Regarding the outside classes, patio and yard, these also suffer from the problem of both being present in many images simultaneously and sometimes they even incorporate parts of house, which falls in the outside view class.

6   Conclusion

This paper proposes Vision Transformers as the state of the art architecture for the task of indoor classification and makes an analysis of the main neural network architectures for image classification and how they perform. Results show that even the most basic Vision Transformers are already able to surpass the performance of the most recent CNN architectures. Despite the results obtained show that the Vision Transformer architecture improved only a little when compared with the ConvNeXt results, the version used for the Vision Transformer was one of the most basic ones and, recently, works involving more advanced architectures, like the Constrastive Captioner [35] are emerging. This means that it is likely that more recent Vision Transformers like this would produce even better results than those shown in this paper. Future work should consist in testing these recent Vision Transformer architectures, like the Contrastive Captioner, and compare their performance to the present results.

In conclusion, this architecture will be advantageous to Real Estate Agents during the process of promoting properties, absolving them of the laborious task of sorting images with a model that exhibits outstanding performance.

Acknowledgments. This work has been funded by DevScope. The authors acknowledge the work facilities and equipment provided by GECAD research center (UIDB/00760/2020) to the project team.

References

1. Ahmed, E., Moustafa, M.: House price estimation from visual and textual features (2016). arXiv:1609.08399
2. Ali, N., Zafar, B.: 15-Scene Image Dataset (2018). https://doi.org/10.6084/m9.figshare.7007177.v1, https://figshare.com/articles/dataset/15-Scene_Image_Dataset/7007177
3. Boiman, O., Shechtman, E., Irani, M.: In defense of nearest-neighbor based image classification. In: 2008 IEEE Conference on Computer Vision and Pattern Recognition, pp. 1–8 (2008). https://doi.org/10.1109/CVPR.2008.4587598
4. Bosch, A., Zisserman, A., Munoz, X.: Image classification using random forests and ferns. In: 2007 IEEE 11th International Conference on Computer Vision, pp. 1–8 (2007). https://doi.org/10.1109/ICCV.2007.4409066
5. Chhikara, P., Goyal, A., Sharma, C.: Re- tagger: A light-weight real-estate image classifier. In: Amini, M.R., Canu, S., Fischer, A., Guns, T., Kralj Novak, P., Tsoumakas, G. (eds.) Machine Learning and Knowledge Discovery in Databases, pp. 627–630. Springer Nature Switzerland, Cham (2023)
6. Deng, J., Dong, W., Socher, R., Li, L.J., Li, K., Fei-Fei, L.: Imagenet: A large-scale hierarchical image database. In: 2009 IEEE Conference on Computer Vision and Pattern Recognition, pp. 248–255 (2009). https://doi.org/10.1109/CVPR.2009.5206848
7. Dosovitskiy, A., Beyer, L., Kolesnikov, A., Weissenborn, D., Zhai, X., Unterthiner, T., Dehghani, M., Minderer, M., Heigold, G., Gelly, S., Uszkoreit, J., Houlsby, N.: An image is worth 16x16 words: Transformers for image recognition at scale. In: International Conference on Learning Representations (2021)
8. Espinace, P., Kollar, T., Soto, A., Roy, N.: Indoor scene recognition through object detection. In: 2010 IEEE International Conference on Robotics and Automation, pp. 1406–1413. IEEE (2010)
9. Fei-Fei, L., Fergus, R., Perona, P.: Learning generative visual models from few training examples: An incremental bayesian approach tested on 101 object categories. In: Computer Vision and Pattern Recognition Workshop (2004)

10. Hayat, M., Khan, S.H., Bennamoun, M., An, S.: A spatial layout and scale invariant feature representation for indoor scene classification. IEEE Trans. Image Process. **25**(10), 4829–4841 (2016). https://doi.org/10.1109/TIP.2016.2599292
11. He, K., Zhang, X., Ren, S., Sun, J.: Deep residual learning for image recognition. In: Proceedings of the IEEE Conference on Computer Vision and Pattern Recognition, pp. 770–778 (2016)
12. Koch, D., Despotovic, M., Leiber, S., Sakeena, M., Doeller, M., Zeppelzauer, M.: Real estate image analysis: A literature review. J. R. Estate Lit. **27**, 269–300 (2019). https://doi.org/10.22300/0927-7544.27.2.269
13. Li, J., Huang, S., He, R., Qian, K.: Image classification based on fuzzy support vector machine. In: 2008 International Symposium on Computational Intelligence and Design, vol. 1, pp. 68–71 (2008). https://doi.org/10.1109/ISCID.2008.51
14. Liu, Z., Mao, H., Wu, C., Feichtenhofer, C., Darrell, T., Xie, S.: A convnet for the 2020s (2022). ArXiv:abs/2201.03545, https://arxiv.org/abs/2201.03545
15. Lu, L., Toyama, K., Hager, G.: A two level approach for scene recognition. In: 2005 IEEE Computer Society Conference on Computer Vision and Pattern Recognition (CVPR'05), vol. 1, pp. 688–695 (2005). https://doi.org/10.1109/CVPR.2005.51
16. Marée, R., Geurts, P., Piater, J., Wehenkel, L.: Biomedical image classification with random subwindows and decision trees. In: International Workshop on Computer Vision for Biomedical Image Applications, pp. 220–229. Springer, Berlin (2005)
17. Mazurov, M.: House rooms & streets image dataset (2022). https://www.kaggle.com/datasets/mikhailma/house-rooms-streets-image-dataset. Accessed 12 Dec 2022
18. Mokhairi, M., Engku Fadzli Hasan, S.A., Nur Shazwani, K.: Comparison of image classification techniques using caltech 101 dataset. J. Theor. Appl. Inf. Technol. **71**(1), 79–86 (2015)
19. Nascimento, G., Laranjeira, C., Braz, V., Lacerda, A., Nascimento, E.R.: A robust indoor scene recognition method based on sparse representation. In: Mendoza, M., Velastín, S. (eds.) Progress in Pattern Recognition, Image Analysis, Computer Vision, and Applications, pp. 408–415. Springer International Publishing, Cham (2018)
20. Oliva, A., Torralba, A.: Modeling the shape of the scene: A holistic representation of the spatial envelope. Int. J. Comput. Vision **42**(3), 145–175 (2001)
21. Papers with code: Image classification on imagenet (2022). https://paperswithcode.com/sota/image-classification-on-imagenet. Accessed 12 Dec 2022
22. Quattoni, A., Torralba, A.: Recognizing indoor scenes. In: 2009 IEEE Conference on Computer Vision and Pattern Recognition, pp. 413–420 (2009). https://doi.org/10.1109/CVPR.2009.5206537
23. Roberts, L.G.: Machine perception of three-dimensional solids. Ph.D. thesis, Massachusetts Institute of Technology (1963)
24. Russell, B.C., Torralba, A., Murphy, K.P., Freeman, W.T.: Labelme: a database and web-based tool for image annotation. Int. J. Comput. Vision **77**(1), 157–173 (2008)
25. Smith, S.M., Brady, J.M.: Susan-a new approach to low level image processing. Int. J. Comput. Vision **23**(1), 45–78 (1997)
26. Sullivan, E.: Facial Recognition Technology (2021). https://leg.mt.gov/content/Committees/Interim/2021-2022/EconomicAffairs/Meetings/September2021/facial-recognition-technology.pdf

27. Szummer, M., Picard, R.W.: Indoor-outdoor image classification. In: Proceedings 1998 IEEE International Workshop on Content-Based Access of Image and Video Database, pp. 42–51. IEEE (1998)

28. Tan, M., Le, Q.: Efficientnet: Rethinking model scaling for convolutional neural networks. In: International Conference on Machine Learning, pp. 6105–6114. PMLR (2019)

29. Vailaya, A., Jain, A., Zhang, H.J.: On image classification: City images vs. landscapes. Pattern Recognit. **31**(12), 1921–1935 (1998). https://doi.org/10.1016/S0031-3203(98)00079-X, https://www.sciencedirect.com/science/article/pii/S003132039800079X

30. Vaswani, A., Shazeer, N., Parmar, N., Uszkoreit, J., Jones, L., Gomez, A.N., Kaiser, L., Polosukhin, I.: Attention is all you need. Adv. Neural Inf. Process. Syst. **30** (2017)

31. Wang, W., Dong, S., Zou, K., LI, W.S.: Room classification in floor plan recognition. In: 2020 4th International Conference on Advances in Image Processing, pp. 48–54. ICAIP 2020, Association for Computing Machinery, New York, NY, USA (2021). https://doi.org/10.1145/3441250.3441265

32. Wang, Z., Sacks, R., Yeung, T.: Exploring graph neural networks for semantic enrichment: Room type classification. Autom. Constr. **134**, 104039 (2022)

33. Xiao, J., Ehinger, K.A., Hays, J., Torralba, A., Oliva, A.: Sun database: Exploring a large collection of scene categories. Int. J. Comput. Vision **119**(1), 3–22 (2016)

34. Xiao, J., Hays, J., Ehinger, K.A., Oliva, A., Torralba, A.: Sun database: Large-scale scene recognition from abbey to zoo. In: 2010 IEEE Computer Society Conference on Computer Vision and Pattern Recognition, pp. 3485–3492. IEEE (2010)

35. Yu, J., Wang, Z., Vasudevan, V., Yeung, L., Seyedhosseini, M., Wu, Y.: Coca: Contrastive captioners are image-text foundation models (2022). arXiv:2205.01917

36. Zhou, B., Lapedriza, A., Khosla, A., Oliva, A., Torralba, A.: Places: A 10 million image database for scene recognition. IEEE Trans. Pattern Anal. Mach. Intell. (2017)

Author Index

A

Abdelhamid, Yasser   II-467
Agirrezabal, Manex   II-3
Ahmed, Areeg   II-467
Albuquerque, Hidelberg O.   II-93
Alegre, André   I-227
Aleksandrov, Martin   II-401
Ali, Muhammad   II-483
Alonso, Eduardo   II-38
Alves, Ana   II-438
Alves, António Correia   I-299
Andrade, Cesar   I-365
Andrade, Thiago   I-215
Antonov, Nikolai   I-483
Antunes, Luís   I-55
Aslam, Zaheer   II-483
Atkinson, Colin   I-158
Ayub, Nasir   II-483
Azab, Shahira   II-467
Azevedo, Pedro   I-467

B

Bach, Joscha   II-15
Baghcheband, Hajar   I-337
Baghoussi, Yassine   I-288
Baião, Ana Rita   II-325
Baj, Giovanni   II-222
Baltazar, André Rodrigues   II-338
Barbati, Giulia   II-222
Barbosa, Agostinho   II-260
Bellas, Francisco   I-3
Bento, Carlos   II-438
Biloborodova, Tetiana   II-234
Boné, João   II-311
Bortolussi, Luca   II-222
Branco, António   I-441
Brazdil, Pavel   I-415
Brosnan, Bríd   II-234

C

Cabaço, Gonçalo   I-227
Calleo, Alberto   II-30

Campos
Campos, Ricardo   I-378, I-402
Campos, Vasco   I-378
Cardoso, Henrique Lopes   I-441, I-454
Carneiro, Gabriel A.   II-351, II-388
Carrino, Stefano   II-497
Carvalho, Alexandra M.   II-325
Carvalho, Tânia   I-55
Cătărău-Cotuţiu, Corina   II-38
Cavaco, Sofia   I-171
Cerveira do Amaral, Filipe   I-389
Chakrabarty, Dalia   I-184
Chaves, Pedro   II-311
Cheema, Sehrish Munawar   II-483
Chrestien, Leah   I-495
Christian, Bielenberg   II-548
Clausen, Christian Skafte Beck   II-511
Coelho, Paulo Jorge   II-483
Coelho, Pedro   II-298
Coelho, Teresa   II-286
Coletti, Roberta   II-247
Cordeiro, Nuno Pablo   II-118
Cortez, Paulo   I-311
Costa, Dinis   II-364
Costa, Joana   II-364
Costa, Nuno   I-239
Costa, Pedro Reis   II-325
Cotofrei, Paul   II-497
Cozman, Fabio Gagliardi   I-428
Crista, Vítor   I-29
Crompton, Helen   I-3
Cunha, António   II-351, II-388
Cunha, João M.   II-64
Cunha, José Boaventura   II-338
Cunha, Luís Filipe   I-402
Cunha, Paulo Rupino   I-92
Curioso, Isabel   II-298

D

da Costa, António Ribeiro   II-426
da Silva, Daniel Queirós   II-376
da Silva, Nádia F. F.   II-93
Dahroug, Ahmed   II-453

de Carvalho, André C. P. L. F.   II-93
De Martin, Juan Carlos   I-79
Delmoral, Jessica C.   I-263
Dias, João   II-118, II-142
dos Santos, Filipe Neves   II-338, II-376
Dreyer, Jonathan   II-497
Duarte, André V.   II-413
Duarte, Fernando Fradique   I-121
Duraes, Dalila   I-3

E
Edelkamp, Stefan   I-495
Esteves, Bernardo   I-133
Estima, Jacinto   I-92

F
Fajarda, Olga   I-146
Faria, Pedro   II-182
Faria, Tiago   I-106
Fernandes, Carlos   II-535
Ferreira, Paulo J. S.   I-251
Ferreira, Rui Miguel Frazão Dias   I-67
Filipe, Vítor   II-376
Fragata, José   II-298
Freitas, Alberto   I-29
Freitas, Luís   I-171
Freitas, Pedro Miguel   II-131, II-157

G
Gabora, Liane   II-15
Gama, João   I-215, I-365
Gamechi, Zahra   I-29
Georg, Rottenwalter   II-548
Ghorbel, Hatem   II-497
Giannuzzo, Anaïs   II-52
Gomes, Luis M.   II-274
Gomes, Luís Mendes   II-131
Gomes, Luís   I-441
Gomes, Luis   II-169, II-195
Gonçalves, Carlos   I-311
Gouveia, Feliz   II-523
Grilo, António   I-67
Guede-Fernández, Federico   II-298
Guerreiro, Maria   II-523
Guerreiro-Santalla, Sara   I-3
Guimarães, Tiago   II-260

H
Hassan Muhammad, Shamsuddeen   I-415

Howard, Daniel Anthony   II-511

J
Janda, Josef   I-511
Janota, Mikoláš   I-483
Jonker, Richard Adolph Aires   I-146
Jorge, Alípio   I-378, I-402, I-415, II-286
Jørgensen, Bo Nørregaard   II-209, II-511
Jozi, Aria   II-169

K
Kailas, Siva   I-349
Karakaya, Ziya   I-29
Katharina, Obermeier   II-548
Kessel, Marcus   I-158
Kimura, Risa   I-16
Kokkinogenis, Zafeiris   II-426
Komenda, Antonín   I-495

L
Labarta, Tobias   II-401
Lambert, Marian   I-158
Lau, Nuno   I-121
Lobo, Afonso   II-260
Londral, Ana   II-298
Lopes, João   II-260
Lopes, Jorge   II-523
Lopes, Maria S.   I-199
Lopes, Marta B.   II-247, II-325
Lopes, Rui Pedro   I-146
Luo, Wenhao   I-349

M
Ma, Zheng   II-209, II-511
Macêdo, David   II-93
Machado, José M.   II-274
Magalhães, João   I-467
Maia, Maria João   I-67
Manso, João   I-227
Marcel, Tilly   II-548
Marcelino, João   I-227
Marques, Nuno   I-227
Marreiros, Goreti   I-29, II-169
Martinho, Diogo   I-29
Martins, Bruno   I-389
Martins, Pedro   II-64
Martins, Tiago   II-64
Matos, Sérgio   I-146
Mauá, Denis Deratani   I-428

Melo, Duarte I-263
Melo, Francisco S. I-133
Melo, Rui II-142
Mendes-Moreira, João I-251, I-288, II-286
Mikulecky, Peter I-41
Mondragón, Esther II-38
Moniz, Nuno I-55, I-239
Montenegro, Larissa II-274
Morais, Raul II-351, II-388
Moreira, António Paulo I-199, II-338
Moreira, Nídia Andrade II-157
Moreira, Rui S. II-523
Mota, Bruno II-182
Moussa, Sherin M. II-453
Murta, Rafael II-64

N
Nakajima, Tatsuo I-16
Naz, Ammerha II-483
Neves, José I-29
Nogueira, Ana Rita I-299
Novais, Paulo I-3, I-29, II-157, II-311

O
Oliveira, Adriano L. I. II-93
Oliveira, Arlindo L. II-413
Oliveira, Hugo Gonçalo II-3
Oliveira, José Luís I-146
Oliveira, Lino I-275, I-323
Oliveira, Pedro II-77
Oliveira, Sérgio I-227
Oliveira, Tiago II-311
Ormazabal, Aitor II-3
Osório, Tomás I-441

P
Paseri, Ludovica II-105
Pedroto, Maria II-286
Peixoto, Carolina II-325
Peixoto, Hugo II-260
Pereira, Artur I-121
Pereira, Pedro José I-311
Pevný, Tomáš I-495
Pinto, H. Sofia I-389
Pinto, José I-299
Pinto, Tiago II-169, II-561
Pires, Ivan Miguel II-483
Pirozelli, Paulo I-428
Portela, Filipe II-535

Poudel, Roshan I-146

R
Rahman, Mohamed Abdel II-453
Ramos, Carlos II-182, II-561
Ramos, Daniel II-182
Ramos, Rui I-275
Rebelo, Sérgio M. II-64
Reis, Luís Paulo I-121, I-337, II-523
Ribeiro, Bernardete I-106, II-364
Ribeiro, Bruno II-195, II-298
Ribeiro, Rita P. I-215, I-365
Rijo, Sara II-311
Rocha, Victor Hugo Nascimento I-428
Rodrigues, Arlete I-251
Rodrigues, Beatriz II-535
Rodrigues, Cláudia II-438
Rodrigues, Eduardo M. I-288
Rodrigues, João I-441
Rodrigues, Tiago Ferreira II-376
Rondina, Marco I-79
Rosário, Luís I-171
Rosato, Ludovica II-30
Rossetti, Rosaldo J. F. II-426
Roy, Gargi I-184

S
Santos, Filipe I-199
Santos, Jorge II-64, II-298
Santos, Manuel Filipe II-260
Santos, Pedro A. II-118, II-142
Santos, Ricardo II-298
Santos, Rodrigo I-441
Satoh, Ichiro I-16
Scagnetto, Arjuna II-222
Schuster, Thomas I-158
Sciolla, Jacopo Ciani II-105
Sec, David I-41
Semedo, David I-467
Shaji, Nirbhaya I-215
Silva, Ana II-311
Silva, Catarina I-106, II-364
Silva, João Miguel I-299
Silva, João I-441
Silva, Joaquim I-171
Silva, Manuel F. I-199
Silva, Vítor II-523
Silveira, Igor Cataneo I-428
Skarga-Bandurova, Inna II-234

Soares, Carlos   I-337
Soares, Daniela   I-311
Soares, Salviano Pinto   II-338
Sousa, Afonso   I-454
Sousa, Armando Jorge   II-376
Sousa, Inês   II-298
Sousa, Joaquim J.   II-351, II-388
Sousa, Ricardo   I-299, I-467
Souza, Ellen   II-93
Štekerová, Kamila   I-511
Strauss, Daniel J.   II-234
Šucha, Přemysl   I-483
Sulun, Serkan   II-77
Sycara, Katia   I-349

T
Tavares, Diogo   I-467
Teixeira, Ana Cláudia   II-388
Teixeira, Rúben   II-561
Texeira, Ana   II-351
Tolnai, Balázs András   II-209

Torres, José M.   II-523
Tse, André   I-323

V
Vale, Zita   II-169, II-195
Vasco, Miguel   I-133
Veiga, Bruno   II-561
Veloso, Marco   II-438
Verborgh, Philippe   I-171
Vetrò, Antonio   I-79
Viana, Paula   II-77
Vieira, José   II-535
Vinagre, João   I-263, I-275, I-323
Vinga, Susana   II-325
Vitório, Douglas   II-93

W
Warrior, Kane   I-184

Z
Zanchettin, Cleber   II-93